Ski Mountaineering in Scotland

Second Edition published in 2025 by
Scottish Mountaineering Press.

Copyright © The Scottish Mountaineering Club.

All rights reserved. No part of this publication may be reproduced, stored in or introduced into a retrieval system, or transmitted, in any form or by any means (electronic, mechanical, photocopying, recording or otherwise), without the prior written permission of the publisher.

ISBN 978-1-907233-49-4

A catalogue record for this book is available from the British Library.

Skiing, hillwalking, mountaineering and ski-mountaineering are activities with a danger of personal injury or death. Participants in these activities should be aware of and accept these risks and be responsible for their own actions and involvement. Route descriptions in this guide are made in good faith, and are checked where possible by the authors. The Scottish Mountaineering Club, the Scottish Mountaineering Trust and Scottish Mountaineering Trust (Publications) Ltd (trading as Scottish Mountaineering Press) do not guarantee the accuracy of any information provided in this guide, and it is not warranted that any route will be safe at any time. The nature of the ground taken by a route may change over time. This guide is prepared for the assistance of participants in planning their own activities. Participants remain responsible for all aspects of their own safety and should consult other sources of information such as up-to-date maps and weather forecasts and experienced guides, as well as making real-time assessments of all risks, and taking such other steps as safe skiing, hillwalking, mountaineering and ski-mountaineering requires in the circumstances.

The authors, editors, friends and assistants involved in the publication of this guide, the Scottish Mountaineering Club, the Scottish Mountaineering Trust and Scottish Mountaineering Trust (Publications) Ltd, can therefore accept no liability whatever for damage to property, nor for personal injury or death, arising directly or indirectly from the use of this publication.

Design & Layout by Gino Di Meo Studio.
Maps by Christopher Smith-Duque.
Cover photograph by Al Todd.

Printed & bound in China by Latitude Press.

Maps are derived from Ordnance Survey OpenData™
© Crown copyright and database right 2023

Distributed by Cordee www.cordee.co.uk.
For details of other SMC guidebooks visit
www.smc.org.uk/publications

Ski Mountaineering in Scotland

Edited by Colwyn Jones

Scottish Mountaineering Club
Skiers' Guide

Introduction	Preface and Acknowledgements	8
	How to use this Guide	10
	History	14
	Safety	18
	Access	28
	Equipment	32
Chapter 1	**South Scotland**	40
Chapter 2	**The Campsies to Loch Tay**	70
Chapter 3	**Central Scotland South**	112
Chapter 4	**Central Scotland North**	144
Chapter 5	**East Scotland**	164
Chapter 6	**North-East Scotland**	206
Chapter 7	**West Scotland South**	250
Chapter 8	**West Scotland North**	312
Chapter 9	**The Northern Highlands and the Isle of Mull**	352
	Index	386

Overleaf: Sgùrr an Iubhair
© Robbie Hearns

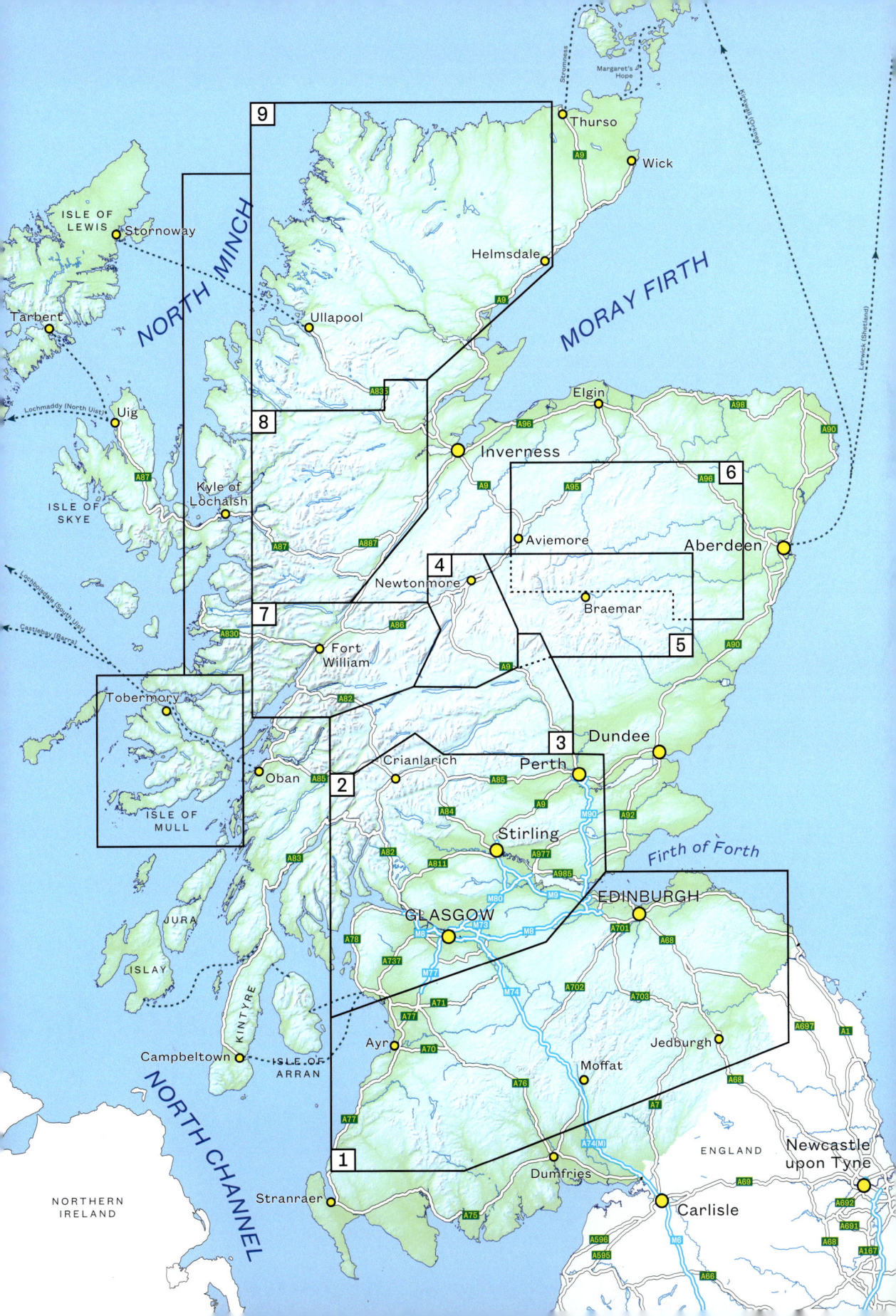

Using this Guide and Enjoying the Hills

Introduction

Preface to the Second Edition

Welcome to the second edition of *Ski Mountaineering in Scotland*. This revised, expanded and rewritten guidebook has multiple aims, but the central objective is to inspire and promote safe participation in what is for many a fulfilling and rewarding activity. Although a seasonal pursuit, ski mountaineering, also called backcountry skiing or ski touring, can quickly become a passion, despite the unpredictable nature of Scottish weather and snow conditions, which usually guard people against full-time obsession.

Throughout this guidebook, all mention of, or reference to, skiing and skiers should be interpreted as including snowboarding and snowboarders.

Users of this guide should be aware of the sometimes considerable risks of leaving controlled ski areas and venturing off-piste. However, ski mountaineering is one of the best, most immersive ways to enjoy Scotland's stunningly beautiful mountains in winter, their splendour greatly enhanced by gleaming hillsides, snow-filled gullies and white-bordered ridges. Even the most tedious peat hag can be transformed into magnificent terrain under snow.

Typically, ascending a peak on skis or snowboard involves similar time and effort to summer hillwalking, but the downhill experience is not comparable. A knee-jarring plod is transformed into an eagerly anticipated, exciting, swift, three-dimensional, kinetic experience – a long-lasting euphoria which, although not guaranteed, is entirely legal and after which you can safely drive. Welcome to ski mountaineering in Scotland.

The First Edition of *Ski Mountaineering in Scotland*

Over 35 years have elapsed since the publication of the first edition of *Ski Mountaineering in Scotland* in 1987. Editors Donald J Bennet and William (Bill) Wallace (also mentioned in route descriptions) are sadly no longer with us.

Bennet died after a long period of illness. His obituary in the 2013 *SMC Journal* (*SMCJ*) commented on his 'commitment to the dissemination of accurate and authoritative information through guidebook writing and publication'. Thus, he lives on through many of the carefully crafted ski mountaineering routes in the first edition and updated in this second. By way of contrast, his co-editor, Bill Wallace, died with his skis on! His obituary published in *The Scotsman* newspaper on 2 March 2006 stated, 'He did one last sweeping, elegant turn on the snow, stopping beside his companions and died instantly of heart failure. It was a culmination he would have wished for himself.'

Below: Approaching the summit of Cairn Gorm (skiers, Kev Neal and Gordon Pearson) © Al Todd

Editor's Dedication

I dedicate the work that I contributed in creating this guidebook to Ann MacDonald.

Acknowledgements

In addition to the authors of each ski route and the many photographers, I acknowledge the help of the following people in completing this ski mountaineering guide: Rab Anderson, Angus Armstrong, Davie Black, Justine Carter, Bunty Campbell, Jim Eccles, Duncan Gray, Adrian Hart, Jamie Johnston, Bruce Kerr, Ann MacDonald, Douglas McKeith, Heather Morning, Jennifer Mullen, Tom Prentice, Niall Ritchie, Kenny Scoular, Brian Shackleton, Alan Sloan, Phil Smith, Ian Smithson, Iain Sneddon, David Stone, Ian Taylor, Mick Tighe, Al Todd, Roger Wild and Noel Williams.

How to use this Guide

Skiing involves the discerning use of gravity once the skier reaches suitable snow for descent, and this force is universally available across all of our Scottish hills. There are around 150 routes in this second edition, grouped into nine geographical areas, from Southern Scotland to the far north.

Each route description starts with a summary box of details of the main summit(s) as follows:

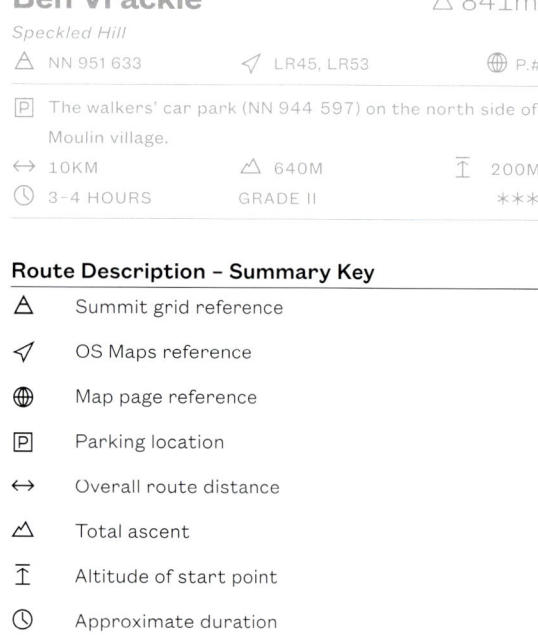

Route Description – Summary Key

△	Summit grid reference
◁	OS Maps reference
⊕	Map page reference
P	Parking location
↔	Overall route distance
△	Total ascent
⊥	Altitude of start point
◷	Approximate duration
✱✱✱	Rating

As in the 1987 edition, 'The routes described in this guide are for the most part the logical ski routes in normal winter conditions.' Obviously, abnormal snow conditions may force parties to choose alternative routes, and invariably the ski mountaineer must make route-finding decisions based on the snow conditions and snow cover encountered. The distances quoted are for the complete tour from start to finish. The height climbed is the total vertical height, including any intermediate tops and reascents in the course of a traverse. The time given is based on the judgement of the route author and is the time that should be taken by a reasonably fit party in average conditions without any long stops. A small number of routes with a predicted time using a form of Naismith's rule are mentioned in the text.

The technical difficulty of a tour, which refers to its most difficult passage and not its average difficulty, may be equated to the difficulty of alpine pistes approximately as follows:

Technical Difficulty Ratings

II	Blue run
III	Red run
IV	Black run (or steep or rocky terrain requiring the carriage of skis)

The terms used in this guide generally refer to the direction of travel of the skier. Note that this is opposite to the convention used in climbing guides. There are no ski routes above normal winter climbing grade II in this guidebook.

Route Ratings

✱✱	Modest
✱✱✱	Good
✱✱✱✱	Very good
✱✱✱✱✱	Excellent

The rating system is an attempt on the part of the authors and editor to convey the quality and difficulty of the tours described. The quality, character and ambience of a tour are indicated by a scale which may be interpreted approximately, as above. One-star tours are not included in this book. Recognising that these ratings are approximate and subjective, readers may prefer to ignore them and form their own opinions. It is far more important that ski mountaineers develop their own judgement based on experience. Only then will they enjoy the freedom of the hills and the pleasure of skiing over them.

Route Diagram Key

P (blue)	Indicates a designated car park. These are typically large, may have marked parking bays, often a parking charge and may even be cleared of snow in winter.
P (outline)	Off-road parking is usually a tarmac or gravel lay-by and, again, may be cleared of snow in winter.
P (black)	On-road parking will have very limited space on a gravel or grass verge and may require the clearing of snow before you can safely park. Driving off may also be difficult.
—	Described routes
----	Path
....	Track
○→	Start point
→○	End point

Hill Categories

▲	Munro; 3,000ft (914.4m) and higher
△	Munro Top; 3,000ft (914.4m) and higher, less prominent summits than Munros
●	Corbett; 2,500ft (762m) to below 3,000ft (914.4m);
◆	Graham; 600m to below 762m;
■	Donald; Lowlands, over 2000ft (609.6m)
⊗	Other summit

Below: The west slopes of Saddle Yoke looking across the valley to Swatte Fell (skiers, James and Kerstin Kinnaird, and Linda Biggar) © John Biggar

The route diagrams have been created using Ordnance Survey OpenData, and all the routes have been successfully skied. The solid red lines show the main route described, with orange lines indicating alternatives. For the first time, several public transport options are included. Car parking symbols are those now used throughout Scottish Mountaineering Club (SMC) climbing and hillwalking guides.

Summit altitudes are based on the latest known valid measurements but recent improvements in GPS triangulation means they may vary by a metre or two. The routes are based on the Ordnance Survey Landranger (LR) 1:50,000 scale maps, with some features from the 1:25,000 scale maps. Note that the map diagrams may be missing recently added features as since writing this guidebook new access tracks, dams, bridges, footpaths, ditches, deer fences, windfarms, buildings, etc. have been created. Ski mountaineering in Scotland takes place within our actively developing country.

Below: Mòine Mhòr
(skier, Jonathan Preston)
© Sarah Atkinson

History

A short history of skiing in Scotland. From the introduction in the 1987 edition. (Original by Donald Bennet and William Wallace, updated by Colwyn Jones.)

It is now almost 100 years since the publication of the first of the SMC's guidebooks (as distinct from guidebook articles in the *SMCJ*). In this time the range and numbers of these books have steadily increased to reflect the widening range of activities and interests of climbers, and their improved skills and techniques. The original edition was the first SMC guidebook to recognise the status of ski mountaineering in Scotland. In the past this status was somewhat undermined by the feeling among some mountaineers in Scotland that the use of skis in mountaineering was not quite a respectable part of their sport, possibly because of the association with the less demanding pleasures of downhill skiing. However, ski mountaineering has been established and enthusiastically pursued by some eminent Scottish mountaineers in the past hundred years. It is appropriate to mention,

Below: Early motorised access to Beinn Ghlas, Ben Lawers range
© SMC Archive

very briefly, a few of the personalities and events of those early years.

In 1892, Will W Naismith, generally regarded as the founder of the SMC, is reported to have used skis on the Campsie Hills, and he described his experiences with enthusiasm to fellow members of the Club.

> *For the sake of any uninitiated, it may be explained that skis (pron. "shes") are wooden snow-skates, 7 feet long (213cm) and 3 to 4 inches wide, largely used throughout the northern parts of Europe and Asia (see Dr Nansen's 'Across Greenland'). The best are made of ash or plane, and cost, with fastenings, about £1, but a light serviceable pair of pine can be had for a few shillings by writing to Messrs Hagen & Co., Bergen. On 12 March, shortly after a considerable fall of snow, M. T. G. and W. W. N. climbed the Campsies behind Milton, and followed the crest of the ridge for two miles to the Meikle Bin. From that commanding point, after a snow shower had passed, a grand view was obtained of the Highland mountains all dressed in white, the Ochils, Firth of Forth, tops of Arran hills, &c., &c. On the return journey the same route was followed. The skis were not of much use when ascending, but upon level ground, and especially where the snow was soft, better progress was made with their aid than without them, while a very slight gradient was sufficient to get up tremendous speed during the descent. When the angle was too steep to risk, the skis were slipped off and turned into an improvised toboggan. At one long slope, some 300 yards in length, and inclined at a general angle of 15°, an hour was enjoyably spent, the snow being in perfect order for ski-ing firm underneath, with a powdering of drifted snow on the surface. This snowbed was crossed by one or two small ridges which imparted a switchback element to the sport, somewhat puzzling to inexperienced amateurs. Of course the party came to grief several times, but they returned home well pleased with their experiment. Skis might often be employed with advantage in winter ascents in Scotland, or rather descents, for although Norsemen skate up as well as down hills, few men in this country are likely to acquire such facility as to use them when going uphill, but they can be easily towed up, as they weigh only a few pounds. In the Alps it is not unlikely that the sport may eventually become popular, particularly with the blasé climber who has "done" everything in the ordinary way, and the individual ambitious of beating all previous "times" in the descent of easy mountains, such as the Breithorn, Cimi di Jazzi, or even Mont Blanc. In the event of the rope proving impracticable, a slight acquaintance with a glacier would reduce the risk from hidden crevasses to a minimum; and as for a gaping bergschrund, an expert would simply fly over it. It is probably no exaggeration to say that a good man on skis could descend safely from the top of the Breithorn to the end of the Théodule Glacier in half an hour.*

— WW Naismith, from 'On the Campsie fells with Norwegian "skis."' *SMCJ*, Vol 2, no 2 (May 1892), p90.

JH Wigner was another early enthusiast who made a ski ascent of Ben Chonzie in 1904, and at the Easter Meet that year WR Rickmers endeavoured to teach some members of the SMC to ski on Ben Nevis, but his efforts were rather thwarted by continuous rain, a problem which modern Scottish ski mountaineers may recognise. After the meet Rickmers presented 11 pairs of skis to the SMC, but apparently none have survived to the present day, unlike at least one celebrated ice axe of the same period. Harold Raeburn, the owner of that axe, was also a skier, but not an enthusiastic one, possibly because his efforts were largely confined to the Pentlands and other low hills, and he saw little prospect of using skis on the higher mountains. He caused consternation one night in Edinburgh by skiing down the tramway lines to Morningside Station on his way home from an expedition to the Pentlands.

The Scottish Ski Club was formed in 1907, and it and the SMC had many members in common. At the SMC's Easter Meet in 1909, Naismith and Allan Arthur carried their skis up Ben Nevis from the Càrn Mòr Dearg Arête, and then ran and crashed their way down the slopes of the Red Burn. Naismith's enthusiasm for this activity prompted him to write in the same year, addressing his fellow members of the SMC who, like their modern counterparts, looked askance at ski mountaineering: 'Will the younger members who have not yet tried skiing allow an old fogey to urge them to take up a sport which bids fair to become a formidable rival of the axe and rope during winter months?'

It seems that at the time there was, as there still is, some divergence of opinion between the merits of Alpine and Norwegian skis and bindings, and the techniques best suited to these two types of equipment. Rickmers had been brought up in the Alpine school, and the skis which he presented to the SMC were the Lillienfeldt model, designed by Zdarsky and the forerunner of modern Alpine skis: short, rigid and heavy. Raeburn, on the other hand, favoured the longer, lighter Norwegian skis which were suited for travel over the level and gently undulating country characteristic of Scandinavia, and this may explain why he was unenthusiastic about using them on steep hills. Nevertheless, he seems to have found them quite suitable for skiing along tramway lines, just as many Nordic skiers nowadays prefer to ski along prepared tracks.

From about 1910 onwards two men emerged as the founders of ski mountaineering in Scotland: Allan Arthur and Harry MacRobert. Their articles in the *SMCJ* indicate the enthusiasm of these and other pioneers of this sport, and the widening range of hills that were being climbed and traversed on skis. At the SMC's Easter Meet in Aviemore in 1913, parties crossed the Cairngorms from Glenmore Lodge to Derry Lodge and returned over the Glen Feshie hills. Many of the active ski mountaineers in the SMC were also members of the Scottish Ski Club, thus forming a bond which grew as ski mountaineering developed, culminating in the Bennet/Wallace guide in 1987.

In 1932 the Scottish Ski Club built a small hut in Coire Odhar below Beinn Ghlas, one of the Lawers peaks. This hut became a focal point for skiers but was finally removed in 1999 after sustaining storm damage. Development of skiing centres elsewhere in Scotland from 1956 onwards drew skiers away from the simple pleasures of Ben Lawers to the ski tows and chairlifts of Cairn Gorm, Glenshee and Meall a' Bhùiridh.

One ski mountaineer whose activities in Scotland spanned the years before and after the Second World War was Willie Speirs. He imported his first pair of skis from Switzerland in 1928, learned to ski on the Campsies and was still active 40 years later. His expeditions in Scotland between 1928 and 1965 included Meall a' Bhùiridh in 1932, possibly the first ski descent of the mountain which, 25 years later, was a focal point in the development of mass downhill skiing in Scotland. It must have been a great descent down the north-east corrie of that mountain with not another person or ski-lift pylon in sight.

The years since the Second World War have seen increasing numbers of mountaineers turned skiers, and skiers turned mountaineers, but for 20 years growth in the sport was unspectacular. Its proponents were not given to publish their achievements and enthusiasms widely, and the mountaineers among them were inhibited by the feeling that prevailed among their 'hard' fellow mountaineers that the development of downhill skiing in Scotland was something with which no true mountaineer should have any dealings.

The first traverse of the four Cairngorm 4,000ft mountains in 1953 by Norman Clark was a landmark, and in the north-east the Adam Watsons, father and son, were active skiers over all the hills of Deeside from the low tops of Bennachie and Clachnaben to the high Cairngorms. The younger Adam's traverse of Ben Avon and the five highest Cairngorms in 1962 was an outstanding feat, and an eloquent demonstration of the potential of Nordic skis in the Cairngorms, given the right conditions.

The standard of ski mountaineering was also improving, aided no doubt by the developing downhill facilities in Scotland, and the growing number of skiers going to the Alps for both downhill and mountain skiing. No one exemplified these standards better than John Wilson, whose style, skill and unerring route-finding ability saw others follow him up the ridges and down the corries of Ben Lawers, often in storms and whiteouts, at touring meets of the Scottish Ski Club.

The publication by Malcolm Slesser in 1970 of his book, *Scottish Mountains on Ski*, was a revelation of the great range of ski mountaineering possibilities in Scotland, and stimulated much interest. Slesser was among the first to attempt the Scottish Haute Route (p.289), the traverse on skis from the Deeside hills to Ben Nevis (or vice versa). This long and demanding expedition requires a week of good weather and snow cover, neither of which is likely in Scotland, and adverse conditions foiled many attempts until Mike Taylor and David Grieve traversed from Ben Avon to Ben Nevis in March 1978.

In 1982, Chamonix mountain guide Jean Franck Charlet arrived in Scotland to ski on Ben Nevis at the invitation of the late Hamish MacInnes. The plan was a live outside TV transmission for the BBC. Poor weather prevented the broadcast, but in rehearsal, using two fixed ropes for abseil, Charlet did ski down *Good Friday Climb*: a Grade III winter climb on the North Face of Ben Nevis. No one has claimed a second ski descent, so Charlet's achievement remains unrepeated.

In the 1986 *SMCJ*, Martin Burrows-Smith postulated that, as with new climbing routes, first descents of 'extreme' ski routes should be recorded. Justification for the proposal was an impressive list of more than 30 Scottish gullies he had claimed, although he was not always the first.

The first account of an annual SMC ski mountaineering meet was in 1988 at Kiltarlity. The weather was recorded as 'not perfect', but the snow cover above 1,500ft was continuous and superb. Sgùrr na Lapaich (Glen Strathfarrar) was traversed on the Saturday, and Tom a' Chòinich and Toll Creagach in Glen Affric the next day. Since then, regular annual ski meets have been held, except during disease outbreaks (foot and mouth and COVID-19).

The Scottish Ski Club installed the first permanent ski lift on Meall a' Bhùiridh (Glencoe) in 1955. Skiing in December and January was then considered too austere, and it opened to the public in late February 1956 – the first commercial ski centre in Scotland. Lifts were also installed at Glenshee (a T-bar on Meall Odhar, 1957) and Cairngorm shortly afterwards (1961), the Lecht in 1977 and Nevis Range opening in 1989. The arrival of ski instructors and training and experience of locals in these areas saw a few adventurous individuals starting to explore off-piste potential, not only around the resorts, but also across Scotland, a movement that, despite global warming, continues today – meeting ski mountaineers or observing their ski tracks across Scotland during winter has now become commonplace.

With a couple of recent exceptions (2012 and 2017), there was a succession of excellent if short snowy winters in Scotland from 2008/9 through to 2021, but recent winters have been more variable. There has been an increase in people skiing steep gully lines, with downhill skiers increasingly seeking out quieter slopes.

March 2021 also witnessed the first non-stop round of all of the 18 Cairngorm Munros in under 24 hours. Finlay Wild completed the 105km tour (estimated 6,000 metres of ascent) in 18 hours and 50 minutes (*SMCJ*, vol.50, no.213, p.17-23, 2022).

Another recent European import is ski mountaineering racing (Skimo), which, according to Mountaineering Scotland, 'combines athletic skiing with mountaineering skills, incorporating technical ascents and descents'.

There are different types of courses, ranging from vertical sprints, where racers skin uphill over a set distance, to courses that have short steep sections which require the racers to put their skis on their backpacks – all combined with technical downhill sections.

The (Scottish) races are short (60–90 minutes) and are held towards the end of the normal ski piste day. Each race is exclusively designed around the specific resort, using extensive ski patrol knowledge to ensure racers ski the best conditions in a secure setting.

Competitors have an essential equipment list, they all start at the same time, and the fastest person to complete the course is the winner.

Now the role ski mountaineering plays in the wider sport is well established, not only in Scotland, but to a much greater extent elsewhere. One has only to look at the journals of the European Alpine clubs, and books and magazines on Alpine climbing, to realise that in the Alps in winter, spring and early summer, ski mountaineering is the predominant activity. In Scotland the role of ski mountaineering is perhaps less important because although it may be more pleasant, it is rarely essential to use skis to access ice climbing areas unless in exceptional conditions of very deep, soft snow.

Those who have become 'addicted' to ski mountaineering in Scotland would claim that this combination of skiing and winter mountain walking brings added interest, enjoyment and excitement to both sports. As Sandy Wedderburn, another highly talented SMC climber and skier, says in his book, *Alpine Climbing on Foot and with Ski* (1936), it is a sport which 'has added a new and most delectable pleasure to mountain going'. Greater interest and importance is attached to correct route selection and the discovery of new, untracked and possibly challenging downhill runs gives the skier far more excitement than they are likely to find on the beaten piste. Sometimes the skier will find it easier than the walker to reach the summits, but it would be wrong in general to claim that skiing offers a faster, easier ascent – it all depends on the snow conditions. Going downhill, of course, the situation is quite different, and the skier should not only be much faster but smoother, with the added thrill of speed. The only disadvantage is that this pleasure is all too brief, and before long skins have to be put back on skis for the next uphill climb.

Below: Bentley Shooting Brake, Ben Lawers
© Tom Weir Collection, SMC Archive

Safety

Ski mountaineering is almost always undertaken as a discretionary leisure pursuit; very rarely is it essential, and security and wellbeing must be your prime consideration. Participants should be aware of and accept the inherent risks and take responsibility for their own actions and involvement. Travelling in mountains during winter is never without risk.

Travel

As this is a guidebook for Scotland, there are no tours included where you ski in or out from your accommodation (camping or bothying excepted); some form of travel is always required. For the first time we have included routes with alternatives to travelling by car, namely trains and buses. Nevertheless, car travel is likely to remain the main method of accessing skiing for most people, and with winter driving there are additional safety issues to consider even before you leave home. Driving in winter, even at our modest Scottish altitudes, and often on quiet roads, can be hazardous. Winter tyres in good condition, snow chains, snow socks and 4-wheel drive can mitigate some of those hazards. You should also practise how to fit and use these safely. The first time you try to fit snow chains/socks should not be in an emergency or a blizzard!

When fitting snow chains or snow socks, get off the carriageway to avoid the risk of collision. A passing driver may well see your parked vehicle but may not see a crouched figure beside the front road wheel. Often the banks of snow at the side of a ploughed road result in a narrow passage, making a collision more likely. Similarly, if you have to dig snow out to safely park your car, then take care that you do not create a hazard by obstructing the highway or risk being struck by a passing vehicle. Pack a suitable robust shovel with a long enough handle and a metal blade.

Sometimes cars get stuck in snow and running the engine may keep the occupants warm while awaiting rescue. However, this risks carbon monoxide poisoning (now less likely with catalytic converters, assuming they are in good condition). A diesel car will tick over for well over 24 hours (often days) at idle on a full fuel tank while you await rescue or the snow melts! Getting stuck in snow in an electric vehicle (EV) may be more problematic as the batteries will quickly lose charge if used to heat the interior of the car. EVs lose around 30–40% of their range at freezing temperatures and that reduction in capacity will also apply to how long the

Above: Sgùrr a' Chaorachain with Skye visible in the distance
© Al Todd

battery can operate the vehicle's heater. Consider packing a warm sleeping bag, flask, stove and some emergency food when travelling.

Weather
Two external factors which determine the character of any Scottish mountain in winter are snow and weather conditions, and they influence a ski mountaineering day as much, if not more, than a day walking, climbing or downhill skiing. It must be stressed that the illustrations in this guide are not representative of typical Scottish conditions; the sun does not shine all the time, nor are the mountains always white!

Ski mountaineering has traditionally been a late winter or spring activity after thaw-freeze cycles have settled the snowpack. Snow conditions are such a vital factor in ski mountaineering that they should be considered carefully before setting out. The variation of snow type – ice, névé, crusted snow, spring snow, powder snow, windslab and porridge, to name a few – has a great bearing on the pleasure and safety of the day. These conditions can vary according to the orientation of the mountainside you are planning to ascend and descend, and conditions on opposite sides of a mountain on any given day can be very different. You should take into account not only the weather that day, but also during the preceding week, in particular the amount of snow or rainfall, the wind strength and direction and temperature changes. With these in mind, it should be possible to predict snow conditions and choose a mountain route that will give good and safe skiing. For example, strong winds during and soon after snowfall can leave the windward side of a mountain and its exposed ridges blown clear, while leeward sides may have big accumulations of windslab and large, dangerous cornices. Warm south-westerly winds will soon strip the snow off slopes facing in that direction, while cycles of freezing and thawing will produce hard snow or ice, which may make even gentle slopes potentially dangerous for skiing.

Many of the routes in this guide will only be in condition after a substantial fall of snow, usually requiring a northerly, north westerly or easterly airflow. Scottish westerlies, travelling across the Atlantic from warmer and humid regions, rarely produce enough snow for skiers and usually give rain, which reduces any existing snow cover. Therefore, irrespective of the time of year, if snow falls then seize the moment, go out and ski on it! Ski routes on lower-level hills often have grassy hillsides which can be skied with shallow snow, perhaps after a single heavy snowfall. So early season snow favours routes, usually day tours, on lower peaks with a limited depth of snow. Higher hills are naturally rockier, and enough snow has to accumulate through the winter season to cover boulders and allow continuous ski travel. Sufficient snow also has to collect in gullies to render them skiable, so higher peaks and skiing gullies remain a later season target.

Avalanches

'No snowflake in an avalanche ever feels responsible' – disputed source.

The eternal search for fresh powder snow, the freedom it offers, and the beauty of the mountains, account for many worldwide avalanche deaths each year. Off-piste and backcountry skiers trade the euphoria experienced during skiing with the risk of avalanches and other mountain hazards.

Avalanches in Scotland are not as rare as many people believe, and the risk must be taken seriously. The Scottish Avalanche Information Service (SAIS) Winter Report 2021/22 showed that around 30–40 human-triggered avalanches have been reported each year in Scotland since 2009 among skiers, walkers and climbers, with up to eight fatalities a year (2012/13). Remember that the 2020/21 figures were artificially low owing to travel restrictions introduced during the COVID-19 pandemic.

Most backcountry avalanche victims trigger the avalanche themselves, and everyone venturing onto the hills in winter, especially skiers, should be familiar with the principles of snow structure and avalanche prediction.

As snow falls and lands on a hillside, it is subject to a constant gravitational force. It stays in place when the pull of gravity is opposed by the strength of the internal snow structure. Snow is composed of flakes, crystals or particles with a varying amount of air trapped within it; the more air, the lower the density. The low density and viscosity of fresh snow allows the skier or boarder to surf through powder, which cannot be found (early morning fresh tracks aside) within patrolled downhill ski resorts.

If the weight of snow exceeds the strength of internal bonds between flakes, then the snow slides and settles. Avalanches in maritime climates, such as that found in Scotland, typically occur during or immediately after storms, with slides in the new layers of snow. The greater the volume of fresh snow, the higher the risk, especially in the days following heavy snowfall until the snow has consolidated and stabilised in the relatively warm temperatures. Rain may subsequently soak into the snowpack, thereby increasing the overall load, and rain may lubricate an icy surface, increasing the chances of the heavy, wet snow above the ice avalanching.

The stormy nature of our maritime climate moves snow around continuously and can lead to a build-up of large cornices and thick layers of snow on sheltered lee slopes – so-called lee-slope deposition. As it blows around, the dendritic structure of snowflakes is lost through simple friction. If these rounded snow particles are deposited on a steep lee slope, the resulting windslab becomes a significant avalanche hazard. Deposition of windblown snow is thought to present the largest avalanche risk.

Slopes between 30–60 degrees with fresh snow, whether fallen or blown, should be considered suspect. Avoiding these slopes is essential and may be as simple as choosing to ascend a ridge rather than a gully. On encountering unstable snow, stop and consider your position. Turning back and retracing your tracks is often the safest option. Digging a snow pit will help you to examine the snow profile and check for different layers of snow with varying degrees of bonding between them, but avalanche prediction is a skill difficult to acquire.

If witness to an avalanche, it is vital to start to search for victims immediately, if it is safe to do so. Unless severely injured, some 80% may survive if found immediately, but fewer than 20% are likely to be alive after an hour. Mark the burial site if known, listen for any sound, look for visual clues, and search for as long as you can until help arrives. A working knowledge of first aid, and especially cardio-pulmonary resuscitation, may save a life, as victims may have stopped breathing and/or be hypothermic.

Understanding mountain weather forecasts is essential for making the best decisions, both before and during your day out. Weather and avalanches are intrinsically linked. During the winter season (typically mid-November to mid-April) SAIS gives detailed daily forecasts of the avalanche hazard for the six most popular areas of Scotland: Lochaber, Glencoe, Northern Cairngorms, Southern Cairngorms, Creag Meagaidh and Torridon. Check conditions by combining weather information with the SAIS bulletin (www.sais.gov.uk) for the area you are interested in. Ask yourself what has been happening in the days leading up to your planned adventure, as this will indicate where the snow is and what the conditions are likely to be on the aspect you want to ski or board.

The following table describes the different categories of avalanche risk using the five levels of The European Avalanche Danger Scale (EADS).

Category	Snow Cover	Avalanche probability
5 **Very high**	Generally unstable	Spontaneous avalanches – **touring not recommended**
4 **High**	Unstable in most places	Avalanches triggered by small additional loads – **touring only recommended on very safe slopes**
3 **Considerable**	Moderate to weak compaction on many slopes	Avalanches triggered by additional loads
2 **Moderate**	Moderate compaction on steep slopes otherwise well compacted	Avalanches only triggered by large added loads
1 **Low**	Generally well compacted and stable	Avalanches triggered by large loads on steep ground

Note: For a much more detailed treatment of avalanches, readers are referred to *A Chance in a Million? Scottish Avalanches*, by Bob Barton and Blyth Wright, published by the Scottish Mountaineering Trust in 1985. See also:
- Scottish Avalanche Information Service (www.sais.gov.uk)
- European Avalanche Danger Scale (www.avalanches.org)

Route choice

Exploration of new routes and lines is an essential, everyday and enjoyable part of ski mountaineering. Skiing in Scotland is perhaps more conditional on weather than elsewhere in Europe. Regular gales deposit large amounts of snow as windslab and unstable cornices, and strip snow from ridges and faces. The thin ribbon of snow remaining after high winds and warmer temperatures is often the only ski route available for both ascent and descent.

The safest route may not be the shortest nor the most logical (especially when viewed with hindsight). Often the safest descent route will be dictated by the snow you encounter on ascent. Avoid terrain traps such as the steep sides of gullies, or where windslab or drifts accumulate. Also avoid long traverse lines across a hillside, or if one cannot be avoided, aim to stay as high as possible. Slopes with trees and rocks showing are less likely to avalanche, although the slopes above them may do so, and must be carefully assessed.

If you are faced with a risky slope, the best advice is to turn back! If your collective decision is to continue, then ski into key areas one at a time and maintain distances with a minimum of 10 metres between skiers. Those who are stationary should watch the single skier, and ski from a safe place to the next (hopefully) safe place, typically below a rock, outcrop or trees, or onto a flat area of snow.

Navigation

Navigation on skis is a serious challenge, particularly in poor visibility and complete snow cover. Bad weather brings with it all the problems of mountain navigation which are familiar to mountaineers, but may not be so familiar to downhill skiers, who rely on piste markers for guidance. A cautious line should be followed, keeping well away from potentially corniced edges. At times you may have to take skis off and walk, or keep skins on to reduce speed when descending a slope that would otherwise require turns. If in doubt about your ability to navigate, consider a lower route and/or choose your days carefully.

Map and compass are essential along with, of course, the well-practised skills associated with regular use. Ordnance Survey 1:50,000 Landranger Series maps are the standard mountaineers' maps in the UK. A compass mounted on a wrist strap outside your anorak sleeve is particularly useful when both hands are holding ski poles. However, the skier will often find it hard or even impossible to ski on a compass bearing as steep slopes, minor crags and patches of bare scree and rock will force detours from the correct line. The effects of such detours must be allowed for.

Judging distance in descent in poor visibility is particularly difficult, and electronic gadgets will help with this. An altimeter should be capable of showing height changes of a few metres and can help fix your position by relating to contour lines on the map, provided it has been correctly set before starting out from the foot of the hill. In high winds, however, local pressure variations on mountain summits can cause an aneroid barometer to overestimate the height.

It might also be prudent to carry electronic backup in the form of GPS or, as a minimum, the OS Locate app, which will provide you with a six-figure grid reference and altitude should you become disorientated. 'Slope aspect' is a key tool in the conditions described above.

Assessing slope angle is essential to assess avalanche risk. Gradients of slopes can be calculated from the map by measuring the distance between contour lines. For 1:50,000 scale maps, the following table gives gradients and the very approximate relationship between slope angle and the difficulty ratings used in this guide.

Distance between adjacent thick index (50m) contour lines*	Angle of slope	Approximate equivalent rating of ski difficulty**
2mm	27°	IV
3mm	18°	III
4mm	14°	III
5mm	11°	II
6mm	9°	II
8mm	7°	I
10mm	5°	I

* Ordanance Survey Landranger series 1:50,000 scale.
** Note that these are not winter climbing grades.

For comparison purposes, the average gradient of some well-known downhill ski runs in Scotland are given.

Spikes, Back Corries, Nevis Range	35°
Tiger Run, The Cairnwell, Glenshee	27°
White Lady, Cairn Gorm	20°
Main Run, Meall a' Bhùiridh, Glencoe	18°
Fiacaill Run, Cairn Gorm	15°
Coire Cas, Cairn Gorm	13°

Above right: Caenlochan glen, east face of Glas Maol
© Michael Salt

There are also online mapping websites which have layers that can be turned on to show shaded areas where slope angles become critical (usually more than 30 degrees). They are useful for pre-planning ski routes and especially after fresh snow.

River Crossings
Water is powerful, even when flowing calmly, so care is needed if you have to cross it. If there is a bridge shown on the map, it is usually best to use it, even if that means walking up or downstream for a distance.

Check ice or snow bridges over streams and rivers to ensure they will support your weight. Skis distribute the weight over a larger area, but make sure your climbing skins do not get wet.

If you have to wade, find a calm section, and unhook your rucksack waist and chest straps so that if you fall into the water, you can get rid of your pack so it won't weigh you down. Use ski poles to determine if your next step will be stable and to enable you to always have three points of contact on the stream bed.

If you know that there is a river crossing on your route, it is a good idea to take a pair of well-fitting lightweight shoes to cushion sharp rocks. If it doesn't seem safe, don't risk it. It is better to turn back than to end up wet and cold.

Cold When Skiing

The best snow for ski mountaineering is when the temperature is well below the freezing point of water. Strong winds and a high windchill factor are typical in Scotland, so it is essential to make sure you are more than adequately clothed. Always take a warm hat or a ski helmet and at least one spare pair of gloves and/or mitts. When skiing, take care to look out for snow or ice falling off trees, cliffs, communications towers, wind turbines etc.

Frostbite

The lower the temperature and the longer anyone is exposed, the more severe frostbite becomes.

Frostnip: During the early stage of frostbite, you may experience pins and needles, throbbing or aching in the affected area. Skin in the affected area will become cold, numb and white. The fingers, nose, ears, cheeks and toes are most commonly affected. Frostnip should be treated immediately by warming the affected areas.

After frostnip, prolonged exposure will damage more tissue. The affected area will feel hard and frozen. Once tissue has thawed, the skin will turn red and blister, usually with pain, swelling and itchiness. This is superficial frostbite, as it affects the top layers of skin and tissue. The skin underneath the blisters is usually still intact, but treatment is required to minimise permanent damage.

If exposure continues, skin goes white, blue or blotchy. Damage to underlying tendons, muscles, nerves and bones starts. Deep frostbite needs urgent medical care. It is likely that over time some tissue will die (tissue necrosis), and the necrotic tissue may have to be amputated to prevent infection.

The long-term effects of frostbite may include increased sensitivity to cold and numbness in the affected body parts, most commonly the fingers reduced sense of touch and persistent pain.

Hypothermia

Hypothermia is a drop in body (core) temperature below 35°C (95°F). Normal body temperature is around 37°C (98.6°F). Hypothermia can be serious if not treated. Give first aid if you think someone is hypothermic. The early signs include:
- shivering
- cold and pale skin
- slurred speech
- fast breathing
- tiredness
- confusion

These symptoms suggest mild hypothermia, where body temperature is between 32–35°C. When core temperature drops to 32°C or lower, people usually stop shivering completely and may lose consciousness. This is now a medical emergency.

Off-Piste Skiing

In a resort, skiers can go where they choose thanks to the groomed pistes, defined boundaries and signs warning of any dangers, no matter how small. In contrast, security off-piste relies on you and the collective actions of your fellow skiers. All of the ski routes in this guidebook involve skiing off-piste. Indeed, to fully adhere to the Mountaineering Scotland tourer's access code, you should avoid ascending pistes and ski tow lines in ski resorts. Skiing off-piste into the mountains requires mountaineering skills, but can be made safer through good organisation, group discipline and careful route choice.

Off-piste skiing should not be a solitary activity. Ideally ski in groups of three or more people of similar fitness and ability. Three well-equipped people are the minimum that can manage an accident involving a single casualty. In both ascent and descent, the more experienced skier leads the group, or perhaps skis at the rear if a second knowledgeable skier can lead.

The leading skier chooses the route, usually after discussion, and should stop to discuss any perceived dangers. The group should plan and introduce regular stops to ensure no one gets left behind. Safety may require action to ski with a reasonable distance between individuals. Ski one at a time or from a point of relative safety to the next perceived safe stopping point. When the lead skier stops, perhaps to avoid a hazard such as a cornice or hole in the snow, the remainder of the group should stop just behind and above them.

Off-Piste Rescue

Off-piste skiing can lead to two broad categories of accidents: falls and avalanche burial. The approach to off-piste rescue is common to all mountain accidents.
1) Make sure all involved in any rescue stay safe. The worst possible impact on a safe casualty evacuation is to double or triple the number of casualties.
2) Ensure that the victim of the accident is protected from any further danger, including hypothermia. If you suspect there is serious injury, try not to move the individual.

3) Make sure the victim is secure and cannot fall again or slide down the slope. Assess the risk of a further avalanche. Crossed skis in the snow 5m above the victim will alert any following skiers to the accident ahead.
4) Call for help. If there is a mobile phone signal, dial 999 for emergencies. Some mobile phones can now access satellites for emergency calls. Mountain Rescue is typically coordinated by the police in Scotland, but the emergency operator will be trained to respond to the information you provide. Give concise information about the location and injuries of the casualty and any assistance available at the accident site. If there is no mobile phone signal, and no one has an emergency beacon then someone will have to leave to raise the alarm or find a signal. It is better to stay with the victim, but in a party of two, it may be necessary to leave to summon help. Leave the casualty warm and comfortable in a sheltered, well-marked place. Other groups of skiers or climbers may have a an emergency beacon, a VHF radio or a satellite phone, especially if they are professionally guided, so it is worth asking everyone you might pass while going for help.
5) Rescue may involve a manual stretcher evacuation by a Mountain Rescue team, motorised evacuation (4X4, skidoo, quadbike or piste-basher, if accessible) or helicopter.
    a. A landing site for a helicopter must be as flat as possible, although no pilot will attempt to land on an unsuitable site. A winch rescue may be an option if a safe site is not available, as is often the case in Scotland!
    b. Tie everything down first (rucksacks, skis etc.). Pull down your hat, put on your gloves and wear your ski goggles. If something blows away as the helicopter approaches, leave it. If you chase loose items, the pilot may abandon the landing attempt.
    c. Use the standard helicopter rescue signals. Make yourself visible with your back to the wind and both arms in an extended 'Y' shape. Tell all others to crouch together next to the victim and gear.
    d. As the helicopter approaches you from downwind, maintain your position but drop down onto one knee once the pilot has seen you. You may be the pilot's only fixed point of reference, as the snow disturbed by the rotors reduces everyone's visibility.
    e. Once the helicopter has landed, follow all instructions from the crew. The pilot may or may not stop the engines and rotors. If you see no directions, stay in position.

Do not approach until or unless instructed or directed by the helicopter crew. It is more likely that a crew member will disembark and come to you. A helicopter is always approached from the front and loaded on the left (port) side.

Ticks

Ticks in Scotland can carry Lyme disease, and tick-borne encephalitis virus (TBEV) has been reported in the UK. Because of the milder climate, ticks are active throughout the year. If walking through vegetation late in the ski season, it is worth wearing long trousers with elasticated ankles, or applying insect repellent. Check for ticks at the end of the day and remove any found. An early indication of Lyme disease is a circular, outwardly expanding skin rash around the site of the bite. If you see this, see a doctor as soon as possible. There may be two phases associated with TBEV infection. The first phase is influenza-like symptoms, including fever, headache and fatigue. In a small number of cases this can lead to a more serious second phase that involves the central nervous system, potentially leading to meningitis, encephalitis and paralysis.

Safety Notes
By Heather Morning

Travelling on skis in the Scottish mountains can provide some of the most rewarding experiences of your life. But the often fickle and changeable conditions here favour the opportunist. The preparation is vigorous, the ascent more so, but the returns are immense for those willing to put the time and effort in.

Planning is key to achieving those amazing big descents or classic journeys, ensuring you are best placed to grab those rare opportunities when conditions are just right.

Most mountain safety advice will start with kit, weather, route ideas etc. But reflecting on why people get into difficulties (based on statistics from Scottish Mountain Rescue) starts with us, looking at human behaviour and how we interact with the world around us based on previous life experiences and complex social interactions.

This is known in psychology as heuristics: mental shortcuts that allow people to solve problems and make judgments quickly and efficiently. These rule-of-thumb strategies shorten decision-making time and allow people to function without constantly stopping to think about their next course of action, but they have both benefits and drawbacks.

Although they feature highly in current avalanche education, experience has shown that awareness of heuristic traps is something that even the most experienced can learn from, across all of their mountain decision-making.

The main heuristic traps are listed below, and as we become aware of them, we can take steps to avoid them.

- **Familiarity:** You know the area like the back of your hand and have skied the slope many times; it has always delivered great results, and you have never known anyone to be avalanched there – even though it is a 35-degree angle and on an aspect and altitude showing as a considerable avalanche risk today. You still commit and drop over the edge. But today might just be the day the slope avalanches. Consider another aspect and/or take precautionary measures (one member of the party at a time etc).

- **Over-commitment to a goal:** This is also known as being 'goal-oriented'. You have announced you are going to ski a route, gully or summit and after all that time and effort, you carry on, despite all the warning signs: poor visibility, windslab, fatigue, diminishing daylight ... The list is endless. The key is to take the blinkers off, see the bigger picture and make a value judgement not just based on 'the goal'. A positive way of not slipping into this trap is to plan several objectives for your day, so that as conditions change, you can adapt accordingly.

- **Peer pressure:** However comfortable we feel within a group, we are all exposed to peer pressure. No one wants to be the 'party pooper' or to be viewed as the weakest link. It is crucial to foster a culture of openness and honesty within your group so that everyone can contribute to decision-making and feel comfortable speaking out when they think things aren't right.

- **Scarcity:** This one is particularly relevant for Scottish conditions. Some lines rarely come into condition, and ensuring you are in the right place at the right time with the right people is a juggling act. You might get there and realise that the wind has picked up, forming windslab on that slope you planned to ski. There's a lot of pressure to ignore the obvious warning signs that conditions are not right. Combining scarcity with peer pressure and being goal-oriented is a potentially lethal combination.

- **Social proof:** Just because someone has skied a line before, or you can see tracks and/or people on the slope, does not mean that the line is safe. Make your own decisions based on the best information available to you at the time.

- **Expert halo:** It's not unusual for someone within a group to present as more experienced and knowledgeable than others. It might be that this person just has the loudest voice and the least experience! It's everyone's responsibility to make sure that they are involved in the decision-making process. And finally ...

- **Safety equipment:** It's easy to allow safety equipment to cloud your judgement. Does wearing that transceiver or airbag make you feel safer and influence your decisions?

In summary, heuristic traps can lead to even the most experienced people defying logic, knowledge and common sense in pursuit of their goals. Awareness of this tendency towards mental shortcuts and guarding against it could save your life.

Other Planning Resources

Weather and Conditions
Internet: There are numerous forecasts, and people often have their own favourites.
- BBC: www.bbc.co.uk/weather
- Mountain Weather Information Service: www.mwis.org.uk
- Met Office Mountain Forecast: www.metoffice.gov.uk
- Scottish Avalanche Information Service: www.sais.gov.uk

Other sites include:
- www.metcheck.com/uk
- www.yr.no (hourly weather maps)
- www.metvuw.com (six-hourly weather maps)

Radio:
- BBC Radio Scotland has the Highland News at 07:55 Monday to Friday, which ends with a very accurate forecast for the Highlands region. They also broadcast an excellent forecast for climbers, hillwalkers and sailors at 19:04 Monday to Friday, 07:04 and 22:04 on Saturday, and 07:04 and 20:04 on Sundays.

TV:
- BBC1's Reporting Scotland at 06:50 and 18:55 provides a good forecast for hillgoers.

Route Planning

Up-to-date conditions and ideas on route choice can be accessed at:
- British Backcountry:
  Facebook group: Britishbackcountry
  www.british-backcountry.co.uk
- Scottish Backcountry:
  www.facebook.com/ScottishBackcountry

Navigation

- Additional navigation information can be viewed at www.mountaineering.scot.
- Winter-specific navigation courses are available, provided by Mountaineering Scotland:
  www.mountaineering.scot

Equipment and Skills

It is assumed that people using this guide will have a working knowledge of the necessary equipment and skills required for ski journeys in the mountains. However, for information on this check out the snow sport touring pages on the Mountaineering Scotland website, which include numerous tips and YouTube videos on kit and ski techniques.

South east flank of Morven (skier, Fiona Neal) © Kevin Neal

Access

In 1993 the "Letterewe Accord" was struck between outdoor organisations and Paul Fentener van Vlissingen giving walkers and climbers unlimited access to his land, in exchange for a pledge of responsible conduct. This was the model for Part 1 of the Land Reform (Scotland) Act 2003 which gives people the right to access most land and inland water in Scotland, but these rights only apply if they behave responsibly while doing so, thereby complying with the Land Reform legislation. Land managers also have a legal duty to manage their land responsibly to allow responsible access.

Access rights are given for activities including hiking, climbing, skiing, camping, running and cycling, but don't include access with motor vehicles like cars, motorbikes or campervans. These access rights and responsibilities are explained in the Scottish Outdoor Access Code: www.outdooraccess-scotland.scot.

The key principles to remember are:
- Respect the interests of others (including businesses)
- Care for the environment
- Take responsibility for your own actions

As a skier in Scotland you can access most areas of land outwith the grounds (curtilages – usually the gardens, business premises, farmyards) of properties. Please also avoid areas where your presence might disturb livestock, or where stalking, forestry, windfarm construction or other operations are taking place.

Snowsports Touring and Walking in Managed Resorts in Scotland

Many ski tours in this second edition set off from some of Scotland's five managed ski areas, often because the approach roads end at altitude. Cairngorm, Glencoe, Glenshee, The Lecht and Nevis Range resorts all welcome tourers. Most run ski mountaineering events and they are keen to ensure this activity does not impact the safety and enjoyment of their downhill snowsports customers. Resorts have a business to run and take great pride in providing a quality experience for their paying customers.

In recent years with the growth in popularity of snowsport touring allied to a lack of snow, problems have occasionally arisen between different user groups and the operators of the five Scottish ski centres.

Where signed or touring/walking routes exist, please follow the route markers or reasonable advice from the ski patrol. For your own safety and the safety of other users, avoid crossing or going uphill on managed slopes while downhill skiing is taking place. Avoid ascending and descending slopes while the surface is being groomed. Resort operations may continue 24 hours a day, including during bad weather and whether the ski area is officially open or closed. Remember that after closing, the runs will have been prepared for the next day. Consider where you might be leaving tracks and how it affects the piste.

If you are unsure where to go within the resort area, ask a member of staff or ski patrol. They will be happy to help and will have information on the best and safest areas to ski.

You are encouraged to consider taking advantage of any touring ticket offers for ease of uplift through the managed areas.

In summary, you can walk, ski or snowboard wherever access rights apply but only where this does not interfere with the running of the business or downhill skiing use of ski resorts. Please minimise your impact on the environment, on other users, and on ski resort management operations.

Safety in Resorts

Mountaineering Scotland has produced a tourers' access code with the endorsement of resort managers and users to raise awareness of tourers' access rights and responsibilities and help everyone to stay safe, which is available on their website.

Within resort boundaries, you are bound by the International Ski Federation's Code of Conduct. Those skiing or snowboarding downhill have the right of way. Be especially aware of other skiers and snowboarders approaching from above who may not expect you to be there, especially in changeable weather (it is Scotland after all) and poor visibility.
- Respect all warning signs erected by the resorts, keep away from lift lines (even when they are closed) and stay out of roped-off areas. Ski resorts are not as safe when they are closed.
- Be alert for snowmobiles, piste bashers, groomer cables and other equipment. Stay clear of all grooming machines – do not assume the driver/operator can or has seen you. Grooming machines operating at night may use winch cables which are difficult to see and which may not be directly above the machine.
- Do not attempt to use a ski lift unless you have a valid lift ticket. Never get on a lift if it is unmanned as it might stop and may not start again.
- If there is no marked uphill route, stay outside the snow fence.

- Keep dogs under close control at all times. Dogs can be seriously injured by skis or snowboards and vice versa.
- Do not dig snow holes within resort boundaries. (Yes, this really has happened!)

Stalking, Shooting and Lambing

- **Deer stalking:** From 2023, male deer stalking can take place all year round. Most red deer stag stalking will continue to take place between July and mid-October, with increasing activity from August to mid-October. Red deer hind (female) stalking takes place from the 21st of October to the 15th of February. For up-to-date info on the area you want to ski go to: Heading For the Scottish Hills. There is no stalking on Sundays.

- **Rough shooting:** Shooting of rabbits, hares and pheasants etc. occurs in the winter months. If you suspect this is going on, then ask if it is alright to proceed.

- **Lambing:** It is important to avoid disturbing sheep during the lambing season, from March to May. Dogs should be kept on a lead near livestock throughout the year.

Fauna and Flora

Do not disturb nesting birds, especially the rarer species, such as golden eagle and peregrine falcon, between 1 February and 31 July. Wilful disturbance of nesting birds is a criminal offence. If convicted you face a maximum of £5,000 fine, six months in prison and confiscation of equipment (possibly including your car, skis, boots, avalanche transceiver, etc.).

Footpath Erosion

Part of the revenue from the sale of this and other SMC books is granted by the Scottish Mountaineering Trust as financial assistance towards the repair and maintenance of hill paths in Scotland. However, it is our responsibility to minimise our erosive effect for the enjoyment of future hill users.

Railway Crossings

Scottish access rights secured under the Land Reform (Scotland) Act 2003 don't apply to railway lines. Great care should be taken crossing railway tracks throughout Scotland. Always use underpasses, bridges and level crossings.

Below: Ptarmigan on the south side of Cairn Gorm (skier, Sophie Nicholson)
© George Reid

Camping, Litter and Pollution

Winter camping and snowholing enhance ski mountaineering. There are no crowds, and you can experience the beauty and tranquillity of a pristine winter environment. Responsible wild camping is permitted under access legislation, but do not camp near houses or in cultivated fields. When camping, take care not to cause pollution, and bury human waste carefully out of sight and far away from any habitation or watercourse. Avoid camping in ruined buildings and take everything home that you brought with you (and perhaps any rubbish you might find) and dispose of it properly. Leave as little trace of your stay as possible.

Cairns

The proliferation of navigation cairns detracts from the feeling of wildness and may be confusing rather than helpful for route-finding. The indiscriminate building of cairns on the hills is discouraged.

Bothies

The Mountain Bothies Association maintains bothies in many remote areas of Scotland. Information on these and the Mountain Bothies code of use can be found on www.mountainbothies.org.uk.

Car and Bicycle Use

Many roads in the mountains are single-track. Be courteous to other road users and pull over to allow overtaking – the car behind might have a doctor, fireman or coastguard responding to an emergency. Do not park in passing places or drive along private roads without permission. When parking avoid blocking access to private roads and land or causing any hazard to other road users. The use of bicycles is covered by access legislation (above). Bicycles can cause severe erosion when used 'off road' on footpaths and open hillsides and should only be used on vehicular or forest tracks.

Mountaineering Scotland

Mountaineering Scotland is the representative body for climbers and walkers in Scotland. One of its primary concerns is the continued free access to the hills and crags. Information about bird restrictions, stalking and general access issues can be obtained from the Mountaineering Scotland website, where you will also find contact details if you encounter problems with access.

High Public Road Access in Scotland

Accessing snow can be made easier by using public roads to get up high. Three of the four highest roads have large ski car parks (Glenshee, The Lecht and Cairngorm) allowing mid- and late-season access to many ski routes.

The highest Scottish road is the A93 Cairnwell Pass (670m) between Braemar and Spital of Glenshee. The pass benefits from a large fee-paying car park serving the Glenshee ski resort and can be accessed at various points from the roadside.

The A939 Cockbridge to Tomintoul road is the second-highest at The Lecht ski resort (644m). The route traversing Carn Ealasaid (p.223) is accessed from the road, which regularly features on winter news bulletins as it is often the first road to be closed by snow.

The third-highest Scottish road is the Bealach na Bà pass (626m). As far as is known, no ski routes have been recorded on this unclassified road.

The Cairngorm ski road reaches 610m at the upper car park and is one of the few high points that can be reliably reached by public transport, and the fourth-highest in Scotland (see Chapter 6).

The fifth-highest road is an unclassified (and unploughed) single-track road called the Lochan na Làirige. It connects Edramucky on Loch Tay with Bridge of Balgie in Glen Lyon and kisses the 550m contour (p.119, Ben Lawers). The route up Meall nan Tarmachan also starts from this road about 100 vertical metres lower and south of the high point.

Further south the B797 between Leadhills and Wanlockhead reaches the 468m contour near the (locked) access road to the summit of Green Lowther (p.53). The featured route lies on the opposite face of the peak, but the smooth tarmac summit access road is a possible skiing option with thin snow cover.

The well-travelled A9 Pass of Drumochter (460m) between Dalwhinnie and Blair Atholl has rarely been closed by adverse weather in recent years. Being in the centre of the country the roadside slopes hold snow well and allow vehicle access to a large number of roadside ski routes from convenient parking laybys on the A9 trunk road. Trains and buses disembark at, or near, Dalwhinnie, which lies about 8km north of the Drumochter Pass.

Earlier in the season, when there has been a heavy fall of snow, many other Scottish roads will give good access to countless local hills. Using public transport, the West Highland line transits Corrour railway station at 408m and is the highest point on the rail network, giving access to a number of routes (see chapter 7) and the traverse route from Corrour to Dalwhinnie. Dalwhinnie railway station sits at 351m and gives excellent access to The Fara (p.155).

Below: Coire Fionn, Glenshee © Robbie Hearns

Equipment

This guidebook should not be relied upon as a source of detailed information on skiing and snowboarding equipment. Earlier partisan or tribal division over Alpine Touring or Freeheel/Telemark/Nordic bindings and skis has now been joined by the splitboard revolution for snowboards, or snowboarders using snowshoes for ascents. Ski mountaineering does suggest skis of some kind, but as editor I limit my advice on choosing skis and boards to simply making sure that you pick ones with metal edges.

Types of Skis, Bindings and Boots

Alpine Touring (AT) set-ups are the most popular, largely because of their overall performance on downhill, flat and uphill terrain. The lightest AT set-ups originate from the world of Skimo racing and are as light as other comparable options, including most Nordic mountain touring gear (Skimo gear cannot deliver the same downhill control as more mainstream AT alternatives). Telemark systems cover a wide range of ski, binding and boot combinations from relatively lightweight to heavier downhill-orientated set-ups. Nordic mountain skis differ from AT and Telemark skis because of their 'double camber', which makes them very efficient for the 'kick and glide' technique on rolling hills and plateaux and will often be the best choice for this type of terrain. The double camber, however, makes downhill turns significantly harder.

AT bindings lock the heels down for better control on downhill sections and release the heel for flat and uphill progress. AT boots have rigid soles, and the binding allows the boot to pivot at the toe. Telemark and Nordic bindings are freeheel, meaning the boots are never locked down onto the ski. Flat and uphill travel is facilitated by the boots flexing, in the same way a walking boot flexes.

Alpine Touring

- **Skis:** AT skis have continually evolved ever since they were originally developed, but improved construction methods and combinations of materials have recently accelerated this progression. The trend for ever-wider skis has now plateaued, thankfully, but it has forced manufacturers to consider their side cut and front shovel widths. Ski mountaineering skis vary from around 80mm to over 100mm below the foot. The extra surface area of wider skis helps floatation in powder snow, giving a desirable three-dimensional experience. This does occur in Scotland, just not very often! The main disadvantage is that wider skis are typically heavier and a little harder to manage while skinning uphill on firm snow. The sidecut of a ski is important to consider, as more significant sidecut has been associated – in both ski racers and recreational skiers – with a higher prevalence of injuries to knee ligaments. Overall, knee injuries represent a very high proportion of total ski injuries (as I can personally attest), and continue to be an important consideration in alpine skiing. Using skis with less significant sidecut potentially provides additional protection against injury. Having less significant sidecut is also more efficient when skinning, as the skis will track better in a straight line.

    All ski touring involves off-piste skiing, and a choice then arises of using off-piste or ski touring skis. Both have similar sidecuts, but off-piste skis perform better by holding an edge on harder snow and being more stable at higher speeds. However, they are heavier. Some ski touring skis are now very light but are less technical and perform less well. The lighter option is a huge benefit when carrying or skinning uphill, and your final decision will be a personal choice balancing these factors. For day tours, including most of the routes found in this guide, off-piste skis are perhaps a good place to start.

- **Bindings:** Most AT bindings have an emergency release mechanism to prevent lower limb injuries and must be carefully matched with the boots you choose. Weight is again an issue, and in 1990 the modern pin binding (known as 'tech') was first produced by Dynafit®. The anterior pins eliminated the heavy 'frame' or 'plate' most touring bindings then used to hold the boot toe and heel, although some lighter models are still available. The pin design also reduced the work needed to lift up the heavy plate heel unit with each step. The binding allowed ski touring to go from an activity few would endure, to a sport most could enjoy, although pin bindings can be finicky when used in deep snow. The original patent expired in 2010, and now most ski equipment manufacturers produce a pin binding. Look for a pin binding which includes a toe-piece DIN setting adjustment.

    Most AT bindings have heel risers, sometimes in two or three stages, to raise your foot angle when ascending steeper ground and reduce the strain on your calves.

    There are devices such as Alpine Trekkers or Secure-fix which clip into ordinary downhill ski bindings; many ski mountaineers have a pair stowed in a cupboard, but they are only really useful for short tours. However, they are a good way to introduce a piste skiing companion to ski touring.

Ski bindings often have integral ski brakes, but if not, then ski leashes must be used to prevent runaway skis from being lost or injuring people below you. Even with ski brakes fitted it is still possible to lose a ski, and leashes are more reliable, although there is a theoretical possibility of being injured by a flailing ski in the event of a fall.

- **Harscheisen:** The binding also holds Harscheisen or ski crampons: metal blades which fit to the bindings and allow uphill progress on icy slopes when the grip of your climbing skins starts to fail – a common issue in Scotland.

- **Boots:** AT boots are a cross between a downhill ski boot and a mountaineering boot and are now easily good enough to be used on-piste. Boots typically have a 'walk mode', where the ankle cuff providing the forward cant, or lean required for effective downhill skiing, can be released to allow the skier to stand upright when walking or skinning. Indeed, many piste ski boots now also have this feature. There are many manufacturers with a wide variety of ski touring models; some are made for comfort, others are stiffer and better for steep skiing. Backcountry or off-piste ski boots are also made with the added metal inserts for pin (tech) bindings, so are another option.

- **Ski poles, sticks or batons:** Ordinary downhill ski poles are more than adequate, and are useful for walking when carrying skis. Heavier-duty models should last longer than lighter ones. The baskets of off-piste poles tend to be larger to give better purchase on softer snow, so opt for baskets of 8–10cm diameter (or even wider) rather than the more usual 5–6cm size used for piste skiing. Telescopic ski poles are useful for long traversing ascents (shorten the uphill and lengthen the downhill) and are very light, although the pole adjustment system is considered by many to be just something else to go wrong! Various modern backcountry/off-piste poles have longer handles, sometimes ribbed, thereby avoiding the need for adjustment, but this involves holding the bottom or middle of the elongated handle when downhill skiing. Telescopic alloy poles should be dismantled at the end of the day to allow the sections to dry out and prevent internal corrosion of the tubing. Some poles are now so light that it is no real burden to carry a spare telescopic pole, or a pair if you are snowboarding to help with uphill travel.

- **Climbing skins:** Happily, modern climbing skins are made from mohair (the hair of Angora goats) or nylon, so no seals are now harmed during their production. The skins need to be trimmed to exactly fit your skis so that the metal ski edges are clear for traversing on hard snow. They have a layer of non-setting glue on their fitting surface to attach them to the base of your skis when ascending, and clips at the toe and usually the heel. For descents, the skins are removed and folded, ready for the next climb. Skin wax can be used to prevent snow from sticking to them, which can be a problem when they remain wet from an earlier ascent, or when transitioning up through the freezing level from a wet snowpack lower on the hill.

- **'Approach' shoes:** For spring skiing in Scotland, when snow-lines are receding uphill, or for long approach walks along forestry roads to get to open terrain, a pair of lightweight shoes can be very useful. Your ski touring boots can be carried on your skis, mounted on the bindings. Over any distance of more than a couple of kilometres or height gain over about 200–300m, this system may prove to be more efficient than walking in ski boots, despite the extra weight on your back.

Fell running shoes with good tread are ideal. They are very lightweight and easy to carry in your pack when skiing. As they are usually not at all waterproof it is essential to carry a spare pair of dry socks to change into before skiing.

Snowboards and Splitboards

These days, snowboarders have two main alternatives for touring: use a splitboard which is split into two skis for uphill skinning and then reassembled for downhill boarding, or carry the snowboard, using either snowshoes, short skis or boots (bootpacking) for uphill travel. Carrying a snowboard on your back or in your hands in typical Scottish winter weather (i.e. windy!) can be extremely difficult and needs careful consideration. A splitboard keeps your board on the ground, and with much greater availability, better technology and lower prices these days, this may be the best option.

Choosing a board with some camber, to provide better edge control and easier turning in hard snow, is probably a good idea. Rocker-only boards are good in powder, but realistically pure powder is very unusual in Scotland. Unlike skiers, snowboarders have no real choice about board width, as the downhill board needs to match the width for your boot length. Look for a splitboard with a reliable and easy-to-use system for reassembly, as this can be tricky in a winter blizzard. Ideally, go for one with clamps that are less likely to get bumped or damaged when the board is split into skis for skinning.

Splitboard bindings and interfaces have become much more user-friendly, and many have a 'puck' design. With these systems you slide the binding onto a rail for downhill boarding and attach the toe with clamped pins for uphill skinning. Choose a simple system that will be easy to use in cold conditions and that is not prone to icing up. You'll already be slower than skiers at making transitions! It is recommended that you buy interfaces and bindings together as a package or at least from the same manufacturer. As with ski touring bindings, all splitboard bindings come with heel risers for uphill skinning. Though not essential, consider some form of heel lockdown to make short downhill sections easier (whether with or without skins). Unlike with ski mountaineering equipment, the changeover from walk to downhill mode is on the binding, not on the boot.

Poles are essential for backcountry snowboarders as well, and they absolutely need to be collapsible. Splitboarders won't be able to skin uphill without them, but most of the time on the downhill you will want them stowed in your rucksack. Occasionally it can be helpful to have them to hand for propulsion through short flatter sections of terrain or for balance when stationary, but be aware that finger injuries are possible in harder snow conditions if you have poles in your hand and your hand contacts the snow.

The vast majority of snowboarders use soft boots these days, and for touring they are a better choice than hard boots. They have two major advantages over skiers – you can just use your piste boots and do not need to buy a second pair of touring boots, and, of course, they are much more comfortable to walk in and when skinning.

Being much softer and more flexible than ski boots, snowboarders are likely to need to use boot crampons more often than skiers in the icy conditions common in Scotland. Several crampon manufacturers are now making wide-fitting crampons for snowboard boots, which are worth considering. You'll need C1 crampons with a full strap-on system, as snowboard boots are too flexible for step-in designs. To make sure the fit is good, it is highly recommended to have your snowboard boots with you when buying crampons.

Above: Winter waiting room at Corrour train station, Inverness Backcountry Snowsports Club © Al Todd

Helmet

Ski helmets have become more popular in recent years, and it is now more usual than not to wear a helmet when downhill skiing/boarding. The primary reason to wear a helmet is to protect your head, although no helmet can guarantee freedom from concussion or head injury. They can also keep your head warm, and light construction makes them comfortable to wear. All helmets are CE1077-, Snell RS-98- or ASTM F 2040-certified, ensuring good protection for your head. Many modern helmets have air vents which can be opened to cool you down or left closed to make the helmet warmer. Ski helmets have a strap that goes under the chin to hold the helmet firmly on your head, and to ensure it stays on in the event of a crash. The straps should be adjusted to the correct length so that the helmet is comfortable, and the two ends lock together with a buckle. On most helmets your ski goggles go around the outside of the helmet and can be secured with a goggle mount at the back.

Do not decorate (paint or put stickers on) your helmet without checking with the manufacturer, as the solvent in the paint or adhesive may ruin the safety shell. If a helmet is damaged in any way, it must be replaced. Some manufacturers now make ski touring-specific helmets. Wearing a helmet is recommended in descent.

Digital and Paper Map

These items are essential for navigation and should be carried as standard. Some online mapping resources also show slopes of over 30 degrees, which will be more likely to avalanche. They can often be printed to help with safe route planning. GPS is a very useful tool but cold conditions and an extended day may deplete the battery and care is required to avoid this, hence the need for a map and compass and the ability to navigate in poor visibility. Do not store your compass with your mobile phone, which has components that behave like a magnet.

Ice Axe and Boot Crampons

In addition to harcheisen or ski crampons, practice and competence with an axe and boot crampons are essential, and crampons should be test-fitted to boots before setting out. Although the anticipated conditions on the planned route may not indicate the need for axe and crampons, unexpected conditions, a change of route, a navigation error or a rescue can lead you onto steep or icy terrain. An ice axe and boot crampons are recommended for all ski touring.

First Aid Kit, Survival Bag, Headtorch

As with all mountain activities, a small first aid kit should be carried, including a survival bag, whistle, headtorch, pain relievers, hydrocolloid blister plasters, general plasters and bandages.

Repair Kit

A small multi-tool along with wire, cable ties, thin cord, duct tape (often gently wrapped around a ski pole shaft) can be useful and may allow continued skiing instead of a long walk to your destination in the event of equipment failure.

Mobile Phone, Satellite Phone or Messenger, Personal Locator Beacon (PLB)

Mobile phone carriage is now ubiquitous and, irrespective of your phone network provider, can be used in an emergency to summon help, provided there is general network coverage. If there is none, ascending to the nearest ridge or summit may allow you to use your phone to call for help. A satellite phone or satellite messenger should enable you to raise the alarm when there is no mobile coverage, and to also receive a reply. A PLB will send your location to a central office which will raise the alarm, but you will not receive confirmation that your message has been received.

Carrying a power bank (mobile charger) and lead is a good idea to ensure your mobile phone will continue to function.

Food and Drink

It is important to stay rehydrated and well fed. Ski touring can be just as dehydrating as summer hillwalking, so always carry replacement fluids.

Rucksack

Depending on your planned route, a rucksack of 25–40 litres is good for a day route. It should be big enough to carry skins, Harscheisen, axe, crampons, avalanche rescue kit, first aid kit, food and drink, spare clothing, sun hat etc. Make sure it has a waist belt and a chest strap to keep it in place when skiing. Some rucksacks intended for skiing have accessory straps which pull the shoulder straps tight onto your body, aiding stability. A larger model will be needed if carrying camping equipment. To allow carriage of skis, avoid a sack with side pockets and make sure there are sufficient and robust straps to hold a pair of skis, poles and an ice axe.

Clothing

Clothing should be multi-layered to enable adjustment for changing temperatures due to height, wind or physical effort. Wear a base layer of synthetic fabric or merino wool (avoid cotton, which does not dry easily). Mid-layers can be fleece tops and trousers, and an outer shell made of waterproof and windproof material is essential (jacket with hood and overtrousers or salopettes). A warm hat, gloves or mitts and spares are essential. Goggles are invaluable when travelling into the wind, and sunglasses are required on bright days (even if the sun is not visible). Consider taking a sun hat, suncream and lip salve when the weather dictates.

Avalanche Rescue Gear
Regular training and good equipment will maximise your chances of saving buried avalanche victims. An avalanche transceiver or beacon, avalanche probe and snow shovel are essential safety gear for every ski tourer. All team members must know how to use them to find and recover someone buried by an avalanche.

Avalanche transceivers or avalanche beacons are both a transmitter and receiver in one unit. Since 1986, transceivers have all used 457 kHz for finding people buried under avalanche snow. At the start of the day, all skiers in the group must check that their transceivers are in transmit mode. Transceivers are worn under outer clothing and transmit low-power pulsed radio signals. After an avalanche, if some members of the group are buried, the others switch their transceivers from transmit to receive mode and search for signals coming from the buried people. There are many manufacturers and models on the market, and you must read the instructions and practice in a safe place beforehand.

Transceivers are sensitive to magnetic and electrical interference so they should be worn as far away as possible from items such as mobile phones, radios, GPS, smart watches, car keys, heated gloves etc.

Transceivers are not a preventive measure against possible avalanche burial, and if you have to use one, then an error in route choice has already been made! However, they may reduce the amount of time victims remain buried under snow, hopefully making survival more likely.

With suitable training digital transceivers are simple to use. They take the strength of the signal and the transmitted dipole flux pattern and display both distance and direction to the buried transceiver. They also allow for multiple burial searches as they can differentiate between transceivers.

Several digital beacons are also equipped with an 'extra' frequency called W-Link. This frequency broadcasts additional details to other transceivers capable of receiving the W-Link signal. These include a wearer's 'vital signs' and movements in the victim, such as a heartbeat.

Remember to switch off your transceiver when you are safe at the end of your tour.

A robust metal-bladed snow shovel is essential as the loss of energy in an avalanche often results in the debris snow hardening. It can also be used at the start of the day to clear a parking space at the roadside as required.

Avalanche probes are typically made of light thin walled aluminum alloy or carbon fibre tubing robust enough to probe through avalanche debris for buried victims. They have a central quick release wire which holds the probe rigid when in use and they vary from about 250 to 350cm cm in length.

Airbag System (ABS)
An ABS is an integral part of a safety system built into a skiing rucksack. If caught in an avalanche, the victim pulls an emergency handle on the airbag (essential action which is by no means guaranteed). You need to free a hand from one of your ski poles to pull the emergency handle. Once manually triggered the airbag inflates, thereby reducing the skier's overall density and potentially enabling them to rise to the top of the snow of the avalanche. Often the brightly-coloured airbags reach the surface, allowing companions to find victims more easily. An airbag offers an enhanced level of safety but relies on the victim having the presence of mind to trigger it. The disadvantage is the extra weight carried, although later models are gradually becoming lighter.

Right: Ascending Meall Garbh from the south (skier, Al Todd)
© Graeme Gatherer

Chapter 1

South Scotland

Previous spread:
Buchan Hill
(skier, Craig Cameron)
© Ross Dolder

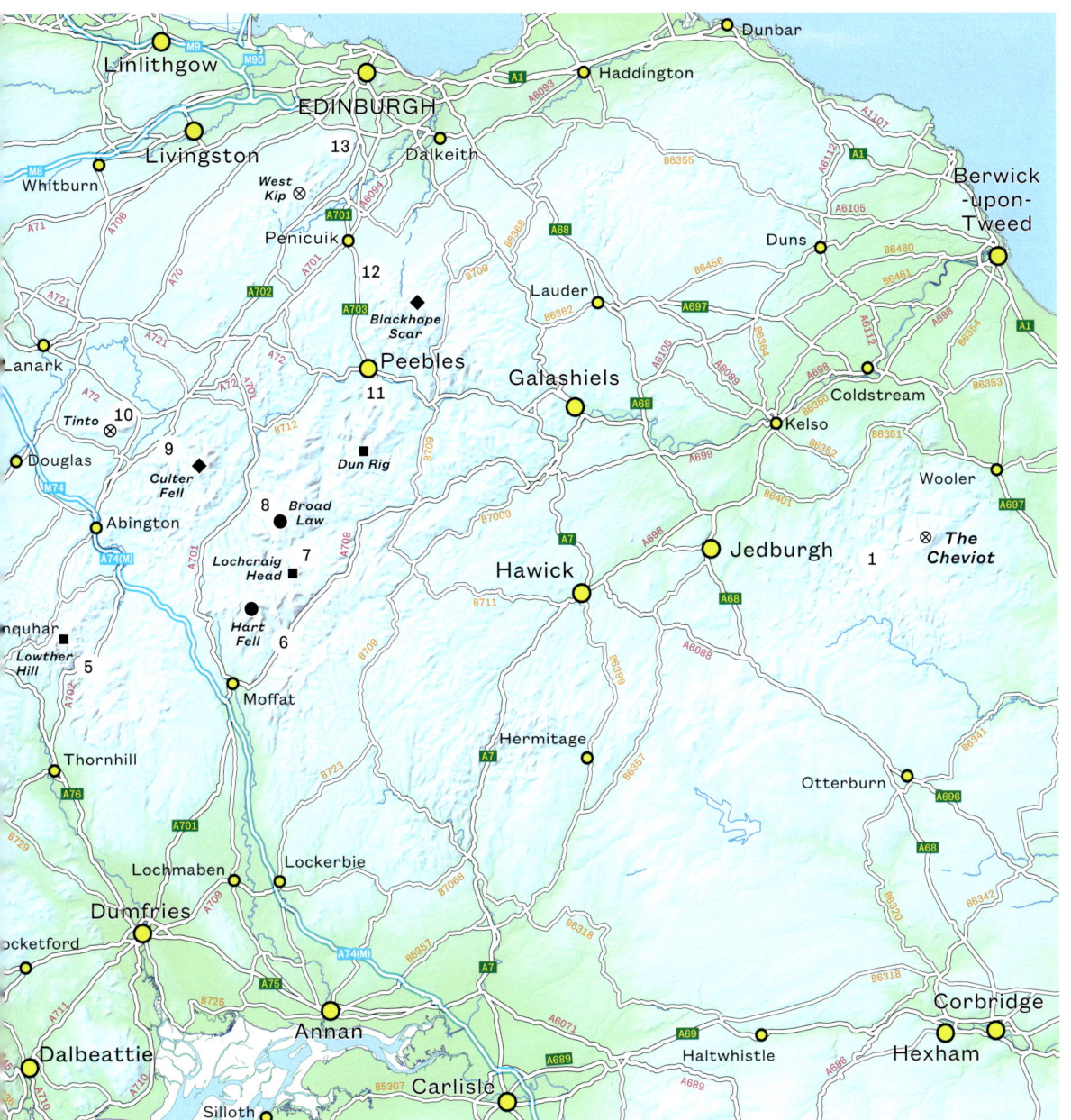

1.	The Cheviot	P.44
2.	The Merrick	P.45
3.	Corserine	P.50
4.	Cairnsmore of Carsphairn	P.52
5.	Lowther Hill	P.53
6.	Hart Fell	P.54
7.	Lochcraig Head	P.54
8.	Broad Law	P.56
9.	Culter Fell	P.57
10.	Tinto Hill	P.58
11.	Dun Rig	P.59
12.	The Moorfoots	P.60
13.	The Pentlands	P.64

The Cheviot

⊗ 815m
△ NT 908 205
↗ LR74, LR80
🌐 P.44

🅿 Up the Bowmont Valley at Cocklawfoot
(NT 851 186/55.4614, -2.2361)

↔ 13KM   △ 575M   ↕ 240M
🕐 5-6 HRS   GRADE III   ★★

By Colwyn Jones

Including a ski tour on The Cheviot in this book might seem misguided as the summit of this sturdy peak actually lies in England. However, one possible starting point lies in Scottish territory at Cocklawfoot. Go down the minor road off the B6401 about 12km south of the village (confusingly called Town Yetholm), close to the north end of the Pennine Way, which ends at Kirk Yetholm. The Cocklawfoot road is single-track with passing places.

An interesting cleft in the north face of The Cheviot is known as Bizzle Crags, and this exposed mass of granite has seen several winter fatalities, including the so-called Bizzle Avalanche on Sunday, 7 February 1988, when hard-packed snow slid beneath a group as they climbed up the side of the crag. Two of the group died, and two others were seriously injured.

Despite path improvements with stone slabs, a summer ascent of The Cheviot is typically a wet, boggy route; therefore, a ski ascent when the ground is frozen has much to commend it. If the roads are passable park considerately on the roadside close to the turning for the farm at Cocklawfoot. Head east on a good landrover track past the farm, then abandon the track to continue east up the steep Mallie Side (452m) and then on to the Pennine Way, roughly following a fence along the border (favouring either Scotland or England as snow conditions or preference dictates). At just above the 700m contour, the Pennine Way turns north-west at a junction of paths and fences (NT 896 193; 743m). Follow a spur that crosses the border to the triangulation station, which is raised on a substantial breeze block plinth, although part of this may be hidden under snow.

To descend, retrace your ascent route as far as the path/fence junction, and from here there are three options: 1. Continue to follow your ascent route to give a good run back down to the farm at Cocklawfoot. 2. If conditions allow, from the path/fence junction head directly west into the valley of the Cheviot Burn and back to the farm. 3. Follow the border fence down to the cairn at King's Seat (531m), then follow the line of the Kingsseat Burn back to the landrover track and so to the farm.

Other starting points (in Northumbria) are from the eastern Harthope Burn and northern College Valley. The College Valley involves a long approach (where a bicycle might help) but with the possibility of a circular tour from the head of the valley. Visiting Bizzle Crag on ascent, take in the summit of The Cheviot and return via The Hen Hole, a similar rocky feature to Bizzle.

Top: The Cheviot above the Bowmont Valley and the Border Ridge
© Colin Lesenger

The Galloway Hills

The Merrick ● 843m
Fingered or Branched Hill

△ NX 428 855   ◁ LR77   ⊕ P.46

P Bruce's Monument car park from Glen Trool village (NX 415 804 / 55.0930, -4.4844).

↔ 14KM   △ 800M   ⊥ 130M
⏱ 6-8 HRS   GRADE II/III   ★★

By Stephen Reid, John Biggar and Ross Dolder

The relatively unknown south-west corner of Scotland contains three major ranges of hills of interest to ski mountaineers. The rounded grassy Moffat and Lowther Hills lie east and west of the M74, respectively, while the more rugged Galloway Hills are found much further west, beyond Dumfries and Castle Douglas. Conditions suitable for ski touring in these compact but unfrequented mountain ranges are not that common but do occur most winters and can occasionally be absolutely magnificent. High grassy plateaux, flanks and ridges make for reasonable skiing given a modicum of snow cover and, while it is usual to have to walk some way to gain good snow, it is not unknown to be able to don skis at the roadside. Many tours and variations have been made in this area – those described here are just a selection of the best.

At 843m and just short of Munro status, The Merrick is the highest peak in the Galloway Hills and an obvious ski mountaineering target. It can be approached from Glen Trool to the south or from Kirriereoch to the west.

From Glen Trool (6–8 hours): A fine route with spectacular scenery and very reliable in its upper half due to the drystone wall, which usually retains a good ribbon of snow in its shade long after the rest of the hillside is brown. Follow the tourist path from Bruce's Monument car park (NX 415 804) and head north along the west bank of Buchan Burn to a point (NX 416 817) where the path diverges from the burn and leads up through woods to the bothy of Culsharg (NX 415 821). From here the track follows the Whiteland Burn through further woods to emerge on open moorland and a junction with a drystone wall (NX 409 836) that runs from Bennan to Benyellary. Turn right (north-east) along this to the summit of Benyellary (NX 414 839) and continue to follow the wall over the Neive of the Spit to a point (NX 419 847) where it turns due north. Carry on north-east to the summit of The Merrick (NX 428 855).

Return may be made by the same route or, if cover is very good, head south-east to a point (NX 438 845) at the north end of the Rig of Loch Enoch. Follow this fine ridge southwards to the summit of Buchan Hill (NX 429 819; 493m) from where a grand ski run south-west returns you to the car park with only the crossing of Buchan Burn to negotiate.

From Kirriereoch (8–10 hours): A more testing route than that via Glen Trool, but spectacular and with the possibility of an excellent steep descent down the West Face of The Merrick. From the public car park and picnic spot (NX 358 866; 170m) near Kirriereoch Loch, follow the track, branching left at a fork, to Kirriereoch Farm gate. Don't enter the farmyard but take the track which passes in front of it and turn right almost immediately. Continue on this track for about 1km to the next junction, just before a bridge over Kirriemore Burn. Turn right, cross the bridge and turn left immediately along a track, which may not

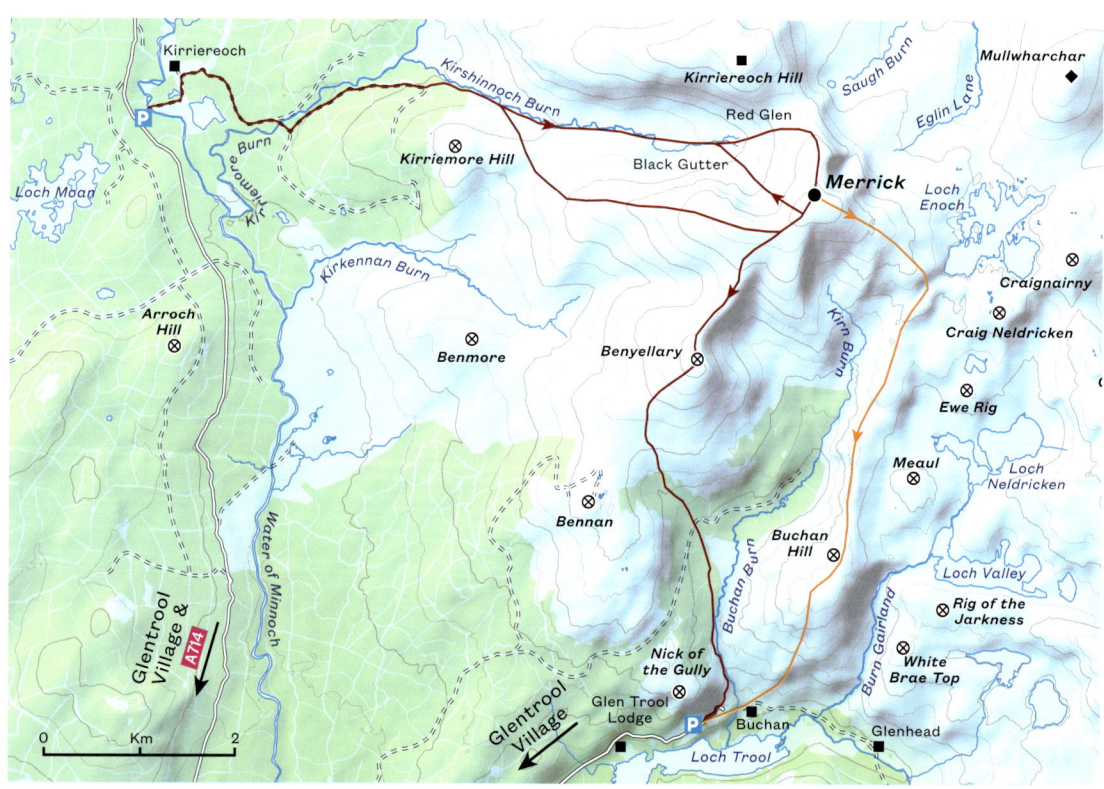

Below: The Merrick (skiers, Kenny Livingston, Dave McNicol and Linda Biggar) © John Biggar

be marked on the OS map, for about 1.5km until it doglegs sharply back on itself (NX 386 868). A firebreak drops down from here to the Kirshinnoch Burn. Follow the burn easily up the valley, passing the spectacular ice climbing crag of the Black Gairy, which lies to the right, until zigzagging up steeper ground at the head of the valley leads to the base of the Little Spear (NX 428 859), the steep north ridge of The Merrick. Exposed skinning/cramponing up this leads to the OS trig point at the summit.

From here there are two main descents. The first, which gives an excellent easy-angled long downhill run, is to follow the west ridge of The Merrick, passing along the top of the Black Gairy to a dip (NX 398 859) just before Kirriemore Hill, then head north-east to Kirshinnoch Burn and rejoin the route of ascent, which is reversed to the starting point. The second is to descend the steep 30-degree West Face of The Merrick, which lies only 50m or so from the summit and slightly south due west of it. This gives probably the longest steep ski run in the Galloway Hills, and certainly the most exhilarating, passing under the Black Gairy to join the route of ascent at Kirshinnoch Burn. The downside of this route is that the remainder of the descent is rather flat, but good route-finding will ensure a minimum of poling is required.

Below: Ron Kenyon skinning past Black Gairy on the way up The Merrick from Kirriereoch © Stephen Reid

Corserine

● 814m

Crossing point of the Rhinns of Kells

△ NX 497 871　　　◁ LR77　　　⊕ P.51

🅿 Forrest Lodge car park, a few miles west of the A713 (NX 553 863 / 55.1495, -4.2725).

↔ 14KM　　　△ 760M　　　↕ 150M
🕒 6-7 HRS　　　GRADE III　　　**

By Stephen Reid, John Biggar and James Kinnaird

The Rhinns of Kells range, being largely grassy on the summit ridges, is better suited to ski touring in marginal conditions than much of the Galloway Hills, and a good day out may be had fairly soon after heavy snowfall. Corserine is the highest summit, and though it makes a good objective in its own right, a most enjoyable day includes it in a tour of the central part of the ridge.

Park at Forrest Lodge car park. Go south-west on foot along the track, passing Burnhead, and continue straight on, heading south on track and path to reach the edge of the forestry and a stile (NX 534 838). Continue steeply up the hillside bearing slightly left to a wall, which is followed over Meikle Lump and on to the top of Meikle Millyea (NX 518 829; 746m). Turn north-north-west and follow the ridge along and over Milldown (NX 511 839; 738m) and Millfire (NX 508 848; 716m). It is probably not worth taking skins off for the slight descents along the ridge before approaching the summit of Corserine.

From Corserine, ski south-south-east until you reach the head of Hawse Burn. Keep west of the fence and lower part of the burn to reach a stile (NX 513 852) and footbridge (NX 515 853) at a point marked 'waterfall' on the OS 1:25,000 map. Cross the bridge and follow a path to a memorial, whence Forest Road (marked as a path on current maps) leads to Burnhead and the car park. This circuit is equally good in reverse.

The Rhinns of Kells Traverse

🕒 (7-8 HRS)

A superb ski mountaineering day in spectacular scenery with many possible extensions and variations. Of course, it can also be done in reverse.

Two cars are required. Leave one car at the Forrest Lodge car park. Travel in the second car north up the A713 through Carsphairn and park on the A713 near Brochloch (NX 538 961; 230m). Follow a vehicle track downhill to cross a bridge over Carsphairn Lane (NX 528 964), then after 400m turn left and begin climbing southwards on a track for about 1.5km until you can break westwards onto the open hill and eventually the top of Knockower (NX 516 943). Continue in a south-westerly direction to the first main summit of the Rhinns, Coran of Portmark (NX 509 936; 623m). The ridge now runs more or less due south over the summits of Meaul (NX 500 909; 695m), Carlin's Cairn (NX 496 884; 807m), Corserine (NX 497 871; 814m), Milldown (NX 511 839; 738m) and Meikle Millyea (NX 518 829; 746m). From this last summit, follow a north-easterly course towards Meikle Lump from where various descents can be made depending on how the snow is lying, but head for the edge of the forestry and a stile (NX 534 838). Once on the track, turn right and take the second left, which leads back past Burnhead to the car park.

Three main alternatives to the route described above are as follows:

1. To shorten the day by about 2 hours, descend directly from the top of Corserine and follow the Hawse Burn (see above).
2. To avoid tedious walking through forestry, park the first car at Clenrie (NX 556 825; 210m), though this gives less opportunity for a steep finishing ski run.
3. The truly complete ridge traverse would require unusually good snow cover and involves finishing over Little Millyea (NX 512 811; 578m) and Darrou (NX 507 801; 479m), then finding your way through forestry to the track junction at NX 496 795 and a bridge over the River Dee. Cross the river, turn left and a further couple of kilometres bring you to the public car park at Craigencaillie House (NX 504 782).

Key

1. Corserine　　　P.50
2. Carsphairn　　　P.52

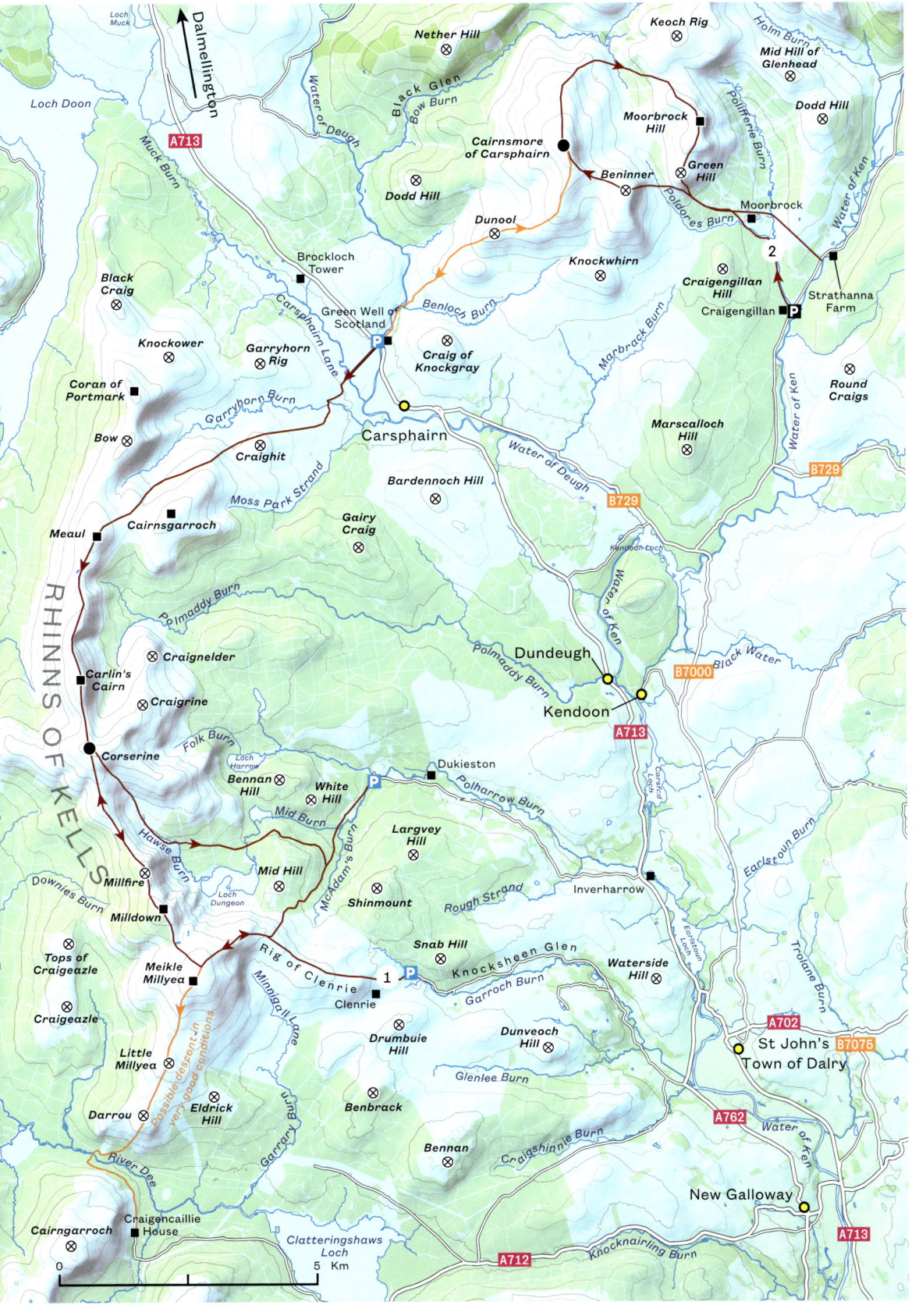

Cairnsmore of Carsphairn ● 797m
Big Cairn of the Alder Glen

△ NX 594 979 ◁ LR77 🌐 P.51

🅿 If from Carsphairn, park in a lay-by off the A713 just north of Carsphairn village at Green Well of Scotland (NX 557 945/55.2242, -4.2694). If via Moorbrock Farm, see the options below.

↔ 8KM   △ 600M   ⊤ 200M
⏱ 4-5 HRS   GRADE II

By Stephen Reid, John Biggar and James Kinnaird

This hill can be a good choice for a shorter day, or after a recent snowfall when the start and finish on the A713 means there are less likely to be access problems.

From Carsphairn: From the lay-by, follow the farm track north-eastwards for about 2km until you reach a small burn on the north side of Willieanna. This leads to a small col (NX 576 959), then more steeply onto the summit of Dunool (NX 580 964; 541m). Go along the flat ridge eastwards (often via a snow ribbon behind the wall), then up onto the Black Shoulder and finally to the summit of Cairnsmore of Carsphairn (NX 594 979; 797m).

The best descents are either by the ascent route, often with a fine steep run off the nose of Dunool, or by the west-facing slopes directly under the summit, to pick up the head of the farm track (NX 578 971) then enjoy a long glide back to the car.

Via Moorbrock Farm: A better option if the snow cover is good and the minor road off the B729 is clear, it takes in three summits and gives some excellent skiing. Two tracks lead to Moorbrock Farm (NX 629 966). The first, from Craigengillan (NX 637 947; 210m), is not so obvious and involves turning off right over an old stone bridge that may not last many more winters. The second lies 500m further along the minor road (NX 640 952) and is better. Follow either track to the farm, go through the farmyard, cross a ford and turn left along a forestry track that skirts the edge of Green Hill (NX 616 973), a southerly outlier of Moorbrock Hill. When almost opposite the broken crag of Beninner Gairy, ski down a firebreak and cross the Poldores Burn. From here, Beninner Gairy may be outflanked by long detours north or south – better to don crampons and make a direct ascent of the rocky ridge to the summit of Beninner (NX 605 971; 710m). A gentle descent westwards and ascent north-westwards leads to the top of Cairnsmore of Carsphairn.

Opposite top: Never mind the Tussocks, Cairnsmore of Carsphairn. (skiers, John Biggar and James Kinnaird) © Stephen Reid

descents. The only drawback is that these slopes are mainly south-facing, so this is definitely a midwinter tour.

With two cars a through-route could be skied in about the same time. From the starting point, climb north and slightly westwards to reach Comb Head, then continue westwards to Cold Moss (NS 898 094; 628m). A shallow descent leads to the peat-hag-filled col at NS 894 098, then climb the south-east flank of Lowther Hill (NS 889 106; 725m) to the buildings on the summit.

There are several good descent lines off Cold Moss and Comb Head, depending on snow cover (3–4 hours return). For a longer option, from the summit of Lowther Hill continue north-east to Green Lowther (NS 900 120; 732m) and return via the same route, or venture further over Peden Head, Dungrain Law, Dun Law (NS 917 137; 677m), White Law and Louise Wood Law (NS 932 153; 618m) to a second car parked on the B7040 1km west of Elvanfoot at a side bridge over Elvan Water (NS 929 174; 310m).

Return by skiing down the long north ridge of Currie Rig before turning east, heading for a gap in the forestry and regaining the forestry track near where it crosses Black Burn. Follow the burn up to a saddle on Moorbrock Hill and head south to the summit (NX 620 983; 650m). A long ski down the south face of Moorbrock Hill regains the forest track, which is followed to Moorbrock Farm and thence the road. With two cars available routes 1 and 2 could be combined to give a fine traverse of the range.

Lowther Hill ■ 725m

△ NS 889 106	◁ LR71, LR78	⊕ P.53
P On the A702, approximately 1km west of the Dalveen Pass high point (NS 906 083/55.3567, -3.7264).		
↔ 8KM	△ 370M	↥ 320M
⏱ 3–4 HRS	GRADE III	**

By Stephen Reid and John Biggar

Lowther Hill, one of the highest points of the Lowther Hills range, makes a good short tour. It can be climbed up gentle slopes from the village of Wanlockhead (NS 873 129; 420m) to the north-west, but the steeper and more interesting terrain to the south near Dalveen Pass makes for better

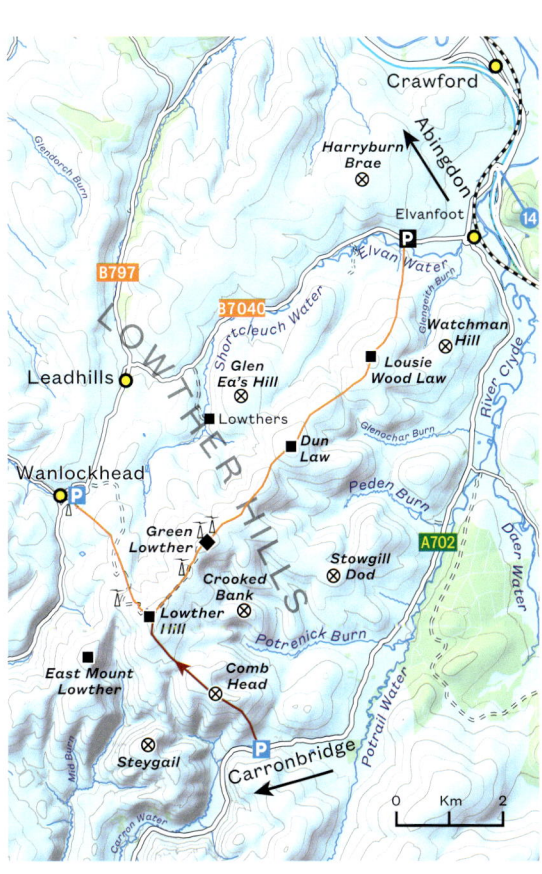

Hart Fell ● 808m

△ NT 113 135 ⌖ LR78 🌐 P.54

🅿 Parking off the A701 at the Devil's Beef Tub (NT 055 127, 55.3993, -3.4931).

↔ 10KM   △ 420M   ⊺ 395M
⏱ 4–5 HRS   GRADE III   ★★

By Stephen Reid, Andrew Wadeson and John Biggar

Snow in the Moffat Hills, as for other ranges elsewhere in the south of Scotland, can be transient and should be taken advantage of immediately. The summit plateaux are broad, flat and quickly wind-stripped, but the slopes are often steep and the corries and gullies (known locally as cleughs) load snow well so that northerly-facing snow patches and wreaths can survive above 700m until the middle of May. When the snow has fallen to low levels, it is possible to enjoy long point-to-point tours. But beware: large avalanches are not unknown in these hills.

One such route traverses the range, taking in a series of hills (Great Hill, Chalk Rig Edge, Spout Craig, Whitehope Knowe and Hart Fell) from the starting point. Navigation is easy, staying near the drystane dykes and fence lines all the way to the 808m OS trig point at Hart Fell (NT 113 135). From here it's possible to return the same way.

Approximately 0.5km south-east of this summit, a 30-degree north-east-facing gully called Nubberry Knowes (NT 122 131) drops down to the traverse east under the slopes of Falcon Craig before the Blackhope Burn foot crossing. If snow cover remains and you're not overly concerned with the state of your ski bases, the final leg can be skied along the Blackhope Farm track with just a little poling out to a second parked car on the A708 (NT 147 098).

Lochcraig Head ■ 802m

△ NT 167 176 ⌖ LR79 🌐 P.55

🅿 Limited roadside parking at the Megget Stone between Talla and Megget Reservoirs (NT 151 203, 55.4698, -3.3436).

↔ 8KM   △ 375M   ⊺ 450M
⏱ 2–3 HRS   GRADE III   ★★

By Stephen Reid, Andrew Wadeson and John Biggar

When the snow-line isn't so low, more reliable terrain can be accessed on northern aspects of the Moffat Hills. A great 2–3 hour out-and-back tour to Lochcraig Head (802m, NT 167 176) affords outstanding views to White Coomb (821m) and the Ettrick Hills beyond, and to Loch Skene immediately below and the tempting ski lines that surround it.

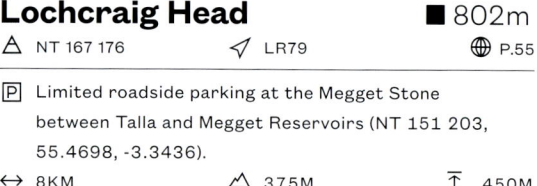

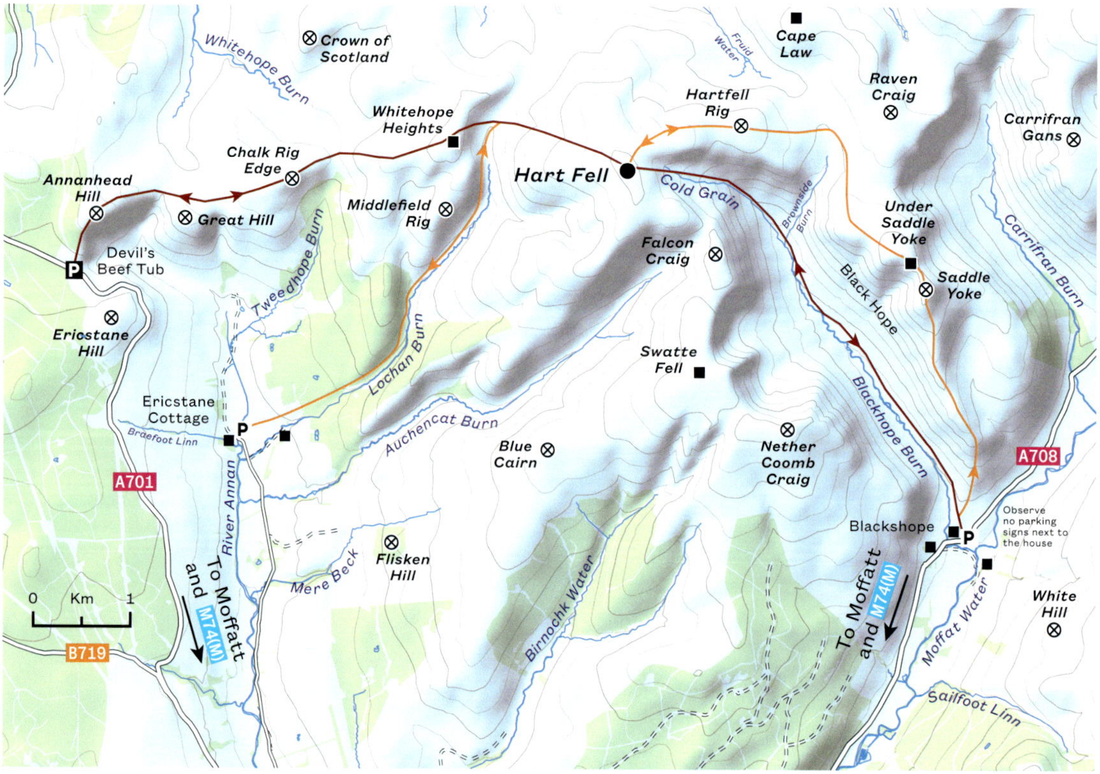

If you have ascended via Nickies Knowe, return via Talla Nick and follow the wide gully through to the drumlins by the side of Talla Water. If your ascent was via Talla Nick, follow the ridge to Nickies Knowe and choose a steep westerly descent line down to the drumlins or the mellower northerly slope via Wood Brae.

Alternatively, Lochcraig Head can be approached from the south-east to give an equally spectacular tour of similar length. Park on the A708 north of the Grey Mare's Tail, just past the county border signs on each side of the road (NT 205 165; 315m). Head up Yearney Knowe between the two plantations with Happertutie Burn on the left. On attaining the top of the ridge, head south-west to Watch Knowe (NT 183 161; 605m) from where the south face of Lochcraig Head lies ahead. Go north across Winterhope Moss and contour around onto the ridge of Lochcraig Rig (NT 177 178; 621m), turning westward to the top of the Lochcraig Head (NT 167 176; 801m).

For a short day, the return journey is more or less via the approach, though much variation is possible. Alternatively, on reaching the top of Lochcraig Head, a full tour of the hills right round to White Coomb could be made, with lots of scope for steeper stuff on the slopes above Loch Skeen.

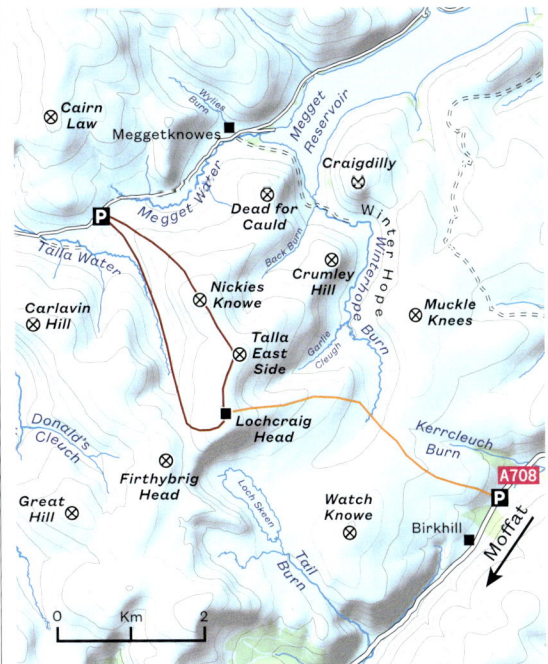

Below: Lowther Hill at the end of a traverse of the range (skier, Linda Biggar) © James Kinnaird

Broad Law

● 840m
△ NT 146 235
◁ LR72
⊕ P.56

[P] Limited roadside parking at the Megget Stone between Talla and Megget Reservoirs (NT 151 203, 55.4698, -3.3436).

↔ 6KM △ 390M ↥ 452M
⏲ 2-3 HRS GRADE II ★★

By Colwyn Jones

This Corbett lies in the core of the bleak winter lands between Peebles and Moffat and rewards the work involved in ascent with a fine downhill ski run. It is a short enough tour to be completed in an afternoon or evening. The ascent starts near the Megget Stone, which may have originally served as a boundary marker between Selkirkshire and Peeblesshire. The stone is a slab of local greywacke only 0.84m high but may originally have been taller. There is space to park a single vehicle at the cattle grid, and there is also a small parking area further along the road in the direction of Talla Reservoir. The Talla Reservoir approach road is disarmingly steep, and might be best avoided by using the Megget Reservoir option.

The sheep fence can be used to guide you north-east up the broad crest over Fans Law, inclining in a more northerly direction over Cairn Law and then remarkably direct (with one small deviation) to the triangulation station on the top of Broad Law. A sizable saucer-shaped radio beacon for aviation navigation (which looks like a 1950s alien spaceship) lies just north of the summit, and there are obvious radio masts nearby, though the cluster does not mark the top.

The summit and south crest used in ascent are likely to have been exposed to prevailing winds, so the descent route will be dictated by the accumulation of snow observed on the way up. With a westerly wind the snowpack may be deeper on the east (lee) side of the fence followed in ascent.

If the road up to the Megget Stone is impassable, or if simply preferred, then a circular tour may be substituted starting from the western end of the Megget Reservoir at the car park (NT 179 219; 345m) where the Linghope Burn drains into that artificial loch. Gain the broad crest west of the Linghope Burn and head north-west over Lamb

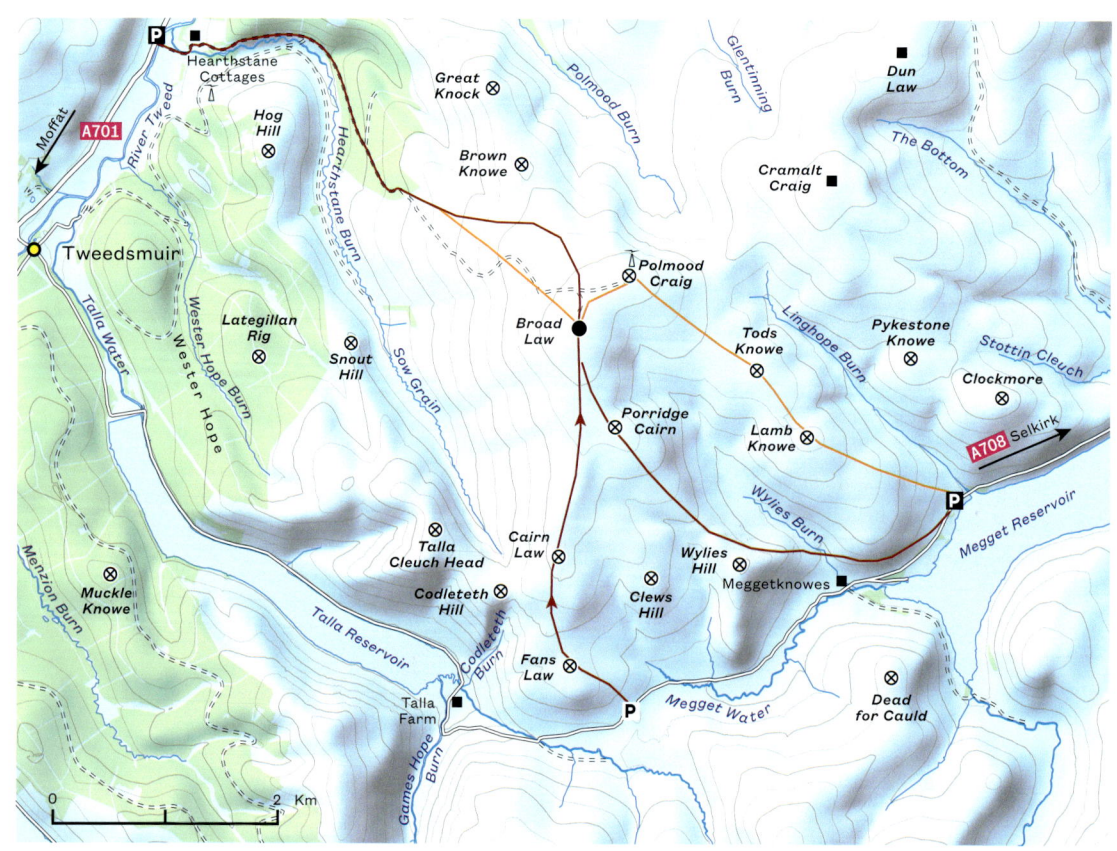

Knowe and Tods Knowe to the 800m contour, then veer west to the summit. Return by the same route or, for the circular tour ski down towards the Megget Stone and return following the snow-covered tarmac road as a guide to reach the Megget Reservoir.

Broad Law can also be skied from the north on the Tweedsmuir side. Roadside parking is on the A702 at the entrance to Hearthstane Estate (NT 109 260; 260m). From there: Distance 8km; height climbed 580m; time 4–5 hours.

This is a longer approach, but the forest track typically holds the snow well, and the track serving the radio beacon almost reaches the summit, allowing simple navigation. The track exits the forest at the 490m contour (NT 130 245). The maintenance track has numerous roadside marker poles to follow, or you can ignore them to take a slightly steeper and more direct line to the summit.

Descent requires you to relocate the forest/track junction (NT 130 245; 490m), possibly slaloming from the summit down through the roadside poles, then ski back down the tree-lined track to return to the car.

Culter Fell ◆ 748m

Hill of the Ploughshare

△ NT 052 291   ◁ LR72   ⊕ P.57

P There are several suitable entries around this hill, but the nearest is 0.5km south of Birthwood in the valley of the Culter Water, 3.5km south of Coulter village (NT 032 305, 55.5590, -3.5365).

↔ 6KM   △ 490M   ⊺ 260M
⏱ 2-3 HRS   GRADE III   **

By Sandy Cousins, updated by Colwyn Jones

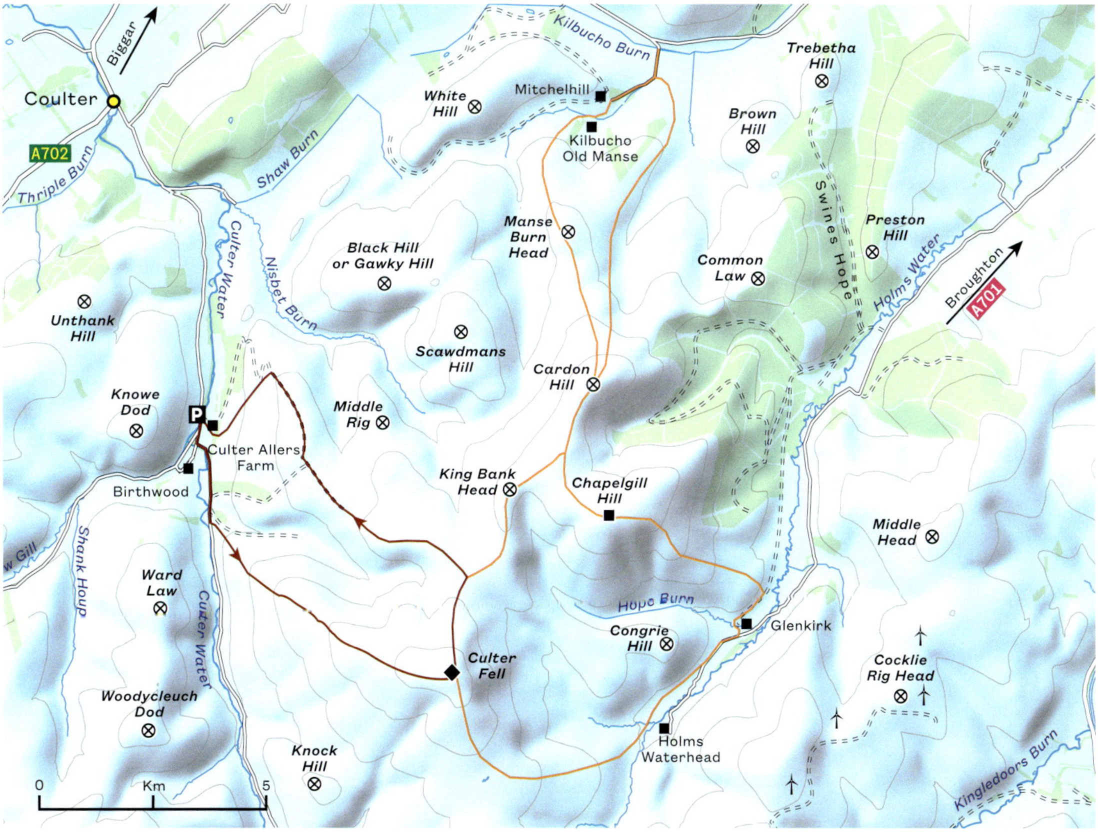

Culter Fell sits surrounded by several lower tops and is the highest point of a large area of many grassy, rounded hills between the valleys of the Clyde and the Tweed Rivers. From the main roads in these two valleys, several minor roads lead up the higher valleys towards Culter Fell itself. The shortest ascent, which can easily be done in a short winter's afternoon, starts from the Culter Water. From Coulter village on the A702 take the narrow road next to the Culter Water to a point 0.5km beyond Birthwood at the foot of Kings Beck. Climb the heathery ridge of the oddly-named Fell Shin, following a track and grouse butts at first to the summit. Ski north along a fence for 500m to a flat col, and then north-east down the ridge on the north side of Kings Beck, but do not ski down into the very steep-sided valley of this stream.

On the north side of Culter Fell a longer tour starts on the public road leading to Mitchell Hill Farm (NT 071 344), south-east of Biggar. An undulating route goes up the north ridge of Cardon Hill, then over King Bank Head, meeting the fence leading to the summit. On the descent from Cardon Hill choose the best route down the northward glens, or down the north ridge, according to the snow conditions.

On the east side of Culter Fell a minor road branching off the A701 at Rachan Mill goes up the Holms Water to Glenkirk (NT 079 294). A circular tour from there takes in Chapelgill Hill and Leishfoot Hill. This traverse is on short grass and heather, giving good skiing without the need for a deep snow cover. There is a steep corrie on the east side of Culter Fell, which should be avoided by skiing south from the summit along a fence towards Moss Law for 1km before dropping east down the shoulder of Leishfoot Hill towards the road end above Glenkirk.

This area of the Scottish Borders is quite different from the Highlands. It may lack the rugged grandeur of the northern mountains, but it has a character of its own, epitomised by the smooth rounded hills which, under adequate snow, are ideal for ski touring.

Tinto ◆ 707m
Fiery or Beacon Hill

| △ NS 953 343 | ↗ LR72 | 🌐 P.58 |

| 🅿 | There are several convenient starting places on the roads around Tinto Hill, but the main route described starts from Fallburn car park (NS 964 374, 55.6197, -3.6455). |

| ↔ 6–8KM | △ 460M | ⊺ 230M |
| ⏱ 2–4 HRS | GRADE III | ✶✶ |

By Sandy Cousins, updated by Colwyn Jones

Tinto is the most prominent hill in the upper Clyde Valley, set among open rolling country which is very different from much of the Scottish landscape. Being less than an hour's drive from Edinburgh or Glasgow, it is very accessible and is encircled by roads: the A83, B7075, and minor roads by Fallburn,

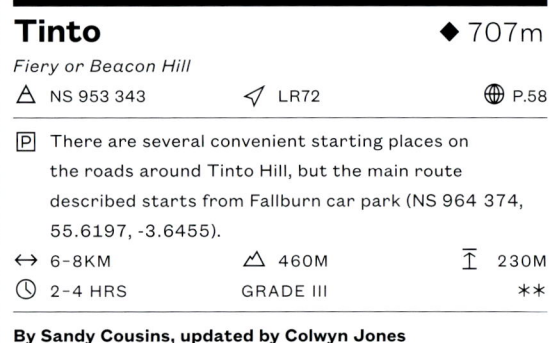

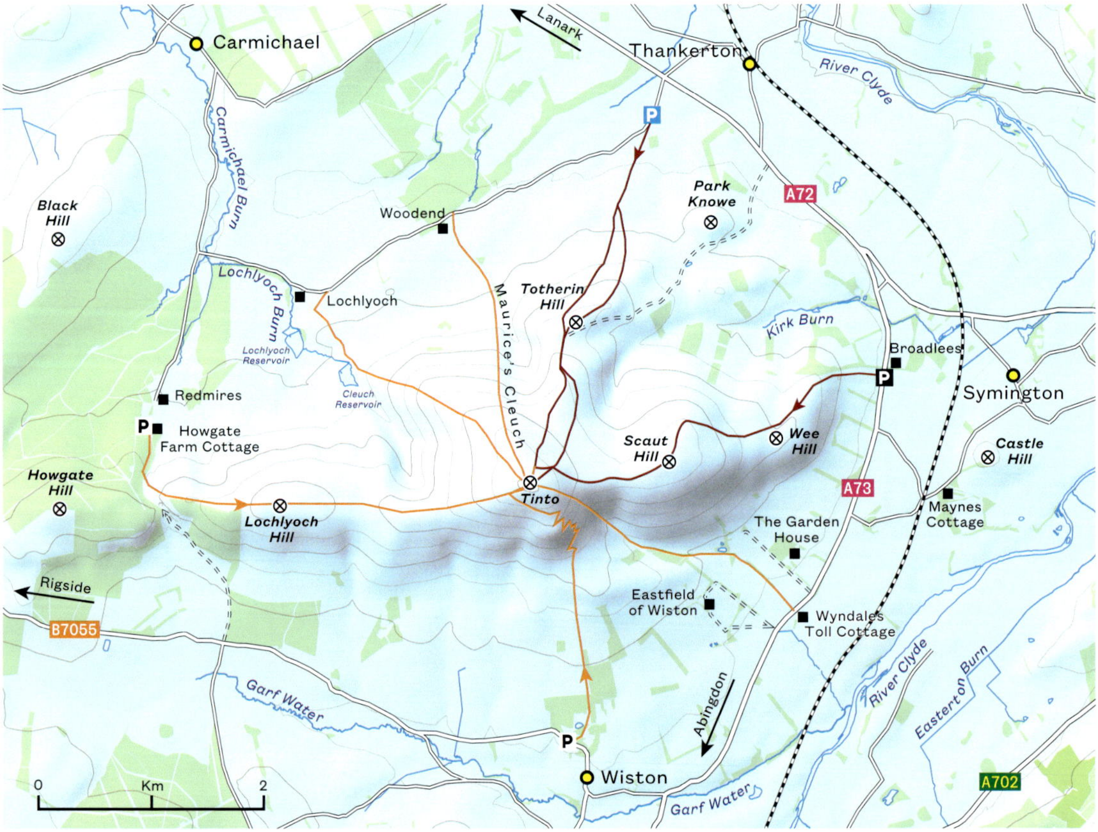

Woodend, Lochlyoch and Howgate Farms. Thus, if the roads have been ploughed, it is a good hill for a short day out, an afternoon or even an evening sortie. Sandy Cousins, in the first edition, wrote, 'I have on one occasion in late February left Glasgow after work, skied up the north side of Tinto to arrive at the summit after sunset and returned to the road by torchlight across smooth snowfields reflecting the last of the alpenglow.'

The best ski route up Tinto always depends on conditions caused by the wind direction during recent snowfalls. It may be worth a circular reconnaissance of the hill to assess the best snow cover. Streams, shelterbelts of trees, walls and fences can often create ribbons of snow when other parts of the hill are bare, and there are possible routes on all sides. If your party has two cars, it may be possible to do an interesting traverse; otherwise, the descent route is likely to be near the ascent.

On the north side, which usually has more reliable snow cover, the road between Fallburn and Lochlyoch Farms gives easy access to the fields, beyond which lies the steeper rounded north-west shoulder of Tinto between the two Cleuch burns. Further east the route starting from the large official car park near Fallburn, up past the ancient hill fort to the shoulder of Totherin Hill and along the fence to the summit, gives good views across the northern slopes of Tinto.

To the west the summit of the road at Howgate Mouth is the highest starting point (approx 380m), and the route follows the ridge over Lochlyock Hill – a good option if there is a fresh west wind blowing.

To the south you can start at Millrig and climb north towards the steep scar of Pap Craig, which must be avoided. This is the shortest and steepest ascent. A good, steep descent can be made south-east from the summit into the high corrie of the Lanimer Burn, ending across moorland and fields.

To the east of Tinto you can start near Broadlees and go up on the south side of the plantation to Wee Hill, then continue south-west along the ridge, following a track over Scaut Hill and along a fence to the summit. The descent can be varied by skiing down the Kirk Burn to St John's Kirk.

The Manor Hills

Dun Rig (Glensax Horseshoe) ■ 744m

NT 253 315   LR73   P.60

P The car park at the south-east edge of Peebles at the end of Glen Road (NT 260 392, 55.6408, -3.1773).

↔ 24KM   △ 900M   ↕ 170M
⏱ 6-8 HRS   GRADE III   ★★

By Bruce Kerr

Although this is a long tour with many flat sections favouring Nordic gear, it has the attraction of traversing most of the high points to the south of Peebles over relatively easy ground. Start at the entrance of Haystoun but take the track to the left, signposted as the Cross Borders Drove Road, leading down towards the Haystoun Burn. This is known as the Gypsy Glen, as historically it was a popular camping spot for travellers using the drove road. Cross the burn and head uphill to follow the drove road southwards, skirting the first hill then going over Kailzie Hill and Kirkhope Law towards Birkscairn Hill. This section of track can hold the snow well if there has been snowfall with an easterly wind.

From Birkscairn Hill a short descent leads to a col before Stake Law. Ascend Stake Law, keeping to the right of the fence line. Follow the fence to the top of Dun Rig (triangulation station) and the high point of the tour. From the top of Dun Rig go south-west, aiming for the 713m spot height. The best snow tends to lie in the hollows on the north side of the crest line. This allows a curving traverse leading to a short descent to the col (marked as Glenrath Heights; NT 243 316). Climb northwards over Middle Hill and Broom Hill to gain the plateau leading to the top of Hundleshope Heights, the final high point and second triangulation station.

Depending on snow conditions there are several possible descents from here. The most convenient is to head north-eastwards towards the ridge marked Dead Side. The west side of the ridge, overlooking Waddenshope Burn, often holds snow. Descend north to the end of the ridge to gain the track. Follow this past Haystoun, perhaps using your head torch, and back to Glen Road.

The Edinburgh to Peebles Border bus service X62 is an option. Note: the earliest arrival in Peebles would be 9:30am at the roundabout outside the BP garage (8:15am from Edinburgh). From the BP garage walk west along Eastgate, heading into Peebles. After 150m, just before the Post Office, turn left into Tweed Brae. Follow this downhill where the road goes right to the edge of a park. Turn left into Tweed Green and follow the edge of the park to the river. Turn left, then right over the footbridge to a pedestrian crossing over Kingsmeadows Road. Cross this into the park and follow the right-hand path to reach Glen Road. Turn left and follow the road to the start of the route at NT 260 392 (20 mins).

The Moorfoots

Blackhope Scar ◆ 651m

NT 315 483   LR73   P.61

🅿 The hillwalkers' car park at Gladhouse Reservoir (NT 292 528, 55.7630, -3.1292) off the minor road connecting the A703 to the B6372.

↔ 16KM   △ 650M   ⊤ 285M
⏱ 6-7 HRS   GRADE II   ★★

By Colwyn Jones

The Moorfoot Hills are a minor range of moderate-height hills south of Edinburgh which form part of the Southern Uplands. Many of the south-facing slopes above the A72 east of Peebles are heavily forested, forming part of the Tweed Valley Forest Park and containing a popular mountain biking centre. The Hills are home to Bowbeat Wind Farm completed in September 2002. The site consists of 24 Nordex N60 wind turbines (80m high, 60m diameter rotors) which lie between Bowbeat Hill, Blackhope Scar and Dundreich Hill. When established the wind farm was Scotland's largest. This tour has been variously described as a fine day out or one providing little reward for the effort involved! The mid-section visits the industrial site mentioned above, which some skiers may find intrusive. Most of the remaining excursion parallels agricultural sheep fencing, which will guide you on the tour unless the snow accumulation is impressively deep.

Access is described from the north using the minor road which connects the A703 to the B6372. Other entry points exist, and a regular bus service from Edinburgh to Peebles can be used: alight at the village of Eddleston to access the area. The length of the approach tracks and undulating terrain favours Nordic ski touring gear. Large, flat peat hags and waterlogged terrain define the Moorfoot Hills throughout most of the year, but when the ground is frozen under snow, progress across these hills may seem easier. This is more likely around January after a good snowfall down to sea level. The Moorfoot Hills occasionally hold a decent depth of snow when the Pentland Hills, being closer to the sea, are less well covered.

From the hillwalkers' car park at Gladhouse Reservoir (NT 292 528), follow the road to Moorfoot Farm and, after traversing the farmyard, continue south towards Gladhouse Cottage. Cross the bridge over the River South Esk and follow the track toward the remains of Hirendean Castle. If there is sufficient snow, continue up the

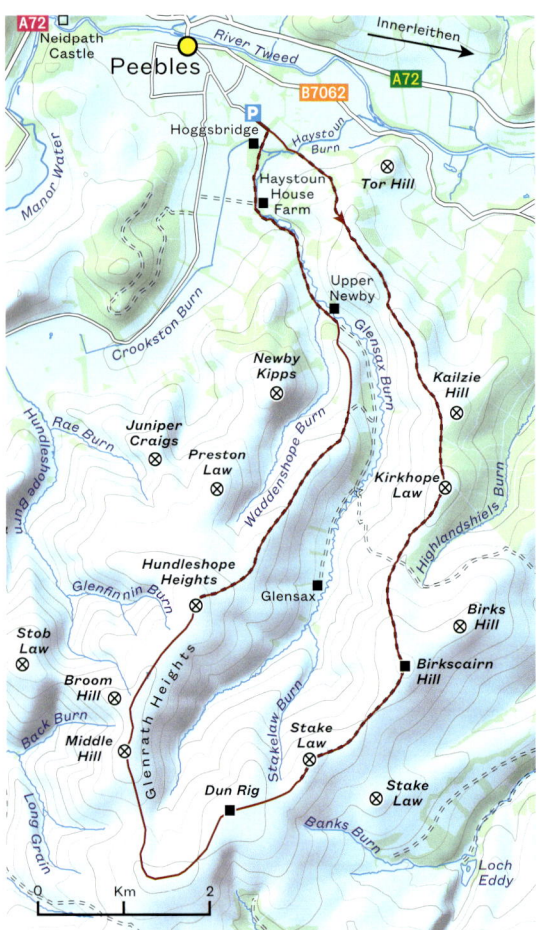

ridge behind the ruin, crossing a barbed wire fence (no stile) at the 400m contour to gradually reach the large flat summit of The Kipps (542m). From the summit continue to a corner of the fence at NT 308 499. In poor snow conditions, it may be better to follow the track on the east side of the River South Esk from Gladhouse Cottage, taking the first left turn (approximately 350m) up onto the broad col and the nearby fence. Once at the fence turn south and follow it over rough ground to the summit of Blackhope Scar (651m), the high point of the tour indicated by a triangulation station.

From Blackhope Scar, follow another fence south-south-west towards Bowbeat Wind Farm. It is not worth any corner-cutting as the fence takes both the best line and may accumulate a good layer of snow. Climbing skins can be removed for this short descent to the 550m contour.

This is the boundary of the windfarm, and skins will be needed to ascend to the summit of Bowbeat Hill (626m). There is a boundary fence or maintenance track, either of which may ease progress and aid navigation. From the summit of Bowbeat Hill or from the highpoint of the windfarm track, it is possible to enjoy another short slope, but the track narrows and steepens, making for an interesting descent.

After reapplying skins continue north through the remainder of the windfarm and exit through a gate in the fence just after the most remote windmill and buildings. Continue north, without a fence to follow, then north-west rising to cross another fence to reach the trig pillar and adjacent small cairn on Dundreich (623m).

The final leg follows the fence heading north-east to the cairn on Jeffries Corse (613m). Once at the cairn, finally remove your climbing skins for the day and continue down the line of the fence. Where the fence turns slightly west, deviate slightly east towards a distant fence going north-east down the broad ridge ahead to the glen floor. Stay on the right side (looking downhill) to avoid a deer fence, and the slope eases over rough pasture

Key

1. Blackhope Scar — P.60
2. Dundreich — P.63

Below: Heading off Dundreich
(skier, Hamish MacEwan)
© Doug Bryce

to bring you back to Gladstone Cottage. Retrace your route through Moorfoot Farm and, depending on the hour, perhaps enjoy the sight of the resident barn owl as you return to the car park.

Dundreich ■ 623m

△ NT 274 490   ⌖ LR73   ⊕ P.61

P Roadside parking off the minor road connecting the A703 to the B6372 at the signpost to Portmore Reservoir (NT 255 514, 55.7507, -3.1880).

↔ 8KM   △ 350M   ⏉ 280M
⏱ 3-4 HRS   GRADE III   ✶✶

By Colwyn Jones

The north-west flank of Dundreich has a reputation for holding fine snow, particularly after a cold easterly wind (a 'Beast from the East'), and gives a good half-day touring in a quiet setting.

Ski up the the access road to Portmore Loch, and after 1km take the east (left) track around the reservoir to its southern end. Continue following the track for a few hundred metres, and after passing a second gate (310m), cross the nearby watercourse and head south-east directly up the slope ahead. This broad ridge brings you close to the flat summit of Brown Dod (1:25,000 OS map; 600m), where the snow-covered, well-worn, flat footpath can be followed easily north-east to the Dundreich summit trig pillar and adjacent small cairn.

Descent is north-west from the summit, and the line uses the optimum snow observed on the ascent. The slope angle in the corrie can approach 30 degrees, so care is required after fresh snowfall; of course, this may be the only time you try to ski here! On reaching the watercourse, follow your ascent route to the reservoir track and shortly arrive back at the car park.

A fine alternative descent (in good weather) if returning to the village of Eddleston is south-west from the top of Dundreich. Initially descend the gentle slope south-west of Brown Dod (1:25,000 OS map) for approximately 400m, then head west towards the steep gully, which often holds good snow. Favour the north-east side when the wind comes in from the east, and the south-west side when the wind comes in from the west, and check the avalanche conditions. When descending via this route it is important to remain above the 350m contour to ensure an easy run back to Portmore Loch.

The Pentlands Traverse

Scald Law
(Nine Mile Burn to Hillend)

⊗ 579m

△ NT 191 611   ⌖ LR66   🌐 P.65

🅿 Nine Mile Burn (NT 177 577, 55.8058, -3.3138).
Limited parking adjacent to the footpath signs.

↔ 13KM   △ 650M   ⭳ 280M
⏱ 5–6 HRS   GRADE II   ★★

By William Wallace, updated by Colwyn Jones

In 2010, a group of SMC members enjoyed superb powder skiing on Caerketton Hill in the Pentlands, some 5km from their back door. However, after the infamous Pentlands wet slab avalanche the next day, by evening the powder snow had transformed into brick-hard boilerplate.

Many of the Pentland Hills may be skied on their own or in groups from the A702 trunk road, which is a busy commuter route and unlikely to be snowbound, although the numerous roadside lay-bys may or may not be ploughed and are likely to be busy.

The traverse is a fine, lengthy day out, but due to the relatively low hills, snow seldom accumulates in sufficient quantity to make the ski traverse possible. It is a glittering prize to be discerningly sought. Nevertheless, the terrain is largely grass-covered, typically on footpaths, which permits skiing on minimal snow cover. Where these popular footpaths are eroded down to rocks, or repaired with stone treads and pavers, the adjacent hillside can often be used, especially in descent. Skis may need to be carried on the lower sections and where paths are followed through gates and over stiles. The route is popular, and the tracks of downhill and cross-country skiers, snowboarders, snowshoers, tobogganists, hillwalkers, dogs, mountain bikers and fell runners may be found in the snow.

To complete the traverse successfully, you must have transport from Hillend, at the Edinburgh city boundary on the A702, to Nine Mile Burn. Infrequent bus services, such as the Edinburgh to Dumfries Stagecoach 101 service from the city centre, can be caught at the Lothianburn Snowsports Centre bus stop on the southbound carriageway just before the ESSO petrol station. Don't worry when the bus diverts to pass through Penicuik, as it re-joins the A702 before Nine Mile Burn.

From Nine Mile Burn follow the signposted footpath (Balerno by Monks Rig and Braids Law) along field boundaries. There are two options at one of the Scottish Rights of Way Society signs (NT 176 580) where the Braids Law option branches off the Balerno route. With sufficient snow either route can be followed as both meet at the col (NT 174 603) before the final ascent of West Kip, and combining them gives a short, pleasant circular tour from Nine Mile Burn. The circle goes up just below Braids Law, might include a visit to the summit of West Kip (south and west slopes can provide good descents), then returns via the line of the Monks Rig footpath.

The second traverse option follows the Balerno route, which continues to reach a stile onto open ground (NT 174 584). Ascend north up the easy broad ridge passing the Font Stone (NT 175 591), which may be covered by snow, to reach the flat top of Cap Law, overlooking some stunted conifers. A new deer fence was installed in 2021 to allow tree planting west of the route. From here, negotiate a short dip and gate at the col before the final steep rise to the top of West Kip (NT 178 605; 551m). Continue north-east over East Kip (NT 183 608), then descend to the col beyond. Make a rising traverse on the best line, perhaps following the obvious footpath, across the north-west slope of Scald Law to the summit (NT 191 611; 579m) – the highest Pentland top and equipped with a triangulation station.

From Scald Law the route continues steeply down deep heather next to the stony footpath, then north-east up over Carnethy Hill. Again the descent slope has a rocky path with adjacent deep heather before you reach a gate and the short rise to the summit of Turnhouse Hill. From Turnhouse Hill the easiest route is to use the line of the footpath to descend east in between two fenced enclosures of wind-blown and stunted trees (mainly larch) via gates and down to a footbridge (NT 228 630) across the Glencorse Burn. Here the track divides at a T-junction. The left branch follows the bank of the Glencorse Burn, upstream past old gravel filter beds and up onto the tarmac road leading to Glencorse Reservoir. The right branch goes downstream and joins the tarmac road towards the Flotterstone Inn, which has a large busy car park. (From here you can return by bus to Edinburgh, or phone for a taxi.)

Go left up the tarmac road towards the reservoir (or right if you took the filter bed path) to a pedestrian gate (NT 225 632). If there is no live firing on the Castlelaw shooting range (perhaps unlikely with good snow cover, unless Arctic warfare training has been instituted), ascend north-east to

Key

1. The Pentlands Traverse: Nine Mile Burn to Hillend   P.64
2. Allermuir Hill and Caerketton Hill   P.67

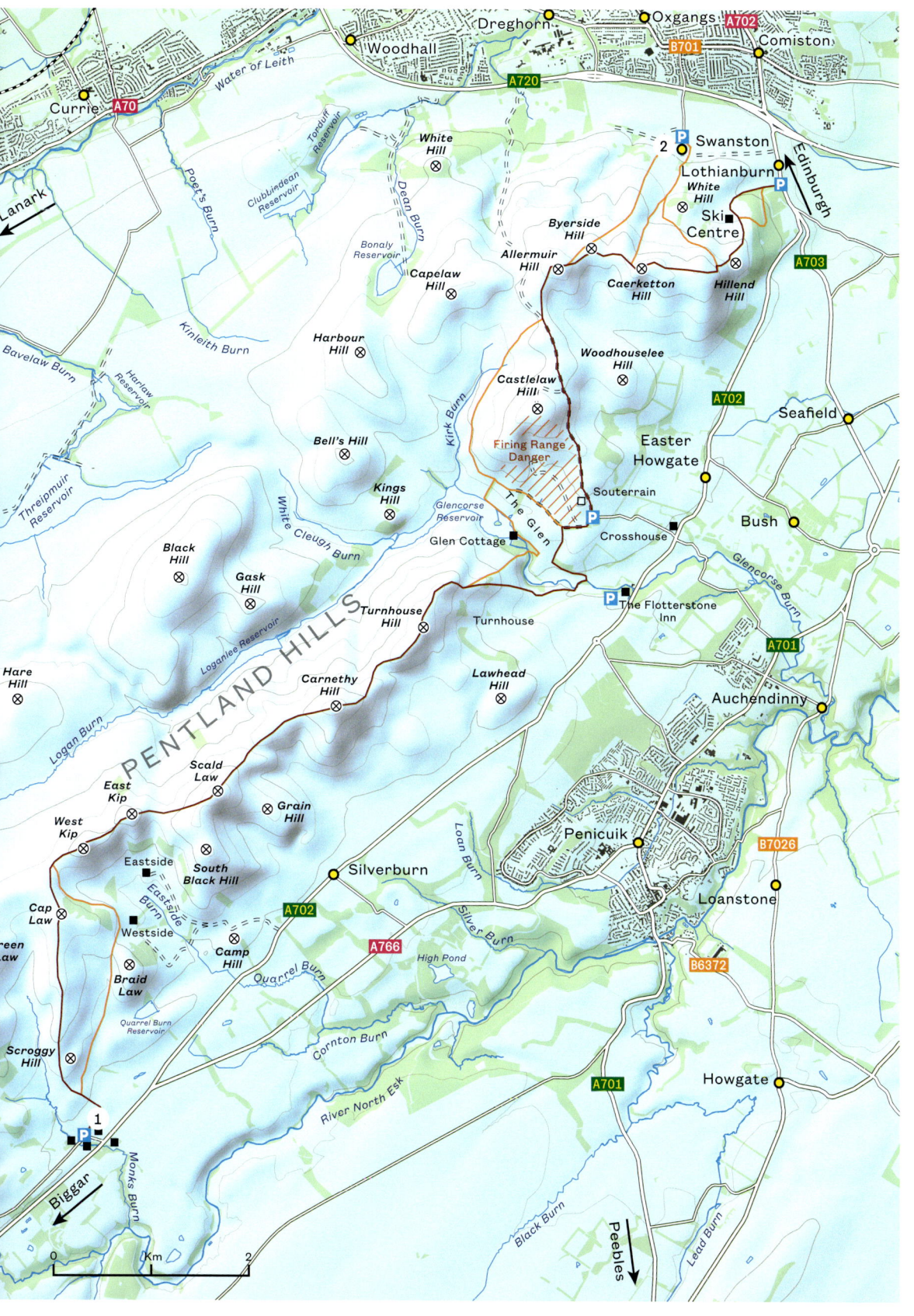

Below: Cap Law
(skiers, Amy Goodill,
Ann MacDonald
and Colwyn Jones)
© Erik Lang

pass the shooting range buildings, then left to join the military vehicle track which passes round the east side of Castlelaw Hill and the souterrain fort. The military track collects drifting snow, so is preferable under limited snow conditions. When there is adequate snow, the alternative route to avoid the firing range (and the better continuation from a second bridge – see below) goes around the west side of the hill starting 300m before the north corner of the reservoir up the side of a shelterbelt (access gate and signage at NT 218 639) where skis may have to be carried initially.

There is a possible feral, direct descent off Turnhouse Hill. At the first (higher) of the two fenced enclosures, follow the fence on either side to the lowest point, then ski north-east down the nose of the slope that guides you to two deer fences enclosing a new rough plantation. Climb the first fence; the second has a pedestrian gate and stile (NT 221 633) and marshals the trees lining the Glencorse Burn. On foot, walk steeply downhill for 150 metres to reach a second

footbridge (NT 223 634). Note that there is no established path. If you choose this second bridge, after crossing, go immediately right over a fence and follow the obvious track to join the footpath from the filter beds, then follow it up steeply through trees to a gate onto the tarmac road. From either route around Castlelaw Hill, follow the respective paths and then continue north over a cattle grid up next to the fence to the Allermuir summit (NT 227 661), then turn east, descend, re-ascend and pass over Caerketton Hill (prehistoric cairn on top) with good views over the city, continuing with a short, steep descent along the ridge and fence until east of the dry ski slope chairlift. To avoid the narrow footpath down through dense gorse bushes, directly below the park bench (NT 246 664) take easier slopes a few metres back and down sharp left towards the Snowsports Centre. Stay on the right of the fence around the alpine coaster (toboggan on rails) down to the access road and then on down to the large car park next to the A702 which also serves as the terminus for Lothian bus service 4. The route may change slightly as this area is earmarked for development as a multi-activity leisure centre with a zipline, food court and retail space, plus a glamping village. From the park bench it was possible to descend to the right, staying out of the gorse bushes and skiing down through trees to turn left and follow the first fence you meet down to the road. However, this option is now more difficult owing to the new trees planted on the hillside. If there is not enough snow cover to ski, then the number 4 bus can be used to return to the city.

and the parking charge is voluntary. The Lothian bus number 4 service and Skylink 400 service both pass nearby. Disembark on Oxgangs Road at the Swanston Road bus stop and walk (or ski) about 1km along Swanston Road, crossing above the bypass to reach the official car park.

From the east end of the car park follow the footpath through the trees, then the thatched cottages on the east side of Swanston Burn. The footpath continues up through gates, crosses the golf course, the burn and finally emerges onto the open hillside. A bealach (NT 232 663; 450m) between Allermuir and Caerketton gives a suitable waypoint. Note there is a lower bealach 250m to the west.

Either summit is accessible from the col by following the fence west and east, respectively. When clear of cloud, the summits typically afford good views over the Scottish capital, the Firth of Forth and the Kingdom of Fife beyond.

Minor crags directly north of the highest Caerketton summit should be avoided in descent as the face will never have a safe build-up of skiable snow, so either return to the first bealach, which gives a fine ski return, or follow the fence east to above the artificial ski slope before descending. Ski left above the fence at the top of the ski lifts back along the footpath to the starting point in Swanston.

From the summit of Allermuir the main footpath to Swanston gives a good grassy line to ski, but at the 350m contour where the path drops down to Swanston Burn, stay on the broad ridge, ski down off the end, crossing fences and bypassing small crags, over fields then the neatly manicured golf course, past the clubhouse and back to the car park.

There are also starting points from car parks at Dreghorn Burn (NT 227 680) and Bonaly Country Park (NT 211 674) with access to the north side of the Pentland Hills. Nordic/cross-country options exist, such as a circumnavigation of Capelaw Hill. Edinburgh bus services 10 or 16 (plus some walking) could be used as neither of these car parks are ploughed as a priority.

Allermuir Hill 493m
NT 227 661

Caerketton Hill 478m
NT 236 662   LR66   P.65

P Pentland Hills Regional Park car park (NT 240 673, 55.8934, -3.2164).
↔ 6KM   △ -300M   ↕ 175M
⏱ 2-3 HRS   GRADE II   ★★

By William Wallace, updated by Colwyn Jones

Short tours, suitable for a morning, afternoon, evening or even a night-time ascent are Allermuir and/or Caerketton Hills. They can be reached by reversing the final leg of the traverse, or perhaps more readily from Swanston village to access the north faces. Roads to the car park at the Swanston new golf course are often ploughed,

Right: Powder day on the Pentlands (skier, Gav Carruthers) © Doug Bryce

Chapter 2

The Campsies to Loch Tay

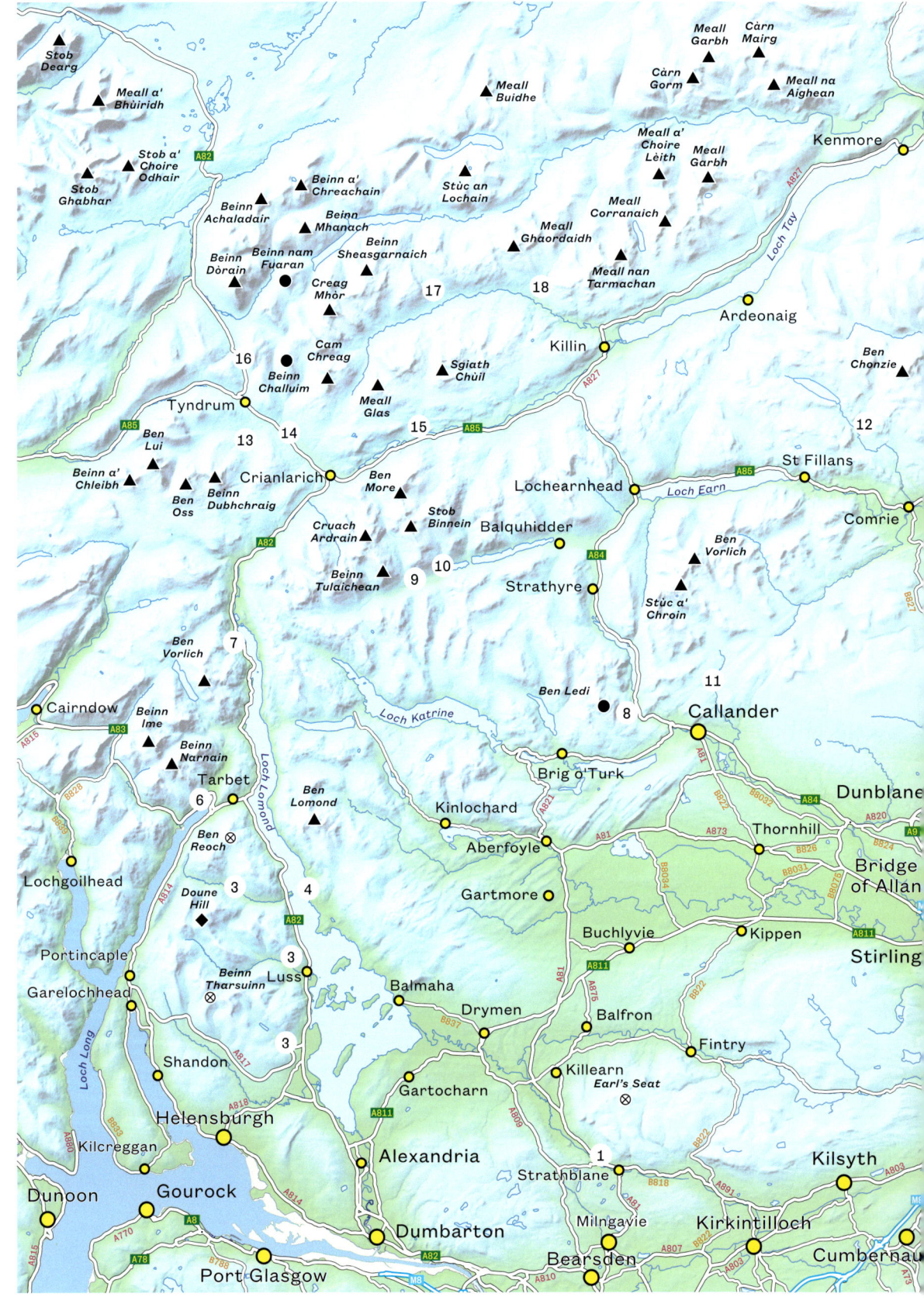

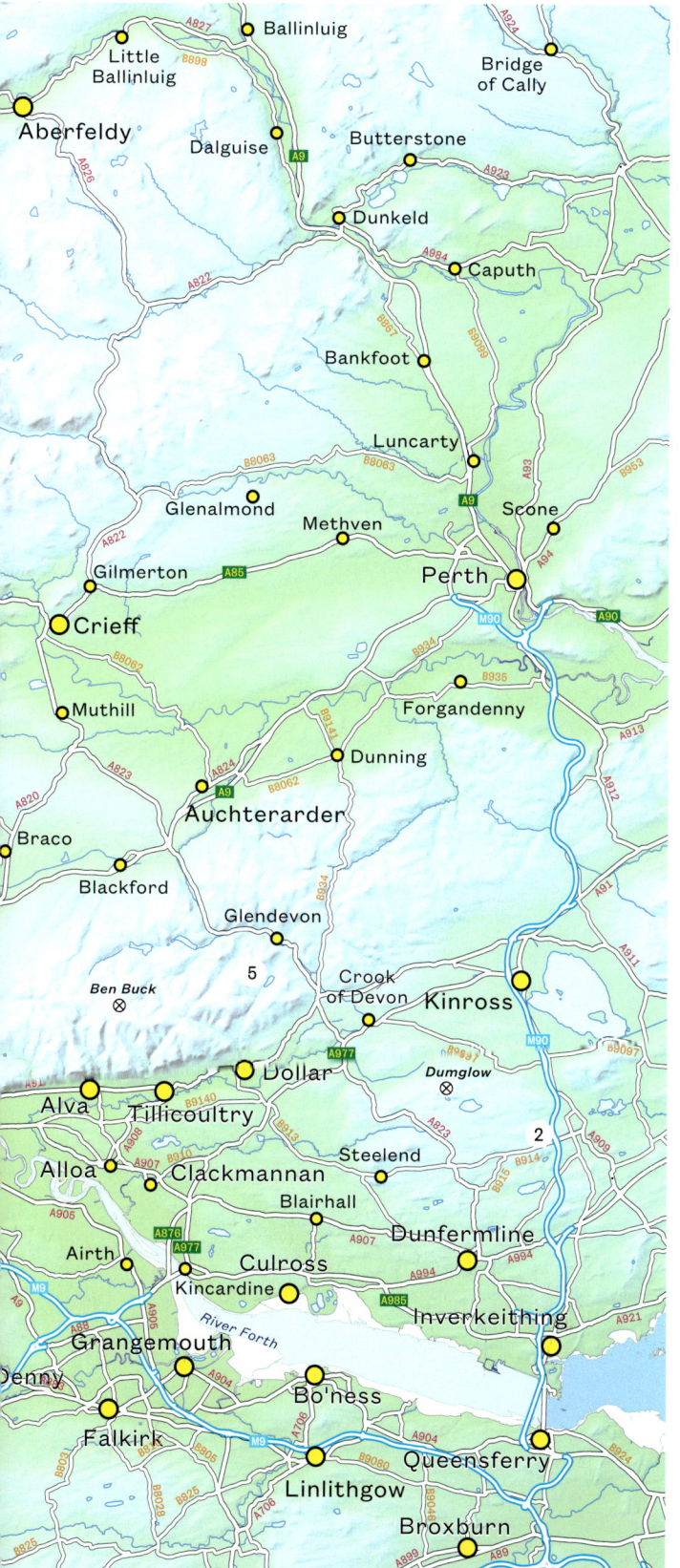

#		Page
1.	The Campsie Fells	P.74
2.	The Cleish Hills	P.75
3.	The Luss Hills	P.76
4.	Ben Lomond	P.79
5.	The Ochils	P.80
6.	The Arrochar Alps	P.83
7.	Ben Vorlich (Arrochar)	P.85
8.	Ben Ledi	P.86
9.	Cruach Ardrain	P.88
10.	Ben More	P.89
11.	Ben Vorlich	P.91
12.	Ben Chonzie	P.93
13.	Ben Lui	P.94
14.	Ben Challuim	P.98
15.	Sgiath Chùil	P.99
16.	The Auch Hills	P.103
17.	Mamlorn Mountains	P.106
18.	Meall Ghaordaidh	P.108

Previous spread:
Ochils Innerdownie
(skier, Al Bird) © Al Todd

The Campsie Fells

⊗ 578m

Earl's Seat

| △ NS 569 838 | ◁ LR64 | ⊕ P.74 |

| 🅿 The B822 Crow Road (NS 627 819/56.0100, -4.2003). |
| ↔ 12KM | △ 650M | ↕ 337M |
| ⏱ 4–5 HRS | GRADE II | ** |

By Donald Bennet, updated by Colwyn Jones

The Campsie Fells are reported to be the birthplace of Scottish skiing. William W Naismith, a founder member of the SMC, skied up Meikle Bin with a companion in March 1892.

They are the nearest hills to Glasgow with potential for skiing, although their character of extensive plateau-like tops surrounded by steep slopes and escarpments makes them more suitable for cross-country rather than downhill skiing. The tussocky grass and eroded peat banks on these tops mean good snow cover is somewhat essential, but such cover is rare as the Campsie Fells reach only 578m. However, when the conditions are right, there are some short tours that are well worth doing over a half day or evening, perhaps if your workplace has closed early owing to fresh snowfall!

The easiest and highest access by car is from the B822, the menacingly named Crow Road from Lennoxtown to Fintry, which crosses the Campsies. At Muir Toll near the source of the River Carron, there is roadside parking, but it may need to be dug out with your snow shovel when snow conditions are optimal; please take care if working at the roadside.

Once parked or dropped off at the top of this road, you can tour both east and west.

A circular traverse east goes over Lairs (518m), Cort-ma Law (531m) and Lecket Hill (547m), which can even be extended to Meikle Bin (NS 667 821; 570m), though forestry has made access to this hill more difficult.

To the west you can do an out-and-back traverse of Holehead (551m) and Hart Hill (522m), starting up the maintenance road to the weather radar station close to the triangulation station on Holehead. This gives good walking access if the snow cover doesn't reach the road. Alternatively, parking at the end of the forest track on the east side of the road (NS 628 816) allows you to nip through a gap in the fence to start the ascent immediately. There are numerous burns and gullies to be worked around on descent.

If transport can be arranged, then as an alternative from the top of Hart Hill you can enjoy a downhill run south to Clachan of Campsie.

The summit of Earl's Seat (NS 569 838), the highest of the Campsies, can be reached in a separate tour from the south either up the long ridge on the south-west side of the Fin Glen over Dumbreck (508m), or from Blanefield, starting up the 'pipe road' and traversing north-west below the long escarpment of Slackdhu to reach easier slopes leading to Clachertyfarlie Knowes (547m) and Earl's Seat.

Parking at the north-west end of the Carron Valley Reservoir on the B818 (NS 673 858) and following the signposted footpath to the summit of Meikle Bin is a better option for this hill. There is a fine initial descent down the grassy north-north-west ridge, then you can retrace your approach on the snow-covered track, with a somewhat tedious return poling along the side of the reservoir.

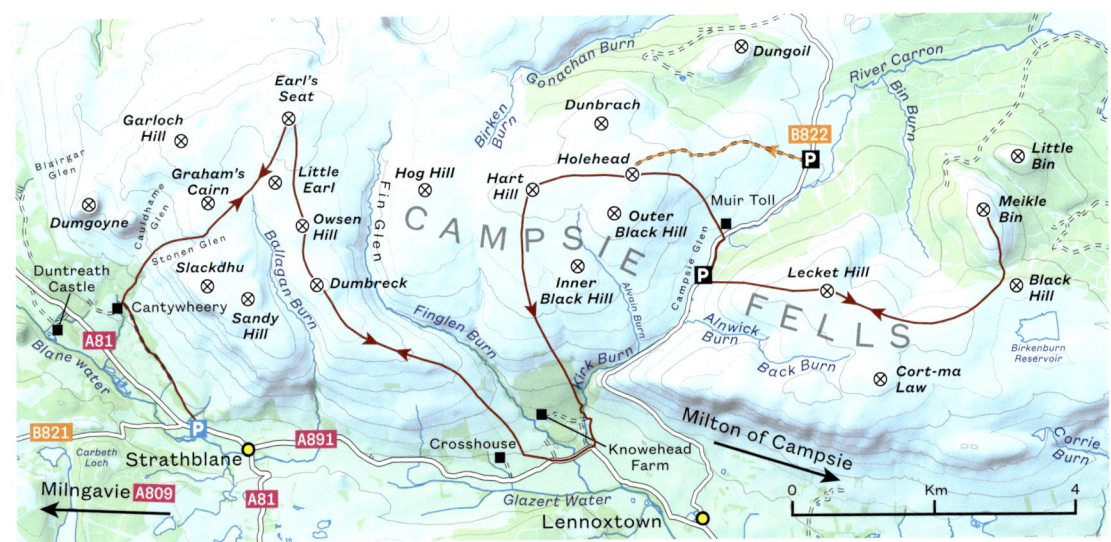

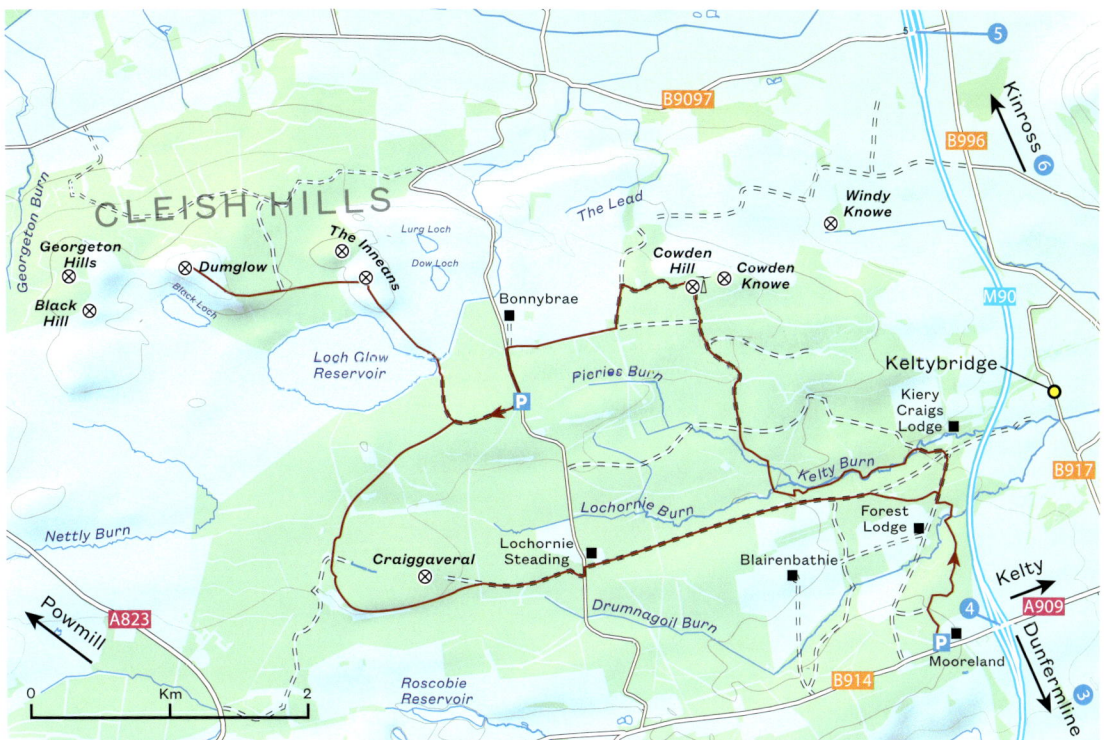

The Cleish Hills

Dumglow ⊗ 379m

△ NT 076 965   ↗ LR58   🌐 P.75

P The upper car park at the entrance to the Forestry and Land Scotland (FLS) visitor centre, Blairadam trails car park (NT 129 937/56.1285, -3.4019) on the B914 just off junction 4 of the M90.

↔ 14KM   △ 200M   ⊤ 210M
⏱ 4–5 HRS   GRADE II   ★★

By Colwyn Jones

Public transport can be used to reach Kelty (Stagecoach X56 service from Edinburgh towards Perth; disembark at the first stop after the M90). Blairadam is on the north side of the B914, some 500m west of Kelty and Junction 4 of the M90. The pavement on the north side of the B914 from Kelty to Blairadam crosses the slip roads from the M90. The slip roads are busy and likely to be clear of snow.

There are a couple of small parking areas at the entrance just off the B914, and a larger main car park 1km down the moderately steep road at the visitor centre. Dumglow is the sole ski route described within the Kingdom of Fife, and the footpaths require only a moderate covering of snow down to sea level, typically early in the year. The Blairadam FLS site has an extensive network of well-made tracks for walking and mountain biking. When covered with snow these tracks running through Sitka plantation favour classic Nordic ski equipment. The tree canopy is so dense in places that it may prevent snow from reaching some paths, which may influence your route choices. Please be aware that pedestrians, dog walkers and mountain bikers may also be out enjoying the snow.

Unusually the day starts with a downhill run! From the car park on the B914 ski north down the steep (for Nordic gear), narrow and twisting route under the dense canopy shading the Fife Pilgrim footpath. Cross a footbridge, go up a slight rise, then take the right fork to soon join the main footpath coming out of the lower car park. If the steep Pilgrim footpath is deemed too technical to begin the day, the gentler tarmac access road down to the main visitor centre could substitute. Continue down the main footpath to a path junction just before the Kelty Burn, a total vertical drop of some 60m and the lowest point of the day, at least with regard to your altitude!

From the junction head west on one of the suitable footpaths, and after just over 1km, turn north to soon continue on wide logging tracks that eventually pass a communications tower. At the tower head west, following the narrow path through trees to reach a hopefully well-frozen boggy section. A short branch leads north-east out of the trees through a metal gate to reach Cowden Hill (285m), where views of central Fife may be visible. Back on the narrow track, continue in a westerly direction, with a left turn at a T-junction, then a right dogleg through a gate at a large dwelling house. After 1km you reach the single-track tarmac road between Cleish Mill (on the B9097, two miles west of the M90 Junction 5) and Greenknowes on the B914. Turn left (south) for 0.5km, where there is a small roadside car park at the track which has been clear-felled on the south side. This car park could also be used as a starting point for a short ascent of Dumglow if the road is accessible. From here, head west along the track to reach a gated junction after 500m. Bear right, remaining on the main track to reach the assorted buildings at the anglers' car park at the eastern end of Loch Glow. Skirt below the low dam at the head of the loch. Go over a wooden footbridge spanning the concrete outflow channel and turn left, following a fence up to a metal ladder stile, which is most unlikely to be under snow. Cross this and leave the main lochside path and counter-intuitively head north-east around the shoulder of the first 336m-high top. From here, descend west through a narrow, steep-sided little ravine on the path leading to the edge of a forestry plantation. An obvious path leads up through the right edge of the trees (the trees on the left of the path have been clear-felled). There is no gate into the wood, but there is a stile in the deer fence. The sheltered path rises through the densely packed conifers, emerging onto a forest road midway up. A modest signpost indicates the Dumglow path as it disappears, continuing ahead into the trees. Light is soon visible at the end of the arboreal tunnel. The path has a steep exit to the plantation at a stile and curves right, climbing gently to reach the summit triangulation station and cairn on the top of Dumglow (379m). Pause here awhile and enjoy views east over Loch Leven and the Lomond Hills and north-west to the Ochils.

The return is gently downhill along your approach tracks back to Loch Glow, then back along the track for 400m to the gated junction. Here follow the branch south-south-west through the cleared trees to reach the margins of a quarry after 1.5km. Turn east and follow the track back, with a final kink to the tarmac road. Cross the road onto a straight forest track heading east and signposted to Blairadam Forest. This leads back to the network of Blairadam footpaths, and from here make your way back to the visitor centre then finish the tour with an unwelcome return uphill to your starting point.

The Luss Hills

By Bill Morrison, updated by Ole Kemi and Colwyn Jones

The Luss Hills offer a large area of potentially good ski touring within easy reach of Glasgow. They are remarkably smooth and grassy, with broad ridges and a general absence of crags, screes and boulders, and there are many possible tours. Glen Douglas separates the two northern hills while the southern group is deeply divided by the cleft of Glen Luss running west from Luss village. The hills only reach a height of 730m, and as the starting points are mostly less than 100m above sea level, there is usually only decent snow cover for skiing in early winter and it is rather unpredictable. On good days the views over Loch Lomond, the Firth of Clyde and the Southern Highlands are very fine. The group includes eight Grahams and is bounded on the east by Loch Lomond, on the south by the A817 through Glen Fruin, and on the west by Loch Long. Access to the hills is possible from the Glen Fruin road and the A82 road up Loch Lomondside, and also from the roads up Glen Luss and through Glen Douglas from Loch Lomond to Loch Long. Public transport options include regular coach services from Glasgow to Luss or the Inverbeg Hotel.

To the west of The Strone and Beinn a' Mhanaich, and north-west of Doune Hill, is a UK military munitions depot (Defence Munitions Glen Douglas) covering an area of 226 hectares with 56 magazines built into a hillside, reportedly capable of storing around 40,000 tons of missiles, depth charges and conventional shells. Despite the Official Secrets Act (1989) rumours that Glen Douglas is used to store nuclear munitions are doubtful; however, this military area is not accessible. Note that the A817 was originally built as a military access road, and no parking, overtaking or stopping on the road was permitted. These restrictions may no longer be rigorously enforced, but the nearby Glen Fruin road provides trouble-free parking.

Beinn a' Mhanaich ◆ 709m
Mountain of the Monk
△ NS 269 946   LR56   🌐 P.77

Beinn Chaorach ◆ 713m
Mountain of the Sheep
△ NS 287 924   LR56   🌐 P.77

🅿 The southern group of Luss Hills can be approached from the Glen Fruin road. Take the A818 from the Arden roundabout off the A82 towards Helensburgh and then the Glen Fruin turn-off at the second roundabout. Follow this minor road to park on the verge of a large lay-by (NS 274 900/ 56.07213, -4.7743) about 250m north of Auchengaich Farm, just before the bridge over Auchengaich Burn. Signage forbids the use of drones in this area.

↔ 12KM   △ 700M   ↕ 280M
⏱ 3-4 HRS   GRADE III   ★★★

Walk or ski on the old reservoir access road on the east side of the Auchengaich Burn. Carefully cross the A817 and continue to the Auchengaich Reservoir. Cross the dam and skin up onto the long easy-angled ridge over The Strone to the cairn on the summit of Beinn a' Mhanaich. The fence and firing range warning signs provide simple navigation up most of the ridge.

Ski about 500 horizontal metres back south along the ridge to a dip, then turn south-east to ski down the slope to the bealach (351m). From here a fence forms a useful guide to ascend south-east up the long ridge of Beinn Chaorach to reach the triangulation station on the summit, the high point of the tour.

The summit fence continues for 1km to the top of Beinn Tharsuinn (656m). Abandon the fence here and descend south-south-west for 1km along the ridge towards Auchengaich Hill (556m), then ski steeply west down the flank of this hill back to the reservoir access road at the Auchengaich Burn, and so to the car.

The southern hills can also be reached from the main A82 road up Loch Lomond at the A718 road junction (NS 353 883). Park considerately, then walk or ski up the private road past Shemore into Glen Finlas. From the head of a small reservoir climb north-west to Creag an Leinibh (657m) and continue over point 693m to perhaps include an out-and-back leg to Beinn Tharsuinn and Beinn Chaorach; navigation is again simplified by the summit fence. Return to point 693m, then follow the ridge first south-east then south to reach the shoulder of the hill called Balcnock (645m). Continue south-east to the unfortunately named Craperoch (462m), then east to follow Finlas Water back to the A817 and shortly back to the car parking spot.

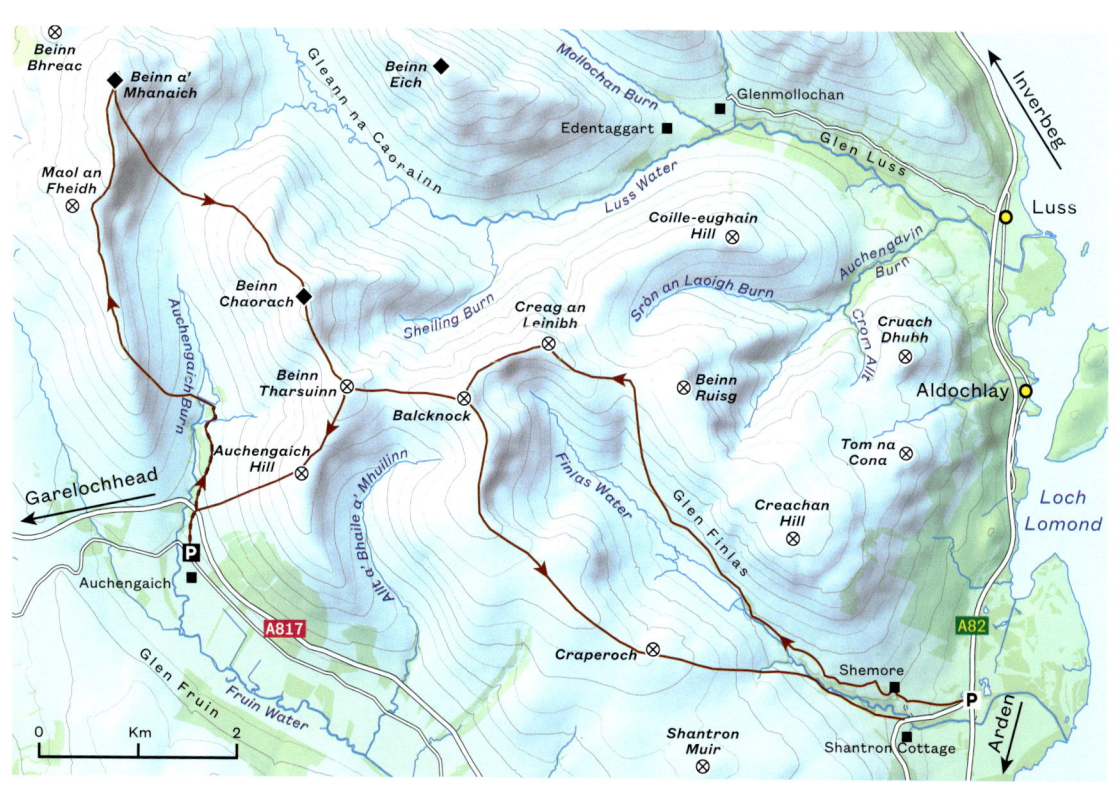

Beinn Eich
△ NS 302 947　　⌲ LR56　　◆ 703m　　🌐 P.78

Doune Hill
△ NS 290 971　　⌲ LR56　　◆ 734m　　🌐 P.78

Mid Hill
△ NS 321 962　　⌲ LR56　　◆ 657m　　🌐 P.78

🅿 Ski or walk up Glen Luss to the farm at Edentaggart.
↔ 20KM　　△ 1,150M　　↕ 150M
⏱ 6-8 HRS　　GRADE III　　**

Beinn Eich, Doune Hill and Mid Hill form three sides of Glen Mollochan, branching off upper Glen Luss. Looking up the glen from Luss village, the conical shape of Beinn Eich is very distinctive, with the ridge of Doune Hill behind. On the north side of the glen the ridge to Beinn Dubh rises directly from Luss and continues to Mid Hill. It is possible to drive up Glen Luss to the end of the public road near Glenmollochan Farm, but there are few parking places which anyway may be hard to use if there is snow down to the lochside. It may be better to park in the large pay and display car park in the centre of Luss, especially as the parking is free out of season!

From the farm at Edentaggart follow the footpath up the fine east ridge of Beinn Eich (703m). Continue north-west along the ridge to pass Beinn Lochain then curve round a slight dip at the head of the glen to reach the triangulation station on the summit of Doune Hill (734m), the highest point of the Luss Hills, and of this tour. A return by the same route allows the skier to stay high for as long as possible before the run down to Glen Luss.

An alternative, more energetic route traverses Doune Hill with a lengthy descent east from the first dip north of the trig pillar. Avoid the line of any streams flowing down to the bealach (230m) on the north side. At the bealach, reapply climbing skins and climb the 400m up the east ridge of Mid Hill to finally turn north (623m) to reach the summit (657m). After catching your breath, travel north-east, then very soon east, and then south-east around the head of Glen Striddle to the summit of Beinn Dubh. Helpfully a fence traverses the summit and this is followed to the 500m contour from where the route descends the south-east ridge at a satisfying and consistent gradient all the way back to the village of Luss.

If the reascent up Mid Hill seems too daunting or the weather has deteriorated, then from the bealach head down following the track on the north side of Glen Mollochan with a return along the Glen Luss road.

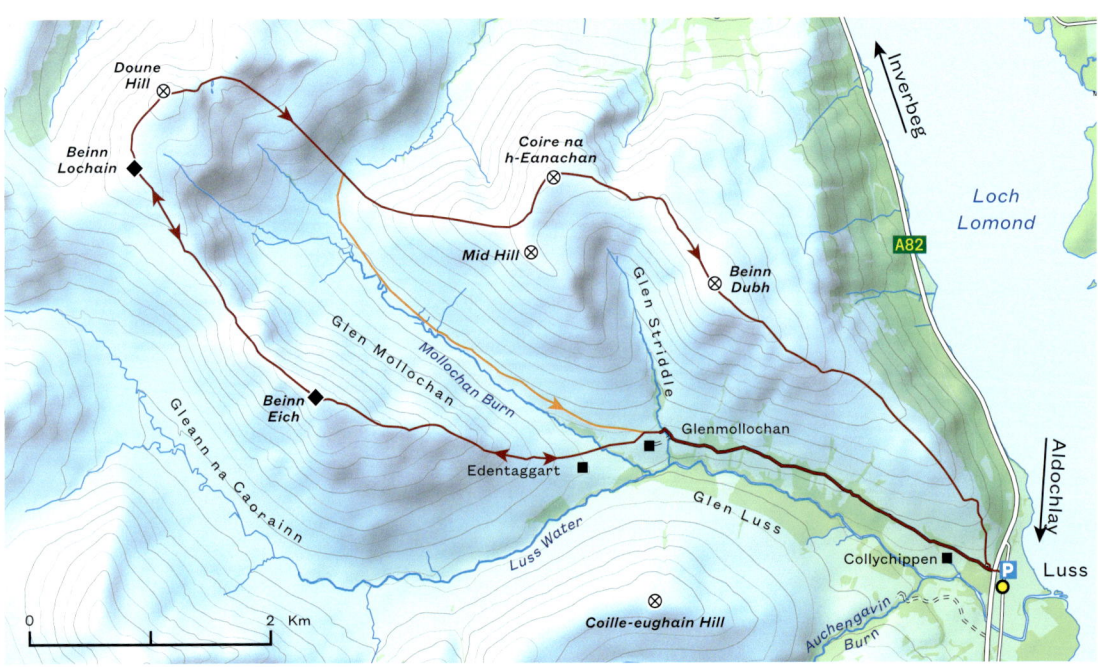

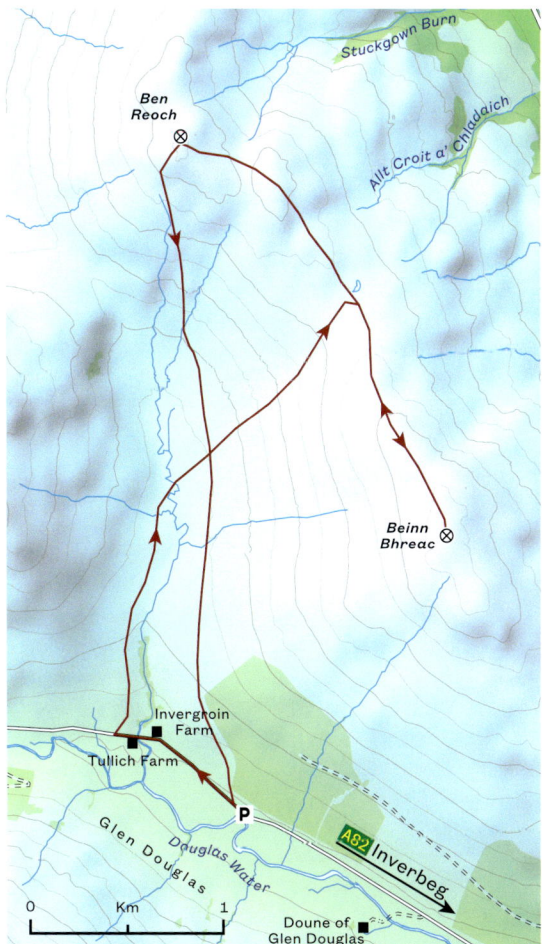

The initially steep descent is due south from the summit, where some old fence posts might help with navigation. Then follow the watercourse, perhaps favouring the eastern bank or where there is snow, to allow a direct return to the parked cars, or via your access near Invergroin Farm.

Ben Lomond ▲ 974m
Beacon Hill

△ NN 367 028   ◁ LR56   ⊕ P.80

P Rowardennan on the east side of Loch Lomond about 10km north-north-west of Balmaha (NS 360 986; altitude 10m). There is an alternative start at Blairvockie Farm (NS 377 968/56.1366, -4.6128) 2.5km south-east of Rowardennan.

↔ 13KM   △ 970M   ⊥ 10M
⏱ 4-5 HRS   GRADE III   ★★★★

By Donald Bennet, updated by Colwyn Jones

Ben Lomond, well known as one of Scotland's most popular hillwalkers' mountains, is also a surprisingly good skiers' peak. However, as the ascent starts barely 10m above sea level, it is a ski tour which should be reserved for a day when the snow-line is very low. Overall, the skiing on the long middle ridge is easy, but the last few hundred metres to the summit are steep and can give good but not unduly difficult skiing. These upper slopes face south-west and may therefore have very variable conditions.

The best starting point will depend on the level of the snow-line. If it is above 200m, the simplest start is to carry skis up the well-engineered path from the pay and display car park and toilets at Rowardennan. It leads east-north-east through the forest and crosses a track and footbridge onto the open hillside at the foot of the south ridge of Ben Lomond below Sròn Aonaich.

If there is snow down to loch level, then two better approaches are possible, which, unlike the path mentioned above, give good skiing much earlier at lower levels. One route starts just north of the Rowardennan car park at Ardess cottages and goes east up the wooded hillside onto the higher open slopes. Above 200m bear north past Tom Eas, then north-east to Sròn Aonaich.

The other starting point is at Blairvockie Farm, 2.5km south-east of Rowardennan. Follow an upland track to the east of the wooded Coille Mhòr Hill, and after 2km leave this track and continue north up Sròn Aonaich. Once on the long south ridge of Ben Lomond, where the three routes described converge, there is an easy and in places almost level approach to the upper cone of the mountain.

Beinn Bhreac ⊗ 681m
Speckled Mountain

△ NN 321 000   ◁ LR56   ⊕ P.79

P On the hills to the north of Glen Douglas is a good short tour starting near Invergroin Farm at a small parking area below conifer trees (NS 310 987/56.1510, -4.7223).

↔ 8KM   △ 750M   ⊥ 110M
⏱ 2-3 HRS   GRADE III   ★★

Ski up the road, past the farm and cross the bridge over the burn. Go across fields on the right and through another couple of fences/gates to the open hillside. Pass some small waterfalls and at about the 200m contour, or before if possible, cross the burn draining from An t-Sreang and aim towards a col (525m) between Beinn Bhreac and Ben Reoch. Once the ridge is gained, turn right to visit the triangulation station on the top of Beinn Bhreac (681m). Return to the col and then ski past the small east top (632m) to the cairn on the summit of Ben Reoch (661m).

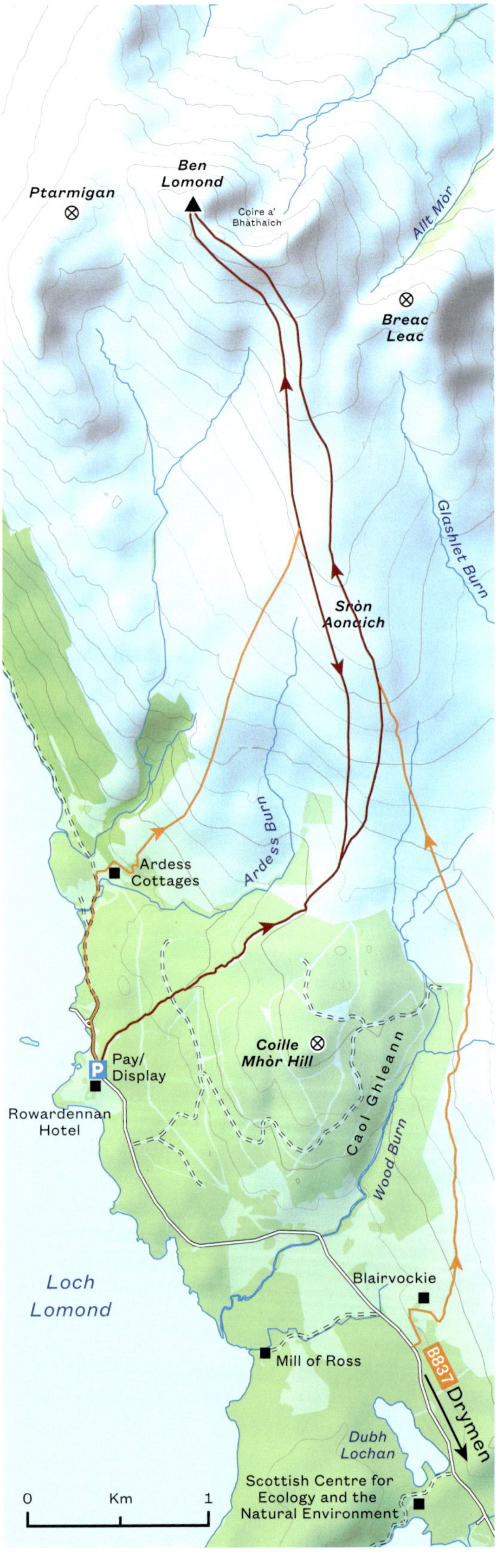

As the ridge begins to steepen, bear north-north-west (not following the line of the path) and gain height by a rising traverse and a few zigzags up the south-west face. This climb ends on the summit ridge not far from the top, and for the last 200–300m go along this narrow ridge and up the short summit dome.

The return is likely to follow more or less the line of ascent, during which you will no doubt have studied the best route for the downhill run. Only the top 200m are steep, and below this there is a long, easy schuss along the broad crest of the south ridge.

The Ochils

These hills are for the opportunist skier, for when the snow arrives it does not usually stay for long. The skiing is mostly over gently undulating hills, which in summer are entirely grassy. Nordic skis are suitable, especially if the plan is to travel rather than seek out steeper descents, which can also provide entertainment for the Alpine skier or snowboarder. Such is the featureless nature of these hills that a clear day is desirable; otherwise be prepared to challenge your navigation skills in poor visibility.

Several ski tours are possible over the wide, flat-topped grassy summits of the Ochils. The longest and most satisfying is the complete traverse from Glen Devon to Sheriffmuir, or vice versa. There are also shorter tours, starting for example from Dollar, Tillicoultry or Alva on the south side of the Ochils and also visiting Blairdenon Hill from the Sheriffmuir road.

The Ochils Traverse ♦ 721m

Ben Cleuch

△ NN 902 006	⌖ LR58	🌐 P.81

🅿 The A823 in Glen Devon at the car park opposite Glendevon Castle at the foot of Glen Sherup (NN 972 051/ 56.2278, -3.6595).

↔ 23KM	△ 870M	⊤ 230M
⏱ 6-8 HRS	GRADE III	★★★

By Gerry Peat, updated by Chris Ravey and Colwyn Jones

If road conditions permit, and you have two cars, leave one for the return on the unclassified Sheriffmuir road at the small stand of trees close to Lairhill (NN 833 027), where there is good parking beside the road; altitude 314m. In the fortunate event that the road is blocked by snow, there are several options for parking along the unclassified road that leads up from Dunblane past the MacRae Monument (NN 815 019).

Start the traverse in Glen Devon opposite Glendevon Castle and follow the signposted forest tracks through the conifer plantation towards Glensherup Reservoir, then swinging back eastwards, eventually onto a smaller footpath through the trees and onto the north-east ridge of Innerdownie. Follow the wall south-westwards along the ridge to the summit of Innerdownie (NN 966 031; 611m).

Alternatively, follow the north-east ridge of Innerdownie in its entirety from Burnfoot, accessed via a footpath and bridge over the River Devon from the A823 just west of the Tormaukin Hotel. Innerdownie can also be ascended via the slopes on the north-west side of Glenquey Reservoir, starting at a lay-by beside the Castlehill Reservoir (NN 997 033) and following the farm road to Glenquey.

Leaving Innerdownie, continue south-west past Bentie Knowe, following the ridge to Whitewisp Hill, then westwards to Tarmangie Hill. An easy run west leads down to the next col, followed by a level traverse west-south-west across the flat Skythorn Hill to Andrew Gannel Hill. If the tour is to include all of the Ochil 2,000ft summits, a diversion to King's Seat (648m) can be made between Tarmangie and Andrew Gannel, with an ascent of the north ridge of King's Seat from the river junction towards the top of the Glen of Sorrow. Descending north-westwards from King's Seat allows Andrew Gannel to be ascended via its east shoulder.

From Andrew Gannel Hill, a broad ridge, with the obliging fence, leads west to the summit of Ben Cleuch (721m), the highest of the Ochils. Halfway between Andrew Gannel and Ben Cleuch there is the option to follow a fence southwards and visit The Law (638m), another 2,000ft summit.

If there is enough drifted snow you may need to use your snow shovel to create adequate shelter from the wind around the stone wall surrounding the trig pillar on Ben Cleuch. The views are superb on a clear, crisp winter day, with a backdrop of the Highland mountains to the north and views across the Firth of Forth towards the Pentlands and Tinto to the south.

From the summit of Ben Cleuch (NN 902 006) ski west-north-west then north-north-west to the summit of Ben Buck (679m) using the fence to navigate if it is visible. Ben Ever (622m) is another summit over 2,000ft, and you can tick it by going south from Ben Buck, then traversing back northwards to the end of the Alva landrover track (NN 888 010). The next section needs accurate

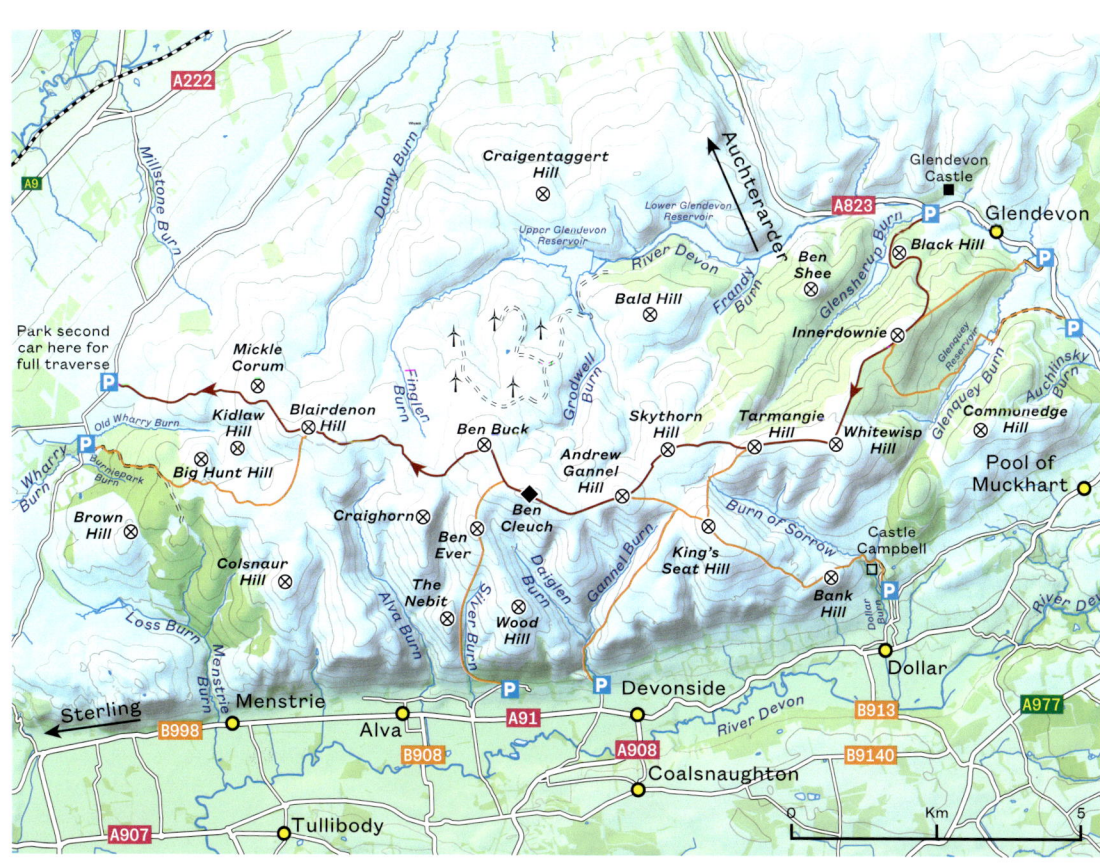

navigation, having few identifiable features. From Ben Buck head west to cross a vague col at the top of the Alva landrover track, then head north-west across the peat hags, crossing a fence in the vicinity of a 560m ring contour, to gain the broad eastern ridge of Blairdenon Hill (NN 865 018; 631m), where three fences meet. From Blairdenon summit follow the fence westwards along the broad ridge towards the minor summit of Greenforet Hill (613m), passing the memorial (if not buried by snow) to a pilot who was killed when a de Havilland Tiger Moth plane crashed here in August 1957. At Greenforet Hill continue north-west towards the summit of Mickle Corum (594m). Either bag the summit and ski the steep west slope of Mickle Corum towards Glentye Hill (481m) or descend towards Glentye Hill from the col between Greenforet and Mickle Corum. From the summit of Glentye Hill, ski through the recent tree plantation down the west slope towards the Sheriffmuir road at the small stand of trees at Lairhill.

Numerous shorter excursions can be enjoyed in the Ochils, often joining the route of the 'grand tour' from convenient access points along the A91 Hillfoots road. King's Seat Hill (648m), for instance, can be ascended from Dollar via Castle Campbell. A starting point of Mill Glen in Tillicoultry can give a pleasant circular tour by heading along the path on the south-east side of Gannel Burn, taking in King's Seat Hill before heading back north-westwards to Andrew Gannel Hill and Ben Cleuch, returning to Mill Glen via The Law. The hill track on the east side of The Nebit above the village of Alva gives easy access to a path up the south-west shoulder of Ben Ever. The hill track can be accessed either from Alva Glen or from the Ochil Hills Woodland Park. From Ben Ever it is only a short distance to Ben Cleuch around the headwall of Daiglen Burn.

For those wanting a shorter trip from the western edge of the Ochils, Blairdenon Hill and Colsnaur Hill (553m) can also be accessed from the bridge at NN 828 016 on the Sheriffmuir road. From here the Jerah forestry track can be followed eastwards and south-eastwards for approximately 2km to a vague col south-west of Big Hunt Hill. Leave the track here to go north-east for around 600m, then follow the broad ridge generally east and south-eastwards for a further 1,500m to reach the well-defined fence line which runs between Colsnaur and Blairdenon Hills. Good navigation may be required in poor visibility. The fence line can then be followed either southwards to Colsnaur Hill or northwards to Blairdenon Hill. Return following the route of ascent influenced by the prevailing snow conditions, or follow the return described for the full traverse via Mickle Corum.

The Arrochar Alps

by Ole Kemi

The Cobbler and the wider Arrochar Alps are scenic mountains well known amongst hillwalkers and climbers, but they also provide excellent ski mountaineering. Rising dramatically west and north of Loch Long and Arrochar, they are especially convenient for Central Belt residents, and the jagged skyline of The Cobbler, in particular, is inspiring and exciting.

Opposite: Beinn Ime heading for the A83 (skier, Douglas Sloan) © Alan Sloan

The Cobbler ● 884m

Ben Arthur

△ NN 259 058　　　🧭 LR56　　　🌐 P.83

🅿 An Socach/Succoth A83 pay and display car park by Arrochar (NN 294 049/56.2064, -4.7504).

↔ 10KM　　　△ 890M　　　⊥ SEA LEVEL

🕐 4-5 HRS　　　GRADE II　　　★★

By Ole Kemi

The start from Loch Long offers the best views of The Cobbler and the Arrochar Alps, and may be reached by public transport.

From the car park, zigzag up a good path through the lochside forest. At an altitude of 100m follow a landrover track left/south-west for 70m before breaking right. Soon you will emerge from the forest, The Cobbler in front of you. The path passes the Narnain boulders, after which a left-branching path leads directly to the southern, steep aspects of The Cobbler's North and Centre Peaks, while a right-branching path offers a mellower ski approach towards Lochan a' Chlaidheimh and the bealach between Beinn Narnain and The Cobbler (628m). Here, turn south-south-west up gentle

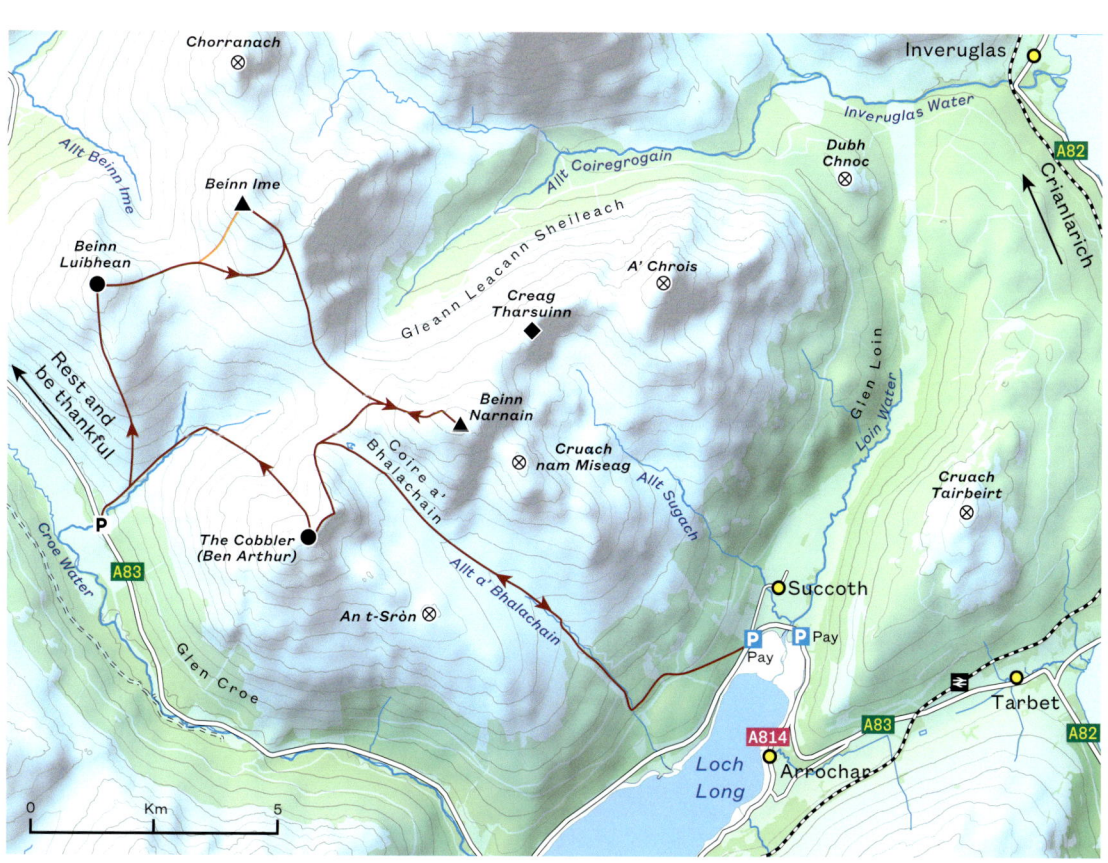

slopes that soon narrow to a broad ridge leading up to the North Peak. Either bypass or take in the North Peak but continue to the Centre Peak and the main summit of The Cobbler (NN 259 058). Be aware that the summit ridge is often very icy and has steep cliffs to the south-east.

The return follows the ascent line, with open, gentle slopes suitable for skiing, but some boulders and outcrops that must be negotiated. In good snow conditions, an eastward descent line after and north of the North Peak leads to gully lines and steeper slopes that have been skied before. Other descents follow the steep slopes south-east from the col between the North and Centre Peaks along the stepped path. Alternatively, bypass with care the Centre and South Peaks to the west to follow the broad ridge south-east to An t-Sròn (614m) before returning to the path.

Beinn Luibhean ● 858m
Hill of the Little Plants
△ NN 242 079   ◁ LR56   ⊕ P.83

Beinn Ime ▲ 1,011m
Hill of Butter
△ NN 255 084   ◁ LR56   ⊕ P.83

Beinn Narnain ▲ 926m
Hill of Notches
△ NN 271 066   ◁ LR56   ⊕ P.83

The Cobbler ● 884m
△ NN 259 058   ◁ LR56   ⊕ P.83

P A small car park on the A83 Glen Croe/Rest and Be Thankful road, just below a bridge (NN 242 059/ 56.2139, -4.8349). The car park accommodates 3–4 cars with careful parking; alternative lay-bys are a short distance in either direction.

↔ 13KM   △ 1,580M   ↕ 170M
⏲ 6–8 HRS   GRADE III   ★★★

This route benefits from a higher start point, sees less traffic, takes in two Munros and two Corbetts, and remains high throughout the day. While longer,

Below: Ben Lomond from Ben Vorlich summit with Loch Lomond © Mike Dixon

it is potentially kinder to the bases of your skis in marginal snow conditions due to grassier slopes at lower altitudes.

From the car park, cross the gate and bridge, and follow a steep path up left/north of the burn. At an altitude of 250–300m, leave the path and head north up steep slopes that soon become a wide ridge with small, easily bypassed outcrops to reach the summit of the Corbett Beinn Luibhean (NN 242 079). Continue by descending east to Bealach a' Mhargaidh (1:25,000 OS map) before ascending Beinn Ime by traversing east to reach its south ridge at around 800–850m. Follow the ridge north-north-west or take a more direct, but steeper, north-east line from the bealach; either way, reach the high point of the day and the first Munro (NN 255 084). Beware of steep slopes east of the ridge. Return south-south-east to Bealach a' Mhaim (637m) before ascending east-south-east up the gentle slopes that take you to the summit of Beinn Narnain (NN 271 066) and the second Munro.

Before reaching the bealach upon return, veer left/west to Lochan a' Chlaidheimh and the bealach between Beinn Narnain and The Cobbler (628m). Here, continue south-south-west up gentle slopes that soon narrow to a broad ridge leading up to the North Peak of The Cobbler. Thereafter, continue to the Centre Peak and the main (and final) summit (NN 259 058) for the second Corbett. Beware that the summit ridge is often very icy and has steep south-east drops. From here, return to the car park by finding a north-north-westerly descent line down broad, grassy slopes until you reach the burn. Cross this just below a dam onto its right/north side, where a path leads back to the A83. This descent is on good slopes with few hazards, providing comfortable skiing as long as snow cover allows, but the ground below is typically wet underfoot.

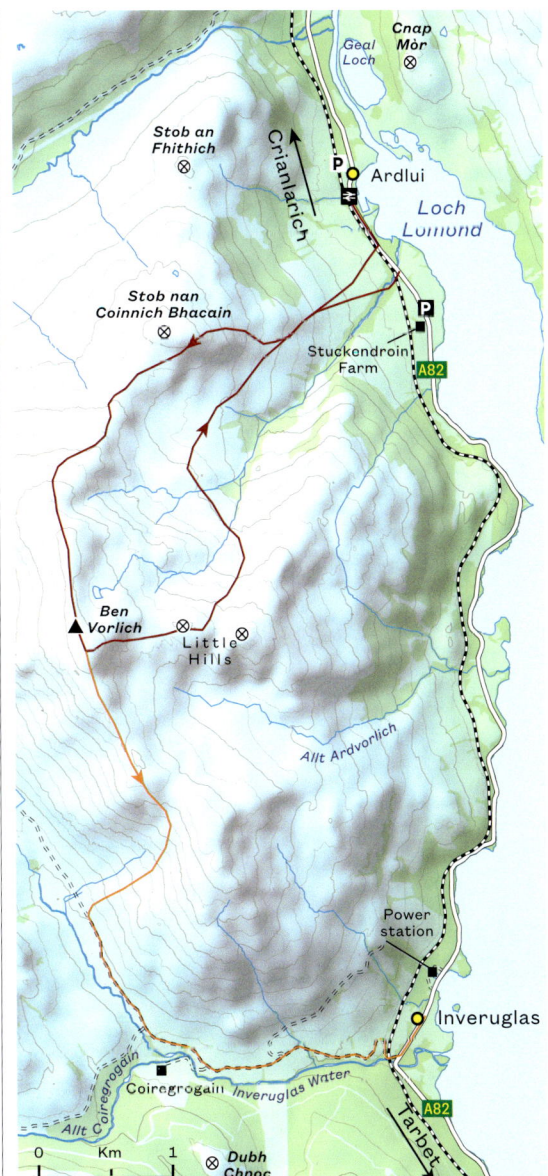

Ben Vorlich ▲ 943m
Hill of the Bay

△ NN 295 124	⌖ LR50, LR56	⊕ P.85
P Ardlui (NN 316 155/56.3025, -4.7224) on the A82.		
↔ 10KM	△ 950M	⊺ 15M
⏱ 3-4 HRS	GRADE II	★★

By Colwyn Jones and Ole Keml

Ben Vorlich is a broad-based, twin-topped mountain situated on the north-east bank of Scotland's largest freshwater loch (by surface area), Loch Lomond. A pleasant ski ascent following the summer track towards Loch Sloy and the long south ridge starts from the large pay and display car park at Inveruglas (NN 323 098), just north of the Loch Sloy Power Station (buses from Glasgow; café and toilets). However, an interesting ski route starts north-east of the peak at Ardlui Marina.

The train station is a good starting point, particularly if you arrive by rail; alternatively, there is limited parking on the A82 opposite the hotel. Head south on the A82 to the second railway underpass to the south of the Ardlui Station subway entrance (the first underpass is conveniently signposted as not leading to Ben Vorlich). Alternatively, roadside parking can be found on the east side of the A82 north of the entrance to Stuckendroin Farm (NN 322 147). Parking here avoids the short walk along the busy A82.

Once you have passed below the railway by either route, the open hillside leads south-west through scattered birch woods to Coire Creagach. At the 500m contour a shelf traverses south and can be used to ascend the minor top, Little Hills, 808m (NN 303 124). From this outlier head west and follow the best line to the triangulation station. However, the true summit is 200m north of the trig pillar, atop a small crag.

As is often the case, the safest descent is probably the ascent route. However, an alternative is to head north over the second twin summit and, following the broad ridge around the top of Coire Creagach, pick your way down to the subsidiary top of Stob nan Coinnich Bhacain (647m), then head north-east back to either Ardlui Station or Stuckendroin Farm.

A complete traverse of the peak from Loch Sloy Power Station to Ardlui is possible with two cars or by taking a bus to Inveruglas and returning by train from Ardlui.

Ben Ledi ● 879m

Hill of the Gentle Slope or *God's Hill*

△ NN 562 097   ↗ LR57   ⊕ P.86

P With good snow cover, the best ascent (according to Wallace) starts at the Dam Road car park at the end of the public road (NN 531 073/56.2358, -4.3709), 1km north-north-west of Brig o' Turk, 10km west of Callander. A slightly longer but more attractive start is from the Woodland Trust Lendrick Hill car park at the Glen Finglas Gateway on the A821 (NN 546 065/56.2291, -4.3461). The starting point for the south ridge is the Iron Age fort car park (NN 602 073/56.2380, -4.2565) on the A821 about 3km west of Callander, opposite the road signposted to Invertrossachs. Alternatively, start at the main Ben Ledi car park off the A84 south of Loch Lubnaig on the Rob Roy Way.

↔ 9KM   △ 770M   ⇅ 100M
⏱ 3–4 HRS   GRADE II   ★★

By William Wallace, updated by Colwyn Jones

Ben Ledi is a prominent and accessible hill in a unique position on the southern edge of the Highlands. It commands extensive views across the Central Lowlands and gives a rewarding ski ascent in crisp, clear conditions when there is good snow cover low down. Starting points for all three routes

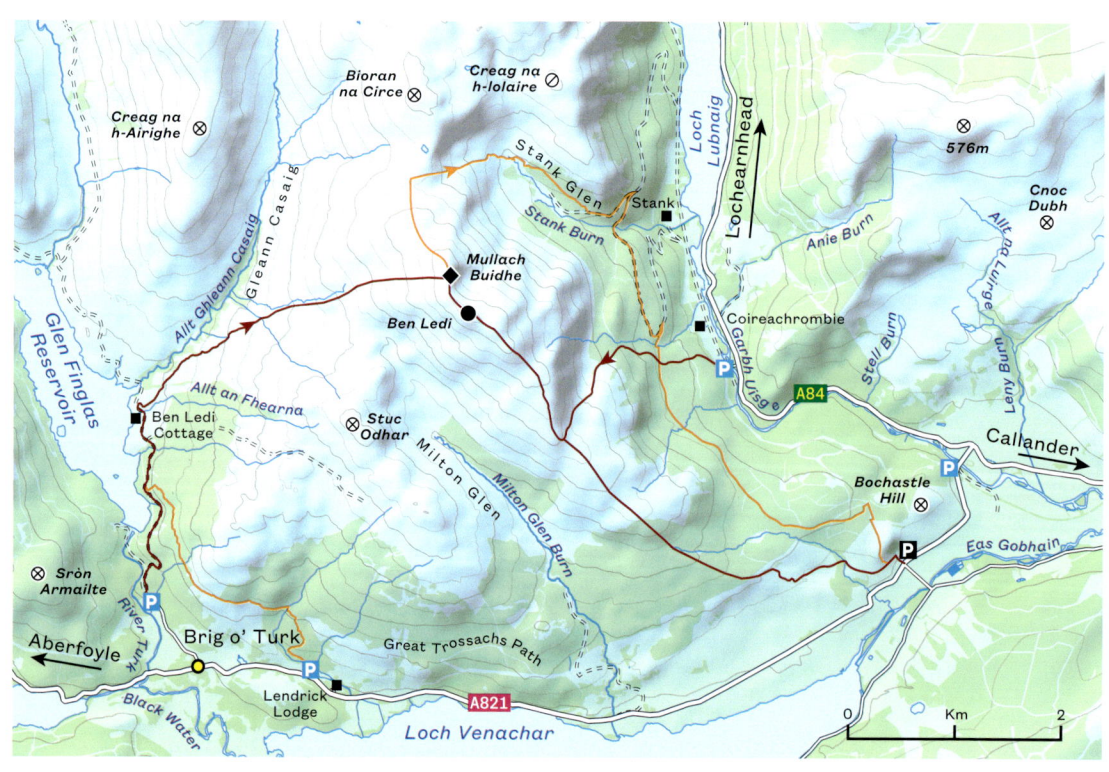

Above: Ben Ledi (skier, Doug Bryce) © Eaton Beaver

described below are not much more than 100m above sea level.

The Brig o' Turk route starts 1km north-north-west of the village at the end of the public road, south of the Glen Finglas Reservoir dam. Take the right fork up the private tarmac road, which climbs high on the east side of the reservoir for 1.5km to the agricultural buildings at the foot of Gleann Casaig. The alternative start from Lendrick Hill car park follows the footpath north over the Great Trossachs Path footbridge for a short distance, but soon turns west and contours the hillside to meet the tarmac road above Glen Finglas Reservoir and on to the buildings of Gleann Casaig. Continue north-east up this glen along a good hill track high on the south-east bank of the stream to a high point (360m) at NN 544 099, taking care with the stream crossings. Then climb due east up the easy-angled hillside, which gives a pleasant ascent and steepens when the summit ridge is reached north-west of the trig point on Ben Ledi.

The route described in the first edition from the derelict Coilantogle Farm no longer has safe roadside parking, but space for 4–5 cars is available about 1km towards Callander at the Iron Age fort car park (NN 602 073). Go up 100m and turn left onto the excellent Great Trossachs Path through regenerating woodland and an access gate in the deer fence. After about 1km, at a path crossroads (NN 592 072), turn right to follow a faint path north-west up the hillside, past a ruined sheep fank towards the south-west corner of the forestry plantation where there is both a vehicle and pedestrian gate (NN 588 073). Good snow cover is desirable here as the vegetation is troublesome on this south-facing and deer-free slope. Continue uphill along the west side of the mature plantation to a short steepening, above which (at about 420m) the south-east ridge of the hill is visible. Ski up the crest of this wide ridge to a second deer fence with a gate (NN 576 080). There is also a rudimentary stile if deep snow prevents the gate from being opened. Join the main Ben Ledi footpath at the 580m contour as it follows the south ridge, which has alternate level sections, two dips and short steeper rises, to pass a memorial cross and the boulder sculpture park, just before the trig pillar. The cross is a memorial to Police Sergeant Harry Lawrie BEM, who was a member of the Killin Mountain Rescue team.

He was fatally injured in a Wessex helicopter crash in February 1987 while searching for an injured climber on Ben More.

A third ascent route starts from the large Ben Ledi car park (NN 586 092; 125m). Follow the well-signposted summer footpath to Ben Ledi. The steep, narrow path is busy and is, in places, a stone staircase, so it is unsuitable for skiing or skinning, but it quickly reaches the margins of the forest at 400m, where skiing is more amenable, so it may be a better choice with suitable snow cover. The track turns south to avoid crags and sweeps round onto the south ridge to join the summit route described from the Iron Age fort.

Descent of these three routes is by your ascent route. However, when conditions are safe the Loch Lubnaig route could allow you to traverse the peak. Continue north from the summit, over a minor summit and down the north ridge to reach the Bealach nan Corp (1:25,000 OS map; 650m). This translates as 'Pass of the Dead' and is the high point on an old coffin road from Glen Finlas to St Bride's chapel.

From the bealach follow the south bank of the burn draining the area. Aim for the summer stile (NN 564 111) over the deer fence, and a derelict low fence, then go down to a path junction. Take the path over Stank Burn and follow the narrow track down to a forestry track. If you are walking by this point, then go right on the waymarked footpath that will deliver you to the lochside and a flat walk back to the main car park. However, if there is sufficient snow, continue skiing straight downhill on the wider forestry track to the next junction. Turn right, then re-cross the Stank Burn for the final unwelcome vertical ascent of 70m over less than 1km. From the crest of the track ski down to meet the well-made main footpath and follow this back to the car park. This narrow track will likely be busy with walkers, so diplomatically avoid all obstacles before you are finally spat off the track close to the car park.

If your party has two cars, or an accommodating driver, a very nice traverse of Ben Ledi can be crafted by combining two of the three ski routes described above, when conditions allow.

A steep, extreme ski descent is very occasionally possible down Ben Ledi's Central Gully when there is a good build-up of snow. Central Gully is classed as a Grade I winter climb, but the date and identity of either the first climber to ascend or skier to descend the route is unknown. The condition of the snow in the gully is best assessed by climbing up it. From the main Ben Ledi car park take the footpath and, as it leaves the trees, cross first a low fence, then the burn, allowing a traverse to the foot of the gully (NN 573 092). This is only at an altitude of about 450m, so cold conditions are essential for safe snow. There are narrow sections in the lower part of the route. Avoid the gully late in spring or in mild temperatures when there will be a significant wet slab avalanche risk. The ascent is typically a slog up deep snow, after which you are faced with a right or left finish. The left exit (looking up) has a central rocky pinnacle (which may be banked out) and is steep and best avoided with skis strapped to your rucksack! The right exit allows a safer finish, although the top of the gully is steep and can host a large and hazardous cornice (NN 570 093; 680m), which can pose an avalanche risk. The top of the gully is still 200 vertical metres from the summit of Ben Ledi and the upper slopes of the hill may hold a large volume of snow. As with any gully or slope, careful assessment of the avalanche risk is required before attempting to climb up or ski down.

Beinn Tulaichean ▲ 946m
Hill of Hillocks

NN 416 196   LR51, LR56   P.89

Cruach Ardrain ▲ 1,046m
Stack of the High Part

NN 409 212   LR56   P.89

P The car park on the minor road 700m east of Inverlochlarig Farm and 9km west of Balquhidder (NN 446 184/56.3329, -4.5151).

↔ 12KM   △ 1,020M   ↕ 130M
⏱ 5-6 HRS   GRADE III   ★★★

By Donald Bennet, updated by Colwyn Jones

These two peaks south of Crianlarich are steep, rugged and craggy, but they give a very interesting tour with some good skiing on their upper slopes and along the high ridge connecting them. Beinn Tulaichean is really a minor summit on the south ridge of Cruach Ardrain. The approach is west of Balquhidder along the single-track road beside Loch Voil.

Proceed west along the road to the farm where the track on the west of Inverlochlarig Burn allows direct access to the south-east slopes of Beinn Tulaichean. The gradient is easy at first, but the hillside steepens and higher up it is necessary to zigzag and eventually, as you approach a line of crags, make a long rising traverse west to reach the broad, easy-angled south ridge. Continue up this, passing a little rocky knoll on the east, and in 600m reach the summit of Beinn Tulaichean.

Ski north-north-west down along the broad ridge, which gives easy running to the col at about 820m. Here, re-apply climbing skins for the ascent of Cruach Ardrain. If the snow cover on the ridge leading north-north-west is poor, it may be better to ski up the shallow gully immediately to its east. At the top of the ridge (or gully) turn right (north-east) and climb the last short slope to a little plateau with two cairns. The summit of Cruach Ardrain is 100m further north-east across a dip.

Return by the ascent route to the 820m col. On the descent the gully will probably give a better run than the ridge, unless the latter is well covered with snow. In good conditions, however, the gully gives delightful skiing. From the col it is feasible to return over Beinn Tulaichean and ski down the ascent route, and this might be the preferred option on a fine afternoon, giving you the chance to enjoy the splendid views south and south-west to Ben Lomond and the Arrochar Alps.

The alternative, which gives a quicker descent to low ground, is to ski east from the col into the Inverlochlarig Glen. At first the skiing is easy, but lower down the terrain is broken up by streams, little gullies and crags, and there is no advantage in keeping high on the west side of the glen. If there is snow cover low down, it is best to ski fairly directly down to the track in the glen and enjoy a long, easy schuss to Inverlochlarig.

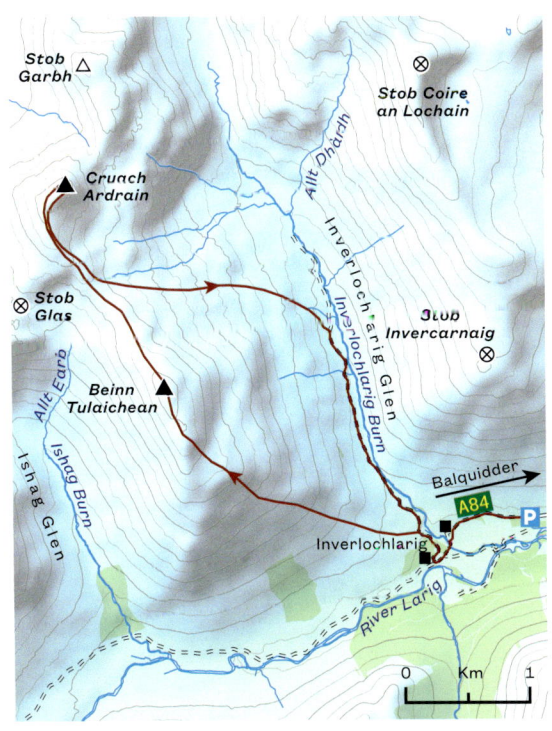

Stob Binnein ▲ 1,165m
Conical Pointed Hill or Anvil Hill

NN 434 227   LR51, LR57   P.90

Ben More ▲ 1,174m
Big Hill

NN 432 244   LR51   P.90

Near the west end of Loch Doine, 7.5km west of Balquhidder (NN 460 192/56.3404, -4.4920).

↔ 12KM   △ 1,350M   ↕ 160M
⏱ 7-8 HRS   GRADE IV   ★★★★

By Donald Bennet, updated by Colwyn Jones

This route was classed by Bennett as one of the finest ski traverses in the Scottish mountains, crossing two of the best known and highest peaks of the Southern Highlands. Not only are the scenery and character of the mountains very fine, but the skiing itself is full of interest and, in certain conditions, may be quite difficult. The traverse follows well-defined ridges, which in places are steep-sided and corniced, so this is a route for those who are competent in both skiing and winter mountaineering. It demands great caution in icy conditions or bad weather, particularly in poor visibility. On a fine day, however, it has few equals.

The complete traverse of Stob Binnein and Ben More can be done equally well from south to north, or vice versa. The south-to-north traverse described here is probably the better choice. It goes up the long south ridge of Stob Binnein over the lower Top of Stob Coire an Lochain (NN 438 220; 1,068m), drops 300m to the col, the Bealach-eadar-dha Bheinn (pass between two bens), reascends the same height to Ben More and finally descends its north-east ridge to Glen Dochart. Variants of this route can shorten the traverse or allow a return to the starting point to avoid the need for two cars.

The southern starting point is 7.5km west along the road from Balquhidder to Inverlochlarig. Leave the road at the cottage on the west side of the Allt Carnaig and climb north-west up Glen Carnaig, crossing two or three small stream gullies. Alternatively use the walkers' car park (NN 446 184) 1.5km further along at the end of the minor road.

Pass below the crags on the east side of Stob Invercarnaig and reach the lowest point of the ridge between it and Stob Coire an Lochain by an easy-angled and normally uncorniced slope. Continue north-north-west up this ridge, which becomes steep-sided and corniced on the right, but given adequate snow cover presents no difficulties and leads directly to Stob Coire an Lochain.

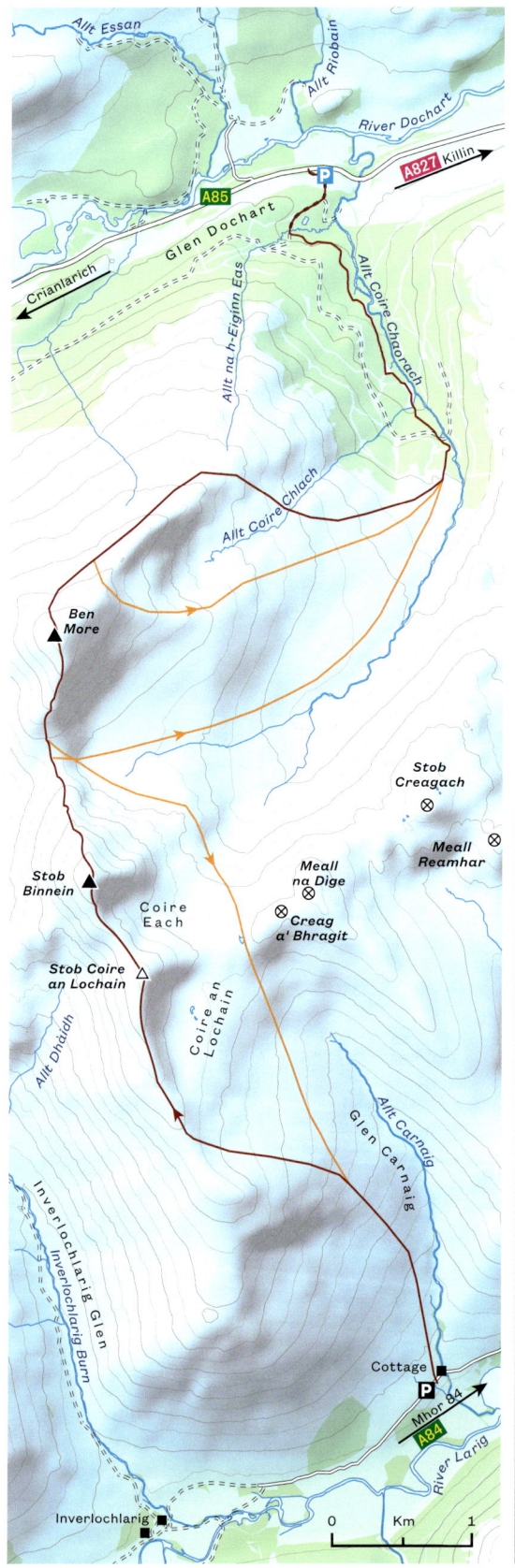

Beyond this Top the ridge is broad and smooth for a few hundred metres, dropping slightly before rising, increasingly steep and narrow and with a large cornice on the right, towards the summit of Stob Binnein (NN 434 226; 1,165m). The last 50m are too steep for skis, and crampons and an ice axe may be needed to reach the summit, where a small cairn stands at the south edge of the little sloping plateau.

The next section of the traverse may well give the best skiing of the day; equally, it may provide the most testing, depending on the state of the snow (or ice) on the north-north-west face of Stob Binnein. Ski down on the west side of the north ridge, possibly close to the ridge or further west on the broad face of the mountain, which drops with unrelenting steepness to the head of the Benmore Burn far below. Bennett mentions an exhilarating yet safe run with a complete cover of firm névé; on another occasion, icy snow barely thick enough to cover the stony slope gave a most unnerving descent which demanded the utmost caution.

The Bealach-eadar-dha Bheinn is a wide, flat col with an easy drop on its east side to the head of Coire Chaorach. The ascent to Ben More is steep; north at first onto the ridge, then north-east up the ridge, gradually curving round north past some little crags which look prominent from below. The summit is a large crag.

The descent of the north-east ridge of Ben More starts easily along the broad, easy-angled crest, but soon a short, rocky step must be negotiated. The skiing is easy again until the ridge narrows at Sròn nam Fòrsairean, where you can either descend south-east into Coire Chaorach or continue a descending traverse on the steep north-west flank below the rocky crest to regain the ridge in a few hundred metres. Both routes call for care.

The densely planted trees of the Ben More Forest are not far below, and you should aim for a gate in the forest fence about 0.5km west of the Allt Coire Chaorach. Just below this gate (NN 458 254), a track goes down through the forest, with a few zigzags and a crossing of the Allt Coire Chaorach low down before reaching the A85 in Glen Dochart. With good snow cover you can ski right down this track, a fitting end to a great day.
It is possible to go direct from the Bealach-eadar-dha Bheinn to Glen Dochart down Coire Chaorach, skiing easily along the north-west side of the burn to the tree line to meet the traverse route. This is much shorter and easier than the traverse of Ben More (12km; 1,020m; 6 hours). To return from Ben More to the southern starting point, ski back down the south ridge to the Bealach and then east to the head of Coire Chaorach. If snow conditions are good on the south side of Ben More, you can leave the

ridge two-thirds of the way down to the Bealach and ski steeply south-east between small crags to the head of the corrie, a short and exhilarating run. Once in Coire Chaorach, which forms a level bowl below the east face of Stob Binnein, traverse south-east then south with a slight climb to reach the col between Meall na Dìge and Stob Coire an Lochain. On the south side of this col a long, easy run down the wide open spaces of Glen Carnaig leads back to the starting point (13.5km; 1,380m; 7–8 hours).

Ben Vorlich ▲ 985m
Hill of the Bay

△ NN 629 189　　◁ LR51, LR57　　🌐 P.91

Stùc a' Chroin ▲ 975m
Peak of the Sheepfold

△ NN 617 175　　◁ LR51, LR57　　🌐 P.91

P Braeleny Farm (NN 637 108/56.2697, -4.2030) at the end of the public road from Callander up the glen of the Keltie Water (past Bracklinn Falls).

↔ 19KM　　△ 1,150M　　⊺ 220M
⏱ 7–8 HRS　　GRADE IV　　★★★

By William Wallace, updated by Colwyn Jones

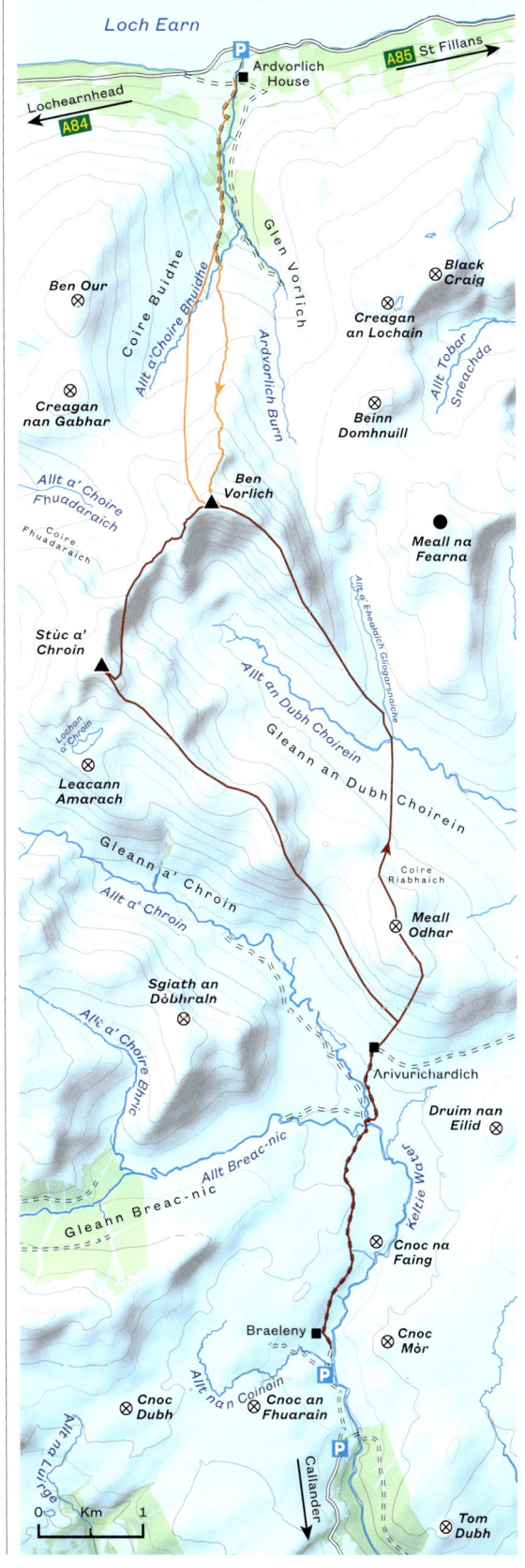

The circuit of these two mountains from the south is a fine and quite long expedition, the highlight of which is the traverse from Ben Vorlich to Stùc a' Chroin. The traverse across the east face of the latter below a series of steep buttresses and gullies is the crux and should only be attempted by experienced mountaineers equipped with ice axes and crampons. It is, however, an excellent ski mountaineering passage in an impressive setting.

The public road going up from Callander past the Bracklinn Falls car park is a steep single-track with gates, and it is not ploughed. Take extra care driving up towards the start, which may be complicated by local people walking their dogs in the area. From the car park south of Braeleny Farm, walk or ski 3km up the new private road north towards the steading at Arivurichardich. Helpfully the ruined bridge over the Keltie Water was reinstated when the hydroelectric scheme was established.

The route continues north, diagonally up the west slopes of Meall Odhar to the north-west end of a broad bealach at the foot of the south-east ridge of Stùc a' Chroin. Easy open slopes then lead north-east down into the Gleann an Dubh Choirein where the burn is crossed to reach the foot of the south ridge of Ben Vorlich (NN 644 166). Initially the ridge is broad and easy but it steepens thereafter with several rocky steps which may be passed on the west. The remains of old fence posts first appear at a little col on the ridge and, if visible, are followed to the summit, which has a large cairn. 100m to the north-west along a level crest is a triangulation station, which is often busy.

From the trig pillar the route follows the fence posts, descending south-west to the Bealach an Dubh Choirein. From the bealach climb south-west, still following the line of the fence posts, towards the foot of the north-east buttress of Stùc a' Chroin. Approaching the foot of the buttress the terrain becomes rocky and boulder-strewn. If early winter hillwalkers have left a footpath, then skis might be carried from here to the top of the slope. However, if there is enough snow, you can enjoy a purer ski ascent by bearing left and making a rising traverse south for 100m to the toe of the buttress, where there are many fallen boulders. Continue south below the steep upper rocks of the Stùc, making a descending traverse for about 250m across a very steep and exposed slope. Great caution is needed, and in hard snow or when the avalanche risk is high it is advisable to take off skis and traverse on foot using an ice axe and crampons. Halfway across the traverse, where the angle eases, ski down more easily to a flat area of huge fallen boulders below the crags. At this point the technical difficulties are over. Continue skiing south on a rising traverse along a broad shelf which leads to the south-east ridge of Stùc a' Chroin, then turn north-west to climb to the summit, turning the steep section of the ridge on the west if the rocks on the crest are not well snow-covered.

In good snow conditions the descent of the south-east ridge is an excellent run. The route initially follows your uphill tracks but then diverges to continue down the ridge, which is almost level at two points, to reach the broad bealach of the uphill route at around 580m. It then follows the outward route down across the west slopes of Meall Odhar to Arivurichardich and finally back to Braeleny Farm.

There are other shorter, separate and easier ski tours on these two mountains for those who prefer to avoid the difficulties on the east face of Stùc a' Chroin. The ascent of the Stùc itself is most easily done from Braeleny Farm by following the route described above to the bealach at the foot of its south-east ridge, and climbing along this ridge to the summit. The return by the same way completes an easy tour.

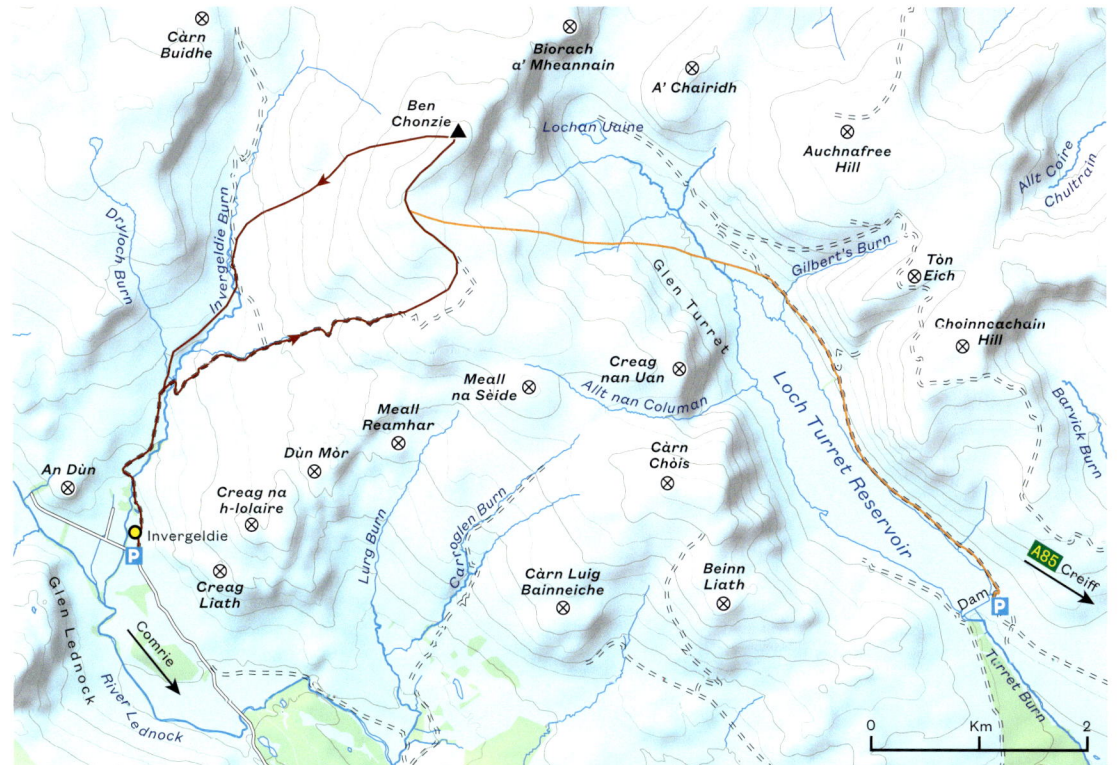

The shortest ascent of Ben Vorlich by itself is from Ardvorlich on the south side of Loch Earn. Follow the track south up the west side of Glen Vorlich to the foot of Coire Buidhe and continue in the same direction up the north ridge of Ben Vorlich. The ridge steepens at its top where the west ridge is joined just before the summit. The descent can be varied by skiing west then north-west from the summit to the bealach at the head of Coire Buidhe, and then down this corrie to rejoin the uphill route.

The ascent of Stùc a' Chroin from Loch Earn (or Loch Lubnaig) by Glen Ample cannot be recommended as there are extensive forestry plantations in this glen, and the north-west ridge of the Stùc (by which the ascent might be made) is steep and craggy.

Left: Glen Turret to Ben Chonzie © Jamie Thin

Ben Chonzie ▲ 931m
Mossy Hill

△ NN 773 308	⌖ LR51, LR52	🌐 P.93

P In Glen Lednock near Invergeldie Farm (NN 740 274/ 56.4213, -4.0397); or In Glen Turret at the Loch Turret dam (NN 821 265/56.4155, -3.9125).

↔ 13KM	⌂ 710M (510M FROM GLEN TURRET)	⊺ 350M
⏱ 4-5 HRS	GRADE II FOR BOTH	✶✶

By Neil Mather, updated by Colwyn Jones

One of the closest Munros to the population of central Scotland, Ben Chonzie is deservedly popular. It is very accessible and, whilst not having any notable features, provides splendid views of the Lawers range, Schiehallion and all the major summits of the Southern Highlands. However, it does not hold much snow late in the season, and its abundant heather means a firm snow base is necessary for good skiing.

If approaching from Comrie by Glen Lednock, the large car park at Invergeldie Farm is the best starting place. Follow the track going north from there for around 1,500m on the west side of the Invergeldie Burn to an obvious crossing below a concrete dam (NN 746 287). Continue to follow the shooting track, which leads east-north-east until, with sufficient snow cover, it is possible to head north-east by steeper slopes to reach the broad south ridge of the mountain. Follow the fence north-west and then north-east (NN 766 302) to gain the substantial summit cairn.

There are two possibilities for the downhill run: either by the ascent route or by descending west from the summit to the head of the Invergeldie Burn, after which follow the best line down the glen until you can regain your uphill tracks.

The alternative route to Ben Chonzie, which gives a more interesting ascent and leads into the crag-girt eastern corrie above Lochan Uaine, is from Glen Turret. Taking the private road from Crieff up to the Loch Turret dam, continue along the track on the north-east side of the loch until, near its head, the track begins to climb uphill. Continue near the lochside past the rhododendrons of the old lodge to the head of the loch. From there start an easy climb west-north-west diagonally across the hillside below small crags and continue in the same direction up the big east-facing corrie until the summit ridge, not far south-west of the summit.

The traverse of Ben Chonzie by the two routes described is a fine expedition, but it requires two cars or a helpful non-skiing driver. The featureless character of the mountain makes accurate navigation essential in bad weather, particularly if the snow is deep enough to bury the fence posts along the summit ridge.

A word of warning about skiing across frozen lochs and reservoirs in hard frost conditions when they may be expected to be safe: as may well be the case with reservoirs, if water has been drawn off and not replaced naturally by streams, the surface ice may be unsupported and much thinner than one might expect, and consequently dangerous to ski across.

Beinn a' Chleibh ▲ 916m
Hill of the Creel or Chest
NN 251 256   LR50   P.94

Ben Lui/Beinn Laoigh ▲ 1,130m
Calf Hill
NN 266 263   LR50   P.94

Ben Oss ▲ 1,029m
Hill of the Loch Outlet or Elk Hill
NN 287 253   LR50   P.94

Beinn Dubhchraig ▲ 978m
Hill of the Black Rock
NN 307 254   LR50   P.94

P At a parking place in Glen Lochy on the of the A85 road (NN 239 278/56.4099, -4.8553).
↔ 19KM   ▲ 1,650M   ⌶ 190M
⏱ 7–8 HRS   GRADE III   ★★★★

By William Wallace, updated by Colwyn Jones

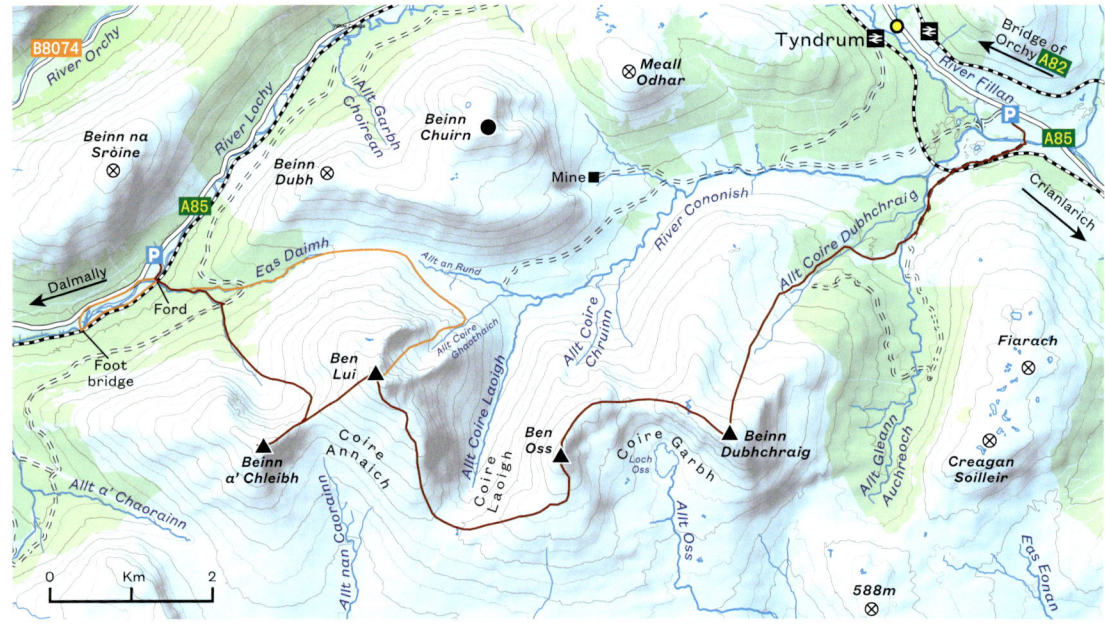

This splendid group of mountains provides one of the best ski tours in Scotland. Individually, Ben Lui and Beinn Dubhchraig can provide very good out-and-back tours from the ends of the traverse. Central Gully on Ben Lui offers a steep ski descent when conditions are safe (see details below).

Ski tourers with sufficient stamina to cope with 1,650m of climbing on skins will wish to complete the traverse of all four mountains. This may be undertaken in either direction, but as the finest downhill runs are usually on the west-to-east traverse, this is the direction described.

From the car park ford the River Lochy just upstream from where the Eas Daimh flows into it. As there are no stepping stones, some parties may prefer to walk 1km downstream to a footbridge (NN 229 270). Once on the south side of the river, follow a good path on the north side of the Eas Daimh through the forest. In 0.6km cross the Eas Daimh and climb close to the stream which drains the Fionn Choirein. Due to the steep hillside and the proximity of the forest to the stream, it may be necessary to carry skis for a short distance in places. At the top of the forest, the angle eases and the deer fence is crossed at a stile close to the stream.

Continue straight up the corrie to reach the headwall, which, although not excessively steep, does have several small rocky outcrops which may be avoided by a left-to-right traverse finishing exactly on the col. Although it need not form part of the traverse, some report that it is satisfying to climb 140m west-south-west to the summit of Beinn a' Chleibh and then return to the col.

From the col the climb up the south-west ridge of Ben Lui is straightforward for 240m, above which the ridge is both steeper and rocky. To avoid the rocks, traverse to the right for 100m, then ascend in the same direction to join the south-east ridge not far from the summit. The summit is an excellent viewpoint, particularly if there are parties climbing Central Gully.

From the summit there is an exhilarating run of 420m down the south-east ridge. Some care is required, however, particularly when the snow on the crest of the ridge is confined to the precipitous east edge. The col at the foot of the ridge is wide with several hillocks, which could be confusing in poor visibility.

From the col ascend east then north-east, gaining 200m up an undulating ridge to reach the steeper summit cone of Ben Oss. Turn north and climb 100m to reach the summit. From there ski down a gently inclined ridge north-north-east to a small col followed by a short climb to the east (avoid putting on skins). The final slope down to the next col follows a long scoop which holds snow well.

The west shoulder of Beinn Dubhchraig, which rises east of the col, is rocky and requires a good covering of snow for an easy ascent. Once on top of this shoulder, turn south-east to climb the final ridge to the summit.

In good snow conditions the descent from the summit of Beinn Dubhchraig down Coire Dubhchraig to the Old Caledonian pinewood at its foot is a very fine long run, although recent forestry plantings in the lower half of the corrie will inevitably spoil it in future. Ski steeply north from the summit and soon reach easier slopes at the head of the Allt Coire Dubhchraig. Continue easily in long schusses down the north-west side of this stream, crossing three fences, and ski through the pinewood to a footbridge at its north-east corner. 200m east of this bridge a track leads over the railway and down to the A82 road in Strathfillan.

Finally, retrieve the car you left in Glen Lochy. A second car, a friendly driver to give a lift or the Glasgow–Oban bus are possible solutions to this problem.

N.B. Central Gully (top NN 266 263) on Ben Lui has been regularly skied as a steep descent. Please check that no one is climbing up the gully and the various branches before descending on skis. Descent of the gully brings you to the wrong side of the hill for an easy return to a car parked in Glen Lochy. Instead, take a long, flat traverse above the 430m contour north-west to the bealach leading down to the Eas Daimh.

- Approximate start height: 1,130m
- Approximate descent: 400m
- General aspect: north-east
- Climbing grade: I

Below: Descent of Beinn Dubhchraig (skier, Dave Anderson) © Hamish MacEwan

Beinn Challuim ▲ 1,025m
Calum's Mountain

△ NN 386 322   ↗ LR50   🌐 P.98

🅿 Kirkton Farm road-end (A82) in Strath Fillan (NN 355 281/56.4169, -4.6674).

↔ 11KM   △ 960M   ⊥ 170M
⏱ 4 HRS   GRADE II   ★★

By Donald Bennet, updated by Colwyn Jones

Appropriately in winter, when the birch trees lining the verges of the A82 are bare, the summit ridge of Beinn Challuim can be clearly seen from the Crianlarich bypass and then on the north-east side of Strath Fillan as you drive north. From the starting point, the appearance of the peak from the strath is of wide lower slopes rising at an easy angle. Above, the rounded dome of the south top hides the summit.

Beinn Challuim gives a pleasant ascent on skis with good slopes for the downhill run. It is one of the easiest Crianlarich hills for the skier, and in good conditions poses few problems. Only the last part of the ridge between the south top and the summit is narrow and exposed. The only other problem might be route-finding in bad visibility, for the south-west side of the mountain is remarkably featureless. On a fine day, however, this is a short and easy tour with grand views of the surrounding mountains.

Kirkton Farm is probably the best starting point, and parking is available in a large car park on the northbound side of the A82, opposite the farm entrance. Follow the track (part of the West Highland Way) past the old St Fillan's Priory graveyard and, just beyond, carefully cross the West Highland Railway Line at a gated level crossing (NN 361 288). Once on the hill the fence of the plantation guides you up a steep path. If there is good snow cover, keeping slightly north of the steepest rise is an option, as the deer fence of a regenerating native woodland enclosure blocks progress. However, there are two rudimentary stiles, take the lower at NN 367 292. After an easy climb to approximately 650m pass west of a knoll on the ridge, Creag Loisgte (burned, scorched or seared crag), and cross another fence to reach a broad, flat col below the upper slopes of Beinn Challuim. In bad visibility a line of fence posts rising above the north-east side of the col may be a useful guide. In clear weather, however, you can ski anywhere up the broad ridge to the south top (NN 386 315, 998m) where the descent starts. A few metres north of this top is a narrow, level hollow, and on its north side the ridge continues, dropping slightly and then rising more steeply to the large summit cairn. In good conditions it is quite possible to ski along this ridge, but in a high wind or white-out, it might be more prudent to walk.

The return follows the ascent route. The skiing is easy, with wide open spaces down which you can choose your own run. Note that in bad visibility it is all too easy to ski off-course on the featureless hillside. In such conditions it might be best to follow your uphill tracks, thus greatly simplifying navigation.

If snow does not reach the A82, an alternative start is at Inverherive Farm in Strath Fillan (NN 370 256). Walk along the farm track and negotiate the level crossing to safely reach Inverhaggernie Farm; continue under the rail bridge and up the hillside to the 350m contour. Glen Lochay offers a possible route from the east with a very long approach to reach the peak. However, this is one for the hardcore as vehicle access up the glen is likely to be difficult if there is enough snow for a ski ascent from the parking area about 1km before Kenknock Farm.

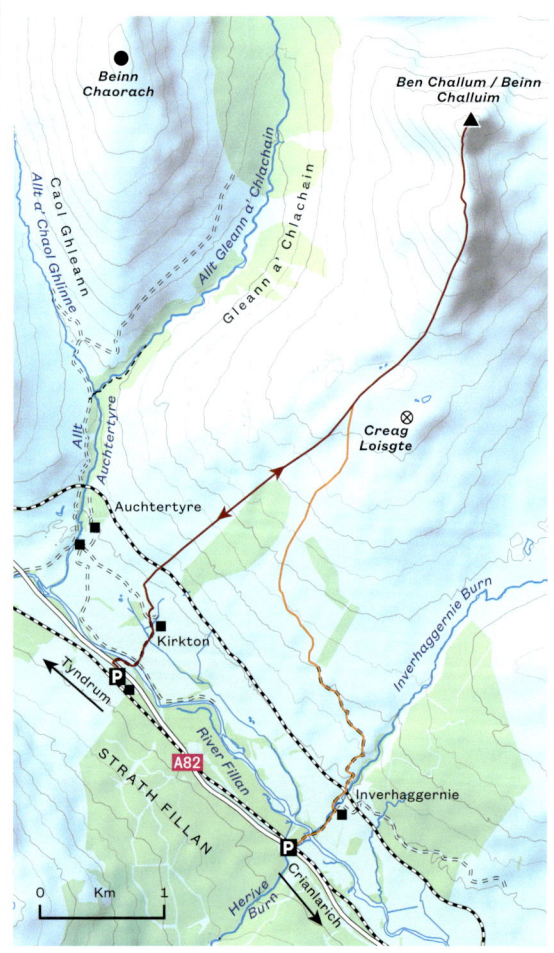

Below: Badour Bridge
(skier, Angus Armstrong)
© Alan Sloan

Sgiath Chùil ▲ 921m
Back Wing, Sheltered Spot
△ NN 462 317   ◁ LR51   ⊕ P.101

Meall Glas ▲ 959m
Green-Grey Hill
△ NN 431 321   ◁ LR51   ⊕ P.101

Beinn nan Imirean ● 849m
Hill of the Ridge
△ NN 419 309   ◁ LR51   ⊕ P.101

| P | At a parking place in Glen Dochart beside the A85 road (NN 448 276/56.4148, -4.5172). |

↔ 20KM   △ 1,400M   ↕ 160M
⏱ 7-9 HRS   GRADE IV   ★★

| P | Alternative starting point: Glen Lochay at the end of the public road parking (NN 477 368/56.4990, -4.4761). |

↔ 16KM   △ 1,200M   ↕ 220M
⏱ 6-7 HRS   GRADE IV   ★★

By Bill Morrison, updated by Colwyn Jones

These three hills lie between Glen Dochart and Glen Lochay and can be climbed from either glen. The southern approach from Glen Dochart is probably the more popular route because of its easy accessibility from the A85, and if there is good snow cover down to the glen it is a perfectly good route. It should be used if the Corbett Beinn nan Imirean is included in the tour. If the snow cover on the southern slopes is thin, or the snow-line is a long way above the glen, then the Glen Lochay approach may have better snow cover on the north-facing slopes, but including Beinn nan Imirean is more difficult from the north.

The circular traverse of these hills can be done in either direction, but it may be better to ski down the west slopes of Meall a' Churain (917m), which give a fine steep run, and then climb up the east side of Beinn Cheathaich, which, being rather rough and studded with boulders, gives less satisfactory skiing. In hard icy conditions the steep sections of these slopes, if taken direct, may require ice axe and crampons, but they can usually be avoided by detours to the north.

From the A85 in Glen Dochart (NN 448 276) walk or ski up the private road north across the River Dochart to Auchessan Farm. Continue up the track behind the farm to the east of the Allt Essan. Crossing fences, the open hillside is reached at around 350m just after a small dam (NN 444 292). Climb the slopes north-east between the rock outcrops of Creag nan Uan and the Allt Riobain for about 2km, crossing a track then towards Sgiath Chrom, heading for the little shallow corrie between that knoll and the rocky prow of Sgiath Chùil. Finally, avoid the steep south face of Sgiath Chùil by a rising traverse across the west side of the peak onto the summit, where the cairn is on the edge of the crag.

After viewing the surrounding peaks, traverse north along the fairly level ridge to Meall a' Churain (918m). The direct descent west from that top gives a very steep and exciting run with a drop of 300m ending at the broad bealach at the head of the Allt Riobain (Lairig a' Churain on the 1:25,000 map; NN 454 325; 609m).

Alternatively, if this descent is unsafe, ski north along the ridge for about 500m to an easier gradient at about the 700m contour and then make a descending traverse south-west to the bealach. This is an easier and safer descent, particularly in icy or avalanche-prone conditions.

From the bealach climb up to the trig point on Beinn Cheathaich (937m), keeping north of the steep rocky slopes immediately below the summit, which is approached up the last 100m of the north ridge. From here ski easily south-west then west along the broad ridge to the high point of the day, Meall Glas.

From that summit, care is needed to find the safe start to the descent. Return east-south-east, along the uphill track, for about 300m, then bear south-east and ski down a steep slope which provides the only feasible ski run through the rocky escarpment on the south side of the hill. Once clear of the crags, ski south-west to the intervening col with Beinn nan Imirean (Lairig Riairein on the 1:25,000 map; NN 425 312; 660m,). From here it is less than 200 vertical metres over 1km to the slabby outcrop forming the summit.

The descent off Beinn nan Imirean follows the broad south-east ridge down onto the southern flanks of Meall Glas, taking the best ski line back to the ascent route through Auchessan Farm.

If you are returning directly to Glen Dochart from the second summit, Meall Glas, then continue through the rocky escarpment on the south side of the hill. The angle soon eases, and the run continues without difficulty, following the general line of the streams which flow south-east towards the Allt Riobain where the uphill tracks are gratefully rejoined.

The starting point on the Glen Lochay side of the hills is at the end of the public road in the glen, just east of Kenknock Farm. Walk or ski west along the private road for 1km and cross the River Lochay at the concrete bridge (NN 466 364). This leads through trees up to where a large hydroelectric pipe goes through the mountain and there is a gate and stile over the deer fence to the open hillside. Previously the derelict bridge at Lubchurran was used, but it is no longer there. Skin south uphill to the 500m contour, then south-east to continue up the broad ridge to Meall a' Churain, where the above route is joined to reach Sgiath Chùil. Continue by the same route to Meall Glas.

The quickest descent is to return to the bealach before Meall a' Churain, from where a north-north-east traverse will return you to the top of the forestry plantation negotiated in the ascent. Once back over the River Lochay it is about 1km back to the car.

A more worthy descent from the summit to Glen Lochay goes north down the wide concave bowl of Coire Cheathaich, which usually holds snow well in its upper part. If the snow cover is good, enjoy a steep run north from the summit followed by an easier slope down the corrie for 3km to a footbridge at Badour (NN 432 349), with a descent of 600m or more. Cross the footbridge then ski (or walk) the 5km back to the car park. The Badour footbridge also allows an out-and-back ascent of Meall Glas and may be a good route choice after heavy snow, as you can plan to avoid east-facing slopes and those of over 30 degrees.

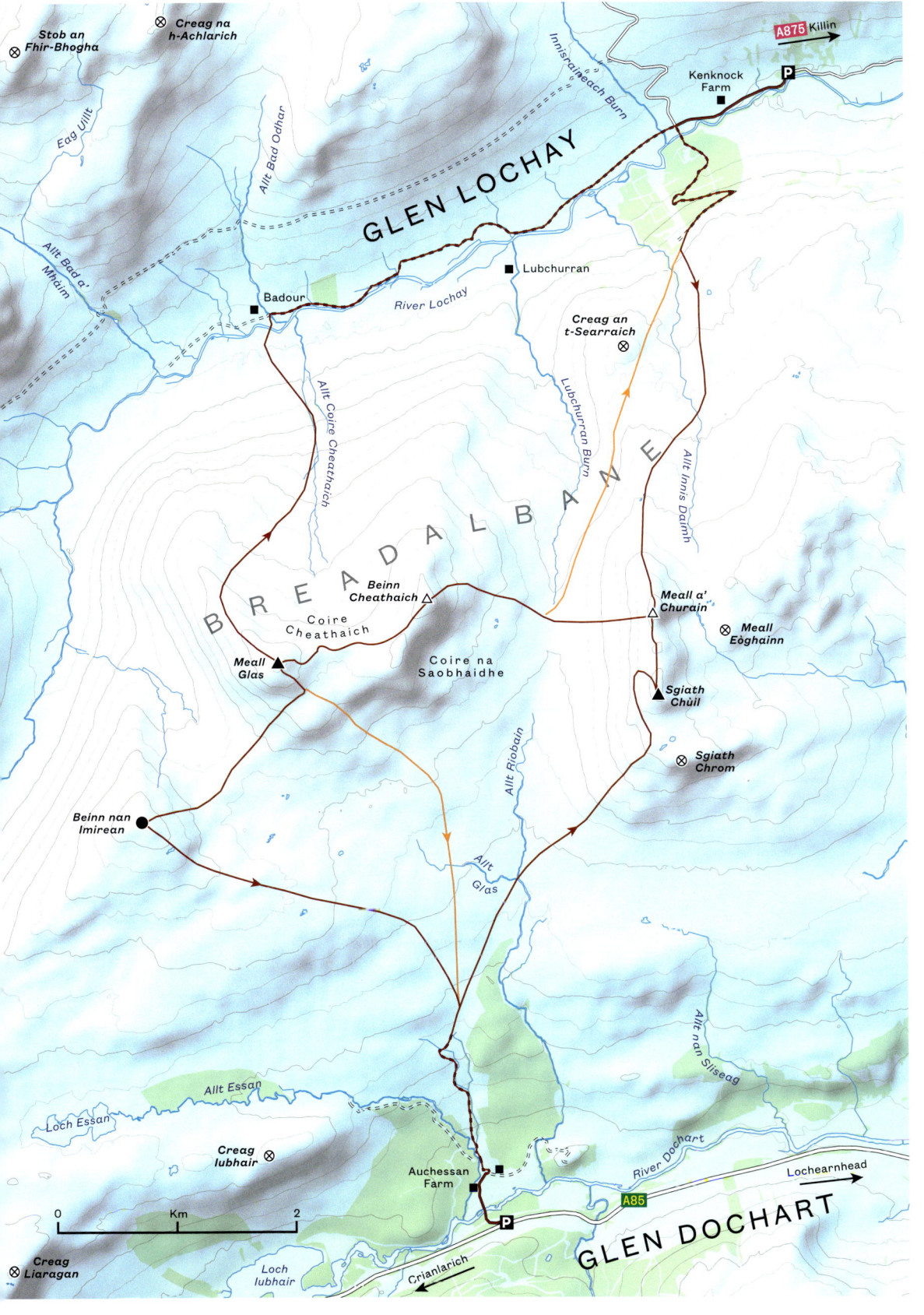

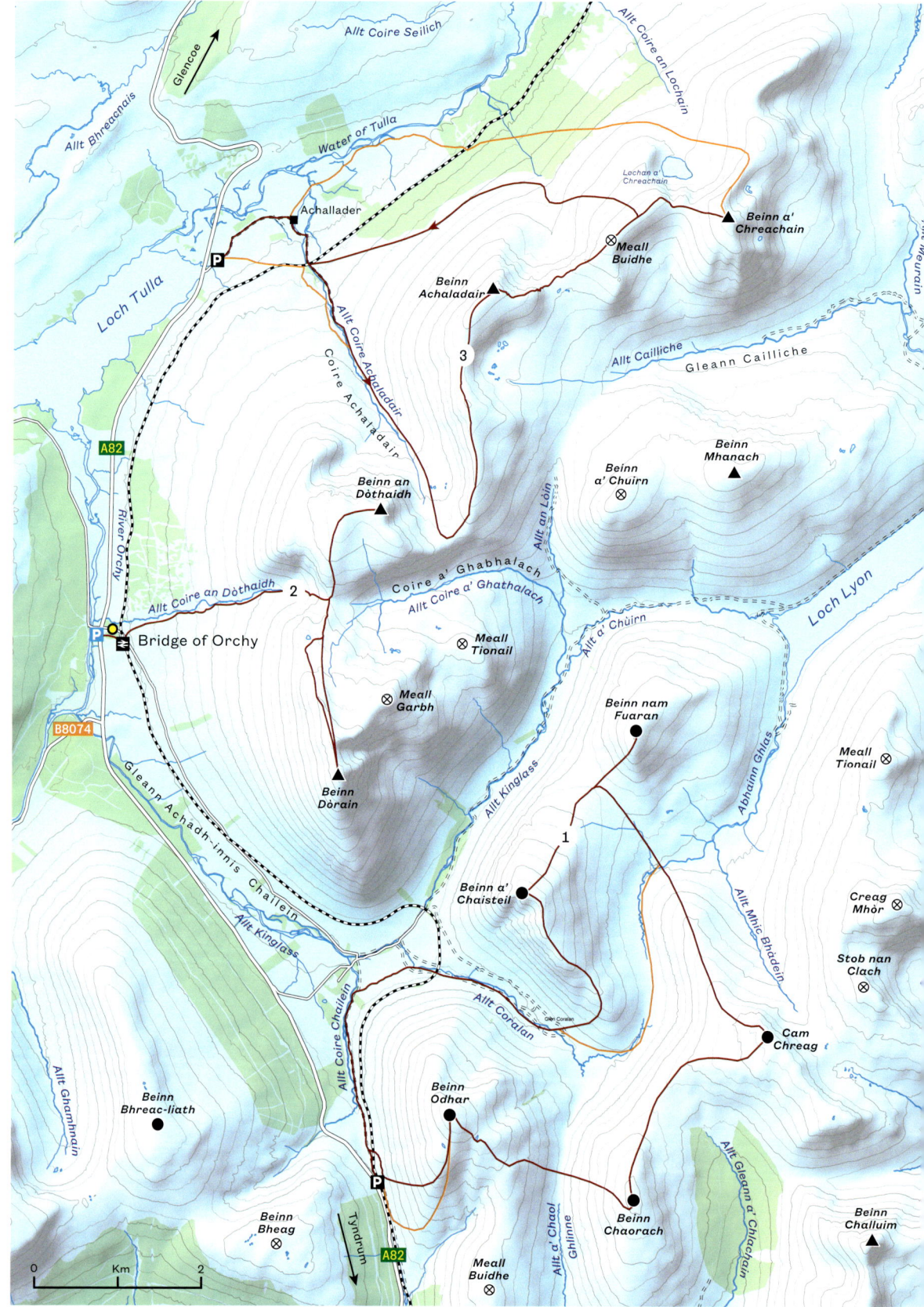

The Auch Hills

Beinn Odhar ● 901m
Dun-Coloured Hill
△ NN 337 338   ⌁ LR50   🌐 P.102

Beinn Chaorach ● 818m
Sheep Hil
△ NN 358 320   ⌁ LR50   🌐 P.102

Cam Chreag ● 884m
Crooked Crag
△ NN 375 346   ⌁ LR50   🌐 P.102

Beinn nam Fuaran ● 806m
Hill of the Well
△ NN 361 381   ⌁ LR50   🌐 P.102

Beinn a' Chaisteil ● 886m
Hill of the Castle
△ NN 347 364   ⌁ LR50   🌐 P.102

P The large car park at the high point of the A82 below Beinn Odhar (NN 328 331/56.4608, -4.7144).

↔ 22KM   △ 2,000M   ⌶ 325M
🕒 8-9 HRS   GRADE III   ★★★

by Niel Craig

The Auch Corbetts sit in a wedge of land bounded by the A82 to the west, Auch Gleann to the north and Tyndrum to the south. They form a unique cluster of five Corbetts that can be linked together naturally to give a long but exceptionally rewarding ski tour. Weighing in at 22km and with some 2,000m of ascent, this is a reasonably long day out by any standards, but as any Scottish ski tourer will tell you, if the right conditions prevail the effort is often rewarded many times over. The substantial height gain should not be considered a deterrent so long as one subscribes to the Newtonian philosophy that what goes up must come down. The tour benefits from panoramas of the Bridge of Orchy and Tyndrum hills, Glen Lochay and beyond – enough to divert one's attention from any uphill sections.

A large car park is conveniently situated on the east of the carriageway at the high point of the A82 (315m) between Tyndrum and Bridge of Orchy. From the car park, a track joins the West Highland Way going under the railway 350m further north and gives access to the lower slopes of the steep west flank of Beinn Odhar. Alternative parking can also be found 1.5km further south, opposite a bridge that crosses the railway and leads directly to the south ridge. Whichever car park is used, on no account should any shortcut be taken across the railway.

If starting at the northerly car park, make a long, rising traverse south on the relentlessly steep west flank of Beinn Odhar to gain access to the more inviting south ridge. This is quite a brutal start to the day, so if you prefer a more relaxed alternative, or the snow conditions are unsuitable, follow the West Highland Way south until the south ridge can be gained more easily. Either way, follow the ridge to the summit, watching out for adits and abandoned lead mine workings at approximately 650m that might be filled with uncompacted snow.

From the summit cairn, descend south-east to a slight levelling, then follow the same line to a larger level area before bearing east-south-east to the bealach between Beinn Odhar and Beinn Chaorach. This line follows the county boundary, so it is possible to ski in Stirling to the south, Argyll and Bute to the north or both simultaneously if you are so inclined. Whichever line is chosen, with good snow cover, this aspect of Beinn Odhar can offer an excellent run.

Continue from the bealach to the trig point of Beinn Chaorach. The west flank of Beinn Chaorach is not as steep as that of Beinn Odhar; however, at this point you will need to decide, based on the prevailing conditions, whether it is best to ascend this slope on skis or on foot.

From the summit follow the broad ridge north-east to the bealach, watching out for occasional loops of fence wire poking out of the snow waiting to catch out the unwary. Pass the site of a small defunct wind turbine at the bealach and continue easily to the summit of Cam Chreag.

From Cam Chreag, strike off into Perth and Kinross, establish yourself on the north-north-west ridge and enjoy the descent to the Abhainn Ghlas. The north flank of this ridge often holds the best snow. On the descent, stop a while to admire the east slopes of Beinn a' Chaisteil across the glen. These slopes offer some magnificent skiing at the end of this tour, so at this point it is probably a good idea to do some homework and scope out the descent route for later in the day.

Key
1. The Auch Hills   P.103
2. Beinn Dòrain (Chapter 3)   P.127
3. Beinn Achaladair (Chapter 3)   P.128

Once off this ridge it is possible to avoid the final two Corbetts if time is short or energy is lacking. If that is the case, follow the Abhainn Ghlas to its source, then the Allt Coralan to pick up a track that passes under the Auch Gleann viaduct and connects with the West Highland Way and the car park.

If completing the circuit, cross the burn at the foot of the ridge just descended and make your way up to a broad bealach of peat hags, which will hopefully be covered in snow, following roughly the line of the Allt a' Mhàim. A small crag and a jumble of boulders guard the summit of Beinn nam Fuaran from the south-west, so it might be quicker to leave skis here and proceed on foot.

From this bealach, a fence line links the last two summits. Once again this follows a county boundary, and this time you can choose between Argyll and Bute in the north or Perth and Kinross in the south (or both) on the way to Beinn a' Chaisteil. This is a long slog at the end of the day, and if you need motivation, think of the descent just around the corner.

Descend the east flank of Beinn a' Chaisteil, keeping in mind the cliffs of the Creagan Liatha on the right if the visibility is poor. At about 500m begin rounding the south-east nose of Beinn a' Chaisteil to make a descent into Glen Coralan, then pick up the track that leads to the viaduct at Gleann Achadh-innis Chailean (Auch Gleann). Follow this to the West Highland Way and continue south to your starting point.

Right: Beinn Odhar north of Tyndrum (skiers, Norman Ritchie, John Ferrie, Brian Williamson, Adam Gibson, Colin MacGregor) © Billy Hood

Chapter 2 | The Campsies to Loch Tay | The Auch Hills

Mamlorn Mountains

Creag Mhòr ▲ 1,047m
Big Rock
△ NN 391 361   ⊿ LR50, LR51   ⊕ P.107

Beinn Sheasgarnich ▲ 1,078m
Sheltering or Peaceful Hill
△ NN 413 383   ⊿ LR50, LR51   ⊕ P.107

P	The end of the public road up Glen Lochay before Kenknock Farm (NN 476 368 / 56.4990, -4.4762).
↔ 20KM	△ 1,260M ↕ 200M
⏱ 7–8 HRS	GRADE III ★★★

by Bill Morrison, updated by Stan Pearson

These two hills lie several kilometres west of the end of the public road up Glen Lochay. Both usually hold snow well and are predominantly grassy hills but lack the clear descent routes ideal for skiing, instead requiring some selective route choice. Beinn Sheasgarnich, in particular, has an extensive area of high corries and broad ridges. The traverse of these hills is a fine but rather long expedition, as you must walk along the private road in Glen Lochay for 5km to reach the foot of Creag Mhòr. Forestry plantation protected by deer fencing in the glen restricts access points. Beinn Sheasgarnich by itself is a relatively short tour, with access assisted by the road (no longer driveable) which leads from Kenknock in Glen Lochay northwards to Glen Lyon. The summit of that road is at 510m, and the ascent from there to Beinn Sheasgarnich up the Coire Bàn Mòr is easy in good visibility. The route combining these two hills sits on the edge of the two OS maps, so printing a centred map is useful.

For the traverse of Creag Mhòr and Beinn Sheasgarnich, however, walk, mountain bike or (if the snow cover is low enough) ski along the rough private road to the junction just beyond Batavaime cottage (NN 421 348). From there follow the track up to the 380m contour, then start a gentle ascending traverse west round the foot of Sròn nan Eun into Coire Cheathaich at about 550m, where two possible routes diverge. The simplest is to continue the curving ascent north-west onto the ridge between Sròn nan Eun and Creag Mhòr, then go along this easy ridge to the prominent cairn on Creag Mhòr. The second choice is to continue up Coire Cheathaich, passing below the impressive craggy slopes on the north-east face of Stob nan Clach (956m) to the bealach 500m south-west of Creag Mhòr, which is easily reached up a broad ridge (9km; 830m; 3.5hrs).

The north-east face of Creag Mhòr is too steep and rocky for skiing, so it is essential to ski north-west from the summit for 500m, then turn north down the Meall Tionail ridge for a few hundred metres until it becomes fairly level at about 820m. At that point ski south-south-east off the ridge down an easy-angled corrie to the bealach at Lochan na Baintighearna (NN 397 367; 1:25,000 map), which will probably be hidden under snow. The south-west ridge of Beinn Sheasgarnich rises steeply above this wide flat col.

The most direct route of ascent starts as a rising traverse up the north flank of the ridge, and higher up you can either aim to reach the ridge 1km south of Beinn Sheasgarnich or continue the rising traverse direct to the summit. This north-facing slope is steep enough to be potentially dangerous in unstable snow conditions, but otherwise it should pose no problems. If it is too steep or unsafe, a traverse from Lochan na Baintighearna bearing east-south-east for just over 1km below rough ground gives access to easy slopes which can be climbed north to reach the broad south ridge of Beinn Sheasgarnich 1km south of the summit.

The return to the public road end in Glen Lochay involves at least 5km of skiing, much of it easy-angled, and good route selection is necessary to maintain downhill momentum. The most direct route is a long descending traverse, south-east at first, then east across the vast southern flank of Beinn Sheasgarnich. Some small crags and peat hags need to be avoided by linking a series of small bowls. Alternatively, ski east down Coire Bàn Mòr and along the Allt Tarsuinn to reach the road between Glen Lochay and Glen Lyon and finish the day by skiing or walking down this road to Glen Lochay.

If returning to Batavaime to collect a bike, there is an excellent run south-west from the south top to the junction of streams at 600m, then south-east down the right bank of the Allt Bad a' Mhàim.

Opposite: Auch Hills (skier, Adam Gibson) © Billy Hood

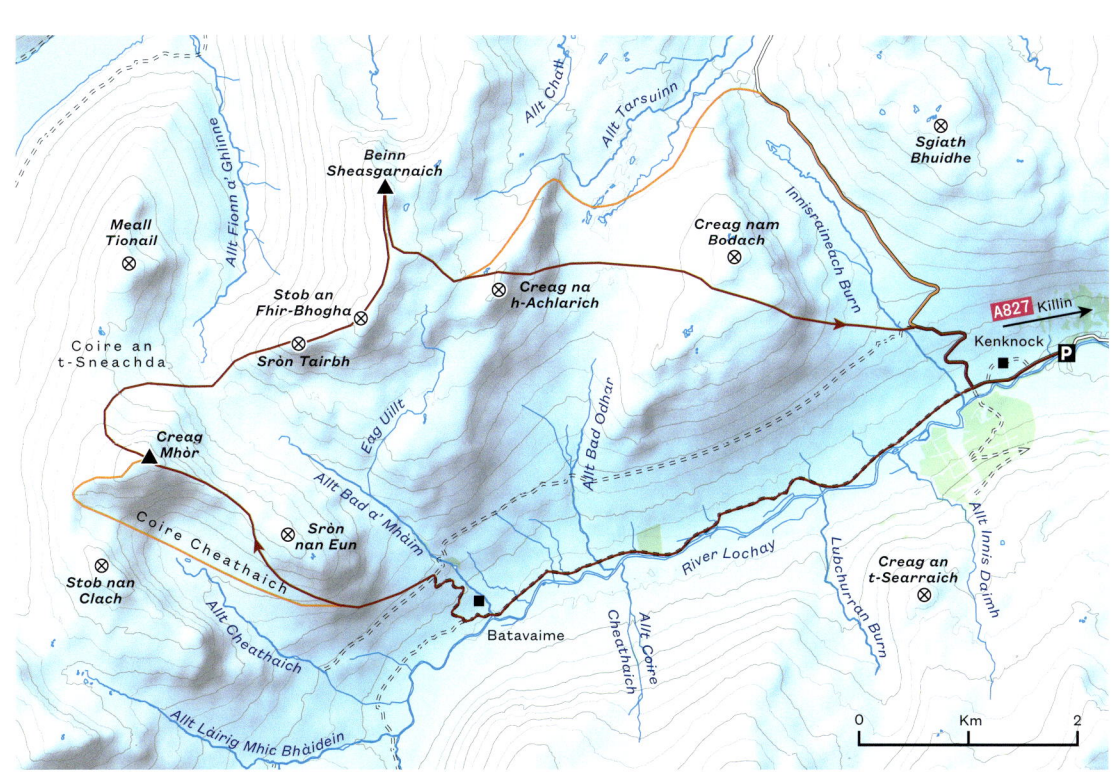

Meall Ghaordaidh ▲ 1,039m

△ NN 514 397 ◈ LR51 ⊕ P.109

P Just west of Duncroisk Farm in Glen Lochay (NN 527 363/56.4960, -4.3952).

↔ 8KM △ 900M ↕ 145M
⏱ 3-4 HRS GRADE III ★★★

by Gordon MacKenzie, updated by Colwyn Jones

Meall Ghaordaidh is situated on the north side of Glen Lochay. Butterfield, in *The High Mountains of Britain and Ireland*, described it as 'Quite the dullest hill in the Southern Highlands.' Although Butterfield meant the dullest Munro – and it is hard to disagree with this judgement – there are drearier hills in the area, but in a good winter the shapely cone of Meall Ghaordaidh provides a fine day's skiing.

Although it may not be the most inspiring of summits, and its distance from any neighbouring Munros makes a longer traverse of two or three mountains impracticable, it does make an excellent short outing on skis. If time has been wasted in a failed attempt to drive up the road to the Ben Lawers National Trust car park, then Meall Ghaordaidh may save the day by providing a suitable, if shorter, alternative.

As with most ski tours, good snow cover down to the road is always an advantage. In the first edition it is recorded that for one ascent, 'The snow-line was at approximately 500m, but it was still possible to put on skis and skins just above the road and ascend along a strand of snow beside one of the burns to the [west] of Duncroisk.'

Parking for about five cars appears to be tolerated in an unusually large lay-by on the minor road off the A827 (NN 526 363) about 6km west-north-west of Killin. The road sees regular residential, agricultural and industrial (water engineer) traffic and is likely to be passable. From the parking space, ski (or walk) east to the well-signposted summer access gate on the road just west of the bridge over the Allt Dhùin Croisg. Follow the landrover track, through gates or over stiles on a couple of deer fences, to the west of the burn.

Once on the open hillside follow the landrover track to a cairn (NN 532 373) which marks the start of the summer footpath to the summit. If the cairn is under snow, a stout metal pole of unknown provenance marks the approximate line of the summer footpath. The easy slopes of the broad south-east flank (or wide shoulder) provide a steady though featureless gradient. Soon you cross a derelict fence (NN 529 378), and a direct line can then be taken to the summit. However, above the 800m contour, the slope steepens and small rock outcrops must be safely negotiated. With fresh snow and a prevailing westerly airflow, windslab may have collected here below the summit. The triangulation station has a well-formed circular stone wall, which may provide some shelter, and on a clear day fine views in all directions, except to the east where Ben Lawers overshadows the summit.

If there is sufficient snow, the line of ascent can be reversed, but the recommended descent is to ski down slightly east of the summit before entering the shallow corrie formed by the most westerly tributary (Allt an Fhaing on the 1:25,000 OS map) of the Allt Dhùin Croisg. This gives a fine run down a more or less steady gradient to the main stream near a sheep fank, from where you will meet the landrover track used in ascent. Follow this back to the road. Alternatively, skiing south directly off the summit, steep and rocky to start, gives a fine run if there is good snow cover. At around 450m, start traversing east to cross an old stone wall (NN 516 378), continue traversing to cross the derelict fence again, and finally return to the original landrover track.

An ascent from Glen Lyon to the north is possible, although if the road is passable you would motor past some fine north slopes of alternative peaks en route. Just before the Cashlie Power Station, cross the River Lyon to the farm buildings at Stronuich (300m), and from behind the house continue into the corrie of the Allt Laoghain. The route of the burn is then followed up to its source at around the 750m contour, that source hopefully under a good depth of snow! From here a steady gradient covers the final kilometre south-east to the summit. Descent follows the line of ascent.

Key
1. Meall Ghaordaigh   P.103
2. Stùc an Lochain (chapter 3)   P.129
3. Meall Buidhe (chapter 3)   P.130

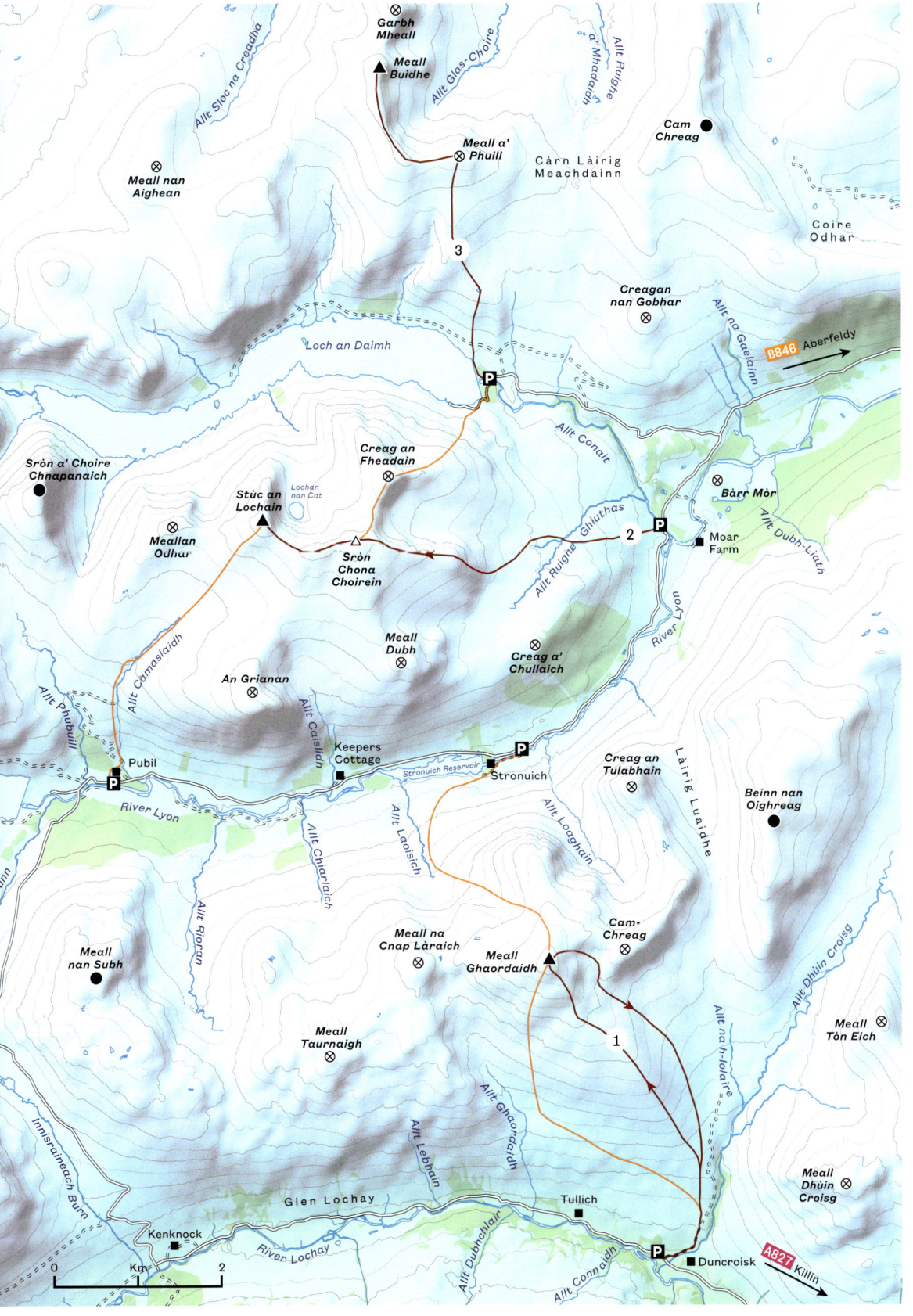

Below: Meall Ghaordaidh, NE shoulder (skier, Adam Gibson) © Billy Hood

Chapter 3

Central Scotland South

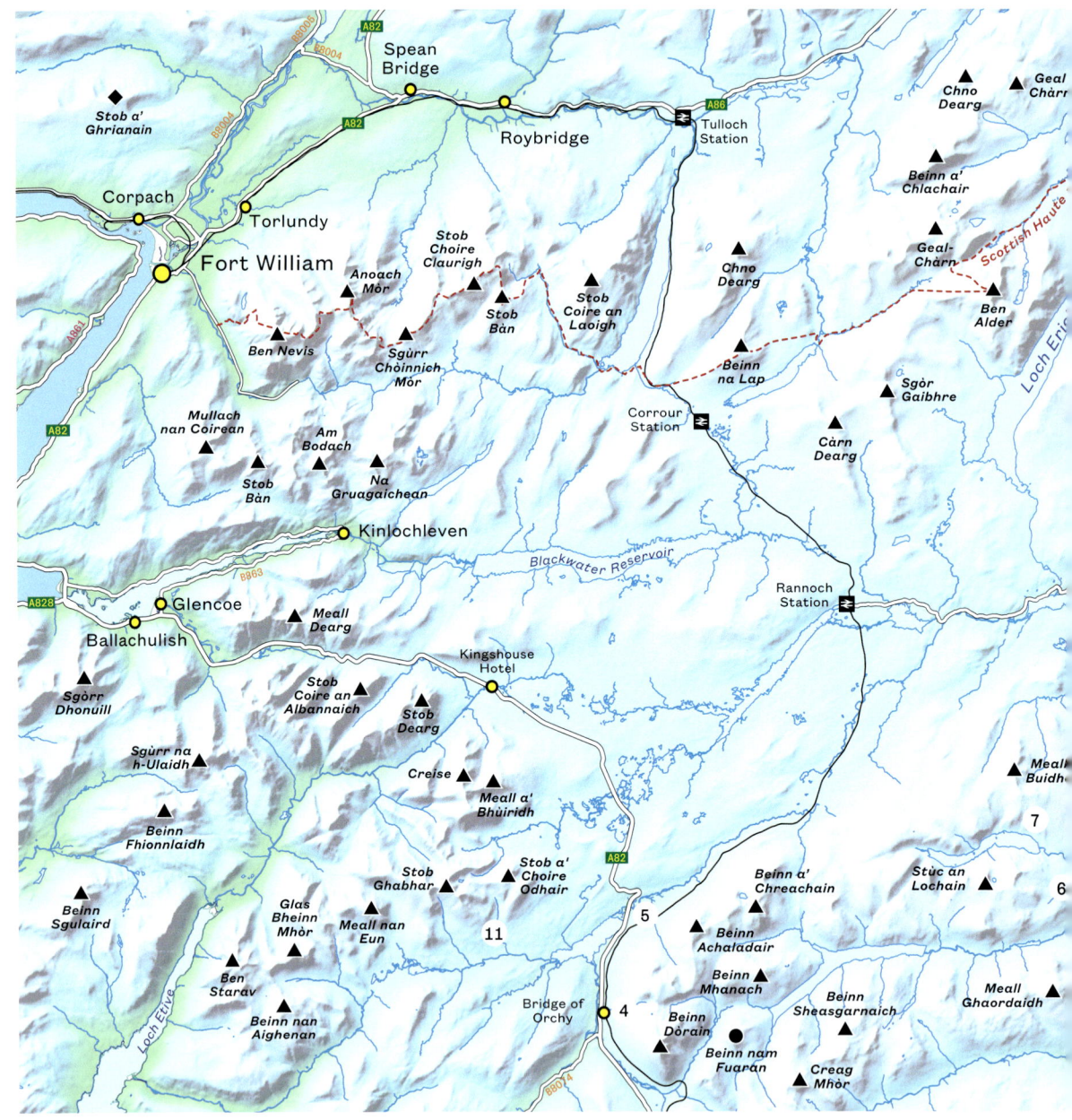

Previous spread: Càrn Liath descent to Monzie (skier, Steve Martin) © Al Todd

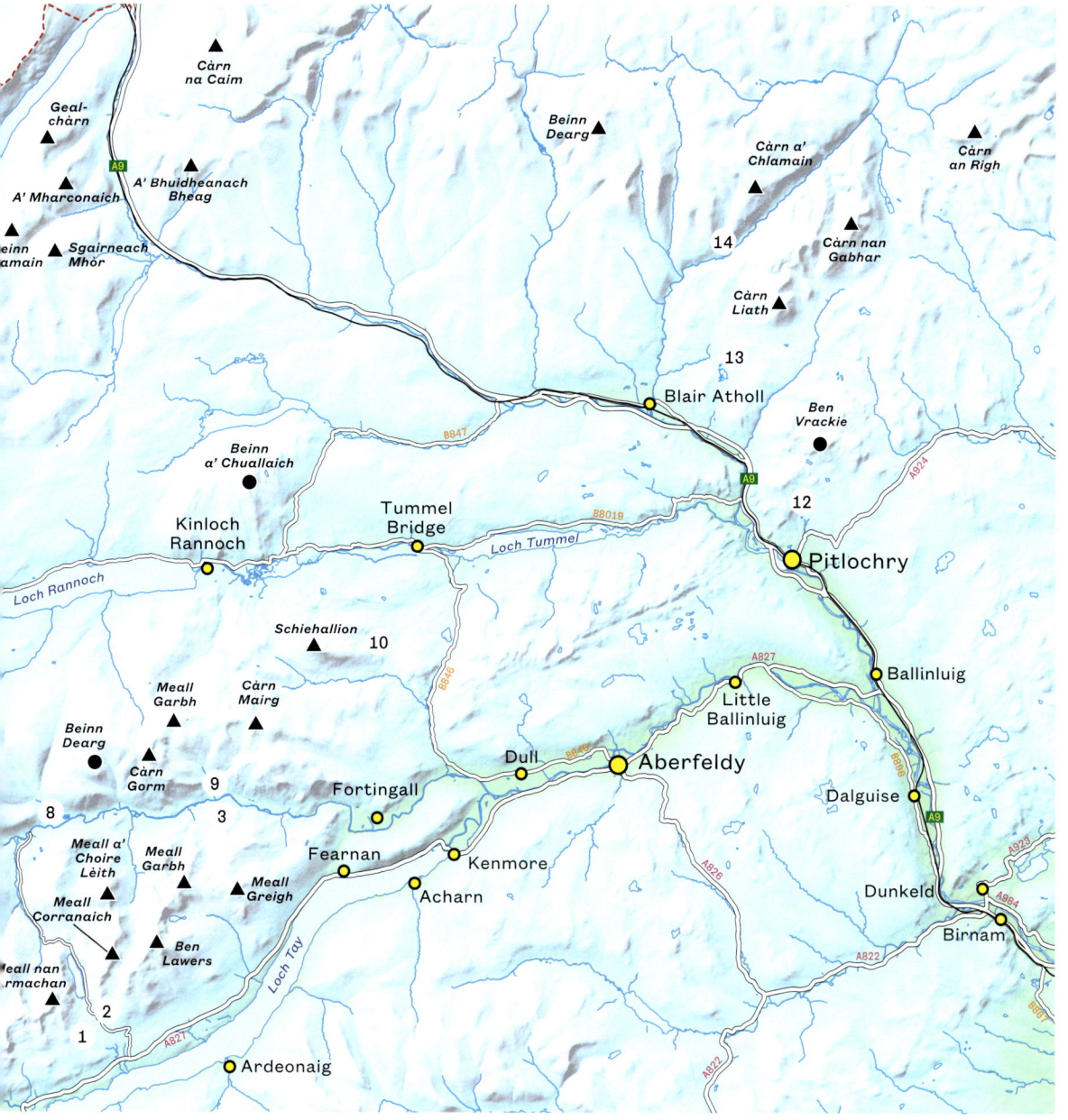

1. Meall nan Tarmachan — P.117
2. Ben Lawers — P.119
3. Ben Lawers North — P.123
4. Beinn Dòrain — P.127
5. Beinn Achaladair — P.128
6. Stùc an Lochain — P.129
7. Meall Buidhe — P.130
8. Beinn Dearg — P.130
9. Càrn Mairg Hills — P.131
10. Schiehallion — P.132
11. Stob Ghabhar — P.134
12. Ben Vrackie — P.138
13. Beinn a' Ghlo — P.139
14. Càrn a' Chlamain — P.141

Key

1. Meal nan Tarmachan — P.117
2. Meall Corranaich — P.119
3. Ben Lawers — P.120
4. Meall Garbh — P.122
5. Allt A' Chobhair Circuit — P.123
6. The Circuit of Coire nam Buidheag — P.126
7. Beinn Dearg — P.130
8. Càrn Mairg Hills — P.131

Meall nan Tarmachan ▲ 1,043m

Hill of the Ptarmigans

NN 585 390   LR51   P.116

P: a) The NTS pay and display car park (NN 609 377/ 56.5111, -4.2613); altitude 420m; or b) the landrover track around Meall nan Tarmachan (NN 605 383/ 56.5164, -4.2682).

↔ 7KM   △ 630M   ⊺ 460M
⏲ 3-5 HRS   GRADE III   ★★★★

By Donald Bennet, updated by Brian Shackleton and Colwyn Jones

There are some good snow-holding corries to the north and south of the summit ridges of Meall nan Tarmachan, but access from the east requires adequate snow cover on the east flank of the south ridge above the road from Loch Tay to Glen Lyon.

From the starting point, climb or ski west up the flank of the south ridge of Meall nan Tarmachan and cross its broad crest to enter the shallow corrie at the head of the Allt Tìr Artair. Ski north up the upper east branch of this burn, which usually holds snow well, towards the col between Meall nan Tarmachan and its south-east Top at the head of the south ridge.

Ahead, to the north-west, the upper slopes steepen, but a wide gully (taken by the summer walking route) provides the route and access to a broad terrace which rises north-east to join the north-north-east ridge of Meall nan Tarmachan just below the summit.

The easiest return is to ski down by the ascent route, taking care in the steep gully down to the col. A pleasant variation is to now ski south-west to the upper west branch of the Allt Tìr Artair and follow this towards 750m before contouring eastwards to re-cross the south ridge and the descent to the road. Alternatively, skin back to the upper east branch of the stream to rejoin the route of ascent.

For a longer day, ski steeply north-west from the summit of Meall nan Tarmachan into Coire Riadhailt for 200m, taking care to avoid small crags not easily seen from above. Skin back up east to regain the north-north-east ridge of Meall nan Tarmachan before returning by the ascent route just below the summit. The return from the north-north-east ridge, described in the first edition as a descending traverse south-east across a steep hillside with small crags, is not recommended.

Meall Garbh Circumnavigation

A circular tour around Meall Garbh (1,026m), which lies south-west of Meall nan Tarmachan, including the main summit, starts from the same parking place as above. Take a more direct south-easterly line on a rising traverse around the south ridge of Meall nan Tarmachan and then west around the south ridge of Meall Garbh towards the disused quarry at NN 574 374, or follow the landrover track on foot or skis to the same point. From there head north up to the high bealach (NN 578 381; approximately 900m) between Meall Garbh and Beinn nan Eachan, which will probably require climbing.

There is a fine, steep ski down the north side using the top of Coire Riadhailt, but excessive enjoyment will result in extra skinning back up in an easterly direction to the lochan just north of the col between Meall Garbh and Meall nan Tarmachan (NN 582 387; 950m). From here it is a routine ascent of 100m to visit the summit of Meall nan Tarmachan.

An alternative descent is to follow your uphill track back to the smaller lochan at the col itself and ski south, steeply down through Cam Chreag, then follow the best line eastwards into the upper east branch of the Allt Tìr Artair (or continue south towards 750m on the upper west branch of the Allt Tìr Artair) and across the south ridge of Meall nan Tarmachan back to the car.

Below: Ascending Meall nan Tarmachan from the South East (skiers, Brian Williamson, Colin MacGregor and John Ferrie) © Billy Hood

Ben Lawers
Hill of the Loud Stream

By Donald Bennet, updated by Brian Shackleton

Ben Lawers is the highest hill in Tayside, and the Ben Lawers area is rightly regarded by ski mountaineers as one of the very best in Scotland, helped by an access road kissing the 550m contour. The area comprises a great range of seven Munros, linked by high ridges and surrounded by many corries to the east of Lochan na Làirige. Since the summits are all above 1,000m and occupy a central position, they gather snow arriving from both the east and the west. This, along with the relative absence of crags and boulder fields and the predominance of smooth, grassy slopes, makes Ben Lawers and the surrounding area ideal for skiing. Skiing is possible with only modest snow cover, but with complete cover it is superb. Combined with the varied and interesting topography of the range, a wide variety of ski tours are available, ranging from the simple ascent of a single peak to the traverse of the main range around Ben Lawers itself.

The most popular starting point for skiing on Ben Lawers is the NTS pay and display car park (NN 609 377; 410m), 2.5km along the narrow road from Loch Tay to Glen Lyon. This car park on the west side of the road replaced the previous one a short distance further north at the former site of the (now removed) NTS Visitor Centre at the foot of Coire Odhar. There is also parking 1km further along the road at the track leading round the south side of Meall nan Tarmachan (NN 605 383). Another slightly higher starting point for tours to the west end of the main range below the prominent cairn (NN 594 416) on the same road, 500m north of the north end of Lochan na Làirige at the high point of the road. It is important to point out that between Loch Tay and Glen Lyon this road is not kept open in winter and may be impassable due to snow or ice, especially on its higher stretches beyond the NTS car park. A fourth but lower point of access to Ben Lawers is from the little village of Lawers on the A827 above Loch Tay, climbing up by the Lawers Burn towards Lochan nan Cat. Car parking is very limited in Lawers but may be possible by enquiry at the Lawers Hotel and payment of a small fee.

The following descriptions of relatively short tours and the traverse of the whole Ben Lawers range illustrate the variety of skiing in this fine area.

Meall Corranaich ▲ 1,069m
△ NN 615 410   ⊿ LR51   ⊕ P.116

Meall a' Choire Lèith ▲ 926m
△ NN 612 439   ⊿ LR51   ⊕ P.116

P a) A small parking area below the cairn at the high point of the unclassified road from Loch Tay to Glen Lyon (NN 594 416/56.5450, -4.2875); or b) It is often easier, however, to start from a lay-by (NN 600 404/56.5350, -4.2780) 1km before the high point of the road and just before a burn with a prominent block 50m above the road. This starting point is also best if planning to ascend Meall Corranaich on its own.

↔ 9KM   △ 700M   ⊥ 550M
⏱ 4-5 HRS   GRADE III   ★★★

If starting from the cairn, head south-east, skiing up the shallow corrie at the head of the Allt Gleann Dà-Eig to reach good snow cover in the sheltered upper reaches of the corrie. This can also be reached from the other starting point by following the burn by the prominent block and ascending north-east and then east into the corrie. Near the head of the corrie bear round north-east, keeping right of an old fence line to reach a small col before the final skin, which may be icy, onto the flat top of Meall Corranaich where the small cairn is near the north-east edge of the little summit plateau.

Ski with care down the easy-angled north ridge, which may have thin cover, and in bad visibility be careful to keep to the east of the upper part of Coire Gorm at the point where the ridge divides after 1km. From the col (approximately 780m), 1km further on is a short climb of 150m to the flat summit of Meall a' Choire Lèith.

Ski south from the summit into the upper part of Coire Gorm. This corrie, known at one time in the skiing fraternity as Charlie's Gully, often holds snow well and gives a pleasant run for a kilometre or so. Do not go right down to the junction with the Allt Gleann Dà-Eig, but make a traverse south-west across rough ground, regaining a little height to cross the flat col (NN 596 419) close to the cairn at the starting point.

Beinn Ghlas ▲ 1,103m
△ NN 625 404 ⌕ LR51 🌐 P.116

Ben Lawers ▲ 1,214m
△ NN 636 414 ⌕ LR51 🌐 P.116

🅿 a) The NTS car park (NN 609 377/ 56.5111, -4.2613); or b) the start of the track around Meall nan Tarmachan (NN 605 383/56.5163, -4.2682)

↔ 11KM   △ 1,070M   440M
🕒 5–6 HRS   GRADE IV   ★★★★

This popular tour, which may be done either way round, shows the best of Ben Lawers and Beinn Ghlas without being unduly long. The approach into Coire Odhar may require skis to be carried up the marked footpath from point a) or can be done on skis from point b), ascending north-east around the end of the south ridge of Meall Corranaich to follow the path to the latest fence until into the corrie proper. There is a gate and stile at NN 613 394 to cross this barrier. The best route up Beinn Ghlas depends on the snow conditions on its south-west side. Either (1) continue up the west of the burn or as snow permits, to around 850m, a short way below the col at the head of the corrie, and ski up north-east to reach the north-west ridge of Beinn Ghlas at around 950m; or (2) cross to the east side of the burn and ski up onto the south-south-west ridge and follow it to the summit; or (3) continue

Above: Meall Corranaich south ridge (skiers, Claudia and Gus MacRae) © Al Todd

across the south-south-west ridge into the shallow Coire a' Chonnaidh and ski steeply up its head onto the south-south-east ridge.

From the summit of Beinn Ghlas ski down the broad crest of the north-east ridge. In good conditions this is an easy run, but in bad visibility care is needed as the flanks of the ridge are steep. This run ends at the col below Ben Lawers, which can also be reached from the col at the head of Coire Odhar by descending a short way on the north side to avoid the end of the Beinn Ghlas north-west ridge before ascending to this same point. The initial part of the ridge from the col onto Ben Lawers is steep and rocky, so may require skis to be carried for a short distance. Higher up it may be best to ascend on the north-west side of the ridge, which can hold snow well, making it possible to ski right up to the big summit cairn and triangulation station.

There are several tempting downhill runs from the summit, not least the steep and exciting 500m descent north-east to Lochan nan Cat, or the equally steep run south to the head of Allt an Tuim Bhric. These are routes for experienced skiers in good conditions.

For those returning to Coire Odhar, however, there is good skiing down the south-west ridge of Ben Lawers to the col (keeping to the north-west side of the ridge). From the col, it may be preferable to return over Beinn Ghlas and from there ski down into Coire Odhar by routes (1), (2) or (3), being mindful that snow conditions are likely to have changed during the day. Alternatively, a return to the col at the head of Coire Odhar is possible on a slightly downhill run across the corrie on the north side of Beinn Ghlas and a traverse around the north-west ridge. From this col there is a choice of routes down Coire Odhar, depending on snow cover, back to the starting point.

A worthwhile variation to this tour, not shown on the map, is to include Meall Corranaich. Starting from point b), the route ascends north-west after crossing the fence in lower Coire Odhar to reach the south ridge of Meall Corranaich. Continue up the ridge, passing the small col before the final steep slope onto the summit of Meall Corranaich. Ski down the north ridge for around 500m until it becomes possible to drop steeply into the shallow corrie on the east side, which can hold good snow. Descend south-east in a line that can be continued uphill on the far side to skin up to the Ben Lawers/Beinn Ghlas col. Continue up Ben Lawers, returning over Beinn Ghlas as described above.

Meall Greigh ▲ 1,001m
△ NN 674 438　　◁ LR51　　⊕ P.116

Meall Garbh ▲ 1,118m
△ NN 644 437　　◁ LR51　　⊕ P.116

P	Lawers village on the A827 road (note that car parking is limited: see introduction).
↔ 14KM	△ 1,110M　　⊥ 190M
⧗ 5-6 HRS	GRADE II　　★★★

The north-east end of the Lawers range opens out between Meall Garbh and Meall Greigh to form a broad ridge on the north side of the Lawers Burn, making the traverse of these two hills a fairly easy ski tour. On a fine day it gives superb views of the great craggy faces of Ben Lawers and An Stùc above Lochan nan Cat, the most impressive part of the range.

If there is sufficient snow cover, it is possible to start at the Lawers Hotel on the west side of the Lawers Burn. The way up leads north-north-west through fields onto the open hillside, eventually just east of a small dam on the Lawers Burn at 600m (NN 663 427). If cover is thin, it may be necessary to carry skis initially using the wooded summer route up the east side of the Lawers Burn. This goes past Machuim Farm by a track above the burn, continuing through woodland and then by more open ground before crossing to the west side of the burn 1km before the dam. Going to Meall Greigh first, ski north-east up the open hillside, choosing one of the snow-filled stream beds which lead up to the broad ridge just west of the summit.

Ski west along the broad ridge – easy going in good conditions but calling for accurate navigation in poor visibility – to reach the 834m col below Meall Garbh. The ascent of this hill goes up an obvious gully, usually well-filled with snow, or up the slopes to its left or right, to reach the north-west ridge, which leads easily to the cairn of Meall Garbh. The continuation of the main ridge south-west is narrow, and there is a fine view along it to An Stùc and Ben Lawers. An Stùc is the only peak of the range which cannot be easily traversed on skis.

The South and Southeast sides of Meall Garbh are steep with small crags, so return by the ascent route to the 834m col, and from there ski down to the Lawers Burn dam by an easy run. Below the dam there is at least 3km more skiing down wide-open slopes, with thin snow cover on the fields above Lawers Hotel sufficient for a prolonged schuss down to the road.

The Grand Traverse of the Lawers Range
△ NN 636 414　　◁ LR51　　 P.116

P	a) The cairn at the high point of the Loch Tay to Glen Lyon road, 0.5km north of the north end of Lochan na Làirige (NN 594 416/ 56.5454, -4.2880), or
	b) the lay-by 1km before the high point of the road at (NN 600 404/ 56.5351, -4.2781).
↔ 20KM	△ 1,550M　　⊥ 550M
⧗ 8-10 HRS	GRADE IV　　★★★★★

The traverse of Ben Lawers range is undoubtedly one of the best ski mountaineering expeditions in Scotland, giving a day of extraordinary variety and interest regarding both skiing and scenery. It links up parts of the three shorter tours described above and, dependent on the route chosen, gives challenging ski runs. The best direction is from south-west to north-east and will require making transport arrangements to start on the Loch Lyon to Glen Lyon road and finish at the village of Lawers on the A828 above Loch Tay. Good conditions are needed to provide a memorable day.

From either of the starting points near the high point of the road above Lochan na Làirige, take the route described above to Meall Corranaich. If the road beyond the dam of Lochan na Làirige is impassable, it is also possible to ski directly up the south ridge of the hill or access the ridge from Coire Odhar (as described above) without difficulty, given adequate snow cover. From the summit of Meall Corranaich, it is may best to return towards the col below the summit before skiing steeply down into the head of Coire Odhar, crossing the corrie to ascend to the north-west ridge of Beinn Ghlas. Continue along the ridge to Ben Lawers as described above.

The next section of the main ridge between Ben Lawers and Meall Garbh leads past An Stùc, a steep, rocky peak which skiers usually bypass on one side or the other. One way is to ski north from Ben Lawers, slightly on the west side of the ridge, past the rocky knoll of Creag an Fhithich, and continue north on a descending traverse across the west flank of An Stùc. The north-west ridge of An Stùc overlooks the head of the Fin Glen, and the descent into this corrie is short but very steep. (The ridge may be corniced on its east side, but there is usually at least one place where this cornice is discontinuous.) Ski down to a big boulder at about 720m in the Fin Glen, and there put on skins for the ascent to Meall Garbh, first by an ascending traverse north-east to reach the north-west ridge, then up that ridge to the summit.

An alternative route from Ben Lawers to Meall Garbh past An Stùc goes down the north ridge to the flattening before Creag an Fhithich. From here, turn right and ski steeply east on a diagonal descent (beware of the precipitous drop on the downhill side) until a clear route appears down to Lochan nan Cat. (The steep descent may be corniced and prone to avalanche, so it should only be attempted if conditions allow.) Contour round the north side of the lochan and climb steeply to Meall Garbh.

The last part of the traverse reverses the route already described between Meall Garbh and Meall Greigh and back to the Lawers Hotel, provided there is good snow cover down to road level. It is probably best, however, to ski due south off the summit of Meall Greigh, more or less directly towards Machuim Farm on the east side of the Lawers Burn, as this may give a quicker descent than crossing to the west side. This descent route provides an easier route for carrying skis when the snow runs out, following the summer path on the east side of the Lawers Burn and through the woodland past Machuim Farm down to the A827. The Ben Lawers Hotel is a short walk west (right) along the road.

Ben Lawers North

By Bob Reid

The Glen Lyon approach to Ben Lawers has much to offer the ski tourer. It presents different challenges from the usual approaches and has a habit of being in condition more often than the mountain's southern flanks. Invervar sits at 200m above sea level in an enclosed section of Glen Lyon, which, aside from height gain, offers other advantages. Snow lingers longer than above the Loch Tay roads, affording touring opportunities more reliably and later into the season.

We are accustomed to thinking of Ben Lawers as a twisting ridge, running west–east (the traverse is described in an adjacent section). However, along its northern flanks are a series of north-facing corries, the westernmost being very substantial indeed. Each corrie provides circular ski tours, starting and finishing in Glen Lyon. Each takes in several of the Munro Tops, offering highly satisfactory means of climbing these very large hills. Each is described in turn.

Allt a' Chobhair Circuit

Meall a' Choire Lèith ▲ 926m
Hill of the Grey Corrie
NN 612 439   LR51   P.116

Meall Corranaich ▲ 1,069m
Crooked Hill
NN 615 410   LR51   P.116

Beinn Ghlas ▲ 1,103m
Green-Grey Hil
NN 625 404   LR51   P.116

Ben Lawers ▲ 1,214m
NN 636 414   LR51   P.116

P Coming from the Fortingall end of Glen Lyon, drive 4.5km past Inverar to Camusvrachan (NN 619 478/ 56.6022, -4.2503), where you can turn south toward a bridge across the River Lyon. Parking is possible on the verge just before the bridge.

↔ 18KM   △ 1,600M   ⊤ 190M
⏱ 7-9 HRS   GRADE III   ★★★★

A demanding high-level circuit of four Munros with the benefit of some superb skiing, including one of the best downhill runs in Scotland. Part of this duplicates the Ben Lawers traverse but is worth including because of the increased likelihood of

Ben Lawers, the awkward section midway to the summit from Beinn Ghlas © Al Todd

snow cover on these north-facing aspects.

From the starting point, head south across the bridge and reach the south Glen Lyon road 250m further on. Head east for 1km past a farm called Balnahanaid until you cross the Allt a' Chobhair burn. On the east bank of this burn a track heads southwards into the side glen. The track starts at 200m above sea level and reliably holds snow. There are crag-strewn slopes on each side of this approach running down from the sentinel peaks of Sròn Eich to the west and Creag Roro to the east. It is a fine entry into a very grand and scenic side glen. After nearly 2km the track ends at a set of shielings marked on the map (NN 625 453). From here a westward-slanting traverse uphill can be made onto the north-east shoulder of Meall a' Choire Lèith. Labelled on the map is an incipient corrie named Coire Bàn, whose left-bounding (south) shoulder provides an excellent ridge ascending to the true north ridge of Meall a' Choire Lèith. A further 500m of skinning southward takes you to the summit itself (5km; 2hrs).

From the summit of Meall a' Choire Lèith follow the ridge south, avoiding Coire Liath to the left (east), toward the col at 770m, 1km further south. The ridge now curves a little to the south-east, before a straightforward ascent south to the summit of Meall Corranaich, 2km further south from the col, with a reascent of 300m.

The south face of Meall Corranaich gives a stupendous steep black run down into Coire Odhar. With less cover, it may be better to go to the col south of Corrannaich and descend east into Coire Odhar as described earlier. Best not to go too far downhill, as there's more ascent to come. Aim for the site of the old ski hut (NN 616 401; 760m) but note that the hut is no longer there. From here it is possible to begin the ascent up the west shoulder of Beinn Ghlas (1,103m). From the ski hut site the 350m steep ascent to the summit of Beinn Ghlas is due east.

The connecting ridge between Beinn Ghlas and Ben Lawers is one of the great delights of Scottish skiing. A rounded, whaleback ridge gently sloping north-east, the direction you need to go, but with steepening slopes on either side as you head toward Ben Lawers. Don't ski off the edge! There is just enough room to make a few turns. This takes you 750m along the connecting Ghlas–Lawers ridge to the col (NN 630 411; 998m). The west ridge of Ben Lawers looms over this col and is steep enough that some will prefer to carry their skis the remaining 500m east to the summit of Ben Lawers at 1,214m.

From the summit of Ben Lawers the circuit heads 750m northwards to the named Top, Creag an Fhithich (NN 636 421; 1,047m). From here a 6km downhill run can be made along the eastern flank of the glen heading north. Maintaining height can be advantageous, depending on the snow cover. Some small crags on the lower north west flank of An Stùc should be avoided. It is possible under full snow cover to ski all the way back to the car park.

An alternative in good visibility and on longer days would be to continue along the high-level ridge past Creag an Fhithich to the summit of An Stùc at 1,118m (due northwards). The north-west spur of An Stùc offers an equally splendid run northwards and downwards to the starting point. It is important to note that both the east and north-east faces of An Stùc are steep and craggy and not ideal ground for ski touring (this ridge overlooking the Fin Glen can be reached directly from Creag an Fhithich by a descending traverse across the west face of An Stuic as described in the Grand Traverse.).

The Circuit of Coire nam Buidheag

Meall Greigh ▲ 1,001m
Hill of the Horse Studs
△ NN 674 438   ◁ LR51   ⊕ P.116

Meall Garbh ▲ 1,118m
Rough Hill
△ NN 644 437   ◁ LR51   ⊕ P.116

P	The small car park at Invervar (NN 665 482/ 56.6069, -4.1755).
↔ 13.5KM	△ 1,100M	⊺ 200M
⏱ 6-7 HRS	GRADE III	★★★

A scenic and satisfying circuit taking advantage of the north-facing slopes above Glen Lyon. There is a splendid high-level linking ridge between the two Munro summits, which feels wilder and more remote than it ought to.

The starting point is the same car park that serves routes on the Càrn Mairg Circuit to the north. If that route looks bare to patchy, southwards might reveal snowier slopes. Head south from the Invervar car park on the track to Dericambus, crossing the bridge over the River Lyon. Once across the river, head east, passing farm buildings (NN 670 476). From here an old stalkers' path zigzags steeply south beside a small woodland at first, then up the hill to the south-west marked as Creag Dhubh. No need to ascend this fully on the outward leg of the tour, trending south instead as the ridge to the summit of Meall Greigh becomes clearer. It emerges as a series of hummocky hills, faint at first but becoming a more defined ridge running all the way to the summit of Meall Greigh itself. The easternmost cairn is the summit. It is 3km from the top of the Creag Dhubh zigzags, at a consistent gradient, which makes for enjoyable skinning at a reasonable pace (4.5km, 2.5hrs).

From Meall Greigh the route lies west toward the summit of Meall Garbh, a further 3km away. At first an enjoyable 200m descent with no particular difficulties takes you to a flattish col halfway between the summits. The col is at an altitude of 834m. From this col it is a fairly steep onward climb on skis, keeping to the ridge, at first broad and heading north-west; then at NN 650 441 swinging south-west and narrowing toward the summit. The climb from the col at 834m to the summit of Meall Garbh at 1,118m is 1.5km with nearly 300m of steep ascent (8km; 4.5hrs).

The descent at first retraces the last 500m of the ascent ridge north-east to NN 650 441. It then continues in a north-easterly direction, descending beyond the ridge, now following the north-east spur of the hill. This is the west side of Coire nam Buidheag where there is a substantial set of shielings. This leads to the Inverinain Burn, which drains the corrie northwards. In descent it is advisable to cross this sooner rather than later, ensuring that you can cross back over Creag Dhubh (554m) without too much reascent before descending back to Dericambus.

If you do end up descending too far down the Inverinain Burn, you can skirt the south edge of the plantations and then descend due east to Dericambus and the bridge across the River Lyon back to Invervar.

Beinn Dòrain ▲ 1,076m
Hill of the Storm
△ NN 325 378   ◁ LR50   ⊕ P.102

Beinn an Dòthaidh ▲ 1,004m
Hill of Scorching
△ NN 331 408   ◁ LR50   ⊕ P.102

P	Bridge of Orchy Railway Station (NN 300 395/56.5171, -4.7640) or nearby car park (NN 297 396/56.5170, -4.7691).
↔ 12KM	△ 1,150M	⊺ 160M
⏱ 5-6 HRS	GRADE III	***

By Bill Morrison, updated by Colwyn Jones

Whether approached by train or the A82 from the south, Beinn Dòrain presents an imposing peak flanked by long, steep slopes that do not typically hold good snow on the west side. To its north, Beinn an Dòthaidh also has uniformly steep slopes round its western perimeter above Loch Tulla. Between them, however, Coire an Dòthaidh gives relatively easy access to the upper parts of both mountains, where there is much good skiing and a selection of short- to medium-length tours which may be extended to Beinn Achaladair (see the following route).

Starting from the large car park at Bridge of Orchy, walk up to the train station, go through the tunnel under the railway, through a gate, cross the West Highland Way and follow the track onto the moor. Skin up on the south side of the Allt Coire an Dòthaidh for 2km. Towards the head of the corrie, about 50m below the col at its head, is a small broken cliff with a shelf above it. The easiest route on skis keeps towards the left (north) under the steep and usually ice-covered crags on the Beinn an Dòthaidh side of the corrie until it is possible to turn right and make a rising traverse south-east up to and along the shelf towards the col (744m). The alternative is to use boot crampons and an ice axe and carry your skis. Before reaching the col bear south up a broad gully with a line of low cliffs on its east side, and reach the broad, easy-angled north ridge of Beinn Dòrain. Ski up this ridge to a false summit, then descend south, dropping 20m and continuing along a narrower ridge with steep slopes on both sides for about 200m to the true summit and the cairn, which in clear weather is a superb viewpoint.

The descent may follow the ascent route on the north ridge all the way back to the col. However, after returning past the false summit, it may be better to take a line further east, skiing down the shallow corrie at the head of the Allt Coire a' Ghathalach. This corrie holds snow well and gives a good run, but do not ski too far down before traversing left to reach the col.

Beinn an Dòthaidh is well protected by crags and steep ground on most sides, but the ascent from the col is easy. Climb north-east on a rising traverse above the crags overlooking Coire a' Ghabhalach to reach less steep slopes as you approach the summit. There are three tops, the middle one being the highest. The drops between these tops along the summit plateau are very small, but at the north edge cornices overhang the cliffs of the north-east corrie. Great care is needed skiing along this plateau in bad visibility.

The simplest return to the col is by way of the ascent route. From the cairn at the col ski down to the shelf 30m below, passing to the right of twin-pointed boulders (above the small cliff mentioned above), and continue north-west on a downward traverse below the big ice-covered crag. Once the slopes below are clear, ski steeply down to easier ground by the Allt Coire an Dòthaidh. Easy skiing along the south side of this stream leads back to the station at Bridge of Orchy. This tour can be extended north-eastwards from Beinn an Dòthaidh by skiing south-east from the summit, then east down the ridge leading to the bealach at the head of Coire Achaladair. There the traverse of Beinn Achaladair and Beinn a' Chreachain, described next, is joined, and continuing over these two mountains to its end near Achallader Farm is a superb, lengthy five-star tour. This is a good trip for fit skiers on a fine day, and the 5km return from Achallader to Bridge of Orchy, above the A82 suggests using two cars. Do not ski along the railway.

Beinn Achaladair ▲ 1,038m
Hill of the Field by the Hard Water
NN 344 432　　　LR50　　　P.102

Beinn a' Chreachain ▲ 1,081m
Bare Rocky Hill
NN 374 440　　　LR50　　　P.102

The large hardstanding car park on the south side of the access road to Achallader Farm (NN 313 438/ 56.5561, -4.7456), 300m off the A82, east of the head of Loch Tulla.

↔ 16KM　　△ 1,300M　　↕ 180M
⏱ 7-8 HRS　　GRADE IV　　★★★

By Donald Bennet, updated by Colwyn Jones

The traverse of these two fine mountains starts and finishes at the large car park. From the car park there is a rough waymarked path to a bridge over the West Highland Railway Line to reach the hillside west of the Allt Coire Achaladair. However, with good snow cover it is often better to ski along to Achallader Farm and follow the smooth and well-made hydroelectric maintenance track south, passing under the railway east of the Allt Coire Achaladair, through a small stand of trees to the dam. From here the simplest route of ascent, although not the most direct, is up the corrie to the col at its head, keeping on the east side of the stream. Attempting to climb directly south-east from the railway to the lowest point of the summit ridge of Beinn Achaladair between its two tops is not recommended. These slopes are long and steep, and if the snow is soft, there will be a distinct avalanche risk.

Once on the col at the head of Coire Achaladair turn north-east then north along a broad, easy-angled ridge to the South Top (1,002m) of Beinn Achaladair. It may not be worth taking off skins for the short descent along the ridge that precedes the final climb to the summit, which is close to the north edge of the mountain, overlooking a long steep drop to the railway line far below.

On the descent to the next col, which links Beinn Achaladair to Meall Buidhe, avoid skiing along the ridge as it becomes steep and rocky lower down and may be corniced on its precipitous north side. Instead, ski south-east from the cairn down easy open slopes, dropping about 150m, then turn north-east and make a descending traverse below the rocky flank of the ridge and above a fence (if visible), which leads north-east to the col at 813m.

Continue north-east up to the broad level ridge of Meall Buidhe (NN 359 438; 978m) and traverse its 1km long flat crest. Then descend east slightly to reach the foot of the final climb of 170m to the summit of Beinn a' Chreachain. The exposed and windswept character of these highest stony slopes means they may have poorer snow cover than the lower hillsides and corries.

One possible descent route from Beinn a' Chreachain takes the north-east ridge for 1km before turning north-west towards Crannach Wood. The crest of this ridge is very narrow at one point, and it should be skied with great caution. With good snow cover this is a perfectly feasible route if it is possible to ski through the wood (which has deer fences to cross), although it is a long walk back past Achallader Farm from Crannach Wood if there is not enough snow low down.

It is usually better to return to the cairn at the north-east end of the level summit ridge of Meall Buidhe. Go about 150m south-west from this cairn along the ridge, then turn right and ski steeply down the north-west face of Meall Buidhe. The upper part of the north-west-facing slope is the steepest, and if it is icy or avalanche-prone the descent should be undertaken with great care. In good conditions, however, this is an exhilarating ski run. Lower down, as the angle eases, ski west in a long descending traverse, retaining height above Crannach Wood. Cross the Allt na Crannaich at about 500m and continue a gradual descent across the lower slopes of Beinn Achaladair to reach the railway, crossing this by any safe option near Achallader Farm. Do not ski along the railway. If there is complete snow cover, the descent from Meall Buidhe gives a 4km run with a vertical drop of 700m.

Below: Skiing north off Stùc an Lochain with the forested island of Loch an Daimh (skier, Hamish MacEwen) © Doug Bryce

Stùc an Lochain △ 960m
Peak of the Small Loch

△ NN 483 448	◁ LR51	⊕ P.109
P	Glen Lyon at the bridge over the Allt Conait (NN 529 446/ 56.5705, -4.3949), about 5km west of Bridge of Balgie.	
↔ 10KM	△ 720M	⫯ 250M
⏱ 5-6 HRS	GRADE III	★★★

By CR Ford, updated by Colwyn Jones and Bob Reid

Stùc an Lochain is rather an isolated mountain lying far up Glen Lyon, separated from its neighbours by that glen and the deep trench holding Loch an Daimh to its north. It gives an interesting ski ascent by its east ridge, with magnificent views in clear weather, but good snow cover is needed to make the rough lower ground skiable.

From roadside parking near the bridge in Glen Lyon at the Allt Conait, ascend west over undulating fenced ground to the Allt Ruighe Ghiuthas, aiming to reach the burn at its confluence with the stream flowing out of Coire an Duich (460m). The corrie is not recommended as a ski route, as the headwall is steep and may be corniced. Cross the burn and bear west to the foot of the steepening east ridge of Stùc an Lochain (550m). Ascend this by a very shallow gully, turning a steeper section by a traverse left, then regain the ridge at the fence along its crest. Follow this to the east Top, Sròn Chona Choirein (NN 493 445; 927m). The broad, undulating summit ridge has a fence and should hold enough snow to give an easy, pleasant traverse above Lochan nan Cat to the foot of the final peak. Note the cairn on a rise approximately halfway along the ridge. The last 100m to the summit is steep and may not be skiable.

On the descent return to the cairn halfway along the ridge to Sròn Chona Choirein, then make a descending traverse east-south-east across a broad, smooth snowfield, which should provide good skiing down to the foot of the east ridge. From there pick the best route through the drumlins along the Allt Ruighe Ghiuthas back to the starting point.

With two cars, a fine tour can be made by continuing the traverse from the summit of Stùc an Lochain. Head south-west from the summit down to follow the Allt Camaslaidh, flowing down to Pubil, 8km up the road from the starting point at the Allt Conait. The run down the Allt Camaslaidh is quite easy, particularly in its shallow upper basin. There are intervening fences to cross, and if the snow level is high, using the west bank allows you to walk down to the track through Pubil to reach the second car.

A late-season alternative climbs Stùc an Lochain from the end of the road which leads to the Giorra dam at the east end of Loch an Daimh at 410m (NN 512 463). This makes for a much shorter ascent of Stùc an Lochain – little more than 600m of skinning up. Head south-west from the start and then follow the fence to the top of Creag an Fheadain (887m). Follow the ridge (and fence) south-south-west to Sròn Chona Choirein (NN 493 445; 927m), then to the summit by following the earlier route described (4.5km; 600m ascent; 2hrs). Descent by the same route allows for a combined ascent with Meall Buidhe (NN 498 499; 932m) on the same day.

Meall Buidhe ▲ 932m
Yellow Hill

| NN 498 499 | LR51 | P.109 |

P Giorra dam forming the east end of Loch an Daimh (NN 512 463/56.5855, -4.4235).

↔ 10KM   △ 600M   ↕ 500M
⏱ 3-4 HRS   GRADE II   **

by Bob Reid

Meall Buidhe is not as dramatic a hill as its southerly neighbour, Stùc an Lochain; however, it makes for an enjoyable Munro day on skis. Under late-season spring snow, both Munros could be skied in a day.

From the dam, climb due north up the shallow Coire Beithe before angling north-west toward Meall a' Phuill (878m). A track at the eastern edge of the corrie can retain snow during leaner snow conditions. Continue west from Meall a' Phuill for 0.5km then head north up the sharpening ridge to the summit, crossing point 917m. A further 1km north along the ridge takes you past smaller cairns to the large summit cairn of Meall Buidhe. Note that at 932m Meall Buidhe is the highest point, even though the OS map shows Garbh Mheall (912m), 0.5km further north, as the main peak. The thoroughly enjoyable descent is by the same route.

Beinn Dearg (Glen Lyon) ● 830m
Red Hill

| NN 609 497 | LR51 | P.116 |

P On the minor road at the splendid car park at Innerwick (NN 587 475/56.5982, -4.3040).

↔ 10KM   △ 630M   ↕ 200M
⏱ 3-4 HRS (2-3 hrs if the climb to the summit is omitted)
GRADE II   **

By Colwyn Jones

With good snow cover, the Corbett Beinn Dearg on the north side of Glen Lyon provides a short and reliable tour with a fine south-west face descent.

The car park lies on the single-track minor road going west up the lengthy Glen Lyon. The road, which follows the River Lyon, regularly carries residential, agricultural, and hydroengineering traffic, so may be passable after heavy snowfall, and the section to the parking place (provided by the Meggernie Estate) is not very steep when driving up the glen from the B846.

Walk east a short distance from the car park, go over the road bridge, past the war memorial to the east side of the Allt Ghallabhaich, and immediately turn left through the pedestrian gate in the deer fence shielding the road. On the side of the coniferous plantation, follow the well-maintained, steadily steep landrover track beside the Allt Ghallabhaich leading up towards the Lairig Ghallabhaich for about 3km, then take the right zigzag branch up through the trees, which should keep you warm.

The track leaves the forest at about the 570m contour, through a derelict gate and close to a similarly ramshackle Larsen trap. From this north-east corner of the plantation head due east up a broad, very shallow valley directly toward the summit about 2km distant. As you ascend, the remnants of a deer fence (metal posts over 1.5m high) start to converge from the left. The fence posts take a 90-degree turn left just before the summit and lead to a first untidy cairn, but the true summit cairn is directly in the line of the old fence posts and is easily found on the large flat hill-crown, if not hidden under snow. This geomorphology means there is no shelter on the top as you prepare for the ski descent. Being a Corbett, the views are somewhat restricted south by Ben Lawers but are open to the north over Loch Rannoch and far beyond, and very pleasing to the eye.

Your descent can follow the well-graded ascent route, but if there is good snow cover, then the south-west slope gives a marvellous ski back to Innerwick, marred only by two irritating sheep fences traversing the hillside (note that parts of the slope approach 30 degrees if skied directly, so check the avalanche risk before choosing this south-facing option).

Ski back along your tracks to the 700m contour, then turn south, aiming towards a cairn (NN 598 494) at the head of the Cùl Làirig. Continue towards the knoll with the 741m spot height, which requires a short climb. Turn south-west from here and descend steadily (approximately 19 degrees) for almost 500 vertical metres until the slope flattens just before a third sheep fence and the gate through the deer fence not far from the war memorial. Being south-facing, the vegetation covering the slope is quite tussocky, hence the need for adequate snow cover.

Turning south at the 700m contour during the ascent will avoid the final tedious kilometre to the top if you do not wish to visit the summit of Beinn Dearg.

Càrn Mairg Hills

Càrn Gorm ▲ 1,029m
Blue Hill
NN 635 500 LR51 P.116

Meall Garbh ▲ 968m
Rough Hill
NN 647 517 LR51 P.116

Càrn Mairg ▲ 1,041m
Hill of Woe
NN 684 512 LR51 P.116

Meall na Aighean ▲ 981m
Hill of the Heifer, also known as *Creag Mhòr*
NN 694 496 LR51 P.116

At Invervar, Glen Lyon (NN 666 482/56.6072, -4.1742).
16KM 1,300M 200M
7 HRS GRADE III ★★★

By Gordon Mackenzie, updated by Bob Reid

This tour provides an interesting high-level traverse around the horseshoe on the north side of Glen Lyon. It has the added incentive of taking in four 'ski-Munros' without too much additional effort, as there is little height loss between summits. A generous snow cover, although not essential, will limit the amount of ski-sole left behind on the boulders abounding sections of the traverse.

Park the car a few metres down the side road to Dericambus opposite Invervar, approximately 8km west of Fortingall (the same car park as for the northern Ben Lawers corries). The circuit can be done clockwise or anti-clockwise, and the wind direction may dictate the chosen option – this particular group of hills seems to attract strong winds. The tour described is long and requires good snow cover; however, it can conveniently be shortened to provide a western and eastern half, ideal for mid-winter days. The expansive corries and ridges south of Meall a' Bhàrr offer excellent descents back to Invervar.

The following describes the circuit in the clockwise direction, i.e. ascending Càrn Gorm first. From the car park turn left up the main Glen Lyon road for 25m, past the phone box until a gate on the right, signposted to the Lint Mill. Go up the marked path right of the mill and turn left along a track north through woods, emerging through a gate to the east bank of the Invervar Burn. There have been forestry operations and work on a new hydroelectric scheme built in 2020. Follow the hydro track on the eastern edge of the forestry plantation on the banks of the Invervar Burn. Once you emerge above the forest at the 450m contour near a dam and footbridge, head up the vague south-east ridge of Càrn Gorm and follow the upper ridge more steeply to the summit cairn (1,029m; 3.5km; 2hrs). The descent north off Càrn Gorm provides a good run with just under 200m height drop to the col west of An Sgòrr (924m). Ski down the north-north-east ridge initially, then move east below its crest for generally better snow. The minor top of An Sgòrr can be avoided by skirting its north-west side. Ascend north-east to reach the line of old fence posts, which should then be followed east to the more northerly of Meall Garbh's two summit cairns – the conscientious may wish to visit both (5.5km; 3.5hrs). Continue east along the line of rusting fence posts (which are at their best when masked by fog crystals) to the summit of Meall a' Bhàrr (1,004m; 7.5km; 4hrs).

From here there is an option of heading south on the expansive snow slopes of Meall a' Bhàrr, having completed half the circuit. Snow conditions permitting, this allows a swift return to Invervar. For the full circuit, continue east for 1km before turning south-east and ascending the narrower bouldery ridge leading to the main summit of Càrn Mairg (1,041m; 9km; 4.5hrs).

Although the skiing over this section is not too exacting, there is much compensation in the superb views of Schiehallion to the north and the spectacular Ben Lawers northern corries to the south. From Càrn Mairg continue the circuit descending east, avoiding boulders and small rocky outcrops for about 0.5km and then turn south-south-east to reach the col (NN 691 503; 840m; 10km; 5hrs). The final ascent of the tour is then south-south-east up the broad north-facing slopes, which lead to the rocky tor forming the main top of Meall na Aighean (981m; 11km; 5.5hrs).

The descent then retraces the ascent route of Meall na Aighean north into the Allt Coire a' Chearcaill. These slopes tend to hold snow well and provide a good ski descent to a small bothy (NN 673 497). Even when the slopes adjacent to the stream are bare, a ribbon of snow often clings to its banks, giving a convenient descent route to the confluence with the Invervar Burn, where the outward route is rejoined for the short descent back through the forest to Invervar (16km; 7hrs).

Schiehallion   ▲ 1,083m

Fairy Hill of the Caledonians

△ NN 713 547   ◹ LR51   ⊕ P.132

🅿 Near Braes of Foss Farm on the Coshieville to Kinloch Rannoch road at the FLS car park (NN 753 557/56.6769, -4.0361).

↔ 9KM   △ 760M   ⥮ 330M
⏱ 4 HRS   GRADE III   ★★

By Neil Mather, updated by Colwyn Jones

An easily identified, isolated and handsome peak from every angle, Schiehallion is both bouldery and heathery, so it is only worth attempting a ski ascent when there is ample snow cover. Given such conditions, it provides a good, if short, expedition in impressive surroundings.

The starting point at the pay and display car park on the north side of the mountain near Braes of Foss is marked by a nearby cairn and plaque to commemorate the work of the one-time Astronomer Royal, Nevil Maskelyne, who estimated the mass and density of the Earth. He also confirmed that Isaac Newton's inverse square law of gravitation was true, which, while essential to downhill skiing, often hinders upward progress!

Take the waymarked path, which leads through the forest then along the edge of the trees onto the open hillside, and continue west-south-west over slopes which become steeper as you approach the mountain's east ridge. The footpath has been furnished with stone steps to remedy erosion, which may prevent a simple ski ascent.

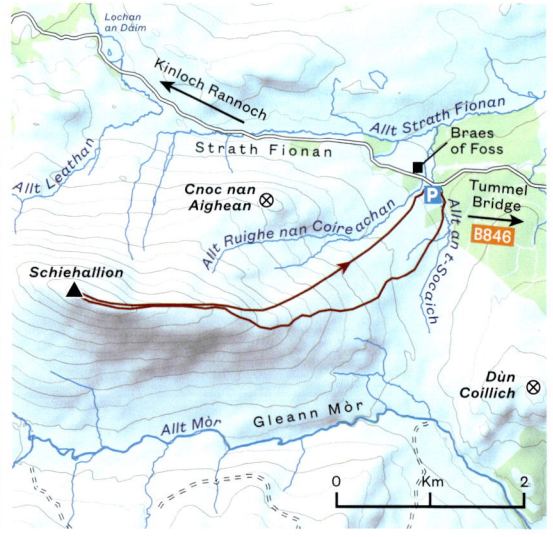

The true ridge is reached at about 800m, and it is then simply a case of following it to the summit. Without a good covering of snow the boulder-strewn crest may prove difficult on skis, and better snow might be found on its north side.

The downhill run will probably be dictated by the need to return to your starting point, so the east ridge can be regained, and while its spine may prove difficult if the boulders are not well covered, good easy skiing can be enjoyed on either side just below the crest.

Lower down it is probably best to leave the ridge at a fairly level place about 300m west of the point where it was gained on the ascent and descend east-north-east by a wide, steep slope directly above the headwaters of the burn which flows down to Braes of Foss. By trending right and keeping to the true right bank of the burn you can use the north-facing slopes, which may well have the best snow cover and allow you to ski right back to the starting point. Alternatively, descend the ridge for a further 300–400m to find easier skiing close to the line of ascent.

Above: Schiehallion (skier, Craig Cameron) © Al Todd

Stob Ghabhar ▲ 1,090m
Goat Peak
△ NN 230 455 ◁ LR41, LR50 ⊕ P.134

Creise ▲ 1,100m
Narrow or Greasy Peak
△ NN 238 506 ◁ LR41, LR50 ⊕ P.134

Meall a' Bhùiridh ▲ 1,108m
Hill of Bellowing (of Stags)
△ NN 251 503 ◁ LR41, LR50 ⊕ P.134

P Victoria Bridge at the west end of Loch Tulla (NN 270 419/ 56.5370, -4.8142).
↔ 17KM   △ 1,570M   ↕ 170M
⏱ 7-8 HRS   GRADE IV   ★★★★★

By William Wallace, updated by Colwyn Jones

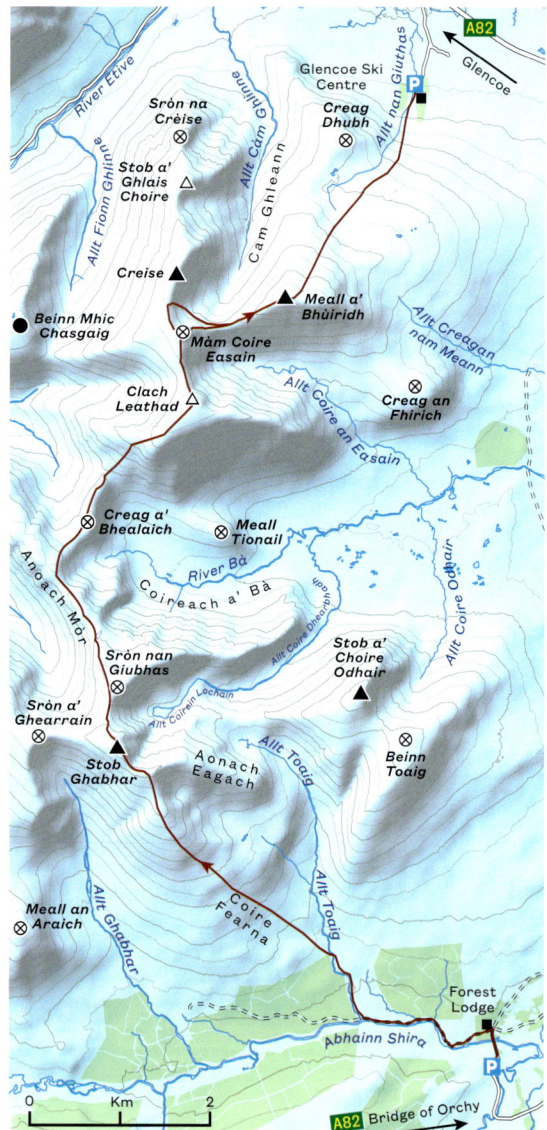

These splendid mountains dominate the west side of Rannoch Moor and, when well covered in snow, give one of the best ski tours in Scotland and a magnificent mountaineering expedition. The traverse should only be tackled by a strong party with mountaineering experience, equipped with boot crampons and ice axes. The most difficult section is the steep slope from the ridge south of Creise down to the col west-south-west of Meall a' Bhùiridh. The broken rocks and considerable exposure on this face do not normally present a major difficulty, but if the snow is hard or icy, the descent of this slope may be quite formidable. As the southern slopes of Stob Ghabhar nearly always hold less snow than the north-east face of Meall a' Bhùiridh, the direction recommended, which gives the best downhill runs, is from south to north. Traversing in the opposite direction, however, means you can use the ski tows of Meall a' Bhùiridh to reach its summit quickly and with little effort.

One requirement for this tour, irrespective of which way you go, is a friendly driver or a second car at the end of the traverse. Alternatively, trains and buses service Bridge of Orchy (6km from Victoria Bridge walking along the West Highland Way) or there is a bus to the White Corries road end.

Turn off the A82 at Bridge of Orchy and drive along the A8005 to the car park just south of Victoria Bridge (NN 270 419). Cross the bridge and turn west, following the private road along the north bank of the Abhainn Shira for 1.5km to the Glasgow University Mountaineering Club Hut beside the Allt Toaig. At this point you will need to decide on the best line of ascent to Stob Ghabhar, whose south-east face appears as a wide corrie between

Opposite: Creise from Meall a' Bhùiridh (skier, Hamish Frost) © Al Todd

the east and south-east ridges, with a waterfall high between them which is best avoided. Normally the best way is across the moorland on the west side of the Allt Toaig to reach the south-east ridge, which is followed to the point where it joins the east ridge. Continue up the crest, keeping well away from its right (north-east) edge, which is often corniced, for 0.5km to the summit.

From the summit of Stob Ghabhar ski north-west for 200m, then north down a broad, easy-angled slope for over 500m towards the distant ridge of Aonach Mòr. Follow this ridge, which has several undulations, but as the ascents are very short it is not necessary to put on skins.

After a further 1.5km, at NN 224 476, descend the north-east side of the ridge down a fairly steep but otherwise easy slope towards a broad bealach. The lowest point of this col, the Bealach Fuar-chathaidh, lies a further 0.5km north-east beyond a small rocky rise. It is a good stopping place, approximately halfway along the traverse.

The hillside north-east of the bealach is steep and has several scoops which hold snow well and can be skied down on the north-to-south traverse. However, going in the other direction it is probably best to carry skis up this section unless the snow cover is good on the slopes to the left, which are slightly less steep. Once on the more level ridge

Above: The col between Meall a' Bhùiridh and Creise (skier, Ben Cooling)
© Al Todd

above, the ascent east-north-east to the summit of Clach Leathad (1,099m) is straightforward.

From that summit the route continues north parallel to the steep edge of the eastern corrie. Neither the descent nor the following ascent are steep, and you can avoid putting on skins. Just under 1km north of Clach Leathad, the route to Meall a' Bhùiridh descends east down a steep, rocky slope. Carry skis initially, but if snow conditions are good, it may be possible to ski down the lower slopes to the col.

An alternative route is to continue north along the level ridge for 1.5km almost to the summit of Creise (1,100m). About 100 horizontal metres south of the summit of Creise there is seldom a cornice on the east side of the ridge. At a point with no rocks below, it is possible to ski down from there, but check the snow conditions as the slope is steep and exposed. After descending 100m traverse right down to the intervening col below Meall a' Bhùiridh.

The ridge from this col to the summit of Meall a' Bhùiridh is quite narrow and may have insufficient snow for an ascent on skis, but it is a straightforward climb. From the summit the top of the upper ski tows is a short distance east, and only slightly lower. If the ski area is still open then ski down the pistes. However, if you have arrived at the summit of Meall a' Bhùiridh late in the day, it may well be deserted and care is needed to avoid any piste bashers grooming the pistes. At the foot of the upper tows bear right past the buildings and ski north-east down to the flat middle slopes of Coire Pollach. Continue north-north-east, skiing easily across the plateau well to the east of the stream draining the corrie, and finally ski or walk down the steeper hillside above the moor to the bottom of the chairlift and the car park a short distance below it.

If traversing from north to south, the summit of Meall a' Bhùiridh can be quickly and easily reached using the ski lifts. From there the west-south-west ridge can be descended on skis if there is good snow cover on the crest. The highlight of the traverse may be the descent from the ridge 1km west-south-west of Clach Leathad down a steep gully to the Bealach Fuar-chathaidh. Finally, if there is good snow cover on the south-east side of Stob Ghabhar, there is a 3km long run from the summit to the glen down fairly easy slopes which are nevertheless full of route-finding interest.

Ben Vrackie ● 841m

Speckled Hill

△ NN 950 632	➚ LR43, LR52	🌐 P.138
🅿 The walkers' car park (NN 944 597) on the north side of Moulin village.		
↔ 10KM	△ 640M	⬍ 200M
⏱ 3-4 HRS	GRADE II	★★★

By Iain Smart, updated by Bob Reid

Ben Vrackie is one of the best viewpoints in the Southern Highlands, with spectacular views out over Strath Tay. The views northwards over the Beinn a' Ghlo massif are also impressive, especially when the hills are in full winter raiment. What this hill lacks in altitude, it more than makes up for in variety and interest. A justifiably popular Corbett, it also makes for a good, short tour in deep midwinter when daylight is limited and the snow may reach the lower glen.

The ascent along the line of the 'tourist path' is as good an approach as any. To reach this, leave Pitlochry by the A924 to Kirkmichael, and immediately after the Moulin Hotel, in the village of Moulin, follow a steep, narrow road on the left to the walkers' car park. The route leads north from the car park on a path through 1km of mixed birch and conifers to a gate. Beyond this an ascending traverse north-east for 1.5km leads to the col at 518m between Meall na h-Aodainn Mòire and Creag Bhreac. From this col, continue on a further rising traverse north-east, 1.5km past Loch a' Choire, and then ascend steeply north to the summit of Ben Vrackie by its south-east shoulder, avoiding the crags immediately south of the summit (5.0km; 620m ascent; 3hrs).

Descent can be made following much the same line. It is particularly pleasant to end the run in the gloaming among the snow-burdened trees above Moulin.

Interesting alternative tours can also be made, either as out-and-back routes, or traverses if using two cars.

The summit of the A924 from Pitlochry to Kirkmichael (NN 986 614) provides one such alternative. From here a less well-frequented ascent can be made (starting at 380m). Climb north-west over Carn Dubh (580m) and Carn Geal (776m), then head west along the interesting east ridge of Ben Vrackie itself, which is narrow in places and requires care (3.5km; 460m ascent; 2.5hrs). Descent is by the same route.

Another alternative exists from above the NTS Visitor Centre at Killiecrankie. Starting at 280m from a farm evocatively named 'Druid' (NN 923 634), a ski ascent can be made heading due east for 3km, then traversing steeply beneath Meall an Daimh (722m) before heading south-west and ascending the elegant west ridge of Ben Vrackie itself (4.5km; 600m ascent; 3.5hrs). Descent is by the same route.

Using two cars would enable a very stylish traverse of Ben Vrackie, combining any two of these three routes.

Right: On the Beinn a' Ghlo traverse (skier, Steve Martin) © Al Todd

Beinn a' Ghlo
Hill of Mists

Càrn Liath ▲ 976m
Grey Hill
△ NN 936 698   ⊲ LR43   ⊕ P.140

Bràigh Coire Chruinn-bhalgain ▲ 1,070m
High Corrie of Round Blisters
△ NN 945 724   ⊲ LR43   ⊕ P.140

Càrn nan Gabhar ▲ 1,121m
Hill of the Goats
△ NN 971 733   ⊲ LR43   ⊕ P.140

| P | Pay and display car park at the cattle grid at the end of the public road on the south side of Glen Fender (NN 906 671/56.7830, -3.7915). |

↔ 24KM   △ 1,640M   ⊺ 340M
⏱ 7-10 HRS   GRADE III   ★★★★

By Iain Smart, updated by Colwyn Jones

Beinn a' Ghlo is a beautiful and mysterious mountain of many peaks, ridges and corries, which extends for 10km on the south-east side of Glen Tilt from Blair Atholl to the wild recesses of the Grampian Mountains far to the north-east. When snow-covered (if driving north Càrn Liath coverage can be assessed from the A9) it gives one of the finest ski mountaineering expeditions in Scotland, and it is very much an expedition, for when you reach the outward end of the traverse at the highest summit, Càrn nan Gabhar, you are a long way from civilisation, and the sense of isolation is strong. The return may be a daunting prospect, particularly if the weather is worsening or darkness is approaching.

The mountain is best approached from Blair Atholl where there is a railway station. The 6km walk to the car park at Loch Moraig, 1km before Monzie Farm, at the end of the public road in Glen Fender, is better by car or taxi (Pitlochry has three taxi companies). At the drop-off point you are high on the moors south-west of Càrn Liath.

From the large pay and display car park, proceed through a gate on the track directly towards the base of this peak. At a small hut, leave the track and climb its steepening slopes by the most suitable route. Snow cover is often thin, for this hillside faces south-west and is very windswept. With good snow cover, however, it is possible to zigzag up without much difficulty, although Harscheisen will be useful if the snow is hard. From the cairn, just beyond the triangulation station on the summit of Càrn Liath, there is a splendid run north then north-east down the crest of the ridge for 1.5km, traversing below Beinn Mhaol on its west side, and dropping 200m to reach the narrow col (765m) below Bràigh Coire Chruinn-bhalgain. From there ascend the steep south-west shoulder to the summit of the Bràigh 300m above.

Continue north-east along the twisting main ridge, dropping about 70m for 1km, then ski east down a good slope, which is steep at the top, for

Key

1. Beinn a' Ghlo   P.139
2. Càrn a Chlamain   P.141
3. Beinn Dearg   P.148

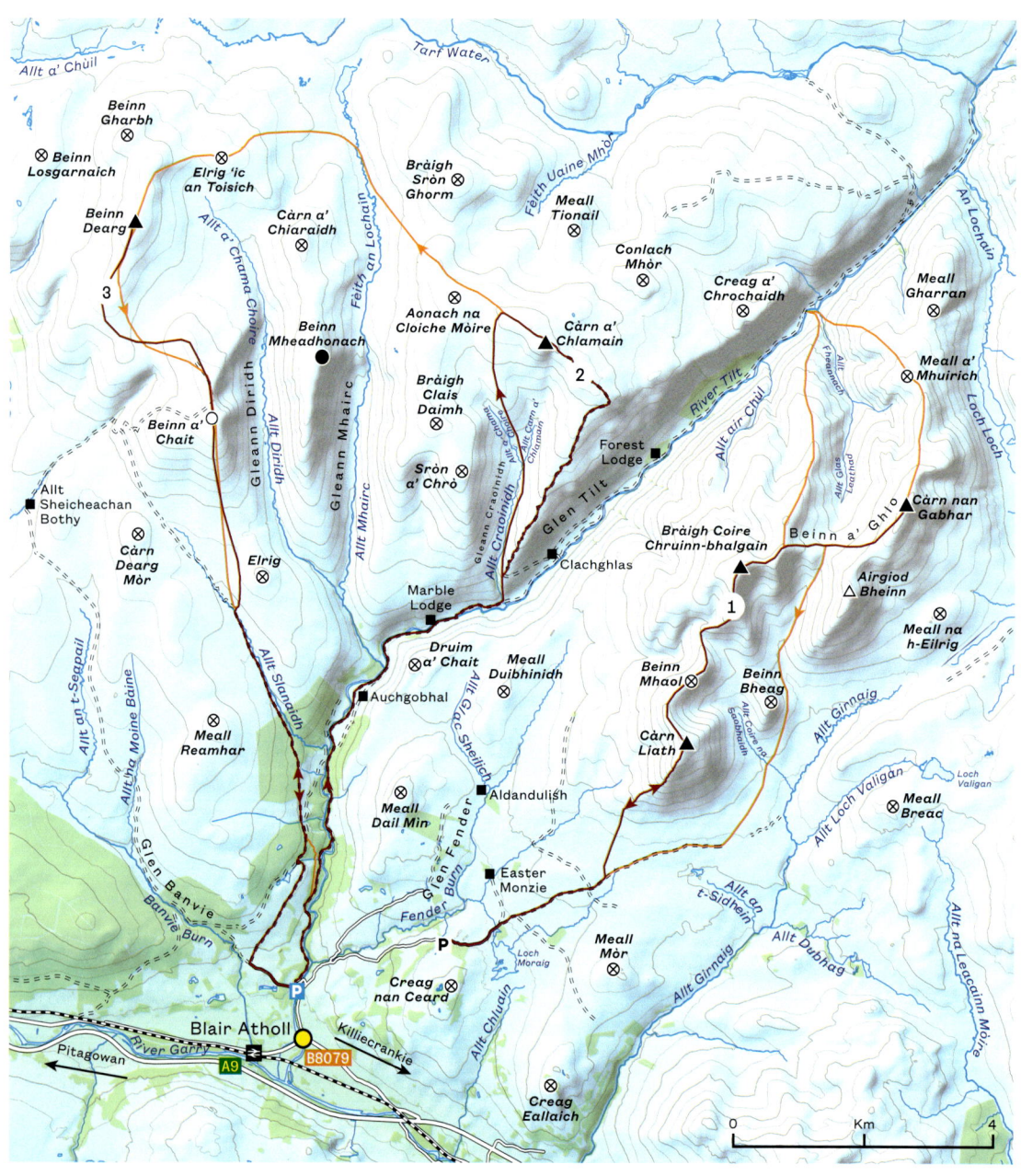

150m to the Bealach an Fhiodha, the col at 847m below Airgiod Bheinn (1:25,000 map). From there make an ascending traverse to the north of Airgiod Bheinn to gain the main ridge running north-east leading to Càrn nan Gabhar, the main summit of the range. Climb about 280m in 2km to reach the second triangulation station of the day.

At this point you are some 12km from the starting point, and there is no easy return. To the north, south and east lies roadless desolation. In good conditions the best route is to retrace your tracks, follow the ridge back again to Càrn Liath and enjoy the thrilling descent from there towards Loch Moraig and (hopefully) the glories of a winter sunset. This is well worth the 420m of re-ascent necessary to reverse the traverse. Another good ending is to ski from Bràigh Coire Chruinn-bhalgain down to Marble Lodge in Glen Tilt, where you can ski or walk out to Bridge of Tilt if you have a second car waiting. If, however, weather conditions are normal, with minimal visibility and a bitter wind blowing, it may be more expedient to return by a lower-level route. Return to the Bealach an Fhiodha, and from there ski south-south-west down the glen leading to the Allt Coire Lagain. Before reaching this stream, at an altitude of about 450m, make a long contouring traverse south-west below Càrn Liath to reach the track between Loch Moraig and Shinagag. This can be a long and weary trudge in poor snow and gathering darkness, and once the track is reached there is still approximately 3km to go to the road end.

Parties staying on the Blair Atholl Estate are permitted access to some of the private roads. A footbridge (NN 956 763) down Glen Tilt, past Forest Lodge, allows you to cross the River Tilt and ascend Bràigh Coire Chruinn-bhalgain or via the north-west ridge of Càrn nan Gabhar as alternative and remote access routes.

Càrn a' Chlamain ▲ 963m
Hill of the Kite or Buzzard

△ NN 915 758	⌖ LR43	🌐 P.140

P	The car park at Old Bridge of Tilt (NN 874 663/ 56.7744, -3.8435), 1km north of Blair Atholl. Parking charges apply.		
↔ 21KM	△ 820M		⊤ 150M
⏱ 6-8 HRS	GRADE II		★★

By Donald Bennet, updated by Colwyn Jones

Càrn a' Chlamain is the highest hill on the steep north-west margin of Glen Tilt, rising directly above Forest Lodge and recognisable from afar by its pointed summit, which appears just above the general level of the hills on that side of Glen Tilt. It is an easy ski ascent, with a lengthy 6km approach along the beautiful lower reaches of the glen. This approach may favour the use of Nordic skis or a mountain bike, or indeed both. Permission to drive up the private road of Glen Tilt from the estate office at Blair Castle is no longer available.

Leave the car park and take the private track immediately opposite along the west bank of the River Tilt. After 2.5km cross the river by the bridge and continue on the east bank until 1km past Marble Lodge at the bridge over the Allt Craoinidh (NN 908 720; 280m).

From this point there are two easy routes up Càrn a' Chlamain, one up the corrie of the Allt Craoinidh, and the other along the broad, smooth south ridge which merges with the south-east ridge near the summit. A circular traverse combining these two routes is probably the best way to do the hill on skis. The 'summer route' by the path from Forest Lodge is not a suitable ski route. A track on the east side of the Allt Craoinidh leads for more than 1km up the corrie, and beyond it the going is very easy up smooth slopes leading west of the summit to avoid an area of steep scree. The broad north-west ridge is reached about 500m from the summit, and you can ski easily along this ridge, passing a rise with a cairn on it that could be mistaken for the top in bad visibility. The summit cairn is a few hundred metres south-east.

Ski south-east from the summit (avoiding steep ground to the south) and in about 300m reach a broad level shoulder. Continue south-east for 500m, then turn south and then south-west to ski easily along the broad ridge directly back to the bridge over the Allt Craoinidh.

It is possible to combine Beinn Dearg and Càrn a' Chlamain in a long day's traverse over the rounded hills north-west of Glen Tilt. The distance between the two hills is about 7km, and midway there is a drop to 640m in Gleann Mhairc.

Overleaf: Càrn a' Chlamain
© Al Todd

Chapter 4

Central Scotland North

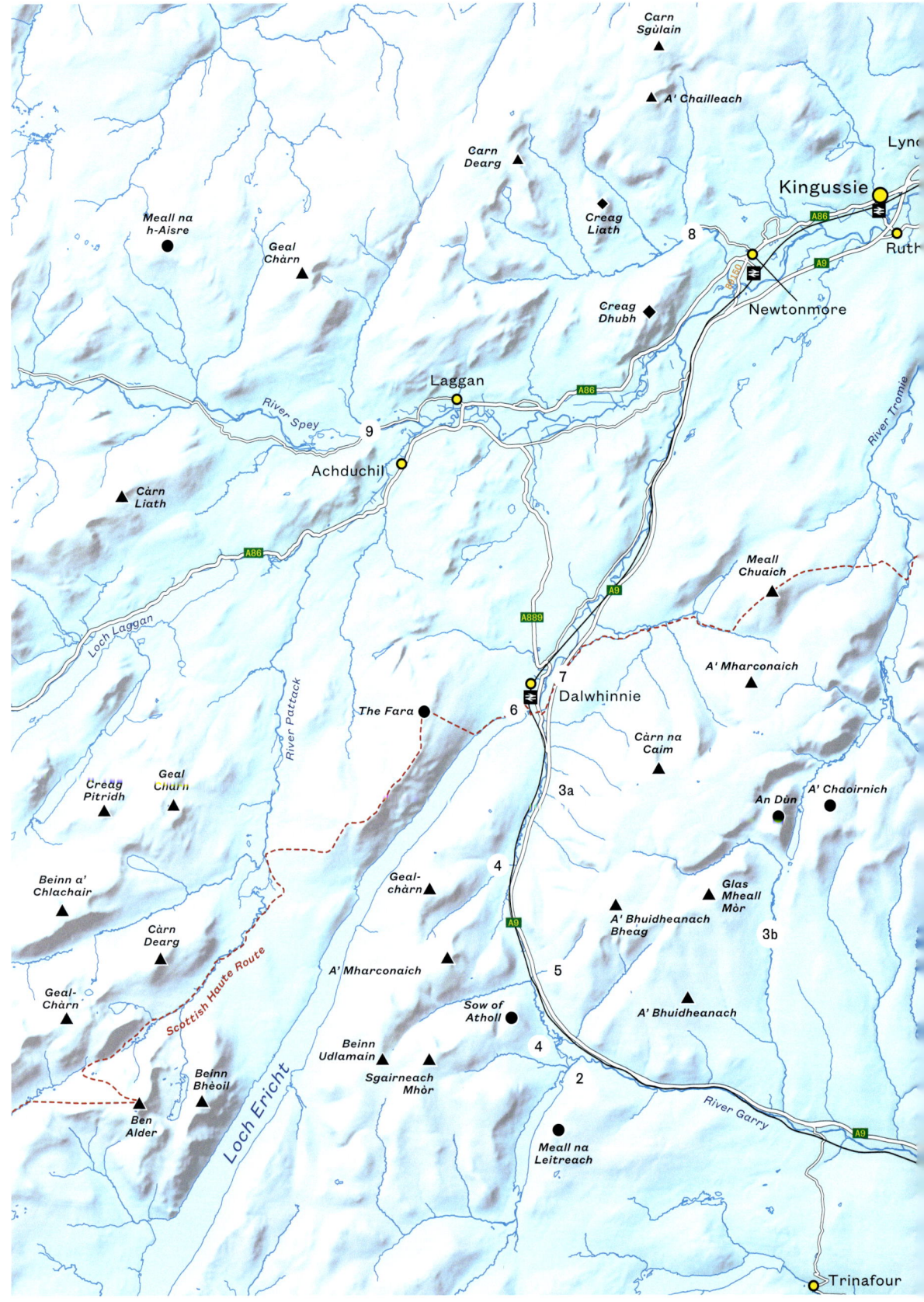

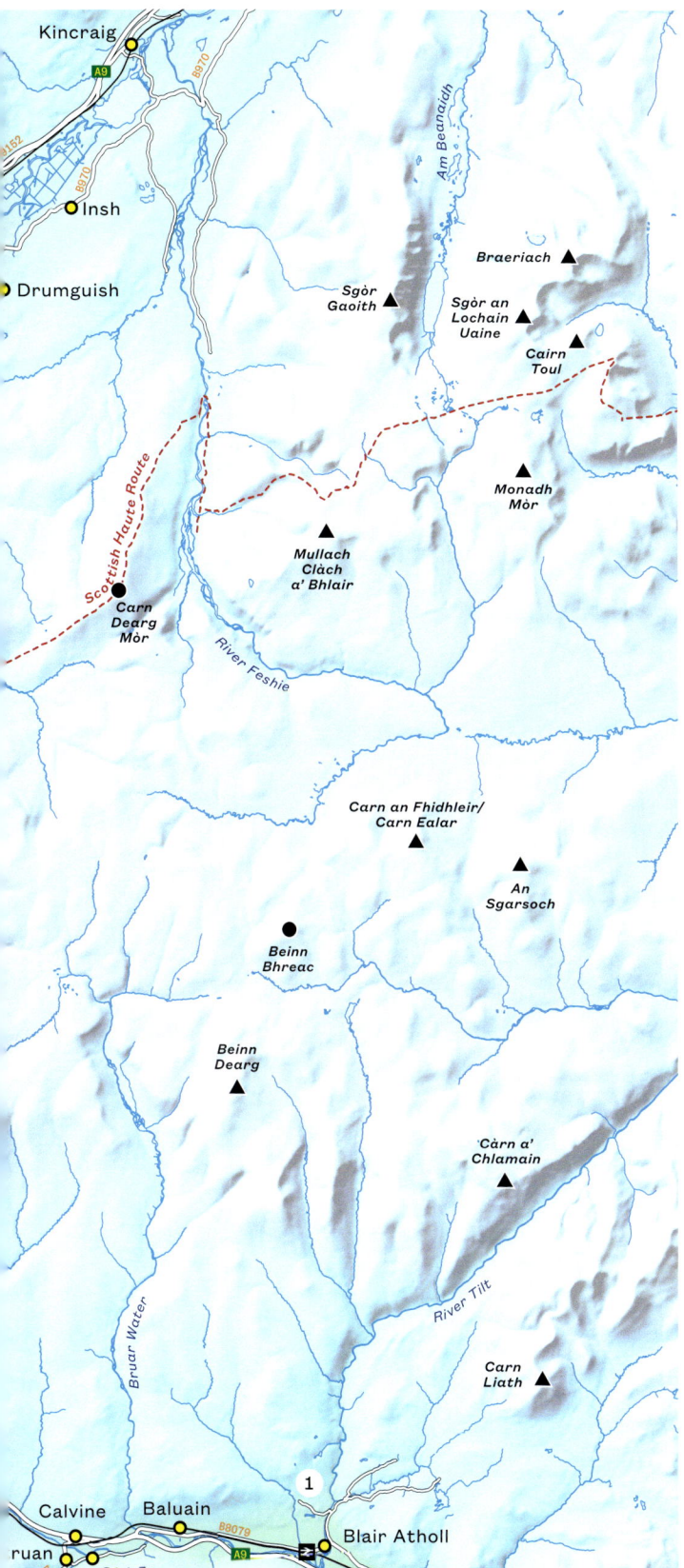

1.	Beinn Dearg	P.148
2.	Meall na Leitreach	P.148
3.	A' Chaoirnich and An Dùn	P.149
4.	West Drumochter	P.151
5.	East Drumochter	P.153
6.	The Fara	P.155
7.	Meall Chuaich	P.158
8.	Monadh Liath	P.159
9.	Geal Chàrn	P.160

Previous spread:
Boar of Badenoch
© Bruce Goodlad

Beinn Dearg ▲ 1,008m
Red Hill

NN 852 777   LR43   P.140

P The large pay and display car park at Old Bridge of Tilt (NN 874 663/56.7745, -3.8436), 1km north of Blair Atholl.

↔ 25KM   △ 1,030M   ↕ 150M
⏱ 6-8 HRS   GRADE II   ★★★

By Raymond Simpson, updated by Colwyn Jones

This remote and isolated mountain lies 13km north of Blair Atholl and is the south-western outpost of the great tract of high, undulating plateau stretching north and east towards Glen Feshie and the Cairngorms. Its ascent on skis is best suited to midwinter days when snow lies low in the glens, making the long approach easy and more spectacular. This is a good tour for Nordic skis, and using a mountain bike to the snow-line might help with the initial approach.

From the car park turn left towards Old Blair. At the crossroads turn right and follow the private road north-east past Blairuachdar Farm and Wood, taking a left fork just before it emerges from the trees, from where there is a fine view up Glen Tilt. A track then climbs into the glen of the Allt Slanaidh through another forest and leads to a small wooden bothy. Beinn a' Chait lies 3km north and it is easier to ascend to about the 850m contour than to traverse the west flank, as the height gained can be used to schuss to the col (NN 854 760) below the summit cone of Beinn Dearg. The top rises 200m above a vast, undulating plateau intersected by meandering snow-choked burns. When you arrive at the triangulation station, the skyline of the Cairngorms seems very distant across this high empty landscape.

From the summit it is worth skiing south-west for 1.5km for the view down Glen Bruar, but unless you decide to return via the bothy in the Allt Sheicheachan to Old Blair (longer and less scenic), do not lose too much height before turning south-east back towards Beinn a' Chait. The Allt Sheicheachan cuts deeply into the west flank of this hill and holds a variety of attractive steep gullies. The slopes are, however, both convex and prone to windslab formation, so unless you are very sure of the snow conditions, give them a wide berth by traversing high up above 800m.

From the south-west shoulder of Beinn a' Chait there is a fine run of 300m down into the Allt Slanaidh, and the return through the woods with views across Glen Tilt to Beinn a' Ghlo is a delightful end to the day.

Meall na Leitreach ● 775m
Hill of Slopes

NN 639 703   LR42   P.149

P Parking just off the A9 signposted to Dalnaspidal adjacent to the level crossing (NN 645 732/ 56.8307, -4.2214).

↔ 6KM   △ 390M   ↕ 400M
⏱ 3-4 HRS   GRADE II   ★★

By Colwyn Jones

The northern slopes of Meall na Leitreach drop steeply to Loch Garry with an eye-catching ridge leading north-east (Sròn na h-Eiteich), which is well observed when travelling on the A9 through the busy Drumochter Pass.

It is convenient to park at Dalnaspidal where there is a level crossing over the railway line. There are several lay-bys adjacent to the level crossing. Parking at the roadside on the A9 avoids a short, steep drive down to the railway line but may be busier.

Beyond the level crossing take the right-hand track (not the track straight ahead into Dalnaspidal Lodge) toward a bridge crossing the Allt Dubhaig burn. Turn off this track just before the bridge and follow the levee alongside the fairly canalised river, heading south-east towards another bridge over the River Garry itself. From this point an incipient path ascends southwards from approximately 50m east of the bridge. From there the ascent is straightforward, continuing due south up the north flank of the hill for 2km, avoiding the steeper north-west slopes. Some sheep fences require careful negotiation. The banks of a stream named Allt nam Plaidean (on the 1:25,000 map) attract a covering of snow in leaner conditions and can be followed. The slope is consistently steep until you reach the undulating plateau at the 700m contour, and the summit is a further 1km south-west (3km; 370m; 2hrs).

The descent simply retraces the ascent route, choosing the best snow cover observed during the ascent.

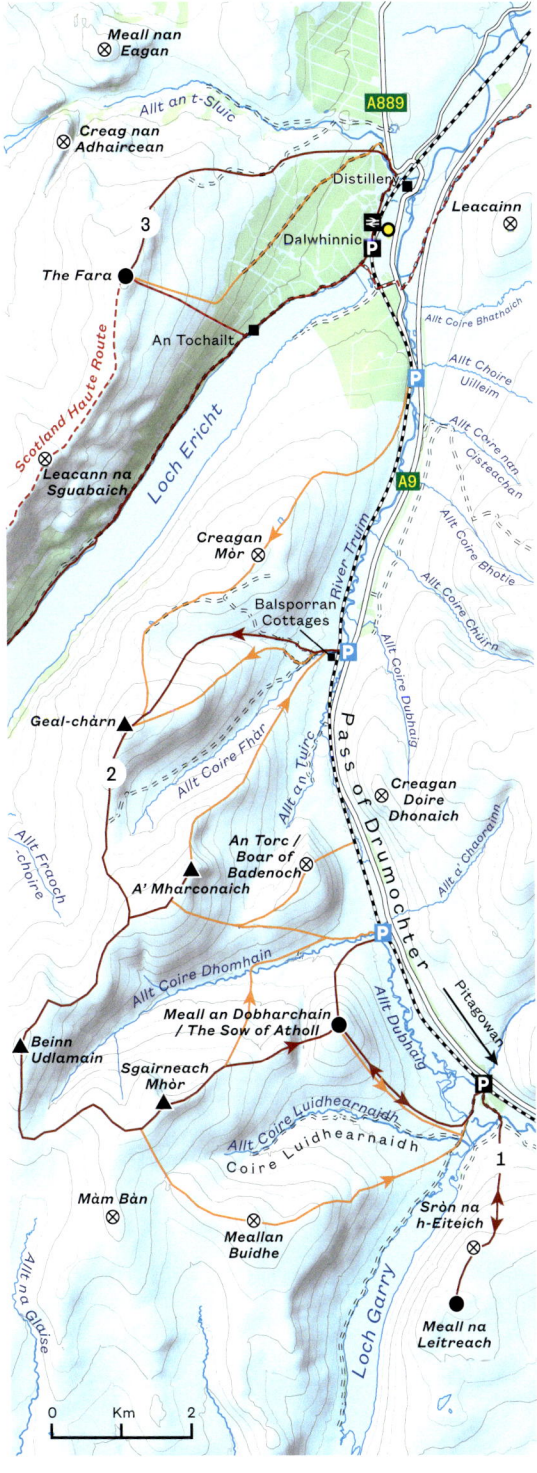

A' Chaoirnich and An Dùn

A' Chaoirnich ● 875m
△ NN 735 807   ◁ LR42   ⊕ P.150

An Dùn ● 827m
The Fort
△ NN 717 805   ◁ LR42   ⊕ P.150

🅿 The A9 east side lay-by (NN 638 821/56.9105, -4.2358).		
↔ 20KM	△ 760M	⫯ 130M
⏱ 7-8 HRS	GRADE II	**

By Bob Reid

These two hills are included partly for completeness but mainly because they are renowned for their snow-holding qualities. They are right at the heart of the Western Cairngorms – which Hamish Brown describes in *The Corbetts* as the 'eroded tableland so characteristic of the Grampians'. Seen from surrounding hills they often present a white, gleaming plateau. They are also very remote: 9km from Atholl and 23km from Tromie Bridge. The Gaick Pass running between the two hills links Atholl to Badenoch. Access can be easier with a mountain bike.

However, the most elegant approach, certainly to An Dùn, is to approach from the A9 on the Drumochter side. Càrn na Caim (941m) and A' Bhuidheanach Bheag (936m) are popular ski Munros known for holding snow. Ascending either of these Munros enables an out-and-back tour, to include An Dùn. From the Càrn na Caim summit, head south-east across the undulating plateau for 3km, crossing Meallan Buidhe (856m), then head for Vinegar Hill (NN 700 804). Now descend east-north-east for 0.5km to the col (NN 710 803) with only a steep final 0.5km to the summit of An Dùn (827m), whose cairn lies at the north end of a 0.5km summit ridge. Return is by the same route (10km; 760m; 4hrs).

A similar, slightly longer out-and-back approach is possible from A' Bhuidheanach Bheag. On a good spring snow day it is also possible to include An Dùn as part of a longer tour in addition to both Munros.

Maol Creag an Loch is an altogether more difficult challenge due to its limited access options. The 8km cycle from the A9 at Dalnacardoch is the most logical but makes for a very long day. Leaving the track 1km before Sronphadruig Lodge just before a small plantation, head north-east up the subsidiary hill of Meall na Spianaig (621m), then follow the narrowing ridge north-east up

Key
1. Meall an Leitrich — P.148
2. West Drumochter — P.151
3. The Fara — P.155

An Sligearnach to reach the plateau. The summit is fully 2km further at first north, then north-east. The spectacular cliffs of Creag an Loch accompany you along the western slopes of the ridge, dropping precipitously to Loch an Dùin – be warned when making wide turns on your descent. This route offers splendid views west across the Gaick Pass to An Dùn (8km cycle and 4km walk; 550m; 4hrs).

Key		
1a.	Càrn na Caim and An Dùn	P.149
1b.	Maol Creag an Loch and A' Chaoirnich	P.149
2.	East Drumochter	P.153

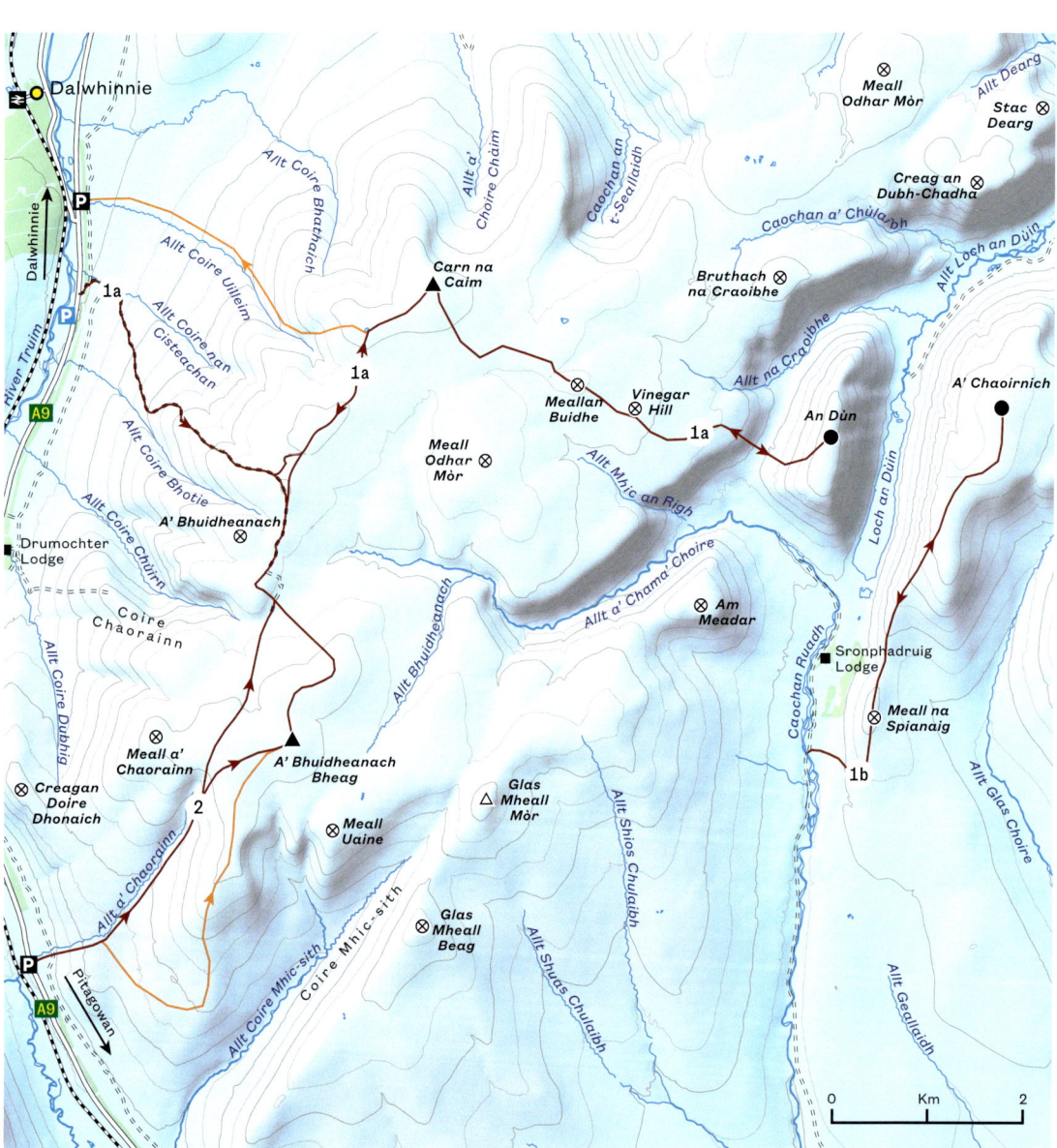

West Drumochter

A' Mharconaich ▲ 975m
The Horse Place
⛺ NN 604 762 📍 LR42 🌐 P.149

Geal-chàrn ▲ 917m
White Hill
⛺ NN 596 782 📍 LR42 🌐 P.149

Beinn Udlamain ▲ 1,011m
Hill of Dark Moss
⛺ NN 579 739 📍 LR42 🌐 P.149

Sgairneach Mhòr ▲ 991m
Big Scree
⛺ NN 598 731 📍 LR42 🌐 P.149

🅿 The car park on the A9 road just south of the Pass of Drumochter summit (NN 630 760).

↔ 18KM   △ 1,350M   ⊤ 450M
⏱ 7-9 HRS   GRADE III   ★★★

By Neil Mather, updated by Colwyn Jones and Bob Reid

This group of hills is obvious from the A9 as you travel south from Dalwhinnie through the Pass of Drumochter. The rounded mass of Geal-chàrn, the most northerly of the group, has some large cairns usually visible on the skyline just below the summit. It is connected to its southern neighbour, A' Mharconaich, which is seen from the north as a graceful, rounded hill whose high eastern corrie is often edged in spring by a rim of snow. The northern slopes of Sgairneach Mhòr form Coire Creagach, a steep and corniced bowl above Coire Dhomhain, at the head of which sits Beinn Udlamain, seen from the road just south of the Pass of Drumochter as a long, level skyline.

The hills tend to be stony on their summits, and the exposed ridges and slopes can often be denuded of snow because of their windswept aspect. Nevertheless, the traverse of the West Drumochter Hills is a fine outing which is possible in most winters, the best conditions previously being found between March and mid-April. For the best downhill skiing, this traverse should be done anti-clockwise round Coire Dhomhain, but the traverse in the opposite direction is almost as good. Wind direction can play a part in assisting continuous snow cover.

The starting point near the Pass of Drumochter is 450m above sea level. Only the ski centres at Glenshee, Cairngorm, The Lecht and Ben Lawers have higher ski roads, a factor contributing to the popularity of these tours. It also means there should be minimal walk-ins and carrying of skis. Traffic cameras covering the Drumochter Snow Gates are available on the internet and can offer good pointers on conditions (see: www.trafficscotland.org).

There is a large lay-by (number 79) on the northbound carriageway of the A9 near the highest point of the Pass of Drumochter. Future road-building plans may mean the A9 becomes a more formalised dual carriageway with pedestrian restrictions; provision for walker car parks and lay-bys will likely be made. At the time of writing, precise details are unknown but please take care at the roadside.

From the existing lay-by head south on the cycle track or the old A9 and cross under the railway through a tunnel (NN 633 750) to reach the landrover track leading up the north side of the corrie. Follow this for 2km, then strike uphill north by good snow slopes heading into the vague col between A' Mharconaich and, to the east, the Boar of Badenoch, until you reach a fence, though this may often be buried under snow. Continue steeply along this fence line heading north-west to the summit plateau of A' Mharconaich. Gain the summit by heading 0.5km north-east along the level and often very stony plateau (4km; 520m ascent; 2hrs).

Geal-chàrn is the outlier of the group by this route and stands 2km further north of A' Mharconaich, to which it is connected by the Coire Fhàr bealach (NN 591 763; 740m). To reach this bealach ski down and west across the north-west flank of A' Mharconaich toward the line of the most westerly tributary stream of the Allt Coire Fhàr, which usually holds snow well. By maintaining a high line of traverse, you may avoid some extra reascent to the bealach. Put skins on at the bealach and ascend the ridge north for nearly 2km toward Geal-chàrn. It becomes stonier as you approach the summit, and the best snow may well be on the east side of the broad crest (7.5km; 280m further ascent; 3.5hrs).

Beinn Udlamain is the next summit. Retrace your earlier tracks across the Coire Fhàr bealach but continue steeply south for 1km to reach the plateau of A' Mharconaich once again. Then ski down the spectacular south-west ridge of A' Mharconaich for 0.5km, on the boundary between Perthshire and Highland, following the fence line to the col at 860m (NN 591 752). From this part of the tour there are spectacular views of the hills of the Ben Alder and Ardverikie deer forests (though there is hardly a tree to be seen) across the deep trench of Loch Ericht. If the ridge is windswept, the best snow may be found on the south-east flank above Coire

Dhomhain, but the fence line heading south-west must be regained to reach the summit of Beinn Udlamain itself at 1,011m (11.5km; 350m further ascent; 5hrs).

The descent of the south ridge of Beinn Udlamain provides an excellent run south to the col marked as Càrn 'Ic Loumhaidh at 810m (NN 580 723). In misty conditions the col can appear vague. It is important to navigate around the head of the Allt Coire Dhomhain, veering from south round to an east-north-east direction and the gentler slopes heading up Sgairneach Mhòr. There is rarely a problem of snow cover here and a direct line east-north-east for 2km to the triangulation station on the summit of Sgairneach Mhòr (991m) can be taken from the col. Occasionally the trig point lies hidden below the surface of deep snow (14.5km; 180m further ascent; 6.5hrs).

The descent from Sgairneach Mhòr to the Allt Coire Dhomhain is the highlight of the tour. Head north-east, at first down the narrow north-east ridge, taking care to avoid the cornices of Coire Creagach on your left in bad visibility, and onward to the first dip in the ridge at 740m.

To avoid The Sow of Atholl (see below), veer left, heading due north, keeping to the west of the tributary burn down to the Allt Coire Dhomhain. With good snow cover, this is a long descent dropping almost 500m over a distance of 3km, and it can provide exhilarating skiing. It is best to cross the stream and return along the track on its north side. If the stream is deep with snow melt and not snow-bridged lower down, it is prudent to aim for a higher crossing point when skiing off Sgairneach Mhòr (18km; 1,330m ascent; 8hrs).

If your party has two cars, an alternative traverse of this group starts at Balsporran Cottages, 4km north of the Pass of Drumochter summit. Lay-bys are available for parking. Cross the railway and follow the path west for 0.3km to the Allt Beul an Sporain. Here you can choose between a direct but exposed route or a more circuitous and less exposed alternative. In good conditions, cross the burn then climb directly south-west up the north-east ridge of Geal-chàrn, passing close to the prominent cairns near the summit (3.5km; 500m ascent; 2hrs). From the summit continue south to A' Mharconaich and complete the tour as described above. However, if it is likely to be windy

on the north-east ridge, some shelter might be found by following the track on the north side of the burn into Coire Beul an Sporain. When the track turns north-west away from the burn, stay high and follow the burn itself west until the slope angle eases. From there a calmer approach can often be made south-west to the summit.

By far the most elegant way to claim the Corbett of The Sow of Atholl (Meall an Dobharchain; 803m) is to complete it as part of this circuit of Coire Dhomain. The Boar of Badenoch can also be included at the beginning of this justly popular and excellent tour – best done in this anti-clockwise direction – since it allows for The Sow of Atholl as a suitably exhilarating finish. First there is the small matter of taking in the Munros – A' Mharconaich, then Beinn Udlamain and then Sgairneach Mhòr. Descend at that point to complete the normal circuit down the north-east spur of Sgairneach Mhòr.

However, The Sow of Atholl gives an alternative splendid descent. Continue onward with the eastwards traverse after Sgairneach Mhòr, passing the marked point 758m (NN 616 737), then cross the steep gash beyond. It is well worth the extra effort. The southern end of the gash affords the most convenient crossing, followed by the short, steep south-east flank of The Sow of Atholl itself, with little more than 0.5km skinning north-east to the summit. Your reward is not just the spectacular views north and south through the Pass of Drumochter but also a hidden gem of a descent. The north flank of The Sow now offers a splendidly steep, black-run descent back to the Allt Coire Dhomain, which is not to be missed and makes for a fitting climax to one of Scotland's most popular ski tours. However, it can be icy and often has a cornice. Variations are available.

The Boar of Badenoch has an even steeper and more adventurous downhill, which is well worth seeking out in suitable snow conditions. A prominent central gully on the east face can catch plenty of snow (as well as the attention of many bored train and car passengers travelling by) and has become a popular descent. Snow conditions can occasionally be very good, but if you are entering this gully from above, great care is needed to assess the stability of the cornice. Repeat as often as the lactic acid build-up allows.

Opposite: A' Mharconaich
(skier, Lisa Fullerton)
© Al Todd

East Drumochter

A' Bhuidheanach Bheag ▲ 936m
Little Yellow Place
△ NN 660 776　　⌖ LR42　　🌐 P.150

Càrn na Caim ▲ 941m
Curved Hill
△ NN 677 821　　⌖ LR42　　🌐 P.150

🅿 Near the summit of the Pass of Drumochter on the southbound A9 (NN 631 760/56.8557, -4.2465).

↔ 13KM　　△ 700M　　↕ 460M
🕐 4-5 HRS　　GRADE II　　★★

By Raymond Simpson, updated by David Buchanan

The A9 gives easy access to these hills from multiple car parks and laybys. Traverses can be made either by using two cars, or a car and a bike (taking advantage of the Sustrans National Cycle Network route number 7 on the west side of the road, east of the railway line). Several bus services can get you to Dalwhinnie, where there is also a train station. Check with operators for timetables and precise locations of the stops. The nearest taxi services are in Kingussie. These hills are particularly attractive for those touring on Nordic equipment, while those on Alpine or Telemark gear can seek out the steeper descents visible from the road.

The area covered by this tour is essentially a high grassy plateau that can be skied under a thin cover of snow. Indeed, it can often be skied when little snow is visible from the roadside, which makes it a good early- and late-season option for those prepared to do some walking.

After parking at one of the many laybys south of Drumochter, ascend the steep slope on the east side of the A9, to the left of some small waterfalls. If you are driving from the south, there is a layby (NN 632 755) opposite the waterfalls and a convenient gate in the fence that runs below the hillside. Pass under the Beauly to Denny power line, and after about 180m follow more gentle slopes and a shallow stream bed, the Allt a' Chaorainn, also known as Jean's Gully (which holds snow for long periods). At the top of this gully, old fence posts lead east for 1km to the triangulation station of A' Bhuidheanach Bheag. More fence posts can help you navigate towards Càrn na Caim. From the summit ski north for 1.5km, initially across the flat plateau and then down to reach a wide col at 830m.

Continue north, ascending gradually for a further 1.5km to reach the 902m knoll. At this point turn north-east, cross another knoll and continue in the same direction across the undulating plateau, gradually descending 30m before the final ascent of 50m to the flat summit of Càrn na Caim. (If you are using the fence posts to navigate, note that they turn south-east just short of the summit.)

To return to the starting point, reverse the outward route until you reach the bealach between A' Bhuidheanach and A' Bhuidheanach Beag. Ascend south-west following a tributary of the Allt Coire Chùirn until you can ski into the top of Allt a' Chaorainn. This gives easy skiing until around the 650m contour. From here, depending on conditions and your skill level, descend to the starting point using appropriate techniques and avoiding the waterfalls.

Alternatively, return west-south-west from Càrn na Caim for 1km to the top of the west-facing slopes on the north-east side of Coire Uilleim. Descend these slopes, which often have a good snow cover, and continue north-west across the moorland to the A9 at the junction with the road to Dalwhinnie. Other options for these hills include the following:

- If there is sufficient snow cover, an alternative start can be made from near the turn-off to Dalnaspidal Lodge just north of the end of the dual carriageway (NN 646 733, limited parking). A gate through the deer fence leads onto the broad shoulder of Fuar Mhonadh, which provides easy skinning to A' Bhuidheanach Beag. If returning via Allt a' Chaorainn, leave the gully before it steepens and take a descending traverse line to the start.
- Parking at Balsporran Cottages (NN 627 793) provides access to steeper slopes that offer options for superb descents. These slopes level off above 900m. The 2km ski across the plateau to the summit of A' Bhuidheanach Beag is a delight for those on Nordic equipment but possibly less fun for Alpine skiers.

Below: Beinn Udlamain heading to A' Mharconaich (skier, Lisa Fullerton)
© Al Todd

The Fara
Ladder Hill

● 911m

△ NN 598 843   ⌖ LR42   🌐 P.149

P A layby north of Dalwhinnie on the A889 (NN 636 858) at a forestry track on the left, just as the road starts to climb.

↔ 10KM   △ 600M   ↕ 360M
⏱ 3–4 HRS   GRADE II   ★★

By Colwyn Jones and Al Todd

This splendid wee hill can be easily ascended from near the village of Dalwhinnie when there is good snow cover. The Fara presents an impressively snowy face looking toward the A9. Often overlooked because of the adjacent Drumochter ski options, it is nevertheless a fine ski hill, whether you are going for the full traverse or simply making repeat descents of its fine east face above the forest. Being close to the SMC's Raeburn Hut, it makes for an excellent short day if the weather is inclement. There are trains from Inverness or Perth. Access by bus involves a 2km walk from a bus stop on the A9 (buses from Inverness and Perth stop there).

The A889 is occasionally closed by snow but is ploughed regularly and roadside parking allows you to follow the landrover track towards the forestry plantation, using a bridge to cross the Allt an t-Sluic. Do not follow the track into the plantation but stay outside the deer fence heading west towards the broad north-east ridge of the hill. A second track, a couple of hundred metres further north on the A889 opposite a quarry, follows the Allt an t-Sluic toward the Allt an t-Sluic Lodge for nearly 2km before fording the burn and heading south-west up the north-east ridge. From here the ridge gains height, giving an ascent of little more than 3km to the large summit cairn, which is visible from the A9.

The simplest descent is by your ascent route favouring the best snow, but the east face of the peak is steep in places and may be corniced, and there have been avalanches in this area with debris often seen after fresh snowfall.

For those arriving by train, the western platform at the railway station does not have a trackside exit. The station exit requires that you cross the footbridge to the east side of the track. There was a level crossing 500m south of Dalwhinnie Station which has been closed, so you will need to walk (or ski) east to the A889 in the village, turn right (south) for 1km to the petrol station, then turn right (west), past the line of Ben Alder cottages to a railway underpass where you can safely cross under the railtrack to reach the north-east shore of Loch Ericht. There is parking just before the underpass where an electronic barrier prevents unauthorised vehicle access. The filling station in the village also provides parking for £3/day (in 2023).

Continue along the horizontal landrover track following the north shore of Loch Ericht, and after about 1km you will reach The Ben Alder Estate gatehouse, The Shieling. Use the pedestrian gate or the adjacent mountain bike access track to continue for another 1km to the next buildings, called An Tochailt Lodge.

Here, abandon the track (NN 615 835), go up through a gate on the right and take the wide, sheltered firebreak steeply up through the forestry plantation onto the open hillside (590m). Harvesting of Sitka spruce has started in some areas. The remains of a fence and wall run perpendicular from the deer fence to the summit, but may be hidden by snow. The summit is obscured by the convex slope above and must be assessed for avalanche risk.

To traverse the hill from the summit, descend by the north-east ridge towards Allt an t-Sluic Lodge. Before reaching the 650m contour, traverse east, crossing the Allt a' Ghiubhais, then take the best snow around the forestry, outside the trees, negotiating fences to shortly arrive back at the A889.

If it is very windy, and it is safe to do so, ski back towards the ascent firebreak, but aim for a gate in the forestry fence 200–250m north-east (left in descent) of the firebreak (NN 610 839). The gate runs through to a landrover track which cuts straight down to the boundary of the plantation. Some poling will be needed at the bottom. Then follow the track onto the A889 and walk south for 2.5km back to Dalwhinnie.

Overleaf: Descent east off The Fara (skier, Lisa Fullerton) © Al Todd

Meall Chuaich ▲ 951m

Hill of the Quaich (cup of friendship)

⛰ NN 716 878   🧭 LR42   🌐 P.158

🅿 A layby on the east side of the A9 at Cuaich (NN 654 867/ 56.8557, -4.2467), north of the Pass of Drumochter. There is also public transport to Dalwhinnie.

↔ 14KM   △ 600M   ↕ 350M
🕐 4-5 HRS   GRADE II   **

By Donald Bennet, updated by Colwyn Jones

Meall Chuaich is rather a solitary hill on the east side of the A9, 9km north-east of Dalwhinnie. In *The High Mountains*, Irvine Butterfield described it as 'A boring hill with an equally drab outlook.' However, it has a searing white solidity in winter providing, after a flat approach, a fine half day's ski touring, particularly early in the season during the shorter daylight hours. It also features as part of Day 5 of the Scottish Haute Route (see p.289).

The route starts from the A9, almost opposite Cuaich cottages. A gated private track leads to a higher track alongside an aqueduct serving the little hydroelectric power station after 3.5km, and beyond it to Loch Cuaich. A thin covering of snow is enough to make this part of the route skiable. Just before reaching Loch Cuaich, turn south-east past a little bothy (often locked in winter), following the track over a broken bridge across the Allt Coire Chuaich.

At a cairn the summer footpath leaves the track up the broad, smooth west-south-west ridge of Meall Chuaich, which gives easy skiing if it is snow-covered. Unfortunately, this side of the hill is most likely to lose its snow under mild south-westerly winds; admittedly, Meall Chuaich does not have the reputation of being a good snow-holding hill. The ridge bears round east, steepens briefly and reaches the wide, flat dome of the summit, which is crowned with a sizeable cairn.

The descent is best made by the route of ascent unless the snow cover is poor, in which case a steeper run south-south-east down a very shallow corrie may give better skiing. On arriving at the track at about the 540m contour, go west, using the track for less than 2km to meet your ascent tracks, then ski back towards your starting point on the A9.

Opposite: A' Chailleach summit (skier, Angus Todd)
© Al Todd

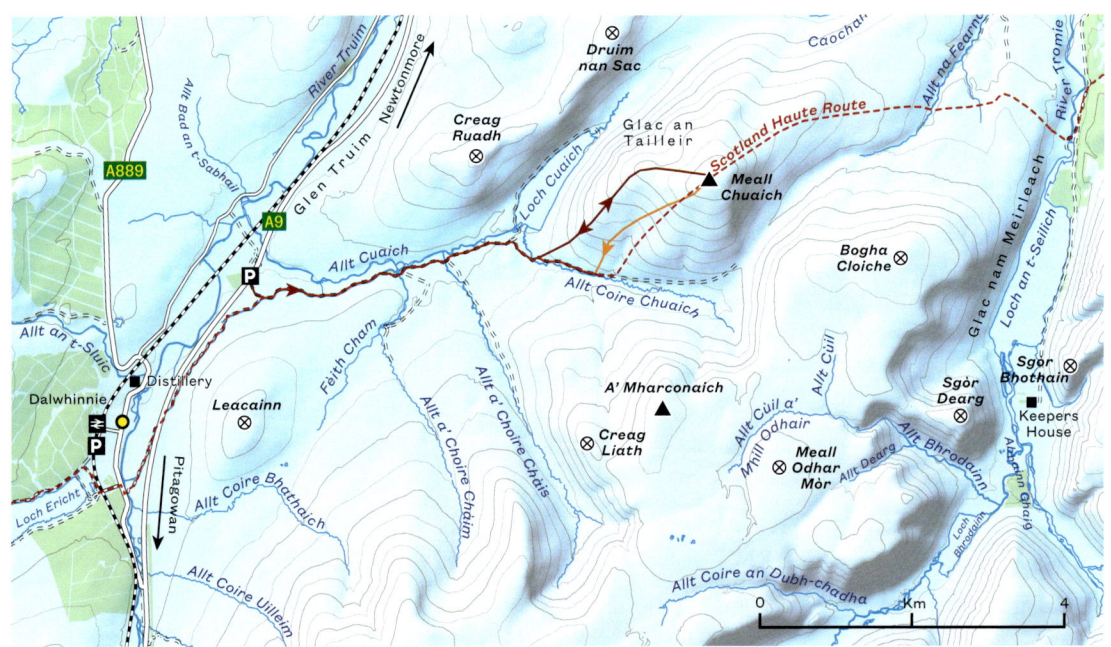

Monadh Liath

A' Chailleach ▲ 930m
The Old Woman
△ NH 681 041 ◁ LR35 ⊕ P.160

Càrn Sgùlain ▲ 920m
Hill of the Basket
△ NH 683 058 ◁ LR35 ⊕ P.160

Càrn Dearg ▲ 945m
Red Hill
△ NH 635 023 ◁ LR35 ⊕ P.160

P The end of the public road from Newtonmore up Glen Banchor near the foot of the Allt a' Chaorainn (NN 692 998 / 57.0703, -4.1577).

↔ 23KM   △ 980M   ↕ 300M
⏱ 7-8 HRS   GRADE II
★★★

By Gordon MacKenzie, updated by Colwyn Jones

The wide undulating plateau of the Monadh Liath north-west of Newtonmore gives an interesting but not too demanding ski tour taking in three Munros with very little loss of height between their summits. Lines of fence posts aid navigation for a long section of the tour across the plateau. Nordic skis are a distinct advantage on this traverse as the nature of the terrain makes attaching and then detaching skins from Alpine skis rather tiresome, and all the climbs and descents, except for the first part of the run down from Càrn Dearg, are quite gradual.

From the end of the public road in Glen Banchor, follow the track north up the east bank of the Allt a' Chaorainn. After 2km cross the burn and ascend north-west past the vintage estate 'Red Bothy' to the ridge between Geal Chàrn and A' Chailleach. From the col climb north-east to gain the first Munro, A' Chailleach, which has a big corrie just east of the large summit cairn.

To minimise the loss of height on the next part of the traverse, ski west for 500m to the head of the Allt Cùil na Caillich before ascending north-north-east to meet the line of fence posts, which is followed east to reach the summit of Càrn Sgùlain. (A warning about skiing more directly from A' Chailleach to Càrn Sgùlain: the Allt Cùil na Caillich, which must be crossed, flows in quite a steep-sided gully, whose northern bank is often corniced.)

Route-finding from Càrn Sgùlain to Càrn Bàn is eased by following a line of fence posts for 6km across the plateau. Four minor summits are encountered on the way, but the height never falls below 850m. The distinctive pointed summit of Càrn Dearg lies 1km south-south-east of Càrn Bàn and is easily reached from the col between them, keeping a safe distance away from the edge of the east corrie.

The descent involves returning a few hundred metres north-north-west to the col between Càrn Dearg and Càrn Bàn and then skiing north-east above a line of rock outcrops down relatively steep slopes to the head of Gleann Ballach.

Continue down the glen on the north-east side of the Allt Ballach for 1.5km and then bear east across the flat ground between Meall na Ceardaich and Creag Liath. Cross the Allt Fionndrigh (steeply banked in places) by a footbridge (NH 659 019) to reach the track on its north-east side. Ski down this track to reach Glen Banchor at a point just east of Glen Banchor Farm and follow the main track in the glen back to the starting point.

Two other shorter ski tours, both suitable for Nordic skis, can be made on the slightly lower hills north-east of Càrn Sgùlain. From Kingussie drive up the road on the east side of the Allt Mòr to the golf course and continue on foot or on skis up the private road past Pitmain Lodge. Eventually the track crosses the Allt Mòr and climbs across the south flank of Càrn an Fhreiceadain (878m), which can be ascended from the track up its broad south ridge.

Several kilometres further north-east, Gealcharn Mòr (NH 836 123; 824m) and Geal-charn Beag (NH 848 144; 741m) can be approached by the hill track which leaves the A9 road at Lynwilg, 2km south-west of Aviemore. This track climbs to the pass between the two hills, and both can be climbed easily from its highest point.

Geal Chàrn ▲ 926m
White Hill

△ NN 561 987   ◉ LR35   🌐 P.161

🅿 The Spey Dam (NN 583 934/57.0104, -4.3350), 3.5km west of Laggan Bridge on the A86 road.

↔ 15KM   △ 650M   ⬍ 280M
⏱ 5 HRS   GRADE II   ✱✱

By Donald Bennet, updated by Colwyn Jones

The English translation of Geal Chàrn, White Hill, suggests this peak will provide a good ski tour. It is the western outlier of the Monadh Liath hills, separated from them by Glen Markie. Typical of the Monadh Liath, it has a flat, featureless summit plateau, but it also has a fine east-facing corrie holding Lochan a' Choire. The rim of this corrie is often impressively corniced in spring, and midway between Geal Chàrn and its south-east top, Beinn Sgiath, the headwall can be split by a big ice-carved gully, the Uinneag Coire an Lochain (1:25,000 map), which, in safe conditions, might give a challenging ski run. This possibility apart, Geal Chàrn is a tour with easy skiing.

From the Spey Dam, park on the south side of the road bridge. Start by going back over the Spey, then north on the track through Crathie Farm. The first 4km of the approach goes up the track on the east side of the Markie Burn. If the snow-line is not low enough, this is a tedious walk carrying skis, so it is worth waiting for suitable conditions. Cross the Markie Burn (no bridge) near the tributary of the Piper's Burn and climb north-west into the lower part of Coire an Lochain. If crossing the Markie Burn is a problem, there is a footbridge 1km further upstream (NN 588 982). Continue north-west, leaving the lochan far to your left, and climb onto Bruach nam Biodag, the broad ridge on the north-east side of the corrie. Once on this ridge move easily west then south-west round the corrie rim up to the level plateau, then bear rightwards to reach the huge summit cairn. In bad visibility a line of fence posts is helpful for finding the cairn. Once on the level plateau near the north end of the corrie's steep headwall, these posts are some distance away to the right (west). Bear south-west to converge with them, then follow them south to the point where the line of posts suddenly turns east. From there the summit cairn of Geal Chàrn is about 100m west.

The return is best made by the same route, and there is plenty of easy skiing back across the plateau, down the corrie and finally, if snow conditions permit, along the track in Glen Markie. Those seeking a more sporting and spectacular

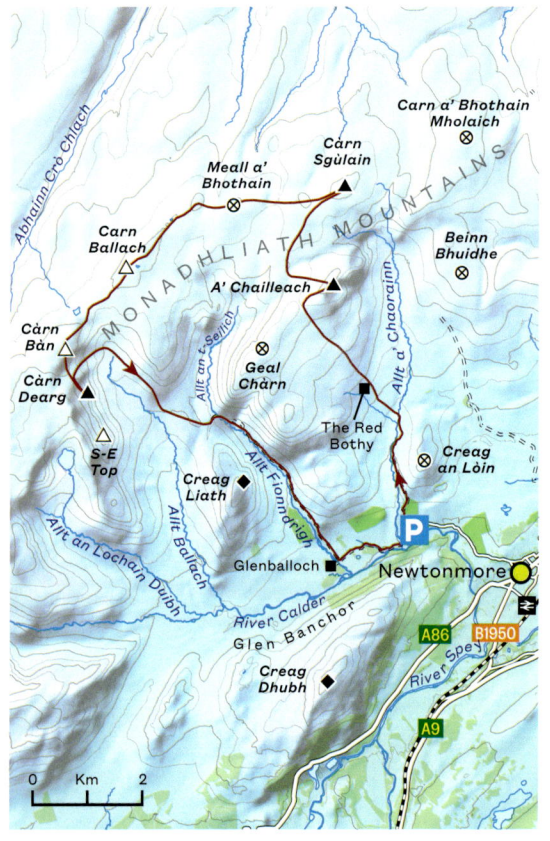

descent might care to try the Uinneag Coire an Lochain, whose top is reached by skiing south-east from Geal Chàrn for 500m. Be warned, however, for the gully is overlooked by steep avalanche-prone slopes and cornices, and it runs straight down to Lochan a' Choire. From the lochan follow the south bank of Piper's Burn, but re-cross the Markie Burn carefully, using all the information you gained on the approach.

An alternative western route starts at Garva Bridge (290m) and is a good option if it is frozen underfoot.

P	Starting point: Parking just before the bridge over the River Spey (NN 522 947/57.0199, -4.4358).
↔ 16KM	△ 650M	↕ 280M
⏲ 5-6 HRS	GRADE II	**

Cross the road bridge and immediately turn right, then follow a track for 450m to the improved track used for installing the Beauly–Denny 400kV overhead electricity transmission line. Go across the metal bridge (under the power line) to the east bank of the Fèith Talagain and continue up a footpath to the 430m contour. The broad south-east ridge of Geal Chàrn then leads directly to the summit.

A return following your ascent can be used, but this white hill has a longer south-east ridge running from the subsidiary top, Beinn Sgiath (887m). Ski south for 500m to the top of the Uinneag Coire an Lochain, then east towards the subsidiary summit. There is no need to skin to the top, and contouring at 850m brings you to the south flank. Descend for 100 vertical metres, then turn east-south-east to follow the ridge to Meall an Domhnaich (608m). A steep descent through the trees is possible, following the power line to return to the metal bridge and shortly thereafter to the car park.

Overleaf: View into the upper reaches of the Spey from Geal Chàrn (skier, Angus Todd) © Al Todd

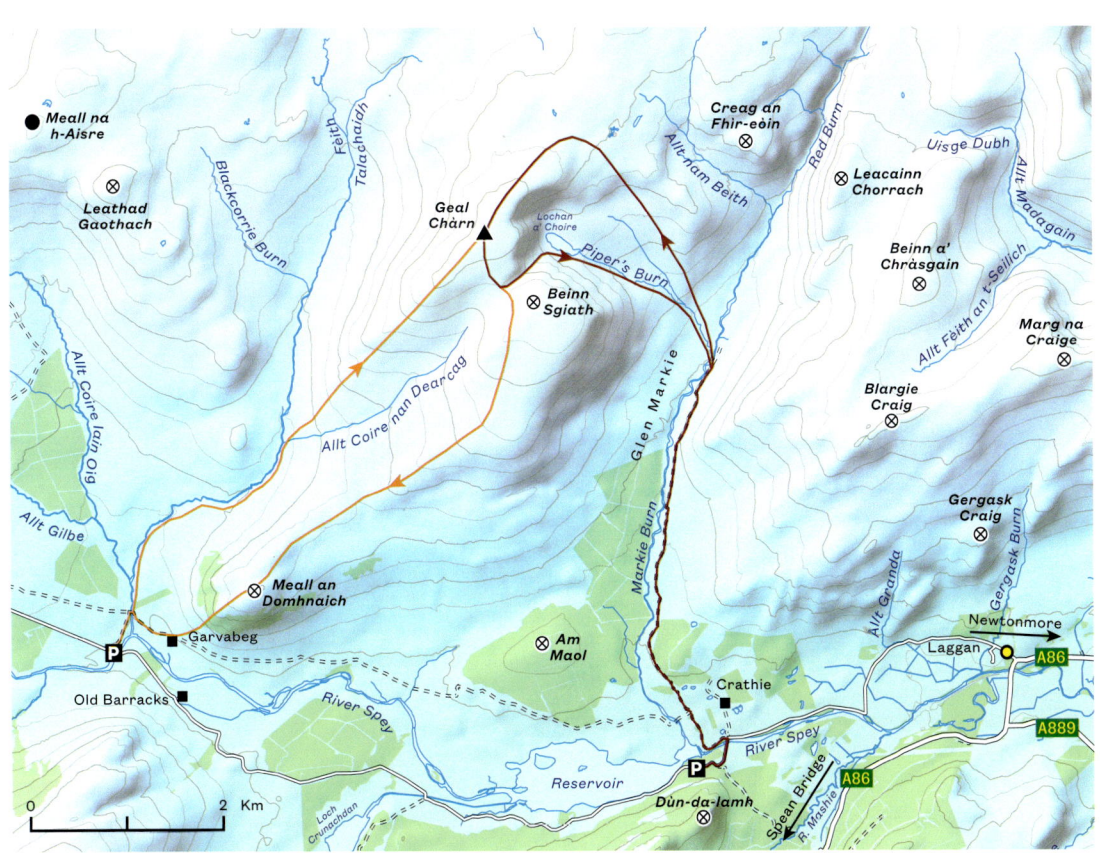

Chapter 5

East Scotland

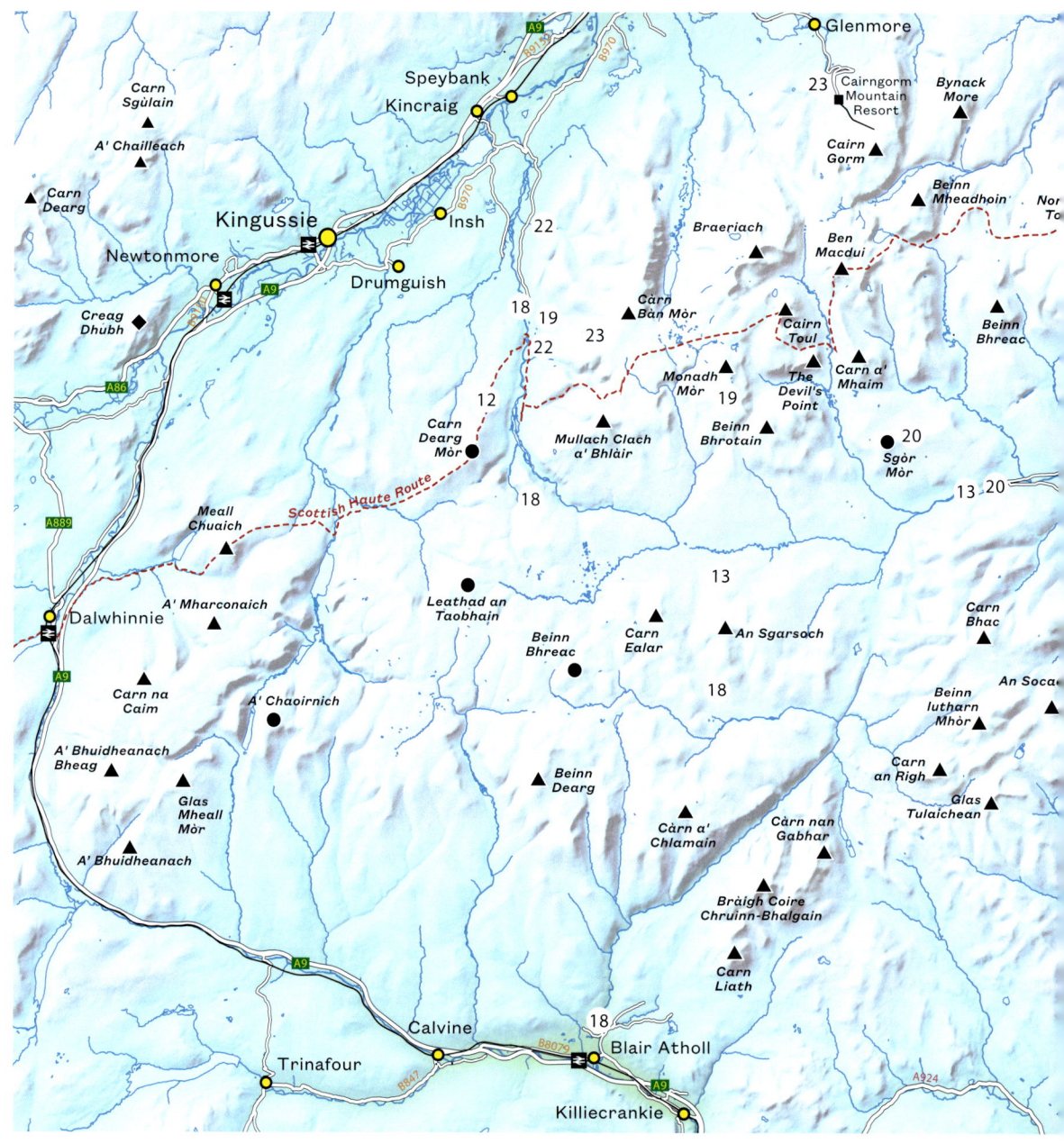

Previous spread: Glas Maol
(skier, Graeme Gatherer)
© Al Todd

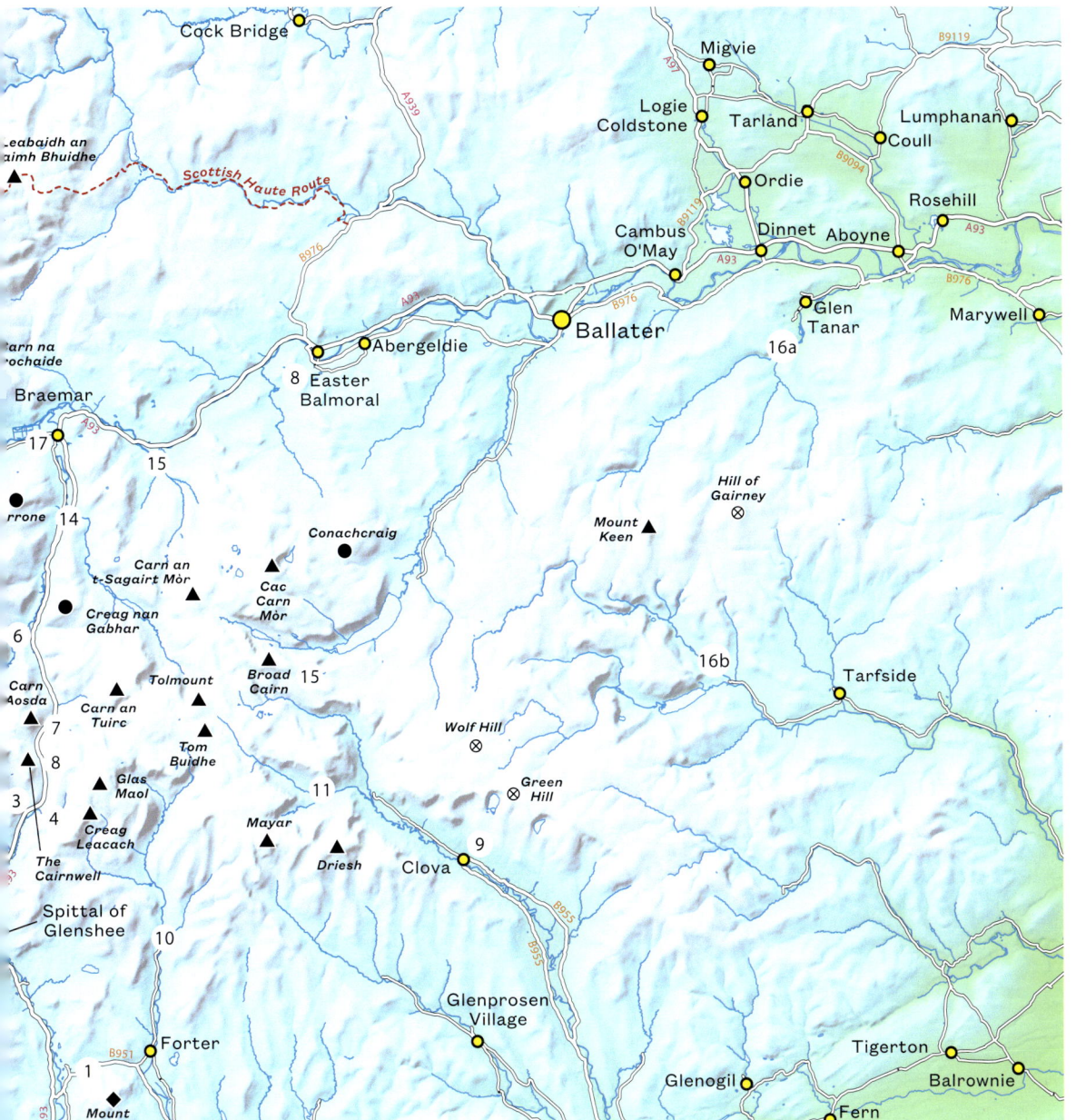

1.	Mount Blair	P.168	13.	An Sgarsoch and Carn an Fhidhleir	P.185
2.	Glas Tulaichean	P.171	14.	Creag nan Gabhar	P.187
3.	The Cairnwell	P.172	15.	Lochnagar	P.187
4.	Creag Leacach	P.173	16.	Mount Keen	P.192
5.	Beinn Iutharn Mhòr	P.174	17.	Morrone	P.194
6.	An Socach	P.174	18.	Ruigh Aiteachain High-Level Tour	P.195
7.	Càrn an Tuirc	P.176	19.	Monadh Mòr	P.197
8.	Glenshee to Balmoral	P.178	20.	Sgòr Mòr	P.199
9.	Greenhill	P.180	21.	Carn na Drochaide	P.200
10.	Mayar	P.181	22.	Glen Feshie	P.200
11.	Glen Doll	P.183	23.	Glenmore to Feshie Traverse	P.200
12.	Leathad an Taobhain and Càrn Dearg Mòr	P.183			

Mount Blair ♦ 744m
Moor Covered Upland Hill

△ NO 167 629   ◁ LR43   🌐 P.168

🅿 Roadside parking by trees at the Perthshire-Angus boundary near the high point on the B951 (NO 158 643/ 56.7633, -3.3781), about 2km east of the A93.

↔ 4KM   △ 410M   ⊺ 362M
🕐 1-2 HRS   GRADE II   ★★

By Colwyn Jones

Mount Blair is a symmetrical cone sitting between Glen Shee and Glen Isla, topped by an obvious communications tower. The fine ski descent of its north slope was probably first found by frustrated winter sports enthusiasts unable to access the Glenshee ski area as the Devil's Elbow road was closed. This modest tour may continue to play this role after a heavy snowfall, often early in the ski season. The nearby A93 is typically well ploughed to allow access to Glenshee and beyond, but after taking the signposted route to Glenisla and Kirriemuir, cross the Shee Water, go through the village of Cray, then drive up close to the high point on the B951. Immediately behind the sign showing you have entered the county of Angus, the parking place has space for about six considerately parked cars. You may need to clear snow for your own parking spot to enjoy the pleasant, short tour to the summit of this Graham, perhaps ascending and descending more than once.

Start the ascent of Mount Blair by going north-east up along the road to a roadside gate which is used by the maintenance team for the large communications tower on the summit. The resulting ATV track should ideally be under a good layer of snow, but the flattened vegetation provides a descent slope of a remarkably consistent gradient up to the 600m contour (approximately 16 degrees on average). You soon reach a sheep fence just before the 550m contour where there is a second gate just above an obtuse-angled fence-line corner. Go through (or more likely over) the snowbound gate and continue directly up, diverging from the fence, to where the slope eases before reaching the surprising variety of summit furniture: the large communications tower, associated buildings, large prehistoric cairn, circular summit indicator and triangulation station. The cairn sits in Perthshire, while the trig pillar and mast are in the county of Angus. The top provides a fine viewpoint, and the stainless steel-clad summit indicator, despite having lost most of its original black lettering, shows the name of the hills you can see: 40 Munros, apparently. One of these pieces of summit furniture will provide shelter from the wind as you remove climbing skins and prepare for the descent. But be careful of any ice falling from the large communications mast.

In poor visibility it is safer to return using your ascent track to navigate, remembering the intermediate gate and fence with a top strand of barbed wire. An alternative or subsequent route is down the wide north-east ridge to point 653m above Creag na Cuigeil (The Whig Rock) above Glen Isla. This part of the hill lives up to its name with somewhat deeper heather, and it requires a good depth of snow. From here follow the north-west ridge back to the B951 and, shortly thereafter, your car.

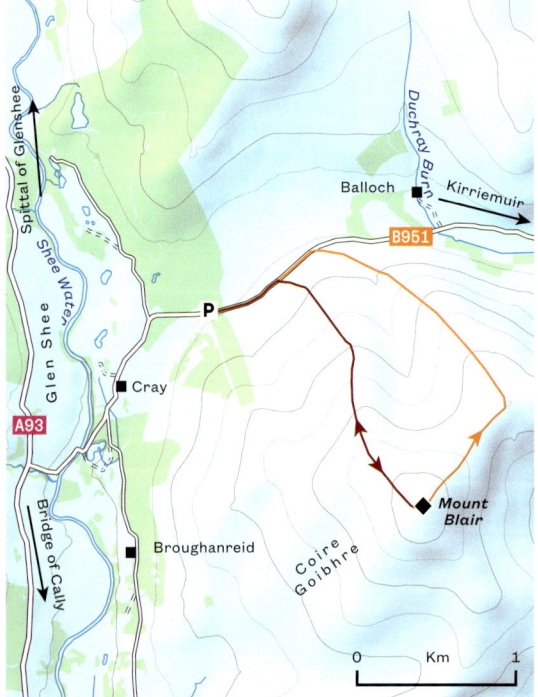

Key

1. Glas Tulaichean — P.171
2. The Cairnwell — P.172
3. Beinn Iutharn Mhòr — P.174
4. An Socach — P.174

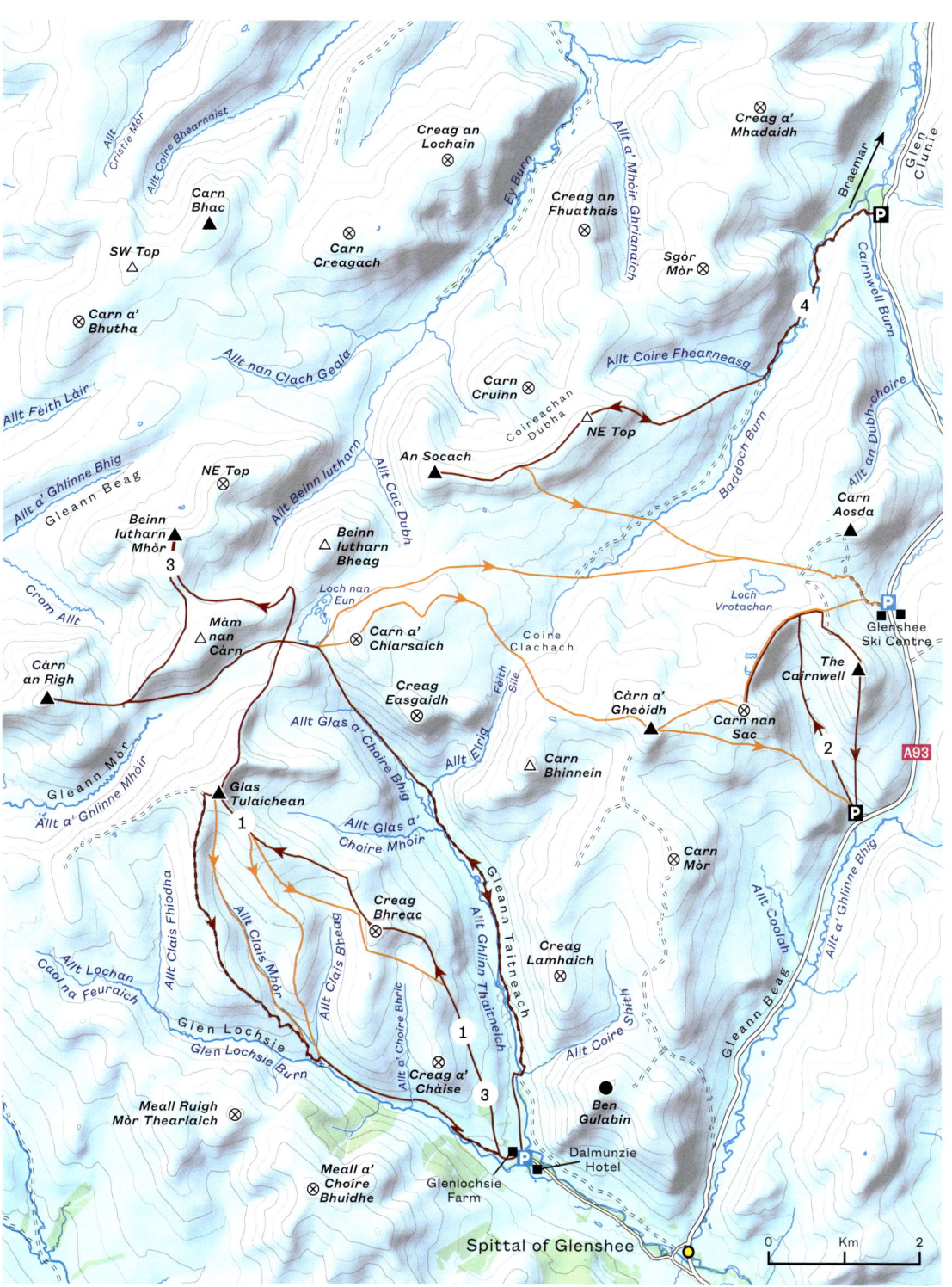

Above: Glas Tulaichean
(skier, Steve Martin)
© Al Todd

Glas Tulaichean ▲ 1,051m
Green Hill

△ NO 051 760 ◁ LR43 ⊕ P.169

🅿 The Dalmunzie Castle Hotel (NO 090 713/ 56.8243, -3.4915).

↔ 15KM   △ 750M   ⊺ 360M
🕒 5-6 HRS   GRADE III   ★★★

By Iain Smart, updated by Brian Shackleton

The easiest ascent of Glas Tulaichean is from Dalmunzie Castle Hotel, where parking may be possible on request for a small fee. After a short approach towards Glenlochsie Farm, which may need to be done on foot, the farm is avoided by a signed diversion on the left, the route of ascent is up the long south-east ridge.

It is best to ski up to the east side of the ridge to avoid steep ground below point 667m before joining the ridge just beyond point 717m (NO 077 734). From here the ascent continues north and then north-west past points 827m and 824m to the more defined ridge leading up to the triangulation station on the summit. The final section overlooking steep ground above Glas Choire Mhòr may be corniced, so care will be needed in poor visibility.

When there is good snow cover down to glen level, it is possible to ski down the broad south ridge to Breac-reidh, or the intermediate ridge between this and the south-east ridge, down to the ruined remains of Glenlochsie Lodge. A good descent can also be made down the corrie of the Allt Clais Mhòr. The line of the dismantled railway offers a direct descent back towards Glenlochsie Farm, but is likely to involve a lot of poling unless the snow surface is slick or there is a favourable wind to assist progress.

If there is insufficient snow lower down, a more reliable descent can be enjoyed by skiing down the line of ascent to around 950m and then south-east into the line of the burn until the burn turns south. From here, make a short ascent on skins to the col between points 824m and 827m. The ski descent can then be continued by following the line of ascent past point 717m. Alternatively, traverse west of point 827m, then descend steeply east by a burn line to flatter ground, which is crossed to join the line of ascent north of point 717m. Return to the starting point following the east side of the ridge.

The Cairnwell ▲ 933m
Hill of Blisters
△ NO 134 773   ⌖ LR43   ⊕ P.169

Càrn a' Gheòidh ▲ 975m
Goose Hill
△ NO 107 767   ⌖ LR43   ⊕ P.169

🅿 A layby on the A93 road 3km south of the ski area (NO 134 756/56.8634, -3.4191).

↔ 8KM   △ 500M   ⎯ 480M
🕒 3-4 HRS   GRADE III   ★★★

By Raymond Simpson, updated by Colwyn Jones

For those wishing to avoid the congestion of the Glenshee ski area, particularly on a weekend, a long ascent (480m to The Cairnwell) may be made starting south of The Cairnwell (NO 134 756) and ascending north-north-west up the glen between The Cairnwell and Càrn nan Sac. The payoff is a longer run at the end of the day.

With good snow cover the most interesting route to Càrn a' Gheòidh starts from the head of this glen at a small col south-east of Loch Vrotachan and follows the ridge south-west over Càrn nan Sac (920m), which may be corniced in places, to where it abuts the summit slopes of Càrn a' Gheòidh. On a fine day the views of the Cairngorms are magnificent, and the first edition stated that there are many sheltered hollows for sunbathing en route. A direct ascent from the starting point is also possible after a steep initial climb north of Creag nan Eun if there is sufficient snow to cover the heather.

For most skiers, Càrn a' Gheòidh is the furthest point west of the tour, from where a fast descent is made north-east to skirt Loch Vrotachan and regain the col leading east into Butchart's Corrie and the option of a run down ensuring you remain outside the pisted slopes (as per ski areas access agreement). If the crests of the ridges are denuded of snow, it is usually possible, even late in the season, to work your way round to the summit from Loch Vrotachan following burns and snow banks on the north-facing slopes.

There are alternatives, however. The simplest descent is south-east from the summit into the Allt Coolah, a long, straightforward run after an initial (100m) steeper section. However, this will involve a 2km return along the A92. The Creag nan Eun ascent route can be used for return, but a finer alternative is to take in the summit of The Cairnwell, arriving as the sun is dipping in the west. From the various communications masts on the top there is the beautiful run either down the south ridge or the convex south-west face, which will return you to your starting point.

This popular short tour can also start from the top of The Cairnwell chairlift, thus incurring the cost of a lift ticket but reducing the total ascent to 130m.

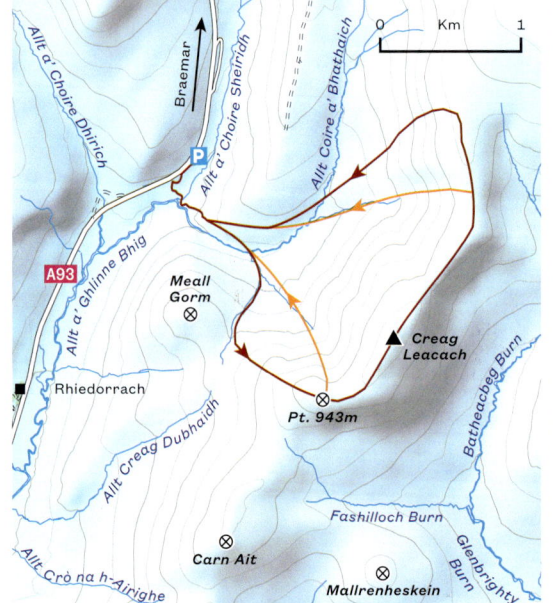

Opposite: En route to Loch Vrotachan and Càrn a' Gheòidh (skier, Esme Todd) © Al Todd

Creag Leacach ▲ 987m
Slabby Rock

△ NO 154 745   ⋌ LR43   ⊕ P.172

P The Connecting Contours car park on the east side of the A93 (NO 139 757/56.8646, -3.4131), just below the Devil's Elbow in Glen Shee.

↔ 7KM   △ 500M   ↕ 500M
⏱ 2-3 HRS   GRADE II   ★★

By Colwyn Jones

The A93 is ploughed to allow downhill skiers access to the Glenshee ski area, but the lower Connecting Contours car park may not have been cleared. This peak delivers a fine, if short, tour and, when conditions allow, a steep descent of the west flank of Glas Maol.

From the car park follow the footpath down and across the Allt a' Ghlinne Bhig to then follow the uphill course of the Allt Coire a' Bhathaich (1:25,000 map) south-east. At around the 550m contour turn south towards the col given a 716m spot height (1:25,000 map) behind Meall Gorm. From the col skin south-east up along the crest towards the south summit (943m). From here continue in a more northerly direction along the summit ridge to the main top at 987m. Continue north-east, traversing the peak following a derelict drystane dyke for a good kilometre to a col with a 933m spot height (1:25,000 map). From the col, or from a cairn 500m further along the ridge if conditions allow, a steep westerly descent regains the line of the Allt Coire a' Bhathaich. Traverse south-west, high across the intervening ridge, Leacann Dubh (Black Slope, but hopefully snowy white), to above your ascent tracks then back to the car park. A visit to the triangulation station on the summit of Glas Maol is less than 1km from the start of this descent.

In poor visibility, or if snow conditions are suboptimal, it is safer to return to the south summit (943m) from where you can ski in a southerly direction back to the track leading to your starting point.

Beinn Iutharn Mhòr ▲ 1,045m
Big Hell's Peak
△ NO 045 792 ⌖ LR43 🌐 P.169

Càrn an Righ ▲ 1,029m
Hill of the King
△ NO 028 772 ⌖ LR43 🌐 P.169

P Dalmunzie Castle Hotel (NO 091 712/56.8243, -3.4912).		
↔ 30KM	△ 1,300M	⊥ 369M
⏱ 10-12 HRS	GRADE III	***

By Iain Smart, updated by Colwyn Jones

These two mountains lie in the remote hinterland between the upper reaches of glens Tilt, Shee and Ey, a long way from the nearest public road – the A93 from Blairgowrie to Braemar over the Cairnwell Pass.

The route described is from the south, starting at Dalmunzie Castle Hotel, 2.5km north-west of Spittal of Glenshee. However, a return to the Cairnwell Pass is possible if travel logistics back to Dalmunzie Castle Hotel have been arranged. Alternatively, access from the A93 just north of the Cairnwell pass via Loch Vrotachan is possible providing you follow the approved route through the resort or purchase a tourers ticket which will quickly take you to a high start point. Access via Glen Ey, though possible, is not considered here as it involves a 14km approach and favours using a mountain bike and Nordic skis, or indeed both, for a long day with limited downhill skiing.

The traverse over these peaks (perhaps including Glas Tulaichean) is an exceptionally fine, long expedition, calling for fitness, good snow conditions and the lengthening daylight hours of spring.

Start behind Dalmunzie Castle Hotel, where parking is possible on request and payment of a small fee at the hotel reception. If planning an ascent of Glas Tulaichean, follow the Glas Tulaichean route to the triangulation station on the summit. From here it is a tricky 2km descent down the north-north-east ridge to a vague col (NO 059 779; 810m) west of Loch nan Eun (790m), a lonely, high lochan in the heart of these mountains. An alternative approach to Loch nan Eun follows Gleann Taitneach north of Glenlochsie Farm, on the west bank of the Allt Ghlinn Thaitneich, for 7km. This saves about 250m of ascent, but the final approach up the line of the Allt Easgaidh to the loch is steep, and snow conditions should be carefully assessed.

From Loch nan Eun ascend the north-east ridge of Màm nan Càrn to the 900m contour and traverse west at this altitude to the col below Beinn Iutharn Mhòr (NO 047 784). A further 1km north with 100m of climbing leads to the large cairn on the summit of this mountain.

Return south to the col and make a descending traverse south-west to the col between Màm nan Càrn and Càrn an Righ (NO 037 772). From there make your way up the east flank to the summit cairn of Càrn an Righ. This is a very remote mountain top, a long way from your starting point; and the equally isolated Fealar Lodge, 3km away to the north-west, is not inhabited during winter.

Ski down the ascent route to the Màm nan Càrn col and traverse east across the south face of this hill to reach Loch nan Eun. From there three possible routes exist. The shortest and safest (perhaps used in ascent) is to descend south-east down the Allt Easgaidh to the bulldozed track in Gleann Taitneach with a return to Dalmunzie Castle Hotel.

There is an alternative low-level route with minimal climbing on the way back to the Cairnwell Pass. This goes round the north side of Càrn a' Chlarsaich to the head of the Baddoch Burn, down this for 2km, then up to Loch Vrotachan and over the col between The Cairnwell and Carn Aosda to reach the ski slopes at Cairnwell. Another possibility, involving much more climbing, is to return over Càrn a' Gheòidh to Glenshee Ski Resort.

An Socach ▲ 944m
The Snout
△ NO 079 799 ⌖ LR43 🌐 P.169

P Roadside parking near the small conifer plantation on the west side of the A93 5km north of Glenshee Ski Centre (NO 138 831/56.9317, -3.4170).		
↔ 14KM	△ 520M	⊥ 420M
⏱ 5-6 HRS	GRADE II	**

By Donald Bennet, updated by Colwyn Jones

An Socach is a long, flat-topped hill between the head of Glen Ey and the Baddoch Burn, several kilometres west of the Cairnwell Pass. Its summit is a broad, crescent-shaped ridge with the highest point at the west end and a slightly lower cairn at the north-east end. It feels especially remote and gives an easy ski tour when approached from the Cairnwell Pass, as described in the first edition. But as this inevitably uses the prepared pistes of the Glenshee ski area for ascent, to avoid contravening the Mountaineering Scotland snowsports touring code, the route described here starts from the A93 where the Baddoch Burn runs into Clunie Water. However, a return to the Cairnwell Pass would adhere to the code.

From the south end of the conifers, take the gated track across Clunie Water to the house at

Baddoch. Some 700m later cross the Baddoch Burn and after around 1km ford the burn draining Coire Fhearneasg. If the burn is not fordable then simply start to climb on the north side of the burn until it is possible to cross onto the broad east ridge of the peak, choosing the best line of ascent and aiming for the cairn on the north-east top (NO 099 805; 938m).

From the cairn there is a fine, high, 2km-long ridge to the true summit and a second cairn, with excellent views to match, although if you prefer it is easy to return and have a pleasant ski back down the Coire Fhearneasg. If snow cover is thin and there are stones and boulders, the best summit route may be on the south side of the ridge, along which a continuous line of snow may form a cornice above the south face. Care is needed not to ski too close to the edge. The small summit cairn stands in the middle of the broad ridge.

The best return is via the ascent route back down the Coire Fhearneasg, following the best snow seen on the way up.

An alternative is to return to the Glenshee ski area, if you can solve the problem that your car is 5km north along the A93. Retrace your approach to the col midway along the summit ridge (NO 092 800). Taking care to avoid any cornices, ski south-east down the wide gully or the slope on its east side where there is the possibility of a good downhill run of almost 400m to the Baddoch Burn. Reapply your climbing skins, cross the track and finally complete the climb of 250m needed to gain a col east of Loch Vrotachan. The last run of the day brings you back skiing outside the snow fences in Butchart's Corrie.

Below: Cairn of Claise
(skier, Graeme Gatherer)
© Al Todd

Glas Maol ▲ 1,068m
The Green Lump
△ NO 167 765 ⌖ LR43 🌐 P.177

Cairn of Claise ▲ 1,064m
Hill of the Hollow
△ NO 185 788 ⌖ LR43 🌐 P.177

Càrn an Tuirc ▲ 1,019m
Hill of the Boar
△ NO 174 804 ⌖ LR43 🌐 P.177

P The south end of the Glenshee Ski Centre car park (parking charges) at the Cairnwell Pass (NO 141 775/ 56.8814, -3.4103). Ski touring around the resort area has become a sensitive issue so follow the Snowsports code or buy a 'ski touring ticket'.

↔ 12KM   △ 600M   ⊥ 660M
⏱ 4–5 HRS   GRADE III   ★★★

By Raymond Simpson, updated by Colwyn Jones

These three mountains, which are very accessible from the A93 at the Glenshee Ski Centre, lie on the western perimeter of an extensive ski touring area that maintains an altitude of 900m for almost 16km north-east to the White Mounth and Lochnagar, and 10km east over the summits of the Angus Hills. In poor visibility, careful navigation is required as skiers have become lost overnight in this wilderness. The described circuit of Glas Maol, Cairn of Claise and Càrn an Tuirc, plus perhaps a short ascent to finish the tour, provides a good introduction to this area, and it is a short day even if you do not use the ski tows.

The Glenshee Ski Centre website has a ski touring page with information, a map and GPX track showing the preferred route for access to the eastern hills and information about parking fees. You can purchase a specific 'ski touring ticket' if using the car park (£18 in 2024), which includes parking and four single uplifts. This would get you over 1,000 metres on Glas Maol if all of the lifts were open!

From the south end of the car park at the Cairnwell Pass, follow the waymarked track for ski tourers up the hillside south of the snow fences delineating ski runs served by tows on Meall Odhar. Continue up onto the summit of this hill (922m), then cross a wide col south-east and ascend the north-west shoulder of Glas Maol, which is steep and intimidating at first but leads to the easier slopes of the summit dome.

Alternatively, you may buy a lift ticket and take the tows in two stages to Meall Odhar, ski down into Coire Fionn and take a further tow up to the head of this corrie at a height of 1,000m, from here it is 500m north to the summit of Glas Maol.

Glas Maol has a triangulation station and is an excellent viewpoint with an open, southerly aspect. The south-facing corrie, which it shares with Little Glas Maol, offers two fine ski runs, and the traverse of the Creag Leacach ridge, which is quite narrow and rocky in places, gives access to steeper skiing in the corrie on the north-west side of that hill.

From the summit of Glas Maol, ski north-north-east before turning east, just above where the snow fences direct downhill skiers back into Coire Fionn, to a broad col. From the col, ascend north-east to the summit of Cairn of Claise. Under most conditions it is easy to follow the line of the fences and the old dyke to Cairn of Claise, although high winds may blast the snow off the most exposed parts of the broad ridge and give frustrating skiing.

The easy descent north from the summit of Cairn of Claise is one of the classic ski runs in the Glenshee area and is followed by a short ascent north-west to Càrn an Tuirc. The summit plateau of Càrn an Tuirc is rocky and often wind-blasted, requiring skis to be carried if visiting its highest point.

To descend, ski north from the summit for a few hundred metres, then north-west at 950m into a shallow, steepening gully, which contains the 'archaeological remains' of an old rope tow and, lower down, the remnants of a ski hut used in the 1950s and 1960s before the Glenshee ski area was established. Either continue down the line of the burn, which turns west then south-west, or more directly, if snow conditions allow, to join the Allt a' Gharbh-choire. Follow this on its north bank to the confluence with the Allt Coire Fionn/Cairnwell Burn where a footbridge leads to the A93 and a small car park. If your party does not have a second car waiting here (or 700m north at another car park on the west side of the road), there is typically enough snow to reapply skins and reascend next to the busy road to the car park.

This circuit can also be done in reverse (clockwise) from either of the two north Glenshee car parks. The ascent of the west face of Carn an Tuirc is steep and can be icy. Thereafter the southward traverse of Cairn of Claise and Glas Maol is straightforward. A variant descent off Glas Maol is to head due north off the summit plateau thus avoiding the ski centre pistes. Head along the edge

---

Key

1.	Carn An Tuirc	P.176
2.	Glenshee to Balmoral	P.178
3.	Creag nan Gabhar	P.187
4.	Morrone	P.194

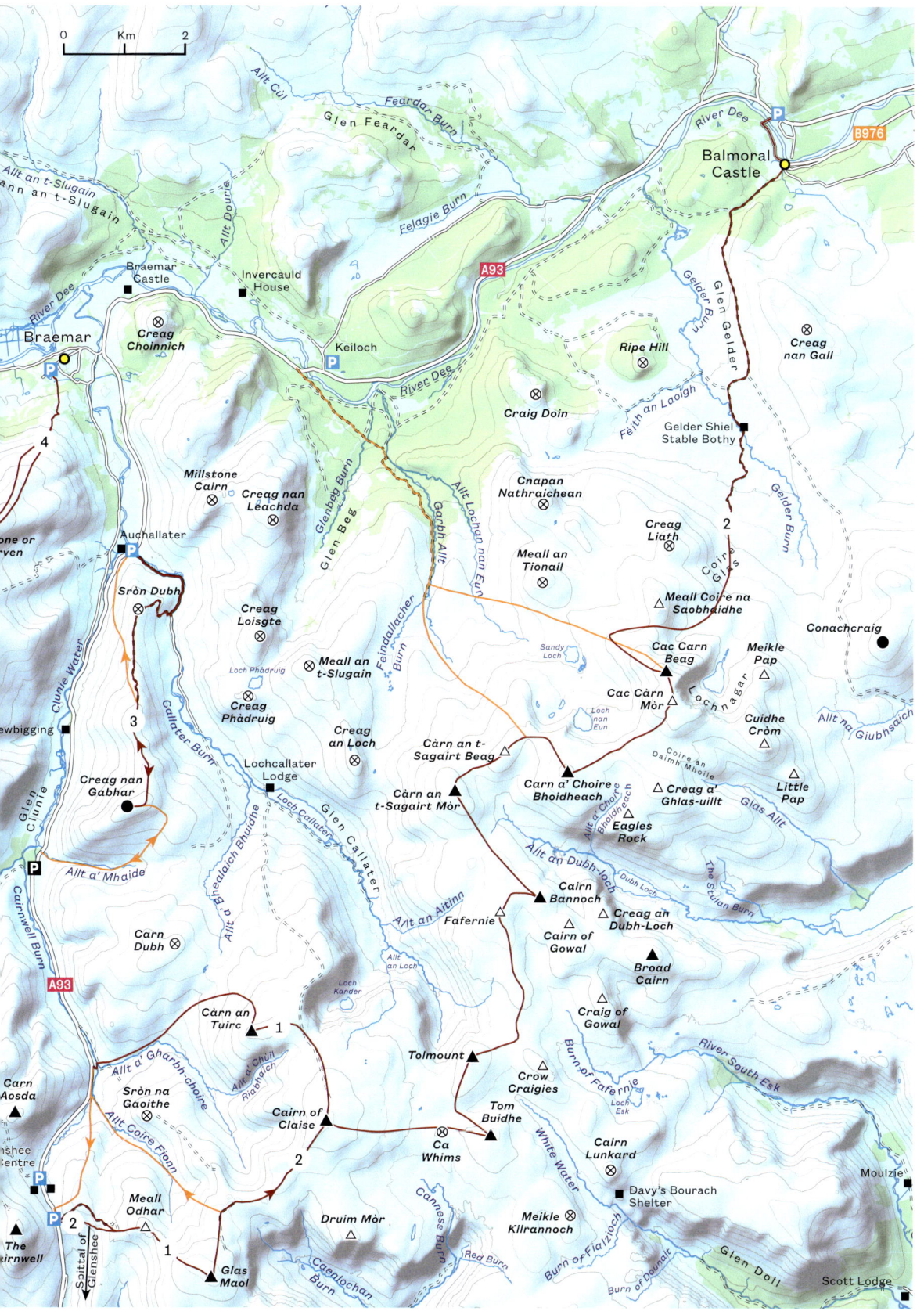

of the Glas Choire on your left, before following the marvellous run north east along the whaleback ridge to Sròn na Gaoithe (814m). A final descent off this top's steep north west face takes you most satisfyingly back to your starting point.

Glenshee to Balmoral

◁ LR43, LR44   P.177

| P | Starting point: The high point on the A93 road (NO 141 775/56.8809, -3.4103). |
| P | Finishing point: Crathie car park (pay and display) and bus stop (NO 264 949/57.0397, -3.2137). |

↔ 36KM   △ 1,360M   ⊤ 670M
⏱ 10 HRS   GRADE III   ★★★★

By Gordon MacKenzie, updated by Roger Wild

This is a superb tour, which initially follows the county boundary line east and north from Glenshee Ski Centre before heading across to Lochnagar and descending to Balmoral and the River Dee. The route ascends eight Munros: Glas Maol, Cairn of Claise, Tom Buidhe, Tolmount, Cairn Bannoch, Càrn an t-Sagairt Mòr, Carn a' Choire Bhoidheach and Cac Carn Beag (Lochnagar).

The 10-hour estimate is based on 4.5kph + 1 min for every 10m of ascent. No allowance has been made for stops or photography. This is a route on which skis can excel, and in good snow and weather conditions some efficient travelling may be enjoyed. The route travels close to some cliff edges, and although the terrain is predominantly undulating, there are a few steep slopes along the way, including the initial climb up to Glas Maol and the final descent from Lochnagar, which require caution with snow conditions and security. The terrain is featureless, and skilled navigation will be required in poor visibility. The compass directions are a general indication of the route, not accurate bearings for detailed navigation. This is a tour to do on a good day when the skiing can be enjoyed to the full and the views appreciated.

The route initially lies on the edge of the ski area, so remember to refer to the Snowsports Touring Code, which can be found online. The Glenshee Ski Centre website has a Ski Touring page with a map and GPX track showing the preferred route for access to the eastern hills and information about parking fees. From the parking area by the high point on the A93, follow the approximate route of the boundary line shown on the map for 1.5km to Meall Odhar (NO 156 773). A minor change in direction takes you to Glas Maol, the first Munro, before turning north and north-east to Cairn of Claise, keeping away from the steep ground at the

Below: The White Mounth from Càrn an Tuirc (skier, Graeme Gatherer) © Al Todd

top of Garbh-choire to the north. Head east for 2km to reach the north side of Ca Whims and then ascend Tom Buidhe, Munro number three. This is an excellent viewpoint from which to appreciate the extent of the high plateau. Keeping as much height as possible, return past the north side of Ca Whims to reach the 890m contour and the boundary line to climb Tolmount. Descend to the col below Knaps of Fafernie. The old drove road from Glen Callater to Glen Doll (Jock's Road) crosses here. In the 1880s the Scottish Rights of Way and Recreation Society (Scotways) took action to prevent the route from being closed. The case went to the House of Lords, where it was shown that the route had long been used by drovers to take sheep from Braemar over the Tolmount to the market via Glen Clova and should not be closed. From the col head north for 2km before turning east to Cairn Bannoch, the fifth Munro. Leaving the boundary line now, head north-west for 1.5km to reach a col and then ascend to Càrn an t-Sagairt Mòr. Leave the summit in a north-easterly direction, traverse over or around Càrn

an t-Sagairt Beag to reach the col on its north-east side, taking care to avoid the cliffs of The Stuic, then turn south-east to the penultimate Munro, Carn a' Choire Bhoidheach. Descend east-north-east for 1.5km and climb to Cac Càrn Mòr, which is on the edge of the precipitous cliffs of Lochnagar. The final Munro, Cac Carn Beag, is a short distance north-north-west, with cliffs to the east of the route. The descent from the summit is steep and requires care. Head west-north-west for 500m to the end of a flattish section before continuing steeply to reach another flattish area near the 910m contour. Traverse along the contour to the col south of Meall Coire na Saobhaidhe, descend east into the corrie of the same name and follow the stream which flows from it to reach the track leading to Gelder Shiel Bothy. Take the track leading towards Prince Albert's Cairn before turning north-east to Easter Balmoral and the B976. The road leads to the bridge over the River Dee and the cark park and bus stop at Crathie.

An alternative route which finishes at Invercauld Bridge on the A93 can be made by continuing west-north-west from the flattish area near the 910m contour (NO 235 866) for 3km to reach the Feindallacher Burn and following the track on its west side, passing the Falls of Garbh Allt and continuing north-west to the Bridge of Dee (NO 186 909) and the main road. There is a bus shelter at the Keiloch junction (NO 188 910), and the bus will probably stop on request. The Invercauld Estate has a car park about 300m up the road towards Keiloch. If leaving a car overnight, it might be wise to contact the estate: office@invercauld.org; +44 (0) 13397 41224.

Another option which avoids the steep descent from Cac Carn Beag is to retrace the outward route to the col (NO 220 852) on the north-east side of Càrn an t-Sagairt Beag, taking care to avoid the cliffs of The Stuic. Now head north-west down the Allt a' Choire Dhuibh to its junction with the Feindallacher Burn and follow the route already described to the Bridge of Dee.

For those wishing to avoid the ski resort, an alternative start can be made from the small car park 2.5kms to the north (NO 147 800). Cross the footbridge below the car park and reverse part of the previous route (Glas Maol etc.) to ascend Càrn an Tuirc and join the original route at Cairn of Claise. The timing is about the same as for the original route.

Transport and accommodation
For the return to Glenshee, you could leave a car at Crathie or take the bus to Braemar and then a taxi to Glenshee (at the time of publication the nearest taxi service was in Ballater). Alternatively, start the trip from Braemar with an early start by taxi to Glenshee. Staying overnight at the Gelder Shiel Bothy may facilitate other options.

- Taxi (based in Ballater): +44 (0) 1339 755654
- Bus service 201: www.stagecoachbus.com
- Rucksacks Bunkhouse, 15 Mar Road, Braemar: +44 (0) 1339 741517
- Ballater Hostel: www.ballater-hostel.com; info@ballater-hostel.com; +44 (0) 1339 753752

Greenhill 870m
NO 348 756   LR44   P.181

The Glen Clova Hotel (NO 328 731/56.8442, -3.1034) on the B955.

↔ 15KM   △ 820M   ↕ 230M
⏱ 5-6 HRS   GRADE II   ★★

By Stan Pearson

Burns and corries may hold the snow well here, offering skiing even when the hills look to hold little snow. Once on the plateau there are many variations over gentle, grassy moorland in almost any direction, with one option described here. Cross-country skiing is a good option.

Ascend the path north from the hotel, or the burn to its east if it has better snow, for 2km towards Loch Brandy. Just before the loch, ascend north-east over a low ridge to the summit of Green Hill. The alternative ascent, which will get you to the snow more quickly if the snow level is high, is to walk up The Snub and then use skis to follow the rim of the corrie of Loch Brandy.

Descend north-west to pick up the Burn of Longshank for 2km to the confluence (NO 349 778). From here head west for 1.5km to Wolf Hill (826m), then back south over gentle terrain to Benty Roads (841m), then a further 2km south-east back to Green Hill. From the summit of Green Hill the descent is south into the Corrie of Inchdowrie. This is steep initially and requires caution. The burn running down to Inchdowrie typically holds the snow well, hopefully close to the B955 and your starting point.

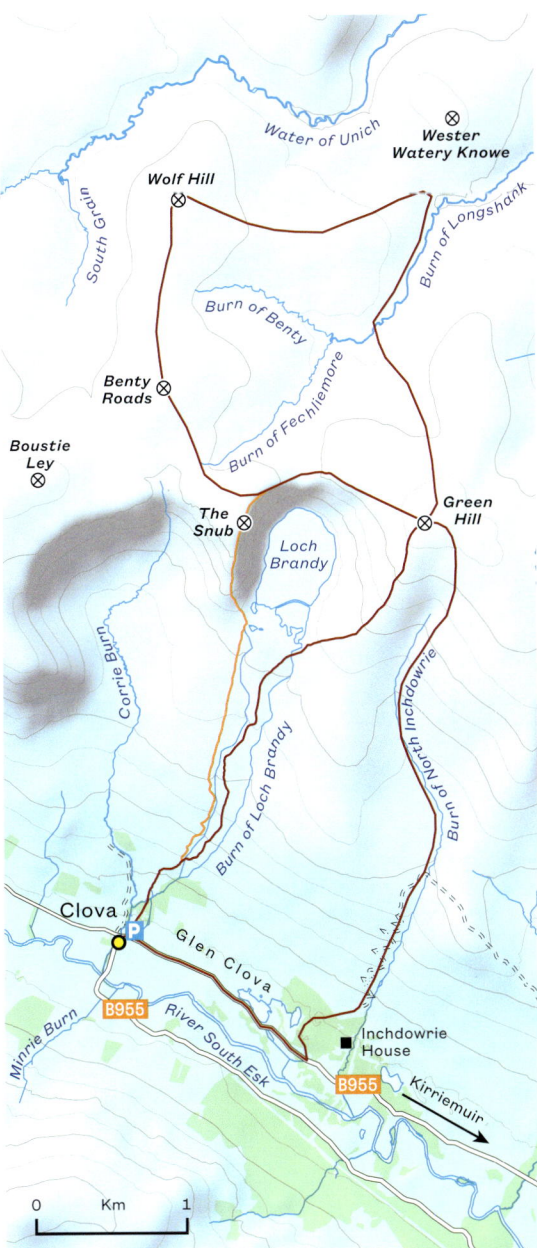

Mayar ▲ 928m
Perhaps *'High Plain'*
⌲ NO 240 737   ⌖ LR43, LR44   🌐 P.182

Driesh ▲ 947m
Thorn Bush or *Bramble*
⌲ NO 271 735   ⌖ LR43, LR44   🌐 P.182

🅿 Auchavan at the end of the public road in Glen Isla (NO 191 696/56.8110, -3.3257); the start of the route is on OS sheet 43; the rest is on OS sheet 44.

↔ 20KM   △ 870M   ⇅ 360M

🕒 7-8 HRS (5-6 hours if Driesh is not included)
GRADE II   ★★

By Iain Smart, updated by Stan Pearson

These two hills are the highest of a large expanse of rounded hills between Glens Clova, Prosen and Isla. They lie close to Glen Clova, but the slopes on that side are steep, craggy and forested, so not ideal for skiing. Glen Isla to the south-west gives a more distant starting point and a long, pleasant ski tour over rolling hills, but beware of navigational errors in bad visibility, which might lead you down to Glen Prosen and a long way from your car.

From Auchavan in Glen Isla cross the river and follow the track past Dalhally and up the south-east side of the Glencally Burn for a further 2km. Continue up the burn on the south side of Sròn Deirg (Red Nose) and reach the plateau 1km west of Mayar. Do not head directly for the summit, as this involves a steep drop down to the Mayar Burn; instead, go north along a fence line for a few hundred metres until an easy descent north-east leads to the flat col 1km north-west of Mayar. From there follow another line of fence posts to the summit.

To continue to Driesh, ski east for 2km to the Kilbo Pass at the head of Corrie Kilbo (1:25,000 map). At this point a path reaches the pass from Glen Doll, but it is not easy to ski up or down this path. To reach Driesh, 150 vertical metres above the pass and 1.5km distant, ascend south-east for 500m to the plateau and then 1km east to the triangulation station on the summit.

From Driesh, return over Mayar from where the descent to Glen Isla is either by the uphill tracks or, if you want a slightly longer route and the conditions are favourable, along the ridge to Bawhelps (830m) and down by the Algeilly Burn. Another much longer variation is to ski north-west from Mayar across the plateau to Dun Hillocks (890m) or even the distant Tom Buidhe (957m), as there is little height loss before heading down the south ridge of Finalty Hill from Dun Hillocks to the Glencally Burn.

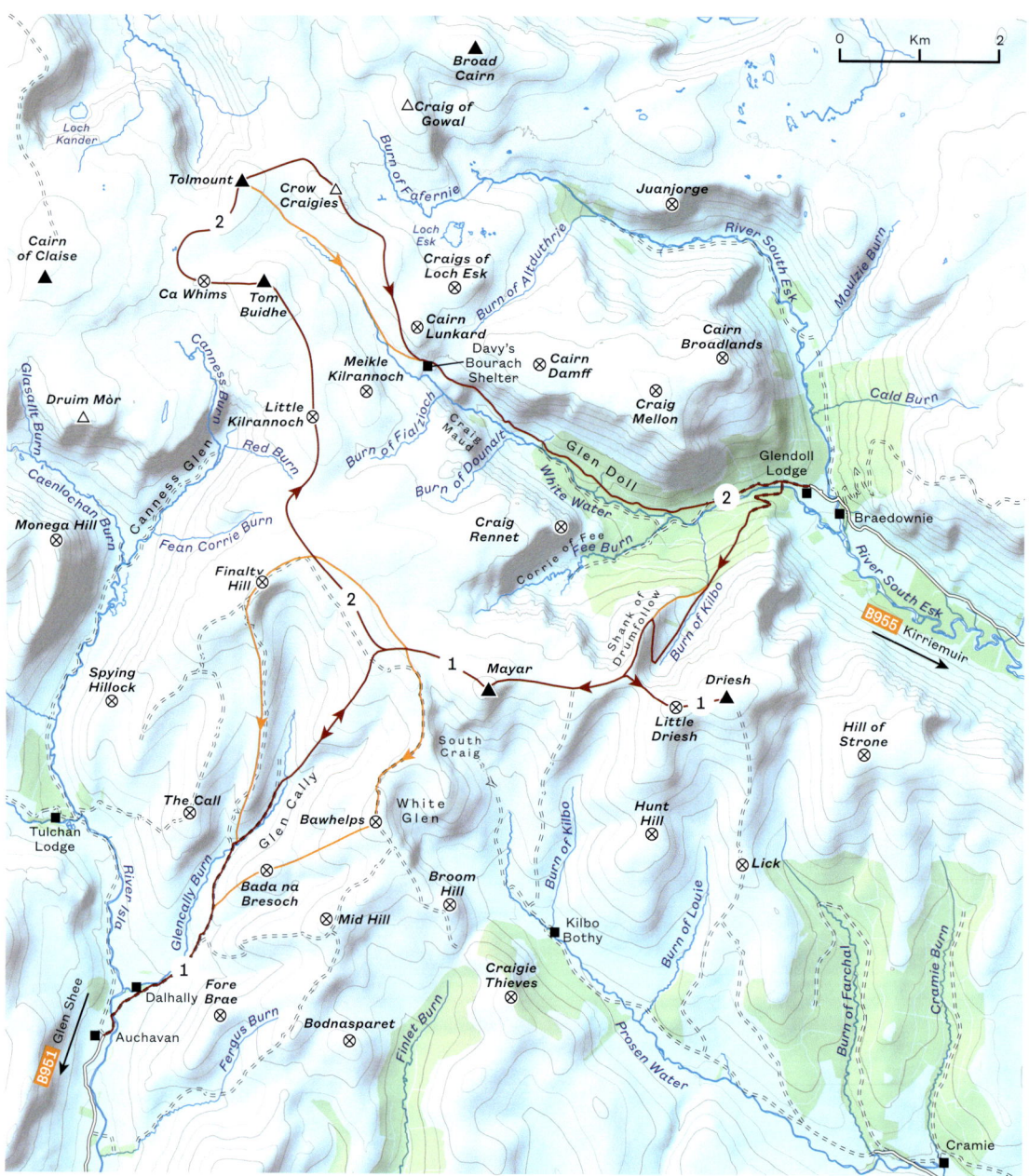

Key

1. Mayer and Dreish from Glen Isla   P.181
2. Mayer and Dreish from Glen Doll   P.183

Glen Doll

Mayar ▲ 928m
Perhaps *High Plain*
- NO 240 737
- LR43, LR44
- P.182

Driesh ▲ 947m
Thorn Bush or *Bramble*
- NO 271 735
- LR43, LR44
- P.182

Tolmount ▲ 958m
Valley Hill
- NO 210 800
- LR43, LR44
- P.182

Tom Buidhe ▲ 957m
Yellow Hill
- NO 213 787
- LR43, LR44
- P.182

- P: The Forestry Commission Glen Doll pay and display car park (NO 283 761/56.8710, -3.1770).
- ↔ 24KM
- △ 1,040M
- ⊥ 260M
- ⏱ 7-8HRS (5-6 hours if Driesh is not included)
- GRADE IV ★★★

By Colwyn Jones and Stan Pearson

This high-level tour from Glen Clova starts up steep, craggy and forested slopes, which are not ideal for skiing, but the difficulties can be walked. Good snow cover down to the car park is needed, but the plateau holds snow well where the wind has not blown it from the underlying rocks. Mayar, and perhaps Driesh, are included, then an easy high route taking in Tom Buidhe and Tolmount, with one difficult descent section. The clockwise option is described, but an anti-clockwise tour is equally possible.

Take the forest track west past the farm to the bridge across White Water and follow the vehicle track for about 1km before turning left up a steep, narrow footpath. The path exits the trees and traverses up the Shank of Drumfollow. If icy there may be better snow for skinning accumulated in the line of the Burn of Kilbo, but if it is safe to do so, try to regain the footpath with some extended zigzags up the west slope from the 650m contour, or simply walk up in boot crampons.

If planning to visit the summit of Driesh, leave the path at the 800m contour going south-east to the col, then continue steeply initially to cover the generous 1km to the triangulation station.

Ski back down to the col, then reapply skins for a comfortable 2km ascent east to the top of Mayar. Continue down the north-west flank of the Munro, then ascend the broad ridge to Dun Hillocks (890m), then go north to the summit of Little Kilrannoch (878m) or contour round the west flank. The summit of Tom Buidhe lies 1.8km further north. A burn-filled valley separates this from the next summit, Tolmount, and, if the snow allows, a height-saving arc can be followed down the north-west flank of Tom Buidhe to a broad intervening col, and then another easy ascent up the south-west ridge of Tolmount to the highest point of the day.

The tributaries of White Water flowing down from Tolmount into Glen Doll give tired skiers easy return slopes down to the 750m contour, where you leave the line of the burn to reach Jock's Road and find the shelter called Davy's Bourach; indeed, you may ski right over the top of it! The next 2km of Jock's Road are steep and rocky and must be skied with care or walked with boot crampons.

On reaching the trees there is a good footpath, with some shorter steep sections that lead back to the original forest track and, hopefully with minimal poling, the car park.

Leathad an Taobhain ● 912m
Slope of the Rafters
- NN 822 858
- LR43
- P.184

Càrn Dearg Mòr ● 857m
Big Red Cairn
- NN 824 912
- LR43
- P.184

- P: Auchlean car park, Glen Feshie (NN 851 983/57.0631, -3.8970).
- ↔ 26KM
- △ 950M
- ⊥ 330M
- ⏱ 7-8 HRS
- GRADE III ★★★

By Bob Reid

Little more than a cairn's height short of being a Munro, Leathad an Taobhain offers a long, elegant ski tour taking in much of the celebrated geomorphology of Glenfeshie, which is increasingly renowned for its rewilding prowess. From the car park at Auchlean head nearly 2km south along a good path on the east bank of the River Feshie, where a footbridge allows access to the estate track on the western side, which leads a further 2km past Carnachuin and Feshie Lodge. Follow the track south until it curves south-west by a ruin (NN 843 917) and ascends towards Lochan an t-Sluic, a further 4km. 200m beyond the lochan is a junction (490m). Follow the left turn (south) and continue along this twisting track for 3km to reach the minor top of Meall an Uillt Chreagaich (847m), then follow the path south-east for 1.2km to the summit triangulation station of Leathad

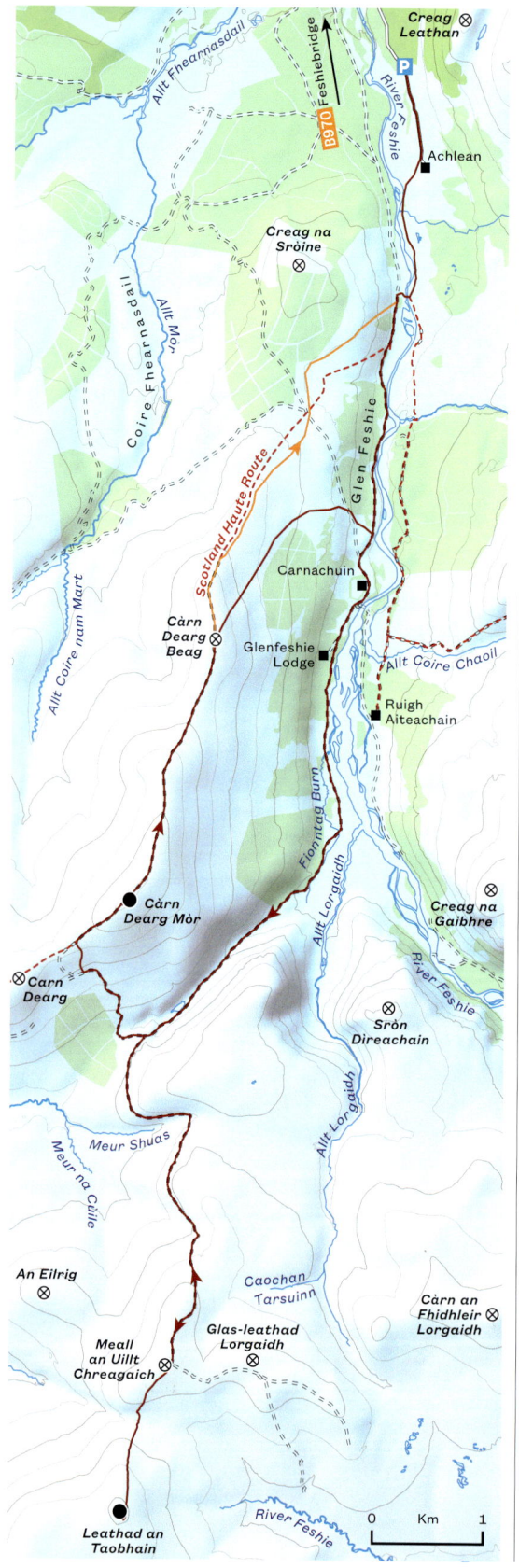

an Taobhain (14km; 680m; 4.5hrs). Note: On some OS maps the summit is shown as point 902m, a further 800m west. This is not the highest point.

Descend via the ascent route. In leaner conditions the track holds the snow well, allowing a relatively straightforward schuss back northwards. Weather and time permitting, there is the option of going over the second Corbett, Càrn Dearg Mòr. From the junction just west of Lochan an t-Sluic, turn west along the track, which soon swings northward up the slopes of Càrn Dearg Mòr, passing a small plantation on the left. The track turns sharply west at the 700m contour, but instead continue straight northwards for a further 0.5km, following the broad summit ridge of Càrn Dearg Mòr (2km from the junction of the two tracks).

A ski descent is now possible, continuing along the main spine ridge of the hill, passing the triangulation station marked Càrn Dearg Beag (694m). A track then offers an easy descent back south-east to pick up the approach route, but in snowier conditions you can continue making a traversing descent north-east toward the footbridge crossing to Auchlean. Climbing Càrn Dearg Mòr on its own also makes for a much shorter ski day, reversing the descent route set out above as a means of approach (10km; 520m; 3hrs).

It is also possible to combine Càrn Dearg Mòr with another Corbett, Meallach Mhòr 769m (OS sheet 35; NN 777 909), which makes for a more substantial ski touring day. It effectively makes a tour of the Allt an Dubh-chadha. Meallach Mhòr is 4km due west from the summit of Càrn Dearg Mòr, following the watershed of the Allt Bhran. There is a drop to an unnamed col (NN 801 904; 540m), but the rounded ridge continuing west is straightforward for nearly 3km, passing a minor summit, Meall an Dubh-chadha (703m), before reaching the summit of Meallach Mhòr. There would need to be significant snow cover for this tour, however. A long, 7km descent option heads north-east, following the track through the Fèith Mhòr to join the descent mentioned above for Càrn Dearg Mòr.

Above: Red House Bothy, Glen Geldie © Al Todd

An Sgarsoch ▲ 1,006m
Place of Sharp Rocks

NN 933 836   LR43   P.185

Carn an Fhidhleir ▲ 994m
Fiddler's Hill

NN 904 841   LR43   P.185

P The Linn of Dee pay and display NTS car park (NO 063 897/56.9895, -3.5432).

↔ 42KM   △ 920M   ⊥ 370M
⏱ 12–14 HRS   GRADE II   ★★★

By Adam Watson, updated by Colwyn Jones

The traverse of these two distant, unfrequented hills is one of the longest day-tours described in this book, regardless of whether you are approaching from the Linn of Dee, Glen Feshie or Glen Tilt. The Linn of Dee is probably the best starting point, and the long, easy gradient from there alongside the River Dee and the Geldie Burn to the foot of the hills suggests that Nordic skis, or indeed inclusion of a mountain bike, may be best suited for this tour.

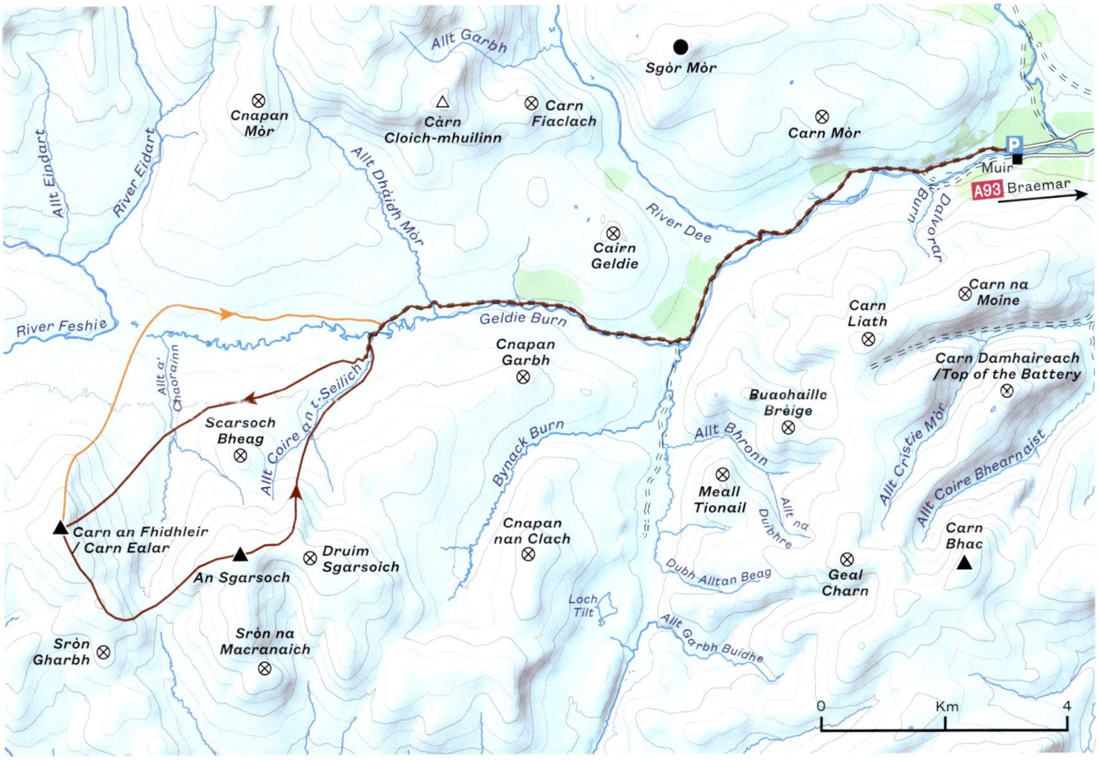

Carn an Fhidhleir stands where the counties of Aberdeen, Inverness and Perth meet, in one of the most remote parts of Scotland. Both hills have mostly smooth, gentle slopes, but the north-east corries of An Sgarsoch are steep and often carry snow cornices. The approach up the Dee and the Geldie takes you into broad, almost bare glens (gated deer fences to encourage tree regeneration have been installed) leading to distant hilltops where there is a great feeling of space.

From the Linn of Dee take the track west up Glen Dee, cross the Dee, then go south-west from White Bridge, passing the new bothy, Ruighe Ealasaid (The Red House), and finally west up the north side of the Geldie Burn. This leads in 12.5km to a point opposite the ruined Geldie Lodge sitting on the south side of the burn. From the Lodge (NN 955 867), a bulldozed track climbs west-south-west towards Carn an Fhidhleir; this track might hold snow and should be followed to its highest point. From there cross the Allt a' Chaorainn and climb south-west straight to the top of Carn an Fhidhleir, 19 long kilometres from Linn of Dee.

If the Geldie Burn at the lodge is high and unsafe to cross, continue along the north side and you can usually find a safe crossing place in 2 or 3km where the burn is much narrower. From there it is easy to head directly to Carn an Fhidhleir, whose summit offers grand views of the wild, bare upper reaches of the Feshie, Tarf and Geldie, and the great bulky Cairngorms to the north.

From the summit, even with patchy snow cover, a good run can usually be found by skiing just on the east side of the broad south-south-east ridge, then making a descending traverse to the 710m col (NN 919 829) below An Sgarsoch. A 300m climb follows to the large cairn on the broad top of that hill. The best descent route is east along the wide ridge for about 1km until good slopes on the north side lead down to the Allt Coire an t-Seilich and Geldie Lodge. Lastly, there are 13km of glen to ski (or walk or cycle) back to Linn of Dee.

Below: Heading into the steeps high above the Clova Hotel (skier, Andy Matthew) © Jamie Matthew

Creag nan Gabhar ● 834m

Goat Crag

△ NO 154 841 ⊿ LR43 🌐 P.177

Ⓟ Auchallater car park, charges apply (NO 156 881/56.9771, -3.3900).

↔ 7KM   △ 450M   ↕ 370M
🕒 3-4 HRS   GRADE II   **

By Bob Reid

Separated from the White Mounth by the narrow slot of Glen Callater, Creag nan Gabhar is a good short day out (perhaps a day-saver in poorer weather) but an elegant mountain ridge to be savoured, with fine views of the higher Munros in all directions.

Start at the pay and display car park by Auchallater on the A93 some 3km south of Braemar. Follow the good track east on the south bank of the Callater Burn for 1.75km until the track splits. Take the right split and skin west up the track, which tackles Sròn Dubh in a steep, uncompromising manner, with zigzags leading to the minor summit (584m). Now head south, following the line of the remnant track along the broad ridgeback of the hill. After 1.75km, where the old track ends, cross Sròn nan Gabhar (722m). The ridge narrows and undulates for a further 1km before steepening south-west toward the summit of Creag nan Gabhar itself (6km; 490m; 2.5hrs).

Descent is initially by the same route. Once past Sròn nan Gabhar there are options to traverse north-west or north-east off the ridge on either flank, depending upon snow conditions. The western flank is the steeper option but has the advantage of taking you directly back to the car park.

You can shorten the day even further by ascending from the A93 at Baddoch (NO 139 834). A path east leads beneath the south flank of Creag nan Gabhar toward the Bealach Buidhe above Glen Callater. After 2km, snow conditions permitting, it is possible to leave the path and traverse first north-east, then north up the south flank of Creag nan Gabhar.

Upon reaching a flattish shoulder (NO 160 839; 730m) traverse north-west for 750m to reach the summit (3.5km; 423m ascent; 2hrs). Descent is by the same route.

Lochnagar

Little Noisy Loch

Broad Cairn ▲ 998m
△ NO 240 815 ⊿ LR44 🌐 P.189

Cairn Bannoch ▲ 1,012m
Hill of the Cake
△ NO 208 843 ⊿ LR44 🌐 P.189

Càrn an t-Sagairt Mòr ▲ 1,047m
Big Hill of the Priest
△ NO 208 843 ⊿ LR44 🌐 P.189

Carn a' Choire Bhoidheach ▲ 1,110m
Peak of the Beautiful Corrie
△ NO 227 845 ⊿ LR44 🌐 P.189

Cac Carn Beag ▲ 1,156m
Little Shit-heap
△ NO 244 861 ⊿ LR44 🌐 P.189

Ⓟ The Spittal of Glenmuick car park (NO 310 852/56.9523, -3.1362), parking charges.

↔ 28KM   △ 1,320M   ↕ 410M
🕒 8-10 HRS   GRADE IV   ***

By Adam Watson, updated by Graham Dudley

This tour makes a magnificent long traverse across the mountains on the south side of the White Mounth from Spittal of Glenmuick to Invercauld Bridge on Deeside. It goes into the wild upper recesses of Glen Muick, above the great cliffs of Creag an Dubh-loch, over the rolling hills of the Mounth and the slopes of Lochnagar and finally down through the grand old pine forests of Deeside. Its length and the distance travelled over high plateau make this a serious day's ski-touring, and one that should be done in good conditions, for winter storms on the high Mounth and Lochnagar are not to be encountered lightly.

From the pay and display car park at Spittal, the route goes along the track on the south side of Loch Muick, through scattered birches below Creag Bhiòrach, to a bridge over the Black Burn. Here fork left up the steep hillside by a track which zigzags up to the plateau above. (An alternative route which continues by a footpath further along the loch shore and then up to the plateau east of Corrie Chash is best avoided as the top part is steep, sometimes corniced and often icy.) Above the Black Burn the track undulates along the plateau edge and then climbs to Allan's Hut (NO 256 808), south-west of Corrie Chash. If the plateau edge and the ridge to the west lack snow, the ground to the south of the track usually holds more.

Beyond Allan's Hut the route leads up to Broad Cairn, and the bulldozed track often holds snow when the stony slopes on either side are snow-free. The top of Broad Cairn is 1.5km west-north-west of Allan's Hut, and the actual summit is an exposed bouldery top which tends to be swept clear of snow, but there are usually big snowfields on either side.

From Broad Cairn (1:25,000 OS map) an easy ski run leads west-north-west to a 934m col, and gentle, usually well snow-covered slopes beyond rise north-west to Cairn Bannoch. The summit is a little rocky top, often peeping out as the only black spot among vast snowfields. The route continues north-west along a plateau to Càrn an t-Sagairt Mòr, where the view opens out to Glen Callater and Deeside. Within 200m of the summit the remains of an English Electric 'Canberra' that crashed in November 1956 can be found, if clear of snow.

From the summit of Càrn an t-Sagairt Mòr head east and descend steeply towards the upper branches of the Allt an Dubh-loch at around 920m elevation. Then ascend the open north-easterly slopes towards the summit of Carn a' Choire Bhoidheach. The summit is featureless with a very small cairn which is likely to be buried in snow. On a clear day the views back down towards Creag an Dubh-loch are spectacular. Continue east-north-east across the plateau, avoiding the corniced cliff-tops of The Stuic above Loch nan Eun.

A line just west of the summer path is the best route to the top of Lochnagar via the large cairn of Cac Càrn Mòr and then the high rocky point of Cac Carn Beag. Be careful of the corniced edge and gullies of the main Lochnagar cliffs and the tops around the Pinnacle and Black Spout.

The steep descent from the summit of Cac Carn Beag heads north-west and should only be considered in good conditions. Take the best snow line heading broadly towards Sandy Loch and then onwards as the angle eases. Follow the line of Allt Lochan nan Eun towards the edge of the forest and Feindallacher Burn and enjoy magnificent views north to Beinn a' Bhuird and Ben Avon. It is best to cross the burn before the fenced forested area. Ultimately you should aim for the track and forest gate (NO 205 880), around 4.3km from the summit. Following the track can give a good run down into Ballochbuie Forest.

At the junction with another older road (NO 198 895), turn right to pass close to the Falls of Garbh Allt on your right, and another brae leads to a fork. The right track goes to the Balmoral stalker's house at Garbh Allt Shiel, and the left goes through old pine forest and past the beautiful hump-backed Old Bridge of Dee to the main road at Invercauld Bridge. From here is a classic view looking back to the Old Bridge and the pine forest leading up to the snowy tops of Càrn an t-Sagairt Mòr and the White Mounth. The pay and display car park is located near Keiloch sawmill on the north side of the A92.

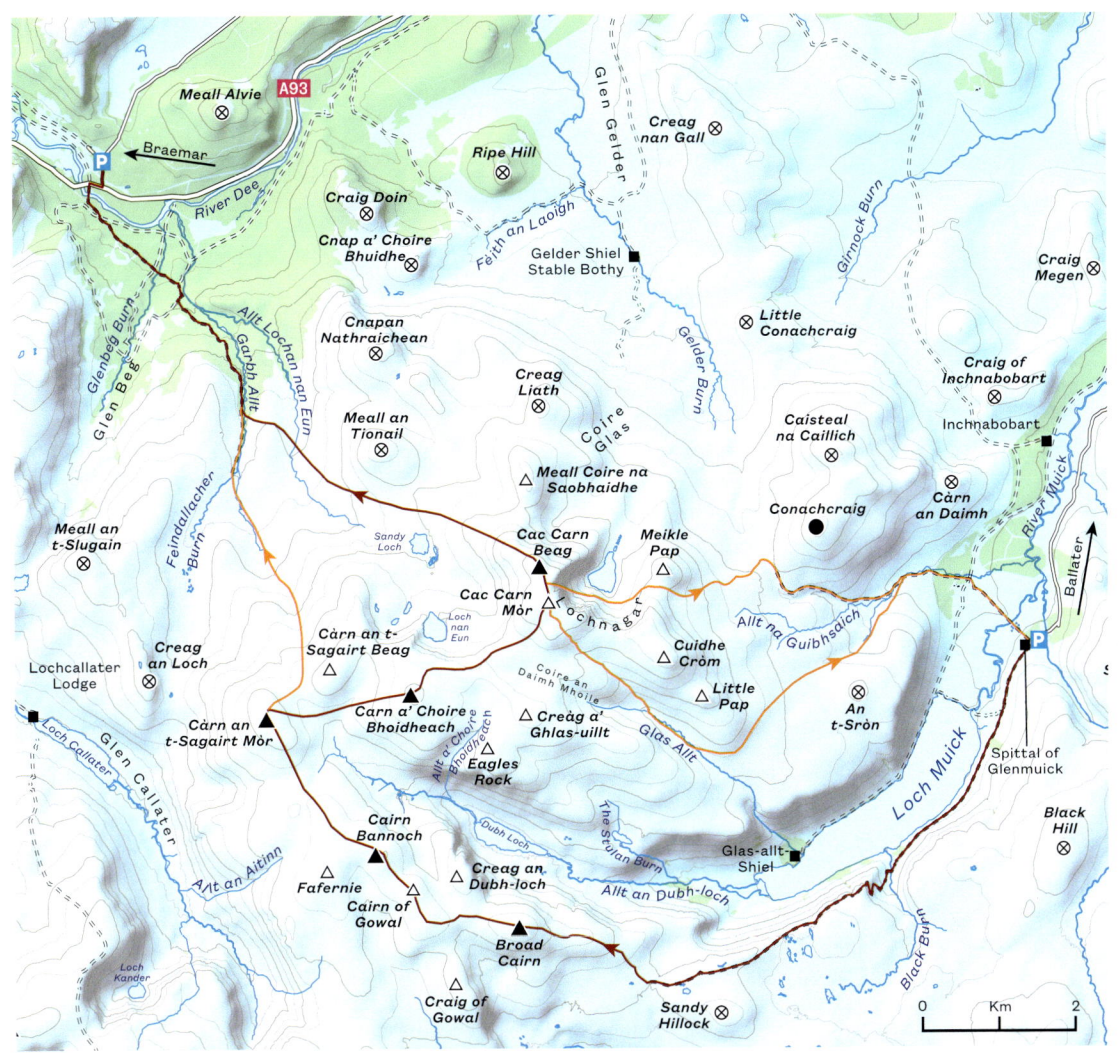

Left: The descent down the Allt a' Choire Dhuibh © Al Todd

Alternative descents:

- (22km and 920m of ascent) From the summit of Càrn an t-Sagairt Mòr, head north-north-east directly across to and down the Allt a' Choire Dhuibh. The slopes are wide and open, and offer good skiing late into the season. When that burn joins the Feindallacher Burn, cross to a footpath, which later passes an old pony shed (NO 204 873) and a wider track down into Ballochbuie Forest, passing the forest gate. The route then continues to complete the traverse to Invercauld Bridge and Keiloch car park.
- (27km and 1,220m of ascent) From the summit of Cac Carn Beag, retrace the route back in the direction of Cac Càrn Mòr then head generally south-south-east and descend towards the broad drainage of Coire an Daimh Mhoile and Glas Allt. After about 2.75km, as the slope begins

to open out, start contouring north-east around the lower slopes of Little Pap in the direction of An t-Sròn. Depending on snow conditions, an alternative higher traverse at around 850m is also possible. Stay west and north of An t-Sròn and follow the line of the small burn that descends to the Allt-na-giubhsaich. Continue descending the drainage, finding the best river crossing to meet the main Lochnagar ascent path. Once on the track return via the Allt-na-giubhsaich Lodge back to the Spittal of Glenmuick car park.

- If conditions are stable, the Black Spout offers a good steep ski descent, taking the obvious deep gully through the cliffs to the corrie. The top of the gully (NO 245 859) can be heavily corniced, particularly on the skier's right (looking down). The easiest access point is usually on the skier's left, where there may be a shallow runnel. The upper part of the gully funnels into a short, narrow, very steep section. This is the most difficult part of the descent, and it can be icy or even bare. The gully then opens out towards the junction with the left-hand branch. The lower section is wider and easier angled. Records indicate that the Black Spout was first skied from just below the cornice by Ashie Brebner in 1954.

Beyond the gully you can either stay high and traverse diagonally across the corrie, aiming for the cairn and mountain rescue box (NO 251 857), or descend directly to the loch. From the east side of the corrie continue eastwards, passing Meikle Pap to the south and onwards following the route of the main footpath and track to Allt-na-giubhsaich.

Right: Late season in the Black Spout (skier, Dave Anderson) © Doug Bryce

Mount Keen ▲ 939m

Monadh Caoin, Gentle Hill

△ NO 409 869 ◁ LR44 ⊕ P.192/193

Southern Approach

P Invermark at the end of the public road up Glen Esk (NO 444 804/56.9113, -2.9104).

↔ 18KM   △ 260M   ⊺ 680M
⏱ 5-6 HRS   GRADE II   ★★

Northern Approach

P Near Glen Tanar House (NO 474 956).

↔ 27KM   △ 180M   ⊺ 760M
⏱ 8-9HRS   GRADE II   ★★

By Adam Watson, updated by Stan Pearson

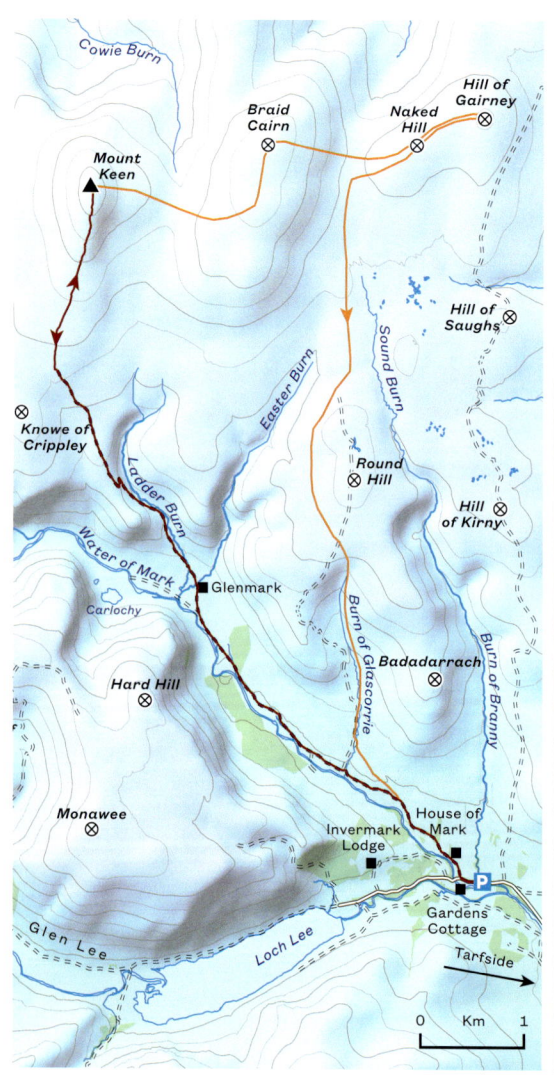

Appearing as a beautiful cone when seen from the north or south, Mount Keen stands out as a more distinctive hill than many higher tops in the Grampians. It is the most easterly of the 900m hills in Scotland and offers very fine views over the low country of Aberdeenshire, Kincardineshire and Angus. It benefits from snow-bearing easterly winds, even if the surrounding plateau does not hold the snow as long as the Cairngorm plateau to the west. The approach chosen may depend on whether you are coming from the south by Glen Esk or from the north along Deeside. A bike can be used for both approaches in less than full snow conditions. Nordic equipment is also an option.

The southern approach is the shortest and easiest, starting at Invermark in Glen Esk. Follow a private road up the north-east side of Glen Mark and reach Glenmark Cottage in 4km, with only 60m of ascent. This is a grand, wild glen with many broken crags and steep slopes above its broad floor. Beyond the cottage, follow the bulldozed track up the Ladder Burn, and then by zigzags onto the open slopes above. From there head straight for the large cairn and triangulation station on top of Mount Keen by the broad, gradually steepening ridge.

The return by the same route usually offers a good run, and it is better not to stray to the east or west as some of the slopes are steep, rocky and often corniced. An alternative return route avoids the steeper slopes of Ladder Burn by heading east over Braid Cairn (887m) and/or Hill of Gairney (756m). From Braid Cairn the best downhill ski option is to head south between Easter Burn and Burn of Brandy to Glas Coire and then take a steeper slope adjacent to the Burn of Glascorrie to the approach track.

A more interesting but much longer route is from Glen Tanar near Aboyne. Good snow cover down the glen is necessary; otherwise, you will have to carry skis a long way. A private road from a car park near Glen Tanar House goes through beautiful natural pine forest up the glen and onto open moorland towards the ruined Shiel of Glentanar. From a point east of the Shiel, a bulldozed track climbs south uphill to 530m, where you should strike off left to head south then south-east round the corrie of Corrach up the steady gradient to reach the rocky top of Mount Keen.

On the descent northwards be careful to avoid the steep, rocky corrie of Corrach, where cornices often build up. The broad ridge to its west gives a good, safe run down the ascent route to the glen and the shelter of its grand pine forest.

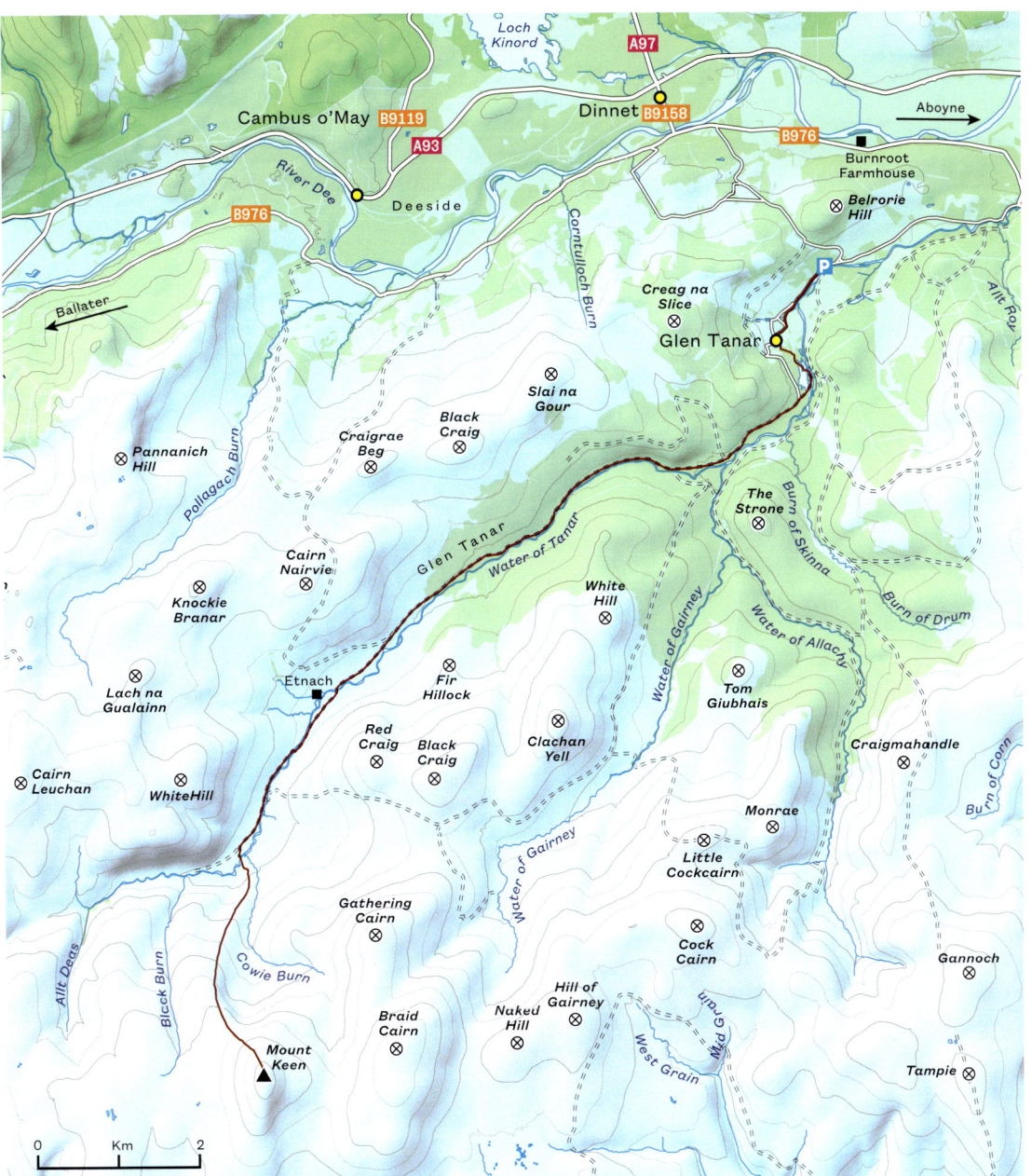

Morrone

● 859m

Big Nose

△ NO 132 886   ⟋ LR43   🌐 P.177

🅿 The duck pond in the village of Braemar (NO 143 910/ 57.0028, -3.4121).

↔ 8KM   △ 520M   ⊥ 375M
🕒 3-4 HRS   GRADE II   ✶✶

By Colwyn Jones

Morrone is a fine peak which can be easily skied from Braemar, giving a reasonable half-day ski trip. It guards the southern area of the village, which means that during the deep midwinter, the peak shades the village from any low sunshine. There are regular buses from Aberdeen to Braemar. The summit of Morrone overlooks Braemar and the adjacent valley of the River Dee. Raise your eyes and there are further views to the Cairngorms, which, on a clear winter's day, makes the ascent worthwhile.

Via Chapel Brae make your way on foot or skis (or drive) from the centre of the village to the large car park close to the duck pond (NO 143 910). From here follow the signposted footpath through the thriving Birkwood Community Woodland (this route may require a short walk). The waymarked path brings you onto the open north-facing hillside. Once clear of the trees the obvious path uphill is somewhat steep initially, but it continues more easily above 750m to the summit, which gives fine views. An assortment of communications towers and associated buildings ruin the summit aesthetics but typically afford some shelter while preparing for the descent, which simply follows the earlier ascent, or perhaps another line on the north flank that has caught your eye.

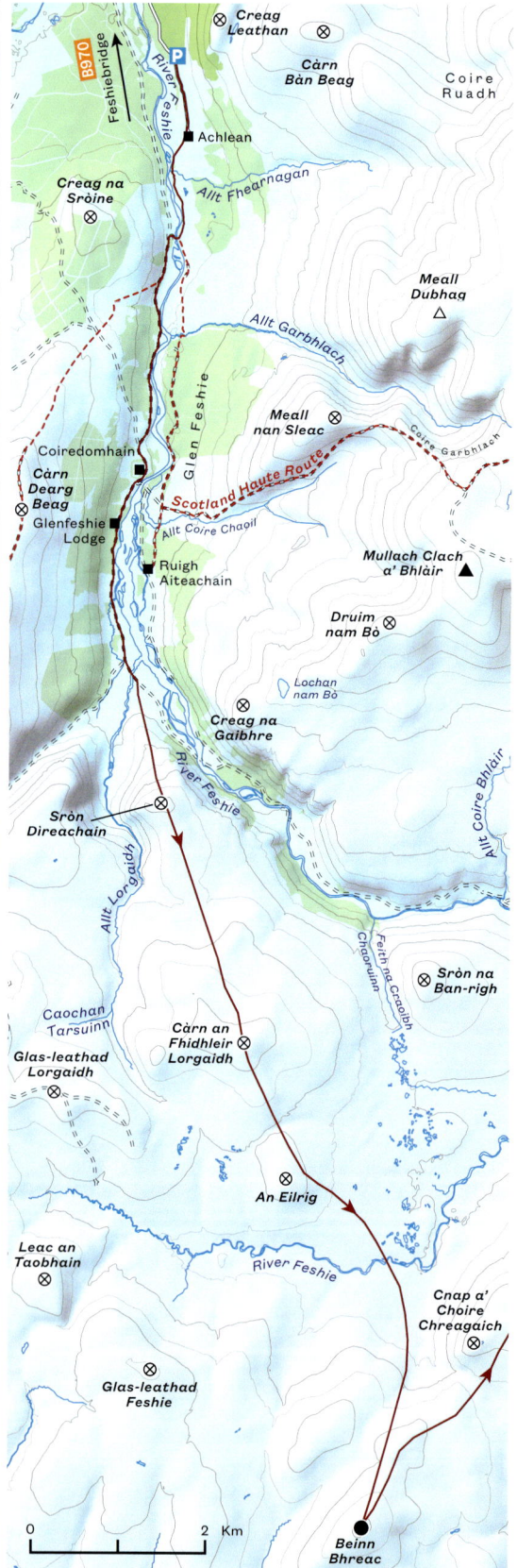

Ruigh Aiteachain High-Level Tour

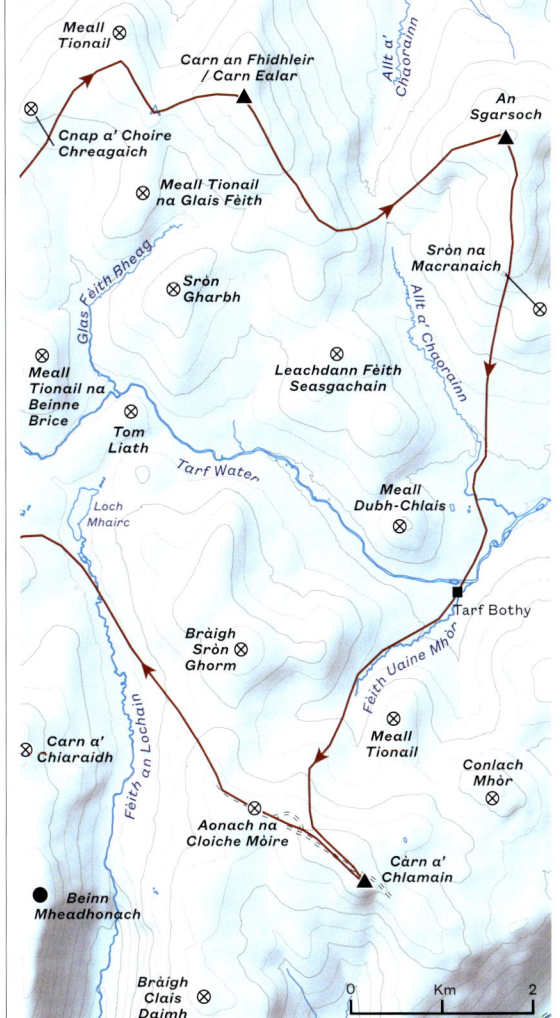

Beinn Bhreac ● 912m
Speckled Hill
- NN 868 820
- LR43
- P.194–196

Carn an Fhidhleir ▲ 994m
Fiddler's Hill
- NN 904 841
- LR43
- P.194–196

An Sgarsoch ▲ 1,006m
Place of Sharp Rocks
- NN 933 837
- LR43
- P.194–196

Càrn a' Chlamain ▲ 963m
Hill of the Kite
- NN 915 758
- LR43
- P.194–196

Beinn Dearg ▲ 1,008m
Red Hill
- NN 852 777
- LR43
- P.194–196

P Starting point: Glen Feshie at the end of the public road from Kincraig at Tolvah (NH 840 000/ 57.07686, -3.9150).

P Finishing point: Blair Atholl Railway Station.

↔ 55KM   △ 2,300M   ⏐ 350M
⏱ 2 DAYS   GRADE III   ★★★★

By Calum Anton

A two-day high-level ski mountaineering trek taking in a Corbett and four Munros, which could best be described as a winter meander through a core of central Grampian summits. It runs north to south in a highly indirect line for some 35 miles, and it was probably first undertaken as a complete ski mountaineering trek by Calum Anton and John Pottie over 17–18 March 1988. In good winter conditions it presents a tour of sheer solitude and never-ending wilderness, unsurpassed anywhere else in the country – a highly rewarding way of gathering some of the more remote and, dare it be said, dull Scottish hills!

Ruigh Aiteachain Bothy (NN 847 927) provides a cosy shelter for an early start but does not solve the problem of crossing the River Feshie to access the logical starting climb up Càrn an Fhidhleir Lorgaidh (via Sron Direachan 1:25,000 OS map) and easy access to good, skiable snows. There are fords, used by the estate, but your starting point onto the hill will depend in part on the height of the river. The start is at the end of the public road from Kincraig at Tolvah, which has some off-road

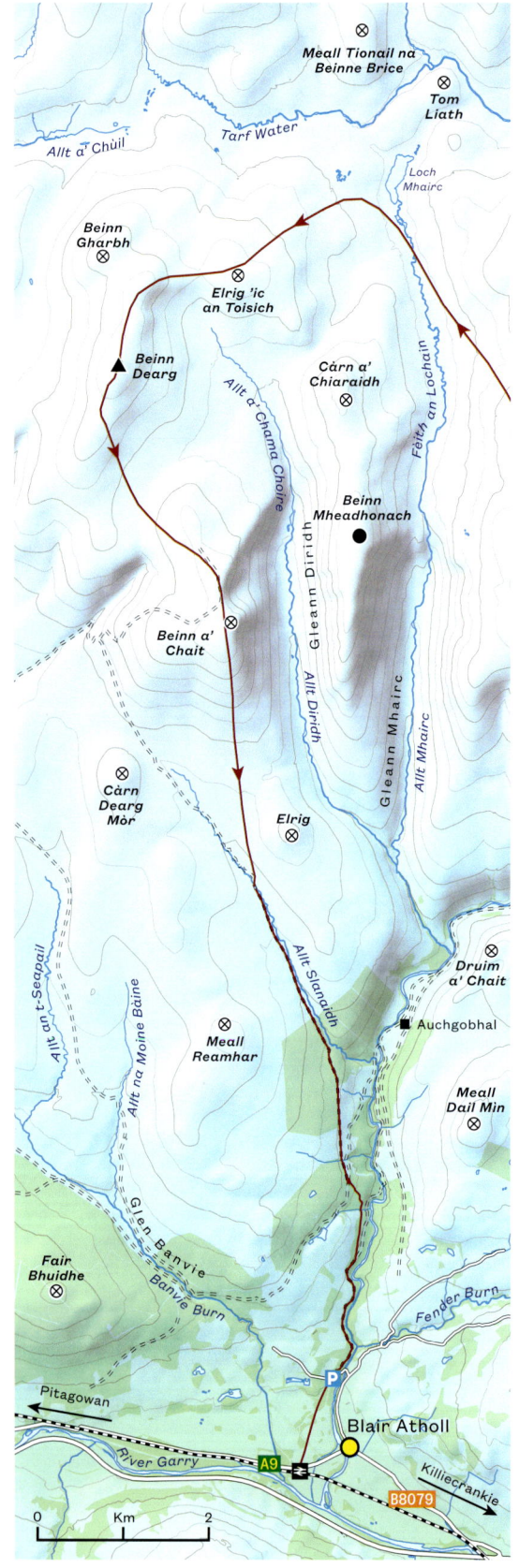

parking (NH 840 000). Follow the private tarmac road on the west bank of the river Feshie, passing Stronetoper, Carnachuin and Glen Feshie Lodge, now on a landrover track, to reach the junction next to a ruin marked on the OS map (NN 843 917). Ford the next stream and start skinning the 300 vertical metres up the north ridge to the summit of Sròn Dìreachain (1:25,000 OS map, 712m). From here it should be skis on all the way to Tarf Bothy, which is now in excellent condition.

Continue up the broad ridge onto Càrn an Fhidhleir Lorgaidh (Cairn of the Fiddler's Path; 849m). Here the space and vista open up, and hopefully it has a blanket of snow. Cross the upper Feshie before heading into the shallow Coire Creagach and onto the watershed around point 845m (NN 872 830). If taking in Beinn Bhreac it is a straightforward 1km south-west from this point.

Returning eastwards there is an easy stretch up onto Carn an Fhidhleir (994m), the meeting of the three counties of Highland, Perth and Aberdeen. All around you is space – to the north the Great Moss with the cliffs of Sgòran Dubh; to the east An Sgarsoch and the head-waters of the Dee with the mass of the Cairngorms; to the south and west rolling hills towards Perthshire.

Head south-east off the Fiddler's summit before descending and traversing down to the bealach below An Sgarsoch's west shoulder. A steady pull soon takes you onto the top (1,006m), named the Place of the Sharp Stones, of which few should be evident in good snow conditions. From here you can see the mass of Beinn a' Ghlo to the south, and the Cairngorms, including nearby Beinn Bhrotain, to the north.

A long run anywhere along the south ridge takes you down to the ruined shieling (NN 928 799) on the lower Allt a' Chaorainn, then across the flat to Tarf Bothy (NN 926 789).

This bothy, renovated in 1992, provides shelter, but a snowhole was used on the previous 1988 trip. Snowholing sounds like a lot of hard work when there is a bothy, but it has much going for it: a fine sense of self-reliance and a choice of terrain for your first run the next morning. By snowholing high on Càrn a' Chlamain at a bealach at the head of Coire Fèidh Uaine, you can enjoy a long uninterrupted run of nearly 4km down to Loch Mhairc the following morning. This bealach (NN 905 766) is the target, allowing a quick out-and-back visit to the summit of Càrn a' Chlamain (963m).

If your plan includes Beinn Dearg, ski down towards Loch Mhairc, then west onto Elrig 'ic an Toisich (885m) which leads directly up onto Beinn Dearg's north plateau top and 1km further south the summit triangulation station (1,008m). Snow conditions on this plateau can vary. It is covered in rough scree, which is fine if well covered, but it is prone to being stripped from the south-west. Once you ski south off the summit, ground conditions improve to give a good run down then across to the west face and summit of Beinn a' Chait (899m), which in turn offers a good descent down its front into the glen of Allt Stanaidh. The length of your walk back to Blair Atholl will, of course, depend on the snow cover extending down this glen.

An alternative descent off Beinn a' Chait could be down into the steep glen of the Allt Sheicheachan and down to the MBA bothy of the same name. However, this and other nearby gullies are known to be unpredictable, being of convex slopes and prone to wind slab accumulation, so please approach with care.

Finishing at Blair Atholl offers almost all you may now desire, including trains both north and south.

Below: Descent northwest from Beinn Bhrotain
© Al Todd

Monadh Mòr ▲ 1,113m
Big Hill

| △ NN 938 942 | ◁ LR43 | ⊕ P.198 |

Beinn Bhrotain ▲ 1,157m
Hill of Brotan

| △ NN 954 922 | ◁ LR43 | ⊕ P.198 |

P	Auchlean car park, Glen Feshie (NN 851 983/ 57.0632, -3.8970).
↔ 26KM	△ 910M	↕ 330M
⏱ 8-9 HRS	GRADE III	★★★

By Raymond Simpson, updated by Sarah Atkinson

This is a lengthy tour across the extensive plateau of the Mòine Mhòr, which often gives good skiing conditions early in the winter and holds snow better than the more exposed high tops. The minor road from Feshie Bridge does seem to get ploughed, although snow tyres and a shovel are advisable.

From the car park head south to the farm at Auchlean then follow the clearly signposted path east up through two gates through the forestry to Coire Fhearnagan and onto the plateau just south

Key
1. Monadh Mòr   P.197
2. Glen Feshie   P.200
3. Glenmore to Glen Feshie   P.203

of Càrn Bàn Mòr. The line of ascent is obvious, and the path often holds snow well. In lean years the Allt Fhearnagan or the Allt Meall Dubhag will provide a snowy corridor to the plateau long after the snow elsewhere in the corrie has disappeared.

From the flat shoulder of Càrn Bàn Mòr descend gentle slopes south-east to the Allt Sgairnich (NN 909 961) but leave this stream where it loses itself in the snow-covered knolls west of Loch nan Cnapan. Pass the lochan to the south and contour Tom Dubh to cross the Allt Luineag at NN 925 954. In lean conditions, it may be necessary to continue north-east to find a crossing. Follow the shallow burn line, crossing a flattening east of spot height 974m direct to any point on the long ridge of Monadh Mòr.

The route chosen will depend on the build-up of snow on the ridge or in the hollows of its west flank. The ridge itself is boulder-strewn, and if wind-blown may not have a good snow cover.

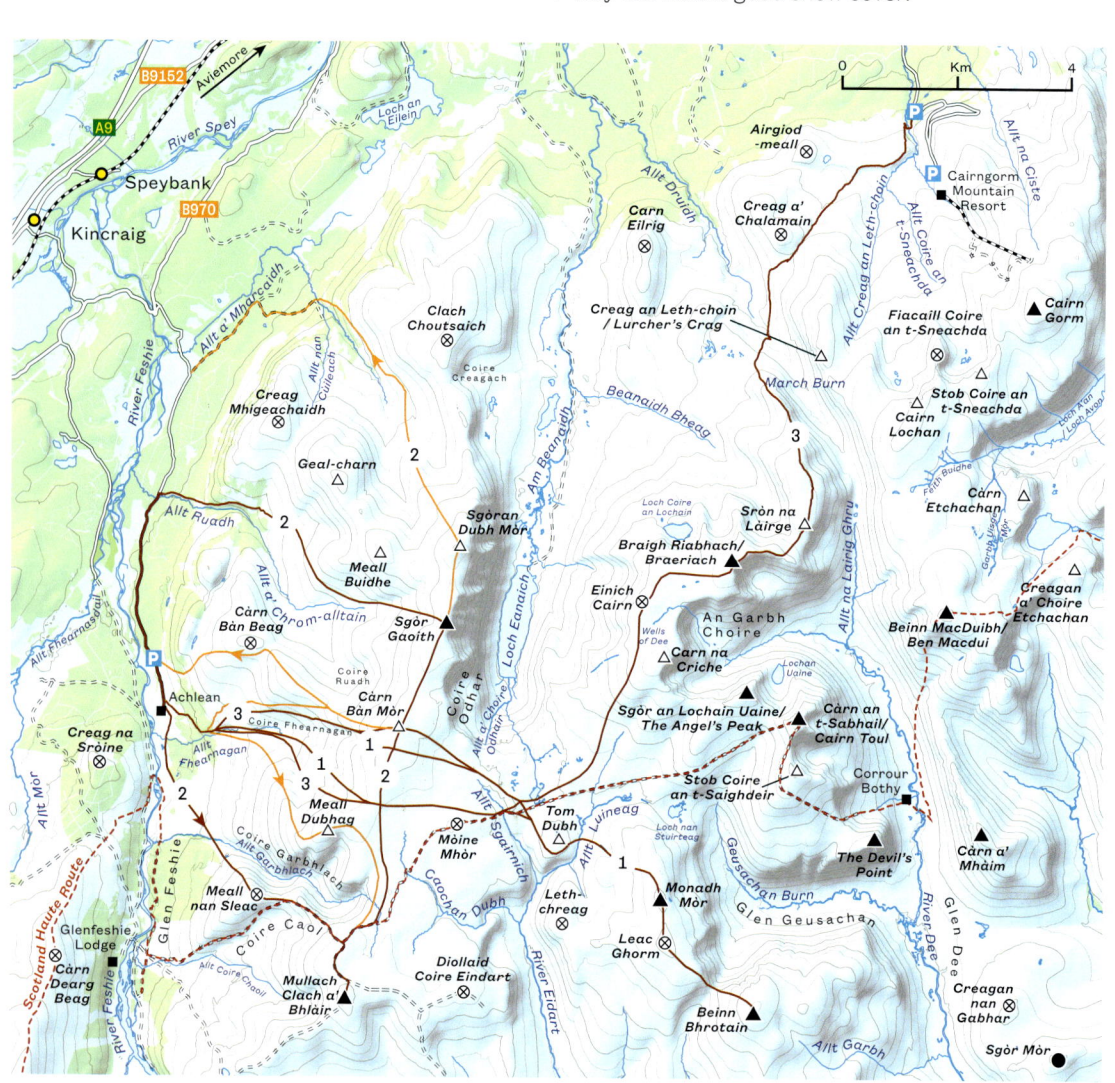

From the summit continue south for just over 1km to another cairn, then ski quite steeply south-east to a narrow col at the head of the spectacular Coire Cath nam Fionn. Care is required in bad visibility. Continue south-east for 1km, at first up a steep slope, then onto the flatter summit dome of Beinn Bhrotain with the triangulation station, where the bouldery nature of the hill makes good snow cover essential for good skiing.

The valley of the River Dee now lies before you, stretching away east to Lochnagar, and you may be tempted by the long run down to White Bridge. However, returning by the way you have come allows you to relish the vastness of the Mòine Mhòr plateau. From the top of Monadh Mòr the right choice of traverse and schuss should take you back to Loch nan Cnapan with minimal effort.

The easiest re-ascent from the lochan goes due west to the col between Meall Dubhag and Càrn Bàn Mòr whence the delightful gully of the Allt Meall Dubhaig, which holds snow well in spring, leads down to the Allt Fhearnagan. A steeper run may be had from the shoulder of Càrn Bàn Mòr into the funnel-shaped gully of the upper Allt Fhearnagan or down the convex slopes of Ciste Mhearad on its south side. Ski on down the Allt Fhearnagan for as far as there is snow; it is not unusual to be able to ski right down to the upper deer fence on a narrow ribbon of snow beside the burn.

Sgòr Mòr ● 813m
Big Peak

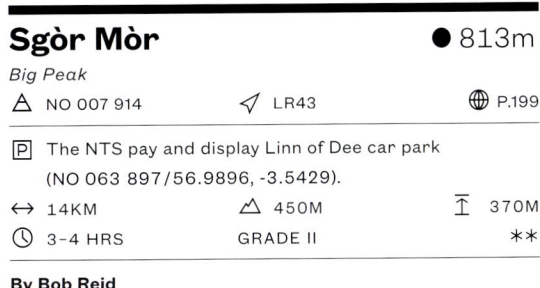

| △ NO 007 914 | ◁ LR43 | ⊕ P.199 |

| P | The NTS pay and display Linn of Dee car park (NO 063 897/56.9896, -3.5429). |

| ↔ 14KM | △ 450M | ⊤ 370M |
| ⏱ 3-4 HRS | GRADE II | ✱✱ |

By Bob Reid

Sgòr Mòr is the highest top of the hill extending westwards from Linn of Dee between Glen Lui and Glen Dee. It is more isolated from its grander Munro neighbours at the heart of the Cairngorm Massif than passers-by would suspect. Glen Lui (Gleann Laoigh) and the Allt Preas nam Meirleach (often used to approach the Lairig Ghru) define the northern aspects of the hill. It offers splendid views of peaks in all directions, with a good ski ascent and descent to boot. The descent slope is south-facing, so needs a good cover of snow over the heather.

From the car park, head west along the White Bridge track for 2km until open hillsides allow a straightforward ascent north following the line of the Allt nan Leum Easain. A gradual traverse north-west passing north of Càrn Mòr (634m) leads to the broad ridgeback of the hill. Head west and cross point 744m (NO 017 916), then continue west for 1km to the summit of Sgòr Mòr (6.5km; 450m ascent; 2.5hrs). Descent is by the same route.

If a traverse of the peak is preferred, then, after starting as above, continue along Glen Dee to White Bridge and take the footpath on the north bank of the Dee. After 2km, the footpath first diverges from the Dee to cross a burn. After crossing this head almost due north up the south ridge of Sgòr Mòr to the summit. Follow the same descent route east, but a diversion, with a short climb to the triangulation station on Sgòr Dubh (NO 034 922; 741m), can be added, with a possible descent through the trees closer to the Linn of Dee.

Carn na Drochaide ● 818m
Cairn of the Bridge

△ NO 127 938   ◁ LR43   ⊕ P.200

P The Linn of Quoich car park (NO 117 910/ 57.0017, -3.4554), at the end of the single-track road passing behind Mar Lodge.

↔ 8KM   △ 490M   ⊤ 329M
⏱ 3-4 HRS   GRADE II   ✱✱

By Colwyn Jones

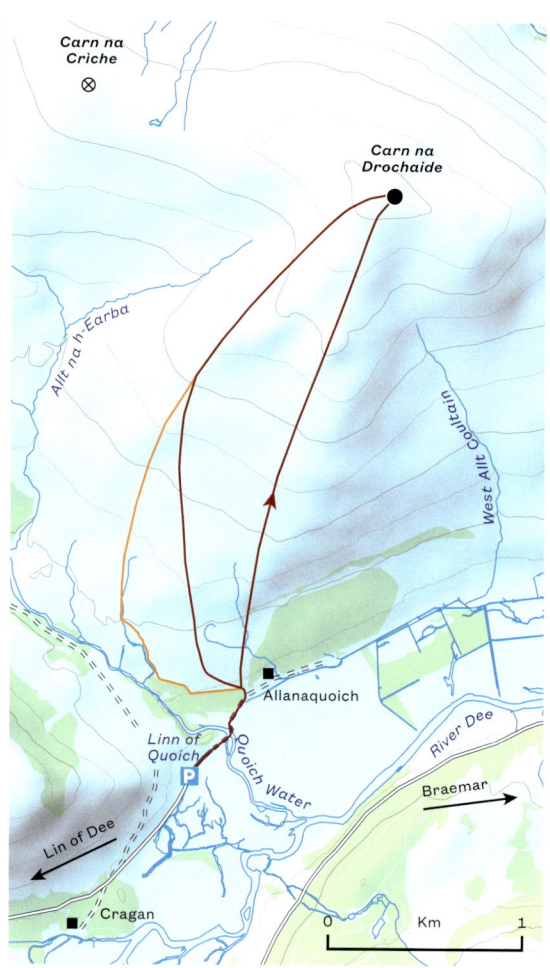

Carn na Drochaide is not a particularly conspicuous peak, but it provides an easy and pleasant half-day ski ascent a short drive from the village of Braemar. The summit is a splendid viewpoint with the southern aspect of the hill giving slopes running down to the level of the River Dee. The summit may be clear when higher hills nearby are in cloud.

Start from the busy Linn of Quoich car park next to the locked gate (parking charges apply). Ski or walk past the locked gate and cross the new alloy Bailey Bridge over Quoich Water to gain the north-east bank. Continue along the vehicle track right (east) to a junction just before a large white/cream house at a fenced enclosure called Allanaquoich. Follow the left branch back west for slightly over 100m to the open hillside. As this approach is south-facing, the slopes have deep heather, so good snow cover is needed for a continuous ski ascent. The south-west slope of the peak has a nice, regular contour pattern, and the even gradient makes it easy to maintain a comfortable rhythm while skinning. However, sometimes you will need to divert slightly to follow the best snow cover. It is usually possible to continue steadily up the south-west flank where the vegetation thins out to quickly reach the large flat summit marked with a large cairn. The lee of the cairn should provide some shelter, and there are several smaller cairns around the rim of the summit area.

The descent follows the best snow encountered on the way up, to shortly arrive back at Allanaquoich, from where some poling will be needed to return to the car park.

Glen Feshie

Mullach Clach a' Bhlàir ▲ 1,019m
Summit of the Stone Plateau

△ NN 882 927   ◁ LR35, LR36, LR43   ⊕ P.198

Sgòr Gaoith ▲ 1,118m
Windy Peak

△ NN 902 989   ◁ LR36, LR43   ⊕ P.198

P Auchlean car park, Glen Feshie (NN 851 983/57.0632, -3.8970).

↔ 24KM   △ 940M   ⊤ 330M
⏱ 8-9 HRS   GRADE III   ✱✱✱

By William Wallace, updated by Colwyn Jones

These hills, which lie on the east side of Glen Feshie, form the western boundary of the Mòine Mhòr (the great moss), a high plateau approximately 950m above sea level which holds snow well. They may be climbed individually from Glen Feshie but are best combined in a traverse which can be done in either direction. However, as the best descents are at the north end of the ridge, the route is described from south to north. The terrain is generally featureless, so accurate navigation is essential, especially in poor visibility.

The end of the public road on the east side of the river in Glen Feshie, 1km north of Auchlean Farm, is the starting point for Mullach Clach a' Bhlàir. Follow the road to the farm then a footpath south, through a deer fence alongside the remnant of old Caledonian pine forest. If there is good snow cover low down, the ascent of Mullach Clach a' Bhlàir can be made through a gap in the woods up the ridge on the south side of Coire Garbhlach, and this is the most direct route.

Ski south across the moor to reach the end of the forest where the Allt Garbhlach issues from the steep-sided corrie. Turn south-east and near the 400m contour cross the river, which may be difficult, or impossible, in spate. Ascend the hillside beyond, climbing parallel to the edge of the forestry plantation at first and then up the steep slopes above to Meall nan Sleac (800m). There is then a short descent to join a bulldozed track where it nears the edge of Coire Garbhlach. Continue up the bulldozed track onto the level plateau, then follow a bearing south for 1km to Mullach Clach a' Bhlàir.

If there is little or no snow on the lower slopes, or burns are in spate, an alternative waymarked footpath goes east from the pine wood up the south side of the Allt Fhearnagan (or along the burn if it is snow-filled) to the foot of Coire Gorm. Ascend this corrie, which usually holds snow well, south-south-east to the summit of Meall Dubhag (998m). The route to Mullach Clach a' Bhlàir is then south-east for 1.5km round the head of Coire Garbhlach, then south-south-west for 2km to the summit.

From the summit there is an easy schuss north-north-east to the stream which flows into Coire Garbhlach. This is followed by a short climb to point 953m and another gentle descent to a wide open stretch of plateau which drains south-east to the River Eidart. The summit of Càrn Bàn Mòr (1,052m) is 2km north and is reached by a long gradual ascent. The top is towards the north end of the flat summit, but in deep snow or mist it may be difficult to find any cairn. If the weather has deteriorated, an early return can be made west from here and includes fences to give a direct descent to the car park, but it is only advised if there is adequate snow cover at the car park level.

Below: Sgòr Gaoith – skinning out from Allt a' Chrom-alltain © Al Todd

The descent to the next col on a bearing north-north-east is only 400m, followed by an ascent of 1km in the same direction along a broad, featureless ridge to Sgòr Gaoith, the highest point of the traverse. Although the summit has no cairn, it is an unmistakable sharp promontory on the edge of the cliffs above Loch Eanaich.

The ski run from the summit will depend on where the snow has drifted in the corries to its west. The most direct descent is down the Coire Gorm a' Chrom-alltain. If you choose the south side of the Allt a' Chrom-alltain, do not ski down to its confluence with the Allt Ruadh, but cross at about the 600m contour and traverse north-west round the foot of Meall Tionail to woods below. Continue north-west along the line of a path into the pine wood and cross a small stream to reach a rough track. Follow this down above the north bank of the Allt Ruadh (1:25,000 OS map) to the road in Glen Feshie, 4km north of Auchlean.

An alternative route down from Sgòr Gaoith goes north along the broad ridge, possibly as far as Sgòran Dubh Mòr (1,111m), and then north-west to the headwaters of the Allt a' Mharcaidh. There is often a very fine run down the corrie between Sgòran Dubh Mòr and Geal-charn. Ski down the slopes on the west side of the Allt a' Mharcaidh, and when you approach the forest bear left and follow a deer fence down to a crossing of the Allt nan Cuileach. On the other side of this stream, at the top of a forest track, continue steeply down it to join a wider forest road. This leads west, and in a further 2.5km the public road in Glen Feshie is reached near Blackmill, 5km north of Auchlean.

Below: Sgòr Gaoith
© Stuart Buchanan

Glenmore Feshie Traverse

Braeriach ▲ 1,296m
Brindled Upland
△ NN 953 999   LR36, LR43   P.198

Einich Cairn ⊗ 1,237m
Fiddler's Hill
△ NN 936 992   LR36, LR43   P.198

Càrn Bàn Mòr △ 1,052m
Big Fair Hill
△ NN 893 971   LR36, LR43   P.198

P Starting point: The Sugar Bowl car park (NH 985 074/ 57.1463, -3.6791). Please note that this car park is pay and display. The car park can also be accessed by public transport. Buses run from the centre of Aviemore.

↔ 23KM   △ 1,320M   ↕ 450M
⏱ 8 HRS (approx)   GRADE III   ★★★★

By Heather Morning

This journey, crossing the high plateau of the Braeriach massif, is one of the best in Scotland, and for a fit, strong team with good navigation skills, it will be a lifelong memorable experience. Good weather is needed as the approach to Braeriach requires detailed navigation close to heavily-corniced corrie rims. Most of the traverse has little threat of avalanche danger; the steepest slopes encountered are during the ascent of the Sròn na Lairige, which tends to be wind-scoured. The traverse also entails some logistical issues as a vehicle needs to be left at the end of the journey at the Auchlean car park near the end of the road on the east side of Glen Feshie. There is no public transport on this road and very little traffic for hitchhiking.

Leave the Sugar Bowl car park, cross the main ski road and take the trail through the trees down to the footbridge (NH 984 071). Continue along the trail for a further 3km into the Chalamain Gap (NH 965 052; 710m). Conditions on this first section are unreliable, and it is doubtful that you will be able to ski through the woodland down to the burn crossing and the traverse along the edge of the moraine. Skis can normally be put on around the burn crossing area at NH 973 062. On a good day the view along this first section across to the Northern Corries is superb. The Chalamain Gap itself is a glacial overflow channel; the floor of the 'Gap' is lined with huge boulders and good snow cover is required to make this skiable. This was also the site of the tragic avalanche in the winter of 2013, when three people died. The avalanche was triggered by a person on the south-east flank of the Gap, and the debris buried the people below – a classic 'terrain trap'.

It is well worth taking your skins off for the 130m descent into the Lairig Ghru (NH 958 037; 600m). The Sinclair Hut, built in 1957 and demolished in 1991, was located on the moraine above this notch. A brass plaque commemorating Angus Sinclair is located on one of the large boulders in the gully. It is well worth refuelling with food and drink here, as the gully will provide the last shelter for a good few hours.

Put skins on again for the long ascent onto Sròn na Lairige. Head 700m south-west for the notch at (NH 956 032) before turning south-south-east for 2.3km to gain the north summit of Sròn na Lairige (NH 963 011; 1,180m) with a height gain of 610m. Caution should be exercised hand-railing the eastern edge of this ridge in poor visibility as large cornices regularly form and last the whole season. Continue south for 500m on flat terrain to the south top of Sròn na Lairige (NH 964 006; 1,184m). It is worth noting that both the north and south top cairns are fairly small and will be buried in some snow conditions. This area is also rocky and may be fairly scoured. A short descent south-southwest leads to the broad bealach at NH 963 002, altitude 1,145m.

Travel 400m south-west to join the main ridge of Braeriach at a small col (NN 961 999 – note the change in prefix of grid references) at 1,195m. Take care here not to overshoot in poor visibility; the corrie rims will likely be corniced. During this ascent, look out for aircraft wreckage from the Bristol Blenheim which crashed in 1945. Most of the wreckage (including propellers) is lower down on the slopes above the Lairig Ghru, but some is visible on this section of the mountain.

The final ascent to the summit of Braeriach can be tricky and serious in poor visibility. The distance to the summit cairn of Braeriach is approximately 900m, bearing west then south-west. Bearings MUST be accurate. The summit cairn (NN 953 999; 1,296m) is small, sometimes obscured by snow and close to the edge. In some snow conditions this section can form a very narrow arête with large cornices to the south and steep ground to the north. In icy conditions it may be advisable to remove skis and put on boot crampons.

The route now takes you across the featureless arctic-alpine plateau of Braeriach. In good visibility, this area is a pure joy to travel over; in poor visibility, accurate navigation remains essential. Head west-south-west for 1.8km, descending 80m then rising 20m onto the summit of Einich Cairn (NN 936 992; 1,237m). There is a cairn at the summit, but there are also other significant cairns in the vicinity that cause confusion. Now head 650m south to the broad bealach (NN 936 986; 1,227m). From here you can enjoy one of the best descents in Scotland down onto the Mòine Mhòr. This is a large expanse of montane heath, undulated with moraines and peppered with small lochans in the summer months. All water features are likely to be frozen and buried, making travel over the area very straightforward.

Pick your line south-west for a 3.2km, 330m descent to Loch nan Cnapan (NN 917 960). The loch is likely to be frozen and skiable, and only identifiable as a large, flat area. The final ascent onto Càrn Bàn Mòr (NN 893 971; 1,052m) is very gradual, heading north-west for 2.6km following the line of the Allt Sgairnich, which holds snow late into the season. The upper reach of this burn line is also a popular snowhole site (NN 898 968), which may afford some shelter in bad weather. The summit cairn is again small and may be buried.

It's all downhill now into Glen Feshie and the road head at Auchlean (NN 851 983). Choose your line (it may well be worth checking it out from the road head when you drop the car off at the start of the day). The three north-west gully lines of the Allt Fhearnagan are locally known as 'Tom, Dick and Harry'; all make great descents, as does the main footpath in good snow cover. Another alternative is to take in Meall Dubhag (NN 880 955) and ski down the north ridge. Descent via any of these lines is unlikely to get you to the roadhead on skis. If the snow-line is high, it may be advisable to carry a light pair of trainers to change into for the remainder of the descent down the main track into the glen and the 1km walk along the tarmac back to your car.

The traverse from Glenmore to Glen Feshie is a committing journey; however, the trip can be shortened at various stages of the route. Descent from Sròn na Lairge can be made northwards down Coire Beanaidh or Coire Gorm. Another great descent from the Braeriach plateau can be made down the west flank of Coire an Lochain. However, this would put you down in Gleann Eanaich with a potentially long walk out. The burn lines running north-west down into Gleann Eanaich west of Loch Coire an Lochain make great ski descents and hold snow late in the season. These lines are locally known as 'The Escalator'. All these routes are steep enough to avalanche, so an assessment of the snow conditions should be made prior to committing to descent. It is not recommended to retreat into the head of Coire Dhondail (NN 926 978; 1,010m), where the stalkers' track is marked on the map, as this corrie's headwall is very steep and a notorious avalanche black spot.

Above: Ascent of Sròn na Lairige (skier, Heather Morning) © Duncan Gray

North-East Scotland

Chapter 6

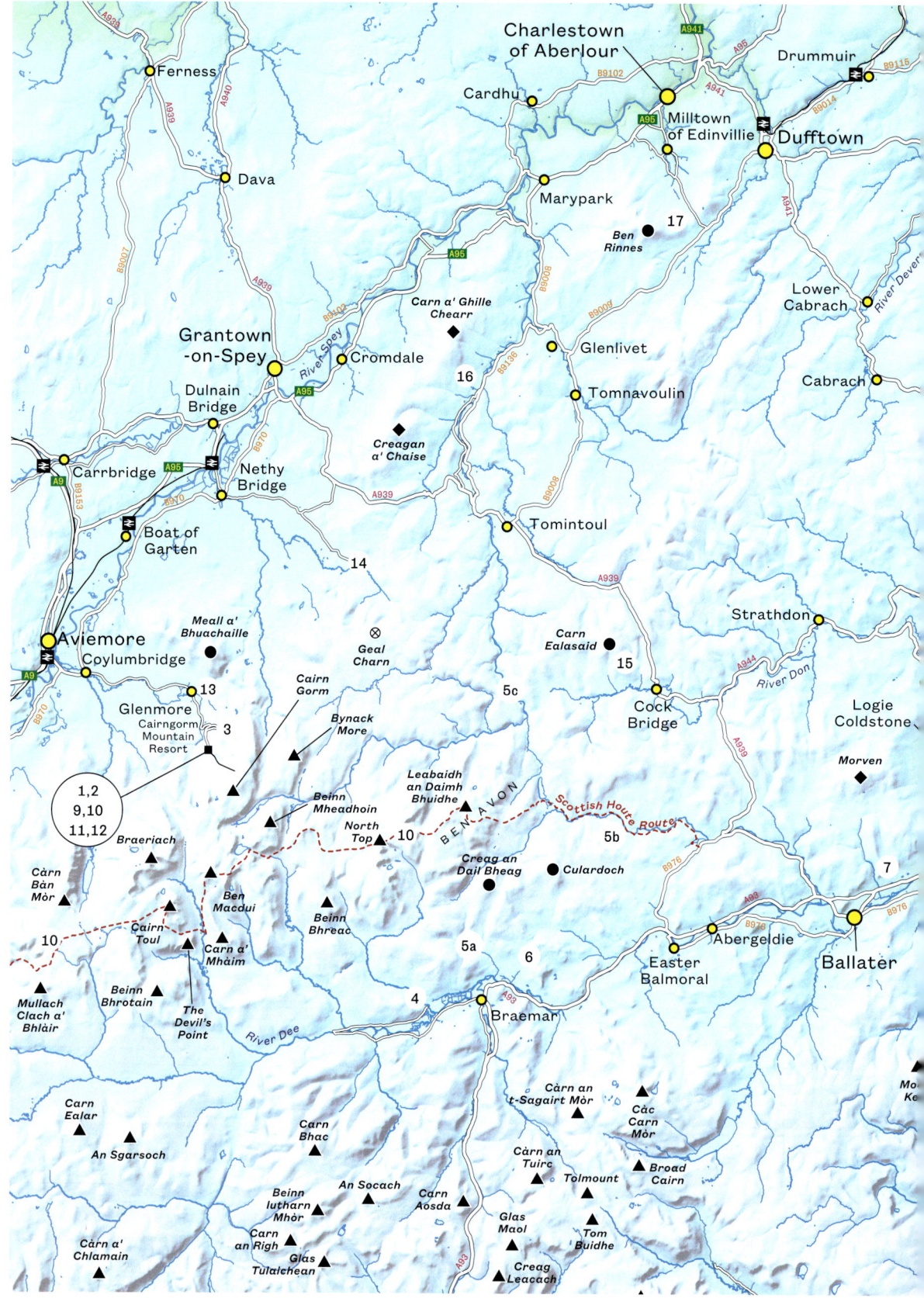

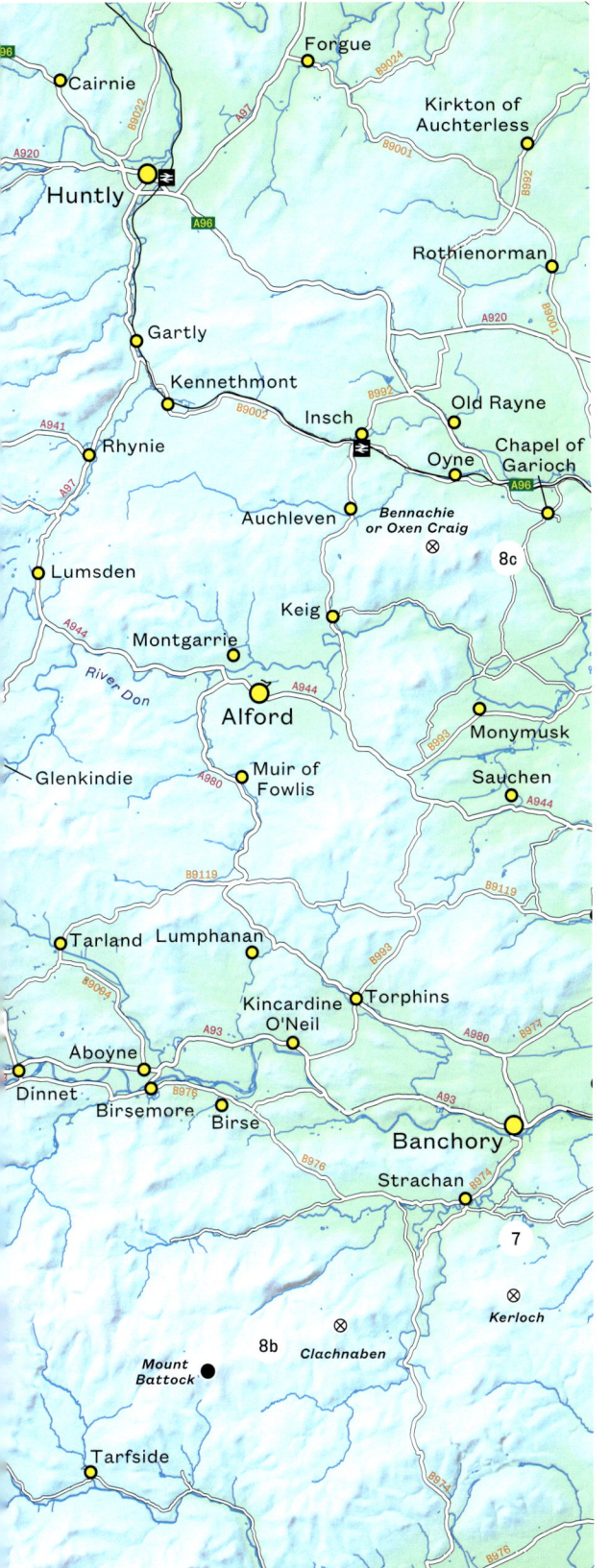

1.	Ben Macdui and Loch Avon circuit	P.211
2.	Beinn Mheadhoin	P.213
3.	Beinn a' Chaorainn	P.215
4.	Beinn a' Bhùird	P.217
5.	Ben Avon	P.219
6.	Culardoch	P.222
7.	Morven	P.224
8.	Lower Dee and Don Hills	P.226
9.	Round of the Northern Corries of Cairn Gorm	P.229
10.	The Cairngorns 5 and 8 tops	P.234
11.	Bynack More	P.238
12.	Creag Mhòr	P.239
13.	Meall a' Bhuachaille	P.240
14.	Geal Charn (Dorback)	P.241
15.	Carn Ealasaid	P.243
16.	Cromdale Hills	P.244
17.	Ben Rinnes	P.248

Chapter 6 — North-East Scotland

Previous spread: On the rim of Coire an Lochain, Northern Corries with the Cairn Gorm summit behind (skiers, Alasdair Stark, Fiona Stark and Angus Todd) © Al Todd

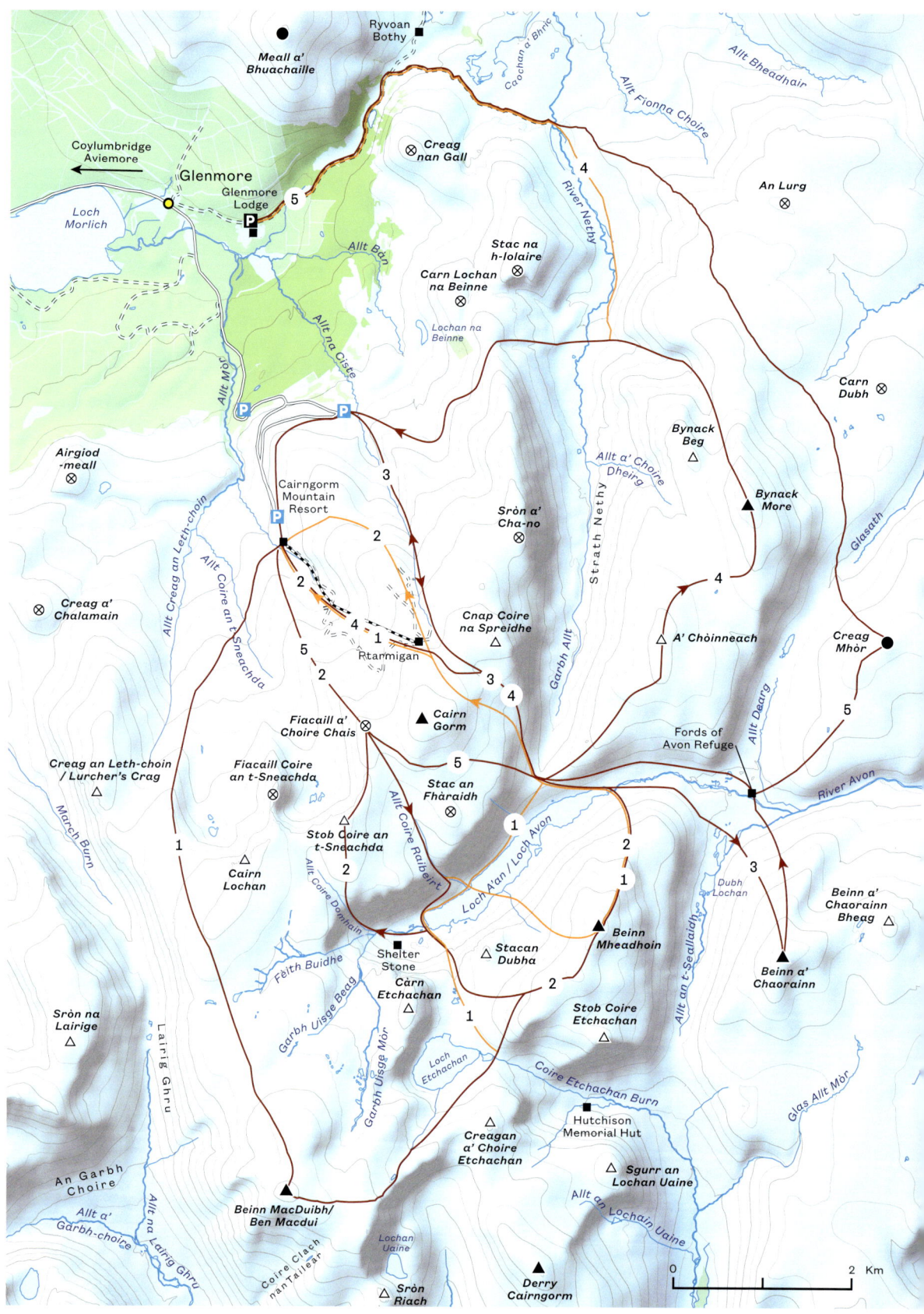

The Ben Macdui Loch Avon Circuit

Ben Macdui ▲ 1,309m
MacDuff's Hill
△ NN 989 989   LR36, LR43   P.210

Beinn Mheadhoin ▲ 1,182m
Middle Hill
△ NJ 024 016   LR36   P.210

P Coire Cas ski car park (NH 989 060/57.1346, -3.6713). Parking charges apply, although parking over the winter may be free. Parking spaces are on a first come first served basis so consider arriving early. www.cairngormmountain.co.uk/parking-at-cairngorm There are regular buses from Aviemore and Glenmore to the ski car parks.

↔ 19KM   △ 1,430M   ↕ 630M
⏱ 6-7 HRS   GRADE III   ***

By Heather Morning

Ben Macdui is the second-highest mountain in the UK and is located in the heart of the Cairngorm plateau. The often featureless plateau is a vast area of rolling arctic tundra, home to ptarmigan, snow buntings and mountain hares. During an average winter it is snow-covered from December through until May, so conditions for ski touring are almost guaranteed. However, wind speeds are often in excess of 40mph, and sometimes vastly exceed this. With limited visibility navigation here is without doubt challenging – choose your day carefully!

From the Coire Cas car park traverse to Lurcher's Gully (NH 976 042; 750m). Cross the lower slopes of the Northern Corries and the burns from Sneachda and Lochain. Later in the season or in poor snow, take a lower route than the normal walkers' track to spot height 1,083m (NH 975 024). This is the same as described in the classic 'Round of the Northern Corries of Cairn Gorm' (p.229).. From the spot height head east-south-east for 1.5km to NH 982 010 at the west end of Lochan Buidhe (1,130m). This line will take you up and over the south-west flank of Cairn Lochan, with a short descent to Lochan Buidhe. Note that steep ground drops away

Key
1. Ben Macdui   P.211
2. Beinn Mheadhoin   P.213
3. Beinn a' Chaorainn P.215
4. Bynack More   P.238
5. Creag Mhòr   P.239

to your right into the Lairig Ghru; care should be taken to avoid this. It is also worth noting that the two lochans shown on the map here will not be visible, but you will see a broad, flat bealach before the ground starts to rise again towards Ben Macdui.

This is a good point on your journey to assess conditions. If they are not favourable, then an option is to head north-east and back towards the car park. Continue east-south-east for 1.1km to NH 985 000 (altitude 1,170m). This point marks the start of the ascent onto the north top of Ben Macdui (1,295m). The north top is normally bypassed by taking a line to the bealach between the north top and the main summit. The bealach is reached by heading east-south-east for 900m to NN 990 992 (1,280m). Do note the change in prefix on the grid reference. The final short leg 300m south-south-west takes you to the summit of Ben Macdui (NN 989 989; 1,309m).

The views are superb looking west over the Cairn Toul–Braeriach plateau with numerous glaciated corries that are often heavily corniced. The summit is clearly marked with a triangulation station perched on top of a huge 5m-diameter cairn. In deep snow the cairn has been known to be buried. There are also many wee howffs near the summit built variously by sappers for the 1847 OS mapping of the peak or military training during the Second World War. The lee of the summit cairn is a good place to refuel, remove skins and assess the journey ahead, taking into account the weather, snow conditions and fitness of the group. Options include a return via your approach route or the Northern Corries route. From here you are committed to completing the journey, which continues through serious and remote terrain.

Leave the summit of Ben Macdui and descend 900m east-south-east to NN 998 988 (1,220m), where the burn line starts (the burn will not be visible, but the depression may be). **Be careful not to overshoot here** as you are approaching the corniced edge of Coire Sputan Dearg. Continue in a north-easterly direction for 2km to the eastern end of Loch Etchachan (NJ 012 003). This is a superb descent on a gradient never exceeding 20 degrees. The loch is generally frozen for several months over the winter and holds ice well into April.

An option from here, avoiding the ascent of Beinn Mheadhoin, is to head north-north-west and drop down the burn line to Loch Avon. Cross onto the north-west bank and continue to The Saddle (NJ 018 033; 807m). Please note that this burn line can form an angle of slope steep enough to avalanche. For those continuing onto the stunning top of Beinn Mheadhoin, take a north-easterly line for 1km up to the first of the tors gracing the

summit ridge of Beinn Mheadhoin (NJ 018 011; 1,163m). With good visibility the summit ridge and tors can be enjoyed as you head initially east then north-east for a total of 900m before reaching the main summit, which is a big granite tor. You will need to take your skis off to climb to the true summit (NJ 024 016; 1,182m).

There are a couple of descent lines to choose from. A steeper option is to descend directly down the north-west aspect from the summit. Care should be taken here to assess the avalanche risk. An easier-angled alternative takes the shallow corrie on the north aspect of the mountain towards the crag of Creag Dhubh. Here the prudent skier will bear east to avoid the crag and steeper ground, and pick a fine line down to the outflow of Loch Avon. (Avalanche risk should be assessed on the lower section above Loch Avon.) The descent off Beinn Mheadhoin is superb, providing 1.7km and 450m of descent in a stunning environment. Often Loch Avon will be frozen; however, the outflow is likely to still be flowing. Either cross the frozen loch (after a risk assessment) or tiptoe across the stepping stones at the outflow. It is worth taking a well-earned rest and refuelling here to admire your tracks and prepare for the big ascent back into the ski area.

Head west-north-west for 700m to The Saddle (NJ 018 033). This slope has a southerly aspect

Above: Skiing a frozen Loch Avon with the Shelterstone beyond (skier, Laura Martin) © Duncan Gray

and fairly low elevation and therefore does not hold the snow well, but there is an established footpath. Large boulders are interspersed with deep heather, providing an entertaining start to the ascent! Conditions above The Saddle should improve underfoot, and an easy skinning line can be taken in a general north-westerly direction for 1.5km to Ciste Mhearad (NJ 011 046; 1,100m), a small corrie (not named on the 1:50k map) which forms impressive banks of snow. There are guaranteed snowholing conditions here throughout the winter, and due to its proximity to the ski area it is very popular. It is likely you will find shelter here, but the lure of a well-earned brew or pint at the Ptarmigan Restaurant might take precedence. A further 300m in a westerly direction will take you to the top of the Ptarmigan ski tow (NJ 008 046). Skins off from here and, if descending 'outwith' the normal ski operational hours, check if there are winch cats operating on the M1 and White Lady pistes. If it is safe to do so, pick a line back down the piste to the car park.

Castlegates Gully

By Colwyn Jones (see Ski Meet Report in the *SMCJ*, vol.40, no.200, pp.526–29, 2000)

Castlegates Gully has been described as 'a cavernous and atmospheric gully separating Càrn Etchachan and the Shelter Stone Crag', but it remains a skiable option during this tour. It holds snow well, is popular and descends for almost 300m towards Loch Avon.

To reach the top of the gully, after leaving the summit of Ben Macdui and after the first 900m of descent at the line of the burn (NN 998 988; 1,220m), either go north along the county boundary line down the broad ridge to reach the summit of Càrn Etchachan (1,120m) or follow the line of the Garbh Uisge Mòr to the 1,050m contour. The top of the gully is 350m north-north-east. Good visibility will help this precise navigation and is also essential to allow you to inspect the gully.

Boulders at the top can be stripped bare, and a short downclimb to the snow may be required. If snow-covered, these boulders can hold 'a peculiar twin-buttressed cornice formed by the wind', which typically allows a safe and moderate entry to the steep gully. Once past the initial narrow 10m, the gradient eases until the gully opens out and the angle increases a little. The exit is through a narrowing in the gully to the wide slope below. From here a boulder-covered traverse east below 800m will return you to the Beinn Mheadhoin track.

An alternative descent to the NW takes you to the entrance to the Shelterstone. Head back to the Cairngorm ski area by the Allt Coire Domhain or the Allt Coire Raiebeirt, being careful of the snow conditions since both routes have been known to avalanche.

Beinn Mheadhoin ▲ 1,182m
Middle Hill

△ NJ 024 016   ◁ LR36   P.210

🅿 Coire Cas ski car park (NH 989 060/57.1346, -3.6713). Parking charges apply, although parking over the winter may be free. Parking spaces are on a first come first served basis so consider arriving early. www.cairngormmountain.co.uk/parking-at-cairngorm There are regular buses from Aviemore and Glenmore to the ski car parks.

↔ 15KM	△ 1,390M	⊺ 630M
⏱ 7-8 HRS	GRADE IIII	****

By Bill Brooker, updated by Colwyn Jones

The start to this tour can be made easier using a 'snowsports touring ticket' purchased from the ticket office at Cairngorm Mountain (£20 in 2024/25), giving access to the Ptarmigan building (NJ 004 049; 1,070m) via two surface tows.

Although less than 6km from the Coire Cas car park on Cairn Gorm, Beinn Mheadhoin is far less accessible than it might appear at first sight, for it is surrounded by deep glens, corries, crags and lochs. The ascent of this Munro takes you into one of the wildest and grandest parts of the Cairngorms National Park and gives an excellent expedition on skis.

From the car park skin up west of all the ski tows and runs, following the Fiacaill a' Choire Chais ridge to its top at point 1,141 m (from the Ptarmigan building the simplest way to this point is over the summit of Cairn Gorm). Continue south-south-east, skiing easily at first, then, if safe, more steeply down Coire Raibeirt to the shore of Loch Avon. The best line on the steep lower section of the corrie is usually on the right (west) side of the burn.

Even if Loch Avon appears frozen, follow the shore south-west and cross the headstream at the lowest safe point. Thread hummocky terrain east below the great cliffs of the Shelter Stone Crag and Càrn Etchachan and turn south up the Allt nan Stacan Dubha (1:25,000 map) towards the Loch Etchachan col. Make sure the snow is safe to ascend. Near the col strike east then north-east up the broad ridge to Point 1,163m and continue along the upper plateau with its granite tors or barns to the summit. Take your skis off to scramble up to the true summit.

Following the ascent route is a fine way back to the lochside and avoids potential problems crossing the eastern outflow of Loch Avon. From the lochside the Coire Domhain footpath can be used for return, especially if there is a skinning track already in place. But an excellent descent run of 450m goes north-north-east off the summit down a wide snow basin. When it steepens at the outcrops of Creag Dhubh, either keep to the right of the rocks or ski down the line of a little stream that penetrates them. Check snow conditions before using this route. A steep run leads down to the foot of Loch Avon, crossing the River Avon near the outlet.

From the foot of Loch Avon climb west for 80m to The Saddle, then north-west much more steeply for 330m. The gradient of this ascent eases halfway up, and you will reach the col between Cnap Coire na Spreidhe and Cairn Gorm. The pistes are a short distance west, and a 600m run down them, perhaps along the Sròn an Aonaich ridge, leads back to the car park.

Diagonal Gully is a wide skiable couloir which holds snow well and descends for almost 300m – unsurprisingly diagonally – towards Loch Avon through the top of the crag called Stag Rocks (1:25,000 map). The top is accessible from both Point 1,141m and high in Coire Raibeirt and, if in condition, can be included in this tour. Diagonal Gully is steep at the top, and an easier entry is usually possible on the right (west) looking down. The gully often has good snow, and being located backcountry to the Cairngorm ski area is popular as a result. If the head of Loch Avon is visible when looking down the gully, then you are likely to be both at the top of Diagonal Gully and enjoying clear weather!

Right: Diagonal Gully (boarder, Robert Thomson) © Nadir Khan

Beinn a' Chaorainn ▲ 1,082m
Hill of the Rowan

| ⛺ NJ 045 013 | 🧭 LR36, LR43 | 🌐 P.210 |

🅿️ Coire na Ciste car park (NH 999 075/57.1466, -3.6593). An alternative start from the upper ski car park (630m) using two ski tows avoids about 500m of ascent. There are regular buses from Aviemore and Glenmore to the ski car parks.

| ↔ 20KM | △ 1,430M | ⫯ 550M |
| 🕐 8-9 HRS | GRADE III | ★★★ |

By Brian Shackleton and Colwyn Jones

This is a long ski tour, best done in late March or April when there are longer daylight hours and when snow conditions can be more reliable and predictable. The tour should not be attempted during or immediately after periods of thaw since crossing the River Avon will not be safe with the river in spate and snow bridges in a weakened condition. Although Beinn a' Chaorainn and its neighbour, Beinn Bhreac, may both be approached from the south from Glen Lui continuing into Glen Derry (as described in the first edition), the northerly approach, described below, provides some memorable skiing and the challenge of a tour into a remote setting in the centre of the Cairngorms.

From the car park, ascend Coire na Ciste on skis to reach the col between Cnap Coire na Spreidhe and Cairn Gorm, to the left of the top of the Ptarmigan ski tow. Ski south-east down into Ciste Mhearad, continuing until the angle steepens before then making a descending traverse south across easier slopes to a stream bed. To avoid an area of

steep slabs at around 950m, follow this stream bed downwards until a further traverse line can be made down to The Saddle at 800m (NJ 018 033). Descend from The Saddle, on foot if necessary, to the east end of Loch Avon and cross the River Avon near its outflow from the loch via stepping stones.

Continue east on skis adjacent to or slightly above the River Avon, and once past the northeast shoulder of Beinn Mheadhoin, turn southeast to cross by the easiest line onto the northwest slopes of Beinn a' Chaorainn. Depending on the condition and depth of the snow, it may be necessary to make a detour to the south around the Dubh Lochan before crossing. Climb the northwest slopes of Beinn a' Chaorainn to the summit cairn (1,082m), which, sitting in the heart of the Cairngorms, offers fine views.

There is now a rewarding ski descent initially north from the summit, then north-west down towards the Fords of Avon Refuge where both the outflow from the Dubh Lochan and the River Avon must be crossed. The first burn should pose no difficulties, and it may be possible to ski with great care across the River Avon via snow bridges; however, be prepared to ford the river by stepping stones in the vicinity of the refuge. Follow the River Avon upstream, then ski uphill by stream beds which may hold snow for around 100m onto A' Chòinneach, before turning west and then southwest to return to The Saddle. If there is good snow cover, it is also possible to ascend in a diagonal traverse to The Saddle after passing the stream beds off A' Chòinneach.

From The Saddle, return north-west by steep slopes to Ciste Mhearad and the col between Cnap Coire na Spreidhe and Cairn Gorm. A final ski down a deserted Coire na Ciste provides a fitting climax to the day, but do check for piste machines grooming the resort snow for the following day.

Below: Fords of A'an stepping stones (skier, Colwyn Jones)
© Brian Shackleton

Beinn a' Bhùird ▲ 1,197m
Table Mountain

△ NJ 092 006 ⌖ LR36, LR43 ⊕ P.217

P Just west of the Quoich Bridge at the pay and display car park (NO 117 911/57.0019, -3.4549) 2km east-north-east of Mar Lodge.

↔ 28KM △ 930M ↕ 330M
⏱ 8-10 HRS GRADE III ★★★

By Adam Watson, updated by Colwyn Jones

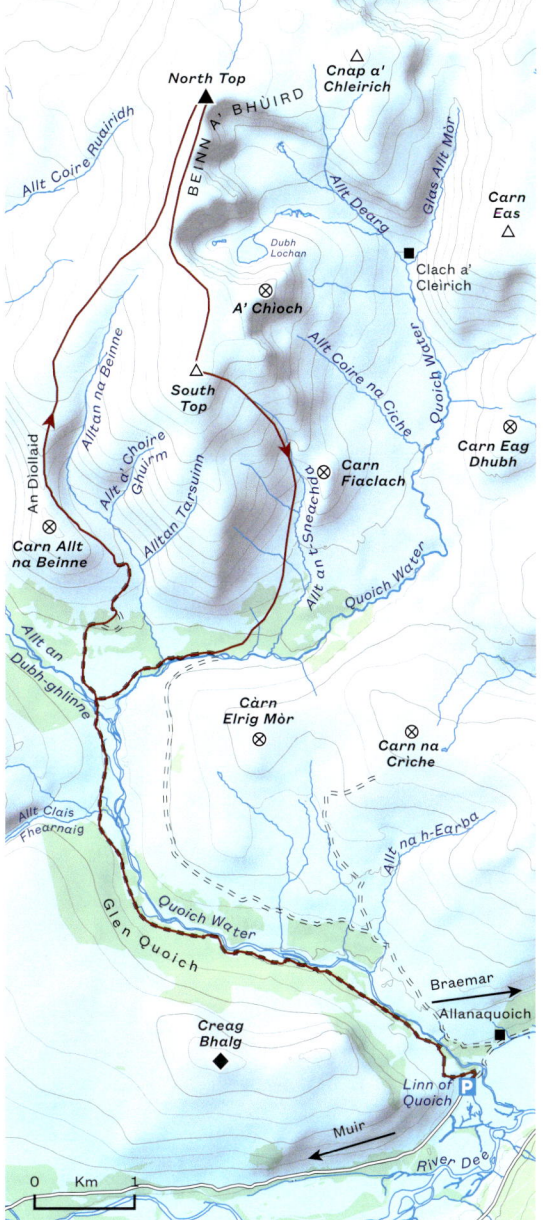

Beinn a' Bhùird offers a magnificent tour through splendid glen and mountain scenery, with a spacious high plateau surrounded by wild, plunging corries. The plateau is very exposed and shelterless, and the cliffs are heavily corniced, so carefully choose the day for this tour and be confident of good navigation.

Starting a short distance west of the bridge over the Quoich Water, follow the bulldozed track on the south-west side of this river through old pine and birch woods. In 5.5km the track crosses the Allt an Dubh-ghlinne at a ford, but on skis you may have to look up or downstream for an easier way across. It is often possible to cross a shallow snow-covered burn on skis when you would break through on foot.

The track continues north, past a junction with the return route, up to and through a pine wood, and climbs in a few zigzags onto the projecting ridge of An Dìollaid (The Saddle). This landrover track originally continued to the plateau, but the NTS has tried to reinstate the original vegetation, and it is now a smaller footpath. Nevertheless, it may well hold snow even if the surrounding slopes are bare, and it continues north across An Dìollaid where, if there is insufficient snow for skiing, a diversion a short distance to the east may give better snow cover. (Take care not to go onto the big steep slope on the west side of the Alltan na Beinne near NO 077 974, which may be corniced.)

The route now goes north-north-east up the broad ridge ahead and crosses the 1,000m contour. Again, its east side tends to hold more snow in the hollow of the Alltan na Beinne, but beware of corniced slopes close to the burn. Eventually you will arrive on the plateau near the col (1,130m) between the North and South Tops where there is a spectacular view down the cliffs to the Dubh Lochan. Gentle slopes lead north across the plateau and so to the North Top, the summit of Beinn a' Bhùird, 13km from Linn of Quoich.

On the return journey there is a good run down the west side of the Alltan na Beinne, but the lower part of this stream east of An Dìollaid sometimes holds little snow. The best return route in safe conditions is south along the plateau to the South Top and just beyond, Point 1,177m (NO 090 979). Continue down slopes west of the Allt an t-Sneachda where there is a continuously steep and exhilarating descent of 550m to the pine wood of Quoich. The pines are open, and with enough snow you can reach the upper end of the track in Glen Quoich (NO 092 952) and follow this west to the Allt an Dubh-ghlinne ford, then back to the Quoich bridge by the outward route.

Ben Avon/Leabaidh an Daimh Bhuidhe ▲ 1,171m

Bed of the Yellow Stag

△ NJ 131 018   ↗ LR36, LR43   🌐 P.218

P Just west of the Quoich Bridge at the pay and display car park (NO 117 910/57.0019, -3.4549) 2km east-north-east of Mar Lodge.

↔ 38KM (24km by cycle)   △ 850M   ↕ 330M
⏱ 10-12 HRS   GRADE III   ★★★

Bill Brooker, updated by Colwyn Jones

The three routes commonly used to reach this remote and huge plateau mountain involve lengthy approaches up the surrounding glens. One starting point is from Tomintoul (NJ 165 176); altitude 350m. No matter which way is chosen, the ski ascent of Ben Avon is a very long expedition, best done in late March or April when the days are long enough.

If road conditions allow, the best way is from the north, where a bicycle may be used for 12km from the car park area (NJ 165 176) 1km from Tomintoul on the minor road leading up Strath Avon. Follow the unmetalled private road on the east bank of the river up Glen Avon. The large gates at Birchfield allow pedestrian and bicycle access, and you should continue to a point about 1km beyond Inchrory. The north-east spur of Ben Avon rises from there, and there is a footpath, but if the slope is denuded of snow it may be better to continue along the road past the Linn of Avon for another 1.5km. If there is suitable snow here then head due south to the small col west of Meall Gaineimh (NJ 164 052; 850m). Keep on the east side of the crest-line past East Meur Gorm Craig to reach the main plateau on Big Brae, then bear south-west to gain Mullach Lochan nan Gabhar (Peak of the Goat Lochan). Alternatively, the same point may be reached by continuing 1km further up Glen Avon (do not cross the River Avon at the bridge) and climbing into Caol Ghleann (Narrow Glen), from the head of which a long-lasting snowfield rises to the plateau. The large summit tor of Ben Avon lies to the south-west across a shallow scoop in the plateau which may be crossed or skirted round its north side. Ben Avon is a lonely and remote summit, especially in winter. The scramble up the summit tor is intimidating, and care is required if attempting to reach the top. The return may be made by either of the two routes described above. That by Caol Ghleann gives a continuous downhill run of 600m from the plateau to the River Avon. The northern corries hold much snow, but they are steep-sided and in places contain crags of Cyclopean aspect. Be watchful for avalanche danger. The plateau itself is complex and demands accurate navigation in poor visibility. Be particularly careful not to ski down either of the streams that converge to fall over a cliff at NJ 159 026.

From the east, Ben Avon may be approached up Glen Gairn, and a bicycle is useful along the estate road for 12.5km from Braenaloin on the B976 (NO 280 999), past Corndavon Lodge to the ruined Lochbuilg Lodge (490m). From there ascend steeply to Càrn Dearg and follow the ridge south-west over Càrn Drochaid, then climb a long slope to gain the main plateau at the striking tor of Clach Choutsaich (Stone of the Coutts). Continue north-west across fairly level ground to join the preceding route, and either traverse across or around the plateau basin to reach the summit on its far side.

On the return leave the uphill route before Càrn Drochaid and ski down the north side of the Allt Phouple (Shelter Burn) into Glen Gairn, a descent of over 600m from Clach Choutsaich. From here it is 2km back to Lochbuilg Lodge.

The third approach to Ben Avon is from the Dee Valley to the south (32km), and it may be the only one practicable if minor roads are snowbound. Occasionally Ben Avon is skied in combination with Beinn a' Bhùird in a lengthy excursion via Glen Quoich (38km). To ski Ben Avon from the south it is more usual to start from near Invercauld Bridge, 3.5km east of Braemar. From the pay and display car park at Keiloch, where the public road ends, take the estate road north-west past Altdourie and, if possible, mountain bike for 8km up the Slugain to reach Glen Quoich. Continue north to The Sneck, the col at the head of this glen between Beinn a' Bhùird and Ben Avon. Climb east steeply from the col and continue north-east for just under 2km across the undulating plateau to the summit. The return may be varied by skiing south-west then south to Càrn Eas and enjoying a steep 400m descent to Glen Quoich.

Key

1. Ben Avon East	P.219
2. Ben Avon North	P.219
3. Ben Avon South	P.219
4. Culardoch	P.222

Below: Ben Avon
(skier, Katie Henderson)
© Gavin Baxter

Culardoch
● 900m
Back of the High Place
△ NO 193 988   ◁ LR36, LR43   ⊕ P.218

Creag an Dail Bheag
⊗ 836m
Crag of the Wee Meadow
△ NO 157 981   ◁ LR36, LR43   ⊕ P.218

P Keiloch pay and display car park (NO 188 913/ 57.0059, -3.3382).

↔ 22KM   △ 800M   ⊥ 322M
⏱ 6-8 HRS   GRADE II   **

By Bill Brooker, updated by Bob Reid

Above: Down the Glas Allt Beag, towards Invercauld with Braemar and Morrone beyond (skier, Gavin Baxter) © Katie Henderson

Culardoch and Creag an Dail Bheag are outliers of Ben Avon, sitting some 7km to its south-east and separated from it by the deep trench of Glen Gairn. Culardoch is a smooth-sided, almost conical hill rising from the 700m contour above the surrounding moors. There are no crags or significant corries, and it is not readily seen from Deeside. Creag an Dail Bheag has a more significant southern spur maintaining height above the glens and culminating at Meikle Elrick (NO 158 954; 709m). Creag an Dail Bheag (863m) is now the recognised Corbett and lies a tedious 0.75km north-west of Carn Liath.

These two hills are not easy to approach on skis, whichever starting point is used. Hillwalkers usually approach the col between the two hills – the Bealach Dearg (NO 180 980; 652m) – and then use that as a second point of departure to gain both summits, each a mere 1.5km east or west from this point. In summer the use of a bicycle is now almost convention. Riding 7km of track from the car park at Keiloch (NO 188 913; 322m) to the Bealach Dearg is relatively straightforward. The Aberdeen–Braemar bus also stops at Keiloch. Assuming bike access is feasible, fat tyres and snow tyres for modern mountain bikes make this possible even when the track is covered with snow (7km on bike from Keiloch; 330m ascent; 2hrs). The ascents of both peaks from the Bealach Dearg are short and sharp. With good snow cover, one alternative to cycling is a long approach on Nordic ski gear, with over half being through ancient Caledonian pine forest.

For Culardoch follow the track for a further 1km as it curves east up the hill to a flattening. Where the track turns sharply north (NO 185 987; 727m), leave the track and continue east for 500m to the triangulation station on the summit. Return by the same route to the Bealach Dearg.

For Creag an Dail Bheag the east ridge of Carn Liath provides a straightforward 1.5km ascent,

with Creag an Dail Bheag 750m further north-west (NO 157 981). Return by your approach line to Carn Liath and the east ridge, which holds snow well and gives a fine return to the Bealach Dearg. Then ski or cycle mainly downhill back to Keiloch.

Creag an Dail Bheag can be approached on skis from the south on rare occasions when the snow is down to the A93. The southern spur mentioned above is accessible from Altdourie (NO 166 931). Tracks through the woods become a path leading up the Glas Allt Beag. Best to divert off this path 0.5km west of Little Elrick where it curves west and continue north up the south flank of Meikle Elrick (3km from Altdourie). From there it is 2km due north up the broad ridge of Creag an Dail Bheag (5km; 500m; 3hrs). This 'ski approach' relies on access from Keiloch to Altdourie – a distance of 2.5km in each direction.

Culardoch can also be skied from the end of the road by Inver at Thistledae (NO 221 937; 310m). Tracks via Auchtavan take you to Culardoch from the south. The same route in reverse gives a good descent off Culardoch with a short final diversion over Leac Ghorm (NO 222 954) before arrival back at your car.

NB: The combination of skis and bike is an essential skill set for the north-eastern hills, and successful deployment facilitates access to many remote hills, particularly the likes of Ben Avon and Beinn a Bhùird.

Morven ● 871m
Big Hill

△ NJ 376 040   ⌕ LR37   🌐 P.224

🅿 On a minor road near Milton of Whitehouse (NJ 411 043 / 57.1268, -2.9763).

↔ 10KM   △ 690M   ⊥ 220M
🕐 3-4 HRS   GRADE II   ★★★

By Bill Brooker, updated by Bob Reid

Dominating the Howe of Cromar and the lowland basin of Kinord, Morven stands at the eastmost extension of the Cairngorms. It offers an easier alternative to the higher mountains when snowbound roads make them difficult to access. The shortest and most attractive approach to the hill is on its east side, where the steep lower slopes hold

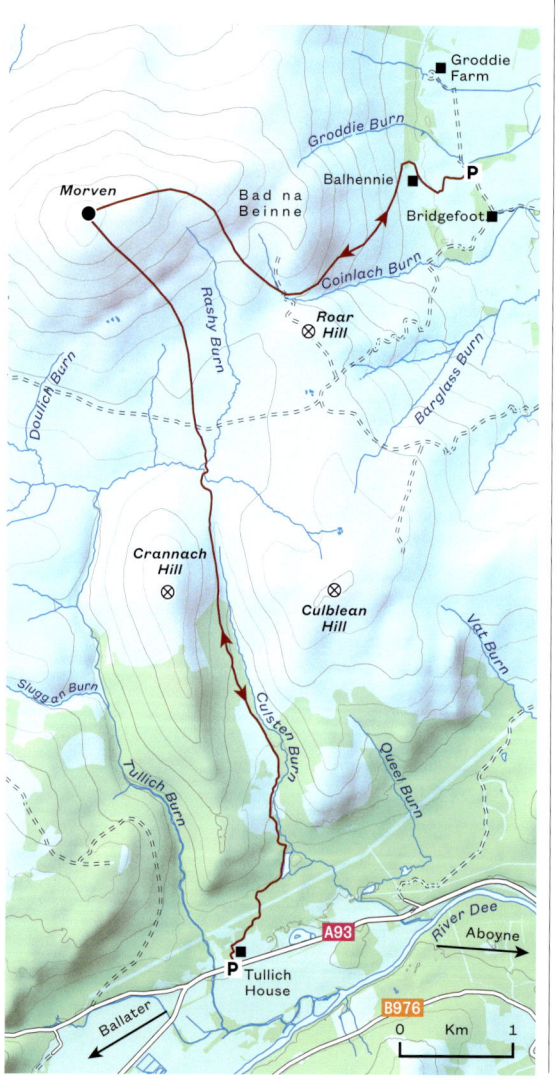

Below: Early morning ascent of Morven (skier, Katie Henderson)
© Jim Savege

snow particularly well. A minor road signposted to Groddie leaves the A97, 1km south of Logie Coldstone, at NJ 433 036 and leads west towards Morven. Approximately 400m past Milton of Whitehouse, an old farm track leads west off the Groddie Road. Please park considerately as there is no car park (NJ 411 043). Follow this old farm track, ascending over undulating slopes, past the deserted farmhouse of Balhennie. The open, steepening hillside invites a rising traverse south-west for some 250m to an easement. Ascending west round the upper basin of the Coinlach Burn, gain the east ridge of Morven. A line of fence posts leads to the triangulation station on the summit, but the last 30m may be too rough for skis unless there is good snow cover (4km; 650m of ascent; 2.5hrs).

Descent is essentially by the same route. Descend south-east, swinging east across the snow-filled hollows between the Rashy and Coinlach Burn headstreams. The steep lower slope may be taken east on the Coinlach side to Ballabeg, but further down the route is intersected by fences, so it is better to diverge north-east to leave the hill at Balhennie and return to the starting point.

An alternative and longer approach well suited to Nordic skis is from the south, leaving the A93 some 2km north-east of Ballater. Start 150m east of Bridge of Tullich. Pass a large barn and go through a gate to join a track passing through the birch woods and young pine trees to enter the glen on the east side of Crannach Hill. Continue up this glen along a track, and at its head cross a col to reach the wide upland basin of the Rashy Burn, beyond which the steepening south-eastern slopes of Morven are climbed to the summit (6km; 680m; 4–5hrs). Under good conditions, descent by the same route gives an excellent 6km run.

The Lower Hills of The Dee and The Don

In the depths of winter, during periods of general snow cover down to the valleys, the lower hills of north-east Scotland offer good, varied hill country for ski touring, and snow conditions that cannot be matched in the high hills. They may also be more accessible than the higher Grampian and Cairngorm mountains when the roads to the latter are snow-bound. These low hills are smooth, lacking cliffs and generally gently sloping, and as a result they are particularly suited to Nordic-style touring. When an easterly airflow brings deep snow, they can become completely white, almost like arctic ice-caps, to a degree seldom seen on the high tops. In places there are scattered trees, birch and pine, regenerating naturally across the lower hillsides, and this gives an unusual character to the landscape, reminiscent of Lapland and emphasising the Scandinavian character of ski touring on these hills.

Clachnaben — 589m
The War Cry of Clan Strachan

NO 615 865 — LR44, LR45 — P.226

Mount Battock — 778m

NO 550 845 — LR44, LR45 — P.226

Greendams, about 1km off the B974 (NO 648 902/ 57.0019, -2.5818).

↔ 25KM — △ 740M — ⌁ 110M
⏱ 6-7 HRS — GRADE II — ★★

By Adam Watson and Bill Brooker, updated by Colwyn Jones

There is a fine tour from Glen Dye south-west of Banchory to Mount Battock. Start just north of Greendams and ski west along a gravel road through the forest beside the Burn of Greendams. A new forest road beyond continues to a stile over the electrified upper deer fence, and a bulldozed track zigzags uphill to Airy Muir, from where there is an easy climb up to Clachnaben with its impressive big granite tor.

Mount Battock lies to the west along a broad, gently undulating ridge with the electrified deer fence on the south for most of the way. Stiles here

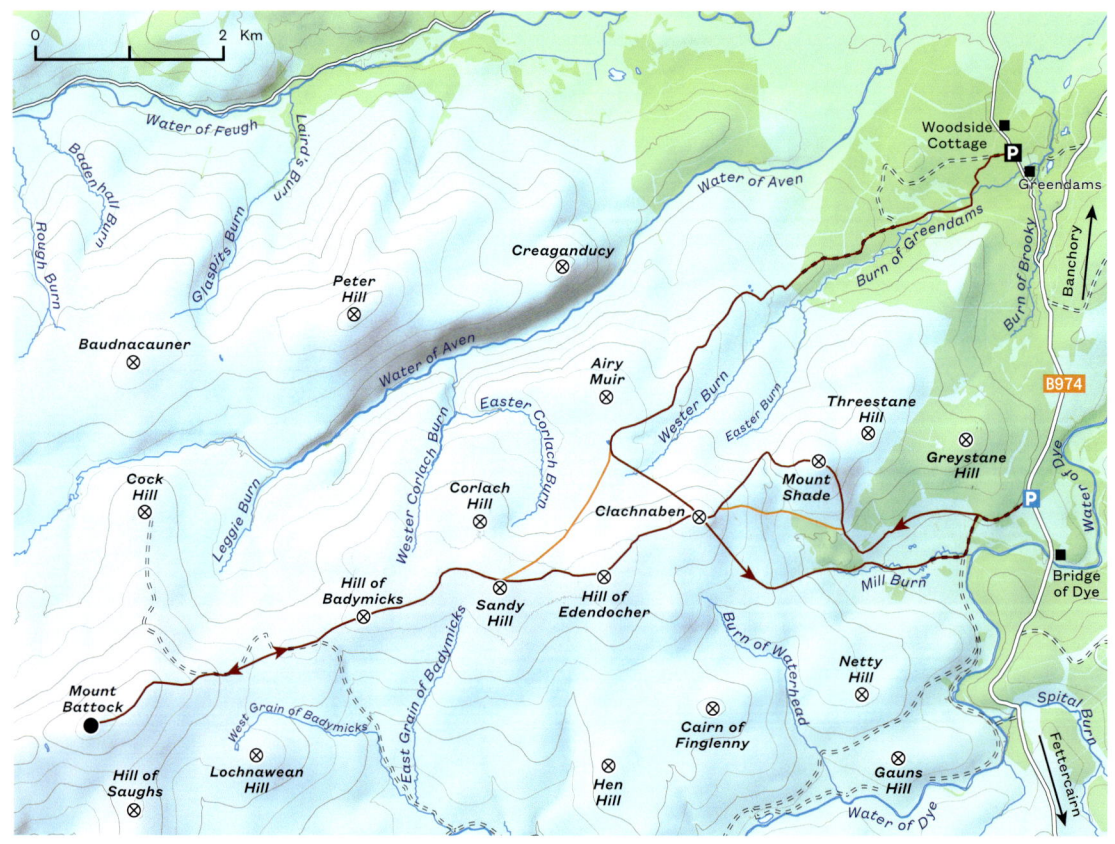

and there offer access at track crossing points, and the wires also break occasionally due to icing. The top of Mount Battock, 7km from Clachnaben, dominates much of lower Deeside and gives fine views into Glen Esk. The return trip offers good runs back, first off Mount Battock, then down to Airy Muir and finally down to and along the forest road.

When conditions are right, Clachnaben by itself gives an excellent half-day tour on Alpine or Nordic skis. Start just north of Bridge of Dye on the B974 (NO 649 867) and go west along a forest track. After leaving the wood, follow a track north-west through a forested area onto the open moor below Threestane Hill. Next, contour round the south side of Mount Shade, or traverse it if snow conditions allow. A prominent glacial meltwater notch known as 'The Devil's Bite' marks the col from which the broad north-east shoulder of Clachnaben leads to the summit. Complete the traverse by skiing south-east and safely step over the electric fence or cross it at a gate/stile where a track comes from the old wood to continue past Miller's Bog towards Glendye Lodge (8km; 400m; 3–4 hours).

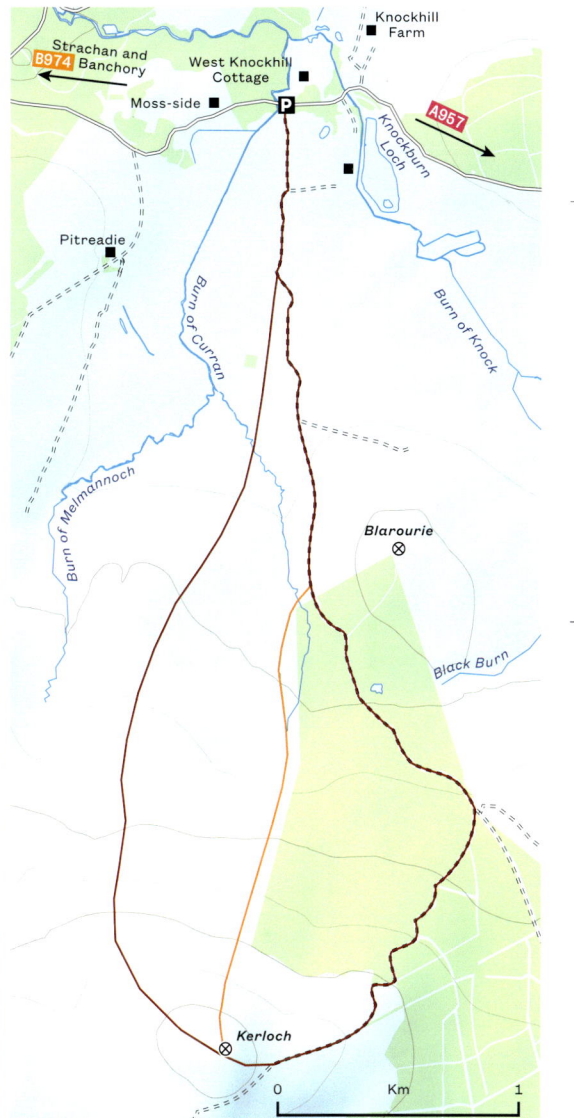

Kerloch

⊗ 534m
△ NO 696 879
⌖ LR45
🌐 P.227

P At a parking area opposite Wester Knockhill (NO 699 916/57.0147, -2.4968), 2.5km east-south-east of Strachan, just east of Moss-side immediately after a road bridge over the Burn of Curran.

↔ 9KM △ 420M ↥ 120M
🕒 2–3 HRS   GRADE II   **

South of Banchory, Kerloch is a fine viewpoint over the low country, and with general snow cover it gives a good short tour. Much of the hill has been afforested, but a track from the starting point can be followed south up the lower moorland, past a radio-controlled model airfield and a quarry, to a gate through the deer fence into Glenskinnan Forest (NO 700 896).

Continue uphill through trees to a track junction (NO 706 889). Ignore the first track turning 90 degrees right, but bear right just before the signpost up long zigzags on a rough, stony, water-eroded footpath, which requires a good depth of snow for skiing, to the cairn and triangulation station on the open summit. The 33 turbines of Mid Hill Wind Farm lie south-east of the summit.

The north face of Kerloch is steep enough to be a worthwhile descent on Alpine skis, provided there is sufficient snow and frost to encrust the marshy ground at the head of the Burn of Curran. The north face can also be used as an out-and-back route if conditions allow. This avoids the rough track described above, which is also narrow in descent but gives little shelter from strong winds.

This ascent is best achieved by turning sharp right along a low fence immediately after the gate into Glenskinnan Forest (NO 700 896). Cross a burn, and at the next deer fence climb over the stile at the padlocked gate. Much of the face appears to have been ploughed for forestry, which is why a good depth of snow is needed for an enjoyable descent. An upper deer fence mars the route, but a gate (NO 697 883) allows access to the steep final slopes. An old low fence going east-north-east from the summit is a useful navigational aid for the descent if the summit is in cloud.

Bennachie
Hill of the Pap

⊗ 528m
△ NJ 663 226 ⇗ LR38 ⊕ P.228

🅿 The car park near Garioch on the north-east of the hill (NJ 691 244/57.3096, -2.5121).

↔ 6KM △ 400M ⇞ 135M
⏱ 2-3 HRS GRADE II ✶✶

Bennachie is one of the most familiar landmarks of the north-east, and it looks particularly fine when snow-covered. In hard winters when big snowfalls have blanketed its rather stony lower slopes, it is one of the most accessible hills for ski touring in this area.

The route from the car park near Pittodrie House north-east of the hill is a good one, ascending briefly through the woods and then across open heather-clad slopes to the top of the hill. Although the highest top of Bennachie is Oxen Craig, and Mither Tap is 10m lower, the latter receives far more visitors because of its spectacular summit tor and Iron Age fort. Reaching it on skis requires very deep snow-cover of rocks. Another route starts at the visitor centre car park near Tullos, south-east of Bennachie, and takes a path west through the forest for 2km before turning north up boulder-strewn ground onto the hill.

With or without Mither Tap, the best ski tour of Bennachie is the complete traverse from west to east over the main tops from the B992 near Towmill, initially following the Gordon Way then ascending to Oxen Craig. From there ski north-east to the car park near Pittodrie, a distance of some 10km and best suited to Nordic skis and those who have access to two vehicles.

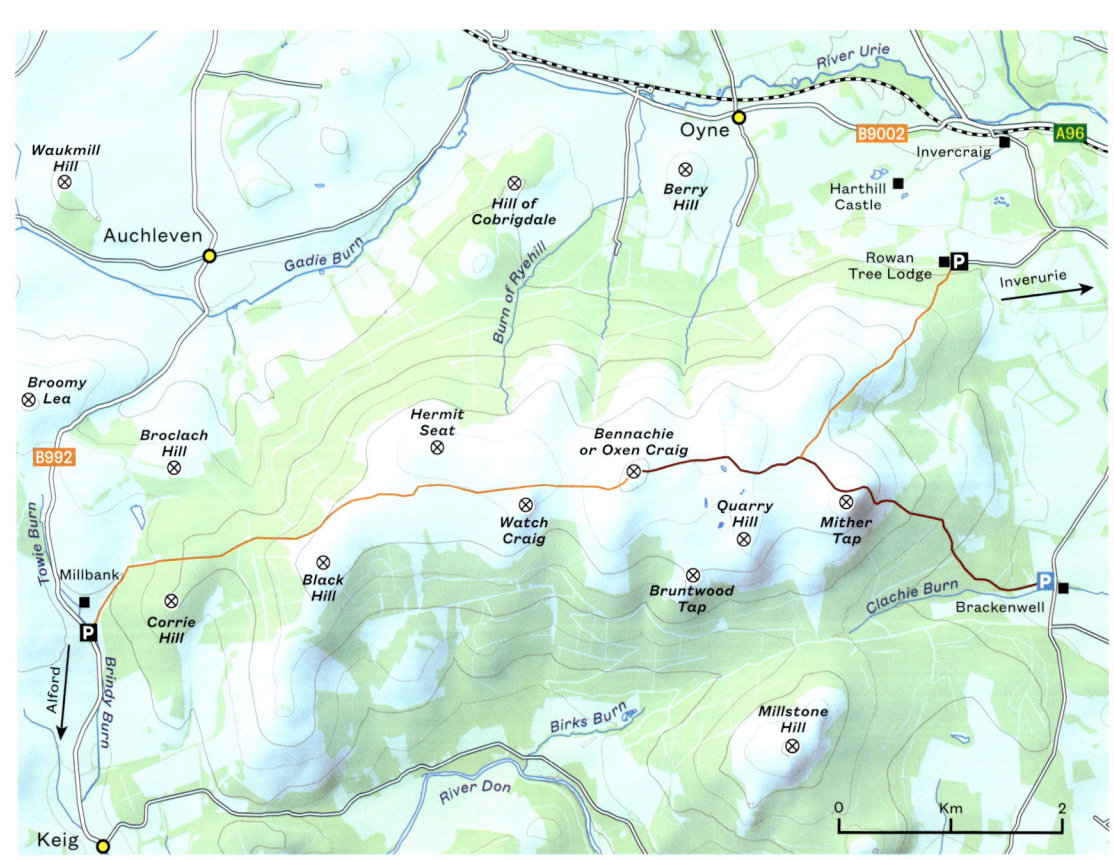

Round of the Northern Corries of Cairn Gorm

Cairn Lochan △ 1,215m
△ NH 985 025   ◁ LR36   🌐 P.229

Stob Coire an t-Sneachda △ 1,176m
Corrie of the Snow
△ NH 996 029   ◁ LR36   🌐 P.229

Cairn Gorm ▲ 1,245m
Blue Hill
△ NJ 005 040   ◁ LR36   🌐 P.229

P Coire Cas ski car park (NH 989 060 / 57.1346, -3.6713). Parking charges apply, although parking over the winter may be free. Parking spaces are on a first come first served basis so consider arriving early. www.cairngormmountain.co.uk/parking-at-cairngorm There are regular buses from Aviemore and Glenmore to the ski car parks.

↔ 11KM   △ 850M   ⊥ 630M
🕐 4-5 HRS   GRADE III   ★★★

By Heather Morning

A round of the Northern Corries of Cairn Gorm must rank as one of the most reliable and accessible ski touring routes in Scotland. It provides the perfect length and difficulty for novice ski tourers with a groomed descent if the route is taken in an anti-clockwise direction. That said, the severity of the weather on the Cairngorm plateau should not be underestimated, and what starts as a clear day may well change quickly and require good navigation skills to travel safely. If following the described route, you should never be on slopes steeper than 20 degrees and therefore an avalanche is unlikely.

With prevailing south-westerly or westerly winds the more usual way round this tour is anti-clockwise directly from the car park rather than using the uplift. This ensures that the prevailing wind is on your back on the exposed high plateau.

As an alternative, this journey can also be made in a clockwise direction using a 'snowsports touring ticket.' These can be purchased from

Key
1. Beinn Mheadhoin   P.213
2. Round of the Northern Corries   P.229

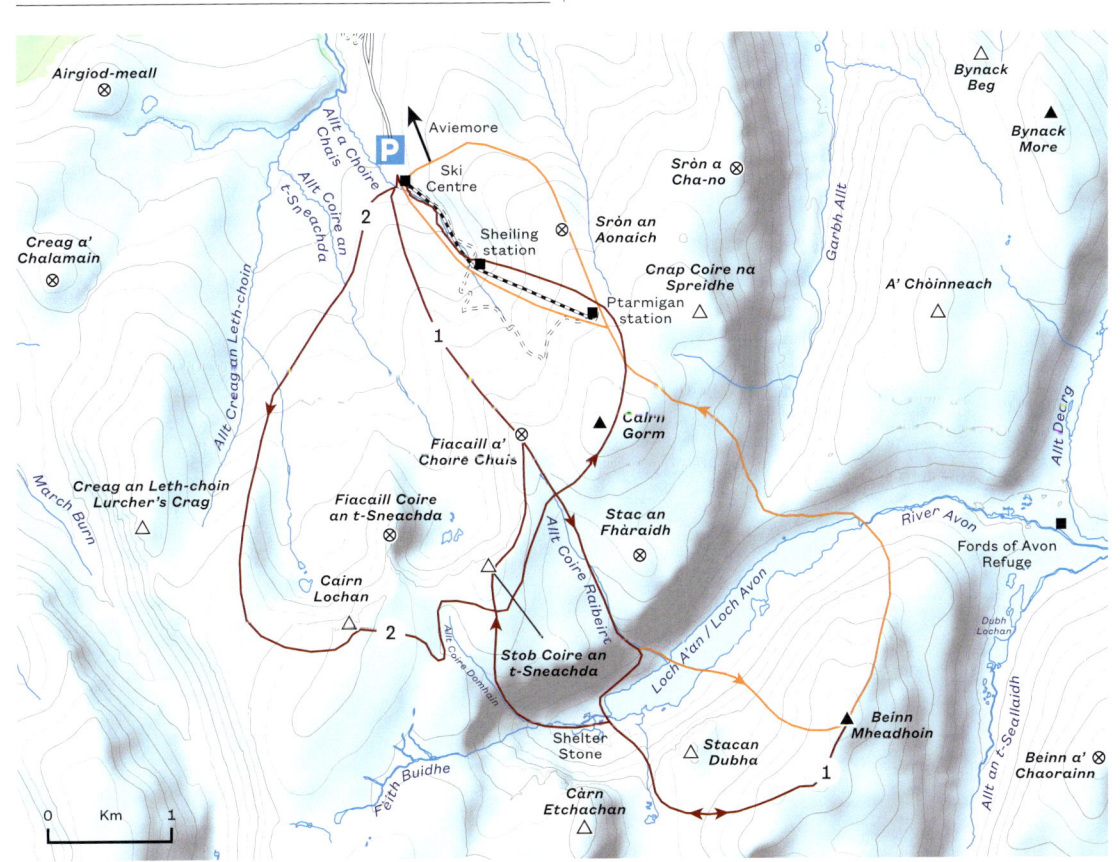

the ticket office at Cairngorm Mountain (£20 in 2024/25), giving access to the Ptarmigan building (NJ 004 049; 1,070m) via two surface tows. Note that at the time of publication, access is not allowed to the Ptarmigan building via the funicular railway.

Anti-clockwise direction:
Leave the Coire Cas car park in an ascending south-west traverse for 2.2km to Lurcher's Gully (NH 976 042; 750m). This line will take you across the lower slopes of the Northern Corries, crossing the burn lines of Sneachda and Lochain with awesome views. In late season or marginal snow conditions a line can often be taken slightly lower than the normal, constructed walkers' track.

At approximately 1.9km there is an alternative line directly up the ridge between Coire an Lochain and Lurcher's Gully to spot height 1,083m (NH 975 024), if snow cover allows. Alternatively ascend Lurcher's Gully until the ground flattens (1,000m), then head south-east to pick up the small cairn at the 1,083m spot height. Here you will be exposed to the full view of the Lairig Ghru and beyond to Braeriach and Cairn Toul.

Continue east-south-east across the flat area and ascend the western flanks of Cairn Lochan (NH 984 023; 1,215m; 0.9km), 20 degrees at its very steepest. If snow cover and visibility are good, then a line close to the corrie rim will provide some excellent views of the crags and beyond. But be warned, in winter the corrie rim of Cairn Lochan is almost always corniced and scoured by strong winds, so the alternative described is a more reliable and safer line for the ski tourer.

It is now possible to take your skins off and enjoy the first descent of the day, heading east for 0.8km to the right-angle in the 1,100m index contour in Coire Domhain (NH 992 022). This is a popular snowhole site for groups and will often offer shelter for refuelling in wild and cold conditions.

Skins on again for the 0.5km east-north-east ascent onto the southern flank of Stob Coire an t-Sneachda (NH 996 026; altitude 1,140m). It is worth noting that the southern flank of Stob Coire an t-Sneachda holds the snow well, whereas the corrie rim is often wind-scoured and stripped. Next, descend east-north-east into Coire Raibeirt to point NJ 002 031 (note the change of grid reference prefix), then take a slightly left-trending trending descent of 0.8km to 1,030m.

The south-south-west flank of Cairn Gorm holds snow well into the spring and is far more reliable than ascending the west aspect of the main hillwalkers' route, which faces west and strips quickly. Ascend north-east to the summit of Cairn Gorm (NJ 005 039; 1,245m) and the high point of the trip with a maximum gradient of 20 degrees.

It is well worth taking shelter in the lee of the stone building (locally known as the Igloo), which is home to a communication mast and meteorological instruments. The building was erected in the mid-1970s to provide weather information for the high plateau area in the aftermath of the 1971 Cairngorms disaster when six young lives were lost. From here 360-degree views can be enjoyed across a wide vista of one of the highest and wildest areas of Scotland. All that remains is to enjoy the rewards of a 610m descent back to the Coire Cas car park.

For your initial descent into the ski area, the most reliable snow cover can be found on the north-east aspect of the mountain in the shallow bowl of Marquis's Well. Descend east-north-east for 700m to a point 50m down from the return wheel at the top of the Ptarmigan T-bar (NJ 007 046; 1,130m), the highest uplift at Cairngorm Mountain. This point is purposefully down the tow line by 50m to allow for any drift off a bearing in poor visibility. Enjoy the piste descent, perhaps taking a break at the Ptarmigan Restaurant for some refreshments!

Clockwise direction:
If uplift is used, taking a clockwise direction provides a shorter excursion for those looking for a less strenuous option. Choose either route described from spot height 1,083m (NH 975 024). However, a steeper alternative would be to descend the 'Twin Burns' area into Coire an Lochain. It is worth noting that the slope here reaches a maximum steepness of 40 degrees, and therefore avalanche conditions should be assessed first before committing to this slope.

Opposite: Starting down Aladdin's Couloir (skier, Ben Cooling) © Al Todd

Below: Skiing into Coire Raibeirt toward Stacan Dubha and Beinn Mheadhoin (skier, Jonathan Preston) © Sarah Atkinson

Below: Heading up Einich Cairn of Braeriach
© Al Todd

The Cairngorms Five and Eight Tops

Cairn Gorm — ▲ 1,244m
Blue Hill
△ NJ 005 040   ◁ LR36   ⊕ P.236

Ben Macdui — ▲ 1,309m
MacDuff's Hill
△ NN 989 989   ◁ LR36   ⊕ P.236

Cairn Toul — ▲ 1,291m
Hill of the Barn
△ NN 963 972   ◁ LR36   ⊕ P.236

Sgòr an Lochain Uaine — ▲ 1,258m
Peak of the Small Green Loch
△ NN 954 976   ◁ LR36   ⊕ P.236

Braeriach — ▲ 1,296m
Brindled Upland
△ NN 953 999   ◁ LR36   ⊕ P.236

P Coire Cas ski car park (NH 989 060 / 57.1346, -3.6713). Parking charges apply, although parking over the winter may be free. Parking spaces are on a first come first served basis so consider arriving early. www.cairngormmountain.co.uk/parking-at-cairngorm There are regular buses from Aviemore and Glenmore to the ski car parks.

↔ 34KM   △ 2,350M   ⊤ 630M
◷ 11.5 HRS   GRADE IV   ★★★★★

By Roger Wild

The Five Tops

This is one of the finest day ski tours anywhere. The route climbs the five highest Munros in the Cairngorms, and in the UK only Ben Nevis is higher. The first recorded traverse was by Norman Clark in 1953. At that time, Sgòr an Lochain Uaine was not a Munro, so the tour was the Four Tops.

There are spectacular views, long climbs with glorious descents and a tremendous feeling of travelling as the skier follows the route across the Lairig Ghru and back again. Some steep and serious ground requires competence with axe and crampons, and experience in assessing snow and avalanche conditions. The terrain is often featureless, and skilled navigation will be required in poor visibility. The compass directions provided are a general indication of the route, not accurate bearings for detailed navigation. This is a tour for a good day when the skiing can be enjoyed to the full and the views appreciated. The route can be followed either clockwise (as described) or anti-clockwise, which may be preferable for Nordic skis.

From the Coire Cas car park either follow the track leading into the corrie, which winds its way up to the Ptarmigan Restaurant, or head east-north-east onto Sròn an Aonaich and continue to the restaurant. Remember to adhere to the Snowsports Touring Code, which can be found online. From the restaurant head up to Cairn Gorm, the first top. From the summit descend west-south-west to the flat col at the top of Coire Cas. Now head south and south-west to reach Stob Coire an t-Sneachda (1,176m) and descend west-south-west to the head of Coire Domhain (NH 992 027). Alternatively, a traverse along the 1,110m contour around the south-east side may provide better skiing. From the head of Coire Domhain head south-south-west for 2km across the south-east slopes of Cairn Lochan to Lochan Buidhe, which may be obscured by snow. Head south, gradually gaining height, and pass to the west of spot height 1,186m, then south-south-east to reach the huge cairn on the Ben Macdui summit, the second top.

The 700m descent from Ben Macdui down to the depths of the Lairig Ghru is one of the finest ski runs in the Scottish mountains, from the second-highest point in Scotland down to what is often the lower limit of the snow-line. The best line to take very much depends on the prevailing conditions. If there is sufficient snow cover a route can be taken south-west from the summit for 500m before turning south to reach the north-west bank of the Allt Clach nan Taillear (Tailors' Burn), then following the bank south-west to the 700m contour. Alternatively, head east-south-east from the summit to the flattish ground at the top of the Tailors' Burn and carefully prospect its steep entry. If the snow is not avalanche-prone, an exciting descent can be made all the way down the burn. A third and possibly safer option is to descend the broad ridge south-east of the burn, cross it at about 800m and continue descending on the north-west side.

If the River Dee is sufficiently frozen or running low enough to cross safely, a direct route can be taken from the foot of the burn up into Coire Odhar. Otherwise, from about 700m, take a descending traverse to Clach nan Taillear (NN 983 965). 'The Tailors' Stone' is where three tailors perished in the snow one New Year's Eve, having wagered that they would dance on the same night in Rothiemurchus and Braemar. Continue to the bridge (NN 983 956) and Corrour Bothy before heading up into Coire Odhar. The snow in the corrie may be unstable or icy, and the lip may be corniced. Take care to find a safe exit from the top of the corrie.

From the relatively flat ground above the corrie, head west-north-west on a steep rising traverse across the south side of Stob Coire an t-Saighdeir (1,213m). The Stob can be avoided on the west side along the 1,150m contour; alternatively climb to the summit and descend to the col on its north side. Continue north-north-east to the summit of Cairn Toul, the third top. If the visibility is good, the view is breathtaking, looking north-east to the route already traversed and west to the wide expanse of the Mòine Mhòr (The Great Moss).

The route for the next 6km travels close to the edge of several corries, all draining into the Allt a' Gharbh-choire, and care is needed, especially in poor visibility. Descend to the col below Sgòr an Lochain Uaine and climb to its summit, the fourth top. Staying well away from the edge, follow the rims of the corries around to spot height 1,265m. Head north then east-north-east to reach the summit of Braeriach, the fifth top. Take care to stay clear of the edge of Coire Bhrochain during the last 200m and approach the summit from its north-west side. The cairn is perched on the edge of the cliffs and may be difficult to discern in deep snow. The route now goes north and then east around the rim of Coire Bhrochain, with steep ground on the north side and precipitous cliffs to the south. In poor visibility the change in aspect of slope may help to identify the north-east-facing slope leading down to the col below spot height 1,184m (NH 963 002). Continue over this and another spot height, and then enjoy a superb ski run down to where the 750m contour crosses the burn in Coire Gorm. Head north-east and north to reach and cross the burn in the Lairig Ghru (NH 957 039). If there is likely to be enough snow in the Chalamain Gap on the east side of Creag a' Chalamain, head up the gradually rising ground into the Gap, bearing in mind that it is a potential avalanche terrain trap. Alternatively climb to the 770m contour on the south-east side of the gap and head east-north-east, traversing along the contours to cross the Allt Creag an Leth-choin and Allt Coire an t-Sneachda, and reach the Coire Cas car park after a magnificent tour.

The Eight Tops

The history of these tours is documented in the *SMCJ* (2011), vol.41, no.202, pp.365–70 and *SMCJ* (2013), vol.42, no.204, pp.461–64. Also well worth reading is *It's A Fine Day For The Hill* by Adam Watson, published by Paragon Publishing. For an account of an 18-Munro tour, see *SMCJ* (2022), vol.50, no.213, pp.17–23.

In 1958 Adam Watson skied the Four Tops, and during the tour he considered whether to continue to Beinn a' Bhùird and Ben Avon to complete a route he had been planning for several years. On that occasion he decided there was insufficient time, but four years later he completed the tour which became known as the Six Tops. The route ascended the five highest peaks plus Ben Avon. Several similar tours were completed over the following decades, and when Sgòr an Lochain Uaine was promoted to Munro status, the route effectively became the Seven Tops, especially as its inclusion only adds about ten minutes to the total journey. Beinn Mheadhoin, a Munro higher than Ben Avon, was not included in the tour. Its inclusion adds up to an hour to the total time, and in 2013 the author completed a circular tour using Nordic skis and ascended the eight highest Munros, starting and finishing on Cairn Gorm, in under 24 hours. In 2021 the Eight Tops tour was repeated by Finlay Wild on ski mountaineering racing (Skimo) equipment in 9 hours 20 minutes.

Ski mountaineering and touring have greatly increased in popularity in the 21st century, driven by various factors, including the improvement of equipment, which make long tours more popular. The modern sport of Skimo has developed lightweight Alpine equipment which compares favourably with its Nordic counterpart with regard to weight. Whichever equipment you choose, the lure of spending long days travelling on skis can be irresistible.

There are several possible route choices for skiing the Eight Tops. The 2013 route starts on Cairn Gorm and descends into the upper part of Coire Cas, crosses the Fiacaill into Coire an t-Sneachda and contours west, slowly losing height until joining the return route of the Five Tops previously described at the 770m contour on the south-east side of the Chalamain Gap (NH 967 051). From here reverse the described Five Tops route as far as the summit of Ben Macdui. Descend east and then north-east to reach the east side of Loch Etchachan and continue north-east to climb Beinn Mheadhoin, the sixth top. The highest point involves a short scramble up a tor. The descent from here requires precise route-finding. Head south-south-west and then south-south-east for 1km to reach the top of the slope above the highest point of Lairig an Laoigh (NJ 033 004). Descending this steep slope could be relatively straightforward, or very icy, or unstable. Now climb east-south-east up onto the Mòine Bhealaidh (Yellow Moss) and head east to ascend Beinn a' Bhùird (North Top), the seventh top. The next section requires care with navigation and negotiating the steep ground leading to The Sneck (NJ 118 010), which is the col between Beinn a' Bhùird and Ben Avon. From The Sneck climb steeply east at first and then turn north-east to reach the summit of Ben Avon.

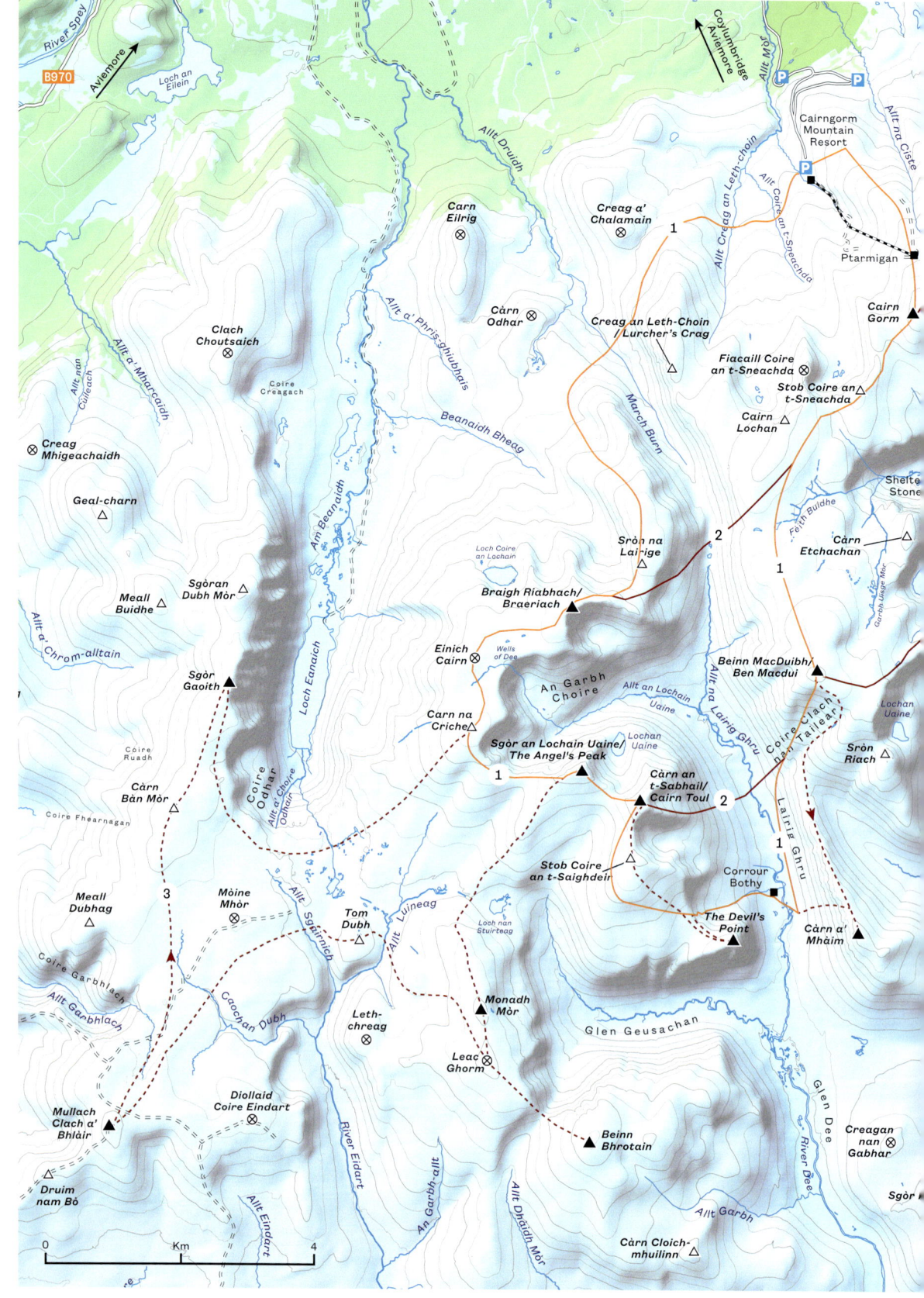

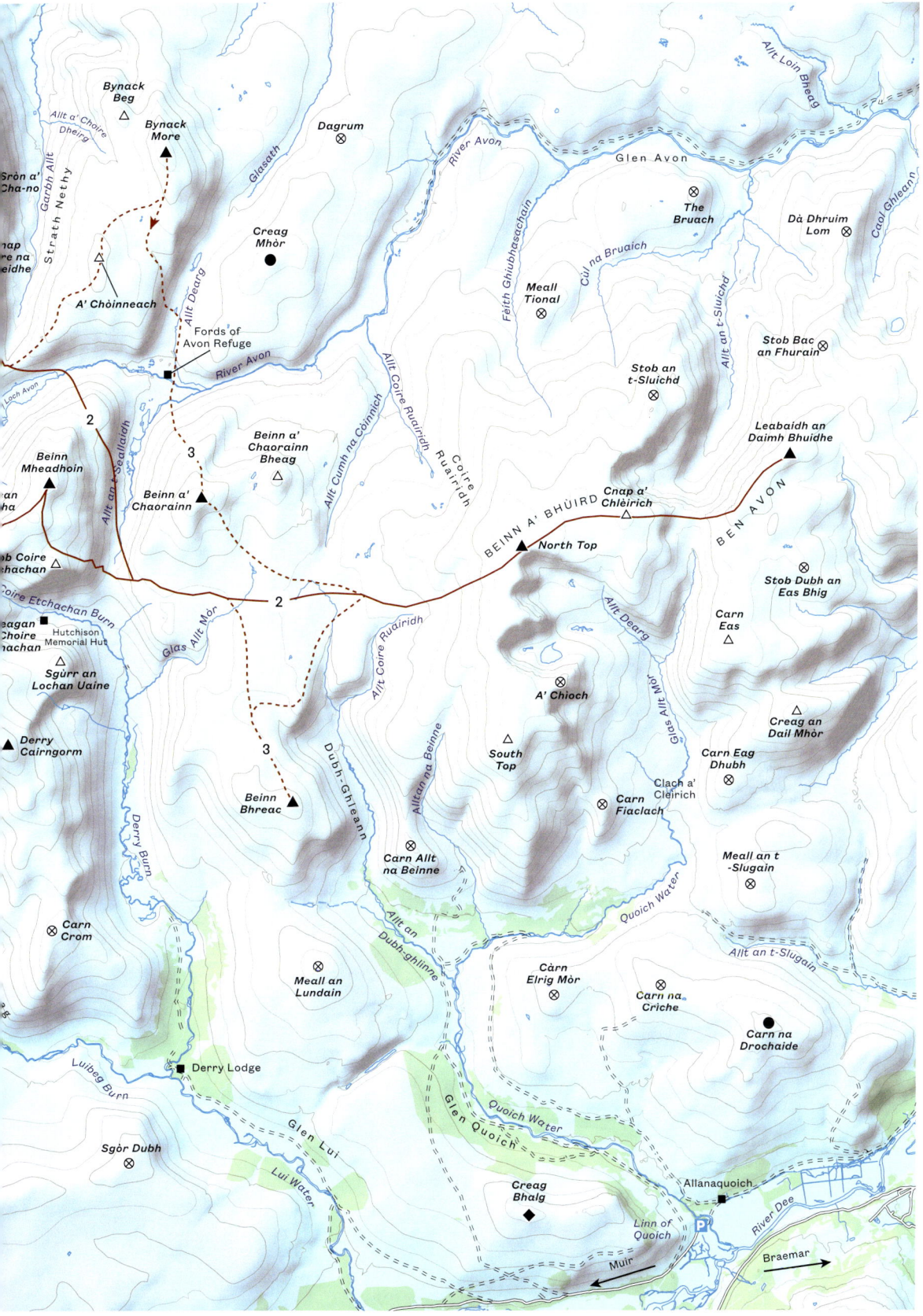

The actual summit is a huge tor named Leabaidh an Daimh Bhuidhe (Couch of the Yellow Stag).

Retrace your tracks back to Beinn a' Bhùird and across the Mòine Bhealaidh to the Lairig an Laoigh. Head north through the Lairig and then contour around the end of the north-north-east ridge of Beinn Mheadhoin to reach the east end of Loch Avon and climb to The Saddle.

An alternative route can be made from Beinn a' Bhùird by contouring around the north side of Beinn a' Chaorainn Bheag. This is a serious and complicated line, especially in the dark at the end of a long day. From The Saddle climb steeply north-north-west until the angle eases and a course can be set for the summit of Cairn Gorm and completion of the tour.

The 2021 route starts and finishes on Cairn Gorm and covers 54km with 3,500m of ascent. The route follows the 2013 route in reverse, ascending Beinn a' Bhùird, Ben Avon, Beinn Mheadhoin and Ben Macdui. From the Lairig Ghru the route ascends directly to Cairn Toul by Coire an t-Sabhail and then follows the Five Tops route as far as Braeriach and the col below spot height 1,184m (NH 963 002). Descend eastwards from the col and then take a descending traverse to the Lairig Ghru at the foot of the March Burn (NH 974 011). This is a steep descent. Ascend the burn to reach flat ground (NH 983 011) and then head north-north-east to the head of Coire Domhain. Continue east and north to the head of Coire Raibeirt before climbing to Cairn Gorm to complete the circuit.

The Cairngorms Munros
A long-distance route ascends all 18 Cairngorms Munros in a continuous circuit, starting and finishing on Cairn Gorm (encompassing all the Munros in Section 8 of the SMC publication The *Munros*).

The first recorded completion was in 2021 by Finlay Wild, who used Skimo equipment, achieving a time of 18 hours 50 minutes. The route covered a distance of 105km and involved a total ascent of around 6,000m. The Munros were tackled in the following order: Bynack More, Beinn a' Chaorainn, Beinn a' Bhùird, Ben Avon, Beinn Bhreac, Beinn Mheadhoin, Derry Cairngorm, Ben Macdui, Càrn a' Mhàim, The Devil's Point, Cairn Toul, Sgòr an Lochain Uaine, Monadh Mòr, Beinn Bhrotain, Mullach Clach a' Bhlàir, Sgòr Gaoith, Braeriach, Cairn Gorm.

Key (previous spread)
1. The Cairngorms 5 Tops   P.234
2. The Cairngorms 8 Tops   P.235
3. The Cairngorms Munros   P.238

Bynack More ▲ 1,090m
Big Cap
△ NJ 041 063   ⊘ LR36   ⊕ P.210

A' Chòinneach △ 1,017m
Mossy Hill
△ NJ 032 048   ⊘ LR36   ⊕ P.210

P Starting point: Coire Cas ski car park (NH 989 060/ 57.1346, -3.6713). Parking charges apply, although parking over the winter may be free. Parking spaces are on a first come first served basis so consider arriving early. www.cairngormmountain.co.uk/parking-at-cairngorm There are regular buses from Aviemore and Glenmore to the ski car parks.

P Finishing point: Either Glenmore Lodge (NH 987 095/ 57.1647, -3.6760), or Coire na Ciste car park (NH 997 074/57.1466, -3.6596).

↔ 16KM/9.5KM   △ 430M/680M   ↕ 630M/1090M
⏱ 5 HRS   GRADE IV   ★★★

By Richard Simpson, updated by Heather Morning

This is a cracking route for those wanting to head out into some remote terrain and take in a couple of major Cairngorm peaks with minimum uphill effort! The route described has the option of using the 'snowsports touring ticket' at Cairngorm Mountain (£20 in 2024/25), which will give you access to the Ptarmigan building (NJ 005 049; altitude 1,080m) via two surface tows. Tickets can be purchased at the main ticket office. At the time of publication, access is not possible to the Ptarmigan building via the funicular railway.

From the Ptarmigan head 450m south-east to the top of the Ptarmigan Tow (NJ 008 045; 1,140m). Then take a south-east bearing for 1.5km to The Saddle (NJ 018 033; 807m). You should get some great turns in heading down the east flank of Cairn Gorm before swinging south-east for a long traverse to The Saddle. Within minutes you are away from the bustle of the ski area into remote terrain, with some great views east across to Ben Avon. Care should be taken to avoid the steeper ground and craggy area running south from NJ 015 036.

A very gradual 2km ascent north-east takes you onto the summit of A' Chòinneach (NJ 032 048; 1,017m). Don't pass up the opportunity to pause during this ascent and turn around to soak in the outstanding view up the Loch Avon basin dominated by the spectacular cliffs of the Shelter Stone Crag and Càrn Etchachan. A' Chòinneach was once classified as a Munro, but in some dim and distant reshuffle it was demoted to a lowly Munro Top. Most importantly it is still a terrific mountain to travel over on skis. A lovely, gentle 900-metre long descent north-east takes you to the broad bealach (NJ 038 055; 940m) before your final ascent onto Bynack More. The most tempting line is to head north-east directly for the 'Barns' (large granite tors), but this doesn't always provide the best line on skis as the ridge is more likely to be scoured. In most conditions a line north-east then north for 1.1km slightly west of the ridge crest will provide a better option to reach the summit of Bynack More (NJ 041 063; 1,090m).

The normal Munro bagger's route to Bynack More (the north ridge) provides a poor ski option. It is far better to descend north-west then north for 2.8km down the Allt a' Choire Dhuibh into Strath Nethy (NJ 025 082; 500m). Be alert to avalanche risk here: the east flank of Bynack Beg often holds a large accumulation of snow, and the burn line is a classic terrain trap. To ski out of Strath Nethy back to Glenmore Lodge via the now-removed Bynack Stables (NJ 020 105) requires good snow cover at low elevation. If there is no snow at this level, then it is advisable to carry a pair of old trainers for the walk out. Strath Nethy is notoriously boggy and you will welcome the surfaced track, which starts at the bridge.

Alternatively, from Strath Nethy it is possible to take a route west for 1.2km up to a notch in the ridge (NJ 014 081; 730m), an ascent of 230m. The gully line with its east-facing aspect holds snow well and leads up to the notch. This leaves a final 1.7km traversing descent back into the lower ski car park at Coire na Ciste (NH 997 074; 530m) and a fitting end to the day. This alternative may also make transport logistics easier. If the ski area is busy and the Ciste car park is in use, then a free shuttle bus continually runs to the upper car park in Coire Cas. Otherwise, it is a short skin, or walk, back to the main car park.

Creag Mhòr ● 895m
Big Crag

△ NJ 057 048   LR36   🌐 P.210

▣ Starting point: Coire Cas ski car park (NH 989 060/ 57.1346, -3.6713). Parking charges apply, although parking over the winter may be free. Parking spaces are on a first come first served basis so consider arriving early. www.cairngormmountain.co.uk/parking-at-cairngorm There are regular buses from Aviemore and Glenmore to the ski car parks.

↔ 18/21km
△ 1,350m if returning by outward route/ 950m if returning via Lairig an Laoigh
⊤ 630m
⏲ 10 HRS   GRADE III   ★★★★

By Bob Reid

This ski tour might be considered to be the pursuit of an ephemeral Corbett by extreme means, though ascent of this remote hill is not easy by any option. It is often an afterthought for folk who have already climbed its near neighbours, Bynack More and Cairn Gorm, without noticing this elegant peak in the foreground because of magnificent distant views eastwards to Beinn a' Bhùird.

There are two approaches, one from the north (described) and the other from the north-east (described as descent). A third even more adventurous option involving a very long cycle would involve the use of Faindouran Bothy, but that is not described here. The best approach is to traverse Cairn Gorm itself – preferably during a good stable weather forecast with plentiful snow cover. This is not a route for poor weather.

From the ski car park, skin up the Fiacaill a' Choire Chais 2km to Point 1,141m (NH 999 039). This can be done in less than an hour by the fit. It isn't necessary to climb over Cairn Gorm for this route – better to traverse across the plateau south-east then east, skirting above Coire Raibeirt and Stac an Fhàraidh to the steep, black-run descent line following the old County Line for 2km toward The Saddle (NJ 017 033; 807m). Careful navigation is necessary, keeping well to the north-east of Stac an Fhàraidh. In poor visibility it is better to go further east, crossing Ciste Mhearad and Marquis's Well before descending all the way to the Garbh Allt with a short re-ascent south-west to The Saddle. The route then continues above Loch Avon for a further 2.5km east to the Fords of Avon Refuge (NJ 042 032; 690m). From there the ascent is a little less than 2km to the summit of Creag Mhòr itself at 895m – a climb of 200m (9km; 750m; 4.5hrs).

Note that reversing this outward route involves a serious amount of uphill skinning, back over the Cairngorm plateau – approximately 4.5km and 500m of re-ascent from the Fords of Avon Bothy. Not impossible by any means, but it needs a strong party, longer daylight hours and good conditions. It is probably necessary to have summited Creag Mhòr before midday. In the SMC book, *The Corbetts*, Hamish Brown notes 'Creag Mhòr may only be a minor summit in the context of the Cairngorms, but these mountains, with their long distances and empty spaces, should never be treated casually.'

From the summit of Creag Mhòr another descent option is to head north along the Lairig an Laoigh to the east of Bynack More. Initially descend steeply from the summit in a north-north-westerly direction. It is little more than a 0.5km descent to the Lairig an Laoigh path where it crosses the Glasath Burn (NJ 051 055) to reach the Fords of Avon Path at a height of 616m. There is a good likelihood this will all be covered in snow. From here the route follows the path north for 2km then north-west for 2km across the shallow Coire Odhar, rising to a height of 800m, before a long, 3km descent can be followed north-east to the Nethy River crossing. The track then leads a further 4km west to Glenmore Lodge and the ski road soon thereafter (12km from Creag Mhòr summit; 200m of re-ascent; 3hrs). This descent route can also be used as a means of ski ascent, assuming wide snow cover.

Meall a' Bhuachaille ● 810m
Herdsman's or *Shepherd's Hil*

△ NH 991 115   ◈ LR36   ⊕ P.240

P The limited car parking area on the roadside, just past Glenmore Lodge (NH 987 095/57.1652, -3.6750); altitude 340m.

↔ 15KM   △ 500M   ⊤ 340M
⊙ 3-4 HRS   GRADE II   ✱✱✱

By Heather Morning and Bob Reid

This Corbett provides a fine day out with splendid views of the Northern Corries and Strathspey. This is also a very useful alternative for those days when the Cairngorm ski road is shut at the ski gates. During exceptional snow winters, Meall a' Bhuachaille turns into one of the most accessible tree skiing venues in Scotland, attracting large numbers of skiers, but make sure you grab it when it comes into condition; rocking horse manure springs to mind! The winter of 2021 delivered with champagne powder. The previous time this rare phenomenon occurred was in 2010. From the summit, the northward-facing slopes into Abernethy also have good snow-holding characteristics.

The best approach is past the Reindeer Centre, a short way beyond Glenmore Lodge. Head north-east on the track, through the locked gate into the wooded glen, round the striking An Lochan Uaine (Small Green Loch, which may well be frozen), then through the deep cleft forming Ryvoan Pass. Take the left-hand track at the fork to shortly arrive at Ryvoan Bothy, altitude 400m. From here head west on the summer footpath which ascends the east ridge of Meall a' Bhuachaille. With good snow cover a suitable ski track should be easily found or created. The large summit cairn may provide some temporary shelter (5.5km; 480m; 2hrs).

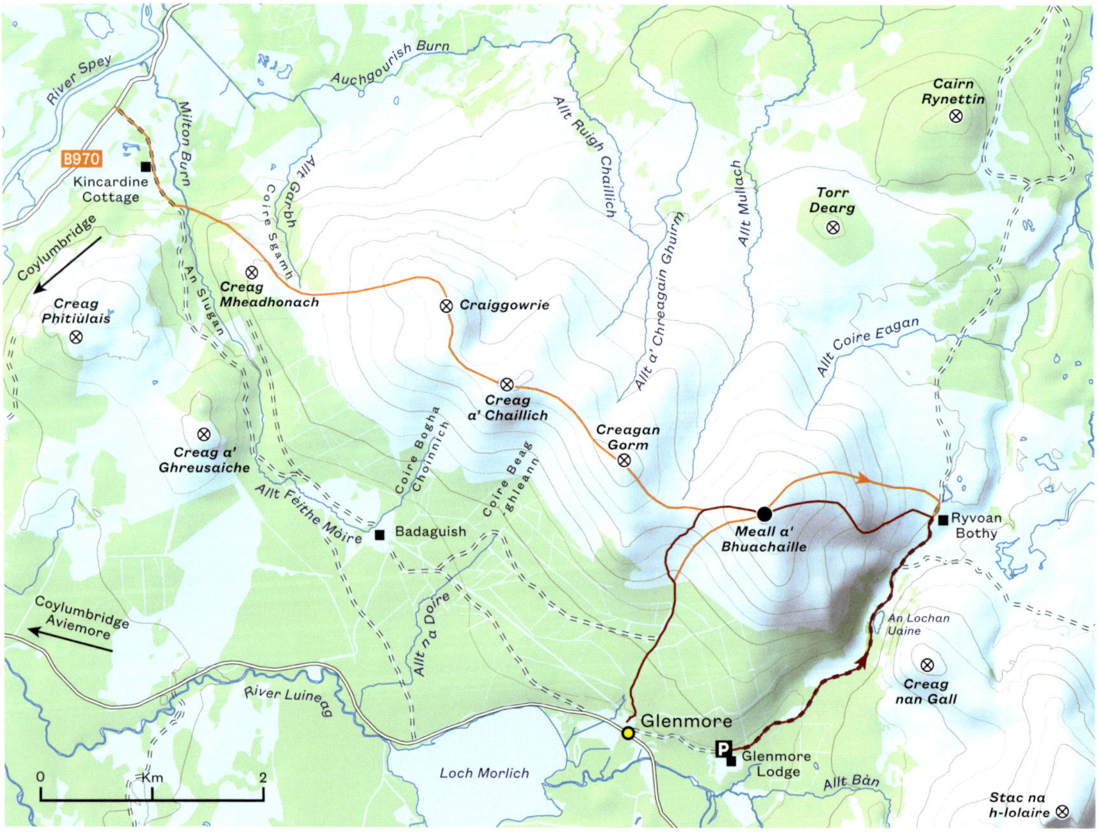

The descent traverses the peak west and reaches the col (NH 984 115) 0.5km further on

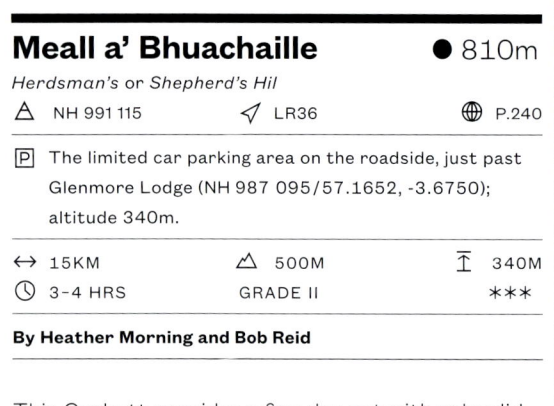

before Creagan Gorm. Follow the line of the summer footpath south, which leads back through the woods towards Glenmore village. If conditions allow ski directly down the wooded south-west flank to the Reindeer Centre.

An alternative onward tour continues north-west over the subsidiary peaks of Creagan Gorm (732m) and Craiggowrie (687m) a further 3.5km along the ridge. Useful deployment of two cars makes return an easy option. Descent south through the forests on the lower slopes is not always straightforward on skis, but heading west-north-west from Craiggowrie leads steeply down across Creag Mheadhonach to Milton and the B970 where there are car parking options, or a walk south for 5.5km back to Coylumbridge to catch a bus.

Other options are to head north down the north-west flank, following the Allt Mullach, or north-north-east down the northern flank above Ryvoan, hand-railing the burn line. All of these descents provide excellent skiing.

Below: Meall a' Bhuachaille (skier, Lucy Dowland) © Tom Weston

Geal Charn ● 821m
White Hill

△ NJ 090 126   ↗ LR36   🌐 P.241

P The car park at the end of the public road going to Dorback Lodge (NJ 077 168/57.2326, -3.5300), easily accessed off the A939.

↔ 12KM	△ 470M	⇕ 375M
⏱ 3-4 HRS	GRADE II	★★

By Bob Reid

One of several 'Mont Blancs Écossais' to go by this name, Geal Charn is an unpretentious hill well suited to a Nordic ski tour. It is a rolling heather-covered hill typical of the lower Cairngorms, and the quality of the skiing is in direct proportion to the depth of snow blanketing the heather. Easily accessible from the Nethybridge–Lecht road, follow the signposts to Dorback 4.5km east of Nethybridge (NJ 047 196), then a further 4km south to Dorback Lodge. Limited parking is available by the roadside near a large agricultural estate building.

Assuming there is snow down to road level (375m) by the lodge, the well-maintained track

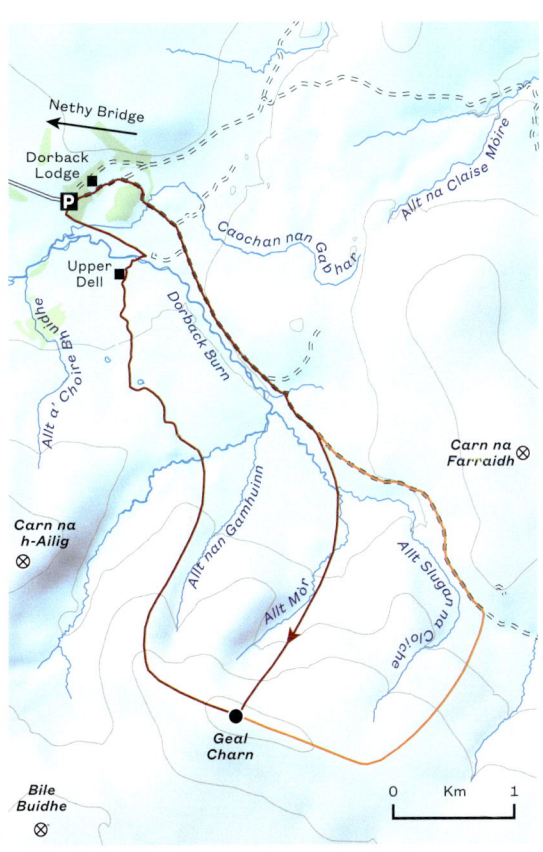

(typical of this busy shooting estate) east of Geal Charn will offer the best ascent. The track follows the east side of the Dorback Burn and it often holds snow well. It is essential to check if the burn can be safely crossed at Upper Dell 700m south of Dorback Lodge for your return leg. After 4km the ascent route leaves the track and turns up the east side of the Allt Mòr burn heading south. This leads into the impressive Coire an Uillt Mhòir. The steep headwalls of the corrie afford access to the summit at 821m, at the centre of a broad ridge running south-east to north-west (6km; 450m; 2.5hrs).

Alternatively, if using Nordic equipment, it may be easier to remain on the track until the watershed, then climb south-west up the less steep headwall gradient to reach the summit.

If it is possible to cross the Dorback Burn, the descent heads north-west from the summit, then north down either side of the Allt nan Gamhuinn, which in turn leads to the track through Upper Dell back to the starting point. Careful navigation may be necessary to safely cross the Dorback Burn using the information you observed on the ascent. If the burn is too high to cross, simply return by your ascent route.

Below: Tree skiing on Meall a' Bhuachaille (skier, Pete Mackenzie) © Al Todd

Carn Ealasaid ● 792m
Elizabeth's Hill

△ NJ 228 117	◁ LR36, LR37	⊕ P.243
P A car park on the A939 (NJ 224 150/57.2199, -3.2861).		
↔ 8KM	△ 460M	⊤ 430M
⏱ 3-4 HRS	GRADE II	**

By Bob Reid

While the hill is better known as The Lecht (the declivity or descending slope), the proper name of Carn Ealasaid or Elizabeth's Hill is shrouded in some mystery. The earliest mapped reference dates back to the mid-19th century, and it may be named after Saint Elizabeth, mother of John the Baptist.

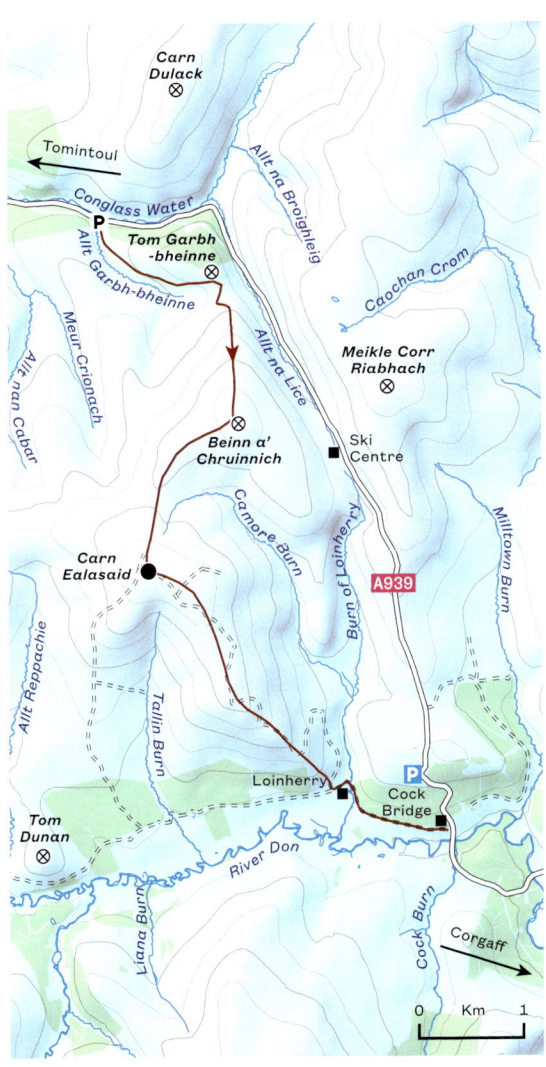

The subsidiary summit of Beinn a' Chruinnich (778m) is in effect the ski centre hill, with the tows heading off this lower summit toward The Lecht Road. The Scottish Ski Touring Code advises not using the pistes as a means of ascent. This is much to the ski tourer's advantage since slightly away from the hubbub of ski uplift is an excellent ski traverse from north to south, taking in both tops. It is best to start at the car park on the south side of the A939, 1km west of the Wells of Lecht (NJ 224 150; 430m). The single-species forests across Tom Garbh-bheinne at this point were felled in 2020, and it will take time for the ground to recover.

Follow the track running south-east from the car park for little more than 1km to a line of grouse butts and the north ridge of Beinn a' Chruinnich (778m). This summit has a communications mast and sits above the northernmost tows of the Lecht Ski Centre. Leave the mechanisation behind, heading south-west downhill, then south toward the col marked with spot height 694m. A short 0.5km reascent then leads to the track across the large flat summit of Carn Ealasaid and the diminutive cairn (4.5km; 360m; 2hrs). On a clear day, you are rewarded with splendid views southwards across Upper Strathdon to Ben Avon, with its granite tors resplendent on the skyline.

This route can be reversed in descent. Alternatively, with the use of two cars, a descent from the summit down the 3km south-east ridge makes for a splendid traverse. There is no public transport, but the road is a busy connection between Aberdeenshire and Highland, so hitchhiking is possible. The south-east ridge finishes abruptly at Loinherry, after which a short 1km stretch of track leads to the main Lecht Road at Cock Bridge.

For a longer day this tour can also be combined with the ascent of Brown Cow Hill or Càrn Mòr in the Ladder Hills on the other side of the Lecht. To have skied all three neighbouring Corbetts in a day would require excellent late-season snow and could arguably be seen as gluttony.

The 'Greater Range' of The Hills of Cromdale

Creagan a' Chaise ◆ 722m
Little Steep Rocks
△ NJ 104 241   ⌖ LR36   🌐 P.245

Carn a' Ghille Chearr ◆ 710m
Hill of the Unlucky or Awkward Boy
△ NJ 139 298   ⌖ LR36   🌐 P.245

🅿 Ballcorach public car park (NJ 154 265/ 57.3215, -3.40516) on the B9186 Strath Avon to Fodderletter road.

↔ 19.5KM   △ 747M   ↕ 230M
⏱ 6-7 HRS   GRADE II   ★★★

By Sarah Atkinson

These fine wee hills nestle between the Rivers Avon and Spey. The Battle of Cromdale took place on the slopes of these hills on 30 April and 1 May 1690, at which the defeat of the Jacobites by government forces effectively ended the rebellion in Scotland. Once home to illicit stills, today these hills are surrounded by many fine whisky distilleries.

The main summits Creagan a' Chaise and Carn a' Ghille Chearr are both classified as Grahams. These summits lie to the south-west and north-east of this mini plateau, respectively. The plateau itself is relatively featureless, and although most of the slopes are gently angled, occasional steepenings lead into terrain traps. Careful navigation is required in whiteout conditions – an error could offer more excitement than the skier intended! The many varying aspects of the ridge lines and gullies mean some good skiing can often be found by observing the wind direction and snow catchment features. The tours described below can be tweaked accordingly. The terrain is mostly heather (occasionally short where grouse moor burning has occurred), bog and some isolated boulder patches. A good depth of snow is required, and with our fickle climate it is rare to enjoy skiing from the road. Note that when the snow cover is good, most gates will need to be climbed over – please do so at the hinge end and with care. Although mountain hares and a sizeable herd of reindeer roam the Cromdales, in winter there is little wildlife to see on these closely-managed hills.

It is worth noting that when there is sufficient snow to enjoy low level skiing here, the roads can be problematic. On the minor roads the snowplough often bypasses the few passing places and gateways. Good snow tyres, reversing skills over a long distance and a shovel are required. Parking at most locations is limited to four or five cars, and you may have to dig out your own parking spot. Please consider farming access.

There are several access points into the Hills of Cromdale, offering pleasant, short tours. From the car park on the west side of the River Avon, follow the 'right of way' north along the bank of the River Avon for 400m, then west past Knock. Continue west then north-west for 2km to the plateau (NJ 130 279). Follow the ridge north-east over Carn Eachie (Horse Hill; 700m), then north-north-west to the summit of Carn a' Ghille Chearr and the triangulation station. There are fine views down to the Moray Firth and across to Morven and Scaraben. To the west over the Dava Moor and Slochd distant hills peek up from Ben Wyvis to Creag Meagaidh. To the east the long line of the Ladder Hills dominates the skyline with Ben Rinnes to the north-east. If conditions dictate it may be possible to descend direct to Knock from here, though the terrain is bouldery in places.

From the summit return to Carn Eachie. Traverse the broad plateau ridge and its many tops (passing an unmissable cairn erected by the people of Cromdale for King Edward VII's 1902 coronation at NJ 107 260), for 6km to the second summit, Creagan a' Chaise. Here there is a magnificent cairn-castle, constructed to celebrate the 1887 Golden Jubilee of Queen Victoria. There is also a trig pillar. The Cairngorm massif dominates the view.

Descend east off the summit, past grouse butts to 450m and pick up the track leading to Milton Farm (NJ 140 248). Alternatively descend into the corrie north-west of spot height 698m and follow a steeper line on the south side of the Milton Burn to pick up the track. From Milton follow the road for 2.25km back to the car park.

The Greater Traverse of The Hills of Cromdale
⌖ LR36, LR28   🌐 P.245

🅿 Park off the A939 at a layby (NJ 061 222/57.2807, -3.5584) and for the finish park off the A95 at another layby (NJ 144 343/57.3919, -3.4252) near the Tormore Distillery.

↔ 19KM   △ 751M (828M descent)   ↕ 430M
⏱ 6-7 HRS   GRADE II   ★★★

Perhaps the most attractive ski tour is a traverse of the entire ridge south-west to north-east from Sgòr Gaoithe (Windy Pinnacle; NJ 076 218; 628m) to Tom a' Chait (NJ 157 332, sheet 28). This would require a car or arranged drop off/pick up at each end. Take a direct line to the first top, Sgòr Gaoithe. Continue along the ridge to the summit, cairn-castle and trig pillar of Creagan a' Chaise (NJ 104 241; 722m). Traverse the plateau ridge and its many tops to Carn a' Ghille Chearr (NJ 139 298; 710m). Descend north-east to Creag an Tarmachain and continue north-east to the broad col at Lagaguish (NJ 163 322, sheet 28). Head north-north-west up the gentle incline to Tom a' Chait (mast) or traverse round to pick up the track on the north-north-west flank. Follow the line of the track leading to the A95 or, livestock permitting, cut left straight across the moorland and field directly to the layby. From the track end it is a 500m walk left along the wide verge of the A95 to the layby.

Cromdale Mini Tours

Creagan a' Chaise from the A939 Grantown to Tomintoul Road

Park in a layby (NJ 061 222/57.2807, -3.5584) or at the snowgate (NJ 066 214/57.2741, -3.5498).

↔ 12KM △ 690M (with the Leth-allt Mòr extension)

This first Cromdale mini tour is also the start of the greater traverse. Take a direct line to the top of Sgòr Gaoithe, then on to the summit of Creagan a' Chaise. Return by the same route, or ski north-west from Carn na Cloiche (NJ 092 221) to the Leth-allt Mòr burn (NJ 081 226). From here either traverse round Sgòr Gaoithe (quite long and undulating) or skin back up to the summit of Sgòr Gaoithe to enjoy another run down to your car.

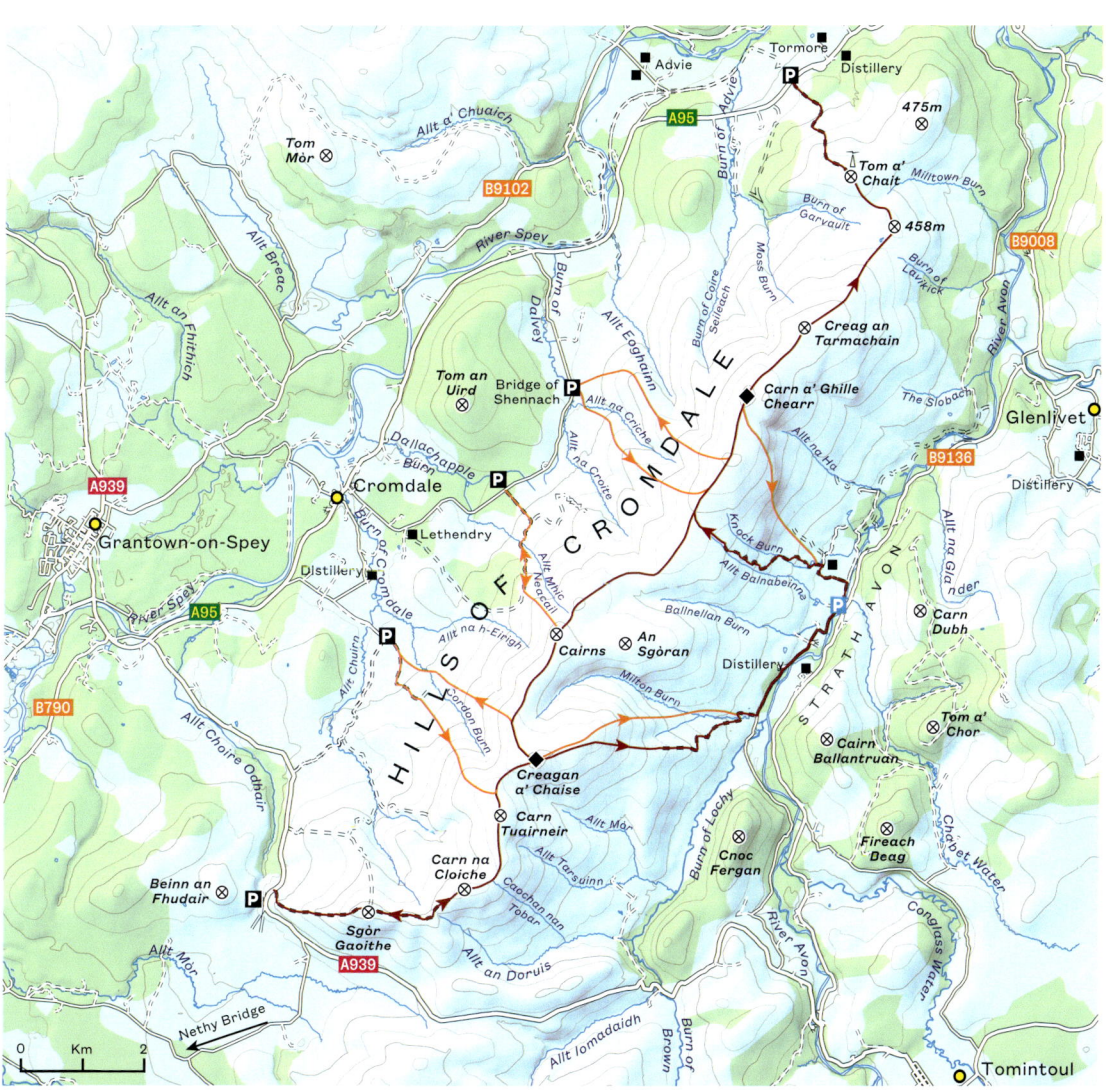

From Cromdale, Balmenach Distillery Road

🅿 Off the A95, the minor Balmenach distillery road. Park near Burnside Farm (NJ 080 261/57.3356, -3.5007).

↔ 8.2KM   △ 484M

Follow the track south-east past the farm to a flattening on the ridge (NJ 086 252). Continue up the ridge trending toward the col at NJ 099 239 and on to the summit of Creagan a' Chaise. From here there is the option to ski down the north-west ridge; however, the better skiing seems to be from Carn Tuairneir following a fence line toward a row of grouse butts (1:25,000 map), then across to approximately NJ 086 246 to pick up a burn leading back to the initial track from Burnside Farm.

From Cromdale, Haughs of Cromdale Road

🅿 Park in a large layby (NJ 096 281/57.3167, -3.5279) near Claggersnich Farm.

↔ 11.2KM   △ 536M

Follow the road 400m north-east to join a track heading south-east between fields. Follow this track as it crosses fields and pass a small patch of forestry to a gate on the right. Continue up the track over moorland to the Clach nam Pìobair (the Piper's Stone; NJ 103 269). Legend has it that a Jacobite piper stood on the stone during the Battle of Cromdale, playing tunes to urge his men on until he was slain. On that cheery note, ascend south-east to spot height 635m (NJ 108 259) and the coronation cairn. Follow the ridge south-west then south-south-

east to the summit. From here retrace your route back to the coronation cairn. You can ski back by the same route, but a better option is to continue along the ridge to the next flat top (NJ 112 266; 610m) and descend north-west between the Allt Mhic Neacail and a fence to an open gateway, then across the moor directly to the gate you crossed earlier to re-join the track at the field boundary. It is possible to tour both summits from this approach, though this involves retracing your route from each and is perhaps less satisfying than the south-east option.

Top: The Jubilee Cairn
on Creagan a' Chaise.
(skier, Jonathan Preston)
© Sarah Atkinson

Carn a' Ghille Chearr from Cromdale, Haughs of Cromdale Road

P Park on the verge (NJ 111 298/57.3504, -3.4780) at Bridge of Shennach.

↔ 10.2KM   △ 511M

Follow the 'right of way' signposted path crossing a burn, then climb south-east up the Cnoc na Seilg ridge (Hill of the Hunting) to join the plateau. Continue north-east over Carn Eachie and on to the summit, where there is a cairn and trig pillar. Return to Carn Eachie, then retrace your route up or descend via the Càrn na h-Iolaire ridge (Hill of the Eagle) to NJ 122 291 where there are a few scattered pine trees. Cross the Allt na Criche here and re-join the path. Both options offer good skiing.

Ben Rinnes ● 840m
Headland Hill

| △ NJ 255 354 | ◁ LR28 | 🌐 P.248 |

🅿 The car park on the minor road north-west off the B9009 (NJ 282 365/57.4122, -3.1961).

| ↔ 8KM | △ 550M | ⬍ 300M |
| ⏱ 2-3 HRS | GRADE II | ★★ |

By Bill Brooker, updated by Bob Reid

Ben Rinnes is the dominant hill in the lower Spey Valley, rising well above its lower neighbours and a prominent landmark from many distant viewpoints. It is high enough to hold snow well, particularly on the flanks of the east ridge, depending upon how the snow has drifted. Being a heathery hill, it needs decent snow cover to give good skiing, but in the right conditions it gives a pleasant short tour, for the B9009 road between Dufftown and Tomintoul passes close to the foot of the hill and provides good access.

If the southern slopes have the better cover, ascend from Glen Rinnes, leaving the B9009 near the Glenrinnes Community Centre (next to the distillery). There is some off-road parking adjacent to the building (NJ 273 341; 278m). Head west, reaching the open hillside after crossing a sheep pasture. Skirt the west end of Benrinnes Wood to gain the east ridge, beautifully named the Scurran of Lochterlandoch. This leads in a further 1km to the summit (3.5km; 540m; 2hrs).

Descent is by the same east ridge, which gives an excellent downhill run, but be sure to turn off the ridge early enough to avoid the Benrinnes Wood descending to the glen.

If the northern side of the east ridge has better snow cover, approach from the side road between Glen Rinnes and Aberlour on the east side of Ben Rinnes, provided this narrow road is not blocked by snow. Parking may be difficult, and you may wish to use the nearby hillwalkers' car park. Start at NJ 282 365 and follow a bulldozed track west for about 1km before turning south to join the east ridge west of Roy's Hill, and thereafter take the main east ridge to the summit (3.5km; 540m; 2.5hrs).

An ascent is also possible from the A95 side, starting from close to the Benrinnes Distillery at Milltown of Edinville. Just south of the distillery a track leads south up the northern slopes of Ben Rinnes past the Tom of Ruthrie from where the water of life (Uisge Beatha) flows. Roadside parking can be found at Upper Lyne but please park considerately (NJ 257 393; 264m). Follow the track south for 2km, climbing to a point high on Baby's Hill. From there head a further 2km south, then south-east, above the Scurran of Well to the summit of Ben Rinnes (4km; 580m; 2.5hrs).

Opposite: Cairn Gorm summit igloo dressed in its winter splendour (skier, Lucy Dowland) © Tom Weston

Chapter 7

West Scotland South

Previous spread: Looking West towards Stob Poite Coire Ardair from Sròn Coire a' Chriochairein
© Oli Warlow

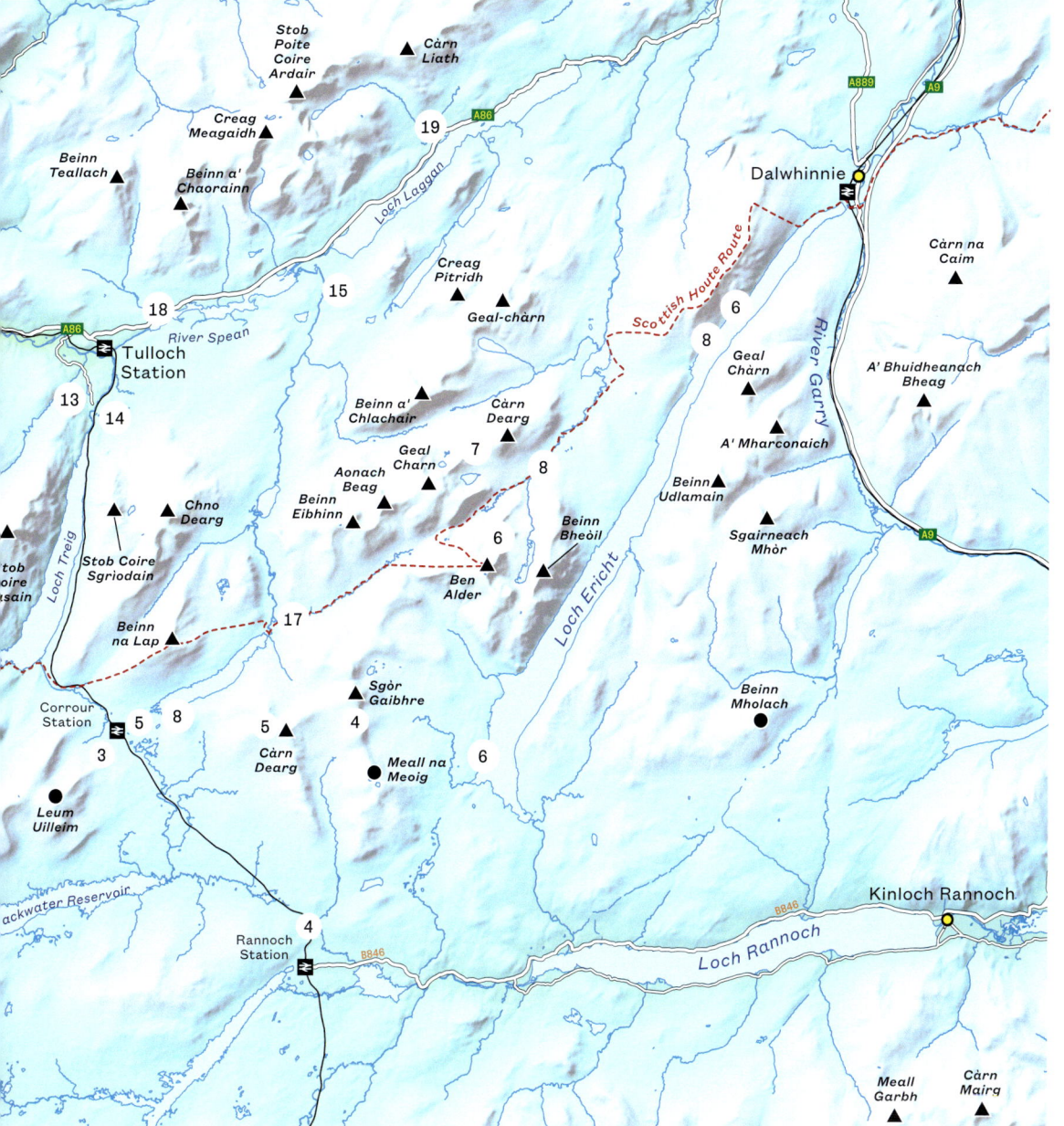

1.	Buachaille Etive Beag	P.254	11. Ben Nevis	P.272
2.	Beinn a' Chrùlaiste	P.255	12. The Aonachs Traverse	P.277
3.	Leum Uilleim	P.258	13. The Grey Corries	P.280
4.	Rannoch Traverse	P.258	14. The Easains	P.284
5.	Beinn na Lap	P.261	15. Chno Dearg	P.284
6.	Ben Alder	P.261	16. Creag Pitridh	P.287
7.	Corrour Ridge	P.263	17. Scottish Haute Route	P.289
8.	Corrour to Dalwhinnie Traverse	P.265	18. Beinn Teallach	P.306
9.	Mamores West	P.267	19. Creag Meagaidh	P.307
10.	Druim Fada	P.270	20. Gulvain	P.310

Buachaille Etive Beag

The Little Shepherd or Herdsman, of Etive

Stob Dubh ▲ 958m
Black Peak

△ NN 179 535   ↗ LR41   🌐 P.254

Ⓟ The NTS car park on the A82 in Glen Coe (NN 188 562/ 56.6627, -4.9580).

↔ 11KM   △ 960M   ↕ 170M
⏱ 4 HRS   GRADE II   ★★

By Colwyn Jones

Buachaille Etive Beag sits comfortably, watched over by a more hearty neighbour, the Buachaille Etive Mòr (Big Shepherd of Etive), on the south side of Glen Coe. The north-east face is too steep and broken to use as an ascent route, but further west

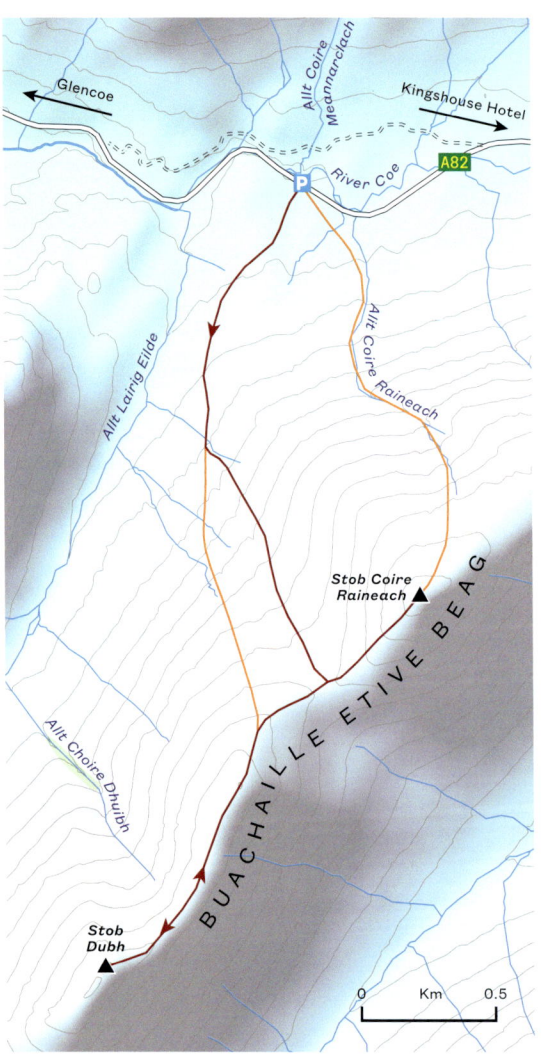

a large car park allows good access to a pleasant ascent on skis, steep in places, but with good descent slopes for the downhill run if sufficient snow has accumulated. The western flank of the peak is rough ground, and a substantial depth of snow is needed for a ski descent back to the well-maintained footpath down the Làirig Eilde, serving the car park. On a fine day this is a short tour with grand views of the surrounding mountains, including south down to Loch Etive.

From the west end of the car park, opposite the beehive cairn, follow the track up to the 310m contour where there is a small descent. Bear left up the hill, and as the footpath has many steps, the choice of ascent is dictated by the best snow cover. Vague hollows on either side of the footpath retain snow and can often be used to good effect. The climb is not trivial, with some steeper sections, but with purpose you will soon arrive at the bealach (750m) between the northern top, Stob Coire Raineach, and the main summit, Stob Dubh. Both summits can be visited with fine views from the northern top (925m). The Allt Coire Raineach (1:25,000 map) drains down a gully on the left side of the north face of this top, and with good snow cover gives a steep and exciting 750m run almost straight back to the car park. The condition of this line can be checked as you approach the car park. The highest point on the 'Wee Buachaille' has an undulating approach ridge, passing over a north-east top (902m) and a steep final slope where skis may need to be carried, or a ski depot fashioned to safely reach the summit.

The return follows the ascent route. The skiing off the summit is steep and exciting, but the subsequent undulating ridge probably needs a bit of poling. The descent back to the bealach, perhaps favouring deeper snow on the right (east) side of the ridge but avoiding any cornices, leads back to the ascent path and fine skiing down the west flank of the peak. If conditions allow, an earlier descent north from the north-east top can give good, steep skiing for the impetuous. The lower flank is rough with many course streambeds, and traversing early in the descent may ease your return to the car.

It is not known whether a traverse of Buachaille Etive Beag has ever been achieved by skiing down the steep, grassy south ridge to Dalness. Such a route would require careful assessment of the snow conditions and would finish less than 100m above sea level where it meets the road in Glen Etive. It is steep (over 30 degrees in places), south-facing, and would require care at the top and foot of the ridge (and indeed throughout the run) to avoid rocks at the top and to cross deer fences down near Dalness. A second car would also be needed.

Beinn a' Chrùlaiste ● 857m
Rocky Hill

△ NN 246 566   ◁ LR41   ⊕ P.255

P Altnafeadh car park on the A82 (NN 220 563/ 56.6647, -4.9060).
↔ 6KM   △ 570M   ↕ 290M
⏱ 3-4 HRS   GRADE III   ★★

By Colwyn Jones

Beinn a' Chrùlaiste forms the north side of eastern Glen Coe. It is somewhat overshadowed by the Buachaille Etive Mòr (Big Herdsman of Etive), but from the summit it affords excellent views of the north face of that iconic Glen Coe peak. The broken south flank is too steep to use as an ascent route, but both the east and west ridges provide a pleasant ascent on skis and a good, if short, day out. They can also be combined to allow a fine traverse of the peak with either a second car or a 4km ski or walk back from the Kingshouse Hotel to the Altnafeadh car park along the West Highland Way footpath. A good snowfall is needed to cover the vegetation on the lower part of the route. For those staying in the photogenic SMC Hut at Lagangarbh, the busy car park at Altnafeadh allows easy pedestrian access to the west ridge. Two waist-high fences must be negotiated next to the roadside trees before you can start up the wide east ridge. At the 640m contour the ridge eases then continues steadily for another 220 vertical metres to the triangulation station on a somewhat undistinguished summit. However, there is a splendid view of Buachaille Etive Mòr, a bleak Rannoch Moor rolling east and brooding Glen Coe. To the north the views of some of the highest Scottish mountains are also very fine.

A simple descent by the route of ascent gives a pleasant ski, or, if you are traversing the peak, set off south-east down the ridge to return to the Kingshouse Hotel close to the right bank of the Allt a' Bhalaich (Boy's burn). Alternatively, from the summit, go north overlooking the Coire Bhalach before following the flat ridge east round to points 708m and 705m, then return south along the left bank of the Allt a' Bhalaich directly to the Kingshouse Hotel for some refreshment.

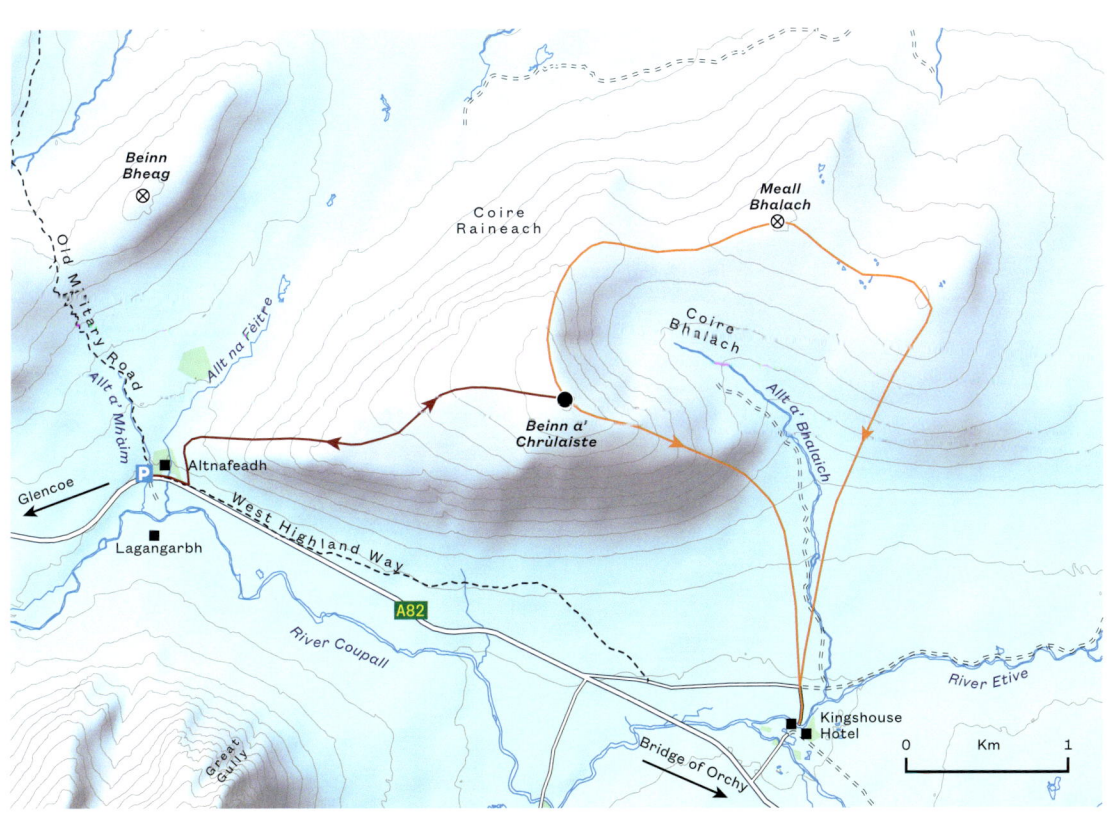

Below: Beinn a' Chrùlaiste
(skier Tom Southworth)
© Al Todd

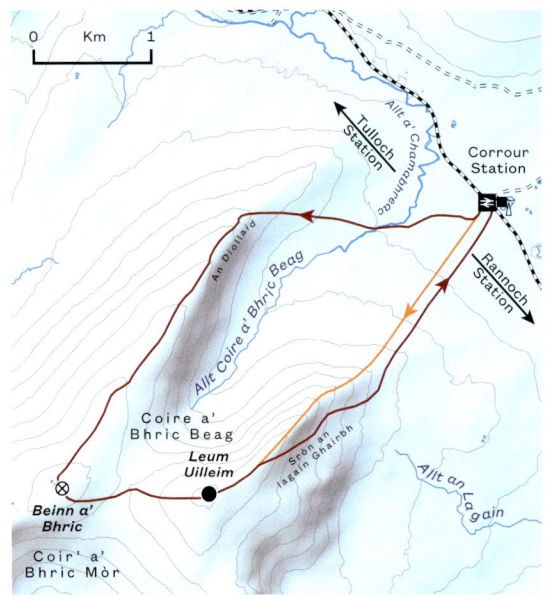

be followed across the Allt Coire a' Bhric Beag draining the corrie to the north-east ridge. This is labelled An Diollaid at the 600m contour, and there is an ATV track which may hold snow leading over Tom an Eòin, then past a cairn to reach the summit of Beinn a' Bhric (NN 318 642; 876m). Turn east, and after a short descent (which is probably not worth removing climbing skins for) it is a 100m steady vertical ascent, avoiding any rocks, to the large summit cairn less than 1km away (909m).

Take in the stunning views across Rannoch Moor, over to Ben Nevis, flanked by the Mamores and the Grey Corries, and even better views towards the great peaks around Glencoe and to the south-east the tidy pyramid of Schiehallion. Descent is a fine run down the north-east ridge, Sròn an Lagain Ghairbh, avoiding any prominent rocks or crags and aiming directly for the railway station. The gradient eases over the final kilometre to the station, or perhaps the start of the outward path, so some poling will be required to finally arrive on the appropriate platform and then board the train home.

Leum Uilleim ● 909m
William's Leap

△ NN 331 641   ⌯ LR41   ⊕ P.258

P Route starts from Corrour Station (parking at Rannoch Station). Note that the Station House Restaurant is closed during the winter and that there is no indoor station waiting room.

↔ 10KM   △ 580M   ⊺ 400M
⏱ 3-4 HRS   GRADE II   ★★★

By Colwyn Jones

Lying south-west of Corrour train station on the West Highland Railway Line, the Corbett, Leum Uilleim, provides a short ski tour on the northern edge of Rannoch Moor. It featured as the backdrop in a bleak scene from Danny Boyle's 1996 film, *Trainspotting*, but this ski tour is far from bleak and provides a pleasant day out with a comfortable train journey to a remote setting.

When the usually boggy peat hags are well frozen, the shortest tour is an out-and-back south-west route straight to the summit. This might be the route of choice if there are only a few hours before the next train home is due. A more satisfying circular tour follows the rim of the north-east-facing cirque, Coir' a' Bhric Beag (Coire of the Little Trout).

Go north along the platform, then turn left to access the open hillside. There are established tracks here on the west of the railway line and, depending on snow conditions, one of these may

Rannoch Traverse

Càrn Dearg ▲ 941m
Red Hill

△ NN 417 661   ⌯ LR41, LR42   ⊕ P.259

Sgòr Gaibhre ▲ 955m
Goat Peak

△ NN 444 674   ⌯ LR41, LR42   ⊕ P.259

P Route starts from Corrour Station (parking at Rannoch Station). Note that the Station House Restaurant is closed during the winter months and there is no indoor waiting room here or at Rannoch Station, where the Tearoom is also closed during the winter.

↔ 19KM   △ 780M   ⊺ 400M
⏱ 6 HRS   GRADE II   ★★

By Chris Ford, updated by Colwyn Jones

These two hills of long ridges and wide corries are at the north-east corner of Rannoch Moor, and they are among the few Scottish hills that are easier to reach by railway locomotive rather than by car. The West Highland Railway Line between Rannoch and Corrour Stations crosses desolate moorland at the foot of Càrn Dearg, and the traverse of the

Key
1. Rannoch Traverse   P.258
2. Beinn na Lap   P.261

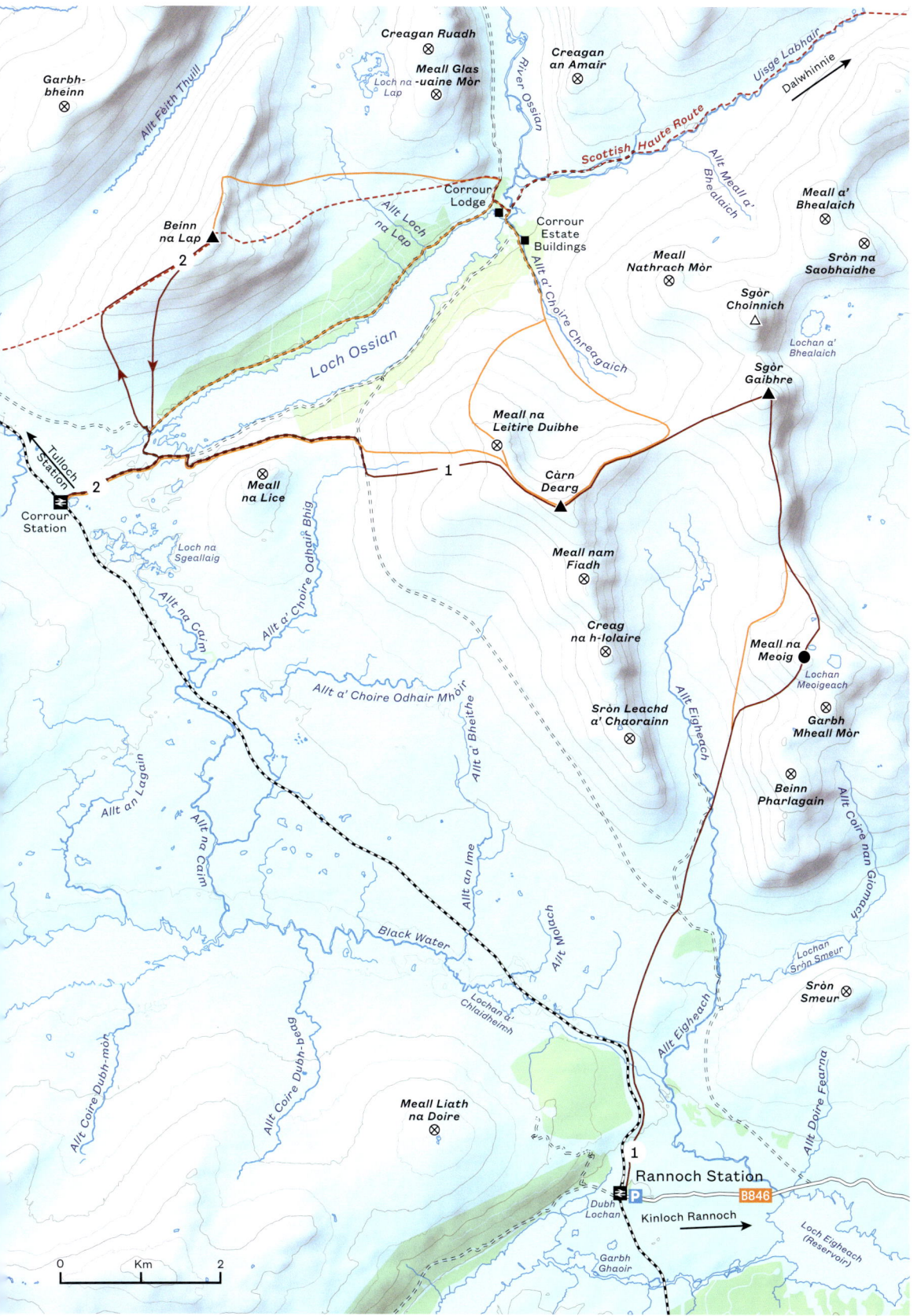

two hills from one station to the other is a fine, logical expedition. The pleasure of this linear tour depends greatly on the conditions, for the hills are undistinguished and there is a lot of very easy-angled skiing. Snow cover down to the moor is essential (Rannoch Station is 300m above sea level). On a clear day the views alone are adequate reward, and on good snow you will enjoy miles of easy ski-running. On a dull day with wet snow, however, there may be prolonged poling down the long glen of the Allt Eigheach on the return to Rannoch Station.

Access to Corrour is dictated by the timing of the early morning trains between Glasgow and Fort William. The time available for the tour depends on the afternoon train passing through Rannoch Station – beware the limited Sunday service!

From Corrour ski east along the track to the head of Loch Ossian, losing a few metres of height. Opposite the youth hostel, leave the lochside track and make a rising traverse for 2km along the improved path round the north side of Meall na Lice. The track turns south at Peter's Rock, a memorial to Peter Trowell, an assistant warden at the nearby Loch Ossian Youth Hostel. He was reported missing in 1979 and his body was recovered from the loch when it thawed several weeks later. Presumably he had fallen in while working at the lochside.

After fording the Allt a' Choire Odhair Bhig, continue east up a wide-open corrie to gain the north-west ridge of Càrn Dearg. This broad ridge provides a gradual ascent of about 1km to the summit cairn of Càrn Dearg (941m). The view west to Ben Nevis and the Mamores is superb. Turn north-east and ski down the broad easy ridge to the Màm Bàn col, then re-apply skins and climb a remarkably constant steeper ridge to the summit of Sgòr Gaibhre (955m).

From here the return to Rannoch Station is 9km, with a drop of 660m. Ski down the south ridge of Sgòr Gaibhre for 2km to Bealach Leathann. If the Corbett Meall na Meoig is included, skin up to the summit just over 1km away. Otherwise take a long, very gradual descending traverse across the west flank of Meall na Meoig and Beinn Pharlagain for 3km to cross the Allt Eigheach. Gain the west bank of the stream and keep to high ground, then pass west of a conifer plantation to shadow the railway 1.5km back to Rannoch Station. Do not follow the landrover track down the glen to the B846, as this requires skiing (or more likely walking) 2.5km along the flat road to the car park at Rannoch Station.

Below: Càrn Dearg
from Corrour Station
© Colwyn Jones

Beinn na Lap ▲ 935m
Dappled Hill

△ NN 376 695   ◁ LR41   ⊕ P.259

▣ Route starts from Corrour Station (parking at Rannoch Station). Note there is only an open bus style shelter, no indoor passenger waiting room. Note that the Station House Restaurant is closed during the winter.

↔ 18KM   △ 550M   ⊥ 400M
⏱ 4-5 HRS   GRADE II   ★★

By Colwyn Jones

Ideally, it may be possible to ski from snow-covered platforms at Corrour Station, passing the Corrour Station House Restaurant (closed November to March) and following the estate road east towards Loch Ossian Youth Hostel. Take the left fork after 1.25km leading to a bridge towards the north-west side of the loch. Almost immediately take the second left fork and shortly leave the track to begin ascending the south flank of the peak. The summer footpath favoured by the many visiting Munroists (often as their final Munro) takes a similar route and may hold a good line of snow. Alternatively, an old landslip just west of the summer footpath may accumulate more snow and permit a better skinning track. The gradient steepens towards Ceann Caol Beinn na Lap (the narrow head of the dappled hill), and moving onto the broad whaleback ridge allows an easy, safe approach if snow has not been stripped from the many rocky areas. This ridge eventually reaches the summit, which has an untidy cairn offering little shelter. (Note that a small walled shelter does not mark the summit.) The views south-west stretch across the beautiful white expanse of Rannoch Moor, while north-west lie the complex mountains of the Mamores leading over to Ben Nevis.

The simplest return is back down the ascent route, choosing the best line of snow seen on the ascent.

The option of a traverse of the peak beckons, with a return to the shores of Loch Ossian after heading east from the summit. Beware, however, as the east flank is initially rocky and may be corniced – care is needed to choose a safe descent line. In poor conditions heading northwards from the top for 800m to the 850m contour should allow you to safely turn east and descend into Coire na Lap (1:25,000 map). From there the gradient flattens somewhat, and cunning is needed to keep your skis running to the track near the end of Strath Ossian. This is close to the striking modernist, four-storey glass and and granite Corrour Shooting Lodge.

From the east end of Loch Ossian there is a good flat gravel track to ski (or walk) the 8km back to the railway station. Make sure that you have sufficient time before the train home, but do not arrive too early, as the warm, comfortable station restaurant is closed in winter, and the waiting room is an open bus shelter style! Skiing up Càrn Dearg on the south side of the loch, by either the north-east or north-west ridge, before returning to the train station gives a very satisfying circular tour. Staying at the eco-friendly all-year-round Loch Ossian Youth Hostel in what feels like a remote and lonely setting is another attractive option.

Ben Alder ▲ 1,148m
Rock and Water Mountain

△ NN 496 718   ◁ LR42   ⊕ P.262

Beinn Bheòil ▲ 1,019m
Hill of the Mouth or *Opening*

△ NN 517 717   ◁ LR42   ⊕ P.262

▣ Cycle from Dalwhinnie village (NN 634 841/ 56.9282, -4.2448, 11km) on the private road along the north-west side of Loch Ericht to Ben Alder Lodge and Loch Pattack.

↔ 26KM   △ 970M   ⊥ 360M
⏱ 8-9 HRS   GRADE IV   ★★★★

By Bill Morrison, updated by Colwyn Jones

Lying between Loch Ericht to the east and the Geal-Chàrn group to the west, Ben Alder, with its mouthy neighbour Beinn Bheòil, occupies a central position in the Highlands, midway between the Lochaber mountains and the Cairngorms. It is a huge flat-topped mountain, prominent in views from the south-west across Rannoch Moor and from Dalwhinnie to the north-east, its great high plateau dominating the surrounding hills and its corries holding snow until early summer.

The approaches to Ben Alder include the route from Dalwhinnie to Loch Pattack, and this is probably the best choice. The first 11km can be covered on a mountain bike, as can the 12.5km approach from the A86 near Inverpattack Lodge. Another good starting point for the ascent is Benalder Cottage, 4km south of the summit, which is reached either from Corrour Station over Càrn Dearg and Sgòr Gaibhre (as described in The Rannoch Traverse), or from the west end of Loch Rannoch by the track to the south end of Loch Ericht. All approaches are exceptionally long, emphasising the remoteness of Ben Alder and adding to the appeal of skiing these peaks.

The entire northern perimeter of Ben Alder, from the Bealach Dubh right round to the Bealach

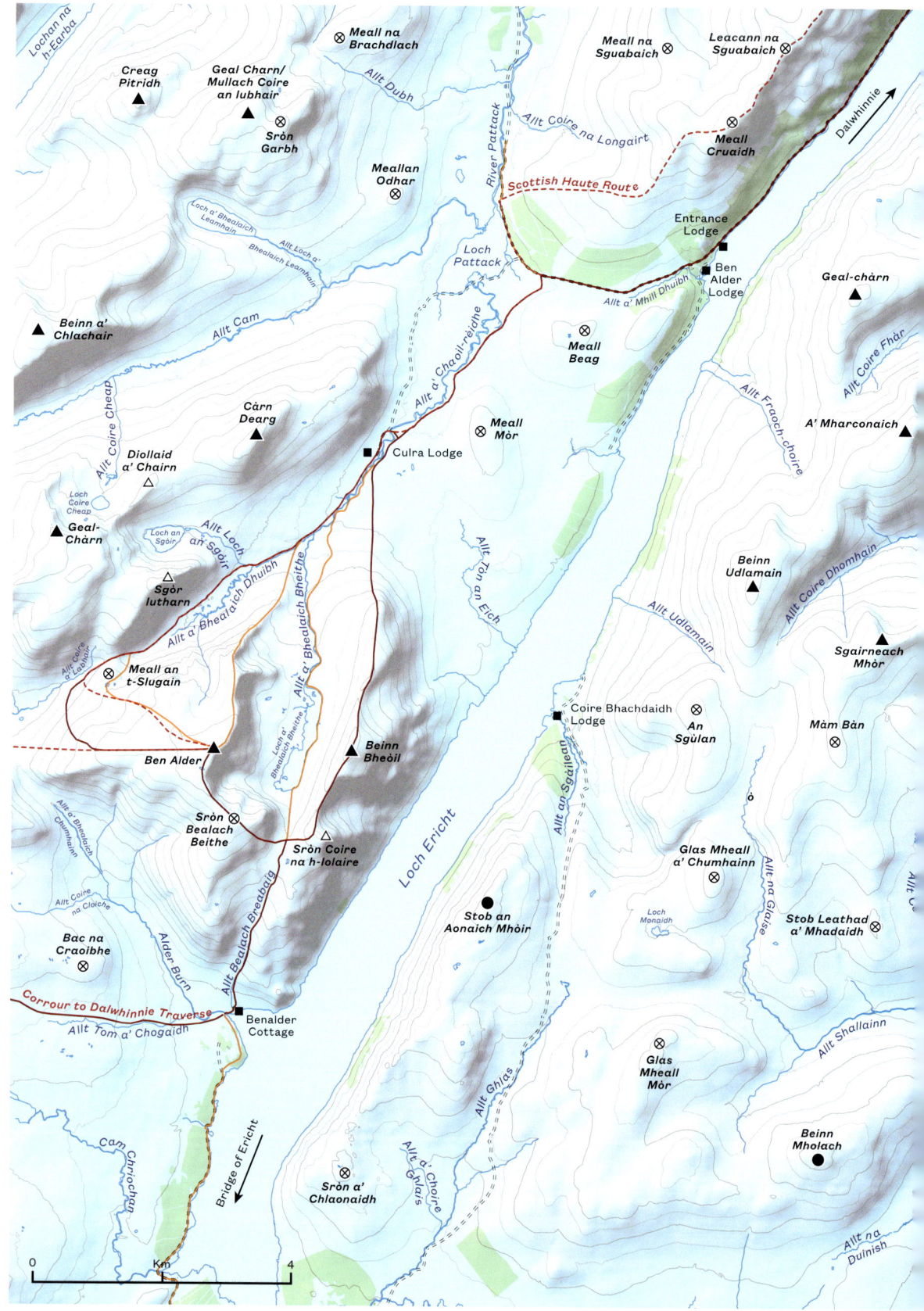

Breabag, is a continuous line of steep crags, rocky ridges and corries, and the ski mountaineer approaching from Loch Pattack must outflank these obstacles to the south unless prepared to shoulder skis and do some serious climbing. The easiest route goes past Culra Lodge to Ben Alder, south-west up the Allt a' Bhealaich Dhuibh to the Bealach Dubh – a splendid pass – then either south-east directly through, or south-west round, the west side of the knoll Meall an t-Slugain and south to reach the broad west shoulder. This is then climbed due east to the triangulation station on the summit.

An alternative and interesting route of distinctly alpine character is the Long Leachas ridge, which drops from the summit plateau directly towards Culra Lodge. The current SMC Ben Nevis climbing guide (which covers Ben Alder) classifies the route as a Grade I winter climb. It should be possible to ski up to about the 800m contour at the foot of the narrow rocky section of the ridge; then you will need to carry your skis on your rucksack and, with crampons on, scramble up the ridge, which is quite narrow and exposed in places. It is best not to attempt this on a windy day! At 1,000m the ridge ends on the summit plateau and the top is 1.5km distant.

From the summit ski south-south-west for 500m, then south-east, keeping well clear of the edge of the Garbh Choire, which often has very large cornices. Continue south-east down the steep slope above the Bealach Breabag, taking care to avoid the crags on the northern part of this slope. At the Bealach Breabag (840m) join the route from Benalder Cottage, which goes directly up the corrie north of the cottage to the bealach and may be continued to Ben Alder by ascending the descent route described above.

From the bealach it is possible to make a direct return to Culra by skiing north past Loch a' Bhealaich Bheithe, either by its west or east shore, and across the lower moor to Loch Pattack.

To complete the traverse over Beinn Bheòil, climb the easy slope north-east from the Bealach Breabag to Sròn Coire na h-Iolaire (955m). From this top go north-west briefly round the edge of the corrie and reach the long ridge leading to the summit of Beinn Bheòil. This ridge is straightforward but does not always hold snow well. From the summit of Beinn Bheòil continue north along the broad ridge for 2km to a level shoulder at 900m, then take the best snow, either on the ridge or its west flank, down pleasant slopes leading to Loch Pattack.

Corrour Ridge

Beinn Eibhinn ▲ 1,102m
Delightful Hill
NN 449 733   LR41, LR42   P.264

Aonach Beag ▲ 1,116m
Little Ridge
NN 457 741   LR41, LR42   P.264

Geal-Chàrn ▲ 1,132m
White Hill
NN 469 746   LR42   P.264

Càrn Dearg ▲ 1,034m
Red Hill
NN 504 764   LR42   P.264

Corrour Lodge (NN 412 697/56.7921, -4.6015) at the east end of Loch Ossian.

↔ 22KM   △ 1,000M   ⊥ 390M
⏱ 8-9 HRS   GRADE IV   ★★★★★

By Bill Morrison, updated by Colwyn Jones

This exceptional range of mountains, 9km long, lies to the north of the Ben Alder group in the heart of the Central Highlands, remote from all public roads. Because of their height and distance from the coast, these mountains hold snow well. They have some splendid ridges which are narrow and steep enough to give demanding skiing, and great corries which are often snow-filled until late spring. This, combined with the inaccessibility and character of these hills, makes their traverse on skis one of the best expeditions of its kind in Scotland.

Points of access include Dalwhinnie to the north-east, Moy on the A86 in Glen Spean to the north, and Corrour Station on the West Highland Railway Line to the south-west. It is advisable to reserve this tour for late winter or spring when the snow on the steeper slopes should be consolidated. Long daylight hours are also necessary if an early morning start in darkness is to be avoided.

For most ski mountaineers a starting point near the foot of the range is desirable. In the first edition, Culra Bothy, 15km south-west of Dalwhinnie, was fêted as the ideal base. However, the bothy is closed pending demolition owing to the presence of asbestos. Wild camping is still an option and works well when combined with a mountain bike approach from Dalwhinnie, although a second night camping would probably be needed to comfortably traverse these hills.

An alternative is to base yourselves on the Corrour Estate where suitable, even desirable, accommodation can be booked around the north-east end of Loch Ossian. There are a number of estate cottages. Even the conspicuous Corrour Lodge, built in 2003, can be rented with a dining room for up to 40 people. Vehicle access on private roads from Moy on the A86 is an added benefit, although if arriving by train at Corrour Station, collection by an estate vehicle can be arranged. Loch Ossian Youth Hostel at the south-west end of Loch Ossian may also be available to hire.

Starting from Corrour Lodge, at the bridge over the loch outflow, take a track north-east over another bridge and open ground to a further bridge over the Uisge Labhair, following its north bank to a small hydroelectric dam. After crossing the bridge over the tributary, the Allt Feith a' Mheallain (470m), the open hillside beckons. Take a direct line up to the Meall Glas Choire (924m). Continue north to the 1,000m contour, then turn east towards the summit of Beinn Eibhinn (1,102m), which is reached after 1km. The views back down Loch Ossian and into Glen Coe are excellent.

From the summit there are steep drops on both sides of the narrow east ridge, and a good covering of snow is desirable. Head east along the ridge, then shortly turn north-east to approach the steep-sided summit cone of Aonach Beag (1,116m) directly. Only 1.5km separates these first two summits, which are welcome successes so early in the day.

Continue east down along the ridge for 500m, then start the ascent to the high point of the ridge, which curves north to reach the summit of Geal-Chàrn (1,132m). Again, this is less than 1.5km from the second summit and is a third welcome success.

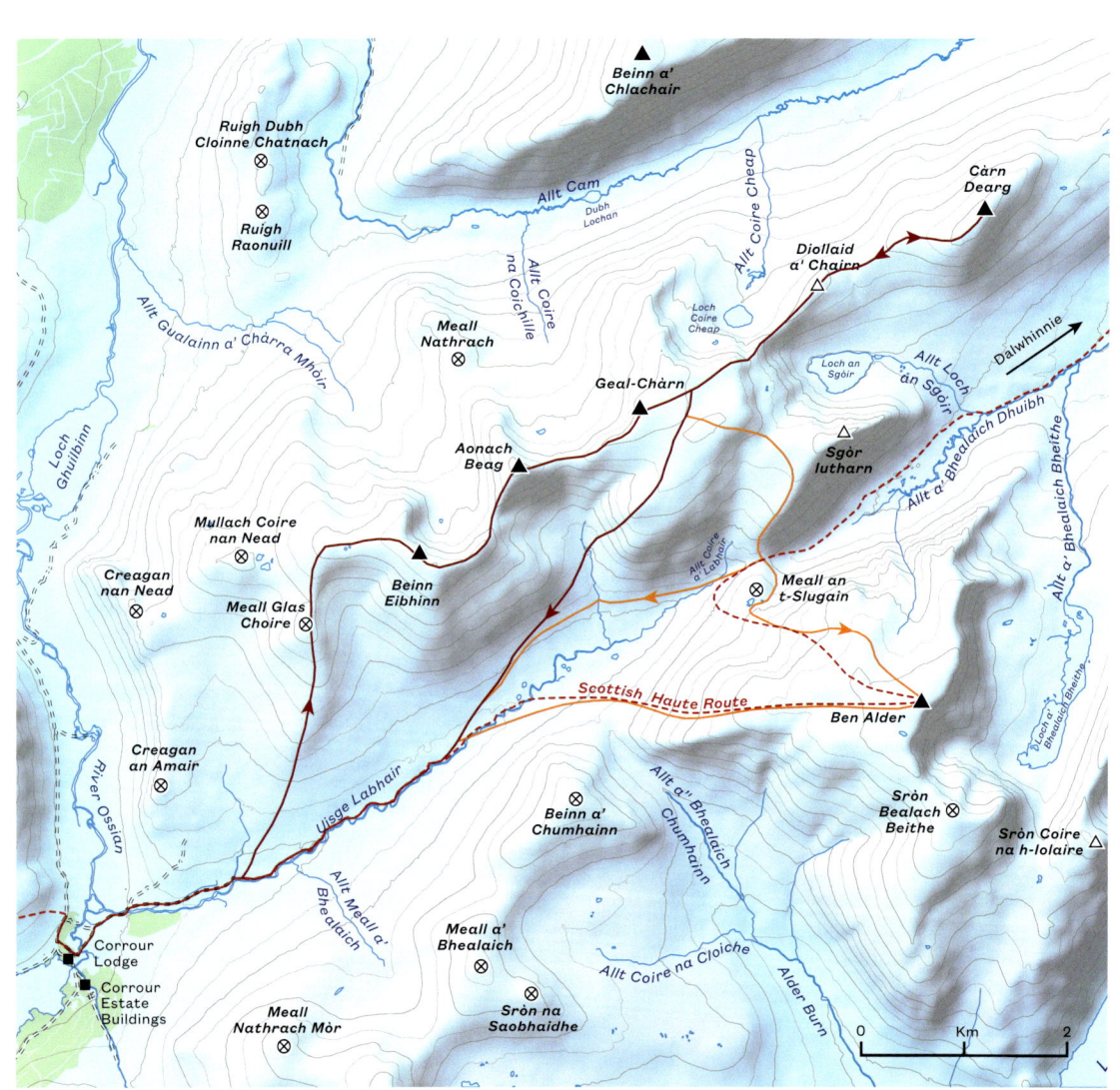

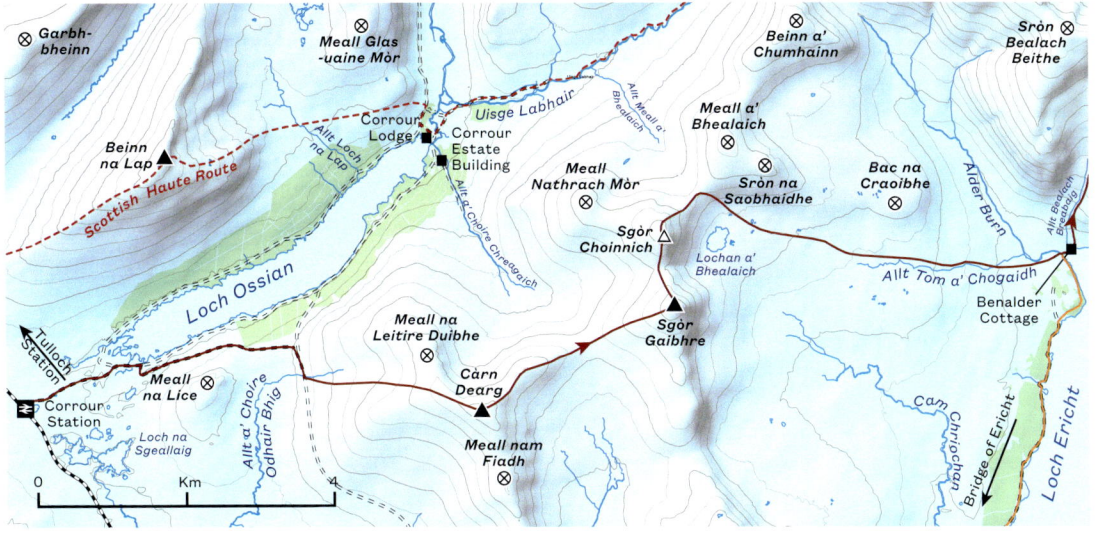

Continuing on to Càrn Dearg involves descent of the narrow, steep, rocky north-east arête (probably best done on foot with an ice axe and crampons), which leads to a saddle where skis can be donned again before continuing north-east along the ridge to Diollaid a' Chairn (925m). The summit of Càrn Dearg (1,034m) is 2km further along a comfortable broad ridge, and while it is soon reached, arrival on this final summit, perhaps late in the day, is also the furthest point from Corrour.

If conditions allow, your return to Corrour is best achieved by retracing your steps up to Geal-Chàrn but aiming for the 1,107m spot height and not the summit. From here descend south-east, then south to Bealach Dubh and return along the north bank of the Uisge Labhair. A steeper and more direct line is possible south-west into the Coire a' Chàrra Bhig, then back to the footpath at the foot of the glen and then the starting point.

During the 2006 SMC ski meet, on arriving at the summit of Geal-Chàrn, the party ignored Càrn Dearg, skied down to Bealach Dubh, crossed onto the opposite side and traversed right, avoiding crags, before skiing directly to the triangulation station on the summit of Ben Alder (1,148m). From the summit a fine 5km descent due west was enjoyed before returning on foot along the north bank of the Uisge Labhair in the gathering darkness to Corrour, for fine company and a good supper.

Corrour to Dalwhinnie Traverse

Càrn Dearg ▲ 941m
Red Hill
NN 417 661   LR41, LR42   P.265/262/149

Sgòr Gaibhre ▲ 955m
Goat Peak
NN 444 674   LR41, LR42   P.265/262/149

Sgòr Choinnich △ 929m
NN 443 683   LR41, LR42   P.265/262/149

Ben Alder ▲ 1,148m
Hill of Rock and Water
NN 496 718   LR41, LR42   P.265/262/149

Beinn Bheòil ▲ 1,019m
Hill of the Mouth
NN 517 717   LR41, LR42   P.265/262/149

The Fara ● 911m
Ladder Hill
NN 598 843   LR42   P.265/262/149

Route starts from Corrour Station (parking at Rannoch Station). Note that the Station House Restaurant is closed during the winter and that there is no indoor station waiting room.

↔ 48KM (18KM / 30KM)   ⌁ 2,480M (930M & 1,550M)
↕ 400M   ⏲ 16-20 HRS (OVER 2 DAYS)
GRADE III   ★★★★

By Colwyn Jones

For some, this traverse recalls a bygone era when access to many parts of Scotland relied on coastal steamers and steam locomotives. This traverse no longer relies on steam but on diesel and links the West Highland Railway Line to the Central Belt–Inverness Line. In the 1983 Eagle Ski Club yearbook, John Harding wrote about the traverse, catching the overnight Caledonian sleeper from Euston station in London, disembarking on Day 1, spending Saturday night wild camping below Ben Alder, then, at the close of Day 2, catching the sleeper back to London to get to the office on Monday morning. Culra Bothy is no longer safe to use, and either using Benalder Cottage or wild camping/snowholing is necessary if you are planning this nostalgic traverse. The route from Corrour to Dalwhinnie is described, but starting from Dalwhinnie and finishing at Corrour Station is equally fine.

The start of this splendid point-to-point traverse is described in the Rannoch Forest tour (p.258), which should be followed from Corrour Station, over Càrn Dearg and on to the summit of Sgòr Gaibhre. From the summit of Sgòr Gaibhre the Dalwhinnie traverse then continues north then east to Benalder Cottage as the destination on the first day of this two-day expedition.

From Sgòr Gaibhre ski down the steep north-north-west flank, then north to the Bealach nan Sgòr and ascend 230m to the summit of Sgòr Choinnich (929m). Avoid the steep east face and ski north then north-east to Càrn a' Bhealaich (NN 448 688; 750m).

From there descend south-east down a steep slope to the corrie north of Lochan a' Bhealaich, from where an easy run of 5km down the Allt Tom a' Chogaidh leads to Benalder Cottage (NN 499 680; 373m). The footbridge over the Alder Burn shown on the 1:50,000 map has been replaced at least once after being washed away by a spate. Benalder Cottage has a wood stove and is reputed to be haunted, although this may have been a ploy by the estate to discourage overnight visitors!

The start of Day 2 involves leaving the comfortable bothy and climbing almost due north for 2km up the line of the footpath to the Bealach Breabag (840m). From the bealach there are options. The simplest route to include the highest point, which is the summit of Ben Alder, is to climb north-west, then north, then north-east around the rim of the Garbh Choire to arrive at the triangulation station and take in the fine views from the large flat summit (1,148m).

The easiest descent is to return to the Bealach Breabag and traverse over Beinn Bheòil. Back at the bealach climb the easy slope north-east from the Bealach Breabag to Sròn Coire na h-Iolaire (955m).

From this top go north-west briefly round the edge of the corrie to reach the long ridge leading to Beinn Bheòil (1,019m). This ridge is quite easy but may not hold snow. From the summit of Beinn Bheòil continue north along the broad ridge for about 2km to a level shoulder at 900m, then on down the best snow, either on the ridge or its west flank, to agreeable slopes leading down to Culra Lodge. An alternative but difficult route to this point from the summit of Ben Alder, of a patently alpine character, is to descend the Long Leachas ridge (Grade I winter climb). There are narrow and exposed sections along the ridge, and skis will need to be strapped to your rucksack when climbing down these sections, so it might be best avoided on a windy day!

From Culra follow the footpath north-east over flat ground to meet the landrover track between Lock Pattack and Ben Alder Lodge. At an agricultural building on the track, it is possible to cross fences behind the barn and climb up the side of the forest to the long, undulating summit ridge of The Fara. This route is the same covered on Day 4 of the Scottish Haute Route tour. If time or the weather dictates otherwise, it may be preferable to ski or walk 12.5km back along the shore of Loch Ericht to Dalwhinnie, avoiding about 500m of ascent.

The three descent options from the summit of The Fara are described in the day tour for that hill (p.155). To complete the traverse, you need to return to Dalwhinnie Station (where, like Corrour, there are seating shelters but no indoor facilities) to wait for the train home. Sadly, the extended high tea at the art deco Grampian Hotel in Dalwhinnie, mentioned by Harding in his 1983 account, is no longer an option as the hotel has since been demolished.

Mamores West

Sgùrr a' Mhàim ▲ 1,099m
Peak of the Breast
⛰ NN 164 667   🧭 LR41   🌐 P.267

Stob Bàn ▲ 999m
White Peak
⛰ NN 147 654   🧭 LR41   🌐 P.267

Mullach nan Coirean ▲ 939m
Summit of the Corries
⛰ NN 122 662   🧭 LR41   🌐 P.267

🅿 Achriabhach or Lower Falls pay and display car park (NN 145 683/56.7695, -5.0370), Glen Nevis.

↔ 16KM   ⛰ 1,650M   ⥍ 60M
🕐 5-9 HRS   GRADE IV   ★★★★
(the Devil's Ridge is a grade I winter climb)

By Finlay Wild

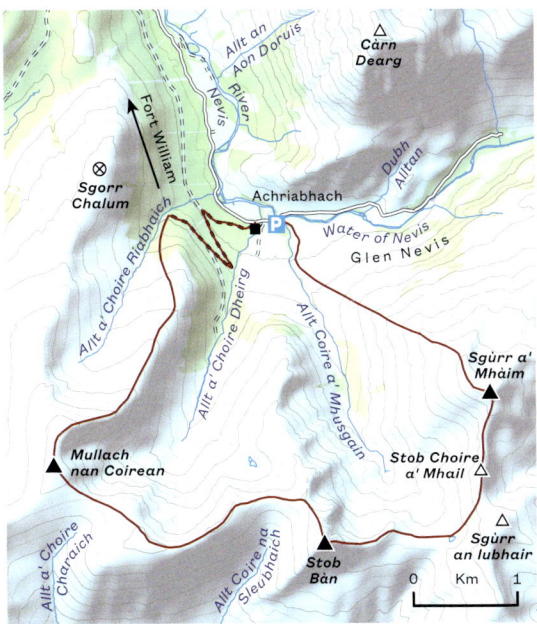

The Mamores is a beautiful and varied range of 10 Munros connected by high and often airy ridges lying south across the glen from Ben Nevis and the Aonachs. Although lower and thus often less reliable than the Ben, in the right conditions there is a wealth of rarely skied routes to be explored. The described route was skied in late January 2021 after a period of snowfall to low level, and takes in the three western Munros of Sgùrr a' Mhàim, Stob Bàn and Mullach nan Coirean. Depending on time and conditions other summits can be added - for example, all 10 Munros were enchained as part of a ski completion of Tranter's Round in 2016 (which also included Ben Nevis, Càrn Mòr Dearg, the Aonachs and Grey Corries in a 60km undertaking).

The Mamores are rough and complex hills requiring stable snow conditions and reasonable weather before embarking on skis - good conditions are elusive. Most will wish to approach from Glen Nevis, although the village of Kinlochleven to the south (accessible via bus from Fort William) gives an alternative access point, particularly for the central and eastern Mamores. Only rarely is the snow-line low enough to make the steep ascent from sea level in Kinlochleven attractive, but if the snow higher up is good, the initial slog may be well worth it!

Drive 7.5km up Glen Nevis and park either at Lower Falls or at a smaller pull-in by the bus stop at Achriabhach. Near Lower Falls Bridge (directly north of the car park) take the southern of two tracks on the south side of River Nevis, going over a stile then through a tall gate to access the hill on an obvious, gently uphill path going south-east, near the east bank of the Allt Coire a' Mhusgain. The path leads to the steep, relentless north-west ridge of Sgùrr a' Mhàim, and you should turn left at a vague junction to ascend this. Zigzagging steeply uphill, go through a gate in a deer fence and follow the track cut deeply into the hill. At some point on this 1,000m climb it should be possible to put skis on, although the steep ridge may need some careful kick turns to make effective progress. Generally grassy in the lower half, there are a few rock steps and bouldery regions, which can mostly be avoided. Higher, there is a slight relenting of the angle at around 850m before a steeper rise over scree (hopefully covered with consolidated snow) to the summit ridge. Cornices and strange wind lips can build up here, as well as on much of the rest of the route - it is advisable to save this route for a good visibility day. Easy escape options from Sgùrr a' Mhàim are limited, so if you decide that the Devil's Ridge or the alternative described below are not suitable, it is best to descend by reversing your route down the north-west ridge, although this is steep and unlikely to make a good ski. In fact if you have doubts about attempting the Devil's Ridge then it is probably best to avoid this tour.

From Sgùrr a' Mhàim descend south towards the narrow and technical Devil's Ridge. This ridge is a summer scramble and Grade I winter climb with exposed drops to each side. It may be possible to ski the initial slopes from the summit towards the ridge, but care must be taken to find a suitable spot at which to replace skis with boot crampons and axe, and possibly a rope for the mountaineering section on foot across the ridge. After Stob Choire a' Mhail the ridge descends gradually to the wider col at NN 164 656 which links to Sgùrr an Iubhair (Peak of the Yew) and possible routes to the Eastern Mamores. Alternatively, if the snow is stable, the Devil's Ridge can be bypassed to the east by skiing the south face of Sgùrr a' Mhàim from around NN 165 666 down to approximately 850m into what feels like a hanging bowl, then loosely following the line of the stalkers' track which traverses south below the Devil's Ridge and climbs more steeply back to the Stob Choire a' Mhail– Sgùrr an Iubhair col.

The grassy slope from the col to the outflow of tiny Lochan Coire nam Mìseach (NN 160 654) sometimes holds good snow, although in leaner conditions take note of the zigzagging stalkers' track which cuts across the slope. The lochan outflow is your best chance of replenishing water supplies. Follow the broader ridge west, which undulates before becoming steeper with cliffs to the north. Powdery drifts were encountered here by the 2021 party, who bootpacked the top part of the ridge as it steepens to gain Stob Bàn. Again, large cornices are common here, and the summit cairn is often totally buried. The north-west flank of Stob Bàn is very rocky, and the snow cover is often lean and unconsolidated. You may have to walk a short way to the small col at NN 146 657.

From here on, the ridge is generally easier, although the more benign-looking map contours do hide some short sections which can require some thought, particularly if there is unconsolidated soft snow and if you are concerned about your ski edges. At NN 130 654 there is a broad summit (917m), then a gentle descent north-west to a col and the final climb to reach Mullach nan Coirean. After summiting, head north then east-north-east to descend a rocky ridge – which again may require a section on foot – before the ridge turns back north-east and becomes broader before reaching a fence at NN 131 672. Stay on the west of the fence and follow it down heathery slopes as it curves east into lower Coire Riabhach. If you can still ski here you have exceptional conditions, and sooner or later skis will need to be carried as you enter the forestry over a stile at around 310m. Follow this winding track down until stone steps deposit you onto a forestry track. From here (NN 134 685) follow the wide track down two corners back to Achriabhach. Assuming there is no snow this low (the 2021 party managed to – just – ski the track to around 100m) it is quicker to take a shortcut path from the corner at NN 140 680 down the edge of the forest in a north-easterly direction back to the glen.

Above: Ascending from Lochan Coire nam Mìseach with Stob Bàn behind (skier, Bjorn Verduijn) © Finlay Wild

Druim Fada, Stob a' Ghrianain

Sunny Peak

◆ 744m

△ NN 087 824   ◁ LR41   ⊕ P.270

P The forestry gate and small pull-in (space for two or three cars) just before Inverskilavulin Bridge (NN 126 831/ 56.9015, -5.0790).

↔ 9KM   △ 750M   ⊥ 60M
⏱ 3–4 HRS   GRADE II   ★★

By Finlay Wild

Druim Fada is a prominent long ridge north of Corpach (Fort William) and an obvious objective for a shorter day when the snow-line is low enough. Its flat ridge runs west for about 5km from its main summit, Stob a' Ghrianain (744m), at the eastern end. The peak is mostly grassy and may therefore be a suitable objective when snow cover is marginal or unconsolidated. There are some steeper shallow corries to the north running into Glen Loy.

Several routes are possible, the shortest involving an ascent of Stob a' Ghrianain from Inverskilavulin in Glen Loy via Coire an Lightuinn, with a descent the same way. Longer outings could start this way but then continue along the 5km undulating grassy ridge – which gives unusual but fine views to Fort William and Ben Nevis – to the western end of Druim Fada at Coille Mhòr (NN 039 821; 635m). You could then return the same way or descend to Gleann Suileag with a finish at Fassfern. The latter option would require extra logistics, for example leaving a car in Glen Loy and a car at Fassfern, or perhaps using the Shiel Buses service 500 from Fort William to Mallaig. Glensulaig Bothy (NN 030 833) could potentially be used as a base.

Approach the hill from Glen Loy (Inverskilavulin), where there is limited parking by a forest gate. Take the forest track in a south-westerly direction, avoiding forks, until it curves south to a prominent

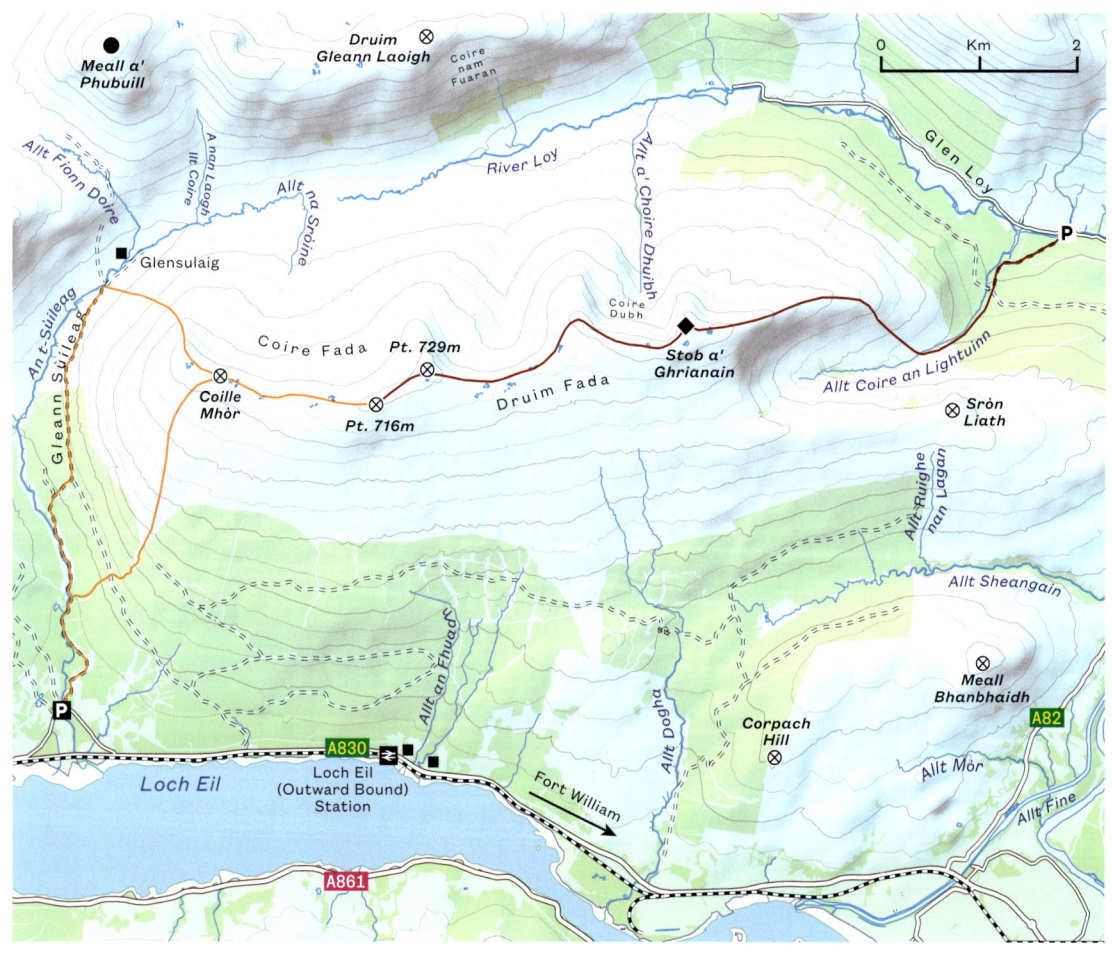

junction (NN 118 826). Take the left-hand (south) junction for a short way, then find a signposted narrow track heading south-west into Coire an Lightuinn near the south bank of the Allt Coire an Lightuinn. This path is boggy and undulating but quickly leads to a gate in the forest (NN 114 821). On the open moor continue on the path heading west to a small bridge which is not marked on the map (NN 112 821). Crossing this, the path continues north-west onto the east shoulder of Druim Fada, then to the summit of Stob a' Ghrianain (NN 087 824).

From here you can either return to Glen Loy via the best ski lines in Coire an Lightuinn, or continue along the Druim Fada ridge to the west top (NN 060 822; 729m), trig point (NN 055 817; 716m) or Coille Mhòr (NN 039 821; 635m). At this point you can retrace your steps back along the ridge to Glen Loy, or (if a second car has been pre-placed or you plan to use the bus from Fassfern) descend the western end of Druim Fada to the forestry track south of Glensulaig Bothy at approx NN 026 827, then ski or walk down Gleann Suileag on good forestry tracks to Fassfern where there is a forestry car park (NN 021 789). Alternatively, it may be possible to ski a descent route south-west from Coille Mhòr to enter the forest at around NN 030 805 and pick up forestry tracks to descend to Fassfern, although the author has not skied this variation.

Below: Observatory Gully, Ben Nevis (skier, Finbar Doig) © Al Todd

Ben Nevis ▲ 1,345m
Venomous or *Cloudy Mountain*

△ NN 166 712　　◇ LR41　　⊕ P.272

🅿 North Face pay and display car park (NN 144 763/ 56.8420, -5.0432) off the A82 at Torlundy north-east of Fort William.

↔ 16KM　　△ 1,315M　　⊥ 30M
⏱ 6-8 HRS　　GRADE IV　　★★★★

🅿 Alternative starting points at Achintee (NN 126 730), Ben Nevis Visitor Centre pay and display car park (NN 122 730/56.8109, -5.0767) or the Glen Nevis Youth Hostel (NN 128 718).

↔ 10-12KM　　△ 1,330M　　⊥ 30M
⏱ 4-6 HRS　　GRADE IV　　★★★★

By Bill Morrison, updated by Colwyn Jones

Ben Nevis, the highest mountain in the UK at 1,345m, offers some of the most durable skiing in the country, but also some of the most challenging. It should always be regarded as a very serious ski mountaineering proposition on account of its height, steep upper slopes, cliffs and weather conditions. If conditions are good, this is a fine expedition with superb skiing and views; in a storm or white-out, Ben Nevis is best avoided, for the problems of navigation on the summit plateau are considerable, and the consequences of errors are likely to be very serious. Completely different snow may be encountered on opposite sides of the mountain, e.g. ice on the steep south-east side above the head of Coire Leis, and loose avalanche-prone powder or windslab at the top of the Red Burn on the north-west side. Ice axe and crampons are essential for this peak, and a rope, helmet

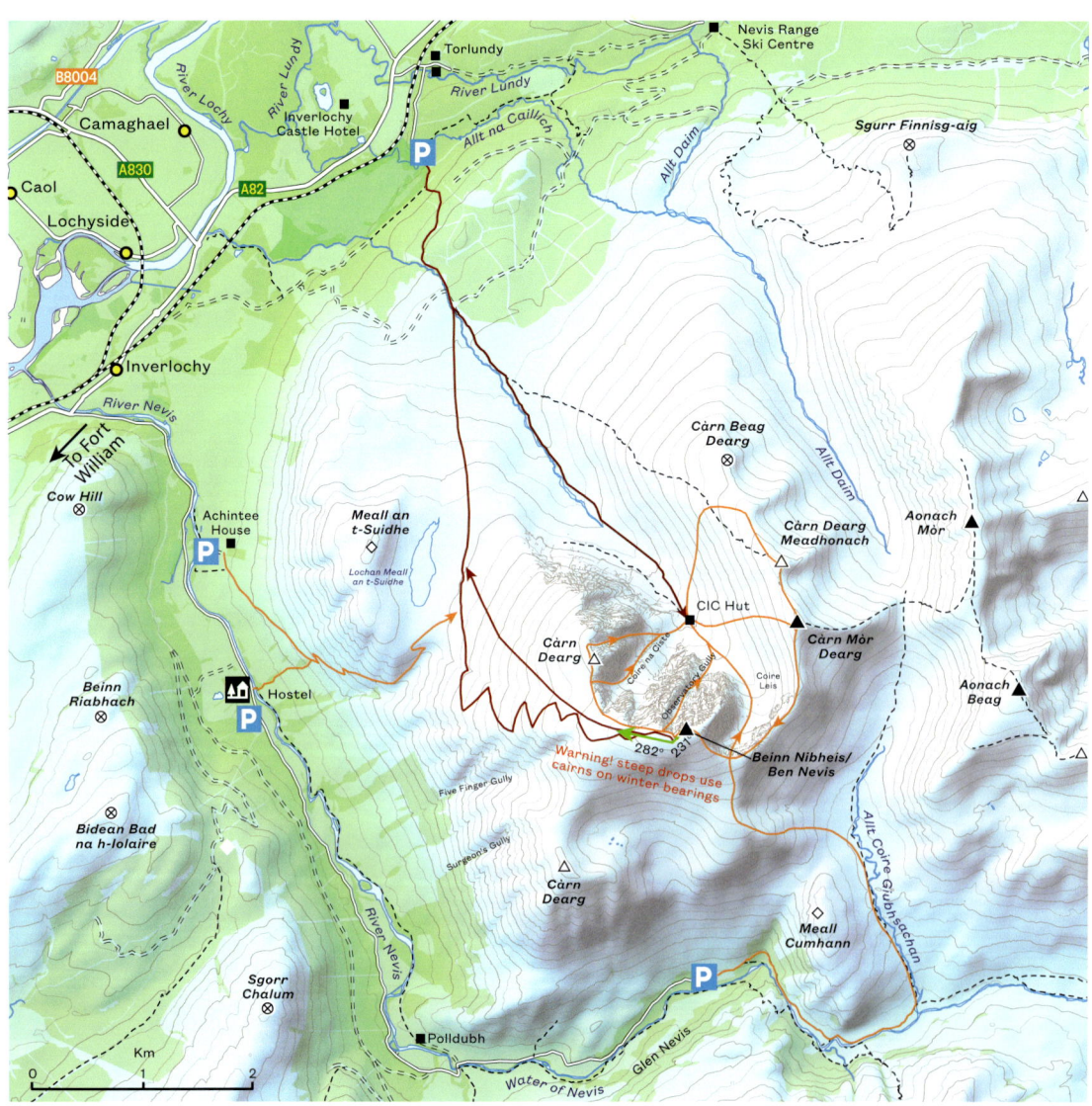

and harness are advisable when planning to ski the gullies.

If there is snow cover down to sea level, the best route starts at the North Face car park, waymarked towards the Allt a' Mhuilinn and onto open hillside at about 300m. Cross the Allt and continue south for 2km to reach Lochan Meall an t-Suidhe (commonly but incorrectly called the halfway lochan, as it is some 100m too low) and a few hundred metres south-east, at about 600m, intersect the main Ben Nevis footpath, which comes up from the starting points in Glen Nevis.

If there is not skiable snow down to sea level, it may be better to start at Achintee or the Glen Nevis Youth Hostel and carry skis up the Ben Nevis path to Lochan Meall an t-Suidhe.

Above the lochan the skier is faced with an ascent of 600m up the wide, steep north-west flank, which has a gradient approaching 30 degrees. At this angle climbing on skis is hard work in anything but good conditions. A route zigzagging upwards between the line of the path and the Red Burn is best, but keep well clear of crags south of the path. The top of the Red Burn ends in a shallow scoop which brings the skier onto easier ground, passing 500m south of Càrn Dearg and heading east towards the edge of the cliffs on the north-east face of Ben Nevis. Before reaching the edge, which is corniced and indented by deep gullies, bear south-east for about 300m and then east for 500m, keeping well away from the cliffs, to reach the deep indentations of Tower Gully and Gardyloo Gully, then bear north-east for 150m to the ruined observatory, triangulation station, indicator post and shelter on the summit, some of which may be entirely covered in snow. A line of cairns marks the summer footpath, which can be used for navigation if visible.

To descend from the summit using the ascent route, ski south-west for 150m to pass the head of Gardyloo Gully, then west for 500m, then north-west towards the head of the Red Burn. (These bearings are crucial. In white-out conditions it is safer to walk, counting paces.) With a low snow-line, the Red Burn can give fine skiing, but it may be cut up by walkers' and climbers' footsteps. Ski down the left or south side initially, then at about 850m, where the burn narrows, cross to the north side and ski north-west down to Lochan Meall an t-Suidhe, thus avoiding very steep convex slopes on the south side of the burn.

For well-equipped, experienced and competent ski mountaineers, there is superb steep skiing to be found on the east side of Ben Nevis.

Steep Skiing on Ben Nevis

By Blair Aitken

One area of Ben Nevis now commonly visited by ski mountaineers is Coire na Ciste on the north-east face. This amphitheatre brings together several classic Grade I and II gullies that have been skied regularly since the 1980s. It does not, however, hold the most sought-after prize: Tower Gully. On the west side of the mountain, more mellow options can be found, but the near-sea-level starting point means that it is often better to search elsewhere for this type of skiing. Having said that, with a low snow-line, the Red Burn makes for a terrific ski.

Access: It is of course possible to access Ben Nevis via the tourist path from the busy car park at Achintee (NN 126 730), but this means arriving at the top of the planned descent route with little information about the snow conditions in the gullies. A better option is to park at the North Face car park near Torlundy (NN 144 763). From here, follow the waymarked Allt a' Mhuilinn footpath to the Charles Inglis Clark (CIC) Memorial Hut (NN 168 722). It will be necessary to walk until at least the hut (it is recommended to wear shoes and carry your ski boots). Ideally, this approach is done the evening before climbing into Coire na Ciste or Observatory Gully, after a night in the hut (see information below).

For safety and out of respect for climbers, it is recommended that Ben Nevis should be seen as a spring skiing destination. During winter the gullies can hold monstrous cornices, unstable wind-deposited snow, footprints and, of course, climbers. Ideally, ski after the cornices have collapsed or slumped back, and the snow has 'corned up' into spring snow. Most skiing on Ben Nevis takes place between March and June, which means higher snow-lines with more walking but potentially less risk, more stable weather and longer daylight hours. It is also easier to book places in the CIC Hut after the winter climbing season has finished.

Ski touring skis and ski crampons can be used, but given the mountainous nature of the terrain it is more important to carry boot crampons and at least one ice axe. For safe entry into the gullies, a rope is advisable. The gullies are often sheltered from the worst of the wind, so bring spare warm layers if you plan to top out onto the summit ridge, where there will likely be significant wind chill. If you are staying at the CIC Hut, you will also need to bring a sleeping bag and provisions (none of which

should be left behind when you leave). There is no need to bring a mattress or stove. An overnight bag can be left in the CIC Hut for collection on the walk out.

Coire na Ciste

Although many single-day visitors will head for the classic Observatory Gully descent, Coire na Ciste offers more varied and enjoyable skiing. It also has a good progression from easier slopes through to some of the steepest skiable terrain in the country.

From the CIC Hut head towards the base of Number Five Gully, then once in line with the lochans in the corrie, traverse south-west into the main corrie directly under Number Three Gully. From here skin west up towards Number Four Gully, making an assessment of the stability of the cornice, snow and rock above you. It is often possible to skin quite far up Number Four Gully, but at some point you will need to switch to boot crampons and an ice axe for the final climb out. Late in the season, a fun alternative is to scramble up Ledge Route. As with most gully skiing, it is worth noting that your first turns of the day will likely be on the steepest slope. If this unnerves you, an easier first descent is recommended. One good option is to skin towards the exit of Number Two Gully and then traverse to the rocky summit above Garadh Gully, below Raeburn's Easy Route and Glover's Chimney. In spring conditions, the ramp of snow from here back to the lochan offers excellent skiing with plenty of space to open the turns up and find your feet.

The easiest gully, and one most commonly skied, is Number Four Gully (NN 158 717). Although steep to begin with, it quickly mellows while twisting its way through the rock before sending you into the wide corrie below. After this descent, conditions will decide what the next gully should be. Number Five Gully is the most enjoyable, and the long, wide entrance offers multiple options for access from above. It then squeezes you into a narrow gully before channelling you out onto the wider slopes above the CIC Hut. This hourglass shape means it is potentially a hazardous terrain trap, and this descent should only be skied when you are sure the snow is stable. Number Three Gully has a similar feel but on a smaller scale. The entrance faces east, and so becomes heavily loaded from the westerly winds, which means it can be surprisingly steep. If this is on your to-do list, it may be necessary to climb from below and ski from a point where the gradient is in your comfort zone.

Beyond numbers Three, Four and Five, there are numerous other challenging gullies that have been skied, but they are normally so steep or rarely in good enough condition that they are not included here. The two exceptions are Number Two Gully and South Castle Gully. These are not for the faint-hearted, but for those confident on steep terrain, their towering walls are alluring. While it is not uncommon to be able to make a complete descent of Number Two Gully, South Castle Gully often has a break near the bottom, making it necessary to climb back up and ski down North Castle Gully or set up an abseil to get back onto the snow below.

Observatory Gully
The Tower Gully and Observatory Gully combination is often used to return to the valley floor after skiing Coire na Ciste, or climbed from below and skied as a single descent. The descent from the top of Tower Gully (NN 164 712) to the CIC Hut is a respectable 600 vertical metres, and linking it with Observatory Gully is one of the most satisfying skis in the country. Later in the season the snow-line and flatter terrain below the exit of Observatory Gully make it a far more pleasant return than walking out from below Number Five Gully on exposed scree.

Another interesting option is to first climb the Càrn Mòr Dearg Arête, possibly making one or two descents into the terrific east-facing bowls, before heading to the Ben Nevis summit and on to Tower Gully. One advantage of this route is that you can change your mind and descend into Coire Leis, where a cairn (NN 170 710) on the ridge marks a safe descent line. Tower Gully hangs above Tower Scoop, and a snow face allows a ski traverse into Observatory Gully, joining it below Gardyloo Gully. The gradient can vary greatly depending on how big the cornice is or has been. In poor visibility, it is vital that Tower Gully is not confused with Gardyloo Gully, and that you know how far back the overhang of the cornice lies. Tower Gully is a no-fall zone due to the exposure of Tower Scoop. In good spring snow, when the entrance has banked out, it is easy to become overconfident: remember where you are!

It should also be noted that Observatory Gully can often be scarred with runnels and peppered with loose rock as you pass below Gardyloo Gully. Even when the rock and snow are deemed to be stable, there is the chance of loose rocks falling from above throughout the entirety of this route.

Opposite: Number 4 Gully, Ben Nevis (skier, Tom Southworth) © Al Todd

Above: South Castle Gully, Ben Nevis (skier, Peter Mackenzie) © Nadir Khan

Below: Number 2 Gully, Ben Nevis (skier, Pete Mackenzie)
© Al Todd

As with all gully skiing, a helmet is a must and vigilance is required at all times.

Another increasingly popular option for competent climbers is skiing Tower Gully after climbing Tower Ridge (made somewhat harder by having skis attached to your back!). This, Scotland's ultimate ski mountaineering route, is now known as the 'Tower Double'.

The best way to ski both Tower Gully and Coire na Ciste is to book two nights in the CIC Hut. Arrive in the evening at the North Face car park, walk in and overnight at the hut. The first day is then spent in Coire na Ciste, and the hut is close enough that you can enjoy a full day on the mountain without feeling rushed. The second day is another chance to explore Coire na Ciste, or to climb and ski over the back of Càrn Mòr Dearg. Both options can then be followed up with a final ski of Tower Gully/Observatory Gully.

NB: The CIC Hut sleeps 26 people and has a toilet, outside running water, a drying room, heating and a fully-equipped kitchen. Booking information can be found on the SMC website.

The Aonachs Traverse

Aonach Beag　　　　　▲ 1,234m
Little Ridge
△ NN 197 715　　　⌖ LR41　　　P.278

Aonach Mòr　　　　　▲ 1,221m
Big Ridge
△ NN 193 729　　　⌖ LR41　　　P.278

🅿 At the car park at the end of the road in Glen Nevis (NN 167 691/56.7774, -5.0007).
↔ 16KM　　　△ 1,300M　　　⌂ 140M
⏱ 6-7 HRS　　　GRADE III　　　★★★★

By William Wallace, updated by Colwyn Jones

Skiing on Aonach Mòr began in the 1930s, mainly by local skiers, but in December 1989, SMC member Ian (Spike) Sykes and his team opened the Nevis Range Ski Resort to the public.

The traverse of these two mountains provides one of the finest tours in the country, but it must be remembered that they are high and subject to rapid weather changes. The traverse needs two vehicles, although with the ski uplift it is also possible to ascend them and then return to the original starting point. Because both mountains have precipitous faces on their east and west sides and huge cornices forming on the edges of the plateaux (particularly on the north-east side of the south-east ridge of Aonach Beag), good visibility is essential for this tour. An ice axe and crampons are essential.

From the Glen Nevis car park follow the excellent path hewn through the gorge to the west end of the Steall meadows. As the car park altitude is only 140m, snow seldom lies for long, and it is normally necessary to walk along the 2km to the ruins at Upper Steall.

Sgùrr a' Bhuic is the prominent peak to the north-east, and the route follows the east bank of the stream which issues from the corrie north of the peak. At first the hillside rises steadily, but it becomes much steeper under the upper slopes of Sgùrr a' Bhuic. Rounding the peak, traverse diagonally upwards across the steep slope to gain the much more gentle slopes of the upper corrie. Cross the bed of the corrie and traverse the south-facing slope diagonally upwards to the north-east to gain the crest of the south-east ridge of Aonach Beag. Follow the ridge first west up several steep sections then, where it flattens, turn north-west towards the summit dome of Aonach Beag. This section of the ridge often has huge cornices, so take care to stay well back from the edge. The final 250m ascent to the summit is up broad open slopes which are not excessively steep. The cairn marking the summit is very small and is usually completely buried under snow in winter. When clear this summit gives fine views in all directions.

The col between the two mountains is 500m to the north-west. As the slope is convex with cliffs to the north and steep broken ground below to the west, accurate navigation is needed in poor visibility. The last 30m down to the col consists of broken rocks and is exposed, so great care is necessary. It is rare that skis can be used here, so anticipate that they will have to be carried. The ascent to the summit of Aonach Mòr is up an easy-angled slope to the north and presents no problem. The summit cairn lies on the west side of the summit plateau.

To return to Glen Nevis, reverse the outward route to Aonach Beag, then descend south, keeping to the west of a shallow gully. There are a few small cliffs at around 750m which should be avoided on the west. Below this cross the stream and descend the outward route to the ruins at Upper Steall.

However, the best way to end the tour is to continue the traverse north along the plateau of Aonach Mòr, which is almost level and narrow between the cliffs to the east and west. After 1km you will reach the patrolled ski resort infrastructure, and it is possible to enjoy pisted runs on either side of the lifts down the line of the Allt an t-Sneachda, which usually holds snow in its upper part until very late in the season. A ski descent of almost 1,000m is possible if the snow extends down to the Nevis Range car park. Just east of the Allt an t-Sneachda, at 370m, there is a stile over, and gate through, the deer fence, which in summer is a mountain bike course leading under the gondola directly back to the car park. The 512 Shiel (N41) bus goes from Fort William Town Centre to Nevis Range, but please check the timetable for up-to-date information.

Out-And-Back Tour

🅿 The Nevis Range ski car park (NN 171 774/ 56.8514, -5.0001). Parking charges apply
↔ 22KM
△ 1,450M (350M if lifts are used)
⌂ 100M
⏱ 8-9 HRS (5-6 hours if lifts are used)
　GRADE III　　　　　　　　　　　　★★★

From the Nevis Range ski area car park (charges apply), the easiest ascent is to take the gondola up to the 650m contour, then the quad chairlift to 920m and finally two ski tows to the 1,190m contour. This approach ensures you avoid breaking the Mountaineering Scotland snowsports touring code by not skinning up any pistes, and deposits you barely 1km from the summit cairn of Aonach Mòr. There is an 8:00am gondola for climbers and ski mountaineers during the winter, and no charge for descending in the gondola. The alternative of skinning (or walking) up from the car park is not recommended, but if chosen the ascent follows the track under the gondola and then continues west of the quad chair beyond the pisted run appropriately named 'Far West'.

Irrespective of your choice of ascent, once at the top of the second ski tow (Summit Button), head south along the wide flat summit plateau (climbing skins required), gaining the few metres in height and the 1km distance needed to reach the summit of Aonach Mòr.

The broad ridge continues south for another 1km to the intervening col (1,080m), and the ascent on Aonach Beag will start on foot. Once over the rocky obstacles it is a short skin of 150 vertical metres up to the large flat summit.

Descent is by the ascent route and as described for the traverse.

As found in most established ski resorts, there are many off-piste runs and, if visibility is good, an alternative and more challenging descent is to return to the summit of Aonach Mòr to ski an itinerary route in the Back Corries called

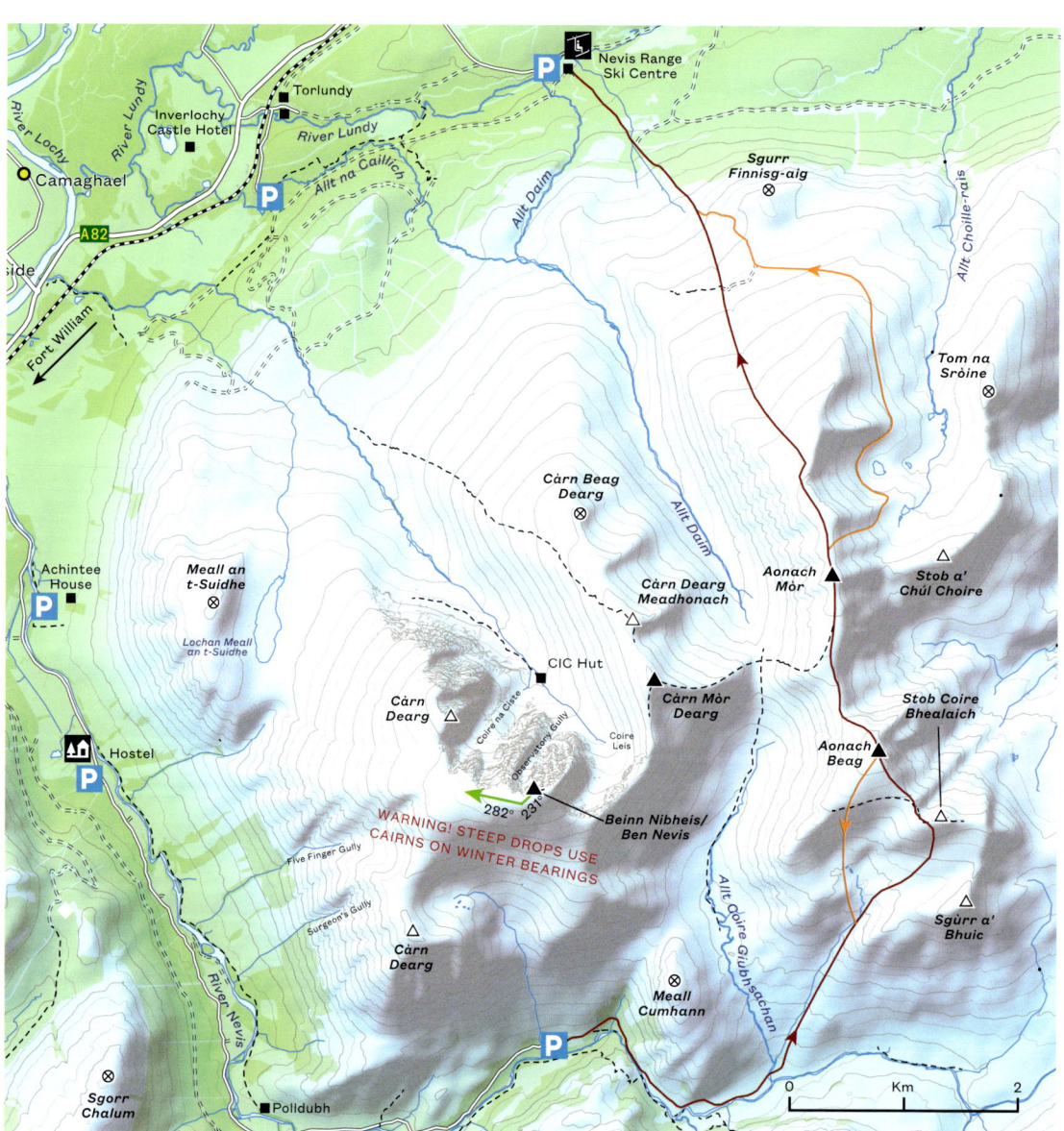

'Spikes'. The route was originally named 'Spike's Fright' after a first descent by Ian (Spike) Sykes, apparently encouraged by colleagues, during a reconnaissance for the new resort.

From the summit cairn of Aonach Mòr, go east for 100m where rocks are usually visible on the edge of the east slope close to the cornice (named Summit Gully on the Nevis Range piste map). This whole corrie is prone to avalanches, so prior assessment of conditions is essential. Move north along the plateau edge (but not too close) for about 300m from the rocks, and if one does not already exist, find a suitable entry point through the cornice down onto the snow of Spike's in the open bowl below. The corrie is initially steep but soon eases to often give excellent skiing. To avoid a reascent with skins, after 200m of vertical descent traverse north to ski to a small col over the intervening ridge to enter the next bowl. Continue traversing around the bowl and over the next ridge, which will bring you under the mothballed Braveheart chairlift. However, from below the chair you should be able to pole/skate following a line of permanent yellow markers to join the main traverse. Safely leave the Back Corries and return to the Nevis Range upper gondola station.

Below: Spikes, Aonach Mòr
(skier, Fraser MacKenzie)
© Ruaraidh MacKenzie

The Grey Corries

Stob Choire Claurigh ▲ 1,177m
Peak of the Brawling Corrie
△ NN 262 739   ⌲ LR41   P.281

Stob Coire an Laoigh ▲ 1,116m
Peak of the Corrie of the Calf
△ NN 239 725   ⌲ LR41   P.281

P	The disused tramway 2km south of Corriechoille Farm (NN 255 788/56.8682, -4.8635).
↔ 22KM	△ 1,350M	⇕ 200M
⏲ 8-9 HRS	GRADE III	★★★★

By Bill Wallace, updated by Colwyn Jones

The high ridge of the Grey Corries, which includes two Munros and does not fall below 980m, provides a superb, albeit fairly long, tour. The traverse may be done in either direction, but as the north-east to south-west direction provides excellent views ahead of the steep eastern corries of Aonach Beag and Aonach Mòr and the topmost cliffs of Ben Nevis beyond, this is the recommended option.

The only practicable approach is from the north. From Spean Bridge follow the narrow public road on the south side of the River Spean to Corriechoille Farm. The unmetalled road which goes past the farm and continues for a further 2km to the south is private, but there appears to be no objection to driving past the farm and parking by the track before a locked gate. Leave the car here and continue up the landrover track which leads south-east through the forest, past 'The Wee Minister', towards the Lairig Leacach. In 1.5km, at the upper

Below: Dusk descent from Stob Choire Claurigh into Coire nan Laogh (skiers, Skiers Mike Cawthorne and Gordon Pearson) © Al Todd

edge of the forest, leave the track and skin up the steep hillside for 200m, heading south-south-west parallel to the edge of the forest. Above this the angle eases slightly, but the gradient is continuous for another 400m south to Stob Coire Gaibhre (958m) on the north edge of Coire na Ceannain. Beyond this top there is a short descent and the ridge narrows. Continue climbing south-south-east, following the steep edge of Coire na Ceannain to the east. At 1,100m the ridge flattens before rising into a narrow rocky crest where it may be necessary to carry skis. The summit of Stob Choire Claurigh is just beyond this crest.

As the open hillside above the forest may be bare of snow, an alternative route follows the line of the 'Old Puggy Line', a disused tramway south-west to a road on the east side of the stream which drains Coire Choimhlidh. Turn south and follow the road for 500m to a dam, then traverse the hillside

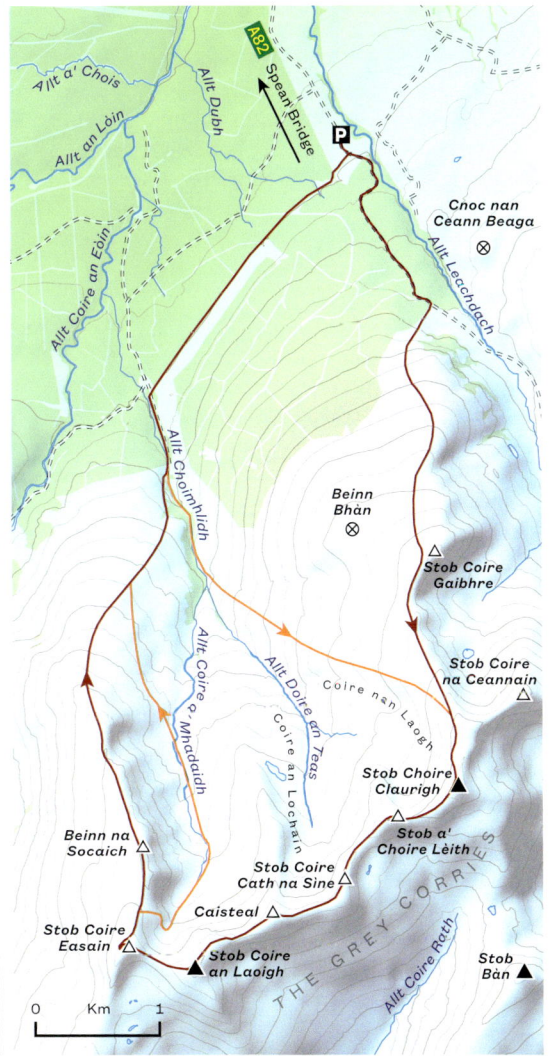

above the stream. 1km beyond the dam several streams converge. Above this the stream beds can hold considerable snow, even late in the season. Follow the south-east course of the stream which drains the corrie under the summit of Stob Choire Claurigh. In the inner corrie there is a steep snow ramp from right to left under the summit rocks, which is ascended to gain the end of the rocky crest mentioned above.

From the summit the ridge to the south-west is broad and easy-angled, thus presenting no difficulty provided there is sufficient snow cover. At 500m from the summit is a col from which it is possible to traverse the south slope to a lower col 500m further on, or alternatively continue along the crest of the ridge, climbing over a minor top, then ski down to the second col. At this point the ridge rises and narrows, and as it is rocky for a short distance it is necessary to carry skis. Beyond the rocky section it broadens again and turns west to climb over a minor summit (1,106m). It then drops 50m before turning south-west to climb 60m to the summit of the second Munro, Stob Coire an Laoigh.

Stob Coire Easain, the next top, lies 500m west-north-west. The descent to the col is 90m and both this descent and the following ascent of 65m are on boulder-covered slopes which require a good covering of snow before they are skiable. On a fine day the view from here of the eastern corries of Aonach Mòr and Aonach Beag is most impressive.

When there is good snow cover, the north ridge over Beinn na Socaich provides the fastest descent, keeping to the west side of the crest (the east side is precipitous). Ski easily along this broad ridge for 2km, then turn north-north-east down open slopes heading north-east to the point where the Allt Choimhlidh flows into the forest. Very little snow is required to make this last part of the descent skiable, as there are virtually no boulders on the grassy slopes.

If there is little snow on the crest of the ridge, an alternative descent is to leave it 500m north-north-east of Stob Coire Easain and ski steeply down into the corrie to the east, which holds snow until late in the season. Continue down the corrie for 1.5km to the 650m contour where it becomes fairly level and the stream drops to the north-east. At that point leave the stream and bear north-north-west on a gradually descending traverse round the base of Beinn na Socaich to join the descent route described above.

Before reaching the forest, cross the Allt Choimhlidh to its east side and reach the end of the road at the dam just below the treeline. Finally, there is a long slog, probably on foot, down the road for 500m and then along the line of the disused tramway back to the day's starting point.

Above: Looking towards the Mamores (skier, Gordon Pearson) © Al Todd

The Easains

Stob a' Choire Mheadhoin ▲ 1,106m
Peak of the Brawling Corrie
- NN 316 736
- LR41
- P.285

Stob Coire Easain ▲ 1,115m
Peak of the Corrie of the Little Waterfall
- NN 308 730
- LR41
- P.285

P	On the minor road from the A86 7km east of Roy Bridge to Fersit near the north end of An Dubh Lochan (NN 348 789/56.8726, -4.7110).
↔ 16KM	△ 1,170M	↕ 240M
⏱ 5–6 HRS	GRADE III	★★★

By Bill Morrison, updated by Amy Goodill and Erik Lange

These two mountains, known as the Easains, are particularly fine, with steep slopes overlooking the fjord-like Loch Treig, the Lairig Leacach and the head of Coire Làire. However, the north-east ridge of Stob a' Choire Mheadhoin gives an easy ascent with a choice of descent routes on its north-west flank (14km; 870m; 4–5 hours). In high winds, progress up the exposed upper ridge can be arduous, especially if the steep final slopes are icy.

From the starting point go south-west across the outflow of An Dubh Lochan and then turn west to reach the line of an old narrow gauge railway track to the right of a rock cutting. The fence line is best crossed at a gate (NN 345 788). Follow the track north-west towards Coire Làire for a short distance, then climb south-west up easy slopes onto the ridge above the plantation on the south-east side of Coire Làire. Traverse the steepening slopes below the crags on the north-west side of Meall Cian Dearg and gain the ridge above at about 800m. An alternative route to this point is to go along the old railway track for 2km to the south-west corner of the plantation and then aim for a small group of trees on the north-west slopes to join the traversing approach. The old railway was used to construct a water pipeline for generating hydroelectric power at the Fort William aluminium smelter and is known as the 'Old Puggy Line'.

Continue up the ridge to the summit of Stob a' Choire Mheadhoin. The ridge leading south-west to the col at 970m and up to Stob Coire Easain is very steep and should only be skied if the snow conditions are excellent, which is not often the case. In icy conditions it may be better to go on foot with an ice axe and crampons. In good snow conditions the avalanche risk needs to be assessed carefully. Returning from Stob a' Choire Mheadhoin, ski down the crest of the ridge for at least 0.5km to get a choice of runs north down to Coire Làire or down the ridge itself. If skiing into Coire Làire, make a long descending traverse above the open birchwoods on the hillside to reach the Old Puggy Line, which has a good surface (if frozen) and a very easy gradient back to the starting point.

Stob Coire Sgrìodain ▲ 979m
Peak of the Scree Corrie
- NN 356 743
- LR41
- P.285

Chno Dearg ▲ 1,046m
Red Nut
- NN 377 741
- LR41
- P.285

P	The end of the minor public road off the A86 in Glen Spean to Fersit (NN 351 783/56.8655, -4.7084).
↔ 13KM	△ 940M	↕ 240M
⏱ 4–5 HRS	GRADE II	★★

By Bill Morrison, updated by Colwyn Jones

The circuit of these two mountains, possibly adding Meall Garbh, gives a fairly easy but satisfying tour with good terrain for downhill skiing. It is best attempted in January or February when snow is down to the road and walking is not required. The big open corrie enclosed by these mountains holds snow well and is sheltered from the worst of the westerly weather by the Grey Corries.

From the end of the public road at Fersit, go east along the private road over two bridges, crossing the River Treig and the West Coast Railway Line, to open moorland 200m beyond the final house. Leave the road near a shed (NN 357 780) and ascend easy slopes south-south-east, following close to the Allt Chaorach Beag. Above 600m the east face of Sròn na Garbh-bheinne looks rocky and unskiable, and an ascent across the north face towards the west, though feasible, is not recommended. Instead, continue along the stream towards Lochan Coire an Lochain to about 700m (500m north of the lochan), then turn west and climb any one of the broad gullies leading up to the ridge between Sròn na Garbh-bheinne and Stob Coire Sgrìodain. These gullies are less steep and rocky than they appear at first sight, and they interlink at various points to give many interesting routes. The ridge up to Stob Coire Sgrìodain is quite rocky, but adequate snow cover will most likely be found on the east side of the crest.

When skiing off the summit of Stob Coire Sgrìodain it is probably best to make a brief detour south-east, then turn south-west to reach the first col (NN 356 740). The next section over two minor tops (958m and 924m) is liable to be bouldery, but beyond there is an easy run down to a broad, featureless col at 900m. From there, Chno Dearg is reached by an easy climb north-east to its prominent cairn on a flat summit which, if windswept, may be rather too bouldery for easy skiing. Meall Garbh is a Munro Top and can be included with little extra effort by climbing south-east from the col to the level ridge where the cairn is on the south top.

The best descent from the summit of Chno Dearg is an almost direct line towards Fersit, giving an exceptionally uniform gradient down wide-open slopes that hold snow well. With complete snow cover there is a 4.5km run with 750m of descent. With less than complete cover the stream beds will probably give the best runs, provided they are snow-filled.

Key
1. The Easains — P.284
2. Chno Dearg — P.284

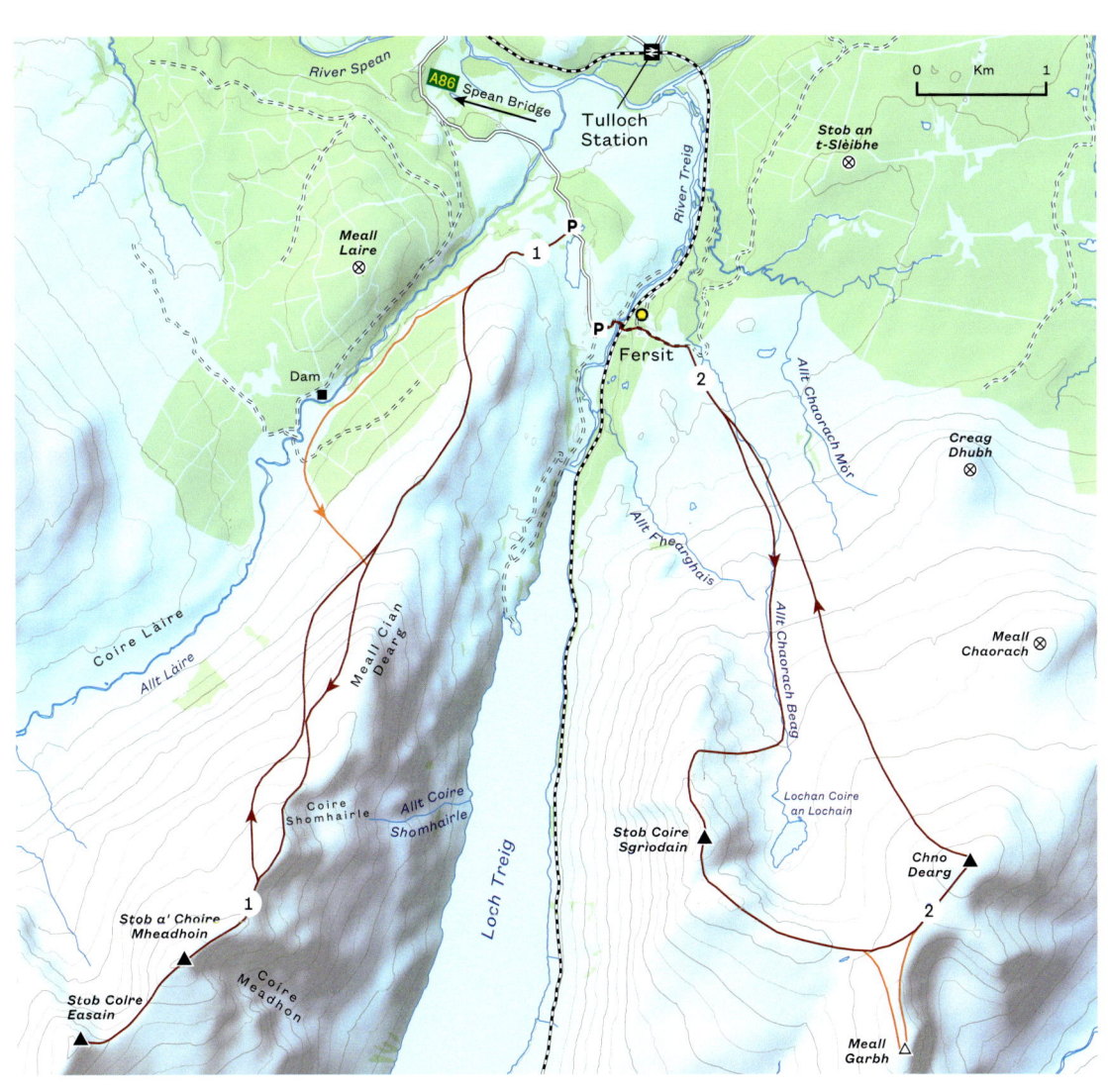

Above: Chno Dearg
(skier, Esme Todd)
© Al Todd

Creag Pitridh ▲ 924m
Petrie's Crag
△ NN 487 814   ◁ LR42   ⊕ P.288

Geal Charn ▲ 1,049m
White Hill
△ NN 504 811   ◁ LR42   ⊕ P.288

Beinn a' Chlachair ▲ 1,087m
Stonemason's Hill
△ NN 471 781   ◁ LR42   ⊕ P.288

P	A large layby on the A86 road through Glen Spean 1km west-south-west of Moy Lodge at (NN 433 830/ 56.9122, -4.5753).
↔ 21KM	△ 1,280M	↕ 250M
⏱ 7–8 HRS	GRADE IV	★★★★

By Gordon MacKenzie, updated by Colwyn Jones

These three peaks are located south of Loch Laggan in the Ardverikie deer forest. They make a fine ski tour over interesting and varied terrain. All the summits are boulder-strewn and need a generous snow cover for good skiing. You would be well advised to carry an ice axe, crampons and Harscheisen on this tour.

The traverse is described in a clockwise direction as the descent from Beinn a' Chlachair gives an excellent finish to the day.

Cross the River Spean by the concrete bridge from the layby and follow the private estate road (through a pedestrian gate in the deer fence) on the east bank of the Abhainn Ghuilbinn for 1km. Then turn east, still following the road, to reach another track which gently rises round the base of Binnein Shuas to a bridge at Lochan na h-Earba (NN 463 813).

On reaching the south-west end of this loch, leave the track and ascend south-east following the line of the Allt Coire Pitridh up fairly easy slopes below Sgùrr an t-Saighdeir. At 550m turn north-east and make as direct a line as possible, zigzagging between small rocky outcrops, to the pointed summit of Creag Pitridh, which gives good views north-west to Binnein Shuas and Creag Meagaidh.

From here descend to the col separating Creag Pitridh from Geal Charn by skiing south at first, avoiding rock outcrops by keeping to their right (west), and then curving east down to the col. The flat summit of Geal Charn has a triangulation station and is easily reached by skinning up straightforward slopes east from the col.

The run from Geal Charn gives almost 300m of skiing down to the pass west of Loch a' Bhealaich Leamhain, the best line being down the west flank of the south-west ridge. The ascent from the pass to the flat north-east ridge of Beinn a' Chlachair can be difficult on skis as the slope is steep, rocky and often icy. Gordon MacKenzie described his ascent of the steepest slopes as being negotiated by sidestepping upwards, using Harscheisen. He reported that this technique can give a sensation of insecurity similar to that experienced while slab climbing. Some might prefer to carry skis and use crampons for this section or make a rising traverse lower down to gain easier slopes near the east side of Coire Mòr a' Chlachair.

Having reached the broad north-east ridge, continue easily along it and turn west above the lip of Coire Mòr a' Chlachair to reach the large summit cairn, not far from the edge of the corrie.

The run down the open slopes of the north-west flank of Beinn a' Chlachair gives 700m of straightforward and enjoyable skiing, having first weaved a way through the boulder-strewn slopes just west of the summit cairn. A track is reached near the ruins of Lùbvan Bothy and is followed north to meet the outward route just west of the artificial lochan on the Allt Meall Ardruighe.

An alternative descent, which can be inspected on the ascent and may give excellent skiing, is down the north-east corrie of Beinn a' Chlachair. From the summit return east then north-east round the rim of Coire Mòr a' Chlachair and ski north-east down a wide unnamed corrie, often well snow-filled, to reach the Allt Coire Pitridh, where the uphill route is joined.

Beinn a' Chlachair and Geal Charn can also be approached from the east, starting at Loch Pattack, which can be reached by mountain bike along the private road from Dalwhinnie past Ben Alder Lodge to the loch. From the south-west corner of the loch, follow the track west to the Allt Cam. Crossing this stream may be difficult or impossible unless the water is low or there is a firm covering of ice. Once on the north side of the stream, Beinn a' Chlachair can be reached by climbing west over gradually rising ground to the final short steep slope leading to the north-east ridge. Geal Charn is climbed up easy slopes to the east of Loch a' Bhealaich Leamhain.

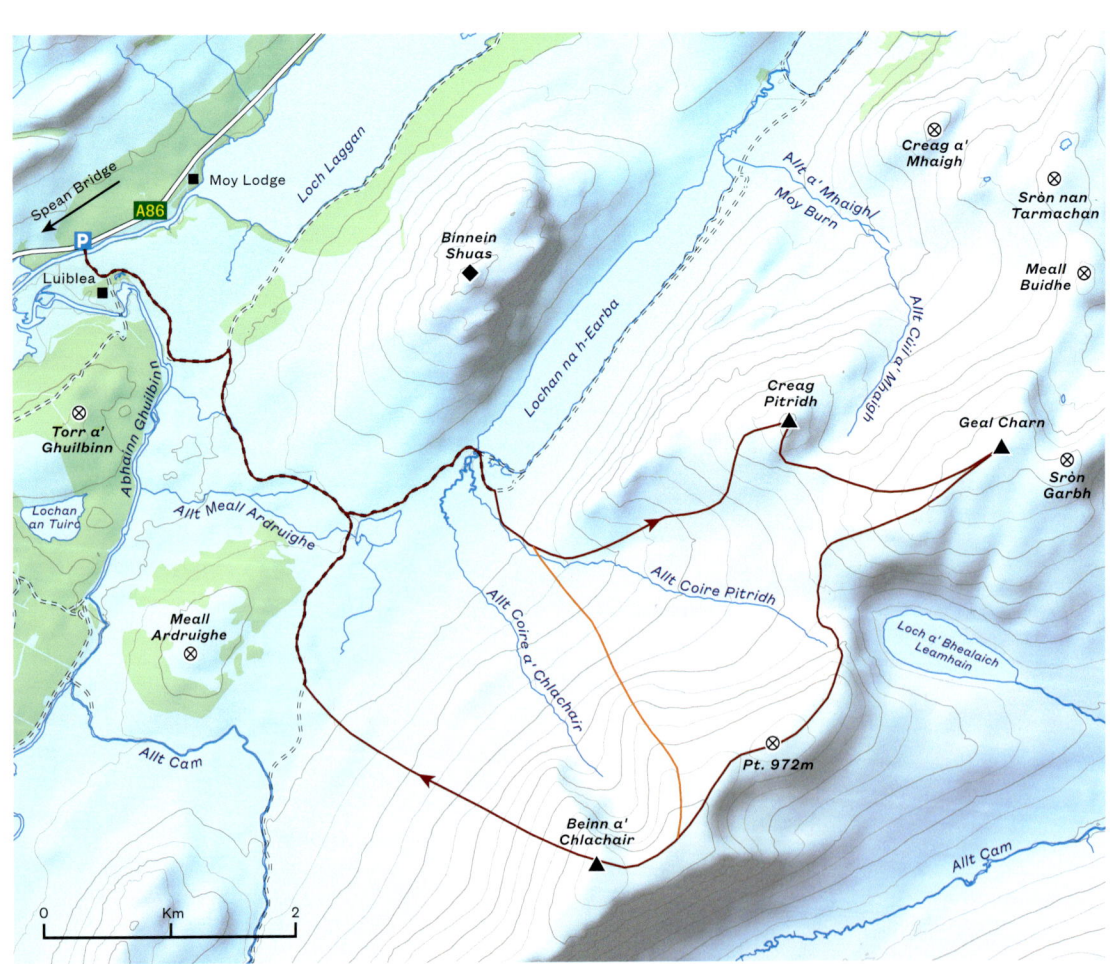

Scottish Haute Route

↗ LR41, LR42, LR35, LR43, LR36, LR37 　　🌐 P.290–301

🅿 Starting point: Glen Nevis Youth Hostel (NN 127 717/56.7997, -5.0676). There is a layby on the east side of the road 150m south of the Youth Hostel.

🅿 Finishing point: Braenaloin on the B976 road (NJ 280 000/57.0859, -3.1892, 370m). There is off-road parking on the east side of the B976 road opposite Braenaloin. If leaving a vehicle for a week, it might be worth informing the folk at the house of your plans. There was a strong mobile phone signal at the time of publication.

↔ 170KM　　△ 10,000M　　⤒ 20M
🕐 7 DAYS　　GRADE IV　　★★★★★

By Roger Wild

This is a high-level traverse across the Scottish Highlands following a direct line along the most significant high ground. The route description is based on a trip made in 2010, which was recorded in the *SMCJ* (2010), vol.41, no.201, pp.1–8.

The route involves sections of steep terrain which require competence with axe and crampons. The peaks included are Ben Nevis; Càrn Mòr Dearg; Aonach Mòr; Aonach Beag; Sgùrr Choinnich Mòr; Stob Coire an Laoigh; Stob Choire Claurigh; Stob Bàn; Beinn na Lap; Ben Alder; The Fara; Meall Chuaich; Càrn Dearg Mòr; Cairn Toul; Ben Macdui; Beinn a' Chaorainn; Beinn a' Bhùird; and Ben Avon.

Public transport: Bus service N41 runs from Fort William to the Glen Nevis Youth Hostel (www.shielbuses.co.uk; +44 (0) 1397 700700). There is a taxi service in Ballater: +44 (0) 1339 755654. Alternatively, walk along the B976 road for 6km to Crathie (NO 264 949) on the A93 road where you can catch bus service 201 west to Braemar or east to Ballater/Aberdeen (www.stagecoachbus.com; +44 (0) 1224 591301).

Accommodation: Rucksacks Bunkhouse, Braemar (www.skiassistant.com/rucksacks-braemar.html; +44 (0) 1339 741517). Ballater Hostel (www.ballater-hostel.com; +44 (0) 1339 753752).

The route can be followed in either direction and may be influenced by the prevailing wind at the time. Another factor is the likely length of any good weather 'window'. If the weather deteriorates in the latter part of the trip it may be better to be on the less technical ground further east than to be battling with the Aonachs and Ben Nevis in difficult conditions. Ideally, there should be complete and consolidated snow cover down to the lowest levels, but this is unlikely and some carrying of skis should be anticipated.

Many variations are possible, including ascending more or fewer hills, different bothies and overnight stays, pre-placed food caches etc. Following a line north of Loch Treig or south of Loch Ericht would offer other routes. Avoiding Ben Macdui in favour of a route further south could create a longer route which finishes further east.

The 2010 party used Nordic metal-edged skis with three-pin bindings and leather boots. The pros and cons of Nordic versus Alpine equipment are discussed in general terms in the chapter on equipment. The most important factors will be personal preference and experience with whichever equipment is chosen. Modern Skimo gear could be a good choice, especially as the ski/binding/boot combination of a Skimo set-up is as light as its Nordic counterpart and maybe even lighter. Other gear taken in 2010 included ski skins, crampons and axes, sleeping bags, mats, bivvy bags and two lightweight stoves, along with maps, compasses, GPS receivers and a simple 'hands-free' system for compass or GPS so that both ski poles could be used while following a bearing. A shovel and spare ski pole were included. The sacs initially weighed 14kg, which included two days' food and cooking gas. Avalanche safety equipment (transceiver, shovel and probe) should also be considered.

There are inevitably many hazards to be negotiated on a journey traversing so much high ground, including cliffs and steep slopes, avalanche terrain, river crossings, weather and poor visibility. Some of these, but by no means all, are mentioned in the description. The ability to navigate in white-out and storm conditions, together with competence on steep ground with axe and crampons, is essential, along with sound judgement about when to take skis off and travel on foot.

Food caches were pre-placed at Lairig Leacach Bothy, Dalwhinnie, Ruigh Aiteachain Bothy and the Hutchison Memorial Hut A vehicle was left at Dalwhinnie, which provided overnight accommodation. The existence of so many good bothies is a crucial factor in the trip, and thanks are due to the Mountain Bothies Association and landowners for the continued provision of the superb shelters along the route. These should be left in the condition you find them, if not better.

The timings given are based on those recorded in 2010. They are the total time, including stops for food and photography and also navigation, which slowed the pace on some poor weather days. The compass directions are a general indication of the route, not accurate bearings for detailed navigation.

Three bothies which were not used in 2010 but which lie close to the route followed are noted here for information: Meanach (NN 266 684), Staoineag (NN 295 677) and Benalder Cottage (NN 498 680).

Evening Approach Prior to Day 1

- ○→ Glen Nevis Youth Hostel (NN 127 717).
- →○ Ben Nevis summit (NN 166 712).
- ↔ 5KM
- △ 1,325M
- ↕ 20M
- ⏱ 3.5 HRS

Ascend Ben Nevis the evening before and bivouac near the summit. Alternatively, make an early start from Glen Nevis (this would make a long day). From the Glen Nevis Youth Hostel, cross the bridge over the River Nevis and follow the line of the main track towards the summit of Ben Nevis. Above the 1,200m contour, the summer path nears the edge of the North Face, which may be corniced. There is a line of cairns on this upper part of the route which avoids the edge until the critical change in direction at the top of Gardyloo Gully (Harvey Maps sells a map which includes information about navigation on Ben Nevis).

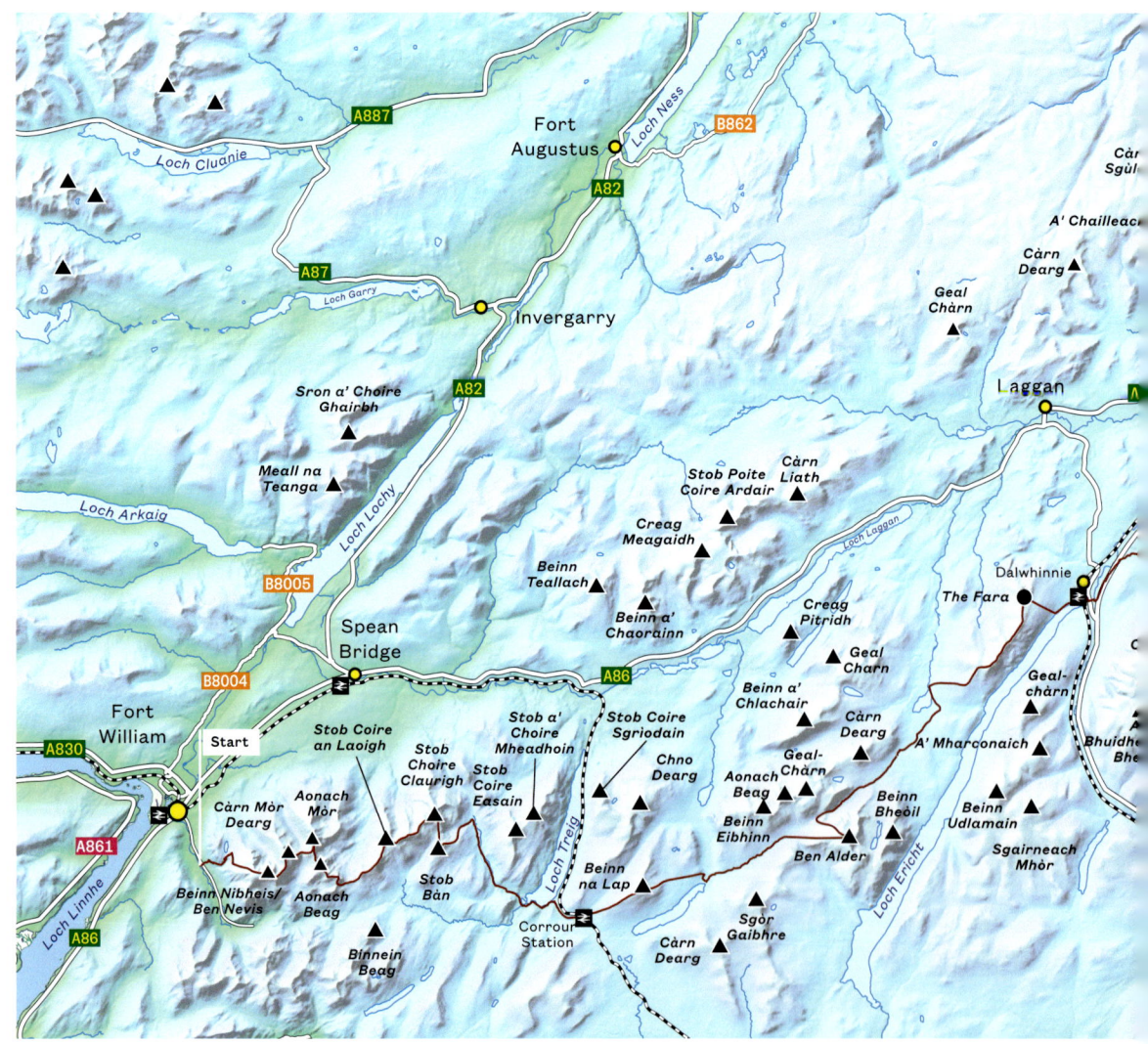

Day 1:
Ben Nevis
Càrn Mòr Dearg
Aonach Mòr
Aonach Beag
Sgùrr Choinnich Mòr
Stob Coire an Laoigh
Stob Choire Claurigh
Stob Bàn

- ⟳ Ben Nevis summit (NN 166 712).
- ⟶ Lairig Leacach Bothy (NN 282 736).
- ↔ 19KM △ 1,850M ⊺ 1,345M
- ⏱ 10 HRS

Food and accomodation: Pre-place food near Lairig Leacach Bothy.

Leaving Ben Nevis summit in a south-easterly direction, descend towards the Càrn Mòr Dearg arête, taking care to avoid the cliffs of the Little Brenva face to the north. Traverse the narrow arête to reach Càrn Mòr Dearg and continue down the steep ridge leading to the col beneath Aonach Mòr (NN 186 722). Climb up steep, broken and serious ground to reach the easier slopes leading to Aonach Mòr summit.

Descend back to the col below Aonach Beag and climb to the summit, steeply at first. From Aonach Beag summit, descend south then east, avoiding the top of the cliffs to reach Stob Coire Bhealaich. About 400m east of the summit there is a small ring contour near the cliff edge (Point 1,048m on 1:50,000 map; NN 206 708).

The descent from here requires care – there are several routes, and any may be icy, corniced or avalanche-prone. Four potential descent points

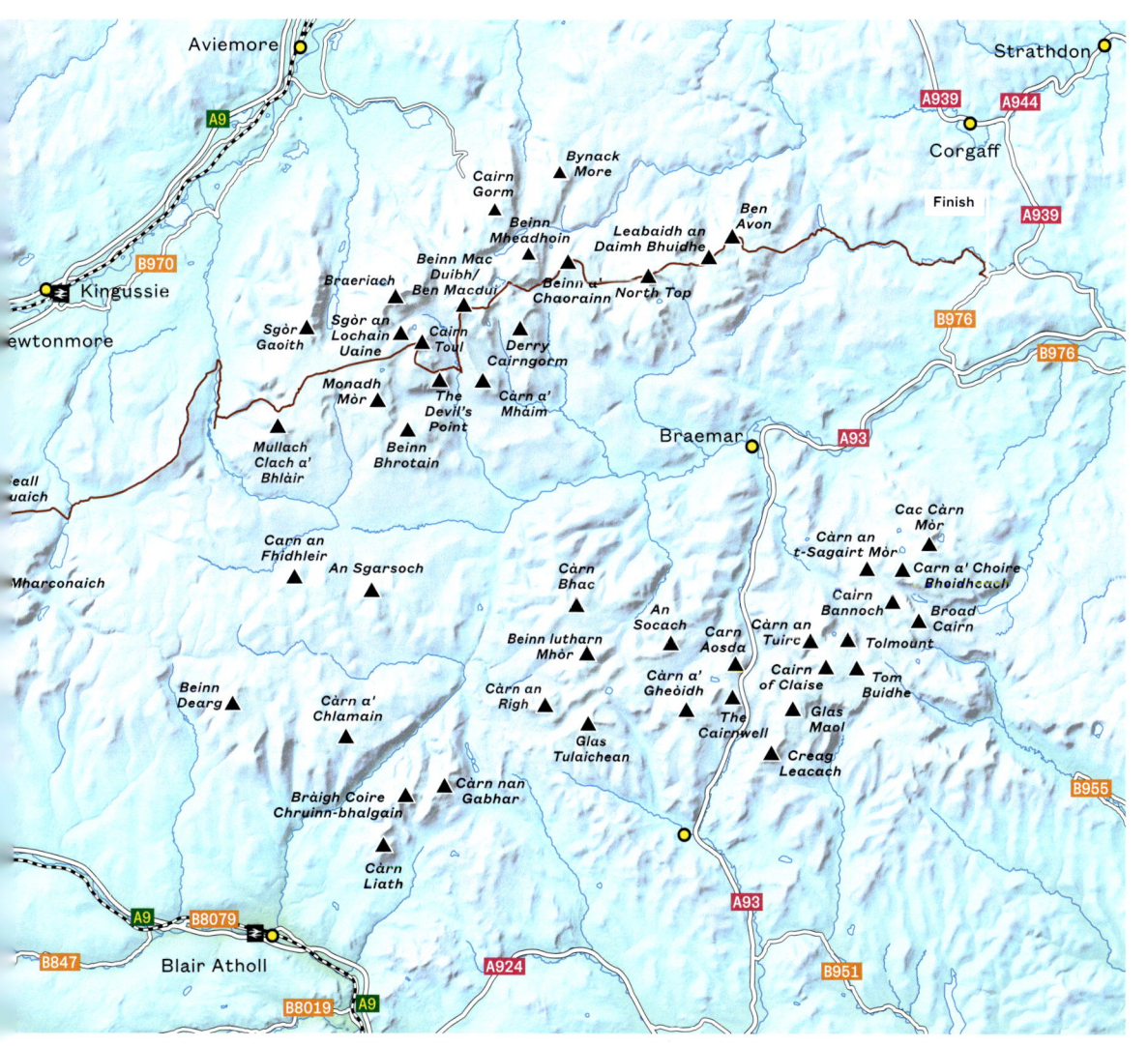

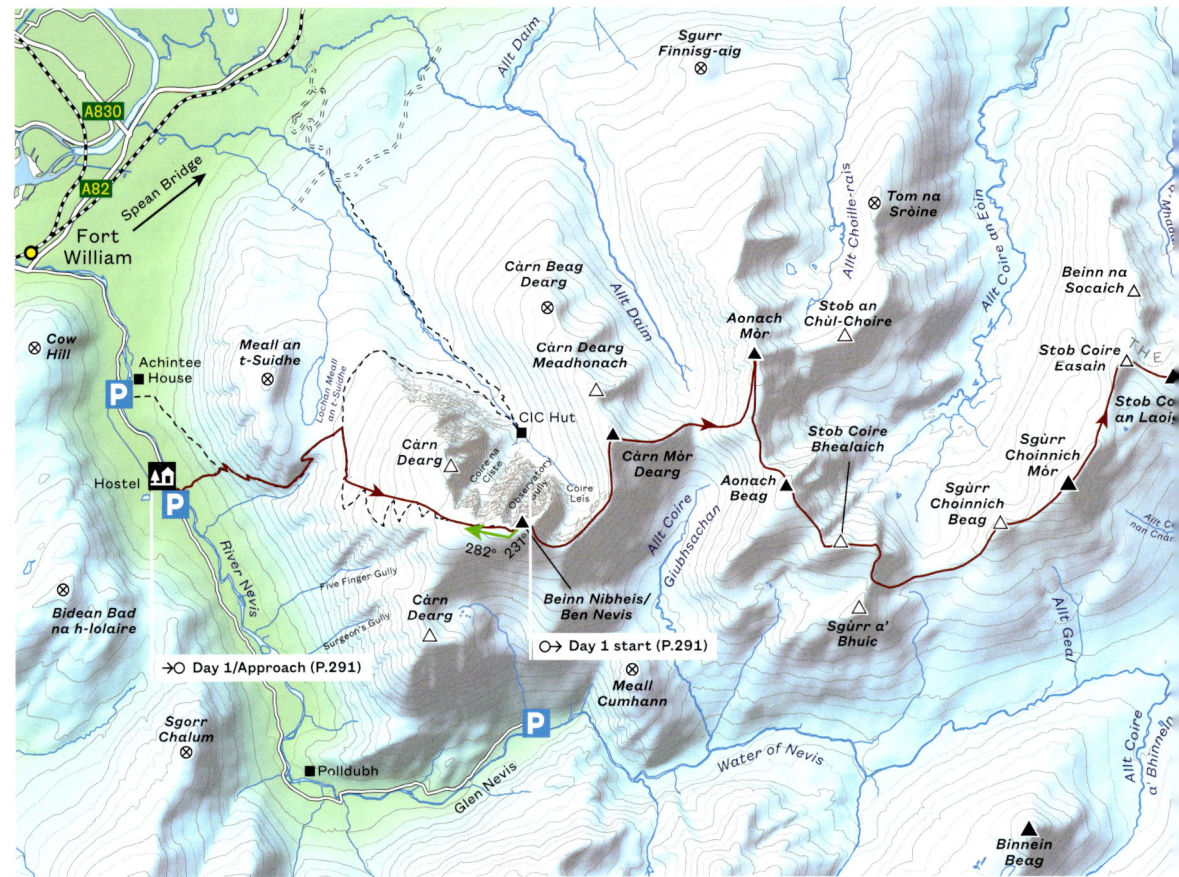

are spaced out along the top of the cliff edge and are shown on the accompanying photograph (see p.291). It may be that none of these options provides a safe descent in the prevailing conditions.

1. From a point just over 100m south of Point 1,048m, a ridge descends towards the wide flat col below Sgùrr Choinnich Beag. This ridge is steep and rocky, and the route changes direction frequently as it zigzags down. It will need to be negotiated on foot, possibly with crampons.
2. Just over another 100m further along the top of the cliffs, a gully descends to the left of a prominent rocky rib.
3. About 150m further along again is the top of a steep slope which leads to a point from which it is possible to traverse to the col. This slope was taken by the 2010 party.
4. About 200m further on, there is a prominent col before Sgùrr a' Bhuic. A gully descends from this col to a point from which it is possible to traverse across to the col.

Now continue over or around Sgùrr Choinnich Beag and up to Sgùrr Choinnich Mòr. Follow the crest and descend a short steeper slope to a flattish col before climbing up to Stob Coire Easain. A turn in the ridge leads to Stob Coire an Laoigh and the remainder of the route is relatively straightforward to Stob Choire Claurigh. Descend south down long open slopes, which hopefully provide good skiing, to reach the col under Stob Bàn. Climb to the summit by traversing around to the west side as the slope steepens. Descend on the east side, taking care to avoid the steep sections, then head to Lairig Leacach Bothy for a well-earned brew.

Opposite: Looking west from Sgùrr Choinnich Beag to Stob Coire Bhealaich and the descent options which are described in the main text. The slope below number 3 was the route taken by the 2010 party (skier, Finlay Wild)
© Roger Wild

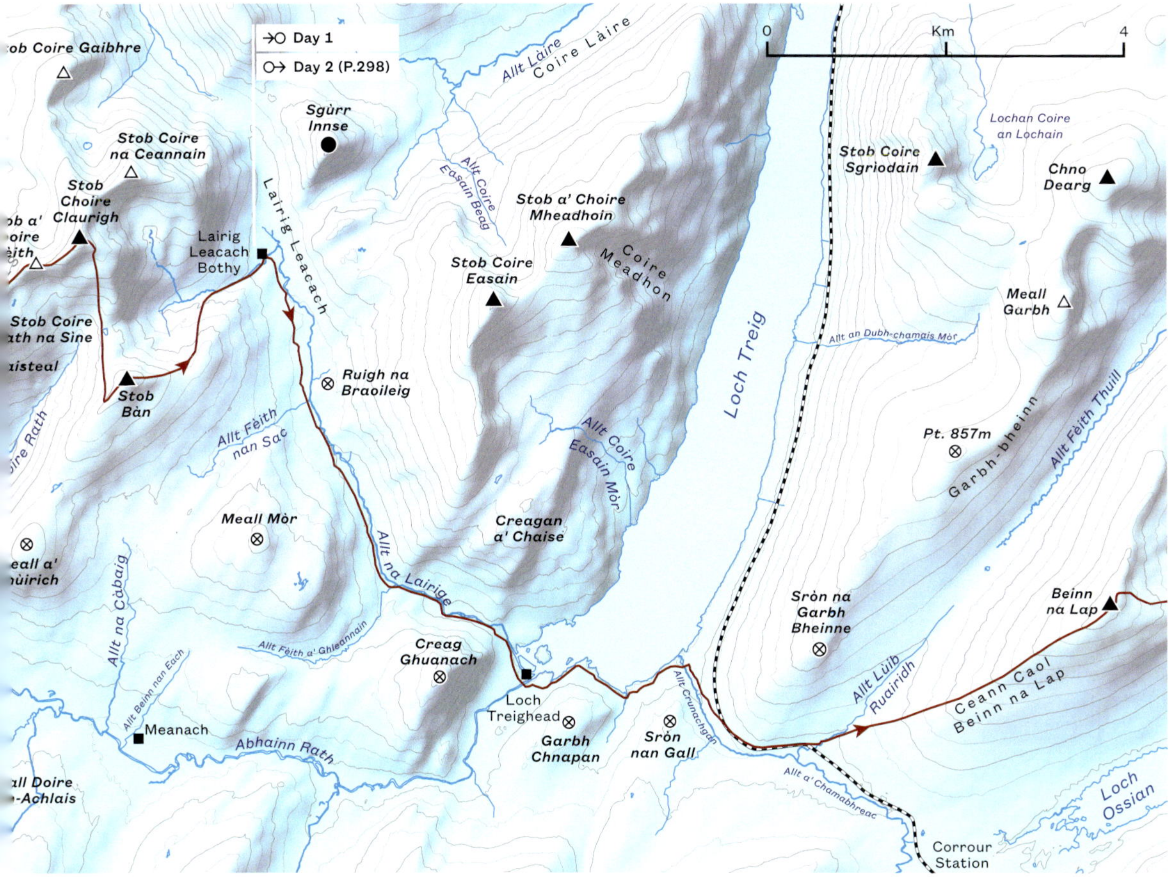

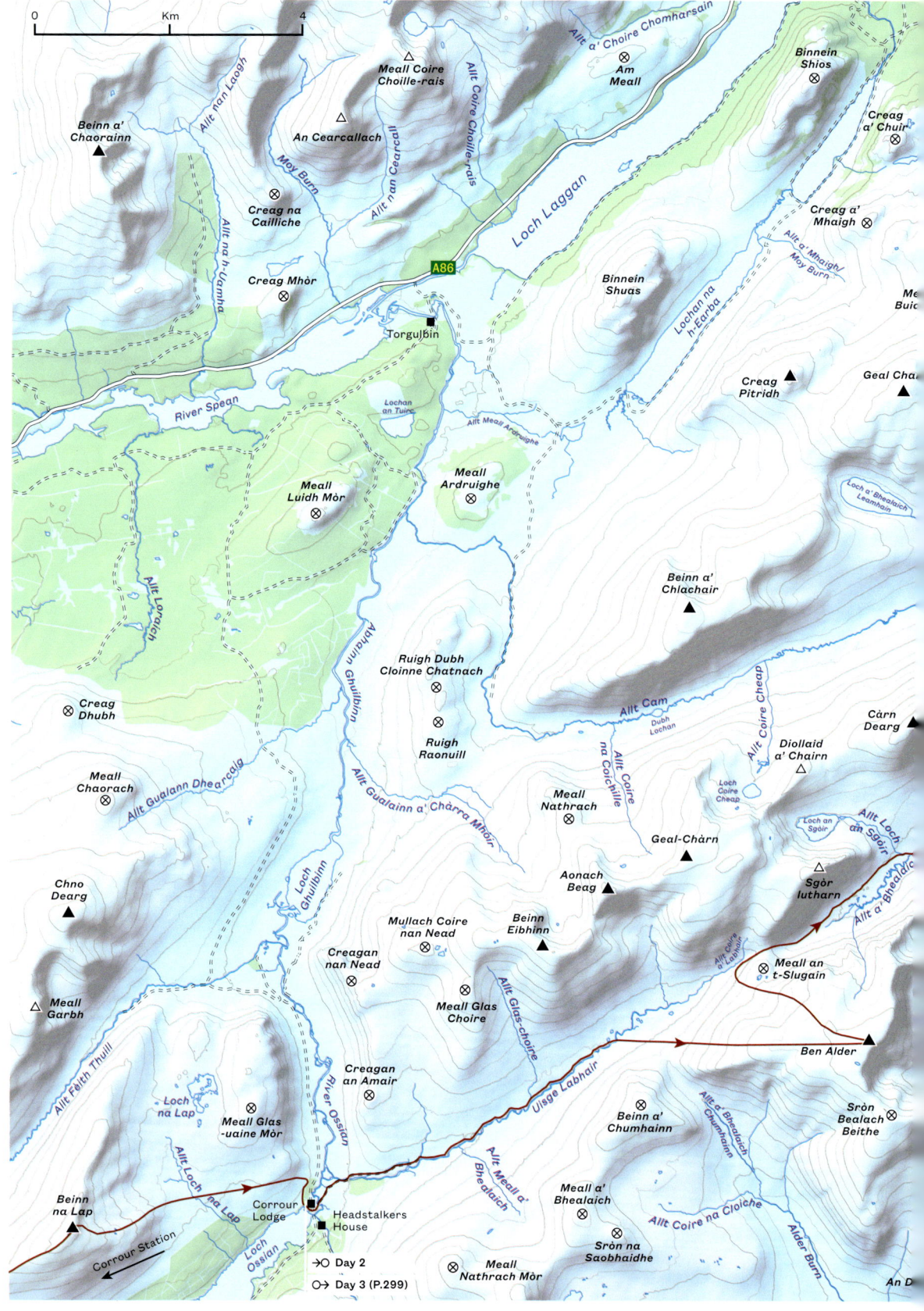

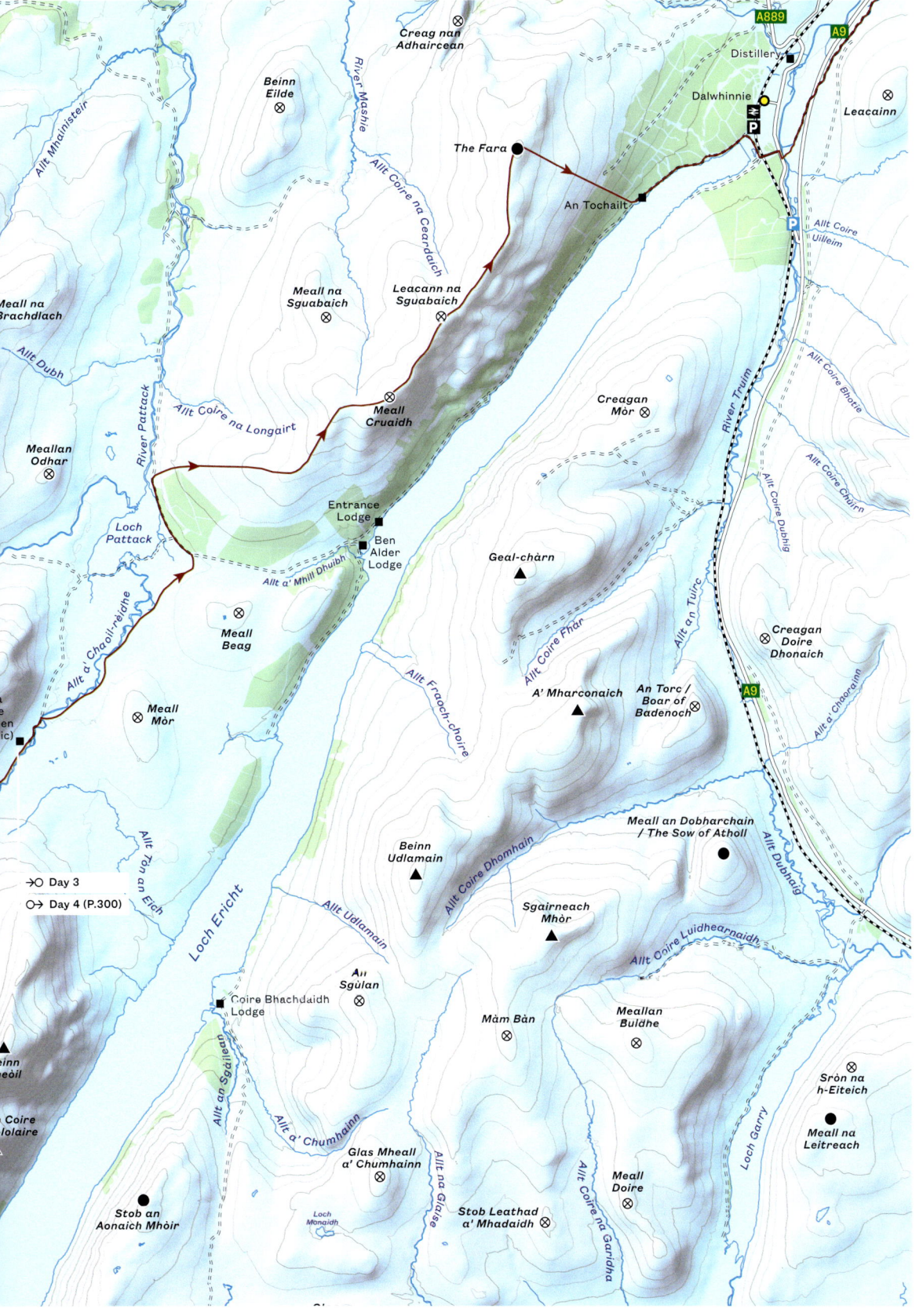

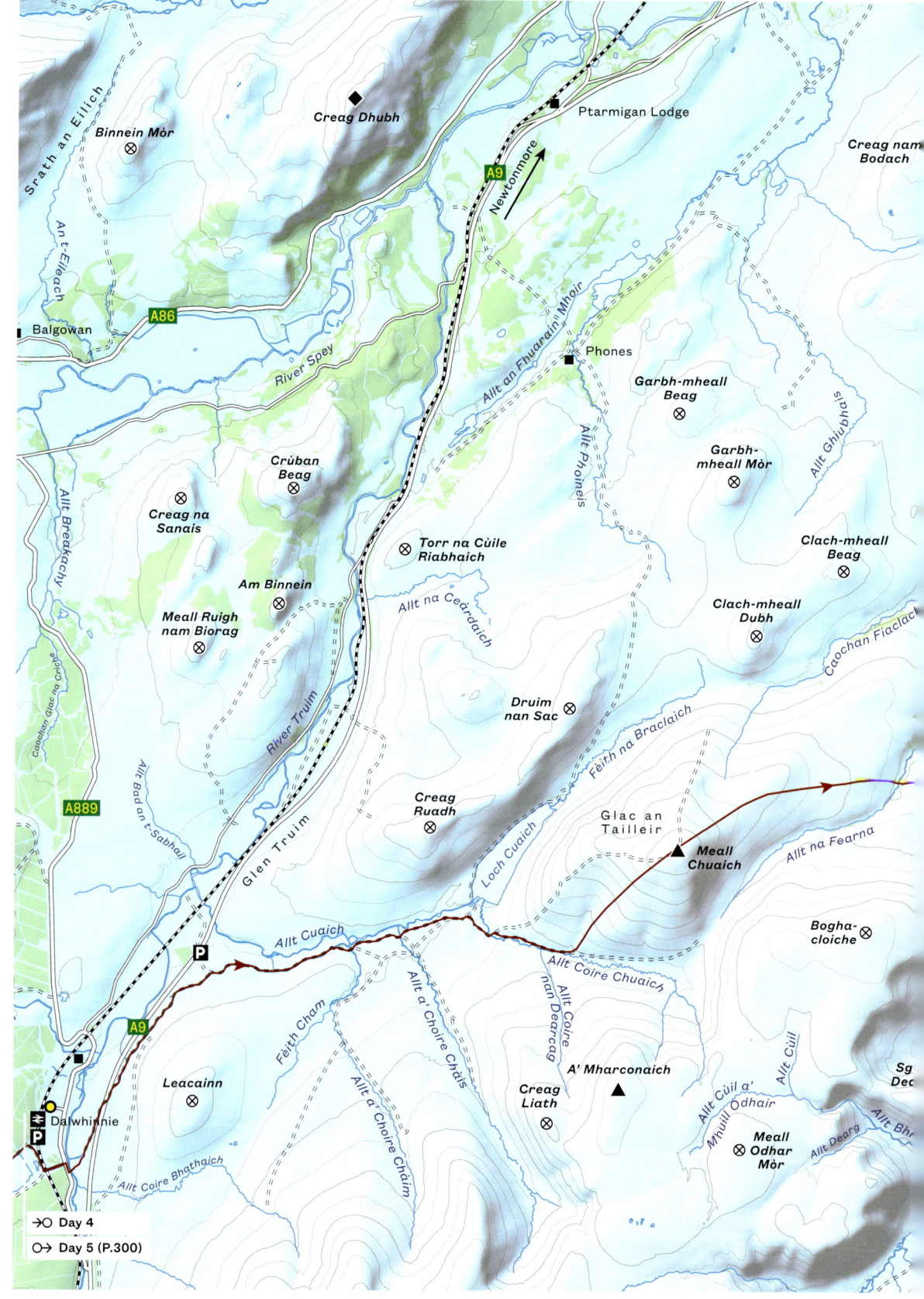

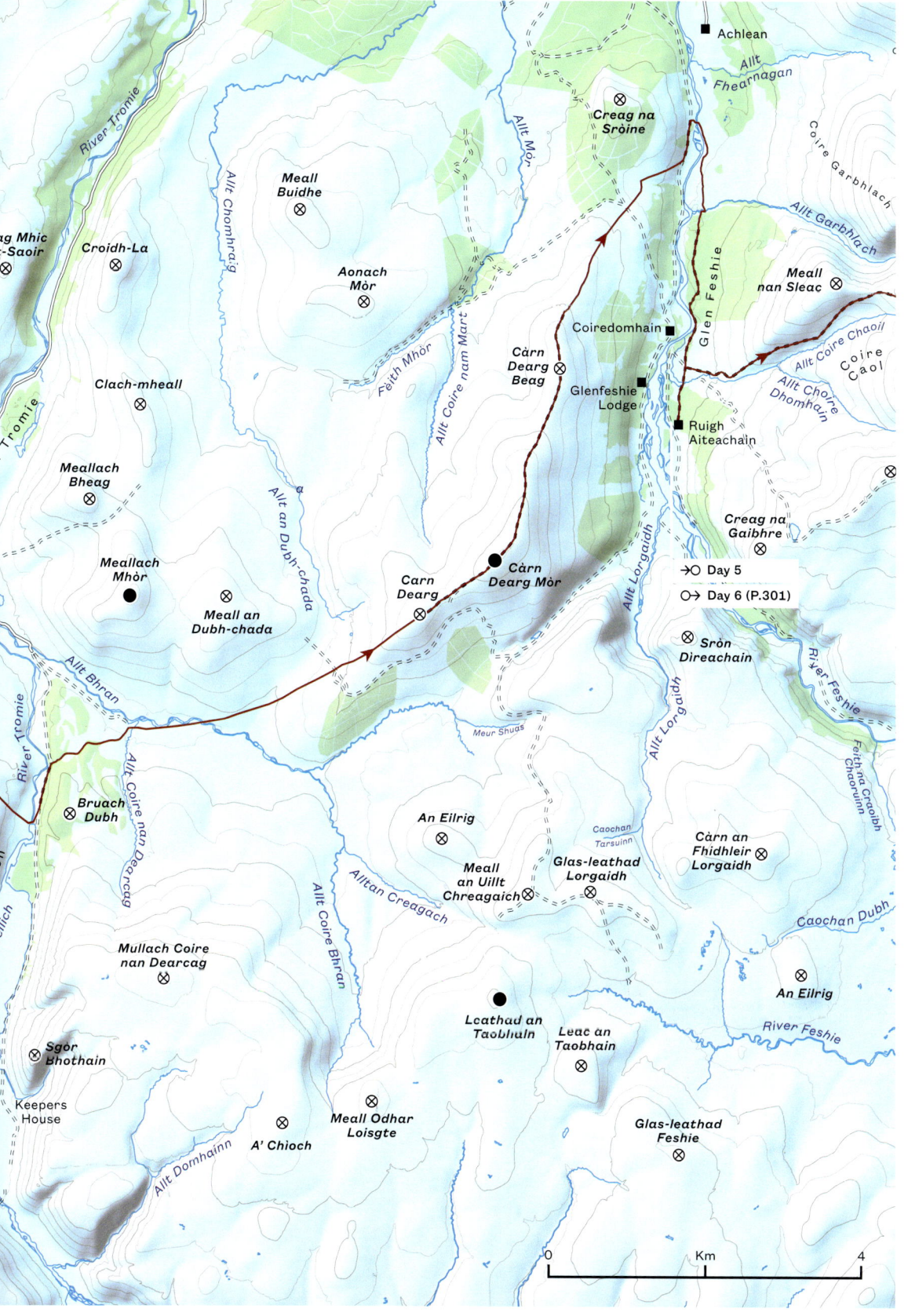

Day 2:
Beinn na Lap

- ⊙→ Lairig Leacach Bothy (NN 282 736).
- →⊙ East end of Loch Ossian (NN 412 697).
- ↔ 18KM   △ 800M   ⊺ 470M
- ⏲ 7 HRS

Food and accommodation: The following are available for this leg of the traverse. Bear in mind that the trip is likely to be spontaneous and opportunistic in order to take advantage of favourable weather and snow conditions, and that booking fixed dates may not be practical. For options 3, 4 and 5, it is wise to check availability in advance.

1. Carry food from Day 1 (or pre-place extra food at Lairig Leacach Bothy for collection) and bivouac at the east end of the loch.
2. Pre-place a tent and two days' food by train to Corrour. This will provide overnight accommodation at Loch Ossian and the tent can be carried the next day for the following night as the bothy near Culra is closed. The tent could be left here for collection later or carried on to Dalwhinnie for use and/or deposit there.
3. After climbing Beinn na Lap, descend to Loch Ossian Youth Hostel. Food could be pre-placed at the Youth Hostel by train or possibly arranged with the hostel staff (www.hostellingscotland.org.uk; +44 (0) 1397 732207).
4. Corrour Estate offers a wide range of accommodation, mainly at the east end of Loch Ossian and also at Corrour Station (www.corrour.co.uk; +44 (0) 1397 707070).
5. After climbing Beinn na Lap, descend to Corrour Station and take the train to Tulloch. Catch the train back to Corrour in the morning and

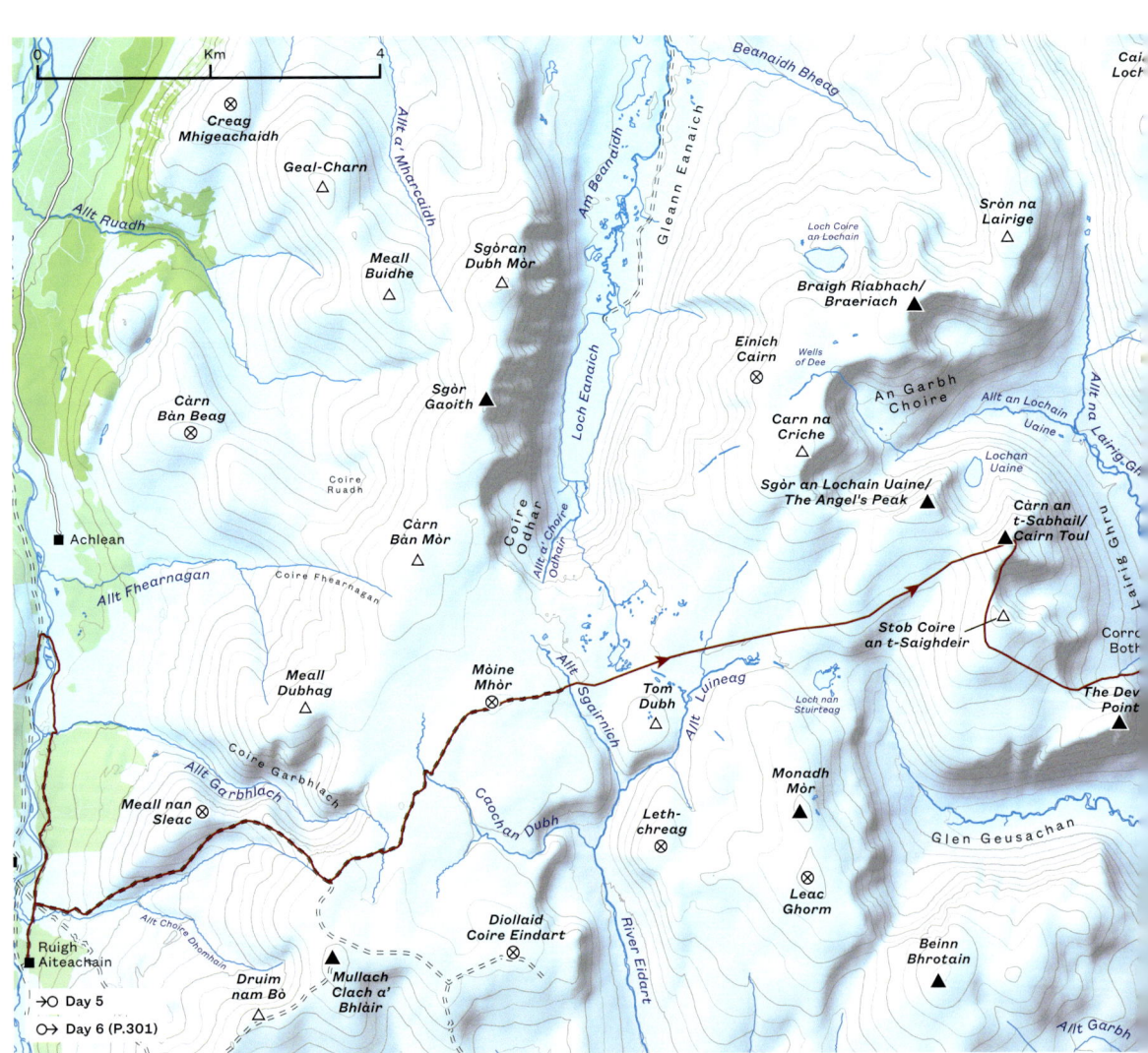

continue to Ben Alder (www.nationalrail.co.uk). Station Lodge at Tulloch is a hostel. Food could be pre-placed at Tulloch (www.stationlodge.co.uk; +44 (0) 1397 732333).

From the bothy, descend south alongside the west bank of the Allt na Lairige to the bridge over the Abhainn Rath near Creaguaineach Lodge (NN 309 688). Cross the bridge, continue along the track to a bridge under the railway (NN 342 681) and ascend the west-south-west ridge of Beinn na Lap. From the summit continue east and lose height slowly to reach the east end of Loch Ossian. It may be best to follow the edge of the forest to reach the track coming from Strath Ossian. It is possible to bivouac in the woods on the south side of the estate buildings or pre-place a tent using the railway.

Day 3: Ben Alder

- East end of Loch Ossian (NN 412 697).
- In the Culra area (NN 522 762).
- 17KM
- 390M
- 900M
- 7 HRS

Food and accommodation: Food can be carried from Day 1 or collected along the way from a pre-placed cache. As Culra Bothy is closed, you will need to bivouac unless alternative arrangements have been made (see option 2 for the previous day). Alternatively, combine this day with Day 4 to finish at Dalwhinnie (a long day).

Follow the Uisge Labhair to below the west ridge of Ben Alder and ascend directly to the summit. Two options are suggested for the descent. In 2010 the visibility was poor and the party headed back west until well clear of the cliffs to the north before

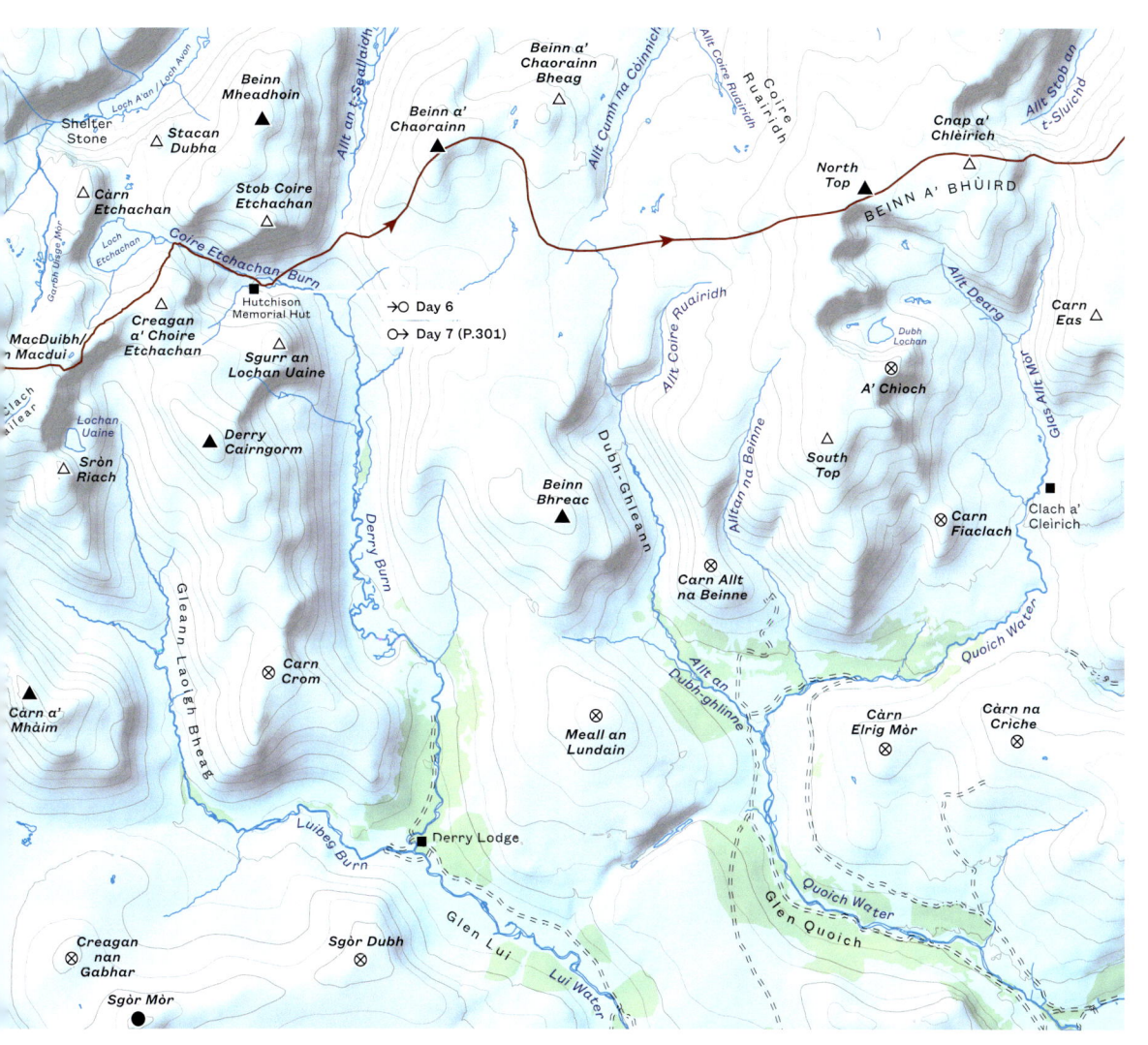

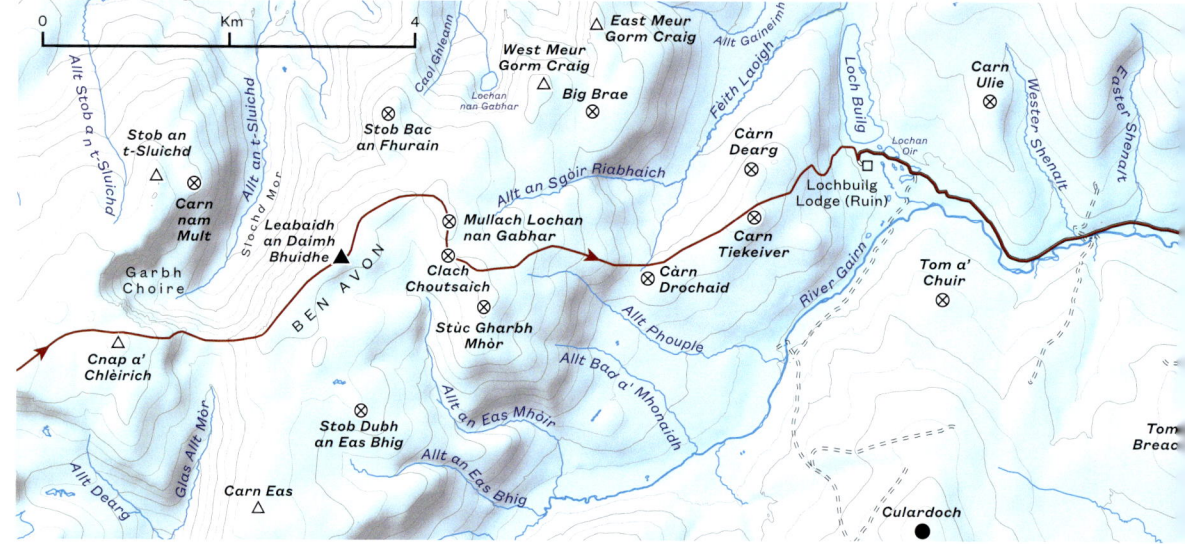

descending to the upper part of the Uisge Labhair and then climbing up to the Bealach Dubh (NN 481 732) and down to Culra. A more adventurous option is to descend on foot down the Long Leachas, a 300m Grade I ridge which descends north-east from the end of the north ridge towards Culra. Competence in descending this grade of terrain is essential.

Day 4:
The Fara

- ↦ In the Culra area (NN 522 762).
- ↣O Dalwhinnie (NN 636 842).
- ↔ 18KM
- △ 700M
- ⊥ 460M
- ⏱ 7 HRS

Food and accommodation: Pre-place food and tent at Dalwhinnie. Alternatively the tent could be carried from Day 3 (see p.298 option 2). Dalwhinnie is situated by the A9, a major arterial road and the only public road crossed during the trip. There is a railway station in the village with trains to Inverness and Edinburgh and buses operate along the A9 to these destinations. The fuel station stocks limited provisions. Accommodation option: Dalwhinnie Old School Hostel, near the railway station (www.dalwhinniehostel.weebly.com; +44 (0) 79601 74462).

In 2010, there was very little snow for the first 4km, but the Allt a' Chaoil-rèidhe was frozen well enough to be skied on and it provided an easy route to Loch Pattack, which was also frozen. Otherwise, decide whether to follow the east side of the river or the landrover track further west, bearing in mind the need to reach the north-east side of Loch Pattack and to cross the ford on the south side if necessary. Ascend by the side of the forest (NN 544 798) and head east to reach the long ridge leading to The Fara. If visibility is good, it might be worth looking across to the following day's route to see where the best snow is. Descend by the firebreak (NN 609 838), which leads to the landrover track by the side of the loch, and follow this towards Dalwhinnie. Just after passing the end of the dam there is a track junction. Turn right (south-south-east) and follow the track to go under the railway bridge and on to Dalwhinnie (the level crossing shown on the map is closed to the public).

Day 5:
Meall Chuaich
Càrn Dearg Mòr

- ↦ Dalwhinnie (NN 636 842).
- ↣O Ruigh Aiteachain Bothy (NN 847 928).
- ↔ 33KM
- △ 1,300M
- ⊥ 360M
- ⏱ 11 HRS

Food and accomodation: Pre-place food at Ruigh Aiteachain Bothy.

Cross the bridge over the River Truim (NN 637 841), follow the track under the A9 towards Loch Cuaich and then carry on along the track on the south flank of Meall Chuaich to reach the foot of a stream at 500m (NN 702 866). An alternative route, which may have better snow, is to cross over the A9 and go around the south and east sides of Leacainn to follow a slight rising traverse to reach the stream. Ascend by the east bank of the stream to reach the

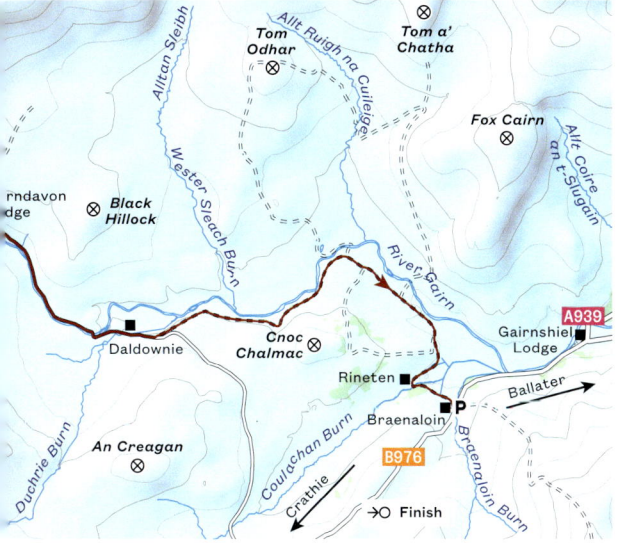

which may be covered by snow (NN 911 957). From the end of the track take a fairly direct line for 5km to Cairn Toul, making best use of the contours and snow and whichever navigational features are deemed necessary. From the summit descend to the col on the north side of the Stob Coire an t-Saighdeir (1:25,000 OS map, point 1,213m on OS 1:50,000 map). In poor visibility, take care to stay away from the cliff edge. Point 1,213m can be avoided by following a descending traverse on its west side until it is possible to take a direct line to the top of Coire Odhar (NN 969 955). The rim of the corrie is likely to be corniced and it might take some time to find the best way in. Once the steep top part of the corrie has been descended, there is a choice to be made. If it is certain that the River Dee can be crossed safely then a direct line can be taken to reach the foot of the Allt Clach nan Taillear (NN 980 975). Otherwise, continue down to Corrour Bothy, cross the bridge (NN 983 956) and head north to Clach nan Taillear (NN 983 965). 'The Tailors' Stone' is where three tailors perished in the snow one New Year's Eve, having wagered that they would dance on the same night in both Rothiemurchus and Braemar. Make a rising traverse to reach and cross the Allt Clach nan Taillear (Tailors' Burn) at 700m and continue up its north side to about 800m. From here another choice can be made depending on the conditions and the inclination of the party. Either climb north then north-east in a fairly direct line to the summit of Ben Macdui, or cross back over the burn and climb the broad ridge on its south-east side to reach flatter ground before turning north-west to reach the summit. From Ben Macdui, descend east and then north-east to reach the east side of Loch Etchachan near the head of Glen Derry (NJ 013 003) and turn east-south-east to the Hutchison Memorial Hut and another well-earned cuppa.

summit of Meall Chuaich, descend the north-east ridge for 1km and then head east to the dam at the north end of Loch an t-Seilich. Cross to the track on the east side of the River Tromie and reach the flattish ground at NN 767 889 and turn east-north-east to the weir on the Allt Bhran (NN 776 893). Cross the river at the weir or further east and take a fairly direct line to the summit of Càrn Dearg Mòr, making the best use of the contours and snow conditions. Descend north-north-east towards Càrn Dearg Beag and continue, crossing a track, to Coire Chrìon-alltain (NN 843 957). Descend to the track to reach the bridge at NN 850 964 (the bridge further south at Carnachuin was not there at the time of publication). Once across the River Feshie head south to the Allt Garbhlach (NN 850 953), which may prove difficult or impossible to cross if it is in spate (upstream may be better). Continue for another 2.5km to Ruigh-aiteachain Bothy.

Day 6:
Cairn Toul
Ben Macdui

- ○→ Ruigh-aiteachain Bothy (NN 847 928).
- →○ Hutchison Memorial Hut (NO 023 997).
- ↔ 27KM　　△ 1,950M　　⏲ 360M
- ⏱ 10 HRS

Food and accomodation: Pre-place food at the Hutchison Hut.

Folllow the ascending track around the south side of Coire Garbhlach to reach the Mòine Mhòr (The Great Moss) and continue to the end of the track,

Day 7:
Beinn a' Chaorainn
Beinn a' Bhùird
Ben Avon

- ○→ Hutchison Memorial Hut (NO 023 997).
- →○ Braenaloin on the B976 road (NJ 280 000).
- ↔ 33KM　　△ 1,250M　　⏲ 700M
- ⏱ 11HRS

From the hut take a gently rising traverse across the south end of the Làirig an Laoigh and then turn east and north-east to climb Beinn a' Chaorainn. From the summit, descend east then south to reach the Mòine Bhealaidh (Yellow Moss) and head east to ascend Beinn a' Bhùird (North Top).

The next section requires careful navigation and negotiation of the steep ground leading to The Sneck (NJ 118 010), which is the col between Beinn a' Bhùird and Ben Avon. From The Sneck, climb steeply east at first and then turn north-east to reach the summit of Ben Avon. The actual summit is a huge tor named Leabaidh an Daimh Bhuidhe on the map (Couch of the Yellow Stag). With the final peak ascended, all that remains is 19km to the end of the tour. Follow a route more or less along the boundary line which is shown on the OS 1:50,000 map. Descend to the landrover track near the south end of Loch Builg (NJ 188 028), then follow it past the closed bothy at Corndavon ruins to the B976 road at Braenaloin.

Single-day trips

The peaks ascended in the Scottish Haute Route can provide many worthwhile single-day trips, and several of these are described elsewhere in the guidebook. Five tours are suggested here:

The Lochaber Traverse

This is Day 1 of the Haute Route. From Lairig Leacach Bothy, follow the landrover track to Corriechoille and the public road to Spean Bridge. A shorter day can be made by using the uplift at Nevis Range and joining the route at Aonach Mòr. The traverse can also be done in the opposite direction.

Beinn na Lap

Accessed by train to Corrour. Ascend the west-south-west ridge, checking to see where the best snow is for the descent back to Corrour.

The Fara

Start from Dalwhinnie and reverse the last part of Day 4. From just beyond An Tochailt Lodge leave the track, go up the firebreak (NN 615 835) and climb The Fara. Descend by the north-east ridge to Allt an t-Sluic and on to the A889 road. Walk 2.5km back to Dalwhinnie.

Meall Chuaich

From Dalwhinnie, follow the route of Day 5 and climb to the summit by the east bank of the stream, which crosses the track at NN 702 866. Alternatively, ascend by the south-west ridge. Look for the best snow to descend by and return along the track to Dalwhinnie. Alternatively, start from near Cuaich on the A9 (NN 654 866) to reach the track already described.

Càrn Dearg Mòr

From the car park in Glen Feshie (NN 850 985) walk south along the road to reach the prominent gated track, which leaves the road just before Auchlean. Follow the track, taking the right fork after about 200m and continue to the Allt Fhearnagan, which may be difficult to cross when in spate. Continue along the main track for a few hundred metres before heading across to the bridge described in Day 5 (NN 850 964) and reverse the route by ascending to Coire Chrion-alltain, Càrn Dearg Beag and Càrn Dearg Mòr. Return by the same route.

Below: Approaching Cairn Toul (skier, Finlay Wild)
© Roger Wild

Overleaf: Traversing the Grey Corries (p.280) (skiers, Mike Cawthorne and Gordon Pearson)
© Al Todd

Beinn Teallach ▲ 915m
Mountain of the Forge

⛰ NN 361 859　　🧭 LR34, LR41　　🌐 P.306

Beinn a' Chaorainn ▲ 1,052m
Mountain of the Rowan Tree

⛰ NN 386 851　　🧭 LR34, LR41　　🌐 P.306

🅿 11km east of Roy Bridge on the A86 road at Roughburn cottages (NN 377 814/56.8950, -4.6658).

↔ 16KM　　⛰ 1,100M　　⊤ 270M
⏱ 5-6 HRS　　GRADE III　　★★★

By Bill Morrison, updated by Wendy MacKinnon

These two mountains give a very pleasant tour, which begins with an ascent of the easy southern slopes of Beinn Teallach, continues along the ridge above the east corries of Beinn a' Chaorainn and ends with a grand run down Coire Clachaig.

Parking is limited to 2–3 cars in a recessed gateway to the forest beside the bridge over the river. Starting from the A86 just east of Roughburn, follow the forest road north-west for 1km. At the time of writing (2023), part of the forest here had been felled. At the junction take a left in a westerly direction. The forest road becomes a path and descends slightly to a farm gate through the wall. Follow the track across flat grassland and cross the several branches of the Allt a' Chaorainn. Crossing this burn is best done low down, although if it is frozen or snow-covered crossing higher up is no problem. Climb north along the west side of the burn to the north-east corner of Upper Laggan Wood, where there is a gate in the fence (NN 365 835), and continue up the broad, easy southern slopes of Beinn Teallach.

From the summit ski north initially down Coire Dubh Sguadaig, then curve round east to reach flat ground at 620m just north of the cairn, at the head of the Allt a' Chaorainn (NN 372 868), where there is also a gate. With good snow cover there is a more direct and very scenic route down through the crags of the north-east face (Tom Mòr) which is not particularly difficult.

The next section needs careful consideration, as it is difficult in poor weather conditions due to the risk of falling through cornices that form in Coire na h-Uamha and around the top of the Allt Bàn. Sadly, several people have lost their lives here, and mountain rescue teams have spent many hours searching for lost walkers and skiers.

Ski up the uniformly steep north-west shoulder of Beinn a' Chaorainn to the North Top (1,043m). Here the east edge is corniced. To keep safe it is necessary to dog-leg and descend initially south-south-west on a bearing of 200 degrees to the west side of the saddle (approx 300m), then head south-south-east up to the main summit (1,052m). To reach the South Top (1,049m), a smaller dog-leg is required to avoid an in-cut gully on the eastern side, which can be heavily corniced.

There are two possible descents. The steeper and more direct route goes down Coire Clachaig and leads to the edge of the now-felled forest. Felling has obscured any route through here, so a better option might be to head west along the edge of the felled area and back to the gate passed through earlier on the ascent. The alternative route from the south Top goes down the south-west ridge, passing north-west of Meall Clachaig to reach the farm gate through the wall at the west edge of the felled forest. From here retrace your steps back to the parking. Tulloch Station (206m) on the West Highland Railway Line is just under 3km from the car park at Roughburn, giving a public transport option but involving a ski or walk alongside the A86.

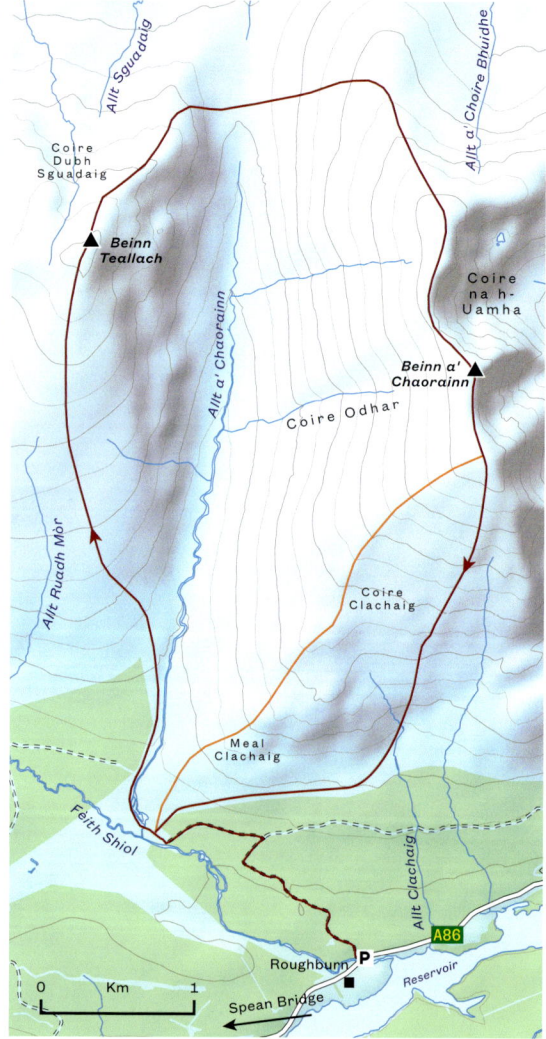

Càrn Liath ▲ 1,006m
Grey Hill
△ NN 472 903　　◁ LR34, LR42　　🌐 P.307

Stob Poite Coire Ardair ▲ 1,054m
Pot of the High Corrie
△ NN 428 888　　◁ LR34, LR42　　🌐 P.307

Creag Meagaidh ▲ 1,128m
Bogland Rock
△ NN 418 875　　◁ LR34, LR42　　🌐 P.307

P	The Creag Meagaidh National Nature Reserve car park near Aberarder Farm on the A86 by Loch Laggan (NN 483 873/56.9516, -4.4961).

↔ 18KM　　△ 1,150M　　⊤ 250M
⏱ 7-8 HRS　　GRADE III　　★★★★

By Donald Bennet, updated by Colwyn Jones

The Creag Meagaidh group is one of the highest mountain massifs between Lochaber and the Cairngorms, and as it is situated far from the western seaboard, it has a good snow-holding record. The traverse of the three Munros and the long horseshoe ridge round Coire Ardair is a fine high-level tour. It can be skied late in the season as it is always above 920m, and on a clear day there are splendid views of the great crags of Coire Ardair. For most of its length the ridge is smooth and broad and the skiing easy, with a very fine descent of 700m at the end of the traverse if snow cover continues down to the road. The most likely problem may be route-finding and navigation in bad visibility, particularly on the vast and featureless plateau of Creag Meagaidh itself.

Starting from the car park by the A86 at Aberarder Farm, follow the waymarked footpath, past the ranger station and public toilets, to the open hillside. Between the 350m and 400m

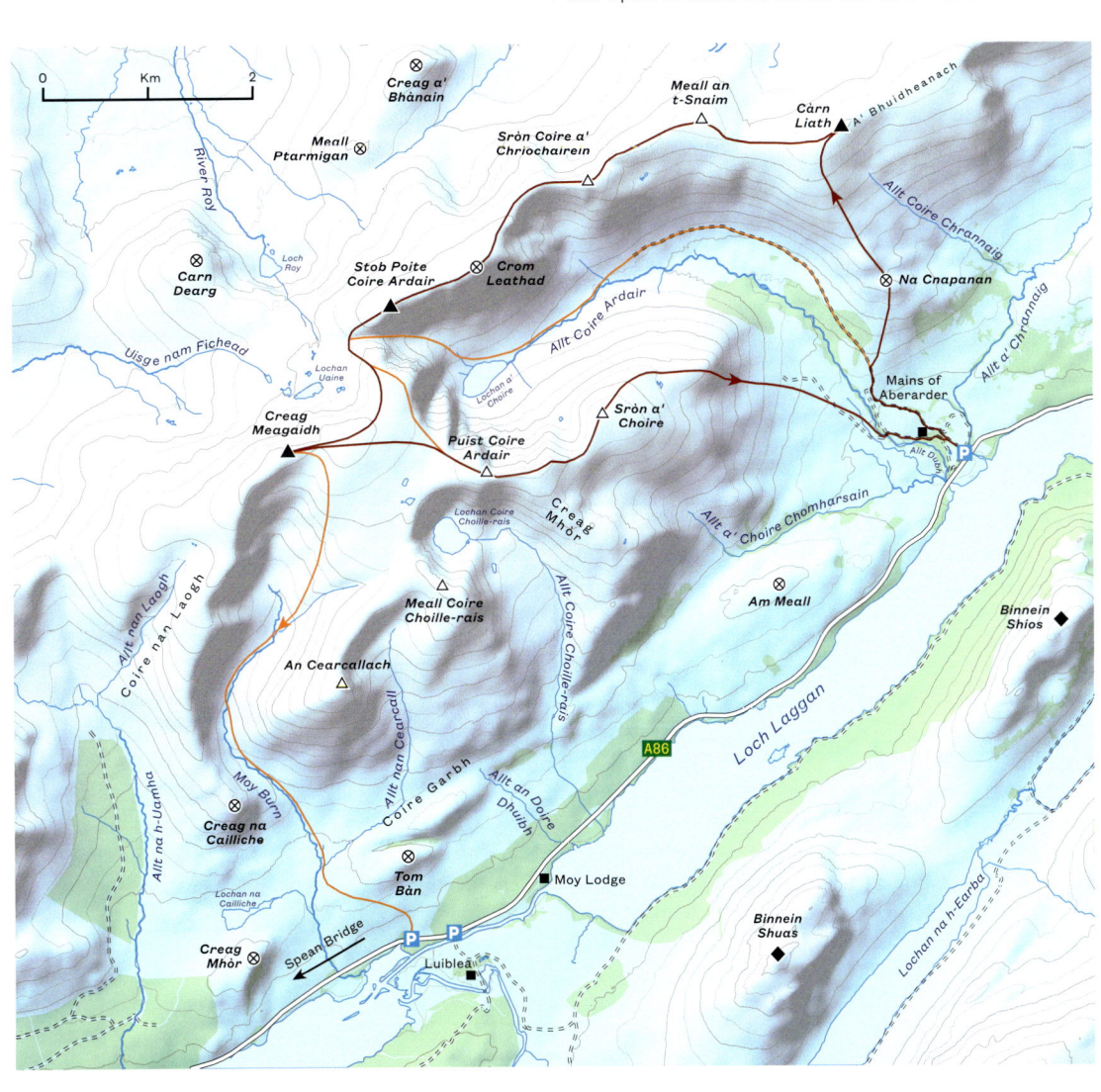

Right: Càrn Liath
(skiers, Angus Armstrong
and Angus Todd) © Al Todd

contours, leave the main path and climb north up the steepening slopes of Càrn Liath to a brief level section of the broad south ridge of this hill called Na Cnapanan (The Buttocks; 625m). Continue up the smooth, featureless slopes with intermittent fence posts leading to the summit, a large cairn on the flat plateau. This ascent route typically gives a fine ski descent but over time regenerating woodland will eventually reduce your downhill options.

Ski west along the broad smooth ridge, descending slightly to a well-defined little col at 920m. The next climb to Meall an t-Snaim (969m) and the need to put on skins can be avoided by traversing horizontally along the south flank of the ridge and descending slightly to reach the next col, which forms a very narrow notch in the otherwise level ridge. In bad visibility or icy conditions, it might be better to stay on the crest rather than traverse below it as described above. From the notch a short, steep climb leads back onto the broad crest, over Sròn Coire a' Chriochairein (991m) and round the corniced edge of Coire a' Chriochairein, following a line of fence posts which continues over another indistinct Top (1,051m) to the summit of Stob Poite Coire Ardair.

Ski west-south-west down a broad easy ridge for about 400m, then turn south and descend more steeply to The Window (Uinneag Coire Ardair), the narrow pass at the head of Coire Ardair. In bad visibility take care not to ski south too soon after leaving Stob Poite Coire Ardair, as there are steep crags north-east of The Window. At this point the traverse can be shortened by skiing east through the pass (where there are often old snowholes which may provide shelter) and descending Coire Ardair, but after the initial steep run down to the lochan there is a long, gradual poling descent for 5km back to Aberarder.

If continuing the traverse, climb south-east from The Window up a steep slope, which may be icy. A visit to the summit of Creag Meagaidh is a fairly flat out-and-back 2km diversion, and a more natural choice might be along the top of the crags of Coire Ardair to your left. If the summit is included, then as the plateau is reached, bear south then west-south-west past Mad Meg's cairn (NN 423 877) to reach the true summit of Creag Meagaidh at another large cairn.

Return due east for 1km to a wide col and climb south-east slightly over the broad hump of Puist Coire Ardair (1,070m) to reach the narrower ridge beyond. This section of the route requires very careful navigation in bad visibility as the plateau is quite featureless and there are precipitous corries to the north and south. If they are visible, there are a few fence posts east of Puist Coire Ardair to aid navigation. Continue east, skiing more steeply down to the level ridge of Sròn a' Choire (1,001m).

It is not necessary to climb to this Top, but a slightly descending traverse east-north-east leads to a small cairn on its south-east shoulder. From there a very fine run goes down the shallow east-facing corrie of the Sròn. This is a vast concave bowl which holds snow well and gives excellent skiing down to the level moor on the south-west side of the Allt Coire Ardair. Continue down this side of the stream almost to Aberarder and cross by a footbridge a few hundred metres west of the farm.

From the summit of Creag Meagaidh, another good and quicker descent route is down the Moy Burn, but it leads to the A86 about 8km south-west of Aberarder. The slopes immediately south of the Creag Meagaidh summit cairn are steep, and the safest route goes south-east at first before turning south-west towards the head of the burn. This may be preferred as a quick way off the mountain in bad weather or approaching darkness.

Gulvain/Gaor Bheinn ▲ 987m
Filthy or Noisy Hill

△ NN 002 875   ⌖ LR40, LR41   🌐 P.310

🅿 Drumsallie on the A830 Mallaig road (NM 960 794/ 56.8614, -5.3472). There is parking on the west side of the A861 between the junction with the A830 and the railway bridge. There is a train from Fort William to Locheilside Station, which is 3.5km east of the starting point. Bus service 500 (and others) from Fort William stops at Drumsallie (see: www.shielbuses.co.uk).

↔ 20KM   △ 1,130M   ⇕ 10M
⏱ 7 HRS   GRADE II   ★★

By Colwyn Jones

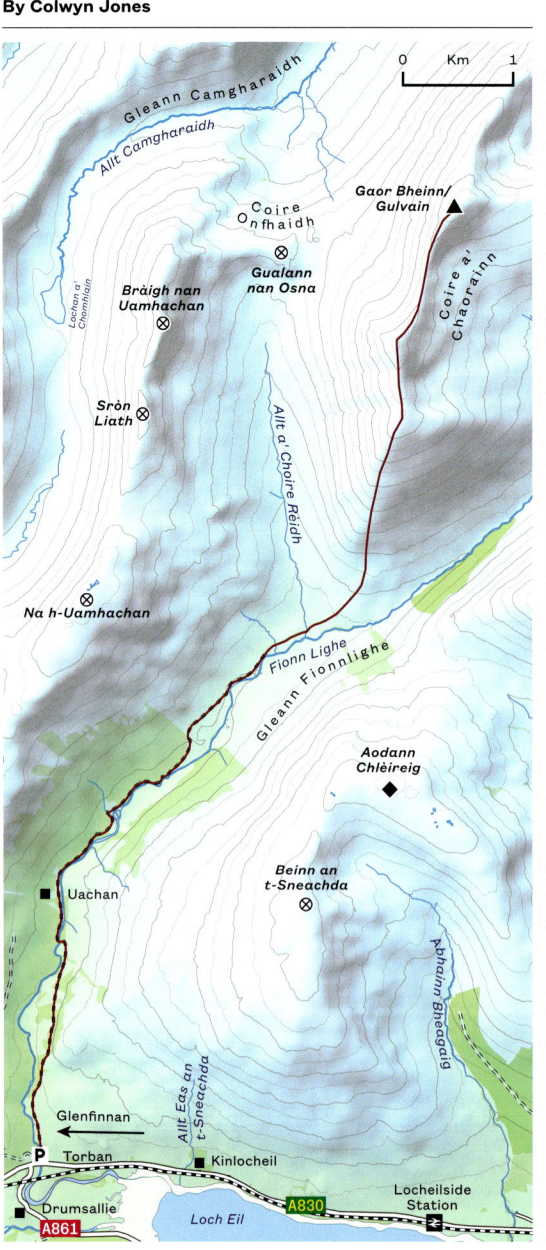

Sitting in the rarely skied moorland between Loch Arkaig and the Fort William to Mallaig road, Gulvain is isolated from other 3,000-foot peaks. When there is snow down to sea level it provides a splendid direct ascent with a fine airy ridge leading to a superb panoramic summit. With the lengthy approach from the south, and when snow conditions allow, a mountain bike might be used to your advantage. From the foot of Gleann Fionnlighe, take the gated landrover track initially rising on the east side of the river and then dropping to cross the river after 2km. The approach of around 6km, mainly in forest and gaining little height, brings you to the open hillside

below the 150m contour and the towering south ridge of the peak.

The next 2km give a 700m vertical gain to the 855m spot height and the triangulation station on the south top (961m) shortly thereafter. There are some steep sections, so keep checking the snow conditions. During the ascent it is also worth checking where the best snow for the descent is likely to be, in particular Coire a' Chaorainn on the south-east side. The true summit lies 1km further north-north-east, and after a short descent, for which it may not be worth removing skins, the graceful ridge leads to the higher north summit and cairn (987m). There are fine views in all directions, to the 'Rough Bounds' of Knoydart, Ben Nevis and Ardgour.

The descent follows the approach route with suitable options following the best snow. If skiing down the slopes on the south-east side, pick a route which will bring you back to the end of the approach track (NM 993 840). Do not descend into the upper part of the Fionn Lighe, as there is much rough ground alongside the burn.

Below: Looking East to the Spey Dam from the Eastern Creag Meagaidh hills (p.307) © Jonty Mills

Chapter 8

West Scotland North

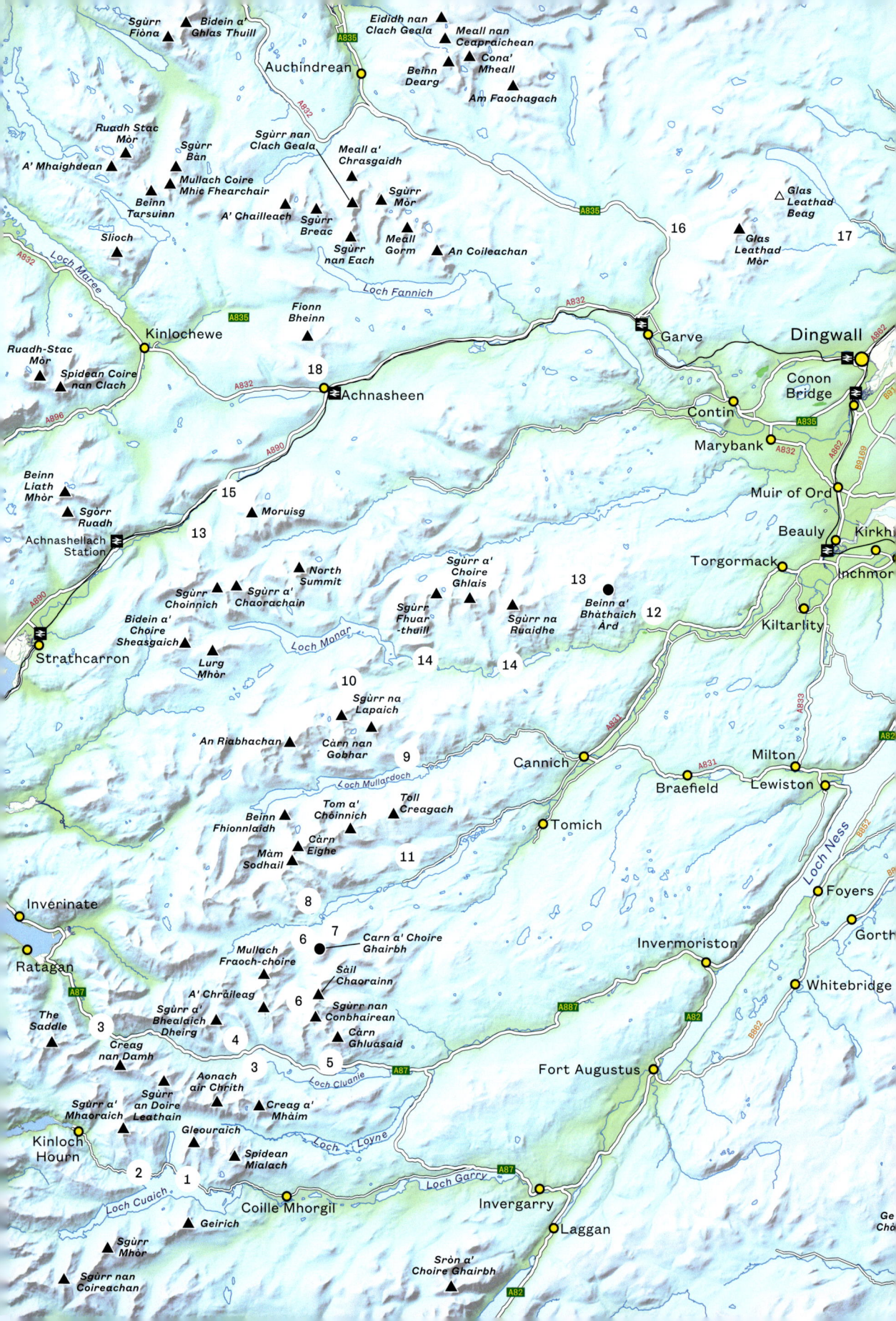

Previous: Sgùrr nan Conbhairean descent into Coire Lair (skier, Al Bird)
© Al Todd

1.	Gleouraich	P.316
2.	Sgùrr a' Mhaoraich	P.317
3.	South Cluanie Ridge	P.318
4.	Sgùrr a' Bhealaich Dheirg	P.322
5.	Cluanie Hills from South	P.325
6.	Sàil Chaorainn	P.327
7.	Carn a' Choire Ghairbh	P.328
8.	Càrn Eighe	P.329
9.	Càrn nan Gobhar	P.330
10.	Sgùrr na Lapaich	P.332
11.	Toll Creagagh	P.333
12.	Beinn a' Bhàthaich Àrd	P.336
13.	Cross Ross-Shire	P.338
14.	Strathfarrar	P.343
15.	Moruisg	P.346
16.	Ben Wyvis	P.347
17.	Ben Wyvis East	P.348
18.	Fionn Bheinn	P.349

Chapter 8 | West Scotland North

Gleouraich ▲ 1,035m
The Roaring
△ NH 039 053　　◁ LR33　　⊕ P.316

Spidean Mialach ▲ 996m
Lousy Peak
△ NH 066 043　　◁ LR33　　⊕ P.316

P Roadside parking on the north side of Loch Quoich (Loch Cuaich; NH 029 030/57.0756, -5.2533).

↔ 13KM　　△ 1,120M　　↕ 215M
⏱ 7-8 HRS　　GRADE IV　　★★★★

By Bill Wallace, updated by Colwyn Jones

Although these mountains are relatively remote, the effort required to reach them is amply rewarded by an excellent traverse and superb scenery. However, as the route described is technically demanding, with steep ascents to both peaks and a very steep descent confined by rocks to the intermediate Fiar Bhealach, only experienced ski mountaineers should attempt the traverse. A good covering of snow is required before this is feasible on skis.

While the southern slopes are predominantly grassy, providing relatively easy routes of ascent and descent, a tour of the ridges along the steep northern edge gives superb views to the Glen Shiel hills and the 'Rough Bounds' of Knoydart, and provides one of the finest traverses in the Western Highlands.

Walk from the road above the north shore of Loch Quoich just west of the Allt Coire Peitireach, where a stalkers' path creates a gap in the rhododendron bushes. Follow this path through a fence and north-west up the hillside following the line of the summer path. If the snow cover allows, at around 500m head north east into Coire Peitireach. Alternatively walk east along the road to the summer descent path and follow the path north-east uphill. Then just above the 400m contour turn northwards under a shoulder into Coire Mhèil. Continue north-west up the stream to level ground south of and below the summit of Gleouraich.

Turn north and climb 100m before traversing north-west into upper Coire Peitireach. The ascent north to the ridge west of the summit is very steep, but this section may be avoided by continuing the traverse to the west before ascending to the ridge. Having reached the ridge, turn east and ascend steeply at first to reach the summit of Gleouraich.

From the summit continue along the ridge east for 500m, descending 70m to a shallow col, then climb 40m to Creag Coire na Fiar Bhealaich. From this top descend east to the Fiar Bhealach (1,006m). Considerable care is required as it is necessary to ski near to the edge of the precipitous northern corrie to avoid a band of low cliffs on the south-east slopes which are not visible from above.

From the bealach the initial ascent 200m south-east is steep and rocky. Thereafter the route is on easier ground, following the edge of the northern corries to the summit of Spidean Mialach.

Key
1. Gleouriach　　P.316
2. Sgurr a' Mhaoriach　　P.317

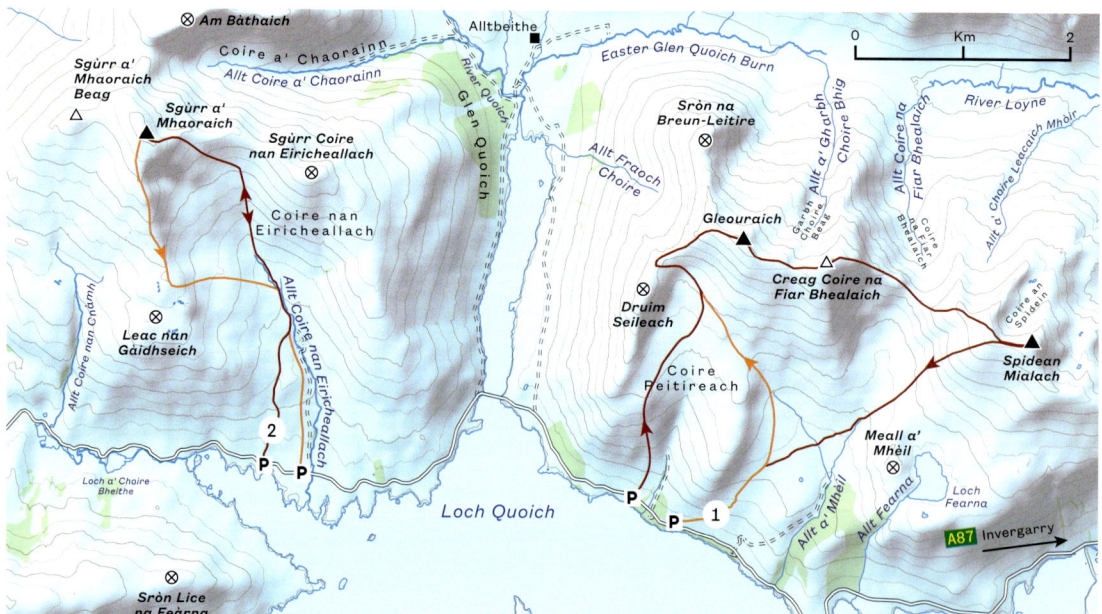

From the summit, at first ski down the easy open slopes to the south-west, aiming for Loch Fearna. After descending 200m, bear west and traverse across the slope to Coire Mhèil. Given sufficient snow, the lower grassy corrie down to the road may be descended at any point.

Recently, two new run-of-the-river hydroelectric schemes have been installed draining into Loch Quoich, and the intake dam maintenance tracks might also be used to ease access to the southern flanks of these fine hills.

Sgùrr a' Mhaoraich ▲ 1,027m
Peak of the Shellfish

⚐ NG 984 065	✦ LR33	🌐 P.316

P	The roadside on the north side of Loch Quoich (Loch Cuaich; NG 993 036/57.0787, -5.3121).		
↔ 8KM	△ 820M	⬍ 210M
⏱ 4-5 HRS	GRADE III	★★★

By Donald Bennet, updated by Alan Sloan

This bulky, isolated mountain to the west of Gleouraich rewards those who venture off the A87 down the single-track road towards Kinlochhourn, with a fine ascent on skis which is shorter and easier than the adjacent traverse of Gleouraich and Spidean Mialach. Although the skiing may be quite uncomplicated, the position of Sgùrr a' Mhaoraich, rising directly above the head of Loch Hourn, makes it a superb viewpoint, and on a clear day few ski tours give such fine views of the western sea lochs and mountains. The final approach to the summit traverses steep-angled ground, so consideration of avalanche risk on this south-facing slope is required.

The original sheltered car parking area near the shore of Loch Cuaich and the stalkers' path just west of the forestry plantation can still be used, but the new maintenance track for a run-of-the-river hydroelectric scheme allows easier access (and perhaps descent) up to the intake dam at about the 350m contour.

Follow the track into Coire nan Eiricheallach (The Irish Corrie). Initially ski easily north, then north-west up to the head of the corrie where the slope steepens under the long east ridge of Sgùrr a' Mhaoraich. Bear up to the left (west) on a rising traverse to reach the east ridge above its rocky part on a ramp at about 830m, where the crest is quite broad. The steep rise above this point can be avoided by a rising traverse left leading onto the upper slopes of the south ridge, which are broad, easy-angled and rise directly to the summit cairn and very fine views.

The best descent may be made by the same route using information gleaned on the approach. Alternatively, ski down the south ridge, though its upper part has many knolls and rocky outcrops, and good snow cover is needed. In good conditions, however, this ridge gives what Donald Bennet originally described as 'very interesting skiing' down to about 650m, where you should bear south-east down towards the lower part of Coire nan Eiricheallach and pick up the track back to your starting point.

Below: An early start on the South Cluanie ridge
© Hamish Frost

South Cluanie Ridge

Creag a' Mhàim ▲ 947m
Crag of the Large Round Hill
△ NH 087 077   ⊿ LR33   ⊕ P.319

Druim Shionnach ▲ 987m
Foxes Ridge
△ NH 074 084   ⊿ LR33   ⊕ P.319

Aonach air Chrith ▲ 1,021m
Ridge of Trembling
△ NH 051 083   ⊿ LR33   ⊕ P.319

Maol Chinn-dearg ▲ 981m
Bald Red Head
△ NH 032 087   ⊿ LR33   ⊕ P.319

Sgùrr an Doire Leathain ▲ 1,010m
Peak of the Broad Oak Grove
△ NH 015 099   ⊿ LR33   ⊕ P.319

Sgùrr an Lochain ▲ 1,004m
Peak of the Lochan
△ NH 005 104   ⊿ LR33   ⊕ P.319

Creag nan Damh ▲ 918m
Rock of Stags
△ NG 983 112   ⊿ LR33   ⊕ P.319

Sgùrr na Sgine ▲ 946m
Peak of the Knife
△ NG 946 113   ⊿ LR33   ⊕ P.319

The Saddle ▲ 1,010m
△ NG 936 131   ⊿ LR33   ⊕ P.319

▭ Parking just east of the Cluanie Inn (NH 079 117/ 57.1560, -5.1766).

↔ 32KM   △ 2,700M   ↕ 220M
⏱ 9-15 HRS   GRADE IV   ★★★

7 Munro route
↔ 25KM   △ 1,900M   ↕ 220M
⏱ 6-12 HRS   GRADE IV   ★★★

By Finlay Wild

The South Glen Shiel Ridge is a classic high ridge linking seven Munros in a linear journey accessed from the A87 in Glen Shiel. In good weather there are stunning views to Kintail, Knoydart and Skye. The route can be extended westward to The Saddle, adding a further two Munros. Equally, splitting the route into two days may be more practical, depending on fitness and conditions.

'South Glen Shiel Ridge Ski Traverse', in *SMCJ* (2018), vol.46, no.209, pp.93-96, describes a fast solo traverse in December 2017 using lightweight Skimo equipment. Conditions were marginal, but the traverse gave a very rewarding and memorable day.

As a ski objective this area is fickle, being both close to the sea and fairly rocky, making good snow conditions elusive. The 2017 traverse utilised an early season window when unconsolidated snow made the skiing technical and awkward. This route requires competent skiing and mountaineering skills and is both physically demanding and committing. As a linear route, consideration must be given to getting back to your start point along the A87 – parties often use two cars.

The 2017 party parked just east of the Cluanie Inn at NH 079 117 and skinned along the old Cluanie-Tomdoun road. Several options exist for gaining the eastern end of the ridge at Creag a' Mhàim. Perhaps the most obvious is to follow the road around Creag a' Mhàim to the east until a track breaks off near NH 101 072 and ascends the south-east ridge of the hill. A more direct alternative is to leave the old road after crossing the stone bridge over the Allt Giubhais at NH 093 094, going over a stile, and then ascending south west before either climbing to the summit directly via the blunt ridge forming the east side of Coirean an Eich Bhric, or taking the corrie to a col at 868m on the ridge west of the summit.

From Creag a' Mhàim there is initially a fairly wide and gentle ridge, but this soon alternates with narrower and sometimes exposed rocky sections. This variability is very much the theme of the day, and careful skinning will likely alternate with sections on foot. As a high ridge exposed to the weather, snow conditions will likely change fairly dramatically throughout the winter, and careful judgement will be required to make safe progress. After Druim Shionnach there is a wide, gentle descent, but then quickly undulating technical sections reappear. After Aonach air Chrith is a rocky, narrow descent – the 2017 party remained on foot for a significant portion of this. For much of the ridge, the remains of an old fence can be a helpful navigational aid. In 2017 most of the descents were difficult as drifts and bare areas along the ridge had created only a narrow area on which to ski, and the snow was often collapsible.

After Sgùrr an Lochain it is possible to bypass the sub-summit of Sgùrr Beag on the south by a descending traverse to the Bealach Fraoch Choire (NG 991 109; 729m), although careful consideration of avalanche conditions would be required.

The ridge west from the seventh Munro, Creag nan Damh, is complex and rocky and will require some progress on foot – indeed, a little way west from the summit is a short steep wall which, in some conditions, will require crampons and ice axe to descend. Once you have descended below around 800m elevation on the west ridge, the angle eases and the Bealach Duibh Leac is reached (NG 968 112; 721m). Here is an obvious point to quit the ridge and descend north-west then north to meet the Allt Mhàlagain (crossed by hidden footbridge at NG 970 134) and the parking at Màlagan (NG 971 139). Again, this is complex ground with the confluence of multiple rivers, and conditions on the day will dictate the best line. There may be several earlier escape options to descend north from the ridge back to Glen Shiel down the many varied corries. These routes would need to be assessed in their own right at the time. Escape south to Glen Quoich would also be possible at several points, but the transport logistics out from Loch Quoich make this option largely redundant.

The 2017 party did not use the Bealach Duibh Leac descent but continued on to add a further two Munros: Sgùrr na Sgine and The Saddle. This section was somewhat more serious, with complex summits and worsening snow conditions.

From Bealach Duibh Leac, continue along the undulating ridge (old fence posts) to the indistinct summit of Sgùrr a' Bhac Chaolais. The route continues west but descends a steep and cliffy section which was negotiated on foot to the col before Sgùrr na Sgine. A substantial wall runs south-west up onto Sgùrr na Sgine's south-west ridge, and this route was used to gain the flank before ascending to the summit. Approximately 500m north-west the route again descends steeply on rocky terrain, and a variety of lines can be used to approach Bealach Coire Mhàlagain below The Saddle. From here the summer route takes a path north-west to meet a wall and follows this to a flatter area just south of the summit. Various lines of ascent are possible on skis; the best option will require consideration of snow conditions on the day.

The Saddle is a complex mountain, and the main ridge to the east joins Sgùrr na Forcan and the Forcan Ridge, which is a summer scramble. Ski descent options are numerous and potentially complex, with much steep ground around. The 2017 party descended the corrie just north of the Forcan Ridge in a north-easterly then easterly direction before climbing back to the col at NG 950 133, ascending Meallan Odhar (610m), then taking the ridge north to meet the stalkers' track which descends to the road. Another option would be to retrace your route from the summit of The Saddle to Bealach Coire Mhàlagain and then descend Coire Mhàlagain north-east to Màlagan. Whichever route is taken, the most suitable finish point is likely to be the parking at Màlagan (NG 971 139).

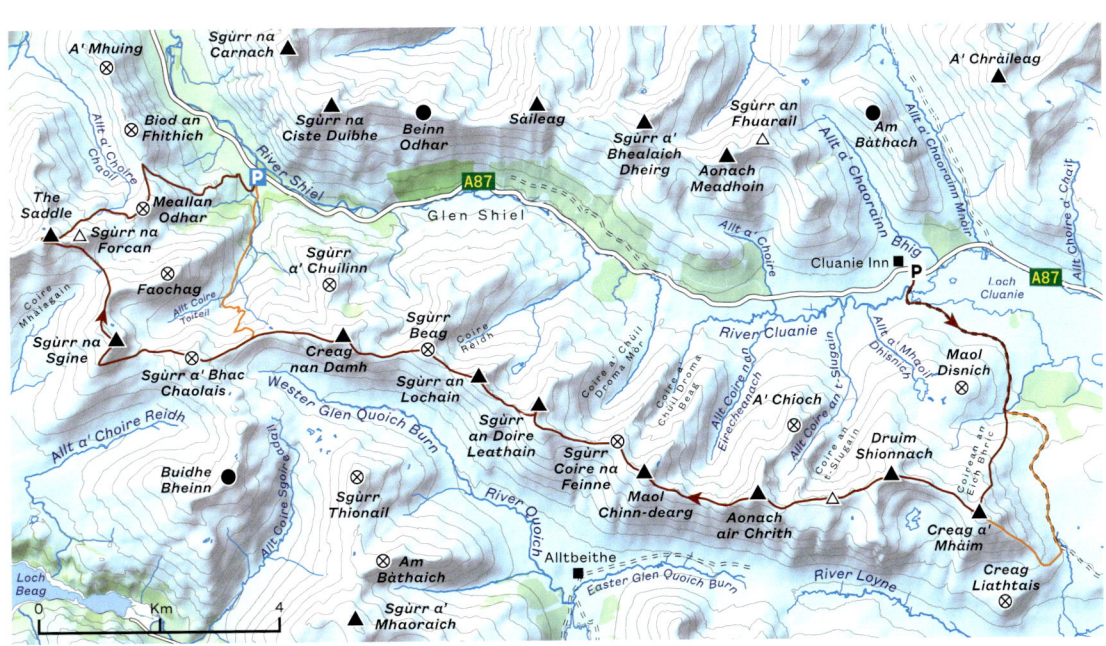

Sgùrr a' Bhealaich Dheirg ▲ 1,036m

The Peak of the Red Pass

△ NH 035 143   ◁ LR33   ⊕ P.322

🅿 On the A87 2km west of the Cluanie Inn, just east of the first forestry boundary. There is a large unpaved layby on the north side of the road (NH 056 114/ 57.1528, -5.2147). The Glasgow–Uig bus service stops at the Cluanie Inn.

↔ 10KM	△ 800M	↨ 237M
⏱ 6 HRS	GRADE III	✶✶✶

By Alan Sloan

Previous: Ski camp on the summit of The Saddle (skier, Dave Mitchell) © Al Todd

Right: Approaching the ridge on Sgùrr a' Bhealaich Dheirg © Alan Sloan

Sgùrr a' Bhealaich Dheirg is the middle of the Three Brothers. It is an accessible ski route from near the high point of the A87 with interesting terrain. Being a trunk road, the A87 is more likely to be cleared than minor roads in the event of a large snowfall. The peak, worthy of the title Sgùrr, is a fine viewpoint with the South Cluanie Ridge to the south and Sgùrr nan Ceathramhnan to the north. There is a 50m scramble to the summit cairn, which may require an ice axe and crampons.

From the car park, travel north on the west side of Allt a' Choire for 800m, then turn west-north-west into Coire Tholl Bhruach. There is a path 100m distance uphill from the burn that is not shown on OS maps. Keeping well above the burn, follow the Allt Coire Tholl Bhruach, turning north then north-west to 750m at NH 039 127. Here make a choice between gaining the col north of point 806m or the col to the north at 827m, depending on snow conditions. In either case, ascend to point 906m before easily reaching the summit ridge to the north-west at 1,030m. Make a ski depot before the short scramble to the summit cairn.

The ascent route also makes a good descent route. Steeper options include skiing directly south-east from point 906m or skiing directly east off point 806m, which may be corniced. The ascent line is then followed without difficulty back to the road.

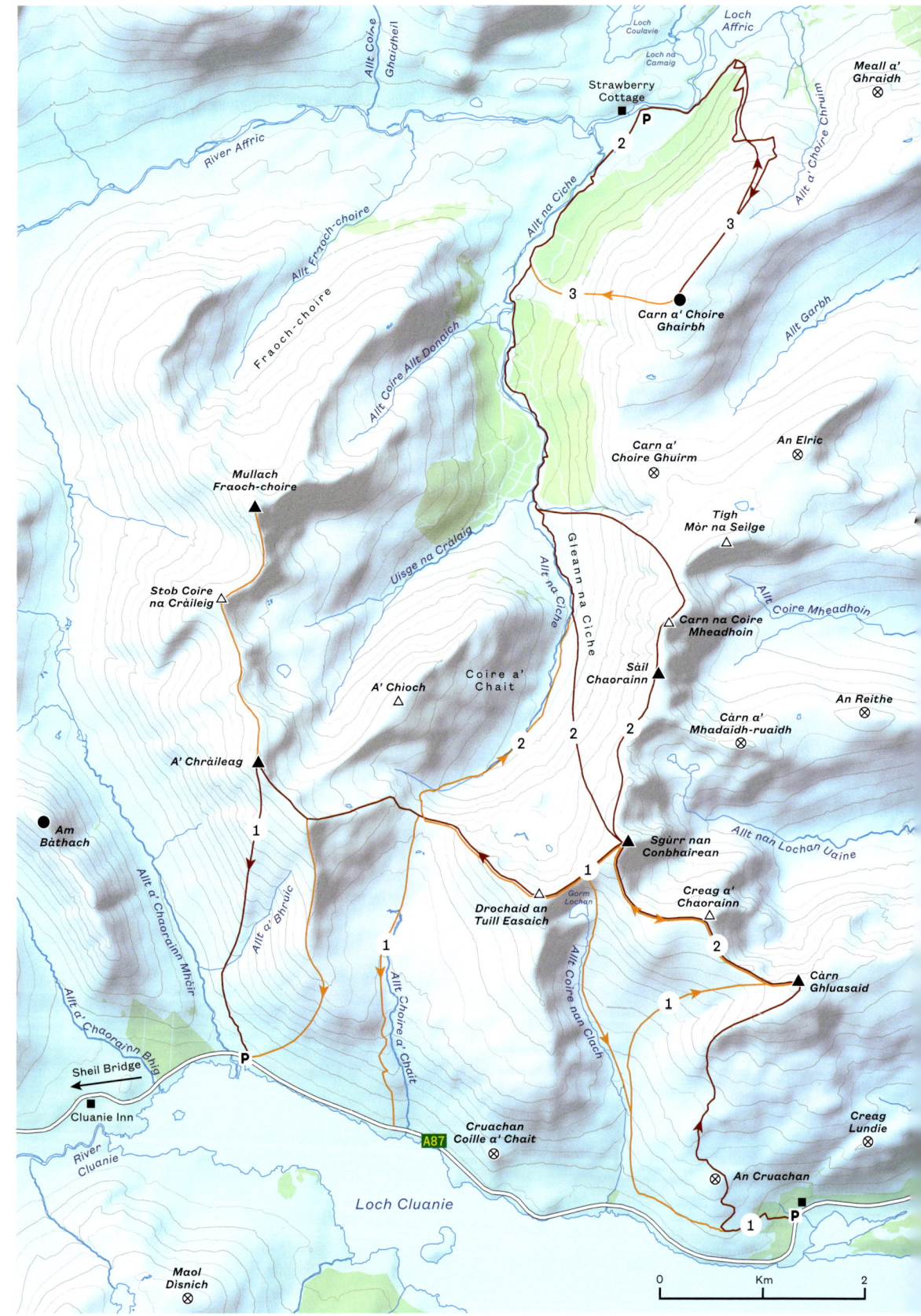

Cluanie Hills from South

Càrn Ghluasaid ▲ 957m
Cairn of Movement
△ NH 145 125　　⌖ LR34　　🌐 P.324

Sgùrr nan Conbhairean ▲ 1,110m
Peak of the Houndsmen
△ NH 129 138　　⌖ LR34　　🌐 P.324

A' Chràileag ▲ 1,120m
The Creel
△ NH 094 148　　⌖ LR33, LR34　　🌐 P.324

Mullach Fraoch-choire ▲ 1,102m
Summit of the Heather Corrie
△ NH 094 171　　⌖ LR33, LR34　　🌐 P.324

🅿 On the A87, 4km west from the Cluanie dam on the north side of Loch Cluanie at Lundie (NH 144 103/ 57.1461, -5.0682).

↔ 18KM　　△ 1,370M　　⊤ 230M
🕐 7-8 HRS　　GRADE III　　★★★★

By Donald Bennet, updated by Colwyn Jones

On the north side of Loch Cluanie at the head of Glen Moriston there is a high range of mountains culminating in A' Chràileag. Their traverse is a very fine ski expedition which fully rewards the long journey to reach them, and there is great pleasure in skiing in this part of the Highlands, surrounded by so many other superb peaks in an area rarely frequented by skiers. The quality of the traverse lies partly in this mountain setting, partly in the character of the peaks, ridges and corries, and partly in the skiing itself, which, although not unduly difficult, is varied and interesting. However, two or three sections require careful navigation when skiing in bad weather. The A87 is a busy road, and two vehicles will be needed for this traverse. The option of an out-and-back route from the Cluanie Inn, accessible by coach, is also described. Coach services are the 915 and 916 (Glasgow–Uig, Scottish Citylink) and service 917 (Inverness–Portree, Stagecoach Highlands/Scottish Citylink).

Leave the large car park, cross the A87 and from a loop in the old road, take the track following the old military road to the mobile phone mast. Behind the mast an old stalkers' track goes north around the knoll An Cruachan (460m). Continue up the steep zigzagging path onto the west-south-west ridge and follow this to the summit plateau of Càrn Ghluasaid. Alternatively, with good snow cover, continue along the old military road and initially follow the line of the Allt Coire nan Clach north up easy slopes on the east side of the burn. After 1.5km bear north-east up the north side of the stream which flows from the plateau of Càrn Ghluasaid, thus avoiding the zigzags of the footpath. Continue easily to this summit where the most prominent cairn (which is not quite the highest point of the plateau) overlooks the wild corries at the head of the River Doe.

Ski west down a broad, smooth ridge, dropping only 60m to a col from which an easy climb of 100m leads to Creag a' Chaorainn (998m). The ridge turns west for a short distance and drops barely 20m before climbing much more steeply in a north-north-westerly direction to Sgùrr nan Conbhairean. The entire ridge from Càrn Ghluasaid to Sgùrr nan Conbhairean is very smooth (the underlying terrain being grass and moss), as are the slopes on its south side dropping into Coire Lair. With good snow cover the coire can provide a short tour and a good return to the car park. Descend westwards towards the col (960m) and an obvious shallow gully gives an easier line through steep ground immediately east of Gorm Lochan. When the angle eases follow the best snow through runnels on the east side of Allt Coire Lair to rejoin your ascent path. The north side of the ridge is precipitous and liable to be corniced.

Ski south-west from the summit of Sgùrr nan Conbhairean down a wide slope which steepens and converges to a little col. At that point the ridge is narrow, with steep drops on both sides, and beyond it rises again very gradually (skins are not needed) for about 200m to the top of Drochaid an Tuill Easaich (1,001m). There, the ridge turns north-west and drops, gradually at first and then much more steeply, to the Bealach Choire a' Chait (approx 730m). You can ski along the crest of the ridge quite easily to the steepening, and then take the south-west flank for a descending traverse towards the bealach. If there is a good snow cover, this descent gives a very good run; otherwise, the ridge and its south-west flank may be punctuated by rocks and boulders, necessitating walking.

The Bealach Choire a' Chait is a wide, flat col, and you can shorten the traverse by skiing very easily south down the corrie. Once at the busy A87 a short walk takes you back to the line of the old military road and a further 4km walk back to the car.

Key

1. Cluanie Hills From South　　P.325
2. Sàil Chaorainn　　P.327
3. Carn a' Choire Ghairbh　　P.328

The ridge to A' Chràileag, however, rises directly from the col, steeply at first, then more steadily until the final steepening leads to the main crest of the mountain 750m south-east of the summit. Check the south ridge here to ascertain the snow cover. The final climb up this broad ridge takes you above the surrounding peaks to the large and splendidly built cairn of A' Chràileag.

From the summit, two fine descents are available:
- Ski directly south then onto a vague ridge which often holds snow on the east side. Continue running back down the south-west flank of the peak to arrive on an agricultural track leading to a small parking place on the south of the A87 (NH 091 120).
- Ski back along the south-east ridge to the junction of the south and east ridges. If you observed good snow cover during the ascent then ski down the south ridge until the 700m contour, when you will need to turn south-west down the very steep slope to reach the A87, hopefully close to the parking place.

Altogether, the run from A' Chràileag to the Loch Cluanie road gives over 3km of very varied and enjoyable skiing with a descent of almost 900m if there is snow down to the loch. It is a fitting end to a grand traverse.

If you are staying at the Cluanie Inn with no car, then an out-and-back tour to A' Chràileag and Mullach Fraoch-choire can be made from the hotel door. The starting point on the A87 is 1.5km east of the hotel at the waymarked footpath on the north side of the road (NH 091 120; 230m). (Distance: 12km; height climbed: 1,070m; time: 5–8 hours; rating: ∗∗∗/IV.)

Go 1.5km east along the side of the A87 to the start of the route up A' Chràileag. Please note that the road is often busy and there is no established footpath. The two road bridges between the hotel and the start must also be used.

The description of the final descent used in the traverse should be reversed, providing a continuously steep route from the 350m contour to the summit. Moving onto the south-east ridge at the 800m contour will ease the final approach to the top.

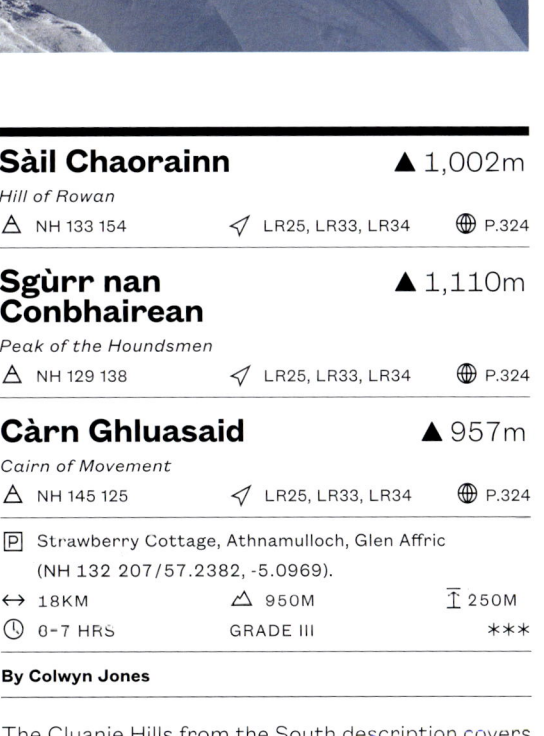

From the summit cairn, continue north along the ridge for 2km towards the summit of Mullach Fraoch-choire. Depending on snow conditions, the ridge narrows and becomes steeper, and skis will need to be carried while using boot crampons and an ice axe. The alternative is to depot the skis where the ridge becomes tricky, visit the summit of Mullach Fraoch-choire, then return to your skis to reverse the ascent route, or use the south-east then south ridge of A' Chràileag to return to the A87 and then the hotel.

Above: Càrn Ghluasaid (skiers, Susan Houstoun and Al Bird) © Al Todd

Opposite: Sgùrr nan Conbhairean (skier, Al Bird) © Al Todd

Sàil Chaorainn ▲ 1,002m
Hill of Rowan
△ NH 133 154   LR25, LR33, LR34   P.324

Sgùrr nan Conbhairean ▲ 1,110m
Peak of the Houndsmen
△ NH 129 138   LR25, LR33, LR34   P.324

Càrn Ghluasaid ▲ 957m
Cairn of Movement
△ NH 145 125   LR25, LR33, LR34   P.324

P Strawberry Cottage, Athnamulloch, Glen Affric (NH 132 207/57.2382, -5.0969).

↔ 18KM   △ 950M   ↕ 250M
⏲ 0-7 HRS   GRADE III   ★★★

By Colwyn Jones

The Cluanie Hills from the South description covers the ascent of some of these hills from the A87, but they can also be successfully visited from the north if staying at the 12-bed Strawberry Cottage, the An Teallach Mountaineering Club Hut.

Strawberry Cottage provides good access to several remote Scottish mountains. It sits at the west end of Loch Affric, north of the River Affric and opposite Athnamulloch steading. Access is by single-track public road from Cannich to the east end of Loch Affric, then, after a locked gate, 8km along a rough track. There is parking within 200m of the cottage, so kit and supplies need to be carried across a footbridge to the hut. Motor access past the locked gate is strictly with permission for two vehicles only. There is accommodation for 12 people, with ample firewood provided for the open hearth. Wild camping in the area is an alternative, perhaps combined with a mountain bike from the Glen Affric pay and display car park (free alternatives exist nearby). Waking up to a crisp, fresh morning at Strawberry Cottage, surrounded by snow-covered mountains, is a must for every aspiring Scottish ski mountaineer.

To ski up this group of peaks, use the landrover track that goes south into Gleann na Cìche, past all of the plantations and deer fences for 4km (NH 122 170; 350m). Once on the open hillside, turn east and choose the best and safest option up the steep slope, with an awkward final 150m up to the 800m contour. The final rise onto the ridge eases and is reached at around 900m. Once on the wide ridge, turn south for a little over 1km to reach the summit of Sàil Chaorainn (1,002m).

There is a shallow descent south from this summit to an intervening col at around the 900m contour, then a 200m rise over a convoluted 1km. This requires careful navigation to reach the summit of Sgùrr nan Conbhairean, the high point of the tour giving good views over Loch Cluanie and beyond.

Càrn Ghluasaid is an eastern outlier (2.5km) which requires an undulating, out-and-back route over Creag a' Chaorainn (998m) to tick the summit.

From the summit of Sgùrr nan Conbhairean, there are two established descent options, in addition to simply reversing your ascent over Sàil Chaorainn. From the summit go north for a few hundred metres, then, when possible, and if conditions allow, follow the steep north-west slope down into the Gleann na Cìche, which typically holds good snow. Before reaching the Allt na Cìche, try to maintain height by a traverse further north towards the end of the trees and the track back to Strawberry Cottage.

With good snow cover, the longer alternative is to turn south-west down to the Drochaid an Tuill Easaich (1,001m) and continue along the ridge to the Bealach Choire a' Chait (727m). From the pass an attempt can be made to follow the stalkers' path down in a north-easterly direction next to the Allt na Cìche and back to your starting point.

Carn a' Choire Ghairbh ● 865m
Cairn of the Rough Corrie

△ NH 136 188   ↗ LR25, LR34   ⊕ P.324

P Strawberry Cottage, Athnamulloch, Glen Affric (NH 132 206/57.2382, -5.0969).

↔ 8KM   △ 650M   ↕ 250M
⏱ 3-4 HRS   GRADE II   ★★

By Colwyn Jones

Glen Affric is one of Scotland's longest and most beautiful glens, containing carefully preserved and regenerating old Caledonian pine forest. This peak is a short tour, easily accessible and suitable for an afternoon if you arrive at the hut around midday, or as a final morning tour if you are departing that afternoon.

To ski up this Corbett, head east back along the landrover track and up the first steep gradient on the south side of Loch Affric to a junction with an old, neglected stalkers' path at NH 142 210. The footpath is steep in places, but a satisfactory skinning track can be successfully established with good snow cover down to the 250m contour. The path zigzags and follows the fence protecting regenerating old Caledonian pine forest up to an altitude of about 500m. Here, where the slope eases, continue contouring east, then up onto the wide ridge at around the 700m contour. Turn west and continue up the broad ridge to the two summits, of which the north is higher at 865m. The summit is surrounded by higher peaks, but on a clear day it gives good views of the many Munros nearby.

Descent can follow the ascent, which has some steep skiing. For the more adventurous, there is a shorter steep route west down the flank of the peak, north of the Allt a' Bhuilg, over a deer fence and down to Gleann na Cìche. However, this option requires good snow cover. On reaching Gleann na Cìche, a landrover track leading north-east back to Athnamulloch finishes a pleasant, short circular tour.

Opposite: Dropping into Coire Leachavie below the steep face of An Tudair (skier, Gordon Pearson) © Al Todd

Màm Sodhail ▲ 1,181m
Hill of the Barns
△ NH 120 253 ⊲ LR25 🌐 P.330

Càrn Eighe ▲ 1,183m
Hill of the File or Notch
△ NH 123 262 ⊲ LR25 🌐 P.330

Beinn Fhionnlaidh ▲ 1,005m
Finlay's Hill
△ NH 115 282 ⊲ LR25 🌐 P.330

P Strawberry Cottage, Athnamulloch, Glen Affric (NH 132 206/57.2382, -5.0969). See Route 120 for further details.

↔ 16KM (25KM) △ 1,100M ↕ 250M
⏱ 6-8 HRS GRADE III ★★★★
(8-10 HRS IF BEINN FHIONNLAIDH IS INCLUDED)

By Colwyn Jones

The two Munros, Màm Sodhail (1,181m) and Càrn Eighe (1,183m), and perhaps a third, Beinn Fhionnlaidh (1,005m), are right behind the hut. Follow the track outside the hut west over a small rise for a few hundred metres, then down to a junction with the circular path around Loch Affric. Follow the footpath north towards Loch Coulavie, but halfway along the loch, cross country to directly zigzag up a shallower slope from the 300m to 630m contour towards a small knoll (NH 119 217), then go north up to Creag a' Chaorainn. Continue over flatter ground up onto the obvious sinuous ridge, with a few undulations, to reach the steeper summit cone of Màm Sodhail and the top. If it has been windy, there may be bare rock on the ridge, but there is often a ribbon of snow allowing the use of skis all the way. An alternative approach, which should only be used if snow conditions are stable, follows the Allt Coulavie up the Coire Coulavie with a steep headwall onto the ridge about 1km below the summit of Màm Sodhail. On occasion cornices atop the headwall have prevented access to the summit ridge.

The next peak is a mere 1km away, but there is a steep descent to the intervening bealach at 1,050m, then an equally steep north-east slope to skin up to reach the slightly more prominent summit of Càrn Eighe and the crowning triangulation station, the highest peak west of the Great Glen (but only just).

If conditions, weather and fitness allow, then you might consider continuing on to Beinn Fhionnlaidh, just over 2km away. The Bealach Beag (832m) is the

lowest point on this leg, but on the return there is a wearying 350m ascent back to the summit of Càrn Eighe, although contouring west below the summit may be possible with the right snow conditions.

The descent follows the ascent route back to the warm, comfortable hut. Alternatively ski down into either Coire Leachavie or Coire Coulavie both of which can provide excellent descent. The initial steep headwalls may form significant avalanche hazards. Coire Leachavie has the advantage of a stalkers track down to the Loch Affric path.

Creag Dubh △ 946m
Black Crag

△ NH 199 350   LR25   P.332

Càrn nan Gobhar ▲ 993m
Hill of the Goats

△ NH 181 343   LR25   P.332

P The end of the public road up Glen Cannich at the Loch Mullardoch dam (NH 220 315/57.3395, -4.9580).

↔ 12KM   △ 860M   ⊥ 250M

⏱ 5-6 HRS   GRADE II   ★★

By Dave Snadden, updated by Colwyn Jones

Below right: Heading along Creag Coire nan Each towards Màm Sodhail (skiers, Fiona Tomlinson, Elliot Marshall) © Al Todd

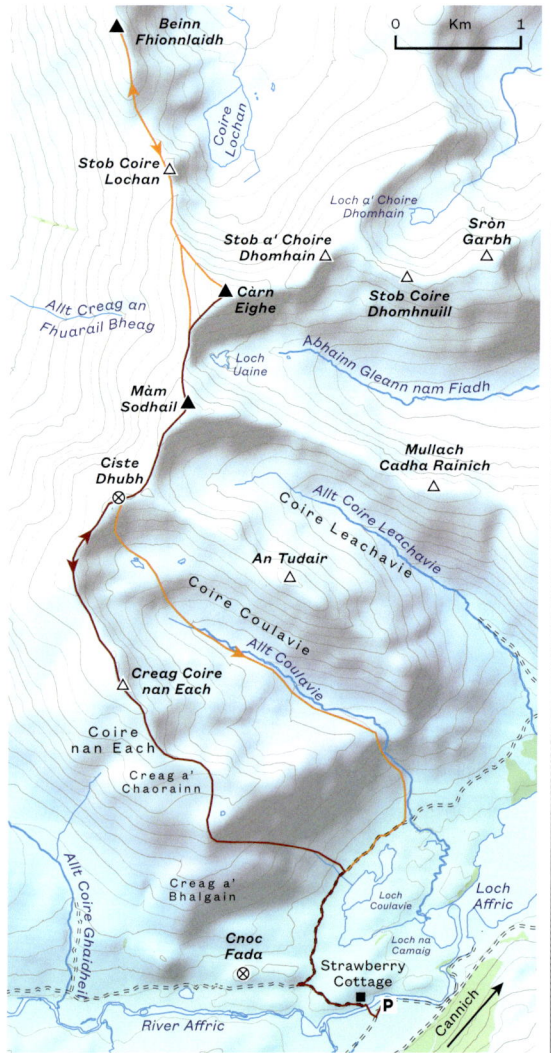

This is the nearest mountain group to the road end at Loch Mullardoch in Glen Cannich. Like many ideal ski mountains, they have rounded contours and smooth slopes, and a tour of the broad ridges encircling Coire an t-Sith gives a pleasant short excursion of no difficulty. This corrie holds snow well and usually gives some good skiing even during years of lean snow cover.

From the Mullardoch dam a footpath goes along the north side of the loch, and it is followed west as far as the Allt Mullardoch. From there a faint path branches off and heads north up the east bank of the burn, leading in 1.25km to the crossing of another small burn. It is quite possible to continue up Coire an t-Sith and make a direct and easy ascent of the south face of Creag Dubh; however, a rising traverse across the lower slopes of the west ridge of point 861m gives access to several steep tongues of snow. The ascent of any one of these is worthwhile, as the gloomy recesses of the corrie are soon left behind, but this route should only be attempted if the snow cover is good.

Once on the crest of the ridge, climb east-north-east until a level traverse north can be made over point 815m (NH 209 344), and then north-west across a shallow col, where a drystane dyke is a useful landmark in thick weather. The ascent to Creag Dubh from the col is simple, though the summit plateau tends to be rocky if there is poor snow cover.

Equally easy is the traverse to Càrn nan Gobhar where the true summit is a small pile of stones 200m north of the more obvious cairn.

There are two possible descents. One goes back to the col towards Creag Dubh and then south-south-east straight down to Coire an t-Sith, but the slope should be treated with care as it is not uncommon to find windslab at its top. Alternatively, a safer route, which gives good skiing but requires better snow cover, goes down the south-south-east ridge of Càrn nan Gobhar to the col below Mullach na Maoile. From there ski down into Coire an t-Sith, cross the burn at a suitable place and rejoin the path back to the lochside.

Key
1. Càrn nan Gobhar — P.330
2. Sgùrr na Lapaich — P.332

Sgùrr na Lapaich ▲ 1,150m
Peak of the Bog
NH 160 351   LR25   P.332

An Riabhachan ▲ 1,129m
The Grey One
NH 133 344   LR25   P.332

The power station in Gleann Innis an Loichel at the end of the road up Glen Strathfarrar (NH 183 381 / 57.3974, -5.0248).

↔ 14KM   △ 1,290M   ⤒ 200M
⏲ 6–7 HRS   GRADE III   ★★★★

By Dave Snadden, updated by Colwyn Jones

Sgùrr na Lapaich is one of the finest mountains at the head of the long glens that penetrate westward from Strath Glass, and its pointed summit and eastern corries can be glimpsed as you approach from the strath. To its west, An Riabhachan is a long level ridge sitting in the heart of the wilderness between Loch Mullardoch and Loch Monar. To ski across these two mountains in the depth of winter is to experience in no uncertain way the isolation and grandeur of this remote part of the Highlands.

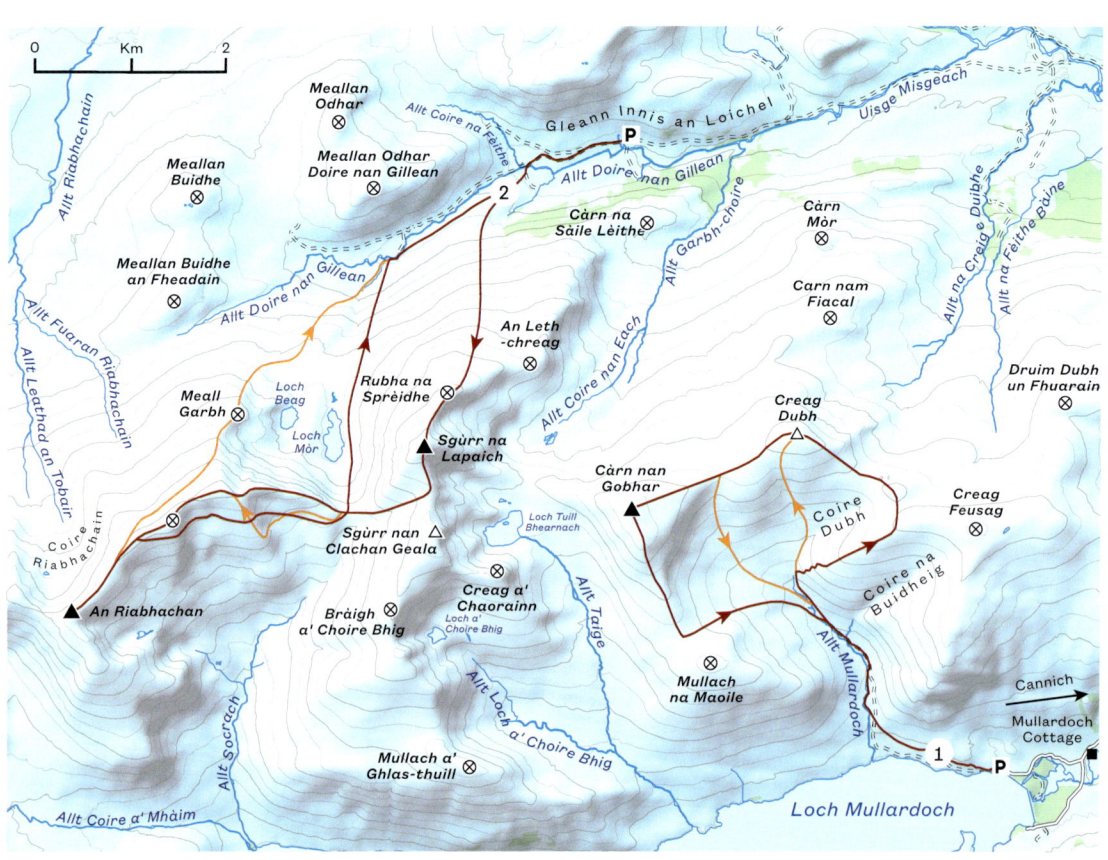

Sgùrr na Lapaich can be climbed on skis from Loch Mullardoch either by itself or in combination with Càrn nan Gobhar. However, the approach along the shores of the loch is tedious, and the traverse from Càrn nan Gobhar involves an ascent of the rugged and precipitous east face of Sgùrr na Lapaich, which, though quite possible, will involve carrying skis up the steepest part. The approach from the head of Glen Strathfarrar is better, and the ascent from there, combined with a traverse to An Riabhachan, gives an excellent expedition into this wild country.

The approach up Glen Strathfarrar is along a private road guarded by a locked gate near Struy in Strath Glass. The key for winter access is the combination for the padlock, which is provided by Mountaineering Scotland. Winter access by car (1 November to 31 March) is available to members of Mountaineering Scotland, subject to conditions. A minimum of two days ahead of your planned visit, either telephone 01738 493942 or e-mail info@mountaineering.scot for details. It should be borne in mind that the road may be impassable due to snow, and the drive from Struy takes much longer than anticipated.

The climb starts from the small power station in Gleann Innis an Loichel, which is reached by driving across the Loch Monar dam and continuing a few kilometres to the end of the road. Proceed west along a rough track for 1km to a small wooden bridge over the Uisge Misgeach (NH 173 379) and follow the track for 200m further to its end. Continue south-west beside a burn for 400m, then turn south and climb the steep slopes above to a large depression on the north side of Sgùrr na Lapaich. This depression holds snow well and gives an easy, though fairly long ascent to the crest of the north-east ridge. From there the ridge is followed in a graceful sweep over a small subsidiary top and up a steepening corniced section to the triangulation station on the summit.

Descend due south for 500m from the summit of Sgùrr na Lapaich to a col 110m lower, taking great care in bad visibility as the slopes to the east are corniced. From there a broad gully gives excellent skiing west down to the col at the foot of the south-west ridge, and if conditions suggest that you should go no further, it is possible to return with a descent north from this col to Loch Mòr. The slopes are steep at first but should pose no difficulty, and from the loch the return to the glen is easy.

The direct ascent of An Riabhachan from the col goes up the east ridge, which is not steep but becomes narrow and exposed in its upper part. An easier alternative is to traverse south-west from the col across An Garbh-choire to reach the south-east ridge and climb this. Both these ridges end at the east top, from where an easy traverse leads along the level summit ridge to the highest point.

Two descents are possible. The first is to return to the east top and descend the south-east ridge, traversing An Garbh-choire to the col between An Riabhachan and Sgùrr na Lapaich, thus joining the alternative descent route mentioned above. It is important not to leave the south-east ridge too soon as the upper part is corniced on its north-east side overlooking An Garbh-choire.

The second descent requires good snow cover but is better in that it goes into remote and bleak country on the north side of An Riabhachan, and in good conditions gives a long and uninterrupted run back to the glen. Ski north-east from the summit by a descending traverse, then a steeper downhill run to a little shallow plateau level with the lowest cliffs above Loch Beag. Descend north of these cliffs to reach the level corrie north of Loch Beag. From there the best route down to the glen will be dictated by prevailing snow conditions, but avoid following the Allt an Eas Bhàin Mhòir as it flows down a steep gorge. A long descending traverse across the lower slopes of Sgùrr na Lapaich may well give the most continuous skiing to end a very rewarding day.

Toll Creagach ▲ 1,054m
Rocky Hollow
△ NH 194 282 ⌖ LR25 ⊕ P.334

Tom a' Chòinnich ▲ 1,112m
Hill of the Moss
△ NH 164 273 ⌖ LR25 ⊕ P.334

P Chisholme Bridge, on the minor road through Glen Affric from Cannich, 3km east-north-east of Affric Lodge (NH 215 242/57.2745, -4.9588).

↔ 15KM   △ 1,100M   ⇞ 230M
⏱ 5-6 HRS   GRADE IV   ★★★

Toll Creagach alone
↔ 12KM   △ 820M   ⏱ 4 HRS

By Dave Snadden, updated by Colwyn Jones

These two mountains give good skiing, often with reliable snow cover until late spring. They can be climbed separately or combined in an excellent traverse. Toll Creagach offers easy-angled slopes, while Tom a' Chòinnich, in marked contrast, has some challenging runs on its steep, snow-holding east face, which should only be attempted by competent skiers who are confident on such terrain.

Start at Chisholme Bridge (on the 1:25,000 map), where the road up Glen Affric crosses the Abhainn Gleann nam Fiadh near the west end of Loch Beinn a' Mheadhoin and there are convenient parking places. Follow the hydroelectric scheme maintenance track west then north for 2km up Gleann nam Fiadh, then, at a junction with a stalkers' path (NH 203 257), turn north-east into a side glen. Mountain bikes might be used to reach this junction. Cross the level floor of this glen to reach the slopes between Beinn Eun and the Allt Coire an t-Sneachda. These slopes can be climbed almost anywhere, giving access to the vast snowy expanse of Coire an t-Sneachda, up which there is a long, tedious plod with little in the way of views to distract. From the corrie it is easy to gain the south or east ridges, and these both lead directly to the triangulation station on the summit of Toll Creagach, where the reward for the laborious ascent is magnificent views to the north and west. If you are not going on to Tom a' Chòinnich, the shortest run back to the road is by the ascent route.

From the summit cairn a line of widely-spaced fence posts leads west down broad slopes to the shallow col before the lower west top (951m). From this col there is a good ski run south down the Allt a' Choire Odhair, and for those with plenty of time and energy the slopes to the north-north-west give an excellent run down towards the Allt Lùb nam Meann; however, this is a long detour on the way to Tom a' Chòinnich, adding at least an hour to the day. The speediest option is to put on skins for the short, shallow ascent to the west top. From there, the descent to the col below Tom a' Chòinnich can be made by skiing down the west ridge, but this

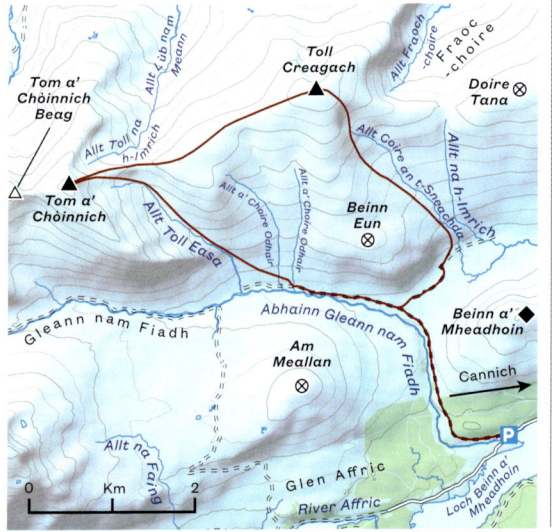

Above: Toll Creagach ascent, Tom a' Chòinnich behind (skier, Dave Mitchell) © Al Todd

ridge is rather rocky and should only be followed if there is good snow cover. A better alternative may well be to ski down a shallow open gully on the south side of the west ridge, and so reach the Bealach Toll Easa (872m).

The climb from the bealach up the east ridge of Tom a' Chòinnich on skis is pleasant and initially poses no difficulties. The final section is steep and narrow, and the last 50–100m may have to be climbed on foot. The summit of Tom a' Chòinnich (1,112m) is marvellous, with steep slopes dropping away on all sides and large mountains all around. The east face is over 1km long and gives several possible ski descents, but the whole face is likely to be corniced, and the first 50m of any descent is precipitous, possibly in excess of 40 degrees. It is usually possible to breach the line of cornices at the point where the east ridge joins the summit plateau near the cairn. The sudden transition from the horizontal summit to the apparent verticality of the descent slopes is quite dramatic, and the seriousness of the descent must not be underestimated as the headwall can pose an avalanche risk. Once the initial slope has been safely negotiated, excellent skiing can be had down the Toll Easa. If the slope is unsafe for skiing, you should retrace your ascent route to the Bealach Toll Easa before skiing down into the corrie.

The maintenance track serving the dam, which is the intake for the run-of-the-river hydroelectric scheme, provides a suitable industrial target for a swift eastern traverse to reach the floor of Gleann nam Fiadh (NH 194 259). From here, continue down the track, past the earlier junction (perhaps collecting mountain bikes) after 1km and back to the road in Glen Affric.

Beinn a' Bhàthaich Àrd ● 862m

Hill of the High Byre

△ NH 361 435   ◁ LR26   ⊕ P.337

P Inchmore car park, 750m west along the minor road on the north side of the River Farrar, from Struy Bridge on the A831 in Strathglass (NH 395 406/57.4272, -4.6764).

↔ 12KM   △ 850M   ↕ 50M
◷ 4 HRS   GRADE II   ✶✶

By Dave Snadden, updated by Colwyn Jones

Anyone driving west on the south side of the Beauly Firth will invariably find their gaze drawn to the shapely peak of Beinn a' Bhàthaich Àrd. A Corbett rather than a high mountain, it nevertheless gives an excellent short, accessible tour. If there is a lot of snow on the roads in Strathglass and the glens radiating from it, then this hill may well be the only ski tour option in the area. It is best climbed when snow cover is low and, being in the weather shadow of the bigger ranges to the west, it often gives a good day when these big mountains are stormbound. There is no public transport available from Struy, but a taxi might be used from Beauly Station, 11 miles away.

Near agricultural buildings and 50m before the locked gate at the foot of Glen Strathfarrar is a rough track which winds its way north through a small forest. Follow this track past fences, across fords, under a power line and up to the tree line that leads to Loch na Bèiste (Loch of the Beastie or perhaps Water Kelpie; 240m). From the east side of the small loch, continue north-west up the stalkers' track on gentle slopes, turning west on top of a knoll, Carn na Gabhalach (713m), then make a short, steep ascent onto Sgùrr a' Phollain (Nose Peak 855m), the north-east shoulder of the main peak.

From here enjoy the short easy, undulating traverse south-west to Beinn a' Bhàthaich Àrd (862m). This traverse presents no difficulties until the last few metres before the triangulation station, where the going is somewhat steep and rocky.

This isolated little summit is a splendid vantage point and commands unobstructed views to the east of the Moray Firth and its associated coastline. For the bold, the drop off the summit to the south-east provides a short but steep and exciting descent to the gentler slopes below. Alternatively retrace your tracks for 200m towards the small col north-east of the summit and reach these same slopes by a more amenable early descent. Further down, the hillside can be skied virtually anywhere, though, depending on the depth and quality of snow cover, you should aim to eventually pass any water kelpies in Loch na Bèiste and safely reverse the ascent route used earlier.

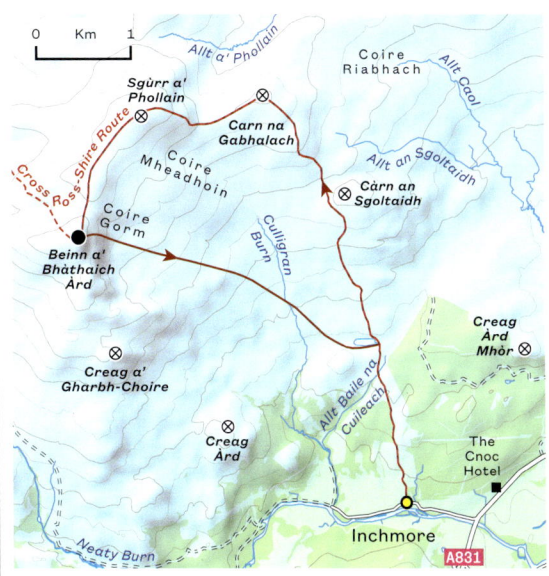

Left: More than adequate snow cover high on the East flank of Beinn a' Bhàthaich Àrd (skier, Helen Tibbs) © Andy Tibbs

Cross Ross-Shire

Craig to Struy High Tops Route

⊿ LR25, LR26   🌐 P.338

🅿 Starting point: Craig Station railway crossing (NH 040 492/57.4912, -5.2729).
🅿 Inchmore, Struy (NH 395 406/57.4272, -4.6763).
↔ 66KM   △ 3,655M   ⇅ 60M
⏱ 2 DAYS   GRADE III   ★★★

By Calum Anton

This is a two-day high-level ski mountaineering trek of seven Munros and two Corbetts, finishing on Sgùrr a' Phollain (a shoulder of Beinn a' Bhàthaich Àrd). It was undertaken on 8–9 April 1983 by Calum Anton and John Pottie.

The peaks included are Sgùrr Choinnich (Kenneth's Peak; NH 076 446; 999m), Sgùrr a' Chaorachain (Peak of the Torrent; NH 087 447, 1,053m), Maoile Lunndaidh (Bare Hill of the Wet Place; NH 135 458, 1,007m), An Sìthean (Fairy Hill; NH 171 454; 814m), Sgùrr Fhuar-thuill (Peak of the Cold Hollow; NH 236 437; 1,049m), Sgùrr a' Choire Ghlais (Peak of the Dun Corrie; NH 259 430; 1,083m), Carn nan Gobhar (Hill of the Goats; NH 273 439; 992m), Sgùrr na Ruaidhe (Red Peak; NH 289 425; 988m) and Beinn a' Bhàthaich Àrd (Hill of the High Byre; NH 361 435; 862m).

The starting point can be reached by train to Achnashellach Station, with a 4km walk to Craig. Overnight accommodation may be available at Gerry's Bunkhouse at Craig to allow an early start on Day 1, and you may be able to arrange a pickup from the station. No public transport is available from Struy, but a taxi can be called from Beauly, 11 miles away. Features on both the 1:50,000 and 1:25,000 maps are used.

The route took two full days, starting at dawn and finishing in near darkness, in the second

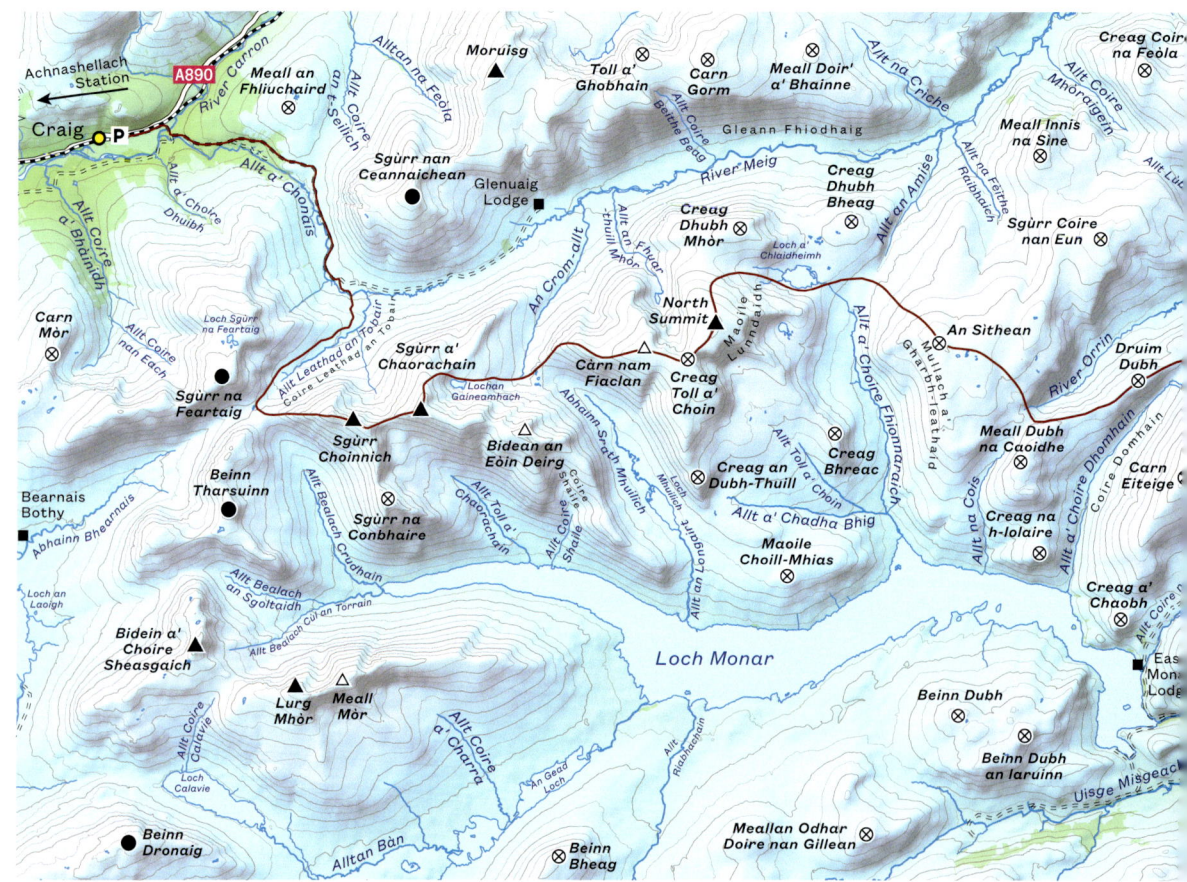

week of April. Snow conditions will, of course, vary. There is no accommodation en route, the overnight requiring camping or snowholing. The latter is recommended as it can be a pleasant way to spend the night at altitude, and you will already be carrying the lightweight snow shovel needed to excavate your den.

This is a very serious ski mountaineering expedition which needs good snow conditions, adequate daylight hours and a fine two-day weather forecast. When first undertaken, it had been several years in anticipation. All overnight gear must be carried, so weight has to be carefully considered.

The start at Craig Station railway crossing takes the track to Glen Uig Lodge. This gate is generally locked, and it is a 1km walk to the start of the climb up through the forestry opposite a mini hydro building. After 2km the track levels off at 300m, and a further 2km takes you to Pollan Buidhe and the junction with the Allt Leathad an Tobair, which joins the main river from the south-west and the Bealach Bhearnais. In most early spring conditions this is likely to be the lowest point where it is possible to don skis. A good skinning grade takes you to the three-way Bealach Bhearnais (600m), where the view opens up. A steep climb east along the inner cornice edge, avoiding the rocky wind-scoured ridge, takes you onto the first of three summits of Sgùrr Choinnich. Depending on conditions, a rocky impasse called Streangan nan Aon Pacan-deug (1:25,000 map) may require you to remove your skis.

From the summit the view all around, particularly north toward Torridon and Achnashellach, and Bidean a' Choire Sheasghaich to the south-west, looks particularly alpine.

How the snow has gathered around this summit may dictate your descent to its eastern Bealach Coire Choinnich. A descent down the southern face of the east ridge crest might be anticipated, but this can be quite bare, and the alternative of following the south ridge for some 450m and doubling back into the south-east corrie gives a

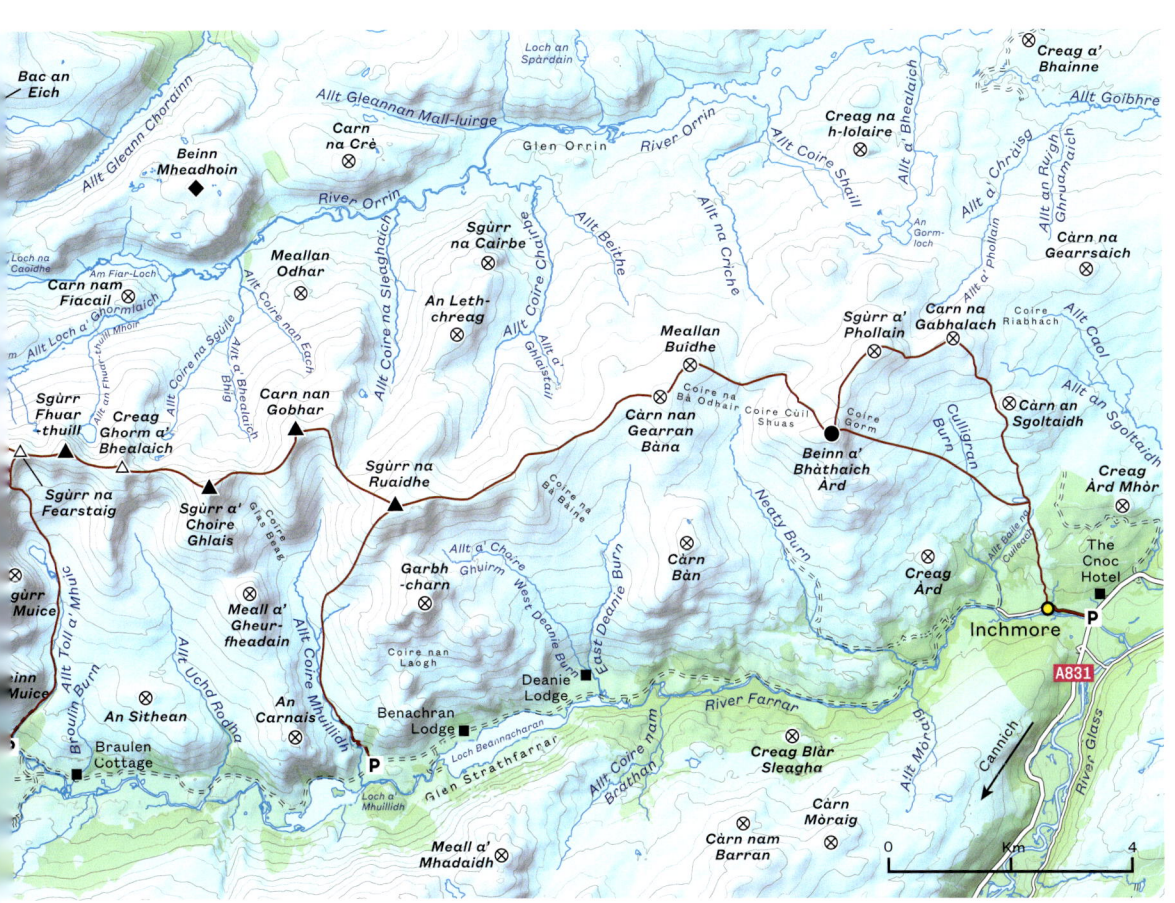

long traverse back to the bealach. From here an uninterrupted skin up the west ridge of Sgùrr a' Chaorachain takes you gently to the triangulation station on the summit.

You may be tempted to go on and include the fine peak of Bidean an Eòin Dearg, but remember your timings. The descent off this peak's north face to the Drochaid Mhuilich is not easy and should be avoided, so if you want to include this top, it's out and back along the ridge before you descend the easy north ridge of Sgùrr a' Chaorachain. This is a fine descent in good conditions, and you can be down past the north of Lochan Gaineamhach to the bealach in minutes. The 1983 party stripped off here in the mid-afternoon sunshine.

With April sunshine comes the softening of south-facing snow, so it may be necessary to carry on up the short climb of the west nose of Càrn nam Fiaclan (996m). Once on the plateau it is easy skinning across all three summits to Maoile Lunndaidh (1,007m), with fine views north-west to Fuar-tholl Mòr (The Big Cold Hole) and its close neighbour, Toll a' Choin (The Dog's Hole).

The descent from here is to the north, then east round south of Loch a' Chlaidheimh, with a good run as far as Torran Ceann Liath and the wide bealach below the north-west flank of An Sìthean. On the 1983 tour the weather turned misty, with a sudden snow shower, which inhibited this descent somewhat. This bealach is the lowest point of the tour (480m) and forms the western edge of a group of slightly lower tops lying against the direction of travel: An Sìthean, Meall Dubh na Caoidhe and Carn Eiteige.

Head south-east onto An Sìthean where it might be prudent at this time of year to maintain a decent height to avoid a climb first thing in the morning and stay on firmer snow. High on An Sìthean is as good a mid-point stop as any, being near halfway and among the lower hills between the two main groups of higher peaks. The name means Place of the Fairies, and you may be well looked after! Choose a good snow bank with reasonable snow to dig into. A snowhole with raised sleeping/sitting shelves, lying parallel to the slope, the entrance perpendicular and only partially closed overnight, should take about an hour to construct, and it is often calm and tranquil inside, whatever the weather outside. A suitable campsite might also be found here.

From An Sìthean, an easy descent leads to its south-east bealach, Clach a' Chomharraidh (588m),

Above: Sgùrr a' Chaorachain with Bidean an Eòin Dearg behind (skier, Kev Neal) © Al Todd

Opposite: Heading towards Carn nam Fiaclan of Maoile Lunndaidh (skier, Mike Cawthorne and party) © Al Todd

then north-east along the Druim Dubh and on to Sgùrr na Fearstaig (1,015m) via its north-west ridge. If it is early- to mid-April, this section before reaching the Strathfarrar Munros is likely to be the most problematic for skiing. The lower steeper slopes of the north-west ridge to Fearstaig are likely to be bare and grassy with little snow-holding potential. Once onto rougher ground above 750m, the 1983 party found better snow to skin to the summit. This point is the start of the chain of tops culminating with Sgùrr na Ruaidhe, the easternmost of the six summits forming the Strathfarrar circuit and also described elsewhere. In 1983 the weather, although calm, was grey and overcast, but it soon cleared to reveal sunshine that stayed for the remainder of the day – the fairies were indeed keeping watch!

In clear conditions there are few difficulties over the next tops of Sgùrr Fuar-thuill and Creag Ghorm a' Bhealaich, and the skiing is good. In poor or misty conditions care should, as always, be taken regarding cornices on the left, which mask some fairly steep drops into the northern corries. Bear south-east initially from the summit before soon following the ridge eastwards down to Bealach Toll Sgàile (1:25,000), the Pass of the Shady Hole.

As the name implies, the ground north of this ridge drops steeply down to the small lochan. Skinning up the north-west ridge of Sgùrr a' Choire Ghlais is straightforward, steepening slightly towards the summit and triangulation station, with fine views opening up all around.

The descent off Sgùrr a' Choire Ghlais has to be the finest of the two days, being generally well snow-covered, quite steep and testing on its upper reaches before easing off to give a long traverse across to the Bealach Sneachda (The Snow Pass; 1:25,000 map; 865m) below the south-west shoulder of your next top, Carn nan Gobhar. A short skin takes you onto its summit plateau and the cairn. There are fine views from here back along the route, with the northern corries particularly impressive and yesterday's Monar Hills in the distance.

There follows a pleasant run from Carn nan Gobhar eastwards initially, then south across the broad bowl to Bealach nam Botaìchean (1:25,000; 767m) before an easy skin on to Sgùrr na Ruaidhe, the last Munro of the trip. This is by no means the final top, however, as you still have to get to Sgùrr a' Phollain, some 9km east from here. After the exhilaration of the day so far, 'no pain, no gain' comes to mind. In reality it is quite a distance, but the skiing is fine, and the ground covered relatively quickly, first east-north-east over Meall Tarsuinn (1:25,000; 912m), followed by Càrn nan Gearran Bàna (764m), Meallan Bhuidhe (766m) and the final drop to the bealach (610m).

There is an easy skin up Coire Cuil Shuas onto Beinn a' Bhàthaich Àrd from the north side (trig pillar). Sgùrr a' Phollain beckons and it is an easy slide of 1.5km north-east to this last top. The final run down is most satisfying and follows any line with the best snow to take you as low as possible. The 1983 party simply followed the Culligran Burn from the upper snowfield down to the House where the laird allowed use of his phone – no mobile phones in 1983 – after expressing amazement at the trip. There is also an established footpath via Loch na Bèiste to the road at Inchmore. It is then a flat 800m walk to Struy on the A831.

Below: On Maoile Lunndaidh
© Al Todd

Strathfarrar

Sgùrr Fhuar-thuill ▲ 1,049m
Peak of the Cold Hollow
△ NH 235 437   ⊲ LR25   🌐 P.343

Sgùrr a' Choire Ghlais ▲ 1,083m
Peak of the Green-Grey Corrie
△ NH 258 430   ⊲ LR25   🌐 P.343

Carn nan Gobhar ▲ 992m
Goat Hill
△ NH 273 439   ⊲ LR25   🌐 P.343

Sgùrr na Ruaidhe ▲ 993m
Red Peak
△ NH 288 426   ⊲ LR25   🌐 P.343

P Glen Strathfarrar at the foot of the Allt Toll a' Mhuic
(NH 226 390/57.4080, -4.9567).
↔ 17KM   △ 1,550M   ⊺ 160M
🕒 6-7 HRS   GRADE III   ★★★★

By Dave Snadden, updated by Colwyn Jones

The high mountain range on the north side of Glen Strathfarrar gives a magnificent ski tour in a wild and lonely setting, crossing four Munros and two subsidiary tops. The traverse is described from west to east, as this should give the best descents on skis.

The approach is along the lengthy private road in Glen Strathfarrar, and access up this road is barred by a locked gate near Struy (NH 394 406). The key for winter access is the combination for the padlock, which is provided by Mountaineering Scotland. Winter access by car (1 November to 31 March) is available to Mountaineering Scotland members, subject to conditions. At least 2 days ahead of your planned visit, either telephone 01738 493942 or e-mail info@mountaineering.scot for details. It should be borne in mind that the road may be impassable due to snow, and the drive up the glen from Struy takes much longer than anticipated.

Having two cars for this trip is a real advantage as the finishing point is 6km along the road from the start. One car should be left at the foot of Coire Mhuillidh (NH 281 386), and the other taken to the starting point at the foot of the Allt Toll a' Mhuic (NH 223 392). From there climb north-east

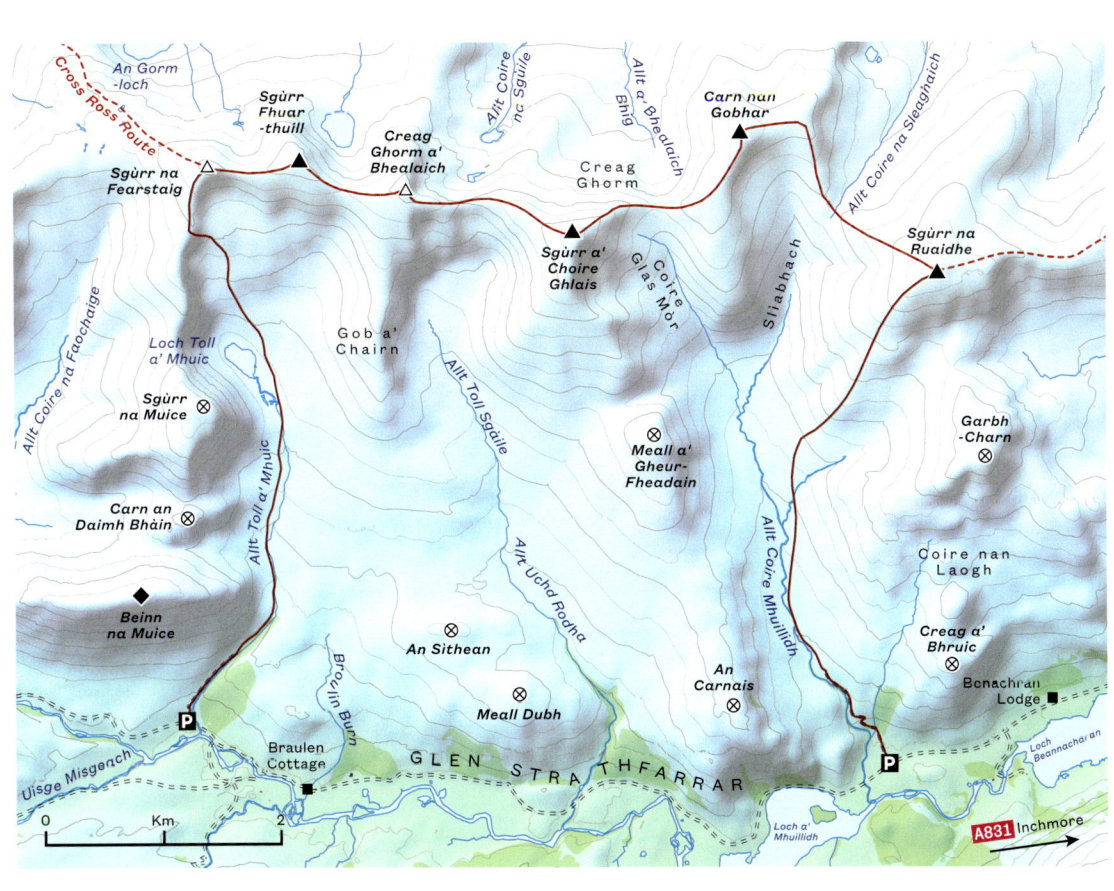

up a landrover track for 1km and continue along the line of the stalkers' path to Loch Toll a' Mhuic. Ascend fairly steep slopes north of the loch until about 800m, where the floor of the corrie becomes more level just below the steep south-east face of Sgùrr na Fearstaig (1,015m). This face can pose an avalanche risk and should be avoided by a short, steep climb west to reach the south ridge of Sgùrr na Fearstaig and then up to its top.

The next section to Sgùrr Fhuar-thuill is straightforward, the descent being short enough to hardly warrant the removal of skins. From its summit (1,049m), ski south-east down the ridge to the next col, taking care to avoid the precipitous and often corniced slopes to the north. The ascent to Creag Ghorm a' Bhealaich (1,030m) by its west ridge should pose no difficulty, but the skiing along this quite narrow section of the ridge is very enjoyable.

In poor visibility the next section of the ridge can be the trickiest of the traverse, as the slopes on both sides are very steep and large cornices can form on the north side. Ski south from the summit at first, gradually veering east to reach the narrow col at the foot of the west-north-west ridge of Sgùrr a' Choire Ghlais. The ascent of this ridge to the summit of the highest peak of the traverse should cause no undue difficulty, although the upper part is quite steep. On a good day the views from the triangulation station are truly magnificent.

The next objective is the col between Sgùrr a' Choire Ghlais and Carn nan Gobhar. The best descent is to ski steeply down the east flank of Sgùrr a' Choire Ghlais and, before getting too low, traverse north-east to the col. From there a short ascent east leads to the flat plateau of Carn nan Gobhar, whose summit is 500m to the north-east. At this point on the traverse the character of the mountains changes quite dramatically, for until now the peaks have been rocky and steep and the ridges narrow, but from here the contours are gentler, the ridges broader, the terrain much less rugged and the summits further apart.

From Carn nan Gobhar ski east for about 500m, then south to the next col. The summit of Sgùrr na Ruaidhe is then easily reached by its broad, smooth north-east ridge. In good conditions there are many fine descents from this hill, the most direct being down the shallow corrie south-west. This gives a fine run into Coire Mhuillidh. With poor snow cover, the gully which drops west-north-west from the summit may give a more reliable descent to the corrie. Finally, a long, easy-angled run south, always keeping on the east side of the Allt Coire Mhuillidh, leads down to the road in Glen Strathfarrar.

Above. Descending the Northwest ridge of Sgurr a' Choire Ghlais, Glen Strathfarrar (skiers, Helen and Andy Tibbs) © Ian Blackwood

Moruisg ▲ 928m
Big Water
△ NH 101 499　　⌖ LR25　　⊕ P.346

Sgùrr nan Ceannaichean ● 913m
Peak of the Merchants
△ NH 087 481　　⌖ LR25　　⊕ P.346

🅿 Glen Carron on the south side of the A890 road (NH 080 520/57.5176, -5.2068).

↔ 11KM　　△ 980M　　↥ 150M
🕒 4-5 HRS　　GRADE III　　★★★

By Dave Snadden, updated by Colwyn Jones

This mountain group can be approached either from the north or the south. The southern slopes are reasonably easy, but the approach to them is rather long and circuitous along the track from Craig in Glen Carron to Glenuaig Lodge up the glen of the Allt a' Chonais. In contrast, the northern flanks are much more accessible from Glen Carron, and the slopes are steeper, offering more challenging skiing. This approach from the north is described here.

Leave the A890 through Glen Carron about 1km west of the west end of Loch Sgamhain, and cross the nearby footbridge over the River Carron. Go under the railway, through forestry gates and then head south-east directly up the slopes to Moruisg. These are gentle and uninteresting at first, but they soon steepen dramatically, and care must be taken gauging the snow conditions and choosing a suitable route between the gullies that fall from the summit plateau. A less direct but easier ascent can be made by traversing east up these slopes to join the north ridge, which leads more easily to the summit cairn. On a good day the hills of Torridon, Letterewe and Achnashellach are seen to good advantage from Moruisg.

From the summit ski south-south-west past point 854m to the col below Sgùrr nan Ceannaichean. The last part of this descent may be rocky, but with good route selection it should be possible to enjoy a continuous run from Moruisg to the col (NH 094 485). On this descent the steep and often corniced crags dropping into Coire Toll nam Bian on your right should be avoided; there is usually no safe route down into this corrie on skis.

Compared with its rounded neighbour, Sgùrr nan Ceannaichean is an interesting and complex mountain. From the col ascend a short ridge west to join the north ridge of the mountain, and follow it to the summit, a small plateau with the highest cairn at its south-east edge. This ascent should not cause difficulty in reasonable conditions; however, the steep final section might be awkward if icy.

The descent route is down the shallow north-west corrie of Sgùrr nan Ceannaichean, but a direct run into the corrie from the summit is not possible because of steep rocks high up. Initially, ski down either the north or west ridge before traversing into the corrie. In poor visibility the route-finding here is very tricky. The easiest option is to ski down the west ridge for 500m where, at an altitude of about 770m, its crest becomes level. Do not go further along this ridge, as it ends above the precipitous west face. Leave the ridge and ski north-east on a descending traverse into the corrie, keeping above the two streams (forming a 'Y') which flow into steep-sided gullies lower down towards Coire an t-Seilich. Cross to the east side of these streams, ski north down the broad slope towards the lower part of Coire an t-Seilich, cross the Alltan na Feòla, then follow the stalkers' path on the north-east bank through a gated area of plantation back to the start.

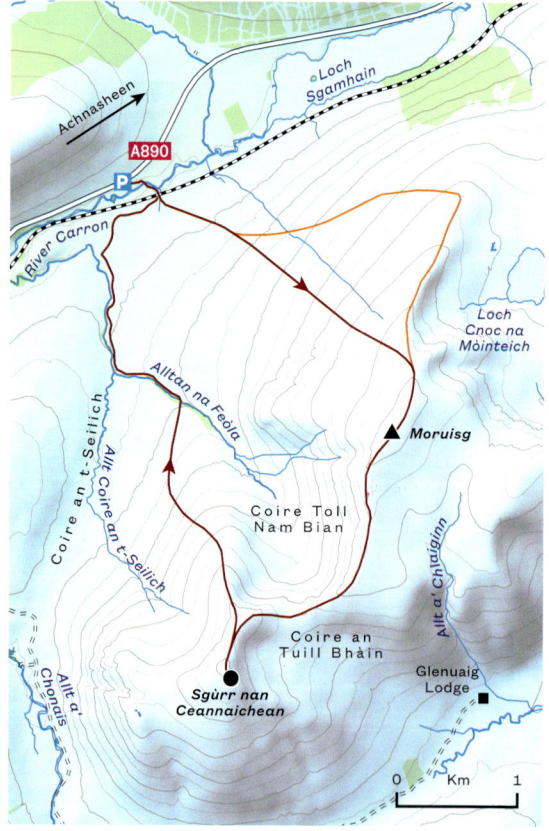

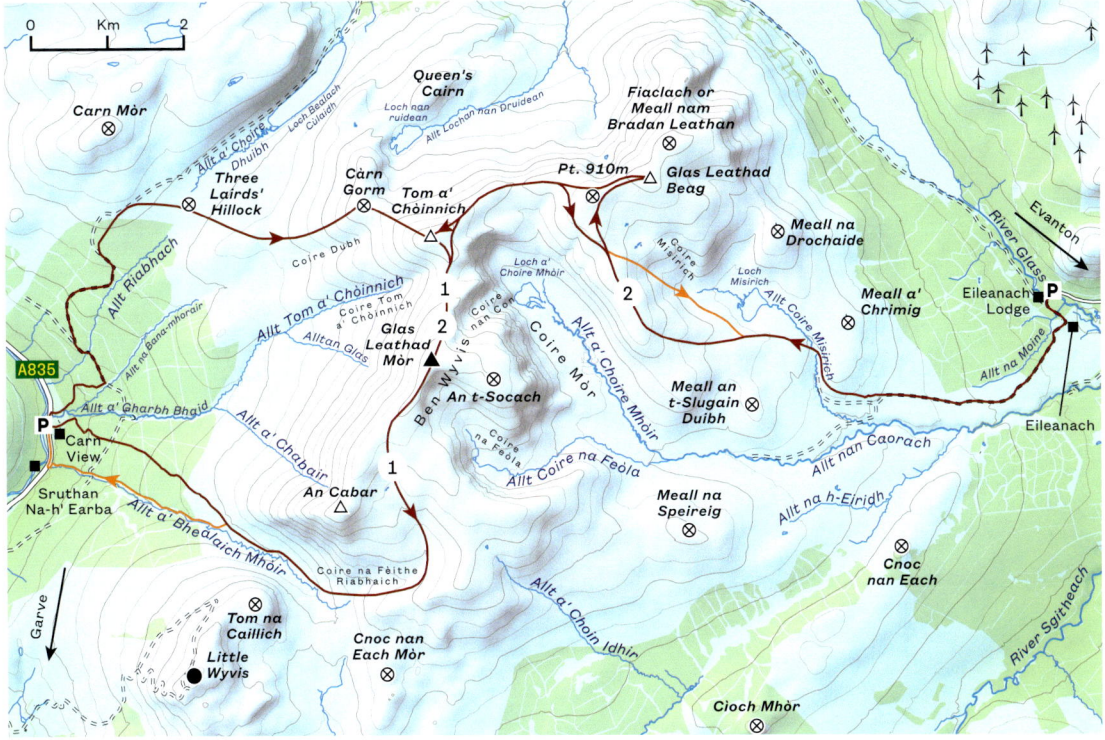

Key
1. Ben Wyvis — P.347
2. Ben Wyvis East — P.348

Ben Wyvis/ Glas Leathad Mòr West Route ▲ 1,046m
Big Grey-Green Slope

△ NH 462 683   ◁ LR20   ⊕ P.347

P Garbat (NH 545 689/57.6859, -4.4424)
at a layby on the A835 from Dingwall to Ullapool.

↔ 17KM   △ 1,000M   ↕ 150M
⏱ 6-7 HRS   GRADE II   ★★★

By Dave Snadden, updated by Colwyn Jones

The massive bulk of Ben Wyvis ranks as one of the most important ski mountains in the Northern Highlands. In the 1970s and '80s there were serious proposals to build a mountain railway on the southern flank and develop a ski resort on the mountain, but environmental concerns and its distance from major population centres posed problems, and it is now a National Nature Reserve. There are many possible routes for the ski mountaineer, all with quite long approaches, though most are technically easy. On a clear day the summit views are unsurpassed.

The western approach from the A835 is the shortest and is described here. The east-facing corries, Coire na Feòla and Coire Mòr, give some exhilarating mountain skiing, best in spring when the snow conditions are stable, but requiring skinning back up after a run. Once on the summit ridge of Ben Wyvis the skiing is superb, for the terrain is smooth and good snow cover turns the grassy corries into vast snow bowls.

Start not at the official Forestry Commission car park but in a layby opposite Garbat (NH 412 679). Walk north across the Allt a' Gharbh Bhaid bridge, and immediately right, follow the track north-east into the Garbat Forest. This new maintenance track for a hydroelectric scheme leads you through the forest. After a few hundred metres there is a locked gate easily passed on either side (NH 415 681; 188m). Continue up the track. Turn left at the first crossroads (NH 419 683), then take a right fork (NH 416 689), go left at the T-junction (NH 422 698), and continue up the road for about 500m, leaving the plantation to arrive at the watershed. Go through a deer fence with a gate (NH 420 705), continue above the edge of the forest (deer fence on your right) and head east towards Meallan Donn (474m). From that point ski up the ridge to join the main ridge of Ben Wyvis between Càrn Gorm and Tom a' Chòinnich. Finally, zigzag steeply up the north-west ridge of this Top where, if clear, you can begin to enjoy fine views (NH 464 700; 953m).

From Tom a' Chòinnich ski first south-east then south-south-west down easy-angled slopes to the col below the highest summit of Ben Wyvis – Glas Leathad Mòr. The ascent to the top from the col is up a broad ridge to the triangulation station (1,046m). On a clear day, savour the magnificent view from the summit before setting off south-west along the broad level ridge. On a stormy day or in bad visibility, however, concentrate on navigating accurately along the featureless ridge.

1km south-west of the summit you will reach the junction of the main ridge leading on to An Cabar and an unnamed ridge branching south-east above Coire na Feòla. Between these two ridges is a wide south-facing corrie, which may well be a vast snowfield. This corrie gives a superb descent, following the curving course of the Allt a' Bhealaich Mhòir, down to the level, narrow defile of the Bealach Mòr. Once through this pass, where some poling may be needed to maintain momentum, bear north away from the stream to reach the forest fence at a gate (NH 430 670; 360m) leading to a firebreak. If there is good snow cover, follow the firebreak down through the forest to the road at Garbat. However, if the snow line is above the road it is better to walk down the official footpath to the road a short distance south of Garbat.

The great north-west flank of Ben Wyvis forms a long concave slope 600m high from the summit ridge down to the upper edge of the Garbat Forest. It presents an obvious and attractive challenge to the adventurous skier, but there is a considerable avalanche risk, and in 1985 a fatal ski mountaineering accident occurred on this slope. Thus, it should only be attempted by expert skiers in good, safe conditions.

Ben Wyvis East ▲ 1,046m
Big Grey-Green Slope

△ NH 462 683   LR20, LR21   P.347

east route

P Eileanach Lodge at the end of the public road (U1991), 4.8km up Glen Glass from Evanton (B817). Park at the forestry track junction (NH 545 689/ 57.6859, -4.4424).

↔ 27KM   △ 1,100M   ↕ 200M
⏱ 6-7 HRS   GRADE II   ★★★★

By Julian Walford

Please note that the Glen Glass road is not ploughed as a priority. It is steep and narrow, with drops down into the river and few roadside safety barriers. The piles of sand on the roadside tell the story. When snowy it requires care and should not be tackled without winter tyres.

Westerly winds often build snow well on the eastern slopes of Ben Wyvis. This route from Eileanach Lodge benefits from a reasonably high starting altitude, then steady, grassy slopes and a track to the foot of the hill at 450m. Though quite long, it offers great high-level ridge skiing, and the continuous descent from the secondary top – Glas Leathad Beag – can be superb.

From the road end, cross the bridge past the lodge and take a track to the left, then turn right and follow the track to the right alongside the forest edge, where snow often lingers. Continue on the track, recently improved for the Allt nan Caorach Hydro Scheme, or alongside it to the south flank of Meall a' Chrimig. Avoid the temptation to climb north over this as the top is an area of degraded peat hags, a skier's nightmare even in good snow. Instead, continue west into Coire Misirich to see where the best snow lies. Climb steadily west on the ridge above the Leacann Bhreac, then north-north-east toward the main east-west ridge. The keen skier will divert north-east to Glas Leathad Beag (NH 492 707; 928m), possibly Scotland's most underrated Munro Top; it would be designated a Munro elsewhere. Meall nam Bradan Leathan, just beyond, could even be skied for completeness – a long-demoted Top just below the magical 3000ft.

Thereafter, ski west towards Tom a' Chòinnich, ascending its west top (again demoted) for completeness and avoiding the steep cliffs to the north. Tom a' Chòinnich itself is still a Top and can be climbed if you are keen or avoided if time is short. Finally, climb south to the triangulation station at the summit, Glas Leathad Mòr (1,046m), where you might meet others who have ascended from the west. On a good day there may be fine views all around. Descend from the main summit north back towards Tom a' Chòinnich, but free-heel to its east from the bealach at 865m up to 910m, before descending the ridge to the east again, down to around 800m. Then skin up again quite steeply 100m to the Leacann Bhreac ridge. If Coire Misirich is well filled, a choice of great descents is now possible, gentler to the south or more steeply south-west. Cross the stream and pick up the ascent route to join the track back to Eileanach.

Fionn Bheinn ▲ 933m
White Hill

△ NH 147 621	◁ LR20, LR25	🌐 P.349

P Achnasheen on the A832 (NH 162 585/57.5794, -5.0750).
↔ 9KM   △ 800M   ↕ 150M
⏱ 3-4 HRS   GRADE II   ★★

By Dave Snadden, updated by Colwyn Jones

This featureless hill is considered by some to be a rather tedious climb in summer. However, its grassy slopes and rounded contours mean that, with good snow cover, it is well suited as a ski mountain and boasts a hitherto secret north face. It is easily climbed from Achnasheen in a few hours and is no more than a half-day tour. Adding the nearby Graham, Meall a' Chaorainn (Hill of the Rowan; 705m), is a simple and satisfying option.

It is usually possible to park considerably in the village of Achnasheen, and passenger trains from Inverness to Kyle of Lochalsh also stop there. The train station no longer has a heated waiting room, merely a bus stop-style shelter.

From the village, go north-east up to the A832, turn left, and after a red phone box take the first right to a road bridge over the Allt Achadh na Sìne to arrive at a gate where signs guide you past a water treatment works to the open hillside. The obvious watercourse in the hillside marks the line of the Allt Achadh na Sìne. A steady climb up either side of this stream leads to a small featureless plateau. The most interesting way from this point is to ascend the broad ridge running up to Creagan nan Laogh. This is a small subsidiary spur 1km south of the east top of Fionn Bheinn. From there it is a simple matter to cross a broad col and climb directly up to the triangulation station at the east top. This top overlooks the Toll Mòr, and this wild corrie is a fine feature of Fionn Bheinn. The traverse round the rim of Toll Mòr is easy, although in poor visibility take care not to ski too near the cornice edge on the north side of the ridge. The main summit of this isolated mountain is a fine viewpoint, with the Fannichs and Letterewe mountains clearly seen.

Two descents are possible. The first is to ski south-east from the summit, then south to rejoin the ascent route at the small plateau mentioned above. Alternatively, the nearby Graham, Meall a' Chaorainn (705m), can be added by skiing south from the summit down the west flank of Creagan nan Laogh. The wide col between the two summits is named Coire Bog, which implies that a ski approach over frozen ground might be preferable.

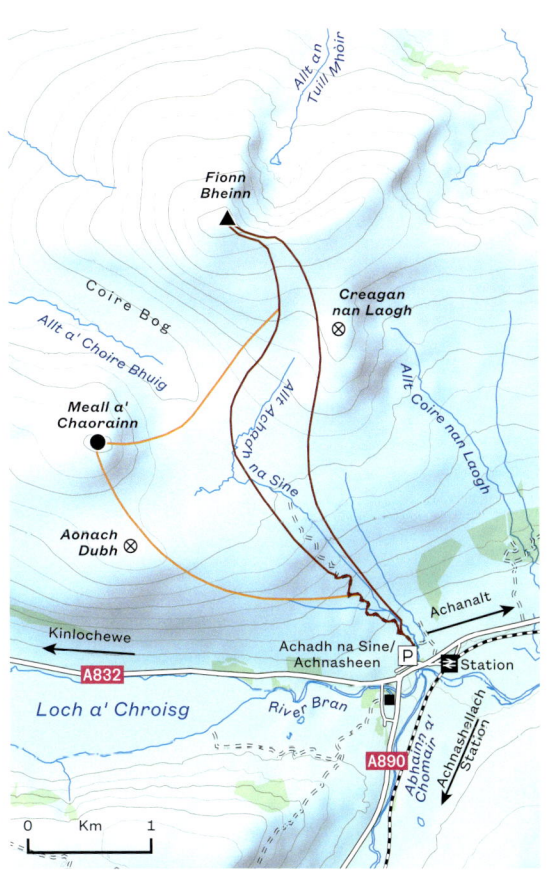

From the col at the 520m contour care is needed, as a direct ascending line west to the small summit cairn (NH 136 604) crosses slopes approaching 30 degrees which may be loaded with an unstable layer or windslab if there has been fresh snow and/or a westerly wind. A circular approach from the south may prove to be safer.

From this accessory summit, initially ski south for 100 vertical metres, then south-east to traverse back towards the ascent route and so to the village of Achnasheen. Both descent options hold snow well and should give good skiing; the choice will depend on the prevailing snow conditions.

From the summit of Fionn Bheinn, Toll Mòr offers a very fine ski descent at a constant gradient of 21 degrees over less than 2km and 650 vertical metres down its remote north face to a landrover track. If conditions allow, the out-and-back nature of this lonely backcountry run means that the simplest return is to skin back up to the summit.

Above: Ascending Fionn Bheinn from the north (skier, Helen Tibbs)
© Iain Rudkin

Chapter 9

North Scotland and the Isle of Mull

1.	Sgùrr nan Clach Geala	P.356
2.	The Fannichs	P.357
3.	Beinn Dearg	P.361
4.	Beinn Enaiglair	P.365
5.	An Teallach	P.365
6.	Seana Bhraigh	P.367
7.	Breabeg	P.370
8.	Canisp	P.371
9.	Ben Klibreck	P.373
10.	Beinn Dhorain	P.374
11.	Ben Hee	P.375
12.	Ben Loyal	P.380
13.	Ben Hope	P.381
14.	Morvern (Caithness)	P.382
15.	Ben More Mull (map on route page)	P.383

Chapter 9

North Scotland and the Isle of Mull

Previous spread: Skiing the NW flank of Sgùrr Mòr © Hamish Kerr

355

Sgùrr nan Clach Geala ▲ 1,093m

Hill of the White Stones

△ NH 184 714   ⌖ LR20   🌐 P.356

🅿 The car park on the south-west side of the A832 (NH 161 761/57.7366, -5.0883).

↔ 21KM   △ 1,500M   ↕ 280M
🕒 7 HRS   GRADE III   ★★★★

By George Reid

How will it come to be, that you are drawn to ski the south-west face of Sgùrr nan Clach Geala? When you first see this magnificent face, a huge white pyramid of snow in the distance, to the north-east of where you stand on the summit of Fionn Bheinn, it will be on your to-do list, guaranteed. Nothing else compares on the horizon, west through to east, and unless your knowledge of the landscape is very good, you will wonder, with impatience, 'What is the name of that mountain?'

Sgùrr nan Clach Geala stands high at 1,093m and offers a wonderfully long descent of around 1.3km, dropping 540m to the bealach at NH 175 076. This is a tour for the pleasure of skiing downhill, and such is the quality of the slope, you'll be eager to ski it twice; the introductory statistics are based on this approach. You don't want to walk any of this journey, and therefore you should wait until there is full snow cover.

The car park is on the left as you travel toward Dundonnell. From here ski 150m down the verge back to the gate at the start of the track (NH 162 760) and then down the track to the south-west. Roughly 200m before the boat house you will discover another track (perhaps not marked on your map) branching off to your left. Take this, as it has a bridge over the stream and leads you into the wood block (easily seen if you switch from map view to satellite view on your phone). Follow the track, which may have less snow on it than the open moor, down to the next bridge, which goes over the river flowing out of the loch.

A path shown on some maps goes roughly southeast from the bridge and then southwards to a ford across the Allt Breabaig at NH 161 741 – don't take

Key
1. Sgùrr nan Clach Geala   P.356
2. The Fannichs   P.357

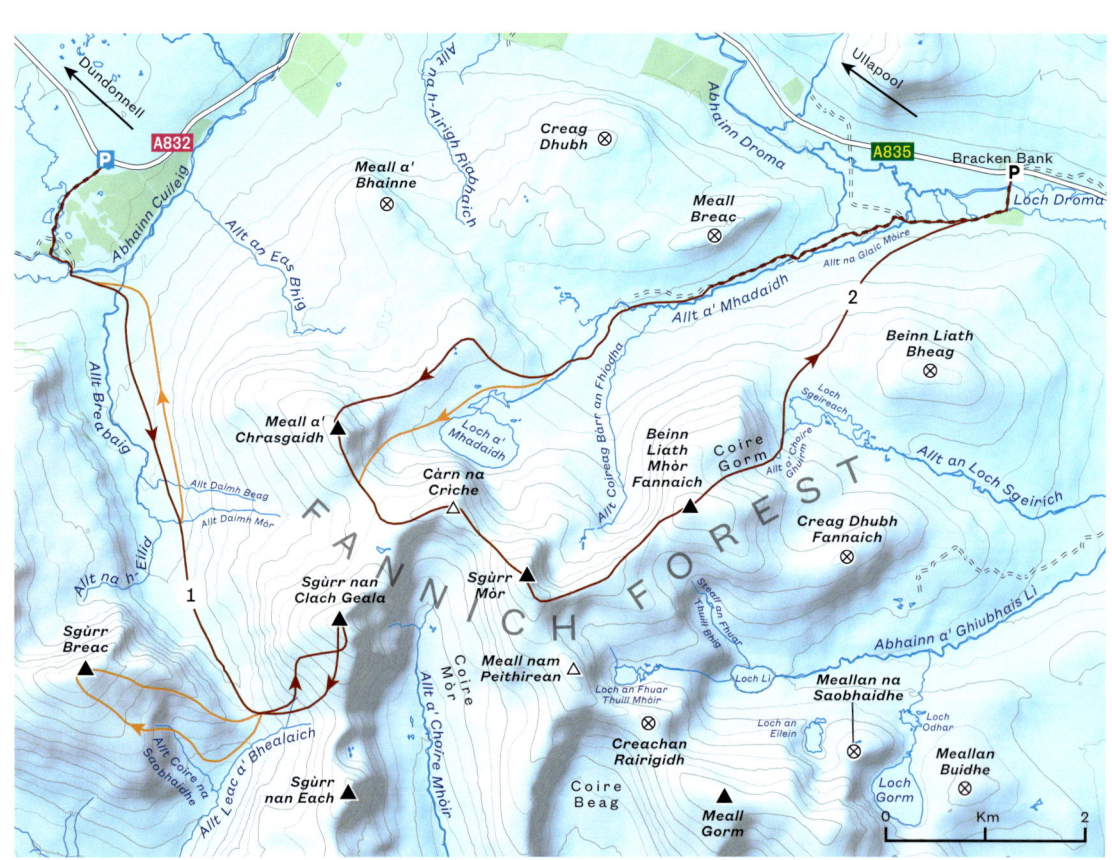

this option! Instead, take a new track that goes in a more east-south-easterly direction from the big bridge at the head of Loch a' Bhraoin toward a new bridge over the Allt Breabaig at NH 163 747; this is best seen from the satellite image on your phone. Once you are across the new bridge and on the east bank of the Allt Breabaig, the fun begins. Head up the long glen, aiming for the bealach at its southern end, some 4km distant. The trick, and the desire, is to make a gently rising skinning track through the undulating terrain which you can follow back at the end of the day without having to sidestep or herringbone up when you are weary and oh-so-very keen to glide home with just the occasional bit of poling.

The magnificent south-west slope of Sgùrr nan Clach Geala is never in view on this approach; it is not until you stop for a well-earned rest at the bealach (550m) that you can start to appreciate the sheer size of this skiers' paradise. Those who have done their homework will have discovered that the angle of the slope is, in places, in the high 20s. There may indeed be a wee bit here or there touching 30 degrees – whatever, it's in the zone where avalanches could occur. The author's ascent in 2021 thankfully featured nothing more than a 'whoomph'. Here is most definitely not the place to get involved in an avalanche! It is well worth making sure you have ski crampons with you: the snow may not be icy, but if the wind has packed it a bit, you may not get enough traction with your skins alone. It isn't steep enough to require multiple kick turns – that's the domain of slopes of 30 degrees and above – but you may require one or two depending on your choice of line.

It goes without saying that if you get a clear day, the view from the summit will be excellent. You'll get to see your vantage point, Fionn Bheinn, where you decided, 'I've got to ski that hill!', and now it is time to ski, ski, ski, hurtling down to the bealach, arriving with beaming smiles and cries of 'More, more, more!'

The descent was a dream; by skinning up the slope you knew exactly where the best ski line would be, and you nailed it. After a well-earned snack in the sun, you get into the groove of your own skinning track and ascend to the lofty height of 1,093m once again. With the extra knowledge from the first descent, you will be able to select another brilliant line down the immense ski field, back to the bealach for more cake and medals.

If variety is the spice for you, or the south-west-facing slope of Sgùrr nan Clach Geala snow wasn't in the best condition, it is well worth considering skiing the south-east aspect of Sgùrr Breac (Speckled Crag; 999m) instead of doing a second lap. This different aspect may provide better snow, particularly the lower part, which is a sheltered bowl and could have the soft snow we seek every winter but find less often than we would like. From the bealach at 550m 'wheech' on down another 100m of altitude to around the 450m contour line (NH 171 701), then ascend up the bowl, weaving through the steeper section onto the upper slopes. If you find the correct line, you can skin up without straying onto terrain approaching 30 degrees. Once again, it is worthwhile referring to a mapping app, which clearly identifies where slopes are steeper than 25 degrees.

All that's left is to follow your approach track back home. If your skinning track has disappeared due to drifting snow, and you are losing height too quickly and envisaging a long poling session lower down the glen, then it may be worth considering hiking up the hill for a short distance. Once you have crossed the stream at NH 168 725, perhaps up to the 400m contour, you are more likely to be assured of a glide all the way back to the bridge.

The Fannichs

Meall a' Chrasgaidh ▲ 934m
Hill of the Crossing
NH 184 733   LR20   P.356

Sgùrr Mòr ▲ 1,110m
Big Peak
NH 203 718   LR20   P.356

Beinn Liath Mhòr Fannaich ▲ 954m
Big Grey Fannaich Hill
NH 219 724   LR20   P.356

P Lochdrum, at the west end of Loch Droma, on the A835 (NH 253 755 / 57.7355, -4.9349).

↔ 17KM   △ 1,140M   ↕ 270M
⏱ 7-9 HRS   GRADE IV   ★★★★

By Dave Snadden, updated by Colwyn Jones and Ian Taylor

The traverse on skis of the three central peaks of the Fannichs is a long, serious, but rewarding expedition. Technically, the hardest part of the traverse is the ascent and descent of Sgùrr Mòr, a fine steep summit whose slopes will require an ice axe and crampons when icy. The approach goes for several kilometres over rough moorland which, if not snow-covered, will entail a tedious walk in and out, so good snow cover down to the road is a great advantage.

Cross the dam at the west end of Loch Droma and follow the track west beside a large concrete pipe. Cross the Allt a' Mhadaidh and continue up its north side along the track to its end 1.5km further on. Ahead the grandeur of the big corries and the peak of Sgùrr Mòr gradually unfolds. Continue beyond the end of the track along the Allt a' Mhadaidh, where the going is rough unless there is good snow cover, and reach Loch a' Mhadaidh (Loch of the Wolf) in a wonderful setting, silent under the forbidding cliffs of Càrn na Crìche.

From the loch there are two possibilities for the ascent to Meall a' Chrasgaidh. The more obvious and easier is to skirt round the north shore of the loch and climb the straightforward but quite steep snow slopes leading to the col between Meall a' Chrasgaidh and Càrn na Crìche. The other route is more interesting and aesthetically pleasing as it leads directly to the summit. Climb north-west from the loch onto the crest of Creag Raineach Mòr (Big Crag of Ferns) and the level lower part of the north-east ridge of Meall a' Chrasgaidh. Ascend this ridge until progress on skis is halted by a steepening. The final 200m is a delightful climb, carrying skis up snow and rocks which are quite exposed but not difficult. Ice axe and possibly crampons will be needed here.

The run south-east from the summit of Meall a' Chrasgaidh gives enjoyable skiing down a broad, smooth ridge to the col at 820m below Càrn na Crìche. There is an easy descent north-east from this col to Loch a' Mhadaidh. Note that once the col is passed, there is no safe descent on the north side of the ridge until Beinn Liath Mhòr Fannaich.

Climb easily to the summit of Càrn na Crìche (961m), from where the best views along the corniced ridge to Sgùrr nan Clach Geala are enjoyed. There is a very short descent south-east to the col at the foot of Sgùrr Mòr. The slopes dropping north-east from here are deceptive as there is an unseen cliff halfway down.

The ascent of Sgùrr Mòr on skis from the col can be problematic and, in icy conditions, unjustifiable. The ridge rising directly to the summit is steep and rocky, and the only feasible ski route is up its east side, which is also steep and very exposed, and should only be tackled with caution. The safest option is to climb the ridge on foot.

The summit of Sgùrr Mòr is an impressive and, in winter, a lonely place; on all sides the snow- or ice-covered slopes fall steeply to glens and corries

far below, and the skier is acutely aware that the most demanding ski run of the day lies ahead.

From the summit, set off in a southerly direction and ski down the ridge for about 200m. If the snow cover is thin, the eroded character of the slope, forming a series of terraces with short steep drops between them, may give some disconcertingly bumpy skiing. At this point the ridge to Beinn Liath Mhòr Fannaich turns off east, still dropping steeply. In poor visibility this ridge can be difficult to find, and meticulous navigation is required as the drop on the north side of the crest is precipitous and the edge usually corniced, and the slope on the south side is also steep. A little lower down the angle eases and the ridge becomes broader, giving a magnificent ski run over a small rise and on to the summit of Beinn Liath Mhòr Fannaich, where the last climb of the day is agreeably short.

Ski north-east off the summit into the northernmost of the two corries on the east side of Beinn Liath Mhòr Fannaich. The initial run off the summit is steep, but lower down there is good skiing on easier slopes. Two-thirds of the way down the corrie, make a descending traverse north under the terminal crags of the north-east ridge to reach the watershed at the north-west end of Loch Sgeireach (Loch of the Skerries). Continue an easy descent north to reach the track by the Allt a' Mhadaidh, with Loch Droma only a short distance away.

A good alternative descent from Beinn Liath Mhòr Fannaich can be used if the Loch Droma track is bare. Ski east from the summit into the more southern of the two corries (Fliuch Choire, 1:25,000 map), which leads to the east end of Loch Sgeireach. From here, a short ascent to the summit of Beinn Liath Bheag gives access to its northern slopes, which often hold good snow, and allows a quick descent back to Loch Droma.

Below: Sgùrr nan Clach Geala and Sgùrr Mòr
© George Reid

Above: Beinn Liath Mhòr Fannaich (skier, Helen Tibbs) © Andy Tibbs

Beinn Dearg ▲ 1,084m
Red Hill
△ NH 259 812 ◁ LR20 ⊕ P.362

Am Faochagach ▲ 954m
Heathery Place
△ NH 303 793 ◁ LR20 ⊕ P.362

Cona' Mheall ▲ 980m
Next Hill
△ NH 275 816 ◁ LR20 ⊕ P.362

P On the A835 at the bridge over the Abhainn an Torrain Duibh (NH 277 743/57.7249, -4.8943) near the north-west end of Loch Glascarnoch.

↔ 22KM △ 1,430M ⊥ 260M
⏲ 8-9 HRS GRADE IV ★★★★

By Dave Snadden, updated by Di Gilbert

This is a magnificent ski mountaineering expedition, seldom undertaken, over remote and rugged mountains. For anyone lucky enough to find it in good condition, it is certain to give a memorable day. Am Faochagach is a fine ski mountain in its own right and offers a variety of excellent ascents and descents. Combining its ascent with a traverse of Cona' Mheall and Beinn Dearg gives a long and demanding tour which should only be attempted by experienced, fit and reasonably fast parties. Good snow cover is essential for this trip, and the snow line should preferably be low enough to allow skiing from the roadside; otherwise, the walk across the rough moor at the north-west end of Loch Glascarnoch is tiresome.

Set off from the A835 in a north-easterly direction towards the Abhainn a' Garbhrain. The river has been reported to pose difficulties in crossing and may require a short wade, but in the grip of a hard winter, it is usually reduced to a trickle. A straightforward climb up slopes to the north-east brings you without difficulty to the long ridge winding its way up to the summit of Am Faochagach. The long haul up to the top is well compensated by the superb sight of Coire Grànda, which nestles between Cona' Mheall and Beinn Dearg.

From the summit of Am Faochagach you will be struck by the dramatic contrast between the gently rolling slopes dropping north-east to Glen Beag and the wild mountain architecture of Cona' Mheall to the north-west. Note that if it has taken more than three hours to reach this summit, you will not complete the trip in the time given and it might be advisable to return. If you choose to go on, you will be rewarded with a long, easy descent to

Key

1. Beinn Dearg   P.361
2. Beinn Dearg West   P.364
3. Beinn Enaiglair   P.365

Loch Prille, traversing on the east side of the knoll of Meallan Bàn. The feeling of isolation on this descent is complete, and at its end Loch Prille (NH 287 815) provides a truly remote setting for an early lunch.

This is the place to contemplate the long climb to Cona' Mheall, for once you have embarked on it there is no way back to your car without completing the traverse of Beinn Dearg. It is possible to bypass Cona' Mheall by ascending the glen to Loch Tuath and then climbing onto the plateau between Beinn Dearg and Meall nan Ceapraichean. However, it is probably just as quick to ascend the east ridge of Cona' Mheall, and it is certainly a finer route.

This is a long and fairly steep ascent of 450m, and good snow is needed to cover the rocky ridge. It is possible to climb on skis to within 30m of the summit, where the final steepening will probably have to be tackled on foot and may require crampons. The ascent is serious

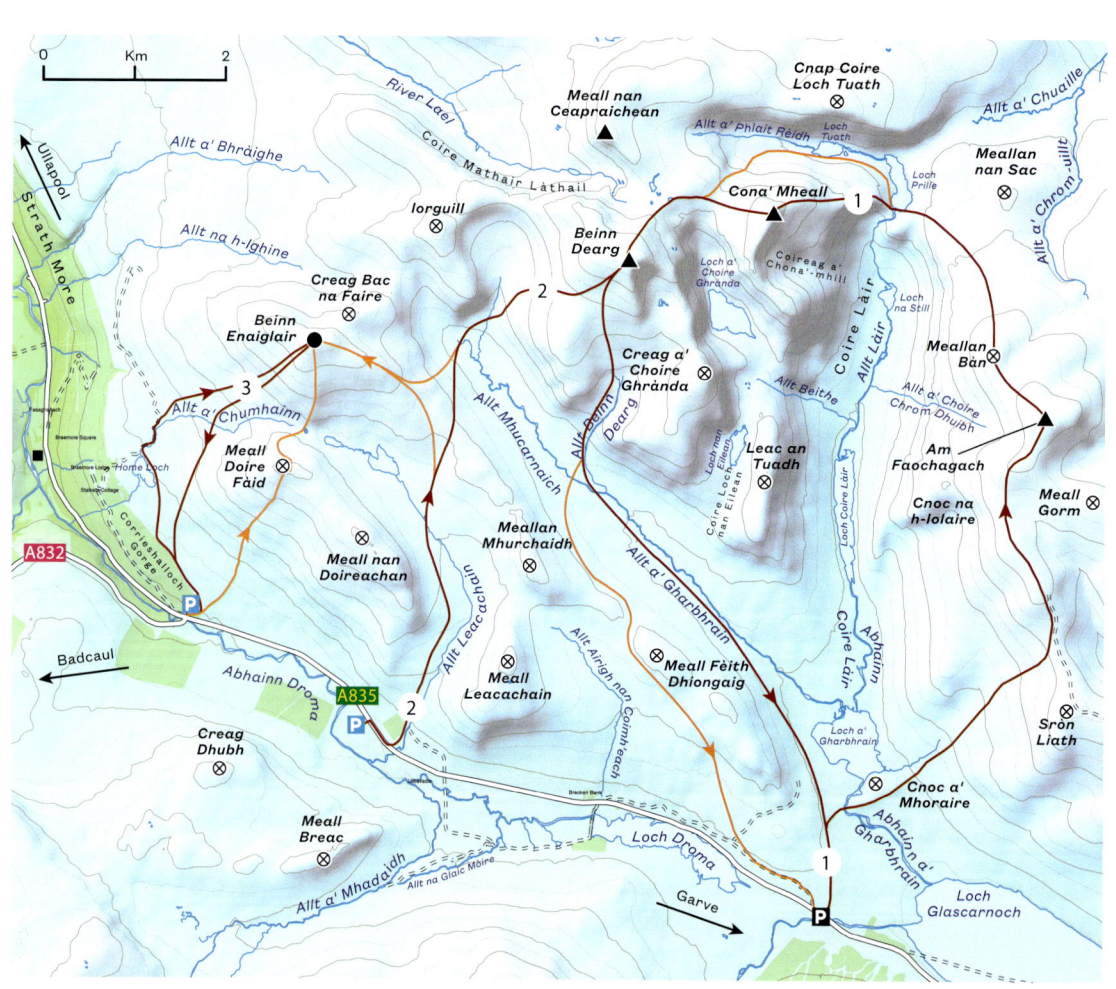

and certainly not place for a slip, especially in icy conditions.

The descent north-west from Cona' Mheall is quite straightforward, though care is required in bad visibility to avoid steep slopes to the north-east and south-west. From the col at the foot of this descent, a short climb west leads to a drystane dyke (NH 263 818). The ridge itself is rocky and the best ascent route lies on the exposed slopes east of the dyke. These slopes are not too steep and should present no difficulty except in very icy conditions. Near the summit plateau the dyke turns west, and the cairn on Beinn Dearg is 200m south of this point.

You are now about to embark on one of the finest downhill runs in the district, and one to be savoured, for the mountain and the view are magnificent. From the summit ski south-south-west down into the snowy bowl between the south and south-west ridges, then along the burn line in the shallow corrie lower down to reach the Allt Mhucarnaich. The vertical descent to this point is over 600m and gives 2km of fine skiing. From here two routes have been reported:

1. Continue south-east along the Allt a' Gharbhrain where the slope may keep your skis running for 4km to Loch a' Gharbhrain, though some poling will be required. At the loch it is worth putting on skins for the last time to traverse the final tedious slopes back to the road.
2. Reapply skins and, on a rising traverse, climb 50 vertical metres to a col west of Meall Fèith Dhiongaig (535m). Then, via the col, aim off in a south-south-easterly direction to pick up one of the burn lines and ski down to the road.

Below: Eastern approach to Beinn Dearg (skier, Steve Martin) © Al Todd

Beinn Dearg West ▲ 1,084m

△ NH 259 812　　　◁ LR20　　　⊕ P.362

P	On the A835, 2km east of Braemore Junction (NH 228 765/57.7439, -4.9781).
↔ 15KM	△ 1,030M　　　↕ 250M
⏱ 6 HRS	GRADE III　　　***

By Ian Taylor

Beinn Dearg is also a splendid individual ski hill, and the most reliable run is often found on the unbroken west-facing summit slopes that lead down into the large bowl of Coir' an Leth-choin (1:25,000 map). This is a magnificent place, remote and seldom visited, and although not that far from the road, access is guarded by the long, undulating south-east ridge of Beinn Enaiglair. If the Abhainn a' Gharbhrain crossing above Loch Glascarnoch is likely to prove too difficult to allow the full tour of the Beinn Dearg range, then this route on the west face is an excellent (and shorter) alternative.

Park at a long layby on the south side of the A835, 2km east of Braemore Junction. This is just west of a small conifer plantation on the north side of the road. Leave the road and climb north-north-east, following the west bank of the Allt Leacachain and contouring round into a flat bowl with the Corbett Beinn Enaiglair at its head. Continue skiing north to the crest of the south-east ridge of Beinn Enaiglair at 620m. This ridge is on Scotland's watershed, with everything on the other side draining into the North Sea despite being less than 10km from the west coast. Drop over the ridge and ski on a descending traverse to the Allt Mhucarnaich and follow this upstream into the wild roughness of Coir' an Leth-choin. Zigzag up the mighty western slopes of Beinn Dearg, passing a large flat area just below 900m, to reach the cairn on the summit. The view in all directions is one to savour before embarking on the superb descent by the same route, hopefully giving 600m of continuous skiing back down to the Allt Mhucarnaich. The only downside is the 100m climb back up to the Beinn Enaiglair ridge before the final descent to the road down the Allt Leacachain. If time allows, an ascent of Beinn Enaiglair (NH 225 805; 889m) can easily be included in the day.

Beinn Enaiglair ● 889m
Hill of Wary Birds

△ NH 225 805 ◁ LR20 🌐 P.362

|P| On the A835 at the Braemore Junction car park (NH 209 777/57.7528, -5.0103).

↔ 7KM   △ 840M   ⏅ 200M
⏱ 3-4 HRS   GRADE III   ★★★

By Di Gilbert

Beinn Enaiglair is a south-west outlier of the Beinn Dearg group, and its west-south-west face provides a fine, often untracked bowl crying out to be skied. The route is easily seen from the Corrieshellach Gorge viewpoint on the A832. Being only 7km from the west coast it is not often in condition – if there is no snow lying on the lower sections, it is probably worth leaving for another day.

From the east end of the Braemore car park follow the signposted footpath through a gate onto the open hillside. Strike a rising traverse line and aim above Home Loch to follow the line of least resistance between Beinn Enaiglair and its neighbouring Graham, Meall Doire Fàid (Hill of the Prophet's Grove). From the bealach, choose the best line to gain the south-west ridge, which takes you to the summit.

An option for more experienced/competent skiers is to ascend the south face of the intervening Meall Doire Fàid (730m). This gives a warming and steady ascent over 500 vertical metres, with improving views to the south. The north side of Meall Doire Fàid drops away steeply, so the descent down this slope is serious, especially the top section. Good visibility is essential since you are skiing onto rock bluffs and ledges down to the Bealach nam Bùthan (1:25,000 map) at the 550m contour where the traversing stalkers' path is likely to be hidden under a good depth of snow. From here, reapply skins for the 350m climb up to the summit of Beinn Enaiglair.

The views from the top are splendid, with sea views and a snow-covered An Teallach as a backdrop for your summit photos. The view down the west-south-west face also delights. From here, simply follow the best snow down to cross the stalkers' path and burn descending from the Bealach nam Bùthan. Stay above the 350m contour higher than the Home Loch where, depending on conditions, you can continue traversing east on the south flank of Meall Doire Fàid back to your starting point.

Opposite top: Beinn Enaiglair (skier, Di Gilbert) © Alison Thacker

An Teallach and Bidein a' Ghlas Thuill ▲ 1,060m
The Forge and Pinnacle of the Grey-Green Hollow

△ NH 069 843 ◁ LR19 🌐 P.365

|P| The walkers car park at Dundonnell track (NH 092 879/ 57.5024,- 5.1253).

↔ 16KM   △ 1,600M   ⏅ 40M
⏱ 8-10 HRS   GRADE IV   ★★★★★

By Al Todd

As far back as the first edition of this guide in 1987, the pioneer steep skiing afficionado, Martin Burrows-Smith, tantalised us with the possibilities on An Teallach. Then later, in 1992, he stated in the *Alpine Journal*: 'An Teallach, for many the best mountain in Britain, has in its two main Coires the finest collection of couloirs in the Highlands. Up to 1,500ft (460m) in height, they are well defined, full of character, and cut through impressively sculptured sandstone walls. Big cornices are rare, so access is relatively straightforward and there is a wide choice of superb descents.'

It's only in recent years, however, that the mountain has been gaining in popularity as a ski destination, with the lure of its complex corries, cliffs and couloirs guaranteeing adventurous steep skiing with fantastic scenery. Snow depth can build remarkably quickly although as a coastal mountain, you need to move quickly, to hit the right conditions since with the arrival of SW winds the snow can vanish almost overnight.

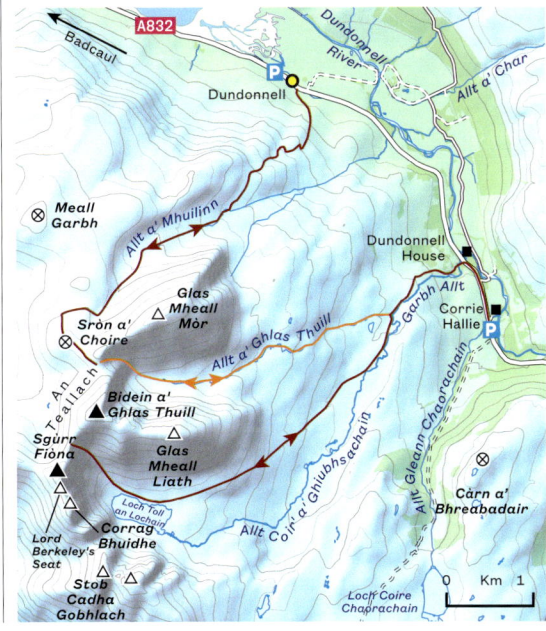

Depending on the objective there are several ways to enjoy the mountain on ski, all approaching from the NE to take advantage of the three east-facing corries and all invariably involving the initial grunt of a hefty bootpack. It's well worth the effort though!

The easiest approach, especially if the main objective is to ski to the highest viewpoint of Bidein a' Ghlas Thuill, takes the walkers' path starting at the mountain rescue post in Dundonnell where there is ample parking available. Cross the road and follow the path steeply up the hillside and round into the lower reaches of Coir' a' Mhuillin. Once the snow is reached, take a line beside the burn which is frequently completely buried and provides a wonderful 3km ski to Sròn a' Choire (863m). From there head south to the col at the top of Glas Tholl and then up the final summit dome, which will require a ski carry and often needing the use of boot crampons and ice axe. You now have a choice of reversing the route to enjoy wonderful mellow skiing or, for the more adventurous, you might be tempted to consider a more challenging descent into either Glas Tholl to the north or Toll an Lochain to the south.

The most popular approach for skiing the steep lines, however starts west of the entrance to Dundonnell House, where a track leaves the side of the road through rhododendrons and past waterfalls on the Allt Coir' a' Ghiubhsachain (Burn of the Corrie of the Pine Trees). Continue along the path west of the burn and follow the best snow up towards the north bank of Loch Toll an Lochain at the 520m contour. The full magnificence of the Coire now stretches before you with several snowy gullies immediately drawing the eye. Most of the obvious lines have now been skied, with the 'popular' route climbing the headwall to the bealach at 900m described as Central Gully in the SMC's *Northern Highlands Central Climbers' Guide*: 'A wide gully which allows a straightforward route up or down from the ridge, cornice permitting.' The only steep section can be bypassed via the easier angled slopes on the north side of the Coire which also give the line of the classic descent as you ski steeply back down to the of the best mountain views in Scotland.

An alternative start, sharing the same approach as the previous route, heads up the north bank of the Allt Coir' a' Ghiubhsachain before then branching off up the tributary Allt a' Ghlas Thuill and into the Glas Tholl corrie. Here a choice has to be made between following the steepening slopes, to the col immediately north of Bidein

a Ghlas Thuill, or branching left and climbing Hayfork Gully, which provides a spectacular 300m winter route through the cliffs. For the former, a straightforward, if steep, ski leads back into the corrie, whilst the latter offers an exceptional gully descent with plenty of character as it snakes a way through the steep cliffs.

An Teallach is a mountain of vast possibilities for advanced skiers who have the necessary winter mountaineering skills. The easier gullies have all now been skied and in a good winter a number of descents can be reported. With the exception of the first described approach however, it is not a place for the faint-hearted and it would be sensible to first familiarise yourself with the complexities of the mountain in summer before heading back for the snow. Also, as in other steep skiing venues, prior to skiing one of the gullies, it should ideally be climbed first to check for any unexpected hazards.

Opposite: Entering an unamed gully on the NE face of Sail Liath (skier, Kev Neal) © Colin Richards

Below: Seana Bhraigh © Mike Dixon

Seana Bhraigh ▲ 926m
Old Mountain

△ NH 281 878	◁ LR20	⊕ P.369
P The Schoolhouse Bothy, Duag Bridge (NH 340 975/ 57.9353, -4.8053).		
↔ 24KM	△ 850M	↕ 100M
⏱ 8–10 HRS	GRADE III	✶✶✶

By Colwyn Jones

Seana Bhraigh is one of the more remote Munros, with dramatic northern cliffs and great wilderness views, poised above the stunning Luchd Choire. It is a special peak which is challenging to ski and has a good reputation for holding snow, and thus a winter visit is all the more alluring.

The SMC *Northern Highlands District Guide* (Strang, 1974) states, 'The north shoulder of Seana Bhraigh often gives a good ski run from the summit to the floor of Strath Mulzie. The upper section is boulder-strewn and requires a fair snow cover, but the lower sections are excellent. A ski approach to the mountain is quite often feasible.' The approach described is up Strath Mulzie from the A837 at Oykel Bridge, where it is possible

to take a vehicle 6km along the unmetalled (and unploughed) landrover track as far as The Schoolhouse Bothy outside the stalking season. During the stalking season you could contact the estate (01403 891765) to check whether an estate gate about 1km before the bothy is locked (NH 347 978). If it is, there is parking at an abandoned quarry by the gate.

From here the track goes a further 8km, past Corriemulzie Lodge as far as a second bothy on the north-east shore of Loch a' Choire Mhòir (Loch of the Big Corrie), Coiremor (Magoo's Bothy; NH 305 888; 300m). Mountain bikes are recommended for this lengthy approach.

If you plan a day visit and the bothy is not on your itinerary, then at a track junction (NH 292 907; 250m), just before the main track crosses the Corriemulzie River (6km from Corriemulzie Lodge), the easiest summit approach up the rough hillside takes a right-hand fork (west of the river). Just before it ends, an ATV track, which may hold snow, ascends right, first south then more directly west-south-west to a rocky knoll (Meallan Odhar, point 626m on the 1:25,000 map). Leave the ATV track here and ascend south to a lochan below point 760m on the Creag nan Gobhar ridge. The small lochan guides you onto the north-east ridge, opening up views to the An Sgùrr ridge across Luchd Choire. The summit cairn on the edge of the corrie is reached after less than 1km. This reverses the description from the earlier SMC *Northern Highlands District Guide* and is option 1 in the SMC hillwalkers' guide, *The Munros* (Anderson and Prentice, 2021, p.332). If visiting the Coiremor Bothy, then crossing the outflow from Loch a' Choire Mhòir (difficult in spate) gives access to the flank of the north ridge, which can then be followed directly to the summit. The views from the top are tremendous and well worth the effort involved in getting there.

If, however, you overnight in the bothy, the next day you may have time to complete a fine round of the corrie, including the remote Corbett, Càrn Bàn (White Cairn; NH 338 875; 845m). From the bothy head south-east into the big corrie but almost immediately leave the loch shore and head uphill due east, avoiding rocky ground, onto the north-west shoulder of Càrn Bàn. The gradient finally eases at the 740m contour, and you should continue along the shoulder over point 779m, then head gently down east for 0.6km (keeping skins on) to a bealach before climbing the final 0.8km to the small cairn on the summit.

Your round continues south from this summit along the ridge for 1.5km to a broad bealach (NH 336 861; 800m). The steep gully running north-west from this point (at the south-east corner of the corrie) has been skied in good conditions. Take care, for it is NOT the gully boasting the waterfall (1:25,000 map; 520m). The correct gully, well seen from the bothy, starts at NH 331 863 at the 700m contour, and the steep snow forming the upper entry must be carefully assessed. If you decide the gully is safe to ski, it provides a direct return to the bothy along the steep-sided big corrie (Coire Mòr). This gully might form part of the return for a suitable day tour after traversing the summit of Seana Bhraigh. A path on the north-east side of the stream about 2km out from the bothy may hold snow and, on ski or foot, will convey you back safely.

Navigation of the corrie round becomes more complex after this point, and the south side of Loch Coire Mhic Mhathain (NH 315 856; 675m) is a suitable waypoint. From here a direct rising traverse west-north-west for 3km to point 906m then gives a simple, short descent, followed by a climb to reach the summit some 1km later. A more aesthetic alternative is to ski along the rim of the corrie, which, while more undulating, affords either tempting or sobering views down into the northern corries of this remote and noteworthy peak.

The first edition of this guidebook mentioned Press On Gully, an exposed Grade I winter climb in Luchd Choire of Seana Bhraigh which has been rarely skied and was reported to give 300m of extreme descent at a reported angle of 45 degrees. Press On Gully is always a very intimidating and serious prospect. It must only be attempted when conditions are safe, and this is best assessed by ascending the gully first to check the snow. The top of the gully often holds a cornice, giving a tricky exit when climbing, and indeed a tricky entry if you do attempt to ski down this gully.

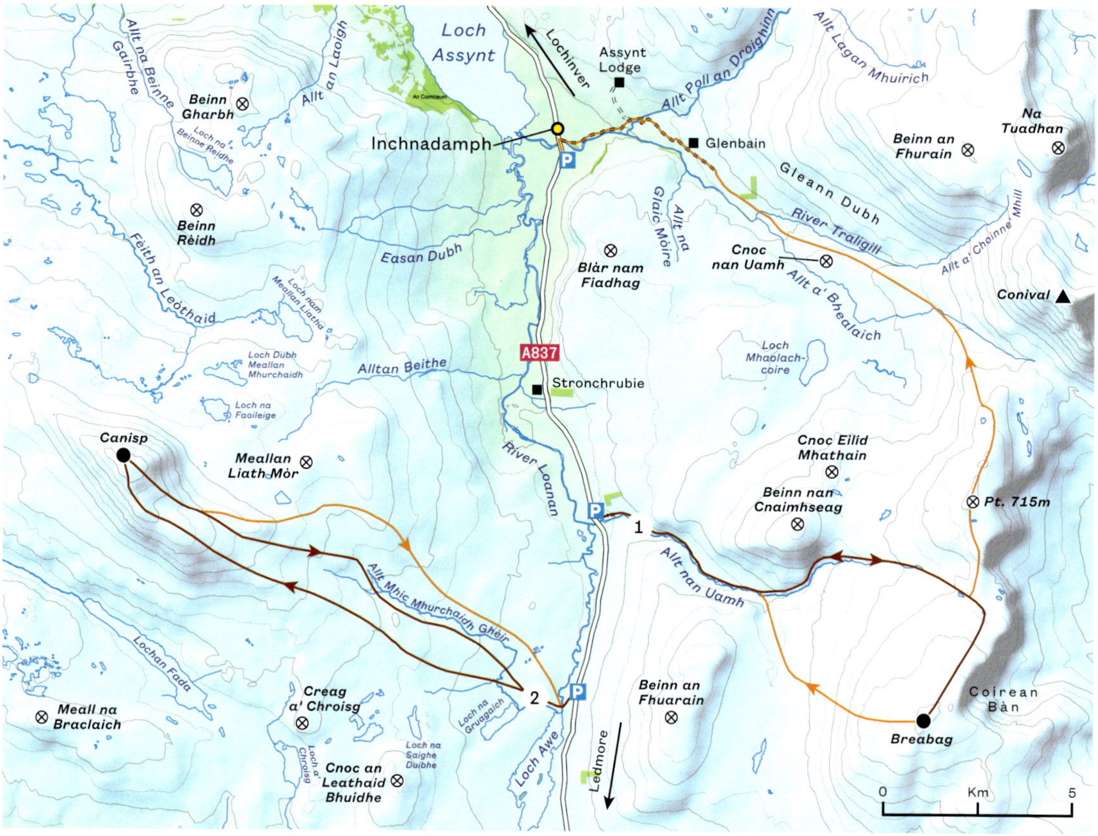

Breabag
Little Height ● 815m

△ NC 286 157 ◁ LR15 ⊕ P.370

ⓟ On the A837 between Ledmore and Inchnadamph at the car park for the Bone Caves (NC 253 179/ 58.1154, -4.9669).

↔ 14KM △ 700M ⊺ 138M
⌚ 5-6 HRS GRADE II ★★

By Colwyn Jones

Breabag is the seemingly impenetrable hurdle barricading the far Northern Highlands as you drive up towards Ledmore junction from Elphin. It can be skied with a combination of good snow cover and an approach from the west, giving a decent tour in remote wilderness.

The Bone Caves car park has a somewhat steep entry from the road if icy, but if you can surmount this small obstacle, plenty of parking is available. From the car park follow the well-maintained footpath signposted to the Bone Caves past the abandoned fish farm and continue up the steadily rising glen containing the Allt nan Uamh. Once past the caves the stream has an impassable waterfall, so assess where the snow is best at the junction. Either climb the slope to the left onto a ledge and carefully traverse above the stream past the waterfall, or turn right up the north-facing Claonaite dry valley, which holds snow well, then turn left onto the broad flank of the hill. The west-facing escarpment has a suitable break allowing you to safely continue up onto the broad ridge. This ridge requires care as it is riven with deep, rocky clefts in places under the snow. The ridge has a low point at around 600m just south of the Bealach an t-Sionnaich (1:25,000 map). Once established on the ridge, assume a southerly track, negotiating the rocky outcrops, which leads to the main summit of this Corbett, just over 1km away with 200 vertical metres of steady ascent.

Descent can follow the approach route, which will be the safe choice in less-than-ideal visibility. However, if on the ascent you observed a suitable snowy descent option skiing directly east off the top, then this will give a steeper, more exciting and direct return to the Allt nan Uamh and back to the car park.

Key
1. Breabag P.370
2. Canisp P.371

A return to the A837 at Inchnadamph (4km north of the Bone Caves; 80m) is possible by traversing the peak south to north – if you have a second car. From the summit, backtrack to the Bealach an t-Sionnaich and go on to Breabag Tarsainn (649m) just before the deep and narrow pass between Breabag and Conival. From here choose the best route northwest off the top to then follow the Allt a' Bhealaich towards Loch Mhaolach-coire, then descend the Gleann Dubh following the footpath along the course of the River Traligill to Inchnadamph.

If the southern ridge of the peak has good snow cover, it can be used as an ascent from the A837 about 300m north of Lyne Farm (NC 248 145; 160m). Park safely at the roadside, then take an easterly rising traverse on open hillside outside the perimeter fence of the farm, then above a few trees high on the northern bank of the Ledbeg River. A small lochan on the ridge is reached after 3km (NC 282 142; 450m). Head north up the south ridge to reach the summit after 2km.

The south ridge just ascended affords a fine descent, but good snow cover observed on the western slopes can provide an exciting alternative 4km return to the farm.

Below: Canisp
(boarder, Jennifer Mullen)
© Will Copestake

Canisp ● 847m
White Hill, from old Norse

| △ NC 203 187 | ⌖ LR15 | ⊕ P.370 |

| P | The roadside car park on the west side of the A837 (NC 250 162/58.0999, -4.9706). |

| ↔ 12KM | △ 690M | ⊤ 160M |
| ⓘ 3-5 HRS | GRADE II | ** |

By Mike Dixon, Colwyn Jones and Jennifer Mullen

Abruptly rising from the surrounding tableland of Lewisian gneiss (reputed to be one of the oldest rocks in the world), Canisp lies close to the coast and is a glaciated, steep-sided ridge running northwest and south-east. The flanks have precipitous crags and scree, which are unsuited for skiing. The peak is perhaps best skied soon after an early season heavy snowfall down to sea level when the avalanche risk elsewhere remains high. Deep snow is essential to cover the abundant rocks and heather found on the slopes of this Corbett. However, the gradient of the route never reaches a critical angle, so it should provide a safe option and may give a super ski down. The starting point is less than 8km north of the excellent Naismith Hut, owned by the SMC. The A837, which sees regular traffic, is usually ploughed and passable after snow, but you may need to use a snow shovel to clear the off-road parking space. A second parking place is available 350m further south, almost opposite a disused quarry (NC 249 158). Choose a clear day, as the views available from the summit are exceptional.

The line of the summer footpath is the shortest and quickest ascent. It starts at the north end of Loch Awe from the car park under telegraph wires and reaches a footbridge across the River Loanan as it leaves the loch. Shadowing the south bank of the Allt Mhic Mhurchaidh Ghèir (Burn of the Son of Fat (Lardy) Murdo), the path should be hidden beneath a good depth, and you can choose the best snow in which to lay in your skinning track. The slot of the Allt Mhic Mhurchaidh Ghèir can develop cornices on the steep box sides in heavy snow, so caution is needed here, especially during the descent. At around the 350m contour head west onto the wide south-east ridge, by which time you will have realised that the slope undulates but still leads steadily to the top. The final 50 vertical metres tend to be icy and, depending on conditions, may require crampons. The summit of Canisp is furnished with a circular walled shelter where the winter panorama is one of the finest in Scotland. The isolated summit gives all-round views of the surrounding moorland, The Minch beyond Lochinver and the well-known mountains of Assynt and Coigach, Foinaven and other peaks of the Reay Forest to the north, and An Teallach and the Fannaichs to the south. Particularly noteworthy is the magnificent close-up of Suilven, one of Scotland's finest and most unique peaks.

The flank of the south-east ridge may sport a cornice, which is best avoided. Descent involves retracing your approach, but by now you should know where the best snow lies to give a fine, safe and swift return to the start. Height might be maintained for longer by taking a more easterly alternative descent route.

Below: Heading up from the Crask Inn, Ben Klibreck (skiers, Alex Reid and party) © Al Todd

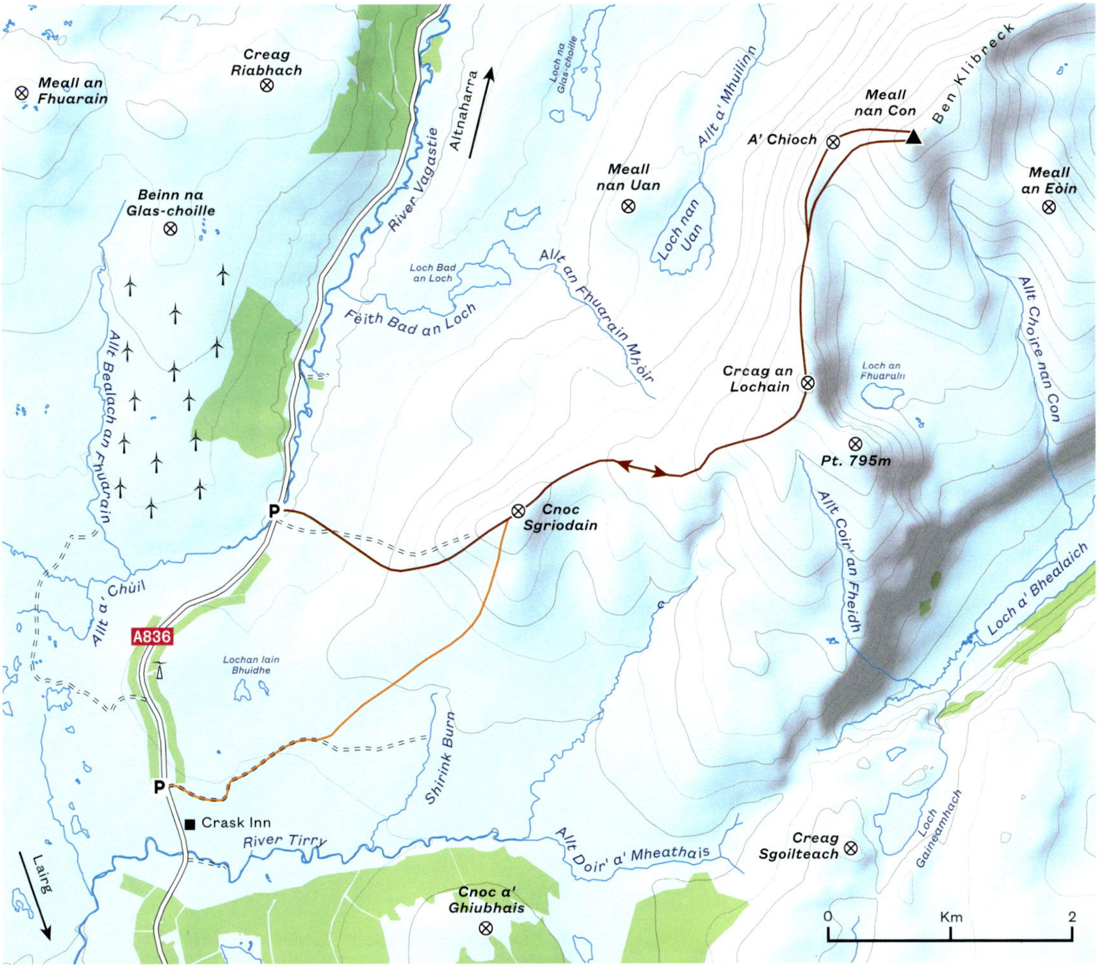

Ben Klibreck ▲ 962m

Hill of the Speckled Cliff

△ NC 585 299 ⌖ LR16 ⊕ P.373

🅿 Allt a' Chràisg Bridge (NC 532 273/58.2108, -4.4976), or any point between Vagastie Cottage and the Crask Inn, depending on snow cover. Parking is limited, with informal roadside parking near the bridge, the Inn, or at unused forest access points. The A836 is a single-track road; passing places should be kept clear.

↔ 17KM   △ 760M   ⊺ 200M
🕒 5–6 HRS   GRADE II   ★★★

By Calum Anton

Ben Klibreck is a fine, solitary hill that is not on the radar of many ski mountaineers, probably due to its relative remoteness. The construction of the 22 turbines, each 125m high, along with associated maintenance road infrastructure at the Creag Riabhach Windfarm on the Altnaharra Estate opposite, will inevitably change the isolated perspective. Klibreck can be readily climbed on skis on a short winter's day with an early start and clear weather. In good conditions, once skis are donned, they should be on all day.

From the bridge, make for the nearest high ground up the south-west slope of Cnoc Sgriodain, which takes you up to 544m. This, with its tall cairn (NC 562 275), offers a fine viewpoint from the north to Ben Loyal and round from Ben Hope and Ben Hee to Assynt. The route ahead climbs onto Carn an Fheidh then Creag an Lochain, with the summit cone of Ben Klibreck's Meall nan Con nudging over the white skyline ahead. A straight schuss down to the bealach takes you to the foot of the unbroken but fairly steep climb to the summit. This is skinnable and brings you out at the summit cairn and toppled triangulation station – a fine viewpoint.

The return route will depend on where the best snow lies. An exit from the cairn, initially to the west with an early sweep round to the south-west face, offers runs-a-plenty across this slope, and will take you to the bealach passed on ascent. The north-west flank of Ben Klibreck is steep, rocky and best avoided; it also drops further away from your starting point. This steep, broken slope continues southwards along and below the bealach, and is not well shown on the 1:50,000 map, so don't be tempted down there.

The recommended route from the bealach is to return along the ridge to Creag an Lochain to maximise the vertical descent over Carn an Fheidh before following the best snow over or around Cnoc Sgriodain and returning to the bridge. However, the 500m slide out and back to the south-east top of Creag an Lochain is worth the fine view down onto Loch a' Bhealaich and Loch Choire, entrenched between the hills and leading the eye far beyond to the distant Flow Country and Caithness.

Beinn Dhorain ◆ 628m
Otter Hill

△ NC 925 156   ◁ LR16   ⊕ P.374

▣ On the Lothbeg to Kildonan road (U2810, 3km off the A9) in Glen Loth, just south of the Sletdale Burn bridge (NC 939 127/58.0905, -3.8016). Park at the side of the road near the hydro intake dam.

↔ 19KM   △ 770M   ⊤ 110M
◷ 4-5 HRS   GRADE II   ★★

By Julian Walford

Beinn Dhorain holds snow well on its gentle southern slopes, giving a good descent in the right conditions. The upper slope was the site of a 350cc AJS motorbike (1947 vintage) engine-driven rope tow in the 1960s, probably the most northerly fixed ski tow in Scotland. It was run by the Caithness Mountaineering and Ski Club, but all that now remains is the flat rock on which it was mounted. With good firm snow a fine loop is possible mostly above 400m, and the gentle gradients benefit from fast skins or waxes giving a good glide.

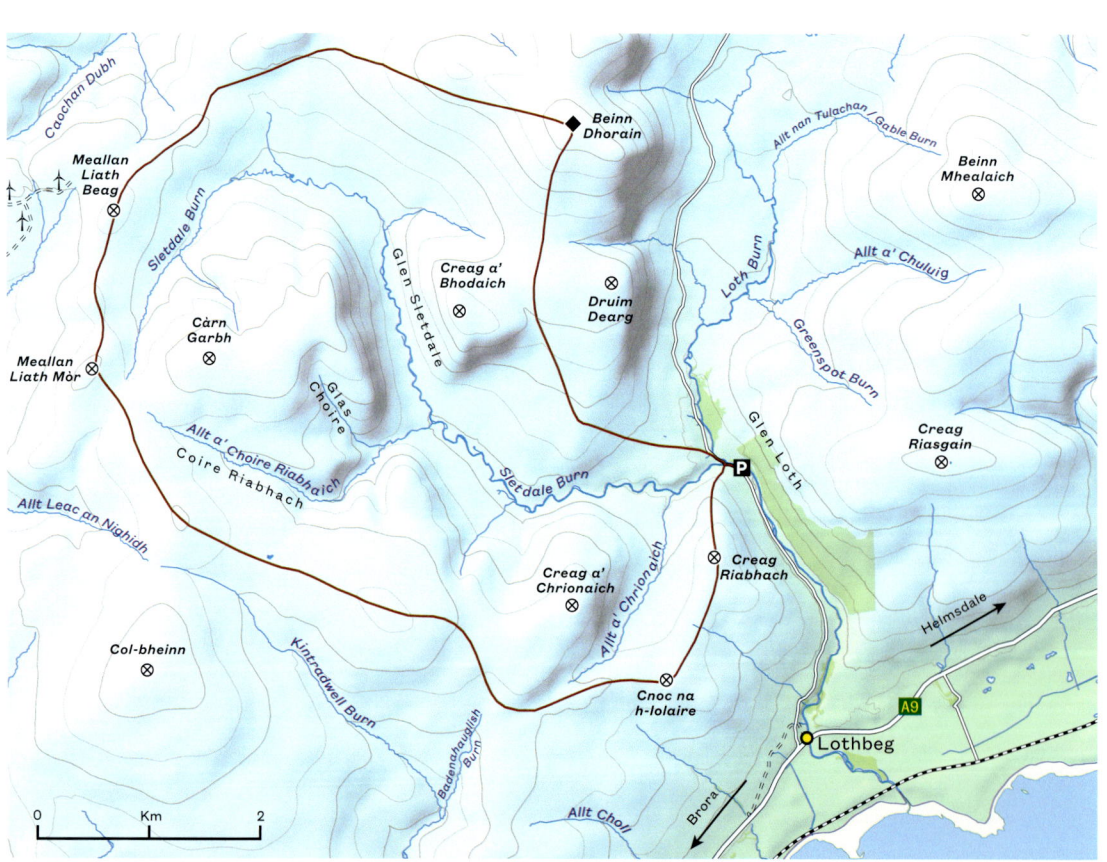

The area can also be reached from the south by mountain bike, from the tracks servicing the Gordonbush Windfarm.

From the Sletdale Burn bridge, climb south up the north ridge of Creag Riabhach to quickly gain height, then continue to Cnoc na h-Iolaire before turning west then north-west to follow the rounded ridge to Meallan Liath Mòr. The horseshoe continues north over Meallan Liath Beag, then north-east past the south flank of The Craggan, and finally east to Choire Mhòr and the Beinn Dhorain summit. Now descend south to the pass between Creag a' Bhodaich and Druim Dearg and the final slope back to the Sletdale Burn bridge.

On a good day there may be excellent views over the Moray Firth to the east, and the wild areas of Caithness and Sutherland to the north and west. For many, the extensive offshore and onshore wind developments are a change in the right direction from the old coal mining just south at Brora. (The colliery supplied mostly local needs and closed in 1974.)

Top: On Bheinn Dhorain (skiers, David Finlay and Fiona Neal) © Kev Neal

Ben Hee ● 873m
Fairy Hill

△ NC 426 339   ◁ LR16   ⊕ P.376

P The A838 at West Merkland at the start of the Bealach nam Meirleach (Robber's Pass, NC 384 329/ 58.2553, -4.7551). Parking is limited.

↔ 12KM   △ 750M   ⊺ 113M
⊙ 3-5 HRS   GRADE II   **

By Colwyn Jones

Sitting on the eastern edge of the Reay Forest, Ben Hee offers a good ski descent over its broad western and southern aspects, if there is adequate snow cover down to the trunk road between Laing and Laxford Bridge. When substantial snow falls, typically from an easterly or north-easterly weather front, approaching from the south-east via the A838 may prove more successful.

The usual walking route to the summit of Ben Hee from West Merkland gives a pleasant moderate ascent, whether carrying skis or skinning. Start from the public road, at a small run-of-the-river hydroelectric station next to West Merkland on the Allt nan Albannach (Scotsburn). Continue north-east for 1.5km along the Bealach nam Meirleach (Robber's Pass) to a stalkers' path that follows the south bank of the Allt Coir' a' Chruiteir (Valley of the Harper). The course of the Allt has a poor record of holding snow deep enough to allow you to criss-cross the stream as the path requires, and perhaps bypass awkward and steeper parts of the stalkers' path. If there is inadequate snow in the burn then the south side of the corrie will need to be used for the ascent, or you may have to walk up the worst parts.

The slope eases at around the 450m contour where a line of modest cairns diverges from the burn onto the even slope on the side of the broad south-west ridge. Of course, these cairns may not be visible in deep snow. Above 650m, swing north-east to climb steadily to the top. Close to the top the grassy slopes give way to a covering of rocks, which may be exposed if wind has blasted the snow. There is a cairn and a walled triangulation station on the summit.

On a cold, clear day the summit gives splendid panoramic views of Ben More Assynt, Quinag, Ben Stack, Foinaven, Ben Hope, Ben Loyal and the mosaic of moorland between them.

The hill provides a steady descent down smooth slopes to the 650m contour where the route of ascent gives a good return to your starting point. An alternative, if there is a good depth of snow, is to follow the south-west ridge over the rocky summit of Meallan Liath Mòr. This involves a short ascent, then a ski down the steep west face directly back to West Merkland. The face is boulder-strewn in places, so it should only be attempted when these grey rocks are well hidden by snow, and any avalanche risk has been judged as safe.

Top: Ben Stack and Arkle from Ben Hee © Mike Cawthorne

Below: Ben Loyal
© Hugh Mackay

Chapter 9

North Scotland and the Isle of Mull

Ben Hee

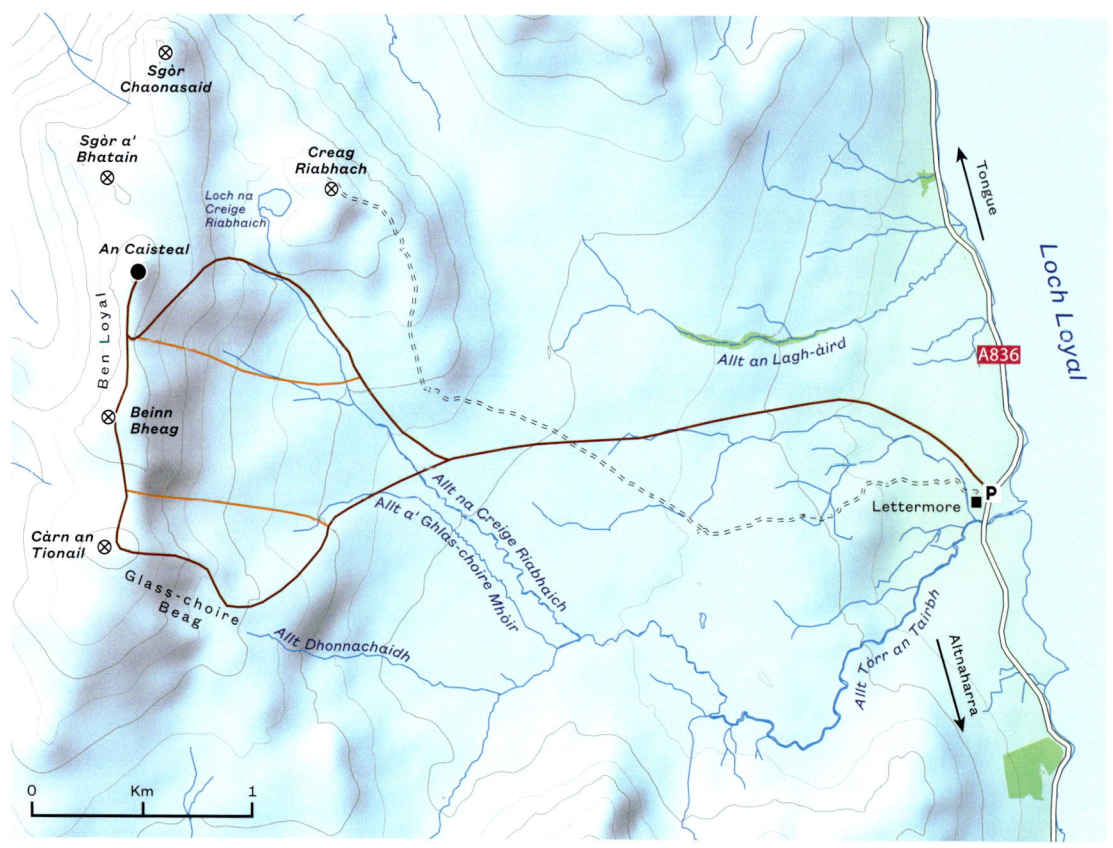

Ben Loyal ● 764m
Law Hill

△ NC 578 488	◁ LR10	⊕ P.380

P Lettermore on the A836 Altnaharra to Tongue road
(NC 616 477/58.3968, -4.3686).

↔ 11KM	△ 650M	⏐ 115M
⏱ 3-4 HRS	GRADE III	★★★

By Julian Walford

Ben Loyal offers good skiing on its eastern slopes with ridges to the north-east and south-east. The upper slopes are quite steep, but on well-conditioned snow they offer a good descent, while the lower slopes are of a steady gradient and snow often builds up alongside the burns. The whole flank is visible from just above the road, so a suitable route can be chosen to account for where snow is lying on the day.

From roadside parking near Lettermore, take the track just north of the house and climb north-west then west, following the small burn. Continue steadily west, assessing the best descent route for later. The flat ground slightly further south is best avoided. Climb north-west alongside the Allt na Creige Riabhaich (1:25,000 map) to near the small loch, then turn south-west to reach the main ridge some 300m south of the summit. Head north, enjoying the views to the summit, An Caisteal (The Castle), which is marked by a triangulation station. Skis will have to be removed to carefully climb the last few metres of these rocky battlements to reach 'The Castle'.

If the snow cover is good, ski south some 1.2km along the ridge to Càrn an Tionail, then ski east down the ridge into Glas-choire Mòr. Pick up the Allt a' Ghlas-choire Mhòir stream edge (1:25,000 map), then leave it to return to the ascent slope.

Alternatively, for a steeper descent, if feasible, descend one of the good snow gullies spotted during your ascent along the flank. The slope above the Allt a' Chaisteil (1:25,000 map) is often well filled.

Ben Hope ▲ 927m
Hill of the Bay

△ NC 477 501   ◁ LR9   🌐 P.381

[P] On the minor road (C1034) between Hope Bridge (limited parking) and Altnaharra. For the northern approach: An Garbh-allt, 8km south of Hope Bridge (NC 462 525/58.4341, -4.6356).
For the southern approach: Allt na Caillich (NC 458 454/58.3710, -4.6377) and Allt Dornaigil (NC 457 451), 15km south of Hope Bridge.

↔ 13–16KM   △ 920M (N.APPROACH)   ↕ 10M
⏱ 3–5 HRS   GRADE II   ★★★★

By Julian Walford

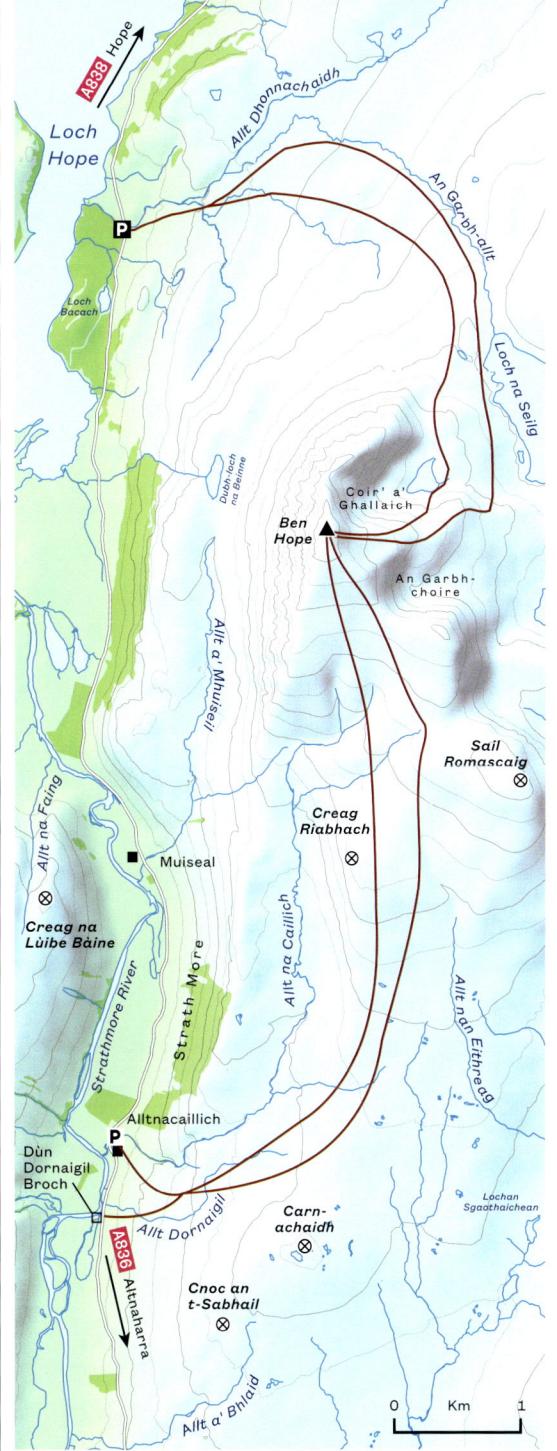

Ben Hope, the most northerly Munro, offers an excellent ski descent on its broad southern aspect, as its flanks, ridges and stream gullies create lee slopes that catch the snow and provide a measure of shelter even in windy conditions. Much of the upper slope is moss-covered and clear of boulders. On a cold clear day, the summit views are usually excellent in all directions: along the north coast towards Orkney, eastwards to the Caithness hills, and south to Sutherland and Ross-shire.

The usual summer footpath from Muiseal is too steep and the low snow rarely usable, but from Allt na Caillich or Dun Dornaigil the slope is gentler, and snow can accumulate in the burns even at low altitude. Climb the steep west flank up to 250m, ideally on skis (otherwise carry them up the path). At this point the snow conditions up the Allt na Caillich and the flanks of Creag Riabhach and Sail Romascaig become clear. Choose your preferred line and climb steadily north all the way to the top. If visibility is not perfect, take great care not to stray too close to the western edge, and once on the summit, carefully locate the triangulation station.

The route down follows the ascent, but in good conditions skiers usually zigzag to maximise the run, veering east towards Sail Romascaig then over to the Allt nan Eithreag. Between the 350m to 400m contour, go west to pick up the Allt Dornaigil (1:25,000 map) to either return to the farm or the ruined broch.

A fine alternative, ideally with two cars, is to traverse Ben Hope starting from the north, then ski out down the route described above. From the roadside parking, climb up east beside An Garbh-allt past the series of nice waterfalls which would be a major tourist attraction anywhere else, then continue to the source, Loch na Seilg (Loch of the Hunt), and ski up the east ridge to the summit. If you are not attempting the traverse, return is by the same route, having spied a suitable line off the east ridge.

Morven
Big Hill ◆ 706m

△ ND 004 285   ◁ LR17   ⊕ P.382

🅿 Braemore car park (ND 073 304/58.2528, -3.5805).
↔ 20KM   △ 550M   ⊥ 150M
⏱ 5-7 HRS   GRADE III   ★★★

By Kev Neal

A trip to an Icelandic paradise, in Scotland! For some, the drive to the very last mountain on the east coast may seem a trip too far. However, those who live in the Highlands, or who are prepared to experience something a little different, could be in for a treat.

Morven, in Caithness, offers stunning skiing with the right winter conditions (a big northerly or easterly snowfall, preferably with a strong ground frost). This will enable the frozen flat approach to become a lovely skin through empty moorland and under big skies.

The best conditions, or rather the conditions worth making this effort for, will have snow almost to sea level. It is recommended you carry snow chains, and it is definitely worth having good snow tyres. Morven is inland and it gets pretty cold at the end of the Braemore road, from where the ski tour starts. From the A9 it is 15km to here along a single-track road, which is not always passable (it relies on locals doing the clearing). There is a small parking area next to the phone box before the wee stone bridge. It can fit about four cars, and you may have to clear a parking space.

From here, you can skin all the way in past Braemore Farm. In suboptimal conditions, a bike might be worth bringing to head along the landover track to the building at Corrichoich (ND 032 296).

The final skin up Morven is pretty steep at 25-30 degrees, taking the south face as the east ridge is rocky. Once at the top you are greeted with views of the Atlantic and Orkney to the north, and to the south, the whole of Scotland!

There are a few descent options, including skiing the south-west-facing open bowl for 500m to the valley floor, or heading down the west side, which, in glorious conditions, will take your breath away.

Note that there are also awesome skis of various lengths off the surrounding peaks Scaraben, Sròn Gharbh and the other Paps.

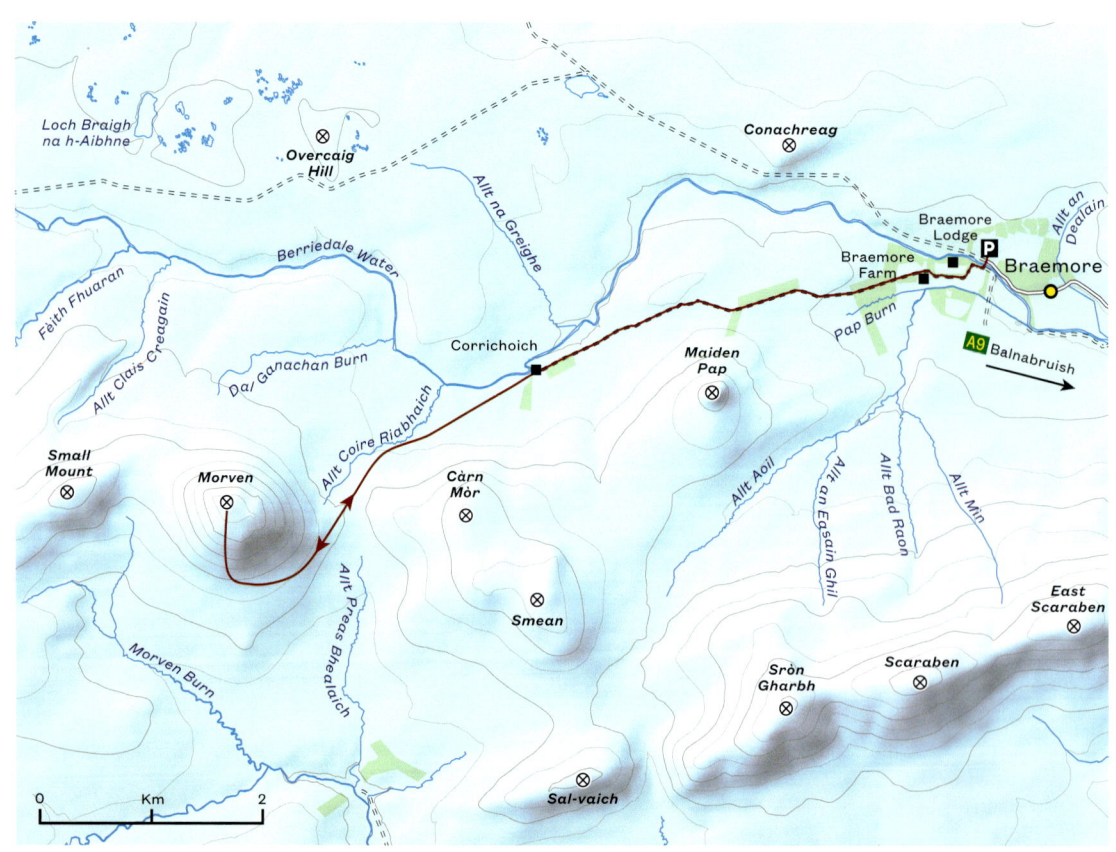

The Isle Of Mull

Ben More ▲ 966m
Big Hill

△ NM 525 331   ◁ LR48   ⊕ P.383

| P | On the B8035 (NM 494 359/56.4491, -6.0673) at the start of the track up to Dhiseig. There is normally ample parking off the road on its north side, opposite the Dhiseig track. |

↔ 12KM   △ 950M   ⊥ 10M
⏱ 5-6 HRS   GRADE III   ★★★

by Jamie Howard

Ben More is the sole Munro on the Isle of Mull, lying to the west of centre of the island. Car ferries operate most days from Oban to Craignure, and from Lochaline to Fishnish. Booking is advisable (www.calmac.co.uk). A car is recommended as public transport to the starting point is almost non-existent. There is a taxi service but you will probably find that the car is quite a lot less expensive! You would be advised to allow for a two-night stay, although there are early and late ferries for those for whom time is of the essence. Prospective skiers would be wise to check snow conditions on Ben More prior to committing to the journey to Mull. Ben More also makes for an excellent winter walking excursion, so be prepared for this eventuality should the snow not be suitable for skiing.

The ski touring route more or less follows the standard walking route up the west ridge. From the starting point, skis will normally have to be backpacked to the snow-line. Ascend the access track towards Dhiseig Cottage, and on reaching trees and the entrance gate for the cottage, turn off up to the right. Go through a field gate and more or less follow the north-east side of the Abhainn Dhiseig uphill. There is a second gate at approximately 50m altitude; thereafter the path meanders along the north-east side of the burn until approximately 250m altitude, when an opportunity to cross over to the south-east side should be sought.

Once on the south-east side of the burn, gradually ascend the ridge on whatever suitable snow there is to where the ridge steepens abruptly at NM 517 334 (750m). You may have to carry skis for this short steep section; however, once on the main broad ridge, it is possible to ski all the way to the large summit cairn. Be prepared to use Harscheisen on this final section. Beware of tracking too far to the north, both on the ridge and once on the summit plateau, as there are steep drop-offs here to catch the unwary. The extensive sea view from the top is superb and an unusual benefit for a Scottish ski tour.

The descent drops back down the west ridge from the summit to a point (NM 521 333). From here, it is worth exploring an option to descend to the south of the ridge, where the snow-holding is frequently better. Either way, gradually work north round to the lower slopes of the ridge, eventually reaching the Abhainn Dhiseig.

Given suitable snow, this makes a superb and unforgettable outing, with fabulous views towards Ulva, Staffa and the isles of Coll and Tiree, and the added possibility of being buzzed by a golden or white-tailed sea eagle!

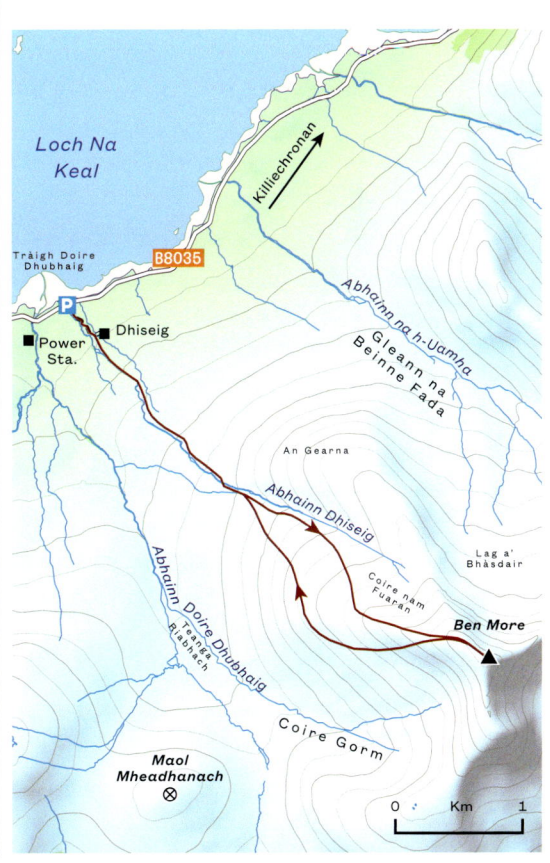

Below: Morven
(skier, Fiona Neal)
© Kevin Neal

Index

A' Bhuidheanach Bheag, 153
A' Chailleach, 159
A' Chaoirnich, 149
A' Chòinneach, 238
A' Chràileag, 325
A' Mharconaich, 151
Allermuir Hill, 67
Allt a' Chobhair Circuit, 123
Am Faochagach, 361
An Dùn, 149
An Riabhachan, 332
An Sgarsoch, 185, 195
An Socach, 174
An Teallach, 365
Aonach air Chrith, 318
Aonach Beag (Corrour), 263
Aonach Beag (Nevis), 277
Aonach Mòr, 277
Aonnachs Traverse, 277
Arrochar Alps, The, 83
Auch Hills, The, 103
Beinn a Bhùird, 217
Beinn a' Bhàthaich Àrd, 336
Beinn a' Chaorainn, 215
Beinn a' Chaorainn, 306
Beinn a' Chlachair, 287
Beinn a' Chleibh, 94
Beinn a' Chreachain, 128
Beinn a' Chrùlaiste, 255
Beinn a' Ghlo, 139
Beinn a' Mhanaich, 77
Beinn Achaladair, 128
Beinn an Dòthaidh, 127
Beinn Bheòil, 259, 265
Beinn Bhreac, 79
Beinn Bhreac, 195
Beinn Bhrotain, 197
Beinn Challuim, 98
Beinn Chaorach, 77
Beinn Chaorach, 103
Beinn Dearg (Blair Atholl/Feshie), 148, 195
Beinn Dearg (Glen Lyon), 130
Beinn Dearg (Ullapool), 361
Beinn Dearg (Ullapool) West, 364
Beinn Dhorain, 374
Beinn Dòrain, 127
Beinn Dubhchraig, 94
Beinn Eibhinn, 263
Beinn Eich, 78
Beinn Enaiglair, 365
Bèinn Fhionnlaidh, 329

Beinn Ghlas, 120, 123
Beinn Ime, 84
Beinn Liath Mhòr Fannaich, 357
Beinn Luibhean, 84
Beinn Iutharn Mhòr, 174
Beinn Mheadhoinn, 211, 213
Beinn na Lap, 259
Beinn nam Fuaran, 103
Beinn nan Imirean, 99
Beinn Narnain, 84
Beinn Odhar, 103
Beinn Sheasgarnich, 106
Beinn Teallach, 306
Beinn Tulaichean, 88
Beinn Udlamain, 151
Ben Alder, 259, 265
Ben Avon/Leabaibh an Daimh Bhuide, 219
Ben Chonzie, 93
Ben Hee, 375
Ben Hope, 381
Ben Klibreck, 373
Ben Lawers, 119, 120, 123
Ben Lawers North, 123
Ben Ledi, 86
Ben Lomond, 79
Ben Loyal, 380
Ben Lui/Beinn Laoigh, 94
Ben Macdui, 211, 234
Ben Macdui Loch Avon Circuit, The, 211
Ben More (Crianlarich), 89
Ben More (Mull), 383
Ben Nevis, 272
Ben Oss, 94
Ben Rinnes, 248
Ben Vorlich (Loch Earn), 91
Ben Vorlich (Loch Lomond), 85
Ben Vrackie, 138
Ben Wyvis East, 348
Ben Wyvis West Route, 347
Bennachie, 228
Bidean a' Ghlas Thuill, 365
Blackhope Scar, 60
Braebag, 370
Braeriach, 203, 234
Bràigh Coire Chruinn-bhalgain, 139
Broad Cairn, 187
Broad Law, 56
Buachaille Etive Beag, 254
Bynack More, 238
Cac Carn Beag, 187
Caerketton Hill, 67
Cairn Bannoch, 187
Cairn Gorm, 229, 234
Cairn Lochain, 229

Cairn of Claise, 176
Cairn Toul, 234
Cairngorm Five and Eight Tops, 234
Cairnsmore of Carsphairn, 52
Cairnwell, The, 172
Cam Chreag, 103
Campsie Fells, The, 74
Canisp, 371
Càrn a Choire Bhoideach, 187
Càrn a' Chlamain, 141, 195
Carn a' Choire Ghairbh, 328
Càrn a' Gheòidh, 172
Carn a' Ghille Chearr, 244
Carn an Fhidhleir, 185, 195
Càrn an Righ, 174
Càrn an t-Sagairt Mòr, 187
Càrn an Tuirc, 176
Càrn Bàn Mòr, 203
Càrn Dearg, 159
Càrn Dearg (Corrour), 263
Càrn Dearg (Rannoch), 258, 265
Càrn Dearg Mòr, 183
Carn Ealasaid, 243
Càrn Eighe, 329
Càrn Ghluasaid, 325, 327
Càrn Gorm, 131
Càrn Liath, 139
Càrn Liath, 307
Càrn Maing, 131
Càrn Maing Hills, 131
Càrn na Caim, 153
Carn na Drochaide, 200
Càrn nan Gabhar, 139
Càrn nan Gobhar (Mullardoch), 330
Carn nan Gobhar (Strathfarrar), 343
Càrn Sgùlain, 159
Ceinn a' Chaisteil, 103
Cheviot, The, 44
Chno Dearg, 284
Circuit of Coire nam Buidheag, The, 126
Clachnaben, 226
Cleish Hills, The, 75
Cluanie Hills from the South, 325
Cobble, The, 83, 84
Cona' Mheall, 361
Corrour Ridge, 263
Corrour to Dalwhinnie Traverse, 265
Corserine, 50
Craig to Struy High Tops Route, 338
Creag a' Mhàim, 318
Creag an Dail Bheag, 222
Creag Dubh, 330
Creag Leacach, 173
Creag Meagaidh, 307
Creag Mhòr (Cairngorms), 239

Index

Creag Mhòr (Mamlorn), 106
Creag nan Damh, 318
Creag Pitridh, 287
Creagan a' Chaise, 244
Creise, 134
Cross Ross-Shire, 338
Cruach Adrain, 88
Culardoch, 222
Culter Fell, 57
Doune Hill, 78
Dreish, 181, 183
Druim Fada, 270
Druim Shionnach, 318
Dumglow, 75
Dun Rig (Glensax Horseshoe), 59
Dundreich, 63
Easains, The, 284
East Dromochter, 153
Einich Cairn, 203
Fannichs, The, 357
Fara, The, 155, 265
Fionn Beinn, 349
Geal Charn (Dorback), 241
Geal Chàrn (Laggan), 160
Geal Charn (Loch Laggan), 287
Geal-Chàrn (Corrour), 263
Geal-chàrn (Drumochter), 151
Glas Maol, 176
Glas Tulaichean, 171
Glen Doll, 183
Glen Feshie, 200
Glen Feshie Traverse, 203
Glenshee to Balmoral, 178
Gleouraich, 316
Grand Traverse of the Lawyers Range, The, 122
Greag nan Gabhar, 187
Greenhill, 180
Grey Corries, The, 280
Gulvain, 310
Hart Fell, 54
Hills of Cromdale, 244
Isle of Mull, 383
Kerloch, 227
Leathad an Taobhain, 183
Leum Uilleim, 258
Lochcraig Head, 54
Lochnagar, 187
Louther Hill, 53
Lower Hills of The Dee and The Don, The, 226
Luss Hills, The, 76
Màm Sodhail, 329
Mamlorn Mountains, 106
Mamores West, 267
Manor Hills, The, 59

Maol Chinn-dearg, 318
Mayar, 181, 183
Meall a' Bhuachaille, 240
Meall a' Bhùiridh, 134
Meall a' Choire Lèith, 119, 123
Meall a' Chrasgaidh, 357
Meall Buidhe, 130
Meall Chuaich, 158
Meall Corranaich, 119, 123
Meall Garbh (Ben Lawyers), 122, 126
Meall Garbh (Glen Lyon), 131
Meall Ghaordaidh, 108
Meall Glas, 99
Meall Greigh, 122, 126
Meall na Aighean, 131
Meall na Leitreach, 148
Meall nan Tarmachan, 117
Merrick, The, 45
Mid Hill, 78
Monadh Liath, 159
Monadh Mòr, 197
Moorfoots, The, 60
Morrone, 194
Moruisg, 346
Morven, 382
Morvern, 224
Mount Battock, 226
Mount Blair, 168
Mount Keen, 192
Mullach Clach a Bhlàir, 200
Mullach Fraoch-choire, 325
Mullach nan Coirean, 267
Ochils Traverse, The, 80
Ochils, The, 80
Pentlands Traverse, The, 64
Rannoch Traverse, 258
Rhinns of Kells Traverse, The, 50
Round of the Northern Corries of Cairn Gorm, 229
Ruigh Aiteachean High-Level Tour, 195
Saddle, The, 318
Sàil Chaorainn, 327
Scald Law, 64
Schiehallion, 132
Scottish Haute Route, 289
Seana Bhraigh, 367
Sgairneach Mhòr, 151
Sgiath Chùil, 99
Sgòr an Lochain Uaine, 234
Sgòr Choinnich, 265
Sgòr Gaibhre, 258, 265
Sgòr Gaoith, 200
Sgòr Mòr, 199
Sgurr a Mhàim, 267
Sgùrr a' Bhealaich Dheirg, 322

Sgurr a' Choire Ghlaise, 343
Sgùrr a' Mhaoriach, 317
Sgùrr an Doire Leathan, 318
Sgùrr an Lochain, 318
Sgùrr Fhuar-thuill, 343
Sgùrr Mòr, 357
Sgùrr na Lapaich, 332
Sgùrr na Ruaidhe, 343
Sgùrr na Sgine, 318
Sgùrr nan Ceannaichean, 346
Sgùrr nan Clach Geala, 356
Sgùrr nan Conbhairean, 325, 327
South Cluanie Ridge, 318
Spidean Mialach, 316
Stob a' Coire Mheadhoin, 284
Stob a' Ghrianain, 270
Stob Bàn, 267
Stob Binnein, 89
Stob Choire Claurigh, 280
Stob Coire an Laoigh, 280
Stob Coire an t-Sneachda, 229
Stob Coire Easain, 284
Stob Coire Sgrìodain, 284
Stob Dubh, 254
Stob Ghabhar, 134
Stob Poite Coire Ardair, 307
Strathfarrar, 343
Stùc a' Chroin, 91
Stùc an Lochain, 129
Tinto, 58
Toll Creagach, 333
Tolmount, 183
Tom a' Chòinnich, 333
Tom Buidhe, 183
West Dromochter, 151

Scottish Mountaineering Club

Established in 1889 the Scottish Mountaineering Club is at the forefront of climbing and mountaineering in Scotland. We want our guidebooks, covering ski mountaineering, hillwalking, scrambling and climbing, to be the first book you reach for when you head for the cliffs, hills and outcrops of Scotland.

www.smc.org.uk/publications

Scottish Mountaineering Press

The Scottish Mountaineering Press exists to promote and share Scotland's natural wonders. We do this by embracing the creativity and art born out of an explorer spirit. Whether it's poetry, photography or prose, our publications capture the moments when nature stuns us into silence and stops us in our tracks.

www.scottishmountaineeringpress.com

Scottish Mountaineering Trust

All profits from Scottish Mountaineering Press books go to help fund the Scottish Mountaineering Trust, a charity that provides grants to projects and organisations that promote recreation, knowledge and safety in the mountains, especially the mountains of Scotland.

www.thesmt.org.uk